THE NANOTECHNOLOGY CHALLENGE

Nanotechnology is the wave of the future and has already been incorporated into everything from toothpaste to socks to military equipment. However, the safety of nanotechnology for human health and the environment is a great unknown, and no legal system in the world has yet devised a way to reasonably address the uncertain risks of nanotechnology. To do so will require creating new legal institutions. This book of essays by leading law scholars and social and physical scientists offers a range of views regarding how such institutions should be formed. Readers will benefit from an accessible synthesis of the available science regarding the health risks posed by nanotechnology, thoughtful analyses of the potential unreliability of public perceptions of such risks, and a range of provocative proposals for creative "Third Way" approaches to regulating nanotechnology. This book is essential reading for anyone who may wonder how we can continue to innovate technologically in a way that delivers benefits and sustains human health and the environment.

David A. Dana is Associate Dean for Faculty Research and the Stanford Clinton Sr. and Zylpha Kilbride Clinton Research Professor of Law at Northwestern University. He is the cofounder and codirector of the Northwestern University Institute for Sustainable Practices and a Faculty Fellow at the Kellogg School of Business, Northwestern University. Dana, the author of more than thirty articles on environmental law and policy, has been published in numerous journals, including *Harvard Environmental Law Review*, *Yale Law Journal*, *Ecology Law Journal*, and *University of Pennsylvania Law Review*. He is a former litigator for the U.S. Department of Justice and for Wilmer & Hale (formerly Wilmer, Cutler & Pickering).

The Nanotechnology Challenge

CREATING LEGAL INSTITUTIONS FOR UNCERTAIN RISKS

Edited by

DAVID A. DANA

Northwestern University School of Law

CAMBRIDGE UNIVERSITY PRESS
Cambridge, New York, Melbourne, Madrid, Cape Town,
Singapore, São Paulo, Delhi, Tokyo, Mexico City

Cambridge University Press
32 Avenue of the Americas, New York, NY 10013-2473, USA

www.cambridge.org
Information on this title: www.cambridge.org/9780521767385

First published 2012

Printed in the United States of America

A catalog record for this publication is available from the British Library.

Library of Congress Cataloging in Publication data

The nanotechnology challenge : creating legal institutions for uncertain risks /
[edited by] David A. Dana.
p. cm.
Includes bibliographical references and index.
ISBN 978-0-521-76738-5
1. Nanostructured materials industry – Law and legislation. 2. Nanotechnology – Environmental aspects. 3. Nanotechnology – Economic aspect. 4. Risk perception. I. Dana, David. II. Title.
K3924.H54N36 2012
343′.0786205 – dc22 2011016702

ISBN 978-0-521-76738-5 Hardback

Contents

Contributors

Kenneth W. Abbott, Professor of Law and Willard H. Pedrick Distinguished Research Scholar, Arizona State University Sandra Day O'Connor College of Law

Jonathan H. Adler, Professor of Law, Case Western University School of Law

Toby Bolsen, Assistant Professor of Political Science, Georgia State University

Linda Breggin, Senior Attorney, Environmental Law Institute, Washington, DC

David A. Dana, Stanford Clinton Sr. and Zylpha Kilbride Clinton Research Professor of Law, Northwestern University School of Law

Daniel Diermeier, IBM Professor of Regulation and Competitive Practice, Kellogg School of Management, Northwestern University

James N. Druckman, Payson S. Wild Professor of Political Science, Northwestern University

Robert Falkner, Senior Lecturer, International Relations, London School of Economics

Kimberly A. Gray, Professor of Civil and Environmental Engineering, Northwestern University

Lyn M. Gulley, Arizona State University Sandra Day O'Connor College of Law

Nico Jaspers, Researcher, International Relations, London School of Economics

Douglas A. Kysar, Joseph M. Field Professor of Law, Yale Law School

Albert C. Lin, Professor of Law, University of California-Davis School of Law

Gary E. Marchant, Lincoln Professor of Emerging Technologies, Law & Ethics, Arizona State University Sandra Day O'Connor College of Law

John O. McGinnis, George C. Dix Professor of Constitutional Law, Northwestern University School of Law

Fern P. O'Brian, Partner, Products Liability, Business Litigation and Life Sciences Group, Thompson Hine LLP, Washington DC

John Pendergrass, Senior Attorney, Environmental Law Institute

Read D. Porter, Staff Attorney, Environmental Law Institute

Douglas J. Sylvester, Professor of Law, Arizona State University Sandra Day O'Connor College of Law

Robin Fretwell Wilson, Class of 1958 Law Alumni Professor of Law, Washington and Lee University School of Law

Laurie Zoloth, Professor of Medical Humanities and Bioethics, Feinberg School of Medicine, Northwestern University

PART I

Introduction

1

The Nanotechnology Challenge

David A. Dana

Nanotechnology has moved quickly from the realm of theoretical science and science fiction to the stuff of everyday life for people across the world. Nanotechnology is deployed in hundreds of products and services and will soon be part of many thousands of products and services. Estimates vary, but nanotechnology is a multi-billion dollar enterprise worldwide now and could become a trillion dollar enterprise in the relatively near term. Everything from socks to tennis rackets to food to surgical techniques to state-of-the-art military technology now may include some form of nanotechnology. If petroleum and plastics formed the infrastructure of the chemical/industrial revolution that transformed countries such as the United States in the last 50 to 100 years, nanotechnology and nanotechnology products may well be the tiny – the nano – basis for the next gigantic revolution in how we live.

As Kimberly Gray explains in her contribution to this volume, *nanoparticles* – extremely tiny particles – have always existed and have been known to exist for a very long time. The nanotechnology revolution began when technologies were developed that allowed nanoparticles to be accurately imaged and manipulated to produce materials having surprising properties of value in a wide range of applications. Nanotechnology is not per se the realm of the very, very small, but of the engineered and manipulated very, very small. Indeed, the promise of nanotechnology is that atoms and molecules of common elements such as silver and carbon can be manipulated into so many shapes and with so many different surface modifications that they can perform a vast array of new functions.

Across the world, national governments have invested heavily in promoting the development of nanotechnology, as have individual states within the United States. The benefits – economic, commercial, environmental, humanitarian – of nanotechnology have been widely touted. "Nano" is cutting edge and transformative, promising to cure cancer and solve the energy crisis. For many in policy-making circles and in private industry, the challenge of nanotechnology to date has been to stay in the race or, better yet, to secure a leading position in the development of the technology. For government officials and investors and business executives, the goal has been to make sure that they and their constituencies share fully in the bounties of this new industrial revolution.

The "nanotechnology challenge" in the title of this volume, however, is not the challenge of how to keep up and win a share of an emerging nanotechnology market. Rather, this volume is addressed to policy makers, citizens, academics, and others who might be interested – and, the essays included here suggest, *should* be interested – in another challenge posed by the nanotechnology revolution. That challenge is simply, how we can we (society) reap nanotechnology's many possible benefits while at the same time avoiding, limiting, or at least being poised to repair damage associated with the human health and environmental risks that this new technology creates.

This nanotechnology challenge is exceedingly difficult – exceedingly challenging, if you will – because the nature of the risks and the magnitudes of the risks from nanotechnology are so poorly understood. Indeed, given the dearth of understanding that we now have, the risks from nanotechnology are likely to remain poorly understood for years to come, even if we do see a significant increase in publically available research in the next few years. The economist Frank Knight used the term *uncertain* to describe risks or possible losses for which too little is known and understood to assign a meaningful numerical probability to the risk of loss.[1] The environmental, health, and safety risks from nanotechnology are without question uncertain risks in the Knightian sense, and so the nanotechnology challenge is not just how to confront risks from a new technology, but also how to confront uncertain risks from a new technology.

Of course, all new technologies pose some conceivable risks to human health and the environment, and, as Laurie Zoloth suggests in her contribution in this volume, genuine scientific uncertainty may be more common than we usually allow ourselves to admit. However, the risks that nanotechnology poses are particularly important ones for us to confront for several reasons, notwithstanding the possibility that, in the end, the risks could turn out to be negligible and to result in very limited, if any, harm, even were they simply ignored. Although we cannot "know" all the possible outcomes associated with nanomaterials and nanotechnology, it is important that decisions regarding nanotechnology development be oriented toward reducing risk.

The remainder of this Introduction sets out, very briefly, the case for why we should confront the challenge of uncertain risks rather than ignoring it. It then explains why current legal institutions are not well-suited for meeting this challenge, and hence why confronting the challenge likely will require new institutions. The Introduction then provides an overview of how the different essays in this volume – written by leading scholars who adopt varied approaches – shed light on the challenge of

[1] *See generally* FRANK KNIGHT. RISK, UNCERTAINTY, AND PROFIT. New York: Houghton Mifflin, 1921.

creating legal institutions for the uncertain health, environmental, and safety risks from nanotechnology.

WHY THE UNCERTAIN RISKS WARRANT ATTENTION

Even if there were not yet any studies suggesting that nanoparticles could cause substantial health harms, there are theoretical reasons for suspecting as much. Notably, their incredibly small size may allow them to migrate to and penetrate into places in the human body where they could cause very serious damage. The worst-case scenarios associated with certain types of nanotechnology are very troubling indeed, as the contributions by Gray and Wilson in this volume detail. For example, studies indicate that nanoparticles in certain inhaled or skin products could pass through the protective barriers that usually protect the brain. There is also some evidence that certain forms of carbon nanotubes, because of their small size and shape, may travel into the lungs when inhaled and lodge there in a way not dissimilar to asbestos. History provides a number of examples – including asbestos, lead, and, arguably, endocrine disrupters released from plastics – in which the ignoring of risks led to disease, death, and irreparable environmental damage.

Moreover, nanotechnologies are being deployed in such a range of contexts that many people in many communities and many environments could be at risk. Purchasers of products containing nanotechnology – especially foods and creams and the like – may be at risk. But so too, and perhaps even more so, are workers all over the world who help produce nanotechnology or handle it. The use, deterioration, and disposal of products and other materials containing nanoparticles could result in bioaccumulation of nanoparticles in non-human organisms and ecosystems in ways that could endanger plant and animal populations and adversely affect food webs that sustain human beings.

It bears emphasis that there is currently no effective way for individuals or communities to remove themselves from these nanotechnology risks. Disposal of nanotechnology into the ambient environment is not tracked, and once they enter the ambient environment, nanoparticles are very hard or impossible to detect with current technology. People therefore have no way of knowing what their environmental exposures are to nanoparticles. Even with respect to consumer products, informed choices are not easy because there are no labeling requirements and no practice of voluntary labels indicating the presence and nature of nanoparticle ingredients. For example, the all-"natural" baby product Burts Bees lotion for children reportedly contains nanoparticles, but the product label contains no indication of that fact.[2] Indeed, nanomaterials have been incrementally incorporated into existing products

[2] *See* Project on Emerging Technologies, June 4, 2007, *available at* http://www.nanotechproject.org/inventories/consumer/browse/products/chemical-free_sunscreen_spf_15/.

for so many years and to such an extent that the nanotechnology revolution could be more accurately dubbed the nanotechnology evolution.

The uncertain risks from nanotechnology deserve attention not just because people and non-human systems could be greatly harmed, but also because it is possible – maybe even likely – that the risks could be reduced or minimized without our having to forego many of the possible benefits of nanotechnology. We do not need to choose flatly between confronting uncertainty responsibly and reaping benefits. One reason this is so is that nanotechnology is highly adaptable and configuration-specific. Thus, if (for example) one form of carbon nanotube may perform a useful function but cause lung damage, it is entirely possible that a minor modification in surface features or charge could deliver the same performance without the same harm. The generation of more information is key – as is the quicker generation of information – to steer us toward less risky forms of nanotechnology and away from riskier ones.

It is also important that we confront responsibly uncertain risks from nanotechnology so that a destructive public backlash is avoided. An incident of highly visible human harm from nanotechnology – particularly harm that could have been foreseen with adequate testing – could shape public impressions and create an environment in which *all* nanotechnology products are treated with suspicion. Corporations that responsibly produce nanotechnology products have a stake in how other participants in the industry act because public perceptions can be very broad-brush and very hard to change once they crystallize.

WHY NEW LEGAL INSTITUTIONS ARE NEEDED TO ADDRESS THE UNCERTAIN RISKS OF NANOTECHNOLOGY

Both in the United States and Europe, the debate over the regulation of emerging technologies has been dominated by two models – a strong precautionary model, in which regulatory approval requires an affirmative showing of safety, and what might be called reactive regulation, in which safety or other studies or regulatory restrictions are mandated only on evidence of the substantiality of a health or environmental risk or actual harm. Neither the precautionary model nor the reactive will work well for nanotechnology, as the contributions by Kysar and Dana in this volume suggest. A new, "Third Way" model of regulation – a more flexible, adaptive, fluid model – is needed for the uncertain risks from nanotechnology. Precautionary regulation would be too slow and cumbersome given the current informational gaps regarding nanotechnology risk and risk assessment and the rapid speed of technological development of new generations of nanotechnology. Nor does there appear to be a strong enough political constituency for strongly precautionary regulation, and certainly not in the United States. Reactive regulation would only come into play too late (perhaps decades too late), when concrete harm may finally be identified and understood. However, by that time, almost nothing could be done to avoid future harms from exposures that had already occurred, and it might be impossible even to assure funding for compensation and repair of already damaged environments.

New legal institutions are required for regulating nanotechnology risks not only because of the limits of the prevailing precautionary/reactive models, but also because nanotechnology cuts across the conventional, organizing lines for regulation of environmental, health, and safety risks. Much regulation is organized around settings (e.g., workplaces) or product or substance types (e.g., new drugs), but nanotechnology involves many, many different settings and a wide range of different substances and products that traverse the usual jurisdictional lines that dictate the agendas of different domestic regulatory agencies.

Moreover, nanotechnology is an international phenomenon: it is produced and used throughout the world, with China emerging as a dominant producer. Because that is so, a cross-national or international regulatory approach – or at least degree of coordination – ultimately will be needed, but there are limited successful precedents for such an approach. At a minimum, we need to think hard about approaches that can work not just in the United States or just in the European Union (EU), but rather that make nanotechnology safer on a global scale.

In sum, the nanotech challenge – the challenge of uncertain risks – is well worth confronting, and it must be confronted with regulatory creativity and innovation. Regulatory solutions cannot be constricted by traditional categories or ways of thinking.

OUTLINE OF THIS VOLUME

This volume begins with the fundamental question – what is nanotechnology and what do we know and not know about risks from nanotechnology? In her contribution, Kimberly Gray argues against five propositions that have been invoked in support of the proposition that our current approach to nanotechnology development involves only negligible risk. She argues against the claims – or as she calls them, myths – that nanoparticles are safe because they are made out of common elements and that they will be unstable and hence ultimately innocuous in ambient environmental conditions. She also argues against another assumption in the public policy debate – that testing for safety will necessarily be very costly and time-consuming.

Addressing the risks of nanotechnology – however that is to be accomplished – will require understanding, trust, and the avoidance of unjustified fear on the part of the general public. Part II of this volume addresses the role of public perceptions. As the Druckman/Bolsen and Diermeier contributions underscore, public perceptions of new technology are often driven by the personal characteristics of the members of the public as much or more than by what is objectively understood or not understood about the technology. Read together, the essays by Druckman/Bolsen and Diermeier suggest that any solutions to the nanotechnology challenge may be constrained if they are delayed until after the public and activist groups develop hostility toward the uncertain risks associated with nanotechnology. Both essays suggest that once a public mindset and attitudes are established, the introduction of new factual information does not readily affect opinion regarding safety or lack of safety. The essays also suggest that any response to the nanotechnology challenge that relies heavily on public disclosure of risks and product labeling must pay careful attention to how lay people process – and sometimes incorrectly process – information regarding an unfamiliar technology such as nanotechnology.

The third and longest section of this volume is devoted to exploring a range of Third Way regulatory solutions to the problem of regulating nanotechnology despite the massive lack of information and hence uncertainties regarding what may and may not be the most problematic forms of nanotechnology and how best to address the most problematic types. The focus of all the essays, in one way or another, is on how we can change the current regulatory regime and incentive structure to encourage the production of more information regarding possible risks from nanotechnology. The essays reflect an awareness that regulatory solutions need to be broad-based, rather than targeted at particular products using nanotechnology, and that there needs to be mechanisms whereby accumulating information can be fed back into and used to improve the regulatory framework.

Dana's contribution on regulatory definitions addresses the question of how a regulatory definition of nanotechnology can take account of gaps in our understanding of risks and how it can keep pace with the extraordinary variety and rapid development of nanotechnology. In a separate chapter, Dana discusses the promise of liability relief as a means to encourage voluntary testing by producers of nanotechnology. Also focusing on creating incentives for private investment in and disclosure regarding safety research, Kysar advocates the use of mandatory environmental bonds for nanotechnology producers. Both Kysar and Wilson emphasize the need for regulation that ensures the creation of a pool of funds for compensation of people and communities that may be harmed from nanotechnology, assuming some harms cannot and will not be prevented.

Explicitly addressing the cross-national and international aspects of the nanotech challenge, Marchant et al. and Adler both argue that "softer," more purely voluntary measures that can form the basis for international coordination may be the best approach to the uncertain risks posed by nanotechnology. Marchant et al. emphasize how soft law approaches may lend themselves to effective international coordination of nanotechnology risks. Adler emphasizes standardized labeling practices that may be voluntarily adopted at first before later becoming mandatory. Both Marchant et al. and Adler acknowledge the limits of voluntary approaches, but both are also wary of heavy-handed regulatory mandates, which they view as likely to chill investment without necessarily increasing social welfare.

The essays by McGinnis and Lin consider very different approaches. McGinnis explores the use of prediction markets (where investors bet on the safety or non-safety of particular technologies) as a way of aggregating available information and guiding regulators facing uncertainty. McGinnis also emphasizes the need not to ignore uncertain *benefits* from nanotechnology as we seek to address uncertain risks from nanotechnology and the need to reconfigure the regulatory state to allow it to act with a speed that matches changes in technology. Lin's essay, unlike the others (with the possible exception of Dana's), does not focus so much on statutory, regulatory, and industry organizational-based reforms, but rather on the potential of courts using common law to address difficult problems when legal institutions cannot do so or require the common law's prompting.

The essays by Wilson and Zoloth take very different approaches to the question of new institutions for nanotechnology. Focusing intensely on one industry (cosmetics), Wilson documents the need for regulation and offers a vision of what that regulation should entail. Zoloth, by contrast, takes a broad view, placing nanotechnology in the context of the deep problem of scientific uncertainty generally and offers general principles that should guide our discussion of new legal institutions.

The last part of the volume brings us back to earth, as it were, analyzing in more detail than the previous chapters where we currently are in terms of the legal treatment of nanotechnology risks under U.S. and European law. O'Brian's chapter is important in offering the perspectives of a leading practitioner who actually counsels companies facing regulatory risks (O'Brian). Porter et al. survey the relevant laws and regulations in both the United States and EU, drawing on a massive research project. Both the O'Brian and Porter et al. chapters suggest that legal reforms on both sides of the Atlantic may be needed to effectively regulate risks from nanotechnology.

It bears note that none of the mechanisms or tools explored in these very different essays are mutually exclusive in any way. There is nothing inconsistent about mandatory testing, liability relief, bond requirements, prediction markets, and/or labeling requirements. They all offer possible advantages, as well as certain possible costs. In the end, the best regime for nanotechnology may blend many of these ideas. Voluntary labeling can exist alongside testing as a quid pro quo for liability relief, just as voluntary or mandatory labeling requirements can be accompanied by environmental bond or insurance requirements. The goals of all these approaches are fundamentally the same – the production of more and better information regarding risk, the use of more testing and monitoring, and the reasoned engagement of the public, all alongside the reaping of nanotechnology's many possible benefits.

As almost all the essays in this volume suggest, the nanotechnology challenge raises issues of relevance beyond the context of nanotechnology. Just as the problems addressed in this volume are not really altogether new and instead reflect the larger tension between protecting ourselves against the dangers of new technology and securing its benefits, the Third Way solutions suggested in this volume could be generalized to address the many risks from existing and new technologies *other than nanotechnology* where information also appears to be inadequately produced. Uncertain risks are characteristic of the nanotechnology challenge, but they are a reality beyond nanotechnology. Addressing nanotechnology responsibly may help us learn how to address the broad array of risks to human and environmental health and safety on our fast-changing planet.

2

Five Myths about Nanotechnology in the Current Public Policy Debate

A Science and Engineering Perspective

Kimberly A. Gray

INTRODUCTION

Global funding for nanotechnology was nearly $12 billion in 2006,[1] and investments in the nanotechnology industry approximately quadrupled from 2004 to 2006. In recent years, overly optimistic forecasters predicted that nanotechnology investments would reach $2.6 trillion by 2014. With the nanotechnology hype cooling a bit, more sober estimates place the global market for nanotechnology at $27 billion by 2013, the result of a compound annual growth rate of 16.4%.[2] These same, more realistic market assessments, however, project that over the next 5 years, electronic, biomedical, and consumer applications of nanotechnology will show very high growth rates between 30% and 60%. Currently with more than $50 billion in products ranging from pharmaceuticals and cosmetics to tools and electronics, we are seeing the transition of nanotechnology as it moves from the lab to the marketplace. According to a nanotechnology-based consumer product inventory conducted by the Project on Emerging Nanotechnologies, as of March 2011, there were 1,317 products produced by 1288 companies located in 30 counties.[3] The lion's share of these products (approximately 60%) fell under the heading of health and fitness and into the subcategories of personal care, clothing, and cosmetics.

This revolution in atomic and molecular engineering promises many environmental and human health benefits, such as dramatic improvements in efficiency, reduced resource use, diminished waste production, and astounding improvements in medical diagnostics and therapeutics. Yet, the risks posed by nanotechnology

[1] Lux Research. (2007). *5th Edition of the Nanotech Report*. http://www.luxresearchinc.com/tnr.php.

[2] A. McWilliams (2008). *Nanotechnology: A Realistic Market Assessment*. http://www.bccresearch.com/report/NAN031C.html.

[3] Anonymous (2009). *Nanotechnology Consumer Products Inventory – Consumer Products*, Woodrow Wilson International Center for Scholars. http://www.nanotechproject.org/inventories/consumer/

to ecological and environmental health have not been rigorously assessed in any organism, at the individual, community or ecosystem scale.[4] Without these data, a meaningful regulatory framework to both protect human and environmental health and safety from the unintended consequences of nanomaterial use and guide ongoing development of nanomaterials cannot be formulated.[5]

The defining characteristic of nanomaterials is their size (at least one dimension of ≤100 nm), which falls into a transitional zone between individual atoms and molecules, and bulk materials. Nanoparticles, a subset of nanomaterials, are defined as having at least two dimensions between 1 and 100 nm.[6] The small sizes, novel shapes, and high surface areas promote unusual and novel physicochemical properties to nanomaterials and make achievable nearly infinite possibilities for surface functionalization, targeted reactivity, and robust material development. The very features, however, that unlock fantastic opportunity for engineering, scientific, and medical applications may also pose serious threats to human health and ecosystem integrity.[7] At this time it is virtually impossible to make predictions about nanomaterials' environmental fate and impact. Subtle changes in size, shape, and surface functionality have profound effects on chemical and physical behavior. Furthermore, we lack the tools and protocols to screen and then interrogate systems at the mechanistic level and to determine dose effects rigorously. Without this basic understanding, we are unable not only to evaluate short-term effects associated with nanomaterial exposure, but also to anticipate unintended, longer term consequences to ecosystem structure and function.

Amidst all this uncertainty, however, we do have sufficient knowledge to rebut certain assumptions that have been invoked by regulators and commentators to avoid or defer considering the question of whether the risks from nanomaterials and nanotechnologies require a more thorough assessment. Based on the well-established

[4] P. J. A. Borm, et al., *The Potential Risks of Nanomaterials: A Review Carried Out for ECETOC*, 3 Particle and Fibre Toxicology (2006); P.J.A. Borm & D. Berube, *A Tale of Opportunities, Uncertainties and Risks*, 3 Nanotoday (2008); R. Chatterjee, *The Challenge of Regulating Nanomaterials*, 42 Environmental Science & Technology (2008); A. Helland, et al., *Reviewing the Environmental and Human Health Knowledge Base of Carbon Nanotubes*, 115 Environmental Health Perspectives (2007); N. Lubick, *Risks of Nanotechnology Remain Uncertain*, 42 Environmental Science & Technology (2008); Andre Nel, et al., *Toxic Potential of Materials at the Nanolevel*, 311 Science (2006).

[5] M. R. Wiesner & J. Y. Bottero, *Environmental Nanotechnology: Applications and Impacts of Nanomaterials*. (McGraw-Hill, 2007).

[6] S. J. Klaine, et al., *Nanomaterials in the Environment: Behavior, Fate, Bioavailability, and Effects*, 27 Environmental Toxicology and Chemistry (2008).

[7] Id.; A. D. Maynard, *Nanotechnology: Assessing the Risks*, 1 Nano Today (2006); D.G. Rickerby & M. Morrison, *Nanotechnology and the Environment: A European Perspective*, 8 Science and Technology of Advanced Materials (2007); M. R. Wiesner, et al., *Assessing the Risks of Manufactured Nanomaterials*, 40 ENVIRONMENTAL SCIENCE & TECHNOLOGY (2006).

scientific and engineering underpinnings of nanoscience, this essay explains and debunks five such misconceptions, or myths. These myths are:

(1) Overall, very small quantities of nanomaterials are needed to produce big effects, and because the Toxic Substances Control Act and other statutes employ a volume or weight threshold for regulation, nanomaterial use is typically in compliance.

(2) In many cases nanomaterials are not new materials; rather, they are only smaller versions of materials already in wide use and deemed safe.

(3) Because nanomaterials are derived from common materials, used in quantities well below harmful thresholds (as determined for common materials), and usually incorporated into products for human application, diffuse environmental and ecological hazards are negligible.

(4) Nanomaterials are not stable under ambient environmental conditions. In the improbable event of large environmental releases, nanomaterials will likely aggregate or become incorporated into larger particulate material, rendering them innocuous. This, coupled with the fact that nanomaterials are used in such small amounts, makes their long-term potential environmental impacts negligible.

(5) Health and safety testing for nanomaterials and nanotechnology products is extremely costly, requires long times, and in many cases is not even feasible. The costs, then, far exceed the risks of nanomaterials to human and ecological health and would quell innovation and diminish the valuable social and economic benefits of this emerging technology.

These mistaken notions persist because there is a fundamental misunderstanding about why materials at the nanoscale behave distinctively, bear unique physical properties, and are potentially many times more reactive than their larger counterparts. Furthermore, although there is a dearth of evidence indicating under what conditions nanomaterials are safe or harmful – the environmental fate, transport and impact of nanomaterials have received only cursory study, and most of this study has been at the mammalian cellular level, not at a system level – lessons from previous industrial revolutions warn us about the many unintended consequences to human health and environmental quality that often accompany rapid and unchecked technological "progress."[8] Products produced for human consumption will leak into their surroundings at various points in their life cycle (production, use, disposal) and over time can gradually accumulate to high levels, with major adverse consequences. We have experienced this time and time again with chemicals such as polychlorinated biphenyls (PCBs), tetraethyl lead, mercury, and combustion products such as

[8] A. D. Maynard, *Nanotechnology: The Next Big Thing, or Much Ado About Nothing?*, 51 Annals of Occupational Hygiene (2007).

dioxins and particulate material. There is no evidence to expect nanomaterials to exhibit markedly different fates.

Because nanomaterial structure can be modified and tweaked relatively rapidly, limits on those nanomaterials found to be dangerous may merely direct further development along a different trajectory in the relatively expeditious production of modified forms that perform similar functions with possibly fewer adverse health or environmental effects. In order for such self-correction to take place, however, screening and testing for deleterious health and environmental effects must be conducted concurrent to product research and development. The very dynamism of nanotechnology development that poses so many challenges for effective regulation may, ironically, also facilitate rapid adaptation and reveal alternative nanomaterial designs in response to regulatory constraints. This can only happen, however, if potential ill effects are recognized in the early stages of nanomaterial development. In this way, then, environmental health and safety regulations can serve to spur innovation and truly catalyze the unmitigated social benefits of new nanotechnologies.

This essay briefly discusses the defining characteristics of nanomaterials, nanotechnology, and nanotoxicity from the perspective of science and engineering to illustrate the flawed logic and inconsistent data on which the *five myths* are based. The toxicology of nanomaterials in various systems and at various scales is reviewed to illustrate the variability of results and the need to evaluate individually the toxic effects of well-characterized nanomaterials. Recent findings about nanomaterial environmental fate and transport are presented to reveal the errors in conventional assumptions and to underscore the need for developing methods to determine the bioavailability of nanomaterials in various ecological systems. Based on our current understanding of engineered nanomaterial behavior combined with historic knowledge of the environmental impacts associated with widely used engineered materials and the emissions of combustion products (e.g., ultrafine particles), strategies to evaluate, if not minimize, the human and ecological risks of nanotechnology are proposed.

BACKGROUND

What Are Nanomaterials?

There are a plethora of sources that provide general as well as highly specific definitions of nanomaterials (see, e.g., the Nanowerk and National Nanotechnology Initiative Web sites[9]). For instance, a Google search on "nanomaterials" yields 1,550,000 hits, and a refined search on "nanomaterials definition" produces 517,000

[9] Nanowerk, *Introduction to Nanotechnology* (2007), at http://www.nanowerk.com/nanotechnology/introduction/introduction_to_nanotechnology_1.php.; National Nanotechnology Initiative, http://www.nano.gov/html/facts/home_facts.html

hits. Simply stated, nanomaterials are defined by their dimensions, one of which must be less than 100 nm, whereas nanoparticles have at least two dimensions between 1 and 100 nm.[10] There are a billion nanometers in a meter. To provide some perspective on such a small scale, the ratio of a nanometer to a meter is the same as a marble to the earth; a 6-foot tall person is approximately 2 billion nanometers, and the diameter of a human hair is about 80,000 nanometers.[11]

Very common materials display startling new appearances and behaviors at the nanoscale and offer transformative applications. For example, at the nanoscale, metal oxides such as iron oxide or titanium dioxide do not scatter light and are transparent, which is attractive for use in cosmetics. In addition, as nanoparticles, these materials develop highly active catalytic properties allowing them to absorb light energy and convert it to chemical energy that can be used in chemical synthesis, pollutant degradation, and solar energy production.[12] Ordinary metals such as silver and gold (Au) undergo surprising changes in color, reactivity, and other fundamental properties (e.g., conductivity, melting point) as their size is diminished to nanometer dimensions. For instance, depending on its exact nanodimensions, gold is no longer shiny and golden in color, but can appear red, blue, or yellow.[13] Nanogold is not even metallic in nature, will not conduct electricity as bulk gold does, and exhibits a trend of dramatically decreasing melting temperature with decreasing size in the nano-range. Furthermore, gold in its bulk state is highly stable, essentially inert, and does not tarnish. In contrast, when gold particles are 3–5 nm in size they are highly reactive and are promising catalysts for oxidation reactions such as the conversion of CO to CO_2, which is an important step in three-way catalytic converters for

10 ASTM (2006), Standard terminology relating to nanotechnology, West Conshohocken, PA, American Society for Testing and Materials, E 2456–06.

11 T.K. Altes, *Is Nano a No-No? Nanotechnology Advances Into Buildings* (2008), at http://www.enn.com/green_building/commentary/32429.

12 H. D. Muller & F. Steinbach, *Decomposition of Isopropyl Alcohol Photosensitized by Zinc Oxide*, 225 Nature (1970); A. Duret & M. Gratzel, *Visible Light-Induced Water Oxidation on Mesoscopic Alpha-Fe2O3 Films Made by Ultrasonic Spray Pyrolysis*, 109 Journal of Physical Chemistry B (2005). A. Fujishima & X. T. Zhang, *Titanium Dioxide Photocatalysis: Present Situation and Future Approaches*, 9 Comptes Rendus Chimie (2006); X. Chen & S. S. Mao, *Titanium Dioxide Nanomaterials: Synthesis, Properties, Modifications, and Applications*, 107 Chemical Reviews (2007); F. Lu, et al., *ZnO Hierarchical Micro/Nanoarchitectures: Solvothermal Synthesis and Structurally Enhanced Photocatalytic Performance*, 18 Advanced Functional Materials (2008). M. D. Hernandez-Alonso, et al., *Development of Alternative Photocatalysts to TiO2: Challenges and Opportunities*, 2, Energy & Environmental Science (2009). J. H. Mo, et al., *Photocatalytic Purification of Volatile Organic Compounds in Indoor Air: A literature Review*, 43 Atmospheric Environment (2009). M. H. Lai, et al., *ZnO-Nanorod Dye-Sensitized Solar Cells: New Structure Without a Transparent Conducting Oxide Layer*, International Journal of Photoenergy (2010). L. L. Peng, et al., *Synthesis, Photoelectric Properties and Photocatalytic Activity of the Fe2O3/TiO2 Heterogeneous Photocatalysts*, 12 Physical Chemistry Chemical Physics (2010). S. C. Roy, et al., *Toward Solar Fuels: Photocatalytic Conversion of Carbon Dioxide to Hydrocarbons*, 4 ACS Nano (2010). Y. Tian, et al., *Core-Shell Nanostructure of Alpha-Fe2O3/Fe3O4: Synthesis and Photocatalysis for Methyl Orange*, Journal of Nanomaterials (2011).

13 E. Roduner, *Size Matters: Why Nanomaterials Are Different*, 35 Chemical Society Reviews (2006).

controlling automotive exhaust and also has use in protective masks for firefighters.[14] Yet, outside this narrow size range, nano-Au is catalytically inactive.

According to a 2011 inventory conducted by the Project on Emerging Nanotechnologies at the Woodrow Wilson International Center for Scholars, the most common nanomaterial in commercial products is silver (55%), followed more distantly by carbon (16%) and titanium (8% – mostly in the form of TiO_2).[15] In the simplest cases, then, and for most of those in commercial use, nanomaterials often bear the same chemical composition as their bulk counterparts. If nano- and bulk materials share the same basic building blocks, their atoms, then can we regard nanomaterials to be truly distinct from their larger sized counterparts? If it is merely size that distinguishes nanomaterials, then are they, in fact, novel materials that necessitate new regulatory attention? Let's consider a striking example of how different materials with the same chemical composition can be by comparing graphite and diamonds. Both materials are made up of carbon, but the arrangement of the carbon differs, producing materials as contrasting as day and night with respect to their color and structural characteristics. Graphite and diamonds, both allotropes of carbon, have grossly different chemical and physical properties and have extremely disparate uses. Let's look more closely at graphite, in which the carbon atoms are typically bonded in an interconnected hexagonal pattern to make up a sheet, called graphene, that is then stacked in layers. Variation in the stacking can alter some properties. If you now peel away a single sheet of graphene (a single layer of carbon atoms arranged in a pattern of hexagons – imagine one-atom thick chicken wire) and roll it up, you would have a carbon nanotube (CNT), yet another allotrope of carbon and probably the most iconic example of a nanomaterial. Because no other element in the periodic table bonds to itself in an extended network with the strength of the C-C bond, it follows that CNTs show incredible strength and stiffness, but they also have very good electrical and thermal conductivity and are highly adsorbent. These novel properties open many possibilities for use in electronics, optics, medicine, aerospace, and architecture. In the case of graphite and CNTs, the size and shape of the atoms' arrangement in the material, not the atoms themselves, make these materials appear, behave, and perform differently. Nanomaterials, then, are new materials because the novel *physical* details of their structure (their size, shape, surface area, bonding structure, etc.), rather than their *chemical* composition, impart new properties and behaviors and hence a multitude of fantastic applications.

So now we come to the question regarding why atoms and molecules, assembled into nanoscale structures, evolve such distinct and extraordinary characteristics. The principles of quantum physics explain that the properties of bulk materials are the average of all the quantum forces affecting all the atoms making up the material,

14 Lehigh University, *Nanogold Does Not Glitter, But Its Future Looks Bright*, Science Daily (2004), at http://www.sciencedaily.com/releases/2004/04/040428062059.htm.

15 Anonymous, *Nanotechnology Consumer Products Inventory – Analysis*, Woodrow Wilson International Center for Scholars (2009), at http://www.nanotechproject.org/inventories/consumer/analysis_draft/.

but this averaging breaks down as particle size and the number of atoms making up the particles are diminished.[16] Two important effects emerge when material size is reduced to nanoscale proportions:

1. Surface area effect – the surface area of a given mass of nanoparticles is hundreds of times greater than that of the same mass of larger (> micrometer scale) particles, and hence many more of the atoms making up the particle are located at the surface.
2. Quantum effect – at the nano-scale, the bonding among atoms is different, as are the energy levels of shared orbitals, producing changes in optical, electrical, magnetic, thermal, mechanical, and chemical properties.

Let's consider surface area effects first. Imagine that we have a beaker containing a suspension of particles, which have a diameter of 2 μm and a mass concentration of 10 $\mu g/m^3$. In a second beaker we have another suspension of particles with a much smaller diameter of 20 nm, but the same mass concentration of 10 $\mu g/m^3$. Let's assume that the particles are spheres and have a density of 1 (1 g/mL). In the case of the larger particles, there would only be 2.4 particles per milliliter of suspension, which corresponds to a surface area of 30 μm^2/mL. In the case of the nanoparticles at the same mass concentration, there would be a million more particles in each milliliter of the suspension (2.4×10^6 particles/mL) with a 100 times greater surface area (3,016 μm^2/mL). Let's say that each beaker contained 1 L of the particle suspension. For the larger particles, then, there would be a total of 2,400 particles with a total surface area of 30,000 μm^2. In contrast, in the beaker of small particles, there would be 2,400,000,000 particles with a total surface area of 3,016,000 μm^2. This comparison illustrates that the same mass of material takes on dramatically different physical features depending on material size, and as we take bulk material to the nanoscale, the number and surface area concentrations skyrocket.

The significance of the surface area effect is both quantitative and qualitative. It is possible to calculate the total number of atoms at the surface with a function, called the *dispersion*, *F*, that scales with size, specifically the surface area divided by volume, or the inverse of the radius. Yet the surface area effect also includes the fact that atoms at the surface of a material are different from those inside the material. The reason for this is that surface atoms have fewer *nearest neighbors*. The electron and orbital geometry of an atom determines the number of bonds it wants to form with its neighbors, which is reflected in a characteristic called the *coordination number*. The coordination requirement of bulk or interior atoms is typically satisfied, meaning that in comparison to surface atoms, bulk atoms are more highly coordinated, form more bonds, and are more stable.[17] At the surface,

[16] Nanowerk.
[17] Roduner.

atoms are under-coordinated and thus display a drive to form bonds to satisfy their coordination requirements (number). Surface atoms tend to be sites of adsorption and chemical reactivity because of their under-coordination and lowered stability. Another consequence of nanomaterials having a higher proportion of atoms at the surface is that they may melt at lower temperatures. Phase transitions, in general, are collective phenomena, and as the number of atoms in a nanocluster is reduced, phase transitions become less well-defined, reflecting more molecular than bulk behavior.[18] Fundamentally, then, a much higher proportion of under-coordinated, less stable, and hence more reactive surface atoms relative to fully coordinated and stable interior atoms accounts for the surface area effect of nanomaterials.

Now, let's turn to quantum effects, which are also related to bonding patterns among atoms or, to put it another way, how electrons are arranged and shared between atoms and molecules in a material. Atoms are defined by the number and ways in which electrons are packaged in their atomic orbitals or electronic shells. Atoms have a discrete set of energy levels (atomic orbitals, shells, or states) at which their electrons are located. Some energy levels are allowed and others are not. The core orbitals occupy a small volume and are localized, but outer orbitals are the ones that are involved in exchanging or sharing electrons with other atoms. If the outer orbitals or shells are completely full, then an atom shows little tendency to participate in chemical reactions and is very stable. Noble gases such as helium, neon, and argon are examples of atoms with exceedingly low reactivity, whose atomic structure is very stable and remains relatively unperturbed when combined together.

In contrast, when a large number of atoms are brought together to form a solid material, the electronic structure of the bulk is a hybrid of all the atoms making it up. The core orbitals of the atoms are unchanged and remain confined or localized, but the outer shells mix or contribute to shared energy states or "bands." These bands are energy levels at which electrons can reside, and each atom of the bulk material contributes its atomic orbitals or states to a band (Fig. 2.1). Thus the width of these energy bands or the "density of states" is a function of how many atoms are added to the material. As a material grows in size, the atomic states of its atoms combine to define a pattern (band structure) of possible energy levels that can be occupied by outer shell electrons (the electrons that are involved in chemical bonds and reactions). As the number of atoms increases to create bulk materials, the density of states at a specific energy level also increases to a point that the energy difference between the bands becomes very small, creating a continuum of energy levels. In other words, as illustrated in Figure 2.1, the discrete nature of atomic energy levels, or states, that characterizes individual atoms transitions to broader energy levels and finally to continuous bands of energy as the number of atoms, and with them, the number of orbitals, contributing to an energy band becomes

[18] Id.

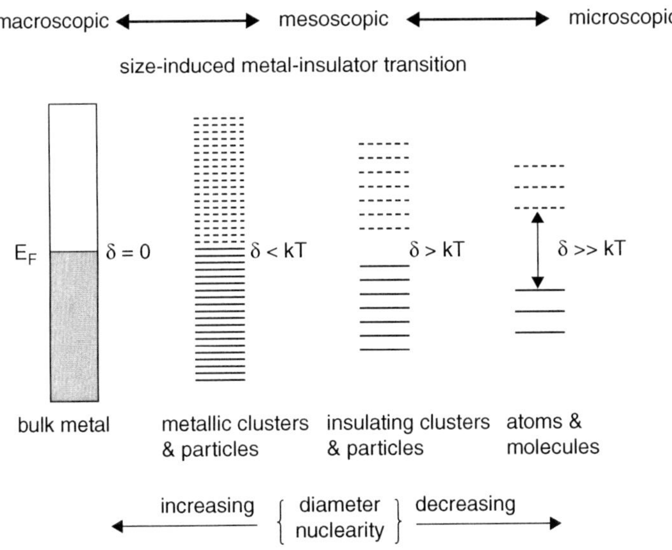

FIGURE 2.1. Effect of atom number and particle size on band structure and density of states. Source: Roduner.

exceedingly large ($>10^{20}$).[19] Why is all this important? Because the band structure of a material determines its electronic, thermal, and optical properties, and the continuum of states created in bulk metals explains their excellent electrical and thermal conductivity.

Because we now have a rudimentary understanding of how increasing the number of atoms alters the band or electronic structure of a solid material, let's consider what happens as we decrease the number of atoms and size of the material. As we reduce the number of atoms, we reduce the density of states in each energy band, which, in effect, narrows the bands and reintroduces a discrete nature to these energy levels (Fig. 2.1).[20] As a consequence of the re-emergence of the discrete band structure, the energy difference between the bands increases with decreasing size. In the case of nanogold, this phenomenon explains the fact that bulk gold is a metal (continuous band structure with delocalized electrons), but at the nanoscale, gold loses its metallic character and becomes a semiconductor, meaning that the band structure tends to take on more atomic-like character with distinct energy levels, a region not populated with allowed energy levels (the band gap), and no delocalized electrons. In order to create mobile charges, it is necessary to excite the electrons

[19] N.W. Ashcroft, Mermin, N.D., Solid State Physics (New York: Holt, Rinehart and Winston, 1976). R. Hoffmann, *How Chemistry and Physics Meet in the Solid-State*, 26 Angewandte Chemie-International Edition in English (1987).

[20] Roduner; P.P. Edwards, et al., *On the Size-Induced Metal-Insulator Transition in Clusters and Small Particles*, in Metal Clusters in Chemistry (P. Braunstien, et al., Eds., Chichester, NY: Wiley-VCH, 1999).

with energy greater than the band gap energy. In fact, by adjusting particle size, it is possible to tune the band gap of a nanoparticle to a particular energy and to visualize the effect by the resulting fluorescence,[21] which produces different color light depending on size (e.g., a smaller particle with a larger band gap may fluoresce blue, whereas a larger nanoparticle with smaller band gap may fluoresce red). When the band gap becomes very large (more atomic-like), the material becomes an insulator. Unlike surface area effects, quantum effects are not smoothly scalable over all particle or cluster sizes. Rather, quantum effects can show discontinuous behavior due to the way electrons fill the discrete band structure of small clusters. With reference to gold again, this explains the fact that there is a narrow size range (3–5 nm) where gold is catalytically reactive, and outside this region, it is essentially inert.

The combined effects of the arrangement, bonding, and energy states of atoms at the nanoscale, then, define the unique nature of nanomaterials. Yet size alone does not account for the transformative and highly tunable properties of nanoscale materials. Novel attributes can also be tailored by varying the shape of nanomaterials or by "decorating" the surface with various types of chemical compounds or functional groups. For instance, it is possible to synthesize a wide variety of nanostructures for ZnO, as shown in Figure 2.2. Nanohelixes, nanoribbons, nanorings, nanowires, nanocages, and nanopropellers of ZnO can be sculpted using a solid-state thermal sublimation process and by controlling the growth kinetics, local growth temperature, and the chemical composition of the source materials.[22] These unique structures support a plethora of novel applications in optoelectronics, sensors, transducers, and biomedical science. Other examples of the power of coupling size and shape are found in cubic, pyramidal, diamond shapes, which can be highly reactive, because corner and edge atoms are even more unsaturated or under-coordinated than simple surface atoms. Corner atoms exhibit the highest affinity to form bonds to adsorbing molecules.[23] For instance, gold and silver nanoparticles can be prepared with triangular, rod-like, or cubic morphologies to special advantage for biodiagnostic, nanotherapeutic, and materials applications.[24] Researchers have probed the architectural effects of such TiO_2 shapes as cubes, rod, stars, petals, and pyramids with the ultimate aim of optimizing the reactivity of photogenerated charges to direct the assembly of a particular shape into organized nanostructures for use in solar cells.[25]

[21] Fluorescence is the emission of light by a substance that has absorbed light or other electromagnetic radiation of a different wavelength. In most cases, emitted light has a longer wavelength, and therefore lower energy, than the absorbed radiation.

[22] Z. L. Wang, *Nanostructures of Zinc Oxide*, 7 Materials Today (2004).

[23] Roduner.

[24] R. C. Jin, et al., *Photoinduced Conversion of Silver Nanospheres to Nanoprisms*, 294 Science (2001); J. E. Millstone, et al., *Observation of a Quadrupole Plasmon Mode for a Colloidal Solution of Gold Nanoprisms*, 127 Journal of the American Chemical Society (2005).

[25] N. M. Dimitrijevic, et al., *Effect of Size and Shape of Nanocrystalline TiO2 on Photogenerated Charges. An EPR Study*, 111 Journal of Physical Chemistry C (2007).

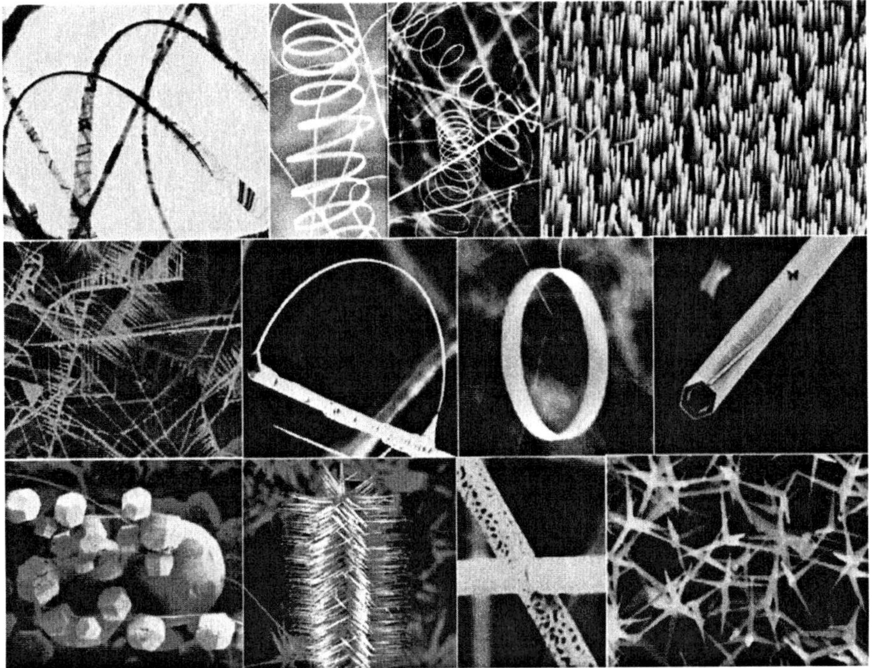

FIGURE 2.2. Examples of the diverse nanostructures synthesized for ZnO. Source: Wang.

Beyond size and shape, there are infinite possibilities created by introducing subtle surface modification or functionalization that allows fine tailoring of both the structure and function of nanomaterials. For instance, biomedical gold nanoparticles stabilized with certain biochemicals (surfactant ligands and specific proteins) show little ability to cross a cell membrane, but when functionalized with oligonucleotides (DNA fragments), they freely cross the cell membranes of more than 15 different cell lines and localize in the interior of the cell or the cytoplasm (the part of a cell enclosed by the cell membrane where most of the cellular activity takes place).[26] Another example is found in the rapidly emerging and expanding field of nanomedicine, which is probably best symbolized by functionalized fullerenes (C_{60}), the hollow nanospheres or soccer-ball shapes of carbon often referred to as "buckyballs." The fullerene structure provides a platform for attaching molecules that then give the nanoassembly a particular and precise purpose, such as targeted drug or gene delivery. In this way functionalized fullerenes are being adapted to a

[26] N. L. Rosi, et al., *Oligonucleotide-Modified Gold Nanoparticles for Intracellular Gene Regulation*, 312 Science (2006); D. A. Giljohann, et al., *Oligonucleotide Loading Determines Cellular Uptake of DNA-Modified Gold Nanoparticles*, 7 Nano Letters (2007); D. S. Seferos, et al., *Locked Nucleic Acid-Nanoparticle Conjugates*, 8 Chembiochem (2007).

wide range of biomedical applications in diagnostic imaging, radiation protection, cancer therapy, and photodynamic therapy.[27]

There are three classes of nanomaterials: natural, incidental, and engineered. Naturally occurring nanomaterials play a critical role in the biogeochemical cycles of earth's materials and have been extensively studied since the early days of earth science and chemistry, hundreds of years ago. For instance, iron, the fourth most common element on earth, exists naturally as nanoparticles in lakes, rivers, ground waters, and soils in the course of weathering, which is the natural cycle of reduction, dissolution, oxidation, and precipitation occurring due to seasonal and other environmental influences. The early study of nanomaterials was referred to as colloidal and interface science, and in this context, nanoparticles were traditionally labeled *colloids*. Many of the scientific connections between this field and modern nanotechnology are discussed by Hans Lyklema in his classic book, *Fundamentals of Interface and Colloid Science*.[28] Incidental nanomaterials are created unintentionally as a result of phenomena such as combustion or material degradation. This, too, is a well-studied area, and much of what we know about the real and potential health effects of nanomaterials comes from the study of the effects of air pollution, particularly the effects of the small particles released by coal-fired power plants and automobiles.[29] The rusting of iron from human-built objects releases nanoparticles in the same way that the weathering of iron-bearing rock does. The vibrant colors of medieval stained glass are the results of artisans of the Middle Ages mixing metallic powders of gold, silver, or copper into molten glass to create tiny metal spheres, which absorb and reflect sunlight in a way that produces rich colors. In contrast to natural and incidental nanomaterials, engineered nanomaterials denote the growing commercial volumes of *controlled* and *uniform* nanostructures that are the products of intentional human design. It is this synthetic control and structural uniformity that not only distinguishes engineered nanomaterials from natural or incidental nanomaterials, but also poses far greater potential threats to human and ecological health.

What Is Nanotechnology?

A practical and general definition of nanotechnology is the following:

> Nanotechnology is the design, characterization, production and application of structures, devices and systems by controlled manipulation of size and shape at the

27 R. Partha & J. L. Conyers, *Biomedical Applications of Functionalized Fullerene-Based Nanomaterials*, 4 International Journal of Nanomedicine (2009).

28 H. Lyklema, *Fundamentals of Interface and Colloid Science* (Philadelphia: Elsevier, 1991).

29 K. Donaldson, et al., *Combustion-Derived Nanoparticles: A Review of Their Toxicology Following Inhalation Exposure*, 2 Particle and Fibre Toxicology 10 (2005). G. Oberdorster, et al., *Nanotoxicology: An Emerging Discipline Evolving From Studies of Ultrafine Particles*, 113 Environmental Health Perspectives (2005).

nanometer scale (atomic, molecular and macromoleculars scales) that produces structures, devices and systems with at least one novel or superior characteristic or property.[30]

Nanotechnology, then, is the ability to arrange atoms and molecules with a level of precision that produces materials and processes that either improve the performance of an existing product or process (e.g., lighter, stronger, more efficient; transparent sunscreens or coatings) or create an entirely new product (e.g., targeted drug delivery, diagnostics, light-emitting diode [LED] lighting). This *nano-construction* can be achieved by both top-down and bottom-up techniques. Some nanostructures are created via the top-down approach by whittling away at larger pieces of material, such as in the case of etching circuits on microchip surfaces or synthesizing certain types of nanotubes. However, it is important to emphasize that this practice is not simply another step in the miniaturization of materials because, as discussed previously, the material takes on entirely new sets of properties at the nanoscale. More and more often, nanotechnology involves bottom-up approaches to the atomic and molecular engineering of new materials. For instance, there are some nanomaterials that self-assemble based on the natural affinity of their atoms or molecules to organize themselves into nano-structures. Nanocrystals of metals and metal oxides are synthesized in this way in the semiconductor or catalysis industry. Positional assembly is an emerging method of targeted control of atomic or molecular arrangement, but is not yet commercial. Although it may sound fanciful now, we could imagine that sometime in the future, molecular robots may be able to transport molecular pieces into a desired position relative to other atomic or molecular features.[31]

As discussed previously, nanoparticles are abundant in nature and are produced by a diverse array of natural processes such as photochemical reactions, volcanic eruptions, forest fires, erosion, biological metabolism, cellular aging, etc.[32] In fact, naturally occurring atmospheric nanoparticles (e.g., aerosols) play an important role in the energy balance of the earth as they absorb and scatter solar radiation. Depending on their size and composition, atmospheric nanoparticles can have either cooling (e.g., atmospheric sulfate nanoparticles) or warming (e.g., soot and carbon black) effects on the earth's climate.[33] Nanotechnology, however, refers only to nanomaterials and nanoparticles that are human made; otherwise it would require the redefinition of much of chemistry, earth science, and molecular biology. Yet, there is certainly an intersection between the natural and human cycles of nanomaterials, and many developments in nanotechnology take inspiration from nature. For instance, the growing interest in geoengineering solutions to global climate change by introducing human-made atmospheric nanoparticles that exert

30 NANOWERK.

31 TECHTARGET, *Nanotechnology* (2011), at http://whatis.techtarget.com/definition/0,sid9_gci213444,00.html.

32 C. BUZEA, et al., *Nanomaterials and nanoparticles: Sources and Toxicity*, 2 BIOINTERPHASES (2007).

33 P. R. BUSECK & K. ADACHI, *Nanoparticles in the Atmosphere*, 4 ELEMENTS (2008).

cooling effects is based on our understanding and ability to predict, as well as mimic, the effects of natural nanoparticles on the earth's climate. Finally, there is another condition that defines present-day nanotechnology. Although humans have exploited nanotechnological phenomena inadvertently for thousands of years in the making of steel or art, these examples of the nanoscale assembly of atoms and molecules were governed by the stochastic or random processing of materials. In contrast, the modern age of nanotechnology is evolving along a deterministic trajectory of directed and uniform synthesis that is informed by an understanding of nanoscale properties and realized by sophisticated tools and techniques to fabricate, characterize, and test them.

One of the most celebrated early visions of modern nanotechnology came from physicist Richard Feynman, who gave a talk on December 29, 1950, to the American Physical Society meeting at Caltech. In his famous address, "There's Plenty of Room at the Bottom – An Invitation to Enter a New Field of Physics," Feynman mused about what could be achieved if we were able to manipulate atoms:

> When we get to the very, very small world – say circuits of seven atoms – we have a lot of new things that would happen that represent completely new opportunities for design. Atoms on a small scale behave like nothing on a large scale, for they satisfy the laws of quantum mechanics. So, as we go down and fiddle around with the atoms down there, we are working with different laws, and we can expect to do different things. We can manufacture in different ways.[34]

Feynman talked about how nanotechnology would allow us to mass produce devices that were perfect replicates, how medical diagnostics and treatment would be revolutionized, and how computers could become smaller, faster, and more powerful. Although he acknowledged the challenges of *scaling down*, because the forces and interactions between atoms and molecules become different at the nanoscale, the principles of physics did not limit the ability to manipulate atoms; rather, he recognized that the limits were the tools to maneuver the atoms or molecules.

Nowhere has the drive to scale down been more dramatic than in the field of electronics. In the mid-1960s, Gordon Moore, one of the founders of Intel, predicted that the number of transistors that could be fit in a given area would double every 18 months for the next 10 years. This prediction, known as Moore's Law, has continued at an astounding pace to far exceed what was originally envisioned by Moore and to produce one of the centerpiece achievements of nanotechnology, nanometer-scale circuitry, which, as Feynman imagined, is smaller, faster, cheaper, and ever more powerful.

What truly distinguishes modern nanotechnology from decades-old abilities to synthesize polymers or create tiny features on computer chips, then, is the ability

[34] R. P. Feynman, *There's Plenty of Room at the Bottom: An Invitation to Enter a New Field of Physics*, CalTech's Engineeering and Science (1960).

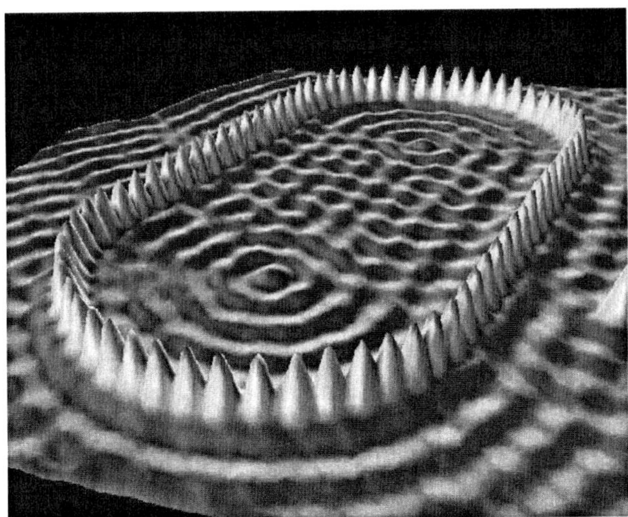

FIGURE 2.3. Electron corrals – iron on copper. Source: http://www.almaden.ibm.com/vis/stm/corral.html.

to image and control these features. Nanotechnology pivots as much on the mechanisms and tools of material design and characterization as it does on the actual production and application of nanomaterials. Modern nanotechnology is all about *knowing* and *controlling* material structure to produce uniform features and targeted effects. Nanotechnology was made possible by the development of tools to image materials at the nano-scale and to determine where atoms and molecules are relative to one another, allowing scientists to relate nanomaterial fabrication to their structure and function.

In 1981, the scanning tunneling microscope (STM) was invented, followed by the atomic force microscope (AFM) 4 years later. The STM, a type of electron microscope, revolutionized the ability to explore, and manipulate, solid surfaces on the size scale of the atom, and its inventors, Gerd Binnig and Heinrich Rohrer of IBM Research in Zürich, were awarded the Nobel Prize in Physics in 1986. STM creates three-dimensional images of a sample by using a stylus, essentially a pointed electrode, to scan over a conducting surface at a fixed distance from it. Extraordinary resolution, anywhere from one tenth to one hundredth of a nanometer, of the surface can be achieved. STMs allow scientists to look at and touch atoms. Researchers have also been able to move atoms around and to selectively break bonds. The topographical image shown in Figure 2.3[35] was created by scientists at IBM who positioned individual iron atoms to build "electron corrals" on a copper surface and to probe the behavior of electrons on these surface structures.[36] AFM

35 http://www.almaden.ibm.com/vis/stm/corral.html.

36 M.F. CROMMIE, et al., *Confinement of Electrons to Quantum Corrals on a Metal Surface*, 262 SCIENCE (1993).

is also a type of scanning probe microscopy that "feels" surfaces with very high resolution (fraction of a nanometer). It was developed to overcome the limitation of STM that required surfaces to be conducting or semiconducting. AFM can image almost any type of surface, including polymers, ceramics, glass, composites, and biological samples.

The tools of nanotechnology, among which various forms of scanning probe microscopy play a prominent role, make possible the fabrication of novel materials possessing nanoscale dimensions in one, two, and three dimensions. Thin films, surface monolayers (one atom or molecule thick surface coating), and engineered surfaces are examples of one-dimensional nanomaterials. These types of materials have been used for decades, but control of their growth and expansion of their use continue to undergo incremental improvements. The main uses of these thin films and surface coatings are in electronic semiconducting devices (integrated circuits, transistors, batteries), optical coatings, and lubricants. For instance, by coating cutting tools or other abrasive surfaces, strength and hardness are enhanced, whereas corrosion and wear are reduced. Because thin film nanostructures can be prepared with extraordinarily high surface areas, they are finding many new applications in dye-sensitized solar cells and fuel cells and, as catalysts, particularly for the synthesis of chemicals and pharmaceuticals.[37]

Two-dimensional nanostructures are best exemplified by nanotubes and nano wires, which have generated great excitement and interest because of their novel electrical and mechanical properties. Carbon nanotubes (CNTs) were discovered in 1991 by Japanese researcher Sumio Iijima and are tubes created by rolling sheets of graphene that have diameters of only a few nanometers and lengths of several millimeters, although recently CNTs of centimeter lengths have been achieved, typically producing aspect ratios (length:diameter) in the range 1,000–100,000. There are single-walled CNTs (one tube) and multi-walled CNTs (several nested, concentric tubes). In general, CNTs display surprising mechanical strength, which, when coupled with their extremely large aspect ratios, create enormously strong and light fibers that are finding a range of applications in reinforced composites, particularly in the construction[38] and transportation industry. Other properties, such as metallic (conducting) versus semiconducting, are a function of the manner in which CNTs

[37] S. M. Paek, et al., *Nanostructured TiO2 Films for Dye-Sensitized Solar Cells*, 67 Journal of Physics and Chemistry of Solids (2006). L. Chen, et al., *Fabricating Highly Active Mixed Phase TiO2 Photocatalysts by Reactive DC Magnetron Sputter Deposition*, 515 Thin Solid Films (2006); L. Chen, et al., *Photoreduction of CO2 by TiO2 Nanocomposites Synthesized Through Reactive Direct Current Magnetron Sputter Deposition*, 517 Thin Solid Films (2009); A. Ignatiev, et al., *Nanostructured Thin Solid Oxide Fuel Cells With High Power Density*, Dalton Transactions (2008); K. H. Yu & J. H. Chen, *Enhancing Solar Cell Efficiencies Through 1-D Nanostructures*, 4 Nanoscale Research Letters (2009).

[38] J. Lee, et al., *Nanomaterials in the Construction Industry: A Review of Their Applications and Environmental Health and Safety Considerations*, 4 ACS Nano (2010).

are rolled (chirality) and their size. Although limited quantities have been produced, commercial production of CNTs is growing, as is their incorporation into a wide range of electronic applications. The ability to tune CNT size and uniformity, and thereby select for certain physical properties, is becoming commercially feasible. Nanotube structures can also be synthesized from other inorganic materials, such as metal oxides. For instance, titania nanotubes can be made by a variety of methods and show potential for use as photocatalysts, in energy storage, for adsorption, and as sensors.[39] Nanowires can be self-assembled from a variety of materials (metallic, semiconducting, insulating, organic, biopolymeric) and composed of ultrafine wires or linear arrays of dots with aspect ratios greater than 1,000. Semiconductor nanowires have displayed amazing optical, electronic, and magnetic characteristics, as illustrated, for instance, by the ability of silica nanowires to bend light around very tight corners. Nanowires are potentially useful in high-density storage and may one day link nanocomponents to create tiny circuits.[40]

Nanoparticles comprise the broad class of three-dimensional nanomaterials. The definition of nanoparticles varies a bit from particles having a diameter less than 100 nm and exhibiting new properties relative to larger size materials to particles having two dimensions in the 1–100 nm range. As mentioned previously, nanoparticles can exist in a variety of discrete shapes or in clusters, such as dendrimers, which are roughly spherical, self-assembled polymeric molecules. Quantum dots, which are semiconductor particles 2–10 nm in diameter that exhibit electron (exciton) confinement in all three dimensions, display highly tunable electronic and optical behavior as a function of their size, which is being exploited in transistors, solar cells, lasers, LED lights, and medical imaging. The majority of nanoparticulate mass exists in nature or is produced inadvertently (incidental nanomaterial), as discussed previously. Although, in comparison, engineered nanoparticles are much less in quantity at the present time, the combination of their uniformity and future forecasted projections of growth is likely to exert far greater effects, either intended or unintended. In general, nanoparticles are currently added to cosmetics, textiles, and paints to improve the performance of established products. Emerging uses are

39 H. H. Ou & S. L. Lo, *Review of Titania Nanotubes Synthesized Via the Hydrothermal Treatment: Fabrication, Modification, and Application*, 58 Separation and Purification Technology (2007). S. Rani, et al., *Synthesis and Applications of Electrochemically Self-Assembled Titania Nanotube Arrays*, 12 Physical Chemistry Chemical Physics (2010). K. L. Schulte, et al., *Effect of Crystal Phase Composition on the Reductive and Oxidative Abilities of TiO2 Nanotubes Under UV and Visible Light*, 97 Applied Catalysis B-Environmental (2010); B. Vijayan, et al., *Effect of Calcination Temperature on the Photocatalytic Reduction and Oxidation Processes of Hydrothermally Synthesized Titania Nanotubes*, 114 Journal of Physical Chemistry C (2010); B. K. Vijayan, et al., *The Effects of Pt Doping on the Structure and Visible Light Photoactivity of Titania Nanotubes*, 114 Journal of Physical Chemistry C (2010).

40 Nanowerk.

targeted drug delivery and catalysts, where nanoparticles can be arranged to achieve very high surface areas and hence reactivity.[41]

Carbon 60 (C_{60}) is the quintessential nanoparticle. Although it was predicted to exist decades before, this new allotrope of carbon was physically discovered in 1985, and in 1995 Harold Kroto, Robert Curl, and Richard Smalley received the Nobel Prize in Chemistry. C_{60} is a closed-cage structure of 60 carbon atoms bonded to create 20 hexagons and 12 pentagons and arranged in the shape of a soccer ball. C_{60} structures were dubbed "buckminsterfullerenes" after Richard Buckminster Fuller of geodesic dome fame, but they are often simply referred to as "buckyballs" or "fullerenes." Fullerenes can be hollow spheres, ellipsoids, or tubes (CNTs) of varying amounts of carbon (e.g., C_{70}, C_{76}, C_{84}, C_{100}). Minute quantities of fullerenes are found in nature as residues in soot from fires or lightning strikes,[42] but this "soot" can be synthesized in larger quantities by sending a large current between two closely stationed graphite electrodes in an inert atmosphere, such as helium, to create a carbon plasma that cools into a sooty residue from which fullerenes can be isolated. Fullerenes have mesmerized scientists for decades and have been intensely researched. Commercial applications, however, have been slow to materialize. One limitation of fullerenes is that they are only sparingly soluble in many solvents, although this can be alleviated somewhat by functionalizing the surface with various chemical groups. Some of the more promising potential applications are in electronic circuits, as tiny ball bearings to lubricate surfaces, and as drug delivery vehicles.

In 2004, more than 2,000 tons of engineered nanomaterials were produced, and the rate of production is expected to rise to greater than 50,000 tons over the next decade.[43] Although the nanotechnology *revolution* has been hailed as the next "general purpose technology" that will have effects on society similar to electricity or communication technologies, in many cases it is more an *evolution* in the gradual improvement of almost all material production, technology performance, and industrial process and, as such, is not a singular innovation as the term *nanotechnology* implies.[44] Given the scale and widespread commercialization of nanomaterials, there is growing concern about the potential and unanticipated consequences of

41 Partha & Conyers. G. H. Li & K. A. Gray, *The Solid-Solid Interface: Explaining the High and Unique Photocatalytic Reactivity of TiO2-Based Nanocomposite Materials*, 339 Chemical Physics (2007); G. H. Li, et al., *A Comparison of Mixed Phase Titania Photocatalysts Prepared by Physical and Chemical Methods: The Importance of the Solid-Solid Interface*, 275 Journal of Molecular Catalysis A-Chemical (2007).

42 L. E. Murr, et al., *Carbon Nanotubes, Nanocrystal Forms, and Complex Nanoparticle Aggregates in Common Fuel-Gas Combustion Sources and the Ambient Air*, 6 Journal of Nanoparticle Research (2004).

43 B. Nowack & T.D. Bucheli, *Occurrence, Behavior and Effects of Nanoparticles in the Environment*, 150 Environmental Pollution (2007).

44 S. Friedrichs & J. Schulte, *Environmental, Health and Safety Aspects of Nanotechnology – Implications for the R&D in (Small) Companies*, 8 Science and Technology of Advanced Materials (2007).

nanomaterials on living organisms and systems. This apprehension is based in part on the fact that naturally derived colloids or nanoparticles have long been recognized to play critical roles in contaminant fate and transport in environmental systems.[45] Furthermore, a good deal of what we know about the acute and chronic human health risks associated with exposure to nanoscale materials comes from the study of diesel exhaust and combustion by-products.[46] Engineered nanomaterials, however, provoke even more trepidation because their uniformity amplifies all their effects, both beneficial and deleterious.

What Is Nanotoxicology?

Nanotoxicology is an emerging discipline that is defined as the science that deals with the effects of engineered nanodevices and nanostructures on living organisms.[47] We can expect the toxic effects associated with nanomaterial exposure to differ from larger sizes of the same material for all the same reasons that nanomaterial properties and performance are modified: (1) much less nanomaterial quantity is required for similar or more often, enhanced behavior; (2) nanomaterials are much more reactive; (3) nanomaterials display greater penetration into cells and through organisms. Yet nanomaterials do not present monolithic environmental risks as some would fear, and we can expect nanomaterials to display widely varying environmental fate, transport, and toxic effects.[48] The challenge is to determine whether, by knowing chemical and physical characteristics, we can predict potential, unintended nanomaterial behaviors and effects.

Nanotoxicity research is highly interdisciplinary and dispersed across a range of fields (chemistry, physics, biology, and engineering).[49] Most nanotoxicological studies tend to focus on in vitro testing of basic nanomaterials without specification of exposure pathways and to emphasize acute toxicity and mortality rather than chronic exposure and morbidity. In other words, most research has yet to grapple with the complex interactions taking place in an individual organism, let alone communities of organisms. Over the last 6 years there have been numerous review articles discussing the potential environmental effects and human health risks associated with nanomaterial exposure.[50] Yet the roots of nanotoxicology extend from the study

45 W. Stumm, Aquatic Surface Chemistry: Chemical Processes at the Particle-Water Interface (New York: John Wiley & Sons, 1987); W. Stumm & J.J. Morgan, *Aquatic Chemistry: Chemical Equilibria and Rates in Natural Waters*, 3rd ed. (New York: John Wiley & Sons, 1996).

46 Donaldson, et al; Oberdorster, et al; K. Donaldson & V. Stone, *Current Hypotheses on the Mechanisms of Toxicity of Ultrafine Particles*, 39 Annali dell'Istituto Superiore di Sanita (2003).

47 Oberdorster, et al.

48 H. F. Lecoanet, et al., *Laboratory Assessment of the Mobility of Nanomaterials in Porous Media*, 38 Environmental Science & Technology (2004).

49 A. D. Ostrowski, et al., *Nanotoxicology: Characterizing the Scientific Literature, 2000–2007*, 11 Journal of Nanoparticle Research (2009).

50 Borm, et al; Wiesner & Bottero; Klaine, et al; Rickerby & Morrison; Buzea, et al; Nowack & Bucheli; V. L. Colvin, *The Potential Environmental Impact of Engineered Nanomaterials*, 21 Nature

of the effects of particulate air pollution on the lungs, where the ultrafine fraction of particles has been shown to display deep penetration throughout the respiratory system and to pose potentially serious injury to lung and other organ tissues by a variety of mechanisms.[51]

Humans have long been exposed to airborne nanosized particles over evolutionary time scales, but over the last 100 years, dramatic and rapid changes have occurred with respect to the nature, proportions, and absolute levels of nanoparticles.[52] The ultrafine particles of interest to pulmonary toxicologists are in the same size range as engineered nanoparticles, less than 100 nm. The ultrafine fraction of airborne particulate material comprise about 70% of the total number concentration of aerosols in a typical ambient urban airshed, whereas these nanoparticles make up only about 1% of the mass.[53] The combustion of fossil fuels emits a wide array of carbon-centered particles, typically associated with metals, such as diesel soot, welding fume, carbon black, and coal fly ash.[54] Extensive study has established that inhalation of these very small particles is highly hazardous to lung tissue and is associated with oxidative stress, inflammation, and cancer. Epidemiological studies have found strong correlations between particulate air pollution, respiratory and cardiovascular diseases, various cancers, and mortality.[55] As a consequence of their small size, with inhalation, nanoparticles are transported and deposited throughout the respiratory tract, where they can possibly be redistributed to other organs. Because ultrafine particles, and nanoparticles in general, are much smaller than cellular structures, they are able to pass through the body's tissue barriers (epithelial [outer] and endothelial [inner] cells) into the blood and lymph circulatory systems and from there reach sensitive target sites such as bone marrow, lymph nodes, spleen, liver, and heart, where they can potentially enter cells.[56] There are also reports of these particles being translocated to and accessing the central nervous system.

Ultrafine air particles are categorized as incidental nanoparticles and exhibit considerable heterogeneity in composition, structure, and behavior. The primary cellular impacts are oxidative stress and inflammation, which are modulated by the chemical and physical characteristics of these nanoparticles. Although the exact mechanisms are not known, oxidative stress, and inflammation are likely mediated in some way by interactions between the large surface areas of nanoparticles and

BIOTECHNOLOGY (2003); J. M. BALBUS, et al., *Meeting Report: Hazard Assessment for Nanoparticles – Report From an Interdisciplinary Workshop*, 115 ENVIRONMENTAL HEALTH PERSPECTIVES (2007); M. AUFFAN, et al., *Towards a Definition of Inorganic Nanoparticles From an Environmental, Health and Safety Perspective*, 4 NATURE NANOTECHNOLOGY (2009).

51 DONALDSON, et al.

52 id. at; OBERDORSTER, et al; BUZEA, et al.

53 BUZEA, et al.

54 DONALDSON, et al.

55 BUZEA, et al.

56 OBERDORSTER, et al; DONALDSON & STONE.

biological systems, but also by the associated metal and organic content of nanoparticulate combustion products. Ultrafine particles may also trigger altered biochemical signaling processes (e.g., Ca^{2+} signaling) and genotoxic effects in cells.[57]

Oxidative stress is a condition in which there is an increased release of oxidation products within the cell. Normally, cells maintain a reducing environment, and minor redox imbalances between respiration and metabolism are routinely adjusted by a number of antioxidant systems that cells have evolved. In the case of air pollutant exposure, however, the generation of reactive oxygen species (ROS), the chemical free radicals causing the redox imbalance (oxidative stress), may exceed the scavenging ability of cells (antioxidant production) or the ability to repair easily subsequent cell damage. Oxidative stress and inflammation are linked. Inflammation is a vital and normal response that cells have developed in response to injury in order to stimulate the regeneration of healthy tissue. In addition, inflammation acts to restore the reducing environment in cells by removing the initial source of the oxidative stress (e.g., phagocytosis of nanoparticles). Yet one of the results of acute and chronic exposure to airborne ultrafine particles is disruption of this repair process (e.g., perturbation of signaling processes of cells), such that inflammation may continue unchecked, leading to disease. ROS generation and inflammation, then, are both a means to combat nanoparticle invasion as well as a cause of injury.

Although there are many differences between the ultrafine particles associated with combustion (incidental nanoparticles) and engineered nanomaterials, the mature field of pulmonary toxicology offers many valuable insights about likely toxic effects caused by nanomaterial exposure and serves as a basis for the expanding field of nanotoxicology.[58] Consequently, although we do not entirely understand the mechanisms and lack predictive knowledge of outcomes, similar biological effects such as the potential for inflammatory activity, oxidative stress response, and genotoxicity are both expected and have been observed in response to ultrafine particles and engineered nanoparticles exposure.[59] Thus parallels between health effects of ultrafine particles and those of engineered nanoparticles should be taken very seriously. Within the context of nanotoxicology and human health, then, incidental nanoparticles comprise a vastly diverse array of materials that stimulate a complex cascade of deleterious cellular events and serve as a model for what can be expected from exposure to engineered nanomaterials.

As previously stated, not all nanomaterials or nanoparticles cause adverse health effects, but in the last decade, knowledge of the potential human toxicity from exposure to engineered nanomaterials has slowly accrued. Buzea and coauthors have described much of this progress in an excellent and comprehensive

57 Donaldson & Stone.

58 Donaldson, et al; Oberdorster, et al.

59 Borm & Berube.

review of the sources, characteristics, applications, health effects, and toxicology of nanomaterials.[60] The importance of the chemical and physical characteristics of nanomaterials cannot be overstated, especially as we try to account for what, at first glance, may appear as contradictory results about the toxic effects of a nanomaterial.[61] Nanomaterial toxicity depends on material composition, size, aggregation, crystallinity, electronic structure, surface functionalization, surface charge, surface coatings (active or passive), and solubility.[62] But nanomaterial toxicity can be enhanced or diminished by environmental factors, such as ultraviolet (UV) activation, pH, ionic strength, temperature, biological modification, and surface adsorption of organic or inorganic chemicals present in the environment. Ultimately, toxicity is determined by an individual's genetic complement, vulnerability, susceptibility, age, fitness, and other comprising factors (e.g., presence of other injuries or diseases, immune compromise, action of other drugs or medications).[63] Because of the complex web of interactions influencing overall toxicity, it is overly simplistic to think that nanomaterial classification by physical features, such as size, will provide a sufficient predictive base; rather, it is essential that the details of nanomaterial structure, behavior, and dose be integrated with exposure details (who is exposed, route of exposure, conditions of exposure, etc.).

ROS generation is the best-developed paradigm for nanoparticle toxicity, particularly via airborne exposure, and oxidative stress is considered a primary mechanism by which nanoparticles could cause disease.[64] In general, oxidative stress is associated with a wide assortment of diseases ranging from cancer to neurodegenerative to cardiovascular diseases, although, as of yet, no clinically identified disease outcomes have been reported for engineered nanomaterial.[65] That said, there is extensive evidence of the co-incidence of nano-debris and disease or injury.[66] Analysis by scanning electron microscopy of tissue and blood samples detected the deposition of micro- and nano-sized particles in patients with orthopedic implants, blood disease, colon cancer and other intestinal diseases (e.g., Crohn's Disease, ulcerative colitis), and lung diseases. What is not entirely clear, however, is whether the cellular uptake of nanomaterials caused the disease or resulted from the disease. For instance, we know that nanoparticle translocation in the body's circulatory systems and into tissue is greater among populations who already have inflammatory diseases

60 Buzea, et al.

61 D. B. Warheit, *How Meaningful Are the Results of Nanotoxicity Studies in the Absence of Adequate Material Characterization?*, 101 Toxicological Sciences (2008).

62 Nel, et al; Buzea, et al.

63 Buzea, et al.

64 Nel, et al; T. Xia, et al., *Comparison of the Abilities of Ambient and Manufactured Nanoparticles to Induce Cellular Toxicity According to an Oxidative Stress Paradigm*, 6 Nano Letters (2006).

65 M. Kovochich, et al., *Principles and Procedures to Assess Nanomaterial Toxicity*, in Environmental Nanotechnology: Applications and Impacts of Nanomaterials (M.R. Wiesner & J-Y. Bottero, Eds., New York: McGraw-Hill, 2007).

66 Buzea, et al.

or broken skin/tissues.[67] In any event, the biocompatibility of materials containing nanomaterials should be revisited in light of the fact that nano-debris has been observed to collect in tissue beyond the site of implant.[68]

The biology of oxidative stress in eukaryotic cells (cells of higher organisms containing complex structures enclosed in membranes, especially the nucleus), particularly mammalian cells, is a hierarchical and complex cascade of cellular responses.[69] For example, ROS generation triggered by nanomaterials may impede fundamental cellular processes such as mitochondrial energy production by disrupting electron flow in the inner membrane of the mitochondria, perturbing the levels and flux of free Ca^{2+} and inducing programmed cell death (apoptosis).[70] There is growing evidence that the mitochondria may be directly targeted by nanoparticles, and mitochondrial damage may be an important mechanism of nanomaterial toxicity.[71] In addition, ROS production modulates intracellular calcium concentrations, activates transcription factors, and induces cytokine (proteins produced by white blood cells that act as messengers to trigger an immune response) production.

Overall, though, the responses to oxidative stress are not linear and are influenced by the type of nanomaterial, dose, and individual susceptibilities. There are, however, a variety of biomarkers that are released along the oxidative stress pathway that would allow for toxicity screening, as illustrated by Nel and coworkers.[72] In this way, toxicity screening was conducted for three metal oxides produced in high tonnage (ZnO, CeO_2, TiO_2).[73] Xia and coworkers found that the metal oxide nanoparticles induced a range of biological responses: ZnO triggered ROS generation and injury, in contrast to CeO_2, which suppressed ROS production and conferred resistance to oxidative stress. TiO_2, on the other hand, although taken up by the cell, showed neither positive nor negative effects. In contrast, Rogers and coworkers found that the antioxidant capacity of nanomaterial-treated human blood serum was significantly reduced (thereby, causing oxidative stress) by nano-TiO_2 (in the anatase form), as well as by nanosilver, a series of nano-carbon black, and fullerene soot, whereas nano-TiO_2 in the rutile form, a type of SiO_2 (Min-U-Sil 5), purified fullerene, and nano-alumina did not reduce antioxidant behavior.[74] Fullerenes (C_{60}) can also induce ROS generation and cytotoxicity, but certain surface modifications

67 Id.

68 Id.

69 Nel, et al; Xia, et al; Kovochich, et al.

70 Kovochich, et al.

71 Id.

72 Xia, et al; Kovochich, et al.

73 T. Xia, et al., *Comparison of the Mechanism of Toxicity of Zinc Oxide and Cerium Oxide Nanoparticles Based on Dissolution and Oxidative Stress Properties*, 2 ACS Nano (2008).

74 E. J. Rogers, et al., *A High Throughput In Vitro Analytical Approach to Screen for Oxidative Stress Potential Exerted by Nanomaterials Using a Biologically Relevant Matrix: Human Blood Serum*, 22 Toxicology in Vitro (2008).

(e.g., attached malonyl groups) promote antioxidant activity.[75] In contrast, Spohn and coworkers carefully studied the extent to which the suspension method and solvent influenced the toxicity of C_{60}-aggregates (nC_{60}) to find that toxicity could be attributed to suspension and solvent effects, not the nC_{60}, itself; that additional rinsing steps could remove the solvent effects before toxicity testing; and that nC_{60} suspended in aqueous solutions had a mild antioxidant effect.[76] An important caveat accompanies these findings, though, in that the size of the nC_{60} aggregates was in the range of 200–500 nm, well outside the official nanoparticle size range. This report underscores the necessity of being mindful of all the nanomaterial/nanoparticle details when comparing toxicity findings. Finally, these examples illustrate that, at this time, nanotoxicity is difficult to predict, but can be evaluated by a tiered testing strategy that couples thorough nanomaterial characterization with toxicity assays.[77]

Either as a consequence of oxidative stress and inflammation or as a direct effect, nanomaterial toxicity injures cells and organisms by damaging proteins, lipids, membranes, and/or DNA, as well as interfering with signaling functions and gene transcription.[78] Nanomaterials have been observed to both stimulate and suppress the immune system.[79] For instance, nano-ZrO_2 exposure triggered enhanced reactivity of macrophages (literally, "big eaters," or white blood cells that engulf and digest cellular and foreign debris in and around tissue) to viral infections, causing excessive inflammation, whereas nano-TiO_2 and SiO_2 exposure depressed the macrophage response, lowering the resistance to viruses and bacteria.[80] In some cases, nanomaterial accumulation in tissue causes the formation of foreign body granulomas, which are chronic masses formed when the immune system attempts to wall off a foreign substance but is then unable to eliminate it.[81] Nanomaterial may also cause the aggregation of platelets leading to blood clots.[82]

There is a direct, if unknown, relationship between nanoparticle surface area and oxidative stress.[83] In a recent review of the size-dependent properties of a wide variety of nanoparticulate inorganic metal and metal oxide materials, Auffan and others sought to identify a critical size, or size threshold, at which nano-imbued properties and cytotoxic effects become significant.[84] They reported that particles

75 NEL, et al.

76 P. SPOHN, et al., *C-60 Fullerene: A Powerful Antioxidant or a Damaging Agent? The Importance of an In-Depth Material Characterization Prior to Toxicity Assays*, 157 ENVIRONMENTAL POLLUTION (2009).

77 XIA, et al; SPOHN, et al; D. BERHANU, et al., *Characterisation of carbon nanotubes in the context of toxicity studies*, 8 ENVIRONMENTAL HEALTH (2009).

78 NEL, et al; BUZEA, et al.

79 BUZEA, et al.

80 M. LUCARELLI, et al., *Innate Defence Functions of Macrophages Can Be Biased by Nano-Sized Ceramic and Metallic Particles*, 15 EUROPEAN CYTOKINE NETWORK (2004).

81 KOVOCHICH, et al.

82 BUZEA, et al.

83 ROGERS, et al.

84 AUFFAN, et al.

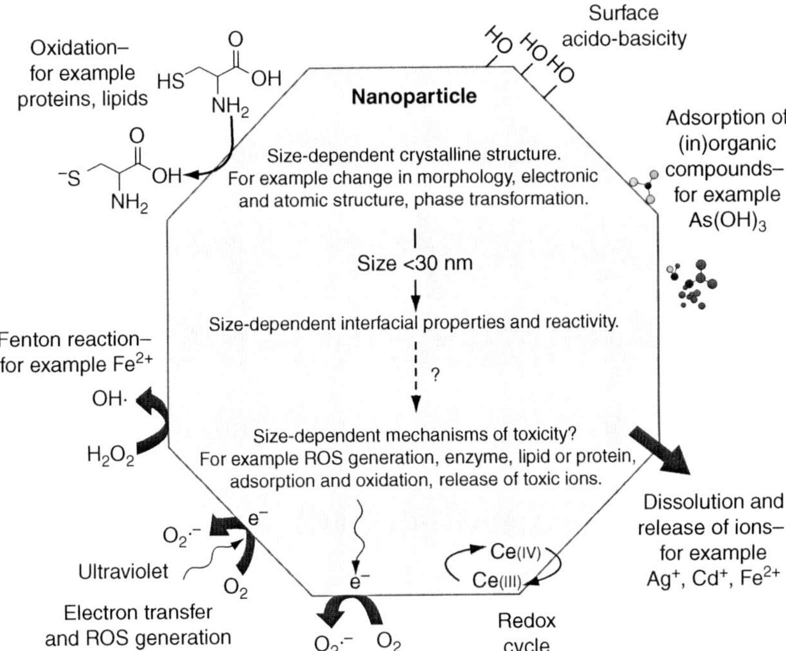

FIGURE 2.4. The potential relationship between the size dependence of the crystalline structure of nanoparticles (typically <30 nm), their interfacial properties (e.g., dissolution, oxidation, adsorption/desorption, electron transfer, redox cycles, Fenton reactions, and surface acido-basicity) and potential mechanisms of toxicity (e.g., the generation of ROS, the release of toxic ions, the oxidation of proteins and the adsorption of pollutants). OH, hydroxyl radical; O_2^-, anion superoxide. Source: Auffan, et al.

larger than about 30 nm did not tend to exhibit properties that were any more deleterious to environmental health and safety than their bulk counterparts. Figure 2.4 summarizes the variety of physicochemical phenomena that can occur at the nanoparticle surface, principally for nanoparticle diameters less than 30 nm, and that is likely related to the exponential increase in the relative number of atoms at the surface, as well as relative surface area. Oxidation reactions and the generation of ROS comprise the majority of the reactions illustrated. The authors propose that the primary criterion for defining and basing regulatory decisions about potential environmental, health, and safety risks should be the novel size-dependent properties of nanomaterials, rather than particle size alone.

Although measurable surface reactivity may show a distinct threshold effect associated with nanoparticle diameter, nanoparticle translocation across tissue barriers does not. Fluorescently labeled polystyrene nanoparticles ranging in size from 50–500 nm were compared relative to their ability to cross the placental barrier and affect the fetus.[85] Polystyrene particles up to 240 nm were taken up by the placenta and crossed the placental barrier, although the viability of the model fetus was not affected. In contrast, however, nanogold particles (<30 nm) coated with polyethylene glycol were not able to traverse the placental barrier under similar experimental conditions. These results pose an interesting contrast to those of Auffan et al. and indicate, at this time, the unfortunate truth that translocation and cellular interactions are likely mediated more by specific surface characteristics than simply size and surface area can predict, and thus they must be assessed individually for each type of nanoparticle.

Given the high areas and adsorptive affinities of nanomaterial surfaces, another route of nanotoxicity may involve nanomaterials as carriers of toxic chemicals into cells.[86] For instance, a group of Swiss researchers found that when human lung epithelial cells were exposed to 20–75 nm of silica that contained small amounts of metals (e.g., $\approx$ 1 wt. % Ti, Fe, Co, Mn) the cells experienced levels of oxidative stress due to ROS formation that varied in direct proportion to their relative catalytic reactivity (e.g., Co, Mn >> Fe > Ti).[87] In contrast, however, the same cells were able to protect themselves from exposure to the soluble salts of these same metals, because their cell membranes create a selective barrier to the dissolved forms of the metal ions. This is an example of a "Trojan horse" effect where metals are carried into a cell on a nanoparticle and toxicity is attributed to the ROS response either promoted by catalytic active sites on the nanoparticle surface or by the dissolution of the metal and release of the ions once inside the cell. The acute cytotoxicity of CdSe-core quantum dots was attributed to this type of effect where the dissolution of CdSe releases free Cd^{2+} inside the cells.[88] Cytotoxicity was mediated by synthesis conditions, UV light exposure, and surface coatings. In fact, the quantum dots could be rendered nontoxic with the appropriate coating, illustrating that toxicity screening can direct design modifications not only to avoid toxicity, but also to improve performance.

The Trojan horse effect applies to a wide variety of chemicals that can piggyback into cells on translocated nanoparticles, thereby triggering a variety of toxic responses ranging from ROS formation promoted by surface sites, the nanoparticle, or the cell to the release of the chemical and subsequent toxic responses (i.e., genotoxicity due to organic contaminants or metal poisoning related to Ag, Pb, and Au dissolution and release, which can inactivate critical enzymes necessary

[85] P. Wick, et al., *Barrier Capacity of Human Placenta for Nanosized Materials*, 118 Environmental Health Perspectives (2010).

[86] J. M. Balbus, et al., *Meeting Report: Hazard Assessment for Nanoparticles – Report From an Interdisciplinary Workshop*, 115 see id. at (2007); L. K. Limbach, et al., *Exposure of Engineered Nanoparticles to Human Lung Epithelial Cells: Influence of Chemical Composition and Catalytic Activity on Oxidative Stress*, 41 Environmental Science & Technology (2007).

[87] Limbach, et al.

[88] A. M. Derfus, et al., *Probing the Cytotoxicity of Semiconductor Quantum Dots*, 4 Nano Letters (2004).

for cellular function).[89] Exactly the same Trojan horse–like behavior, however, is used to great advantage in targeting chemotherapy for cancer treatment, which illustrates that many nanoparticle properties are advantageous under a particular set of conditions, but may pose unintended and injurious effects under altered conditions.

Carbon nanostructures such as fullerenes and carbon nanotubes (CNTs) are the focus of the most extensive toxicological characterization.[90] In a review of CNT toxicity based on animal studies, Lam et al. reported that both single and multi-wall CNTs elicited pathological changes in the lungs and were shown to produce respiratory function impairments.[91] A remarkable range of toxicological results were reported for CNTs by Helland et al.[92] CNTs are a highly heterogeneous group of nanomaterials, but in general they are bioavailable, highly persistent, and possibly accumulate along food webs. Cells have been observed to actively respond to single-walled CNT via immune responses and expression of apoptosis (programmed cell death)-associated genes. At high doses, CNTs are very toxic, but cytotoxicity is markedly diminished at lower doses. The specific fate and impact of CNTs are as variable as their physical and chemical characteristics – a feature common to most nanomaterials.

The diameters of CNTs can vary from 0.4 nm to 100 nm and lengths from nanometers to centimeters. Thus a defining feature of CNTs is their high aspect ratio (ratio of length to diameter), ranging from $10–10^8$, which is significantly greater than that of any other material, but makes them morphologically similar to asbestos. The toxicity of asbestos tends to increase with increasing aspect ratio. Although there are concerns that CNTs may behave similarly, there is no consensus about what best characterizes CNT toxicity.[93] A range of engineered nanomaterials, including CNTs, were rigorously characterized by transmission electron microscopy before a comparison of their cytotoxicity relative to that of chrysotile asbestos, which served as the positive control.[94] In Table 2.1, the results of a simple, short-term toxicity screening test show that CNTs have toxic effects qualitatively similar or slightly greater than asbestos. Nanosilver particles, however, were more toxic than asbestos at lower exposure doses, whereas titania and silicon nitride displayed less relative toxicity under these test conditions. Yet, in another comparison of the cellular toxicity of TiO_2-nanofilaments and multi-walled CNTs (MWCNTs) as measured by acute cytotoxicity on lung cells in vitro, TiO_2-based nanofilaments displayed a

89 Auffan, et al.

90 Colvin.

91 C. W. Lam, et al., *A Review of Carbon Nanotube Toxicity and Assessment of Potential Occupational and Environmental Health Risks*, 36, Crit Rev Toxicol (2006).

92 Helland, et al.

93 Buzea, et al.

94 K. F. Soto, et al., *Comparative in Vitro Cytotoxicity Assessment of Some Manufactured Nanoparticulate Materials Characterized by Transmission Electron Microscopy*, 7 Journal of Nanoparticle Research (2005).

TABLE 2.1. *Comparison of Relative Cytotoxicity Index (RCI) among Common Nanoparticles at Low and High Doses*

Material	Mean Diameter (aggregate, mm)	Mean Diameter (particle, nm)	RCI (at 5 mg/ml)	RCI (at 10 mg/ml)
Ag	1.0	30	1.5	0.8
Ag	0.4	30	1.8	0.1
Al_2O_3	0.7	50	0.7	0.4
Fe_2O_3	0.7	50	0.9	0.1
ZrO_2	0.7	20	0.7	0.6
TiO_2 (rutile)	1.0	Rod shaped 5–15 nm diameter	0.3	0.05
TiO_2 (anatase)	2.5	20	0.4	0.1
Si_3N_4	1.0	60	0.4	0.06
Asbestos – Chrysotile	7	Fibers, 20 nm diameter; High Aspect Ratio (< 500)	1	1
Carbon black	0.5	20	0.8	0.6
SWCNT powder mixture	10	Nanoropes/bundles, 10–200 nm diameter (intermixed with fullerene and iron catalyst)	1.1	0.9
MWCNT powder	2.0	15	0.9	0.8

MWCNT, multi-walled carbon nanotube; RCI, relative cytotoxicity index; SWCNT, single-walled carbon nanotube.
Source: Buzea, et al; Soto, et al.

dose-dependent effect on cell proliferation and cell death, and were found to be more cytotoxic than MWCNT.[95] Furthermore, despite comparable dimensions, marked enhancement of toxicity was produced by surface modification of the titania nanofilaments (acid treatment that replaced Na^+ with H^+). Once again, the precise details of the chemical and physical characteristics of nanomaterials determine toxic effects.[96]

In general, adverse health effects of nanomaterials have been thought to be most highly associated with parameters describing nanomaterial dose, dimension, and durability – the 3 Ds.[97] But it is clear from the discussion presented thus far that

95 A. Magrez, et al., *Cellular Toxicity of TiO2-Based Nanofilaments*, 3 ACS Nano (2009).

96 P.R. Gil, Oberdorster, G., Elder, A., Puntes, V., Wolfgang, J.P., *Correlating Physico-Chemical With Toxicological Properties of Nanoparticles: The Present and the Future*, 4 ACS Nano (2010).

97 Buzea, et al.

this is overly simplistic, and parameters describing mass and number concentration, surface area and surface chemistry, crystallinity, aggregation, solvent and suspension characteristics, and presence of impurities are also very important. Large changes in toxic effects accompany changes in nanomaterial purity, shape, and functionalization. As discussed previously, the primary focus of most nanotoxicity studies has been mammalian systems where mechanisms of biological uptake and toxicity include formation of ROS, disruption of membranes, oxidation of proteins, interruption of energy transduction, and genotoxicity.[98] There is a surprising dearth of information on ecological endpoints[99] and little direct data describing the fate and behavior of nanomaterial in aquatic or terrestrial systems.[100] The literature regarding nanomaterial toxicity on microorganisms is very limited compared with the study of eukaryotic organisms. For instance, mitochondrial damage is identified as a major mechanism of oxidative stress and nanoparticle toxicity, but what are the likely pathways among prokaryotic microorganisms, which lack mitochondria and other subcellular locales of action? Furthermore, even more sparse is the body of work investigating community-level effects that investigate how interactions among populations of microorganisms may be altered, impacting the base of ecosystem structure and function. Finally, if knowledge about the nanomaterial effects on microbial ecology is scant, research on nanomaterial interactions in soils and with plants is virtually nonexistent.[101]

Because nanomaterial production and use are growing rapidly in every sector of the economy, eventual release into the environment over their life cycle is all but certain.[102] The production of fullerenes, for instance, has already reached an industrial scale,[103] and nanoparticulate metal oxides, such as TiO_2 and ZnO, are likely to reach the levels of commodity chemicals in the not too distant future. Nanomaterial fate and impacts on ecological health, however, are anything but certain. The environmental stability of nanomaterial size and reactivity is largely unknown. Few systematic studies have been conducted to determine how abiotic factors such as pH, ionic strength, and anionic, cationic, and organic adsorption influence nanomaterial fate, transport, and, ultimately, bioavailability. The extent to which environmental and biological systems modify nanomaterial properties has not been addressed comprehensively. Finally, the ways in which nanomaterials may affect key biogeochemical functions and food web structure are key questions awaiting answers.

At an elementary level, ecotoxicity assessments begin with understanding nanomaterial behavior in water. For highly aqueous-insoluble materials as C_{60} and CNTs,

98 Nel, et al; Xia, et al; Xia, et al.

99 Borm, et al.

100 Klaine, et al.

101 Nowack & Bucheli.

102 Borm, et al; Wiesner, et al.

103 Spohn, et al.

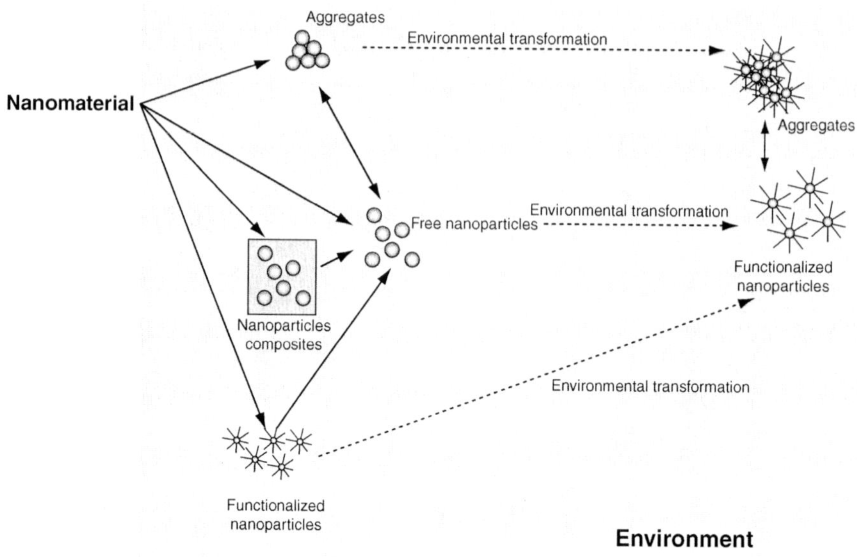

FIGURE 2.5. An example of the environmental processing of nanomaterials in natural waters. Source: Farre, et al.

such study can only be conducted once the nanoparticles are made stable in suspension either by chemically modifying their surfaces or using chemical (e.g., solvents or surfactants) or physical (e.g., sonicating or mixing) dispersants. Care must be taken to tease out the effects of dispersion on observed toxicity.[104] Recent results of basic ecotoxicity tests for a variety of common nanomaterials were summarized by Farre et al and Klaine et al.[105] Although in most cases some acute toxicity or physiological changes were detected, these results are not necessarily predictive of the toxicity that may actually occur in nature. The reasons for this are twofold. First, the testing was conducted on organisms in isolation, ignoring synergistic or antagonistic system-level interactions. Second, upon release to the environment, nanomaterials are likely to undergo environmental processing, which can alter their size and composition and hence their toxicity.[106]

Natural waters contain organic material derived from the biogeochemical cycling of biological materials and serving as a natural dispersant. The adsorption of natural organic material (NOM) is one of the environmental transformations depicted in Figure 2.5[107] that could result in modified nanomaterial aggregation and surface

[104] Id.; M. FARRE, et al., *Ecotoxicity and Analysis of Nanomaterials in the Aquatic Environment*, 393 ANALYTICAL AND BIOANALYTICAL CHEMISTRY (2009).

[105] KLAINE, et al; FARRE, et al.

[106] D.Y. LYON, et al., ECOTOXICOLOGICAL IMPACTS OF NANOMATERIALS, in *Environmental Nanotechnology: Applications and Impacts of Nanomaterials* (M.R. WIESNER & J-Y. BOTTERO, Eds., New York: McGraw-Hill, 2007).

[107] FARRE, et al.

functionalization. It is well established that colloidal stability in natural waters is controlled by the quality and quantity of NOM and further modulated by such environmental parameters as calcium concentration, pH, ionic strength, and sunlight.[108] Although there are few studies on the aqueous stability and aggregation of nanomaterials under relevant field conditions[109], CNTs and nanotitania are readily stabilized in aqueous solution by natural organic material, suggesting that environmental dispersion of these nanomaterials may occur to an extent far greater than originally anticipated.[110] MWCNTs were individually dispersed by NOM for over 1 month, which is greater than that achieved by typical use of a common surfactant under laboratory conditions.[111] C_{60} were also effectively dispersed as aggregates of hundreds of nanometers in aqueous solution in the presence of NOM. In the presence of sunlight and NOM, however, there was an order of magnitude increase in the mass concentration of C_{60} dispersed in water, but even more remarkable was the fact that the C_{60} aggregate size decreased substantially ($<$ 100nm, to as low as 5 nm), possibly due to photochemically driven transformation reactions.[112] Hwang and Li also documented photochemical transformations of nC_{60}, which modified the fullerene surface chemistry (e.g., surface oxygenation and hydroxylation) to increase dramatically aqueous phase solubility and diminish extraction efficiency by toluene.[113] Single-walled CNTs were also found to be photoactive under environmental conditions and to yield ROS, which may promote environmental transformations among constituents present in aquatic systems or mediate ecotoxicological effects.[114]

There is a persistent, a priori assumption that nanomaterial release is presently low, if not negligible, and that if released, nanomaterials are not stable under environmental conditions. However, these proposals are not supported by data. Techniques such as field-flow fraction are only recently being employed to accurately track nanomaterial mobility and fate at low levels.[115] Recent research profiled the fate of nanotitania through an advanced wastewater treatment plant to show that, although the majority

108 C. L. Tiller & C. R. Omelia, *Natural Organic-Matter and Colloidal Stability – Models and Measurements*, 73 Colloids and Surfaces A-Physicochemical and Engineering Aspects (1993).

109 P. Christian, et al., *Nanoparticles: Structure, Properties, Preparation and Behaviour in Environmental Media*, 17 Ecotoxicology (2008).

110 H. Hyung, et al., *Natural Organic Matter Stabilizes Carbon Nanotubes in the Aqueous Phase*, 41 Environmental Science & Technology (2007); R. F. Domingos, et al., *Aggregation of Titanium Dioxide Nanoparticles: Role of a Fulvic Acid*, 43 Environmental Science & Technology (2009).

111 H. Hyung, et al., *Natural Organic Matter Stabilizes Carbon Nanotubes in the Aqueous Phase*, 41 *see id. at* (2007).

112 Q. L. Li, et al., *Kinetics of C-60 Fullerene Dispersion in Water Enhanced by Natural Organic Matter and Sunlight*, 43 *see id. at* (2009).

113 Y. S. Hwang & Q. L. Li, *Characterizing Photochemical Transformation of Aqueous nC(60) Under Environmentally Relevant Conditions*, 44 *see id. at* (2010).

114 C. Y. Chen & C. T. Jafvert, *Photoreactivity of Carboxylated Single-Walled Carbon Nanotubes in Sunlight: Reactive Oxygen Species Production in Water, see id. at* (2010).

115 B. M. Simonet & M. Valcarcel, *Monitoring Nanoparticles in the Environment*, 393 Analytical and Bioanalytical Chemistry (2009).

of titania adsorbed to biomass, 10–100 mg/L was discharged in the effluent.[116] At these levels, other researchers observed that TiO_2 aggregates (nano-anatase) could disrupt carbon and nitrogen fixation by a common cyanobacteria.[117] These results revealed that nanotitania aggregates as large as 200 nm inhibited both cell growth photosynthesis rates and nitrogen fixation activity. In addition, a dose-dependent increase in a stress response protein (nitrogen-rich cyanophycin grana proteins) was also observed, which could serve as a bioindicator of cytotoxicity.

Although 90% of the high commercial use nanomaterials (e.g., silver, ZnO, TiO_2) are removed in wastewater treatment, the nanomaterials become incorporated into the solid material (the "sludge") that is separated from the water and, ultimately, in many cases, is applied to agriculture land as soil amendment (biosolids). Bertsch and other researchers in his lab have shown that earthworms can accumulate gold nanoparticles from soil.[118] In addition, they demonstrated that tobacco plants grown in hydroponic solutions not only accumulated nanogold particles, but caterpillars fed the contaminated plants showed biomagnification of the gold, as evidenced by an order of magnitude increase in gold concentration relative to the plant.[119]

As discussed previously, experiments investigating the dispersion of nanomaterials in aqueous solution under meaningful environmental conditions have revealed a surprising degree of stability in the presence of NOM, as well as marked changes to particle size and surface chemistry. Bacteria (*Pseudomonas aeruginosa*), too, have been shown to disperse aggregates of nano-TiO_2 by preferential biosorption of the nanoparticles onto the cell surfaces.[120] Serious implications are associated with these results – increased stability in solution means that nanomaterials have greater mobility, can be distributed over a much larger area, and have a greater range of biological action. Figure 2.6 delineates the major pathways of nanomaterial fate in aquatic systems, where a ramification of greater water column stability may be higher exposure to filter feeders and fish. Borm and co-authors proposed that filter feeders, which are a unique target group at the base of food webs, may be a good indicator organism for nanoparticle bioaccumulation because of their potential exposure to large quantities of nanoparticles dispersed in solution.[121] Conversely, destabilized

[116] M. A. Kiser, et al., *Titanium Nanomaterial Removal and Release From Wastewater Treatment Plants*, Environmental Science & Technology (2009).

[117] C. Cherchi & A. Z. Gu, *Impact of Titanium Dioxide Nanomaterials on Nitrogen Fixation Rate and Intracellular Nitrogen Storage in Anabaena variabilis*, 44 Environmental Science & Technology (2010).

[118] J. M. Unrine, et al., *Evidence for Bioavailability of Au nanoparticles From Soil and Biodistribution Within Earthworms (Eisenia fetida), see id. at* (2010).

[119] J. D. Judy, et al., *Evidence for Biomagnification of Gold Nanoparticles Within a Terrestrial Food Chain*, 45 *see id. at* (2011).

[120] A. M. Horst, et al., *Dispersion of TiO2 Nanoparticle Agglomerates by Pseudomonas aeruginosa*, 76 Applied and Environmental Microbiology (2010).

[121] Borm, et al.

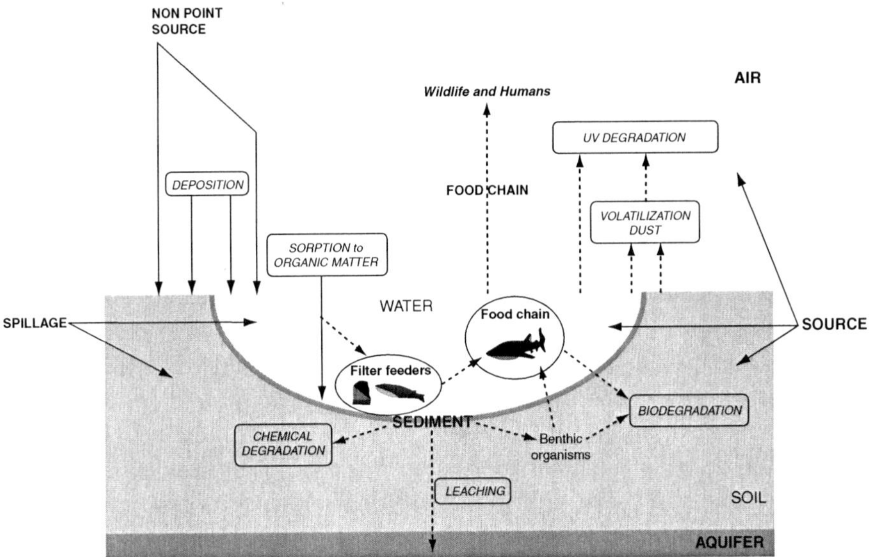

FIGURE 2.6. Potential pathways of fate and transfer of nanomaterials in aquatic systems. Source: Farre, et al.

nanomaterials would aggregate and settle out of the water column to accumulate in the sediments, where they could affect benthic structure and function.

ROS generation is also often invoked to explain nanomaterial ecotoxicity. The toxic effects of nanoTiO_2 are thought to be associated with its ability to generate ROS under illumination, but adverse effects have also been observed under dark conditions for certain formulations depending on size and composition.[122] Evidence of metal dissolution as observed in the cytotoxicity of CdSe or ZnO, for instance, is not found to be associated with TiO_2 toxicity.[123] The ROS mechanism is believed to be maximized in pure-phase anatase nanoparticles at sizes less than 30 nm.[124] One problem with these findings and many other nanomaterial testing results is that the materials tested are often those readily available to the environmental scientist and not the type of nanomaterials known to material chemists and engineers to be the most active and most likely to be developed for engineering applications. Toxicity and ecotoxicity testing needs to be coordinated with the material design and development of the relevant materials.[125]

[122] J. R. GURR, et al., *Ultrafine Titanium Dioxide Particles in the Absence of Photoactivation Can Induce Oxidative Damage to Human Bronchial Epithelial Cells*, 213 TOXICOLOGY (2005); L. K. ADAMS, et al., *Comparative Eco-Toxicity of Nanoscale TiO2, SiO2, and ZnO Water Suspensions*, 40 WATER RESEARCH (2006).

[123] DERFUS, et al; N.M. FRANKLIN, et al., *Comparative Toxicity of Nanoparticulate ZnO, Bulk ZnO, and $ZnCl_2$ to a Freshwater Microalga (Pseudokirchneriella subcapitata): The Importance of Particle Solubility*, 41 ENVIRONMENTAL SCIENCE & TECHNOLOGY (2007).

[124] AUFFAN, et al.

[125] FRIEDRICHS & SCHULTE.

Although research is limited, TiO_2 is among the nanomaterials most widely studied for its ecotoxicological effects. In part, this is because it is easy to procure, is produced in high volumes, and has the potential for widespread environmental release, not only because of its present, nearly ubiquitous use in food, cosmetics, and self-cleaning surfaces, but also due to its potential use in large-scale arrays for photovoltaic cells, photoelectrochemical production of H_2, and rechargeable batteries.[126] As is the case with C_{60} and CNTs, wide variability is reported for the ecotoxicological effects of titania. In a quantitative comparison of the behavioral and physiological responses of Daphnia at sublethal nano-TiO_2 and fullerene concentrations, Lovern et al. reported no statistically significant changes for titania exposure.[127] In a recent review of nanomaterial ecotoxicological effects on fish, Handy et al. reported that no measurements of nanomaterial exposure or accumulation have been made in wild fish populations and that ecotoxicologists lack detailed knowledge about mechanistic interactions.[128] Cytotoxicity studies on fish cells have revealed that ROS (e.g., hydroxyl radical) generated by illuminated TiO_2 induced oxidative DNA damage. Federici and coworkers reported minor toxicological effects on rainbow trout over 14 days of exposure involving oxidative stress, gill injury, and other physiological effects.[129] Scown et al. found that nanotitania accumulated in the kidneys of rainbow trout, but had minimal effect on renal function.[130] In mammalian species, nanotitania exposure, especially that associated with the anatase form, is observed to cause adverse effects depending on nanomaterial surface properties.[131] Nanotitania administered to pregnant mice translocated to the offspring and affected genital/cranial nerve systems.[132]

There is a paucity of data exploring the effects of nanomaterials on microbial organisms. This is a critical gap because microorganisms form the base of food webs. The disinfectant properties of TiO_2 are well established and have been shown to have potential application in controlling biofilm growth.[133] In one of the few

[126] Magrez, et al.

[127] S. B. Lovern, et al., *Behavioral and Physiological Changes in Daphnia Magna When Exposed to Nanoparticle Suspensions (Titanium Dioxide, Nano-C-60, and C(60)HxC(70)Hx)*, 41 Environmental Science & Technology (2007).

[128] R. D. Handy, et al., *Manufactured Nanoparticles: Their Uptake and Effects on Fish-A Mechanistic Analysis*, 17 Ecotoxicology (2008).

[129] G. Federici, et al., *Toxicity of Titanium Dioxide Nanoparticles to Rainbow Trout (Oncorhynchus mykiss): Gill Injury, Oxidative Stress, and Other Physiological Effects*, 84 Aquatic Toxicology (2007).

[130] T. M. Scown, et al., *High Doses of Intravenously Administered Titanium Dioxide Nanoparticles Accumulate in the Kidneys of Rainbow Trout But With No Observable Impairment of Renal Function*, 109 Toxicological Sciences (2009).

[131] D. B. Warheit, et al., *Pulmonary Toxicity Study in Rats With Three Forms of Ultrafine-TiO2 particles: Differential Responses Related to Surface Properties*, 230 Toxicology (2007).

[132] K. Takeda, et al., *Nanoparticles Transferred From Pregnant Mice to Their Offspring Can Damage the Genital and Cranial Nerve Systems*, 55 Journal of Health Science (2009).

[133] E. J. Wolfrum, et al., *Photocatalytic Oxidation of Bacteria, Bacterial and Fungal Spores, and Model Biofilm Components to Carbon Dioxide on Titanium Dioxide-Coated Surfaces*, 36 Environmental

studies of algal response to nanomaterials, Hund-Rinke and Simon observed toxicity produced by nanotitania, but the effects depended on the size, crystalline form, and porosity, and no mechanistic explanations were offered by the authors.[134] Solar cell efficiency has been boosted by incorporating electron transfer from a synthetic chlorophyll analogue to C_{60}, suggesting that in nature there may be potential for C_{60} to uncouple photosynthesis by disrupting the cascade of electron transfer in primary producers (e.g., algae, plants).[135] Finally, to our knowledge, there are no reports concerning ecological responses at the system level due to nanomaterial exposure, in general, or TiO_2, specifically.

According to Christian et al. there are four ways that nanomaterials may impact the environment: (1) direct effects on biota (i.e., toxicity); (2) altered bioavailability of nutrients or contaminants (i.e., Trojan horse effect); (3) indirect effects on the ecosystem (i.e., photosensitized reaction causing oxidation of NOM); (4) changes in environmental microstructures (i.e., modified porosity or particle aggregation).[136] Study of environmental fate and ecological toxicity, however, is hampered by the lack of analytical methods to quantify nanomaterial effects in environmental matrices due to the complexity of both environmental conditions and nanomaterial physicochemical properties.[137] Most assessment methods involve either monitoring a single biochemical reaction or following the response (survival, mutation, reproduction, etc.) of a single organism, but it is paramount that strategies to assess effects on the integrity of links among organisms and overall ecosystem complexity must also be developed.[138] It is imperative that ecotoxicity testing go beyond nanomaterial fate, transport, and single-organism response to determine the mechanisms of bioavailability and bioaccumulation, because these are the processes controlling entry into food webs and, ultimately, risk to human health. At the present time most research is focused on identifying *biomarkers* to provide sensitive signaling of nanomaterial exposure.[139] But *bioindicators* are also needed in the form of key organisms or structural changes in foundational ecological niches, which reflect the health of the ecosystem. Although most research seeks to elucidate lethal endpoints, sublethal effects associated with nanomaterial exposure are also important because they reflect stress on the system, possibly making it more susceptible to other perturbations such as species invasion, climate change, etc.

Science & Technology (2002); S. Ciston, et al., *Bacterial Attachment on Reactive Ceramic Ultrafiltration Membranes*, 320 Journal of Membrane Science (2008).

134 K. Hund-Rinke & M. Simon, *Ecotoxic Effect of Photocatalytic Active Nanoparticles TiO2 on Algae And Daphnids*, 13 Environmental Science and Pollution Research (2006).

135 Borm, et al.

136 Christian, et al.

137 Nowack & Bucheli; Farre, et al.

138 Lyon, et al.

139 Id.

NANO-MYTHS REVISITED

With this basic understanding of what nanomaterials are, why they possess such remarkable properties, how their structure can be tailored to promote specific behaviors and functions, and what types of unintended consequences may accompany the burgeoning commercial uses of nanomaterials, it is time to revisit the five misconceptions about the health and safety of nanomaterials.

(1) Overall, very small quantities of nanomaterials are needed to produce big effects, and because the Toxic Substances Control Act and other statutes employ a volume or weight threshold for regulation, nanomaterial use is typically in compliance.

Rebuttal – Volume and/or weight are the incorrect units of measure for nanomaterials. Nanomaterial surface area, which increases by orders of magnitude for the same weight of material relative to micrometer-sized particles, is one of the primary determinants of nanomaterial activity. The wonder of nanomaterials is that enormous improvements in material performance (e.g., strength, conductivity) and process function (e.g., reactivity, drug therapy) can be targeted by very small quantities. Depending on where the nanomaterials end up, however, these phenomena may unfold not only for desired effects, but also for undesired outcomes. Yet one cannot identify a surface area threshold below which deleterious effects are minimized, because other parameters, such as nanomaterial shape, crystallinity, and surface modification, also exert profound influences, allowing scientists and engineers to tailor further nanomaterial behavior, both positively and negatively. Dose-effect relationships must be recalibrated for nanomaterials with careful attention to the conditions of exposure and susceptibility. The argument that the nanomaterial amounts are too small to matter is the same argument that was used continuously over the last century to discount the risks associated with new chemicals such as tetraethyl lead or pesticides. By now these arguments have been disproved. It is well established that safe levels of many chemicals are difficult to identify, and over long-term commercial use, alarming levels accrue in various environmental media or phases, posing significant exposure risks to threaten ecological and human health.

(2) In many cases nanomaterials are not new materials; rather, they are only smaller versions of materials already in wide use and deemed safe in non-nano forms or combinations.

Rebuttal – At the nanoscale, materials develop entirely new properties and behave uniquely relative to the same atoms packaged as bulk materials (greater than 1 micrometer), because at the nanoscale the behavior of atoms is dictated by different laws of physics – quantum mechanics. Nanomaterials are new chemicals due to the unique arrangement of their atoms; the location (i.e., at surface) and bonding patterns of their constituent atoms differ fundamentally from bulk materials made up of the same (albeit greater number of) atoms. Nanomaterials are new, then, because their atomic and molecular structure and function are novel, not because they are composed of newly discovered elements. The U.S. Food and Drug Administration (FDA), however, invoked this misconceived justification (nanomaterials are not new materials) in its consideration of the regulation of sunscreens that contain nanoparticles. Although the nanoparticles do extend a cosmetic advantage due to their transparency, nanoparticles of TiO_2 and ZnO exhibit strong ROS production in sunlight, which simply redirects cell damage from UV light to free radical exposure.[140] Consumer groups, such as ConsumerUnion.org,[141] have failed to find improved sun protection with the addition of nanoparticles. This example provides a cautionary lesson in that the common nanoparticles found in sunscreens may effectively absorb UV energy, but the mechanisms of energy dissipation (creation of ROS or free radical chemical species) was not considered and is likely as injurious, if not more so, than direct exposure to UV light. A simple surface modification involving the addition of dopants or other types of charge recombination centers, however, can totally eliminate ROS production.[142] This example illustrates another crucial feature of modern nanotechnology – nanotechnology is all about *knowing* and *controlling* material structure to produce uniform features and targeted effects. With knowledge about unintended effects, efforts to redesign and control nanomaterial structure and function can be employed. Finally, nanomaterials are new in the same way the carbon, hydrogen, and oxygen atoms assembled in different number, proportions, and geometries create new polymers. Patent protection is issued based on the unique characteristics of nanomaterials; regulatory oversight of their potentially "new" and unintended impacts on human and ecological health should also be afforded.

(3) Because nanomaterials are derived from common materials, used in quantities well below harmful thresholds (as determined for common materials), and usually incorporated into products for human application, diffuse environmental and ecological hazards are negligible.

Rebuttal – Considering the future projections of production volumes and the fact that nanomaterial use is rapidly becoming diffuse throughout almost all industries, the potential of nanomaterials to leak into the environment is almost certain at some, or all, points along their life cycle, from production to end of use. Among the early emerging applications of nanomaterials are medical, pharmaceutical, and cosmetic products, all of which result in wastewater discharge that provides two points of entry to the environment: (1) separation and concentration into biosolids, which may then be applied to soils and agricultural fields; (2) treated effluent release into receiving

140 G. Wakefield, et al., *Modified Titania Nanomaterials for Sunscreen Applications – Reducing Free Radical Generation and DNA Damage*, 20 Materials Science and Technology (2004).

141 http://www.consumersunion.org/pub/core_product_safety/014360.html.

142 Warheit, et al.

waters and potential uptake into aquatic food webs. The next wave of nanotechnologies is expected to emerge from future energy (e.g., solar cells, batteries) and environmental applications (e.g., water treatment, building insulation self-cleaning surfaces), which will operate at even larger scales of nanomaterial production and will also result in emissions. Although we may not yet know much about long-term environmental and ecological hazards, the small amount of research that is available does not indicate that nanomaterials are inert or negligible in their potential effects. Rather, many nanomaterials exhibit cytotoxicity that may cause serious disruption of ecosystem processes. In the past, the use of potentially hazardous materials (heavy metals, solvents, chlorinated organic compounds, etc.) was justified with similar arguments that their applications were highly controlled, such that environmental risks were both manageable and negligible. Yet these materials leaked gradually into the environment through accidents and emissions to follow pathways similar to those expected for nanomaterials. Over both the short and long term, the environmental, ecological, and human health hazards that accrued from such chemical use as tetraethyl lead and PCBs are indisputable and anything but negligible. Based on this experience, these arguments are spurious, and there is no need to conduct the same experiment all over again for nanomaterials.

(4) Nanomaterials are not stable under ambient environmental conditions. In the improbable event of large environmental releases, nanomaterials will likely aggregate or become incorporated into larger particulate material, rendering them innocuous. This, coupled with the fact that nanomaterials are used in such small amounts, makes their long-term potential environmental impacts negligible.

Rebuttal – Nanomaterials definitely undergo environmental transformation and reprocessing that alter their aggregation and modify their surface chemistry, but there is a significant body of research that reports surprising degrees of dispersion and stability accompanying environmental release. Nanomaterials have been found to piggyback on bacterial surfaces, to be stabilized by interactions with natural organic material, and to show a reduction in aggregate size due to photochemical transformations in the environment. Thus it is incorrect to assume a priori that nanomaterials will become incorporated into larger particles and form inert deposits in soils or sediments. For those nanomaterials and environmental conditions, though, that do promote aggregation, it is unclear that this will render them innocuous and whether these environmental effects are irreversible. The unexpected stability of nanomaterials under environmental conditions and the range of acute toxicity observed in single-organism testing suggest that nanomaterial environmental impacts are not negligible, either in the short or long term. It is not well understood, however, how perturbations to single organisms promote cascading impacts to affect ecosystem structure and function. At the present time there is a pressing need to determine how to conduct nanomaterial cytotoxicity and ecotoxicity testing efficiently and effectively for both short- and long-term risk assessments.

(5) Health and safety testing for nanomaterials and nanotechnology products is extremely costly, requires long times, and in many cases is not even feasible. The costs, then, far exceed the risks of nanomaterials to human and ecological health, would quell innovation, and diminish the valuable social and economic benefits of this emerging technology.

Rebuttal – Nanotechnology is so dynamic and adaptive, that determining the range of "side effects" (both good and bad) will stimulate innovation and discovery and reduce future liability. The savings associated with reduced liability for future environmental and human health damage alone will more than cover the costs of nanomaterial toxicity screening. A tiered approach to comprehensive toxicity and risk assessment is required and must be implemented concomitant to nanomaterial design and development.[143] Because many of the techniques to assess cytotoxic risks are similar to those employed in nanomaterial development, the challenge is associated more with posing the questions regarding what are the unintended consequences that may accompany nanomaterial production and use than how to answer the questions. Standard scenarios of nanomaterial exposure need to be identified. A perfect example is the use of nano-TiO_2 and ZnO in sunscreens and cosmetics. These metal oxides absorb sunlight at the wavelengths that cause skin damage, thus preventing UV light damage to skin. Use of nanomaterials makes the sunscreens transparent, but no one thought to ask the question about outcome – how nanoparticles dissipate the light energy they absorb. It is well established that these semiconducting metal oxides convert radiant energy (sunlight) to chemical energy (highly reactive free radicals) that is very damaging to skin. The solution to this problem is to create energy traps in the nanomaterials, which will dissipate the absorbed UV energy through heat loss and the emission of longer wavelength light. Thus a superior product was eventually developed once full consideration was given to both intended and unintended effects of the nanomaterial behavior. Ecotoxicological risks are more difficult to evaluate than those associated with single-cell responses or biochemical pathways, but knowledge of these risks is critical to the health of the vital life support systems that all life depends on. Ecotoxicity testing is used in the development of pesticides, detergents, and drugs, so it does not present a completely unknown dimension to nanomaterial product development. Finally, the economic benefits attendant to nanotechnology cannot come at the cost of endangered ecological and public health. The evidence compiled to date may be incomplete, but it is sufficient to raise a number of serious concerns about the health and safety of nanomaterials with acute and chronic exposures.

[143] Friedrichs & Schulte.

IMPLICATIONS FOR REGULATION

According to experts, four generations of nanotechnology are envisioned: (1) passive nanostructures designed to perform a single task – the current state; (2) active nanostructures such as multitasking actuators, drug delivery devices, multi-functional catalysts – the emerging state; (3) nanosystems possessing thousands of interacting components; (4) integrated, hierarchical nanosystems acting like mammalian cells or nano-robots.[144] The wonders of nanotechnology are limited only by one's ability to imagine. Yet the nanotechnology revolution is actually more an evolution in the gradual improvement of almost all material production, technology performance, and industrial process, rather than a singular, technological leap.[145] As such, we should expect that nanotechnology will eventually reach most products and industries.

Synthetic control and structural uniformity not only distinguish engineered nanomaterials from natural or incidental nanomaterials, but also pose far greater potential threats to human and ecological health. The novel properties of nanomaterials may present hazards, but they also challenge many of our conventional approaches to assessing toxicity and managing risk.[146] For instance, we do not know whether nanomaterial mass concentration, surface area, or particle concentration or a combination of these should be measured in order to determine exposure and dose,[147] although recent studies have shown that cell and animal toxicity are influenced, at a minimum, by nanomaterial size, surface area, surface chemistry, crystallinity solubility, and shape. Prudent management of ecological risks requires deeper knowledge of nanomaterial stability, mobility, bioavailability, and associated impacts on a wider variety of organisms important to terrestrial and aquatic ecosystems.[148] The details and the extent of nanomaterial toxicity and ecotoxicity (dose effects, metrics of dose, exposure route, target, etc.), however, are largely unknown, especially among non-mammalian species and ecological systems.

There are more than 80,000 chemicals that are currently registered for commercial use in the United States, with only about 530 of these having undergone long-term testing and 70 short-term testing by the National Toxicology program.[149] Nanomaterials will not only substantially add to this burden, but they will also require new testing strategies, because they have different mechanisms of action and toxic endpoints in comparison with conventional chemicals and materials. The volume of anecdotal reports describing conflicting cytotoxic and some ecotoxic

[144] Nel, et al.
[145] Friedrichs & Schulte.
[146] Maynard. (2007)
[147] Maynard. (2006)
[148] Klaine, et al.
[149] Nel, et al.

effects of nanomaterials is growing to a level that may obscure efforts to determine the fundamental and mechanistic understanding of nanomaterial risk to human and ecological health and to find a predictive basis of nanomaterial design, production, and regulation.

> An important lesson we are in the process of learning from nanoscience is that simple classifications of physical behavior (and therefore toxicity) are overly limiting and that we must study toxicology of each material and each morphology, in addition to particle aging, to obtain accurate information to inform policy and regulatory processes.[150]

Life cycle assessment of nanomaterial risks to human and environmental health will extend management responsibility upstream from end-use to material research and development and manufacturing.[151] In order to rigorously conduct comprehensive assessment of these risks, many researchers have called for the development of a tiered testing strategy that is based on nanomaterial properties and behaviors, in addition to nanomaterial size, concentration, or surface area. Although there is no one-size fits all approach to risk assessment, there are four general, key elements to such a strategy: (1) nanomaterial characterization, (2) in vitro screening, (3) in vivo testing, and (4) system level monitoring. First, it is paramount to thoroughly characterize the physicochemical content and properties of nanomaterials and nanomaterial suspensions.[152] The fate, behavior, and ecotoxicology of nanomaterials are closely related to their intrinsic properties,[153] and the results of nanotoxicity investigations offer little insight in the absence of adequate nanomaterial characterization.[154] Second, in vitro testing screens for nanomaterial cytotoxic effects among mammalian cells, as well as environmentally relevant organisms, in order to identify the molecular and cellular basis of toxic responses, such as DNA damage, altered gene expression, changes in cell growth and reproduction, cell death, etc. No single test will predict how nanomaterials behave in organisms or in the environment. It is necessary to conduct broad bioactivity profiles at this screening stage. High-throughput assays are showing great advantage to achieving this task.[155] Third, the cytotoxicity identified in screening tests must be confirmed in vivo at the organism and system level in order to identify both biomarkers and bioindicators of nanomaterial toxicity. Finally, the fourth and probably most difficult stage of a tiered strategy

[150] Buzea, et al.

[151] C.O. Robichaud, et al., *Assessing Life-Cycle Risks of Nanomaterials*, in Environmental Nanotechnology: Applications and Impacts of Nanomaterials (M.R. Wiesner & J-Y. Bottero, Eds., New York: McGraw-Hill, 2007).

[152] Gil.

[153] Christian, et al.

[154] Warheit.

[155] Rogers, et al; R. F. Service, *Nanotechnology – Can High-Speed Tests Sort Out Which Nanomaterials Are Safe?*, 321 Science (2008).

involves environmental monitoring and careful inventory of nanomaterial accumulation and injury among keystone species in critical ecosystems. It is at this stage that potential long-term effects of nanomaterial exposure must be evaluated. In order to develop and implement this type of strategy, improvements in analytical and computational methods are needed. There are limited choices among analytical procedures that have been adapted to messy environmental conditions, and efforts must be made to avoid encountering artifacts when using techniques not tailored to biological/environmental conditions or when extrapolating results to environmental conditions.

The public policy around nanomaterials and nanotechnology must place equal emphasis on knowing both targeted and side effects to human and environmental systems. Full life-cycle assessments must be required, and serious consideration must be given to analyzing the unanticipated consequences of nanomaterial use. Because the degree of structural and functional tailoring of nanomaterial is virtually infinite, rigorous risk assessment that parallels the nanomaterial development process might even serve to stimulate innovation and entrepreneurship. In order for this to happen, though, rapid methods to evaluate nanotoxicity are needed. It is likely that the very tools that facilitate nanomaterial research and development are the very tools that will help determine their safety (e.g., high-throughput screening, genomics, proteomics). The challenge, of course, is how to screen effectively given the enormous number of nanomaterial structural variations and the equally large number of toxicological interactions and endpoints. It is not readily apparent, however, how to conduct comprehensive environmental screening at extended time and length scales that could reveal long-term ecological hazards. And if this were not daunting enough, testing strategies and risk assessments must consider the complexities inherent with exposure to mixtures of nanomaterials.[156] Although there are formidable challenges to be tackled in developing and implementing a tiered toxicity testing strategy, meaningful policy cannot be formulated without reliable and accurate data.

In December 2008, the National Research Council released a report charging that the U.S. government lacked an effective plan to ensure the safety of nanotechnology.[157] A few months later, the U.S. House of Representatives passed the National Nanotechnology Initiative Amendment Act of 2009 (HR 554), which was intended to insure transparency in federal research efforts to understand the potential environmental, health, and safety risks of nanotechnology.[158] No such bill, however, has come up for a vote in the Senate, although the Nanotechnology Safety

[156] Balbus, et al.

[157] R. F. Service, *Science Policy Report Faults US Strategy for Nanotoxicology Research*, 322 Science (2008).

[158] http://www.electroiq.com/index/display/semiconductors-article-display/356916/articles/cleanrooms/top-stories/house-approves-nanotechnology-safety-and-transparency-bill.html.

Act (S.2942.IS) was read twice and then referred back to the Committee on Health, Education, Labor and Pensions in January 2010.[159] The focus of the proposed Senate bill is human health, and its objective is to grant the FDA the authority necessary to study the safety and effectiveness of nanotechnology-based drugs, delivery systems, medical devices, orthopedic implants, cosmetics, and food additives regulated by the agency. This proposed legislation, then, does not address nanomaterial use in products not intended for direct human use or ingestion, nor does it consider the broad environmental risk and, consequently, longer term public health risks that nanomaterials may pose.

Based on our extensive experience with past environmental contaminants and our deep knowledge of the public health threats associated with ultrafine particles, we have a sufficient basis on which to require thorough nanomaterial environmental health and safety testing. The question is not *should* nanomaterials require regulatory oversight, but rather *how* to implement such oversight effectively. No country has yet developed any comprehensive set of nanomaterial regulations aimed at the protection of human and environmental health and safety. Because we lack the political will to establish an effective and objective regulatory framework to determine nanomaterial risks, we face cascading hazards and serious conflicts of interest, particularly if nanomaterial toxicity and ecotoxicity data and risk assessments were to come only from industry.[160] The National Nanotechnology Initiative (NNI) has just marked its 10-year anniversary since it was established to coordinate the federal nanotechnology research and development effort across 25 U.S. Federal agencies.[161] The NNI provides a vision of the long-term opportunities and benefits of nanotechnology, creates a multi-agency framework to ensure U.S. leadership in nanotechnology research and development, and serves as the fulcrum for communication, cooperation, and collaboration as the nanotechnology field has evolved. The organization has succeeded in advancing a world-class nanotechnology research and development program and in educating the public about the promise of nanotechnology to solve some of the most difficult problems facing society. Regrettably, the NNI has not paid commensurate attention to its stated goal to support the responsible development of nanotechnology and to develop both an understanding of potential risks and the means to manage them. The time is long overdue for committing to critical evaluation of the risks and unintended consequences of nanomaterials and nanotechnology. Reducing this uncertainty around nanomaterial use will not only serve to protect public and ecological health, but it will also enhance public acceptance of nanotechnology and accelerate commercialization of its products.

[159] http://thomas.loc.gov/cgi-bin/query/z?c111:S.2942.

[160] Ostrowski, et al.

[161] http://www.nano.gov/

REFERENCES

Lux Research. (2007). *5th Edition of the Nanotech Report.* http://www.luxresearchinc.com/

A. Mcwilliams (2008). Nanotechnology: A Realistic Market Assessment. http://www.bccresearch.com/report/NANo31C.html

Anonymous. (2009). Nanotechnology Consumer Products Inventory – Consumer Products, Woodrow Wilson International Center for Scholars. http://www.nanotechproject.org/inventories/consumer/

P. J. A. Borm, D. Robbins, S. Haubold, T. Kuhlbush and E. Al (2006). The potential risks of nanomaterials: a review carried out for ECETOC. *Particle and Fibre Toxicology*, 3, 35.

P. J. A. Borm and D. Berube (2008). A tale of opportunities, uncertainties and risks. *Nanotoday*, 3(1–2), 58–59.

R. Chatterjee (2008). The challenge of regulating nanomaterials. *Environmental Science & Technology*, 42(2), 339–343.

A. Helland, P. Wick, A. Koehler, K. Schmid and C. Som (2007). Reviewing the environmental and human health knowledge base of carbon nanotubes. *Environmental Health Perspectives*, 115(8), 1125–1131.

N. Lubick (2008). Risks of nanotechnology remain uncertain. *Environmental Science & Technology*, 42(6), 821–824.

A. Nel, T. Xia, L. Madler and N. Li (2006). Toxic potential of materials at the nanolevel. *Science*, 311(5761), 622–627.

M. R. Wiesner and J.-Y. Bottero (Eds). (2007). *Environmental Nanotechnology: Applications and Impacts of Nanomaterials.* New York, NY, McGraw-Hill.

S. J. Klaine, P. J. J. Alvarez, G. E. Batley, T. F. Fernandes, R. D. Handy, D. Y. Lyon, S. Mahendra, M. J. Mclaughlin and J. R. Lead (2008). Nanomaterials in the environment: Behavior, fate, bioavailability, and effects. *Environmental Toxicology and Chemistry*, 27(9), 1825–1851.

A. D. Maynard (2006). Nanotechnology: assessing the risks. *Nano Today*, 1(2), 22–33.

D. G. Rickerby and M. Morrison (2007). Nanotechnology and the environment: A European perspective. *Science and Technology of Advanced Materials*, 8, 19–24.

M. R. Wiesner, G. V. Lowry, P. Alvarez, D. Dionysiou and P. Biswas (2006). Assessing the risks of manufactured nanomaterials. *Environmental Science & Technology*, 40(14), 4336–4345.

A. D. Maynard (2007). Nanotechnology: The next big thing, or much ado about nothing? *Annals of Occupational Hygiene*, 51(1), 1–12.

Nanowerk. (2007). Introduction to Nanotechnology. http://www.nanowerk.com/nanotech-nology/introduction/introduction_to_nanotechnology_1.php

American Society for Testing and Materials (2006). Standard terminology relating to nanotechnology. West Conshohocken, PA, American Society for Testing and Materials.

T. K. Altes (2008). Is Nano a No-No? Nanotechnology advances into buildings. http://www.enn.com/green_building/commentary/32429

H. D. Muller and F. Steinbach (1970). Decomposition of isopropyl alcohol photosensitized by zinc oxide. *Nature*, 225(5234), 728–729.

A. Duret and M. Gratzel (2005). Visible light-induced water oxidation on mesoscopic alpha-Fe2O3 films made by ultrasonic spray pyrolysis. *Journal of Physical Chemistry B*, 109(36), 17184–17191.

A. Fujishima and X. T. Zhang (2006). Titanium dioxide photocatalysis: present situation and future approaches. *Comptes Rendus Chimie*, 9(5–6), 750–760.

X. Chen and S. S. Mao (2007). Titanium dioxide nanomaterials: Synthesis, properties, modifications, and applications. *Chemical Reviews*, 107(7), 2891–2959.

F. Lu, W. P. Cai and Y. G. Zhang (2008). ZnO hierarchical micro/nanoarchitectures: Solvothermal synthesis and structurally enhanced photocatalytic performance. *Advanced Functional Materials*, 18(7), 1047–1056.

M. D. Hernandez-Alonso, F. Fresno, S. Suarez and J. M. Coronado (2009). Development of alternative photocatalysts to TiO_2: Challenges and opportunities. *Energy & Environmental Science*, 2(12), 1231–1257.

J. H. Mo, Y. P. Zhang, Q. J. Xu, J. J. Lamson and R. Y. Zhao (2009). Photocatalytic purification of volatile organic compounds in indoor air: A literature review. *Atmospheric Environment*, 43(14), 2229–2246.

M. H. Lai, A. Tubtimtae, M. W. Lee and G. J. Wang (2010). ZnO-nanorod dye-sensitized solar cells: new structure without a transparent conducting oxide layer. *International Journal of Photoenergy* (Article ID: 497095 DOI: 10.1155/2010/497095).

L. L. Peng, T. F. Xie, Y. C. Lu, H. M. Fan and D. J. Wang (2010). Synthesis, photoelectric properties and photocatalytic activity of the Fe_2O_3/TiO_2 heterogeneous photocatalysts. *Physical Chemistry Chemical Physics*, 12(28), 8033–8041.

S. C. Roy, O. K. Varghese, M. Paulose and C. A. Grimes (2010). Toward solar fuels: photocatalytic conversion of carbon dioxide to hydrocarbons. *ACS Nano*, 4(3), 1259–1278.

Y. Tian, D. Wu, X. A. Jia, B. B. Yu and S. H. Zhan (2011). Core-shell nanostructure of alpha-Fe_2O_3/Fe_3O_4: synthesis and photocatalysis for methyl orange. *Journal of Nanomaterials* 2011 (Article ID 837123).

E. Roduner (2006). Size matters: why nanomaterials are different. *Chemical Society Reviews*, 35(7), 583–592.

Lehigh University. (2004). Nanogold does not glitter, but its future looks bright. *Science Daily*, http://www.sciencedaily.com/releases/2004/04/040428062059.htm

Anonymous. (2009). Nanotechnology consumer products inventory – Analysis, Woodrow Wilson International Center for Scholars. http://www.nanotechproject.org/inventories/consumer/analysis_draft/

N. W. Ashcroft and N. D. Mermin (1976). *Solid State Physics*. New York, NY, Holt, Rinehart and Winston.

R. Hoffmann (1987). How chemistry and physics meet in the solid-state. *Angewandte Chemie-International Edition in English*, 26(9), 846–878.

P. P. Edwards, R. L. Johnston and C. N. R. Rao (1999). On the size-induced metal-insulator transition in clusters and small particles. In P. Braunstien, L. A. Oro and P. R. Raithby (Eds.), *Metal Clusters in Chemistry*. Chichester, NY, Wiley.

Z. L. Wang (2004). Nanostructures of zinc oxide. *Materials Today*, 7(6), 26–33.

L. Wang, D. K. Nagesha, S. Selvarasah, M. R. Dokmeci and R. L. Carrier (2008). Toxicity of CdSe nanoparticles in Caco-2 cell cultures. *Journal of Nanobiotechnology*, (6), 11.

R. C. Jin, Y. W. Cao, C. A. Mirkin, K. L. Kelly, G. C. Schatz and J. G. Zheng (2001). Photoinduced conversion of silver nanospheres to nanoprisms. *Science*, 294(5548), 1901–1903.

J. E. Millstone, S. Park, K. L. Shuford, L. D. Qin, G. C. Schatz and C. A. Mirkin (2005). Observation of a quadrupole plasmon mode for a colloidal solution of gold nanoprisms. *Journal of the American Chemical Society*, 127(15), 5312–5313.

N. M. Dimitrijevic, Z. V. Saponjic, B. M. Rabatic, O. G. Poluektov and T. Rajh (2007). Effect of size and shape of nanocrystalline TiO_2 on photogenerated charges. An EPR study. *Journal of Physical Chemistry C*, 111(40), 14597–14601.

N. L. Rosi, D. A. Giljohann, C. S. Thaxton, A. K. R. Lytton-Jean, M. S. Han and C. A. Mirkin (2006). Oligonucleotide-modified gold nanoparticles for intracellular gene regulation. *Science*, 312(5776), 1027–1030.

D. A. Giljohann, D. S. Seferos, P. C. Patel, J. E. Millstone, N. L. Rosi and C. A. Mirkin (2007). Oligonucleotide loading determines cellular uptake of DNA-modified gold nanoparticles. *Nano Letters*, 7(12), 3818–3821.

D. S. Seferos, D. A. Giljohann, N. L. Rosi and C. A. Mirkin (2007). Locked nucleic acid-nanoparticle conjugates. *Chembiochemistry*, 8(11), 1230–1232.

R. Partha and J. L. Conyers (2009). Biomedical applications of functionalized fullerene-based nanomaterials. *International Journal of Nanomedicine*, 4, 261–275.

H. Lyklema (1991). *Fundamentals of Interface and Colloid Science*. Amsterdam, the Netherlands, Elsevier.

K. Donaldson, L. Tran, L. A. Jimenez, R. Duffin, D. E. Newby, N. Mills, M. W. and V. Stone (2005). Combustion-derived nanoparticles: A review of their toxicology following inhalation exposure. *Particle and Fibre Toxicology*, 2.

G. Oberdorster, E. Oberdorster and J. Oberdorster (2005). Nanotoxicology: An emerging discipline evolving from studies of ultrafine particles. *Environmental Health Perspectives*, 113(7), 823–839.

Techtarget. (2011). Nanotechnology. http://whatis.techtarget.com/definition/0,sid9_gci 213444,00.html

C. Buzea, Pacheco, Ii and K. Robbie (2007). Nanomaterials and nanoparticles: Sources and toxicity. *Biointerphases*, 2(4), MR17–MR71.

P. R. Buseck and K. Adachi (2008). Nanoparticles in the atmosphere. *Elements*, 4(6), 389–394.

R. P. Feynman (1960). There's plenty of room at the bottom: An invitation to enter a new field of physics, in *CalTech's Engineering and Science*, 23(5), 22–36. Available at http://www.zyvex.com/nanotech/feynman.html.

M. F. Crommie, C. P. Lutz and D. M. Eigler (1993). Confinement of electrons to quantum corrals on a metal surface. *Science*, 262, 218–220.

S. M. Paek, H. Jung, Y. J. Lee, N. G. Park, S. J. Hwang and J. H. Choy (2006). Nanostructured TiO2 films for dye-sensitized solar cells. *Journal of Physics and Chemistry of Solids*, 67(5–6), 1308–1311.

L. Chen, M. E. Graham, G. H. Li and K. A. Gray (2006). Fabricating highly active mixed phase TiO2 photocatalysts by reactive DC magnetron sputter deposition. *Thin Solid Films*, 515(3), 1176–1181.

L. Chen, M. E. Graham, G. H. Li, D. R. Gentner, N. M. Dimitrijevic and K. A. Gray (2009). Photoreduction of CO2 by TiO2 nanocomposites synthesized through reactive direct current magnetron sputter deposition. *Thin Solid Films*, 517(19), 5641–5645.

A. Ignatiev, X. Chen, N. J. Wu, Z. G. Lu and L. Smith (2008). Nanostructured thin solid oxide fuel cells with high power density. *Dalton Transactions*, (40), 5501–5506.

K. H. Yu and J. H. Chen (2009). Enhancing solar cell efficiencies through 1-D nanostructures. *Nanoscale Research Letters*, 4(1), 1–10.

J. Lee, S. Mahendra and P. J. J. Alvarez (2010). Nanomaterials in the construction industry: a review of their applications and environmental health and safety considerations. *ACS Nano*, 4(7), 3580–3590.

H. H. Ou and S. L. Lo (2007). Review of titania nanotubes synthesized via the hydrothermal treatment: Fabrication, modification, and application. *Separation and Purification Technology*, 58(1), 179–191.

S. Rani, S. C. Roy, M. Paulose, O. K. Varghese, G. K. Mor, S. Kim, S. Yoriya, T. J. Latempa and C. A. Grimes (2010). Synthesis and applications of electrochemically self-assembled titania nanotube arrays. *Physical Chemistry Chemical Physics*, 12(12), 2780–2800.

K. L. Schulte, P. A. Desario and K. A. Gray (2010). Effect of crystal phase composition on the reductive and oxidative abilities of TiO2 nanotubes under UV and visible light. *Applied Catalysis B-Environmental*, 97(3–4), 354–360.

B. Vijayan, N. M. Dimitrijevic, T. Rajh and K. Gray (2010). Effect of calcination temperature on the photocatalytic reduction and oxidation processes of hydrothermally synthesized titania nanotubes. *Journal of Physical Chemistry C*, 114(30), 12994–13002.

B. K. Vijayan, N. M. Dimitrijevic, J. S. Wu and K. A. Gray (2010). The Effects of Pt doping on the structure and visible light photoactivity of titania nanotubes. *Journal of Physical Chemistry C*, 114(49), 21262–21269.

G. H. Li and K. A. Gray (2007). The solid-solid interface: Explaining the high and unique photocatalytic reactivity of TiO2-based nanocomposite materials. *Chemical Physics*, 339, 173–187.

G. H. Li, L. Chen, M. E. Graham and K. A. Gray (2007). A comparison of mixed phase titania photocatalysts prepared by physical and chemical methods: The importance of the solid-solid interface. *Journal of Molecular Catalysis A-Chemical*, 275(1–2), 30–35.

L. E. Murr, J. J. Bang, E. V. Esquivel, P. A. Guerrero and A. Lopez (2004). Carbon nanotubes, nanocrystal forms, and complex nanoparticle aggregates in common fuel-gas combustion sources and the ambient air. *Journal of Nanoparticle Research*, 6(2–3), 241–251.

B. Nowack and T. D. Bucheli (2007). Occurrence, behavior and effects of nanoparticles in the environment. *Environmental Pollution*, 150, 5–22.

S. Friedrichs and J. Schulte (2007). Environmental, health and safety aspects of nanotechnology – implications for the R&D in (small) companies. *Science and Technology of Advanced Materials*, 8(1–2), 12–18.

W. Stumm (1987). *Aquatic Surface Chemistry: Chemical Processes at the Particle-Water Interface*. New York, NY, John Wiley & Sons, 520 pp.

W. Stumm and J. J. Morgan (1996). *Aquatic Chemistry: Chemical Equilibria and Rates in Natural Waters*, 3rd ed. New York, NY, John Wiley & Sons, 520 pp.

K. Donaldson and V. Stone (2003). Current hypotheses on the mechanisms of toxicity of ultrafine particles. *Annali dell'Istituto Superiore di Sanita*, 39(3), 405–410.

H. F. Lecoanet, J. Y. Bottero and M. R. Wiesner (2004). Laboratory assessment of the mobility of nanomaterials in porous media. *Environmental Science & Technology*, 38(19), 5164–5169.

A. D. Ostrowski, T. Martin, J. Conti, I. Hurt and B. H. Harthorn (2009), Nanotoxicology: characterizing the scientific literature, 2000–2007. *Journal of Nanoparticle Research*, 11(2), 251–257.

V. L. Colvin (2003). The potential environmental impact of engineered nanomaterials. *Nature Biotechnology*, 21(10), 1166–1170.

J. M. Balbus, A. D. Maynard, V. L. Colvin, V. Castranova, G. P. Daston, R. A. Denison, K. L. Dreher, P. L. Goering, A. M. Goldberg, K. M. Kulinowski, N. A. Monteiro-Riviere, G. Oberdorster, G. S. Omenn, K. E. Pinkerton, K. S. Ramos, K. M. Rest, J. B. Sass, E. K. Silbergeld and B. A. Wong (2007). Meeting report: Hazard assessment for nanoparticles – Report from an interdisciplinary workshop. *Environmental Health Perspectives*, 115(11), 1654–1659.

M. Auffan, J. Rose, J. Y. Bottero, G. V. Lowry, J. P. Jolivet and M. R. Wiesner (2009). Towards a definition of inorganic nanoparticles from an environmental, health and safety perspective. *Nature Nanotechnology*, 4(10), 634–641.

D. B. Warheit (2008). How meaningful are the results of nanotoxicity studies in the absence of adequate material characterization? *Toxicological Sciences*, 101(2), 183–185.

T. Xia, M. Kovochich, J. Brant, M. Hotze, J. Sempf, T. Oberley, C. Sioutas, J. I. Yeh, M. R. Wiesner and A. E. Nel (2006). Comparison of the abilities of ambient and manufactured nanoparticles to induce cellular toxicity according to an oxidative stress paradigm, *Nano Letters*, 6(8), 1794–1807.

M. Kovochich, T. Xia, J. Xu, J. I. Yeh and A. E. Nel (2007). Principles and procedures to assess nanomaterial toxicity. In M. R. Wiesner and J.-Y. Bottero (Eds). *Environmental Nanotechnology: Applications and Impacts of Nanomaterials*. New York, NY, McGraw-Hill, pp. 205–229.

T. Xia, M. Kovochich, M. Liong, L. Madler, B. Gilbert, H. B. Shi, J. I. Yeh, J. I. Zink and A. E. Nel (2008). Comparison of the mechanism of toxicity of zinc oxide and cerium oxide nanoparticles based on dissolution and oxidative stress properties. *ACS Nano*, 2(10), 2121–2134.

E. J. Rogers, S. F. Hsieh, N. Organti, D. Schmidt and D. Bello (2008). A high throughput in vitro analytical approach to screen for oxidative stress potential exerted by nanomaterials using a biologically relevant matrix: Human blood serum. *Toxicology in Vitro*, 22(6), 1639–1647.

P. Spohn, C. Hirsch, F. Hasler, A. Bruinink, H. F. Krug and P. Wick (2009). C-60 fullerene: A powerful antioxidant or a damaging agent? The importance of an in-depth material characterization prior to toxicity assays. *Environmental Pollution*, 157(4), 1134–1139.

D. Berhanu, A. Dybowska, S. K. Misra, C. J. Stanley, P. Ruenraroengsak, A. R. Boccaccini, T. D. Tetley, S. N. Luoma, J. A. Plant and E. Valsami-Jones (2009). Characterisation of carbon nanotubes in the context of toxicity studies. *Environmental Health*, 8.

M. Lucarelli, A. M. Gatti, G. Savarino, P. Quattroni, L. Martinelli, E. Monari and D. Boraschi (2004). Innate defence functions of macrophages can be biased by nano-sized ceramic and metallic particles. *European Cytokine Network*, 15(4), 339–346.

P. Wick, A. Malek, P. Manser, D. Meili, X. Maeder-Althaus, L. Diener, P. A. Diener, A. Zisch, H. F. Krug and U. Von Mandach (2010). Barrier capacity of human placenta for nanosized materials. *Environmental Health Perspectives*, 118(3), 432–436.

L. K. Limbach, P. Wick, P. Manser, R. N. Grass, A. Bruinink and W. J. Stark (2007). Exposure of engineered nanoparticles to human lung epithelial cells: Influence of chemical composition and catalytic activity on oxidative stress. *Environmental Science & Technology*, 41(11), 4158–4163.

A. M. Derfus, W. C. W. Chan and S. N. Bhatia (2004). Probing the cytotoxicity of semiconductor quantum dots. *Nano Letters*, 4(1), 11–18.

C. W. Lam, J. T. James, R. Mccluskey, S. Arepalli and R. L. Hunter (2006). A review of carbon nanotube toxicity and assessment of potential occupational and environmental health risks. *Crit Rev Toxicol*, 36(3), 189–217.

K. F. Soto, A. Carrasco, T. G. Powell, K. M. Garza and L. E. Murr (2005). Comparative in vitro cytotoxicity assessment of some manufactured nanoparticulate materials characterized by transmission electron microscopy. *Journal of Nanoparticle Research*, 7(2–3), 145–169.

A. Magrez, L. Horvath, R. Smajda, V. Salicio, N. Pasquier, L. Forro and B. Schwaller (2009). Cellular toxicity of TiO_2-based nanofilaments. *ACS Nano*, 3(8), 2274–2280.

P. R. Gil, Oberdorster, G., Elder, A., Puntes, V., Wolfgang, J. P. (2010). Correlating physico-chemical with toxicological properties of nanoparticles: the present and the future. *ACS Nano*, 4(10), 5527–5531.

M. Farre, K. Gajda-Schrantz, L. Kantiani and D. Barcelo (2009). Ecotoxicity and analysis of nanomaterials in the aquatic environment. *Analytical and Bioanalytical Chemistry*, 393(1), 81–95.

D. Y. Lyon, A. Thill, J. Rose and P. J. J. Alvarez (2007). Ecotoxicological impacts of nanomaterials. In M. R. Wiesner and J.-Y. Bottero (Eds). *Environmental Nanotechnology: Applications and Impacts of Nanomaterials*. New York, NY, McGraw-Hill, pp. 445–479.

C. L. Tiller and C. R. Omelia (1993). Natural organic-matter and colloidal stability – models and measurements. *Colloids and Surfaces A-Physicochemical and Engineering Aspects*, 73, 89–102.

P. Christian, F. Von Der Kammer, M. Baalousha and T. Hofmann (2008). Nanoparticles: structure, properties, preparation and behaviour in environmental media. *Ecotoxicology*, 17(5), 326–343.

H. Hyung, J. D. Fortner, J. B. Hughes and J. H. Kim (2007). Natural organic matter stabilizes carbon nanotubes in the aqueous phase. *Environmental Science & Technology*, 41(1), 179–184.

R. F. Domingos, N. Tufenkji and K. J. Wilkinson (2009). Aggregation of titanium dioxide nanoparticles: role of a fulvic acid. *Environmental Science & Technology*, 43(5), 1282–1286.

Q. L. Li, B. Xie, Y. S. Hwang and Y. J. Xu (2009). Kinetics of C-60 fullerene dispersion in water enhanced by natural organic matter and sunlight. *Environmental Science & Technology*, 43(10), 3574–3579.

Y. S. Hwang and Q. L. Li (2010). Characterizing photochemical transformation of aqueous nC(60) under environmentally relevant conditions. *Environmental Science & Technology*, 44(8), 3008–3013.

C. Y. Chen and C. T. Jafvert (2010). Photoreactivity of carboxylated single-walled carbon nanotubes in sunlight: reactive oxygen species production in water. *Environmental Science & Technology*, 44(17), 6674–6679.

B. M. Simonet and M. Valcarcel (2009). Monitoring nanoparticles in the environment. *Analytical and Bioanalytical Chemistry*, 393(1), 17–21.

M. A. Kiser, P. Westerhoff, T. Benn, Y. Wang, J. Perez-Rivera and K. Hristovski (2009). Titanium nanomaterial removal and release from wastewater treatment plants. *Environmental Science & Technology*, 43(17), 6757–6763.

C. Cherchi and A. Z. Gu (2010). Impact of titanium dioxide nanomaterials on nitrogen fixation rate and intracellular nitrogen storage in Anabaena variabilis. *Environmental Science & Technology*, 44(21), 8302–8307.

J. M. Unrine, S. E. Hunyadi, O. V. Tsyusko, W. Rao, W. A. Shoults-Wilson and P. M. Bertsch (2010). Evidence for bioavailability of Au nanoparticles from soil and biodistribution within earthworms (Eisenia fetida). *Environmental Science & Technology*, 44(21), 8308–8313.

J. D. Judy, J. M. Unrine and P. M. Bertsch (2011). Evidence for biomagnification of gold nanoparticles within a terrestrial food chain. *Environmental Science & Technology*, 45(2), 776–781.

A. M. Horst, A. C. Neal, R. E. Mielke, P. R. Sislian, W. H. Suh, L. Madler, G. D. Stucky and P. A. Holden (2010). Dispersion of TiO_2 nanoparticle agglomerates by Pseudomonas aeruginosa. *Applied and Environmental Microbiology*, 76(21), 7292–7298.

J. R. Gurr, A. S. S. Wang, C. H. Chen and K. Y. Jan (2005). Ultrafine titanium dioxide particles in the absence of photoactivation can induce oxidative damage to human bronchial epithelial cells. *Toxicology*, 213(1–2), 66–73.

L. K. Adams, D. Y. Lyon and P. J. J. Alvarez (2006). Comparative eco-toxicity of nanoscale TiO_2, SiO_2, and ZnO water suspensions. *Water Research*, 40(19), 3527–3532.

N. M. Franklin, N. J. Rogers, S. C. Apte, G. E. Batley, G. E. Gadd and P. S. Casey (2007). Comparative toxicity of nanoparticulate ZnO, Bulk ZnO, and $ZnCl_2$ to a freshwater microalga (*Pseudokirchneriella subcapitata*): the importance of particle solubility. *Environmental Science & Technology*, 41, 8484–8490.

S. B. Lovern, J. R. Strickler and R. Klaper (2007). Behavioral and physiological changes in Daphnia magna when exposed to nanoparticle suspensions (titanium dioxide, nano-C-60, and C(60)HxC(70)Hx). *Environmental Science & Technology*, 41(12), 4465–4470.

R. D. Handy, T. B. Henry, T. M. Scown, B. D. Johnston and C. R. Tyler (2008). Manufactured nanoparticles: their uptake and effects on fish – a mechanistic analysis. *Ecotoxicology*, 17(5), 396–409.

G. Federici, B. J. Shaw and R. D. Handy (2007). Toxicity of titanium dioxide nanoparticles to rainbow trout (Oncorhynchus mykiss): Gill injury, oxidative stress, and other physiological effects. *Aquatic Toxicology*, 84(4), 415–430.

T. M. Scown, R. Van Aerle, B. D. Johnston, S. Cumberland, J. R. Lead, R. Owen and C. R. Tyler (2009). High doses of intravenously administered titanium dioxide nanoparticles accumulate in the kidneys of rainbow trout but with no observable impairment of renal function. *Toxicological Sciences*, 109(2), 372–380.

D. B. Warheit, T. R. Webb, K. L. Reed, S. Frerichs and C. M. Sayes (2007). Pulmonary toxicity study in rats with three forms of ultrafine-TiO_2 particles: Differential responses related to surface properties. *Toxicology*, 230(1), 90–104.

K. Takeda, K. I. Suzuki, A. Ishihara, M. Kubo-Irie, R. Fujimoto, M. Tabata, S. Oshio, Y. Nihei, T. Ihara and M. Sugamata (2009). Nanoparticles transferred from pregnant mice to their offspring can damage the genital and cranial nerve systems. *Journal of Health Science*, 55(1), 95–102.

E. J. Wolfrum, J. Huang, D. M. Blake, P. C. Maness, Z. Huang, J. Fiest and W. A. Jacoby (2002). Photocatalytic oxidation of bacteria, bacterial and fungal spores, and model biofilm components to carbon dioxide on titanium dioxide-coated surfaces. *Environmental Science & Technology*, 36(15), 3412–3419.

S. Ciston, R. M. Lueptow and K. A. Gray (2008). Bacterial attachment on reactive ceramic ultrafiltration membranes. *Journal of Membrane Science*, 320(1–2), 101–107.

K. Hund-Rinke and M. Simon (2006). Ecotoxic effect of photocatalytic active nanoparticles TiO_2 on algae and daphnids. *Environmental Science and Pollution Research*, 13(4), 225–232.

G. Wakefield, M. Green, S. Lipscomb and B. Flutter (2004). Modified titania nanomaterials for sunscreen applications – reducing free radical generation and DNA damage. *Materials Science and Technology*, 20(8), 985–988.

A. D. Maynard, R. J. Aitken, T. Butz, V. Colvin, K. Donaldson, G. Oberdorster, M. A. Philbert, J. Ryan, A. Seaton, V. Stone, S. S. Tinkle, L. Tran, N. J. Walker and D. B. Warheit (2006). Safe handling of nanotechnology. *Nature*, 444(7117), 267–269.

C. O. Robichaud, D. Tanzil and M. R. Wiesner (2007). Assessing life-cycle risks of nanomaterials. In M. R. Wiesner and J.-Y. Bottero (Eds). *Environmental Nanotechnology: Applications and Impacts of Nanomaterials*. New York, NY, McGraw-Hill, pp. 481–524.

R. F. Service (2008). Nanotechnology – Can high-speed tests sort out which nanomaterials are safe? *Science*, 321(5892), 1036–1037.

R. F. Service (2008). Science Policy report faults US strategy for nanotoxicology research. *Science*, 322(5909), 1779.

PART II

Public Perceptions of Nanotechnology Risks

3

Public Acceptance and the Regulation of Emerging Technologies

The Role of Private Politics

Daniel Diermeier

The history of innovation is full of cases in which a new technology, despite its initial promise, quickly encountered substantial public resistance and never reached its economic potential. Examples include nuclear power, genetically modified food, stem cell research, and many others. In some cases, carefully crafted market entry campaigns were derailed by hostile media coverage, creating fear among customers. In other cases, companies were targeted by well-organized activist campaigns. A major reason for these difficulties is the importance of influences and intermediaries. Journalists, experts (real and so-described), regulators, and politicians all shape customer and stakeholder perception about a product, as does the growing importance of peer-to-peer communication through internet channels such as blogs, websites, etc. As a consequence, the relationship between companies and customers is increasingly no longer bilateral and direct, but multilateral and mediated.[1]

The history of genetically modified food products (GMOs) offers an instructive example. Excitement about technological innovation quickly turned to concern, with disastrous consequences for the industry in the European market.[2] Such issues of product acceptance not only pertain to consumer-oriented products, as in the case of, for example, the Flavr Savr® tomato, the first genetically manufactured food product in the United States, but also for business-to-business products, as in the case of Monsanto's Roundup Ready® soybeans, used as an ingredient in many processed food items. In both cases the issue was triggered by worries in the general

[1] Daniel Diermeier, *Reputation Rules: Strategies for Building Your Company's Most Valuable Asset* (New York, NY: McGraw-Hill, 2011).

[2] Daniel Charles, *Lords of the Harvest: Biotech, Big Money and the Future of Food* (New York: Perseus Books Group, 2002); Mark Parry, "Monsanto—The Launch of Roundup Ready Soybeans," Harvard Business Review. Case 9-UV0–321, 2000 and Michael Watkins, "Robert Shapiro and Monsanto," Harvard Business Review. Case 9–801-426.

public about product safety, environmental impact, and the like. In the consumer product case, this may undermine consumer trust, resulting in lower sales. In the business-to-business case, the direct impact may not be on the supplier (e.g., Monsanto) but rather on the branded company that is using Roundup Ready® soybeans as an ingredient for its products, say, candy bars. Concerned about loss of customers, consumer brand companies then will put pressure on their suppliers to ensure that products are "GMO-free," which in turn undermines the sales of the supplier (here, Monsanto). In other words, if there are concerns about a product or technology, these concerns quickly move up the supply chain, undermining the business success of the technology.[3]

Nanotechnology is facing a similar set of challenges as the previously mentioned technologies. In a recent report on future technologies, including nanotechnology, Dr. Doug Parr, Greenpeace International's Chief Scientist, did not mince words: "Any technology placed in the hands of those who care little about the possible environmental, health, or social impacts is potentially disastrous."[4]

In contrast to biotech, nuclear power, or stem cell research, however, the concerns about nanotech products so far have not constituted a significant impediment for nanotech products. Indeed, existing public opinion survey research suggests a fairly broad acceptance of nanotechnology. As discussed in this chapter, not much trust should be placed in these data. Public support for nanotech products is shallow at best and can easily move toward fear and resistance. The typical dynamics of the public reaction to emerging technologies, the factors that influence whether such reaction will be positive or negative, and possible approaches that may influence public acceptance of nanotechnology are discussed.

What makes these challenges particularly daunting is the fact that they can quickly turn to a crisis, if not spotted early, and once they have reached crisis level, effective management is difficult at best.[5] One important reason is that, although companies may have a detailed understanding of their customers, they frequently lack a good understanding of indirect factors that shape customer perception. These include both media coverage (both mass and social media) and the impact of influences such as advocacy and interest groups. Powerful advances in communication technology have made it possible for activist groups to organize and act more efficiently and effectively than ever before. This has led to the emergence of a new channel in the regulation of commerce: private politics.

[3] Of course, these issues can also have regulatory or political impact with public officials responding to public opinion. Here we focus mainly on the issue of customer perception.

[4] Alexander H. Arnall, "Future technologies, today's choices: Nanotechnology, artificial intelligence and robotics; A technical, political and institutional map of emerging technologies" (London, England: Greenpeace Environmental Trust, 2003) p.7.

[5] Daniel Diermeier, *Reputation Rules: Strategies for Building Your Company's Most Valuable Asset* (New York, NY: McGraw-Hill, 2011).

THE EMERGENCE OF PRIVATE POLITICS

It is important to conceptualize challenges to the public perception of an emerging technology not as a "mere" public relations issue. Rather, they constitute an alternative channel for industry regulation that can be just as effective as the regulation of business conduct by legislatures, agencies, and the courts. Baron,[6] Baron and Diermeier,[7] and Diermeier[8] have used the term *private politics* for these phenomena. When we think of politics, we typically think about parliaments, elections, and other public institutions. But there is a growing type of political interaction that, although clearly focused on social and policy issues, operates outside of these traditional institutional environments. Regulation, for example, is usually understood as the result of government action exercised and implemented by legislatures, agencies, and the courts. Yet, in recent years, public institutions are no longer the sole source of constraints on commerce. Instead, political activists and nongovernmental organizations (NGOs) have increasingly succeeded in forcing firms and entire industries to change their business practices by directly targeting companies and their value chains. Issues include environmental protection, human rights, discrimination, privacy, safety of employees and customers, endangered species, animal welfare, and many more. The activists' explicit or implicit goal of this strategy is *private regulation*, that is, the "voluntary" adoption of rules and standards that constrain certain company conduct without the involvement of public agents. In the case of nanotechnology, these may include measures ranging from adopting certain safety protocols all the way to a moratorium.[9]

In many instances, as in the case of nanotechnology, activists do not merely try to change the behavior of one specific firm, but industry practice as a whole. Their weapons of choice range from consumer boycotts to shareholder activism and divestment campaigns. Although sometimes self-regulation is eventually codified in governmental regulation, there are increasingly more examples where industries adopt explicit standards of self-regulation without any reference to governmental actors.

This change in institutional arenas seems to reflect a conscious strategic shift by activists. Many activists now believe that the "long march through the institutions"[10] takes too long and can easily be blocked. Michael Brune, executive director of the Rainforest Action Network (RAN), commented that, "Companies were more responsive to public opinion than certain legislatures were. We felt we could create

6 David P. Baron, "Private politics," *Journal of Economics and Management Strategy*, 12, no. 1 (2003): 31–66.

7 David P. Baron and Daniel Diermeier, "Strategic activism and non-market strategy," *Journal of Economics and Management Strategy*, 16, no. 3 (2007): 599–634.

8 Daniel Diermeier, "Private politics: A research agenda," *The Political Economist*, 14, no. 2 (2007): 1–2.

9 Alexander H. Arnall, "Future technologies, today's choices: Nanotechnology, artificial intelligence and robotics; A technical, political and institutional map of emerging technologies" (London, England: Greenpeace Environmental Trust, 2003).

10 This term is attributed to German activist Rudi Dutschke.

more democracy in the marketplace than in the government."[11] Democracy in the marketplace means that citizen consumers try to create social chance through markets rather than political institutions. If they object to logging in old growth forests, they can impose their will on timber companies by refusing to buy old growth products. Thomas Friedman, a New York Times columnist, characterized this as "globalization activism" in 2001 when he wrote about an international boycott against Exxon Mobil for its stance on climate change. Friedman quoted, Paul Gilding, former head of Greenpeace, who said"

> The smart activists are now saying, 'OK, you want to play markets—let's play.' New York Times columnist Thomas Friedman explained: Lobbying government] takes forever and can easily be counter-lobbied by corporations. No, no, no. They start with consumers at the pump, get them to pressure the gas stations, get the station owners to pressure the companies and the companies to pressure governments. After all, consumers do have choices where they buy their gas, and there are differences now. Shell and BPAmoco (which is also the world's biggest solar company) both withdrew from the oil industry lobby that has been dismissing climate change.[12]

Companies have started to take these challenges seriously, spending significant resources on corporate social responsibility programs and reports, as well as reputation and issue management initiatives, and adopting self-regulatory standards at both the firm and the industry level. Although many such changes in a company are defensive, some companies have tried to take advantage of the presence of concerned constituencies, for example, by branding themselves as socially or environmentally responsible. Well-known examples include BP or Ben and Jerry's (now owned by Unilever).

These issues are highly relevant in the case of emerging technologies such as nanotech. Given their distance from end consumers, nanotech companies are not likely to be the direct target of consumer boycotts. Rather, activists are more likely to target their customers and customers' customers. Such indirect targeting strategies are very common and especially effective if the target is not a specific company, but an industry (e.g., logging), a business practice (e.g., use of prison labor), or an ingredient/product category (e.g., GMOs). In these cases, activists frequently do not target a company directly, but firms in its value chain (i.e., its customers). The RAN sought to end the logging of old growth forests, and rather than threaten Boise Cascade (a paper and wood-products company) directly, RAN threatened its corporate customers. RAN first went after Kinko's, which quickly declared that it would not purchase products made from old growth timber. RAN also targeted home improvement companies, and chose to boycott Lowe's – the number 2 in the U.S. market. One reason for the targeting of Lowe's was the fact that, unlike competing

[11] David P. Baron and Erin Yurday, (2004). "Anatomy of a Corporate Campaign: Rainforest Action Network and Citigroup," Case P42 A, B. Stanford, CA: Graduate School of Business, Stanford University.

[12] Thomas Friedman, "Foreign Affairs; A Tiger by the Tail," *New York Times*, June 1, 2001.

retailers, such as the market leader Home Depot, Lowe's primarily caters to women. RAN reasoned that women would be more sympathetic to its cause than men, which made Lowe's a particularly attractive target.[13]

In the case of nanotechnology, activists would likely not target nanotech companies but focus instead on the downstream segment of the value chain. The campaign would likely highlight broad, immediately relatable concerns such as safety and environmental risks in the context of specific companies that use nanotechnology in their products, especially those directly sold to consumers.

Consider again the example of the RAN. Attractive targets for RAN have a well-known brand and a "public face." RAN chose Citigroup as the first target in its global finance campaign not because it was the industry leader or the worst offender, but because it had a large consumer banking business that could be damaged. Citigroup also had an extensive advertising campaign under the slogan "live richly." Ilyse Hogue, RAN's campaign manager for the Global Finance Campaign, said:

> Citigroup had poured $100 million into its brand image, most recently on its "Live Richly" marketing campaign, which was predicated on the notion that "there is more to life than money." We saw a company that was investing a lot in making the public believe that they operated in line with common social values. Part of Citi's vulnerability was the juxtaposition of what it articulated to the public with what we saw on the ground from Citi's finance activities. (Baron & Yurday, 2004)

After reaching an agreement with Citigroup, RAN targeted Bank of America and JP Morgan Chase, both of which had mergers pending that required regulatory approval.

In the case of nanotech, well-known consumer brands or products are natural choices. Any evidence of specific victims, especially those endowed with special protection by society such as children or the elderly, would be highlighted. One such example could be sunscreen lotions, especially those marketed to children and families.[14]

Of critical importance for the success of corporate campaigns is a high level of media attention. When developing a media communication strategy, there are two basic options available to the activist: paid media and free (or earned) media. Each of these channels has its distinct strengths and weaknesses. Paid media, consisting of direct advertising and other media that the activist has bought the explicit rights to,

[13] For example, Lowe's has wider aisles than Home Depot, which are preferred by female customers. See David P. Baron and Erin Yurday (2004). Anatomy of a Corporate Campaign: Rainforest Action Network and Citigroup. Case P42 A, B, C. Stanford, CA: Graduate School of Business, Stanford University.

[14] For products that use nanotechnology, see the registry maintained by *Project on Emerging Nanotechnologies*, a partnership between the Woodrow Wilson International Center for Scholars and the Pew Charitable Trusts, at http://www.nanotechproject.org/inventories/consumers (accessed on July 25, 2011). A particularly interesting example is the sunscreen Banana Boat. See http://www.nanotechproject.org/inventories/consumer/browse/products/kids_tear_free_spf_30/ (accessed July 28, 2011).

gives the advantage of complete control over the message. However, the drawback is that consumers realize this lack of objectivity, and the credibility of this channel correspondingly suffers. Free media refers to sources such as the news, magazine articles, blog and forum postings, and television reports. The main advantage (other than cost) is the added credibility of the journalist or associated news outlet. The obvious problem is a lack of control: the author may write whatever he or she wishes about the activists, or may misrepresent the activist entirely. Thus a well-coordinated communication strategy is necessary to ensure the success of an activist's message.[15]

The main focus of the activist communication strategy is to cast a negative light on the target organization and to amplify the visibility of the selected message. However, different audiences require unique messages and media channels to reach them. Thus, in order for a communication strategy to be successful, an activist group will need to properly identify its target audiences, develop targeted messages for each group, and leverage the proper media channels.

Crafting individual messages for each audience can present a problem, however. Different messages for different groups may conflict with the values of various target audiences. For example, a message aimed at religiously oriented investors, e.g. pension funds for clergy, that highlights concerns about a company's global labor practices may be less well received by hedge fund investors whose main concern may lie with the cost impact of changing business practices. Even when pursuing targeted media channels for each audience, messages may cross paths, undermining credibility and effectiveness. Manheim succinctly illustrates this problem: "Profit driven behaviors that may not play well on Main Street . . . may play exceptionally well on Wall Street."[16]

Activists circumvent this problem by developing layered communication strategies. This involves focusing on broader, less polarizing issues to communicate through mainstream channels such as television, print radio, and internet sites, while developing more specialized messages for distribution through narrower channels, such as white papers and direct personal communication.

The first audience to consider is *legitimizing agents*. These are groups with generally positive public images who are seen to act with society's best interest in mind. Examples are religious and social advocacy groups and members of the target corporation aligned with the activist's cause who can act as internal agents for change. This group lends credibility to an activist's cause simply by lending their support. Messages targeted to this group tend to focus on greater social issues that the target agent already supports. For a religious organization, this might be improving working conditions in the third world. Without these groups as allies, the general public may interpret an activist's cause as a form of special interest politics.[17] Next come *mediating agents*, composed of journalists, financial and industry analysts,

[15] Jarol B. Manheim, *The Death of a Thousand Cuts: Corporate Campaigns and the Attack on the Corporation* (Mahwah, NJ: Lawrence Erlbaum Associates, 2001).

[16] Ibid.

[17] Ibid.

and celebrities or public figures. As Manheim puts it, the function of this group is to "launder" the campaign (in the sense that these agents are not working in the interests of the union or other advocacy group per se, but that they nevertheless convey its messages) and to broaden their distribution.[18] Messages aimed at these agents often follow a very traditional "storytelling" narrative, with a clearly defined victim, villain, and resolution.[19]

The third group is referred to as *tactical targets* and consists of stakeholders who are able to apply pressure to the target group. As mentioned elsewhere and detailed earlier in this chapter, this group is often risk averse, and, given that there are equal substitutes for their business relationship with the target group, they can be very responsive to activist communication. As noted by Manheim,

> The idea here is to convince the targeted groups that the company has significant failings, and then energize them to take those up with the company's board or management by acting out their normal roles as shareholders, customers, regulators, and the like.[20]

PRIVATE REGULATION

One option for companies that find themselves the target of corporate campaigns is to change their business standards. This can be done reactively (after being targeted) or proactively (in order to avoid being targeted or, at least, to minimize the ensuing damage). Although such change in business practices is, strictly speaking, voluntary, its practical consequences are the same as mandatory regulation by law. If an entire industry chooses to only sell dolphin-safe tuna, it makes no practical difference for consumers and suppliers whether this is done because of a change in international or national law or because of industry self-regulation. Such standards may not be legally binding, but they are self-enforcing as long as the media or activists can impose intolerable reputational damage on a company that fails to comply.

However, important differences remain. For example, legal standards cover the entire industry within the relevant legal domain, whereas self-regulation may only be adopted by a sub-segment of a given industry. On the other hand, private regulation may also cover foreign companies that would be beyond the reach of domestic law. More importantly, the mechanisms that lead to regulation are very different. In the case of public regulation, we have pluralistic competition of interests in public arenas determined by elections, legislative and legal procedures, etc. The adoption of private regulation, on the other hand, is driven by firm and activist strategies competing in market settings. Whether self-regulation will occur and which form

[18] Ibid.

[19] Daniel Diermeier, *Reputation Rules: Strategies for Building Your Company's Most Valuable Asset* (New York, NY: McGraw-Hill, 2011).

[20] Jarol B. Manheim, *The Death of a Thousand Cuts: Corporate Campaigns and the Attack on Corporations* (Mahwah, NJ: Lawrence Erlbaum Associates, 2001).

it will take therefore depends on the details of the strategic interaction between activists and firms.

In order to avoid being targeted by negative campaigns, a firm, for instance, can take proactive measures. The first is to change its practices in the hope of avoiding a campaign.[21] The attractiveness of this strategy in turn depends on whether the activist can or cannot commit to abstain from a campaign once the target makes a concession. Suppose the activist is able to commit to not conducting a campaign if the potential target changes its practices sufficiently. Such a commitment could be credible because of the reputation of the activist. The target would be willing to adopt a self-regulatory practice if the proactive measures are less costly than the harm from the campaign. This gives activists incentive to emphasize maximum harm in a campaign, because it increases the likelihood that a company will self-regulate, without having to spend resources on an actual campaign. Notice that this can lead to multiplier effects at an industry level. If one company takes proactive measures, this can shift the focus of scrutiny to another target and so forth. Indeed, firms may start a self-regulatory "arms race" in an effort not to be targeted.

In order to avoid this self-regulatory race to the top, an industry may then coordinate on adopting industry-wide standards. The U.S. forest products industry did so in establishing the Sustainable Forest Initiative (SFI), which sets standards for forest stewardship. The SFI has more than 200 participants and manages more than 152 million acres of forest land worldwide, including more than 90% of industrial forests in North America. Defining such standards for the industry was easy because the firms had an already-established industry association. Similarly, during RAN's global finance campaign, Citigroup and three other banks developed the Equator Principles to guide the financing of projects in ecologically sensitive areas. Both SFI and Equator Principles restrict a race to the top and can be thought of as a less restrictive form than either public or more stringent private regulation, as is the case in the forest industry's refusal to adhere to the regulations of the Forest Stewardship Council set forth by private NGOs.[22] The strategic benefit of moderate industry-wide standards is that it diffuses the potential reputational harm that can be imposed by NGOs.

Beliefs about whether the target will concede to the activist demands play a large role in whether a firm is targeted in the first place. A potential target may be able to influence those beliefs through its actions. For example, the potential target may establish a reputation for not responding to coercion, challenging government regulations, and fighting lawsuits rather than settling. These actions may have different costs for different potential targets, so the strategies chosen by potential targets can

[21] David Baron and Daniel Diermeier, "Strategic activism and non-market strategy," *Journal of Economics and Management Strategy*, 16, no. 3 (2007): 599–634.

[22] Erika N. Sasser, Aseem Prakash, Benjamin Cashore and Graeme Auld, "Direct targeting as an NGO political strategy: Examining private authority regimes in the forestry sector," *Business and Politics*, 8, no. 3 (2006): Article 1.

reveal information about their type. This also means that one potential target can emulate another, albeit at a different cost.[23]

Because a campaign against a difficult target is more costly to the activist group, corporate campaigns are more likely to focus on soft targets. When softness signals are received, the activist chooses a more aggressive strategy, so the soft firm faces an aggressive campaign. A soft firm thus has an incentive to send the costly signal so as to avoid the more aggressive campaign, essentially mimicking a tough response. The opportunity for a target to develop a reputation thus leads to actions (signals) that may be contrary to the interests of the activist. Activism thus can have perverse effects by encouraging soft types to act tough. That is, potential targets may aggressively oppose threats from both private and public politics so as to signal that they are tough. By voluntarily aligning firm structure with demands of activists through self-regulation and adopting a tough reputation in dealings with activist groups, a firm can avoid being targeted by activist groups, which have practical incentives to seek "worst offenders" with a history of concession.

Once started, corporate campaigns can have three distinct resolutions: campaigns can be resolved by the target conceding to the demand, the activist abandoning the campaign, or the activist and the target bargaining to resolve the issue. However, agreements resolving a campaign are seldom enforceable by a third party, such as a court or other regulator. Although an activist group has as an objective to reach an enforceable agreement, few if any targets will be willing to accept such an agreement. Thus activist groups must seek commitments by officers of the target firms in order to have campaign success. These agreements are easily avoided by management, however. An example of this dynamic in action comes from RAN's campaign against Citigroup. In resolving the campaign, RAN hoped, but failed, to have their agreement approved by Citigroup's board of directors.[24]

Agreements to resolve a campaign must be self-enforcing so that the target does not shirk on its promises and the activist does not make further demands. The principal private enforcement measure of the activist is to resume the campaign. In their campaign against Citigroup, RAN's only instrument for enforcing an agreement is to resume campaign activity, and to date it has not had to do so. The target's enforcement measure is to resume the practices it changed. Thus enforceability of an agreement requires that the parties observe each other's behavior.

To know whether a target is complying with an agreement, an activist must obtain information on the target's practices and actions. RAN uses a variety of monitoring mechanisms. If the agreement pertains to activities in a developing country, it may rely on reports from local activist groups. In the campaign against old growth timber harvesting that targeted Home Depot, RAN used local volunteers to be their eyes

[23] David Baron and Daniel Diermeier, "Strategic activism and non-market strategy," *Journal of Economics and Management Strategy*, 16 no. 3 (2007): 599–634.

[24] David Baron and ErinYurday, "Anatomy of a Corporate Campaign: Rainforest Action Network and Citigroup (A) (B)," Case P42 A, B Stanford, CA: Stanford Graduate School of Business.

and ears. With some training it is possible to distinguish lumber from old growth trees from lumber from younger trees. RAN instructed its volunteers to walk through Home Depot aisles visually checking the lumber and reporting back to RAN on the company's compliance. In RAN's Global Finance Campaign, Citigroup agreed to publish an annual corporate social responsibility report and to report quarterly to RAN confidential data on its implementation of the agreement. Citigroup and RAN also agreed to a "no surprises" arrangement, under which RAN would not criticize Citigroup without telling it in advance, and Citigroup would not violate its environmental policies without telling RAN in advance. This was intended to avoid misunderstandings that could undermine the agreement that ended the campaign.

To resolve a campaign, activists and their targets may create private governance arrangements to which they agree to be subjected. These private institutions may be created to generate information on compliance, address free-rider or other collective action problems, or resolve private politics conflicts. Such institutions govern Internet privacy, working standards in overseas apparel and footwear factories, conflict diamonds, Pacific tuna fishing, and a variety of other practices. These institutions are intended to govern multiple parties, often when monitoring is needed to assess compliance with an agreement. The following example illustrates one of these institutions.

In the early 1990s, U.S. labor unions and activist groups launched a private politics campaign targeting Nike with the objective of improving the working conditions in overseas factories supplying apparel and footwear to the U.S. market. Factory owners and host governments had recognized an opportunity to attract contractors through low costs, and low costs in some cases meant violating wage, labor, and safety laws. Apparel and footwear companies saw lower cost supplies as a source of competitive advantage and put pressure on existing suppliers for lower costs. Low-wage countries recognized their advantage and worked to attract companies. Activists viewed this as a race to the bottom, and U.S. unions saw it eroding what little remaining advantage they had in domestic manufacturing. Activists led a campaign targeting Nike, using allegations of "slave labor."

After nearly six years of protests and small steps by the apparel and footwear industries, the Clinton administration convened the interested parties and challenged them to create a process to ensure that brand name products were produced in a manner that upheld the rights of workers worldwide. Two years later, this Apparel Industry Partnership presented a business code of conduct and a set of principles for monitoring that formed the Fair Labor Association. The FLA combines the efforts of industry, civil society organizations, and colleges and universities to protect workers' rights, independently monitor and improve working conditions, and ensure that labor rights violations are addressed. Currently, more than 25 brand-name companies and more than 200 colleges and universities are affiliated with the FLA. The FLA participants agreed on a code governing workplace practices, including: a 60-hour maximum work week including overtime; minimum wage/market wage (although not a living wage); child workers must be at least 15 years of age; and employees shall have the right to form independent union). The FLA's policy-making Board of Directors has a Chair and equal representation of its constituencies. There are six seats each for industry, civil society organizations, and colleges and universities, and a two-thirds supermajority is required to the code and select the chair. Independent monitoring and inspection of factories was required, with companies selecting a monitor from an FLA accredited list. A plan was required to correct any deficiencies identified, and results of inspections were reported publicly if approved by a majority of the board. The FLA also established a judiciary, the Third Party Complaint Procedure, which accepts and then attempts to resolve complaints from any person, similar to the citizen petition procedures of some government agencies.[25]

As can be seen from these examples, private politics may lead to private regulation that can be as effective as public regulation in shaping business conduct. By definition, private politics is conducted by private entities (NGOs, companies, the media, citizens, etc.). There is no legitimization through public processes of any kind (e.g., election, referenda) other than very general rules about freedom of expression, freedom of association, and so forth. However, little is known about the welfare consequences of private politics. One of the few examples is Feddersen and Gilligan, who show how the presence of activists can reduce information asymmetries compared with a market where activists are not present.[26] Yet studies for specific industries or comparisons with public regulatory mechanisms are sorely lacking at this point.

The effectiveness of corporate campaigns critically depends on the specific features of an industry or product. The case of genetically modified food products offers a template for these dynamics. Biotech companies frequently do not constitute good targets for activists because they lack the brand recognition to trigger significant media interest, a necessary component for the success of activist campaigns. Rather, the potential vulnerability of the biotech industry rests with its customers, such as well-known consumer goods companies who worry about their brand and reputation in a highly competitive market. Once consumer goods companies sense a negative impact on their brands due to the reputational challenges of a key ingredient, they have an incentive to shift suppliers to those that do not face similar problems. This may lead to labeling and standards, even the emergence of premium products that are "GMO-free."

Similarly, nanotech companies will need to win the battle for public opinion if they want to avoid the emergence of a market for "nanotech-free products." The history of controversial technologies has shown that focusing on the technological and scientific aspects is not sufficient. Rather, public fears about safety, environmental, or social impact may lead to private regulation through the mechanism of private politics. Previous technologies of similar impact (e.g., GMOs) have faced significant

25 For a detailed discussion of such mechanisms, see: Jonathan Koppel, *World Rule: Accountability, Legitimacy, and the Design of Global Governance* (Chicago, IL: University of Chicago Press, 2010).

26 Timothy Feddersen and Thomas W. Gilligan, "Saints and markets: Activists and the supply of credence goods," *Journal of Economics & Management Strategy*, 10 no. 1 (2001): 149–171.

challenges in this regard, which has limited their broad adoption. The same process is to be expected for nanotechnology. In the next section, we discuss its specific challenges.

THE PRIVATE POLITICS OF NANOTECHNOLOGY

Nanotechnology is a technology of tremendous promise, yet it has become controversial in recent years.[27] Beyond the significant technical challenges of advancing this emerging technology, public perception and understanding of the field may play the most important role in determining nanotechnology's further development and eventual use and regulation.[28] As discussed in the previous section, public perception will be the main factor driving both traditional political and regulatory processes as well as private politics processes.

The first important fact is that public knowledge of nanotechnology is very limited at best, with more than 80% of Americans reporting knowing either "just a little" or "nothing" about nanotechnology.[29] This suggests that, if asked to make a judgment about nanotechnology, the vast majority of the American public would be relying on incomplete or no information. Such judgments have been shown to strongly rely on (potentially biased) heuristics to simplify the difficult task of making a decision under uncertainty.[30] Further, affective responses in judgment situations are among individuals' first reactions to new stimuli and have the ability to color perceptions and ultimately decisions.[31] Research on the perception of risks associated with the development of nanotechnology support these assertions. Although a majority of Americans confess to knowing little or nothing about nanotechnology, in a survey of attitudes toward nanotechnology, almost 90% of participants polled had an opinion about the risks or benefits, which were largely affect-driven.[32] Additionally, these immediate reactive feelings (either positive or negative) regarding nanotechnology were the most significant indicator of valence toward nanotechnology development. Those who held a negative attitude about nanotechnology would more often report that the risks outweighed the benefits, whereas those holding a positive attitude

[27] Alexander H. Arnall, "Future technologies, today's choices: Nanotechnology, artificial intelligence and robotics; A technical, political and institutional map of emerging technologies" (London, England: Greenpeace Environmental Trust), 2003.

[28] Dan M. Kahan, Paul Slovic, Donald Braman, John Gastil and Geoffrey Cohen, "Nanotechnology risk perceptions: The influence of affect and values," Cultural Cognition Project Working paper No. 22 (New Haven, CT: Yale Law School, 2007).

[29] Peter D. Hart Research Associates, Inc., (2006). Report Findings. Available at http://www.nanotechproject.org/file_download/98 (accessed July 25, 2011).

[30] Amos Tversky and Daniel Kahneman, "Judgment under uncertainty: Heuristics and biases," *Science*, 185 no. 4157 (1974): 1124–1131.

[31] R. B. Zajonc, "Feeling and thinking: Preferences need no inferences" *American Psychologist*, 35 no. 2(1980): 151–175.

[32] Dan M. Kahan, Paul Slovic, Donald Braman, John Gastil and Geoffrey Cohen, "Nanotechnology risk perceptions: The influence of affect and values," Cultural Cognition Project Working paper No. 22 (New Haven, CT: Yale Law School, 2007).

typically felt the opposite. Strikingly, obtaining information about nanotechnology *before* reporting their judgment did not influence their final opinion. That is, contrary to an "updating" approach to judgments, participants' initial attitudes prevailed over new information.[33]

These findings mirror previous research on risk perception.[34] Slovic et al.'s model of risk perception follows dualistic theories of understanding and information processing.[35] That is, risk perception is viewed as two cognitive systems operating concurrently and interactively, each influencing judgments. The first system, the experiential system, allows for quick, intuitive assessments of situations, whereas the second, the analytic system, involves a more protracted and logical method of making a decision. In addition to these two systems, Finucane and colleagues argue that an *affective heuristic* influences risk judgments.[36] That is, feelings and emotions about a given situation provide cues for the appropriate judgment and decision.[37] In the case of risk perception, affective information helps determine both the extent of perceived risks and benefits. Favorable affect is associated with inferring greater benefits and lower risk, whereas unfavorable affect is associated with inferring lower benefits and greater risk. The affective heuristic has been demonstrated empirically to influence risk perceptions in a variety of situations, from toxicity[38] and finance[39] to nuclear power.[40]

As with other immediate, intuitive reactions characterized by the experiential system, affective responses are subject to certain failures and biases.[41] For the

33 Dan Kahan, Paul Slovic, Donald Braman, John Gastil and Geoffrey Cohen, "Nanotechnology risk perceptions: The influence of affect and values." Cultural Cognition Project Working paper No. 22 (New Haven, CT: Yale Law School, 2007).

34 Paul Slovic, Melissa L. Finucane, Ellen Peters, and Donald G. MacGregor, "Risk as analysis and risk as feelings: Some thoughts about affect, reason, risk, and rationality," *Risk Analysis*, 24, no. 2 (2004): 311–322.

35 See, for example, Shelly Chaiken and Yaacov Trope, eds., *Dual-Process Theories in Social Psychology* (New York: Guilford Press, 1999); and Daniel Kahneman and Shane Frederick," (2002). Representativeness revisited: Attribute substitution in intuitive judgment," in *Heuristics and Biases: The Psychology of Intuitive Judgment*, eds. Thomas Gilovich, Dale Griffin, and Daniel Kahneman (New York: Cambridge University Press, 2002), 49–81.

36 Melissa, Finucane, Ali Alhakami, Paul Slovic, and Stephen M. Johnson, "The affect heuristic in judgments of risks and benefits," *Journal of Behavioral Decision Making*, 13, no. 1 (2000): 1–17.

37 Paul Slovic, Melissa L. Finucane, Ellen Peters, and Donald G. MacGregor "Risk as analysis and risk as feelings: Some thoughts about affect, reason, risk, and rationality," *Risk Analysis*, 24, no. 2 (2004): 311–322.

38 Paul Slovic, Donald G. MacGregor, Torbjorn Malmfors, I. H. F. Purchase, unpublished, "*Influence of Affective Processes on Toxicologists' Judgments of Risk*" (Eugene, OR: Decision Research).

39 Yoav Ganzach, "Judging risk and return of financial assets," *Organizational Behavior and Human Decision Processes*, 83, no. 2 (2000): 353–370.

40 Melissa L. Finucane, Ali Alhakami, Paul Slovic, and Stemphen M. John, "The affect heuristic in judgments of risks and benefits," *Journal of Behavioral Decision Making*, 13 no. 1 (2000): 1–17.

41 David Fetherstonhaugh, Paul Slovic, Stephen M. Johnson, and James Friedrich, "Insensitivity to the value of human life: A study of psychophysical numbing," *Journal of Risk and Uncertainty*, 14, no. 3 (1997): 282–300; Paul Slovic, Melissa L. Finucane, Ellen, Peters, E., Donald G. MacGregor, "Risk as analysis and risk as feelings: Some thoughts about affect, reason, risk, and rationality," *Risk Analysis*, 24 no. 2 (2000): 311–322; and Amos Tversky Daniel Kahneman, "Judgments of and by representativeness,"

complicated field of nanotechnology, these concerns are likely to be exacerbated. Even if the relative risks of nanotechnology development are shown to be remote, perceptions have the ability to override logical analyses and inflate the associated risk and underestimate associated benefits.[42] Unfamiliarity is likely to be an added hindrance. Individuals often have evaluations of risk that are contrary to those of scientists and experts based on availability bias, or the likelihood to underestimate the familiar and overestimate the unfamiliar[43] – a common example is assuming more people die in airplane crashes than car crashes after recent widespread coverage of an airplane crash. With risk perception and technology, this leads to overrating the danger of some activities and underrating others. As an example, in an ordering task of the perceived risk of 30 activities and technologies, Slovic reports that lay participants rated nuclear power (an unfamiliar topic) as the most dangerous activity, whereas experts rated it as the 20th.[44] However, when rating a more familiar topic (X-rays), lay individuals considered the activity comparatively quite safe (22nd most dangerous) compared with experts (seventh most dangerous). A similar reaction to nanotechnology could be expected considering the limited exposure of the field to the public.

Views regarding the risks of nanotechnology, and risks in general, however, are not immutable. Even though presenting information about nanotechnology to individuals before they made their judgments did not affect their final decision, receiving information about nanotechnology was related to more polarized views of (un)favorability.[45] That is, as individuals learned about nanotechnology, they used the information to solidify their pre-established position on the debate, conforming the (exact same) information to their specific values, which had originally influenced their affective response. Because individuals are also motivated to find others who share their values, dissemination of information between like others is more likely to lead to the formation of congruent factual beliefs,[46] further polarizing opposing sides of the debate.[47] Risk perception, then, becomes a way of reinforcing

in *Judgment Under Uncertainty: Heuristics and Biases*, eds. Daniel Kahneman, Paul Slovic, and Amos Tversky (New York, NY: Cambridge University Press, 1982).

42 Yuval Rottenstreich and Christopher K. Hsee, "Money, kisses and electric shocks: On the affective psychology of Risk," *Psychological Science*, 12, no. 3 (2001): 185–190.

43 Amos Tversky and Daniel Kahneman, "Judgments of and by representativeness," in *Judgment under uncertainty: Heuristics and biases*, eds. Daniel Kahneman, Paul Slovic and Amos Tversky (New York: Cambridge University Press).

44 Paul Slovic, *The Perception of Risk* (Sterling, VA: Earthscan Publications, 2000).

45 Dan M. Kahan, Paul Slovic, Donald Braman, John Gastil, and Geoffrey L. Cohen, "Nanotechnology risk perceptions: The influence of affect and values," Cultural Cognition Project Working paper No. 22 (New Haven, CT: Yale Law School, 2007).

46 Geoffrey L. Cohen, "Party over policy: The dominating impact of group influence on political beliefs," *Journal of Personality & Social Psychology*, 85 no. 5 (2003): 808–822.

47 Charles G. Lord, Lee Ross, and Marl R. Leper, "Biased assimilation and attitude polarization: The effects of prior theories on subsequently considered evidence," *Journal of Personality and Social Psychology*, 37, no. 11 (1979): 2098–2109.

cultural outlooks, which in turn fuel implicit judgments and affect about the issue.[48] Evidence that cultural outlooks influence views on nanotechnology does exist, with at least one study finding gender and demographic differences in the risk perception of nanotechnology.[49] For example, white participants were more in favor of nanotechnology than African-American participants, whereas men of both ethnicities were more in favor than white and African-American women. Interestingly, there were no reported differences by political orientation, yet there were differences by world view. Those identified as "individualists" (i.e., supporters of the individual initiative) were less swayed by risk arguments than those considered "communitarians," or those conscious of equality or unconstrained pursuit of self-interests.[50]

Much of the evidence surrounding risk perception and nanotechnology suggests that with the proper triggering event, individuals form immediate, affective responses to nanotechnology that are culturally mediated and direct their judgments. Kahan et al. suggest that views of nanotechnology fall along the same ideological lines as other risk-salient issues, such as global warming and nuclear power.[51] These data also suggest that simply presenting information about nanotechnology could potentially be counterproductive, serving only to reinforce and harden existing attitudes. Instead, implementing methods of framing issues that allow for individuals with disparate opinions to reach the same factual conclusions could potentially promote deliberative decisions regarding the advancement of this and other new technologies.[52] That said, using stories, examples, and/or other affect-laden stimuli may have a greater impact on affective intuition than analytical strategies such as scientific studies or probability arguments.[53]

In summary, the findings from the psychology of risk perception suggest a difficult environment for nanotechnology.

1. The public essentially lacks any knowledge of nanotechnology, yet is forming opinions about it.
2. Additional information is largely reinforcing these opinions rather than changing them.

48 Dan M. Kahan, "Fear of democracy: A cultural evaluation of Sunstein on risk," *Harvard Law Review*, 119 (2006: 1071–1109.

49 *Ibid.*

50 Dan M. Kahan, Paul Slovic, Donald Braman, John Gastil, and Geoffrey L. Cohen, G. L. (2007), "Nanotechnology risk perceptions: The influence of affect and values," Cultural Cognition Project Working paper No. 22. New Haven, CT: Yale Law School.

51 Dan M. Kahan, Paul Slovic, Donald Braman, John Gastil and Geoffrey L. Cohen, "Nanotechnology risk perceptions: The influence of affect and values," Cultural Cognition Project Working paper No. 22. New Haven, CT: Yale Law School.

52 Geoffrey L. Cohen, Joshua Aronson and Claude M. Steele, "When beliefs yield to evidence: Reducing biased evaluation by affirming the self," *Personality and Social Psychology Bulletin*, 26, no. 9 (2000): 1151–1164.

53 Paul Slovic, *The Perception of Risk* (Sterling, VA: Earthscan, 2000); and Kimihiko Yamagishi, "When a 12.86% mortality is more dangerous than 24.14%: Implications for risk communication," *Applied Cognitive Psychology*, 11, no. 6 (1997): 495–506.

3. Nanotechnology has certain characteristics that tend to have the public overestimate its risks while underestimating its benefits.

The process of private politics is expected to amplify these concerns and create affective states in members of the public that would further erode trust in the technology. In other words, the current support for nanotech in public opinion is extremely shallow and may erode quickly due to a triggering event (e.g., the Monarch butterfly in the debate on GMOs) or a coordinated campaign (e.g., Greenpeace's anti-GMO campaign in the United Kingdom).[54] Factual information alone is expected to have little impact. This suggests that the role of third parties will be one the critical elements in the battle for public trust.

CREDIBILITY TRANSFER

The use of third parties with high credibility can be critical when trust in a company or technology is low. For example, during the 1990s, Monsanto Corporation successfully used the U.S. Food and Drug Administration to overcome customer concerns about the safety of its genetically modified products in the U.S. market.[55] A similar approach was successfully undertaken by Calgene in the introduction of its genetically modified tomato. The tomato case is instructive because the key for Calgene was to convince not only end consumers that the product was safe, but also business customers such as Campbell Soups, who were concerned about corporate campaigns against its brand.[56]

Interestingly, (moderate) advocacy groups can fulfill the same function as governmental entities in adding credibility. For example, Starbucks Coffee Co. used the environmental advocacy group Conservation International to certify its shade-grown coffee policies. The involvement of activist groups has previously been modeled as a costly signaling game.[57] Endorsements by activists can sustain equilibria where firms differentiate their products with respect to the business practice of concern, as in the Starbucks shade-grown coffee example. Customers are modeled as rational actors using Bayesian updating. The work by Feddersen and Gilligan demonstrates

54 Stories about health concerns are likely triggers. As an example, consider recent research that showed how multiwalled carbon nanotubes inhaled by mice can reach the subpleural tissue of the animal, which may lead to pathogenic changes on the lung surface. See J. P. Ryman-Rasmussen, M. Cesta, A. R. Brody, J. K. Shipley-Phillips, J. I. Everitt, E. W. Tewksbury, O. R. Moss, B. A. Wong, D. E. Dodd, M. E. Andersen, and J. C. Bonner, "Inhaled carbon nanotubes reach the subpleural tissue in mice," *Nature Nanotechnology*, 4 (2009): 747–751.

55 Monsanto tried to replicate this strategy by using the UK Health Ministry as a certifier when it entered the European market, an approach that led to miserable failure due to the fact that the UK government had lost much of its credibility with the public on the issue of food safety during the mad cow disease scandal (Charles, 2002).

56 Daniel Charles, *Lords of the Harvest: Biotech, Big Money and the Future of Food* (New York: Perseus Books Group, 2002).

57 Timothy Feddersen and Thomas W. Gilligan, "Saints and markets: Activists and the supply of credence goods," *Journal of Economics & Management Strategy*, 10, no. 1 (2001): 149–171.

the possibility of credibility transfer in a strategic environment, but does not explore the exact mechanism that is more or less effective. It also relies on rational Bayesian updating by customers, which is difficult to support in the case of nanotechnology given the evidence on the psychology of risk perception previously discussed. Rather, adopting a social psychological perspective, consistent with the literature on risk perception, seems more promising.

In general, corporations are among the least trusted groups in the United States,[58] and various psychological phenomena create difficulties for companies to overcome concerns and build trust. Empirical studies demonstrate that people are more likely to attend to negative information than positive information,[59] find it impossible to withhold judgment even when faced with contradictory and incomplete evidence,[60] and weigh negative information more heavily than positive information when forming opinions of others.[61] Human beings are also chronically suspicious of positive actions and quick to assume ulterior motives.[62] Such biases are particularly problematic for a company, which, as an intrinsically profit-centered entity, almost always has a plausible ulterior motive for praiseworthy acts. For example, one of Nike's first attempts to address negative publicity involved hiring the accounting firm Ernst & Young to assess their business practices in Southeast Asia. The financial relationship between Nike and Ernst & Young greatly reduced the credibility of the independent audit, resulting in continued negative publicity.[63] In contrast, consumer advocacy groups that are wholly independent of the company and whose goals are unsympathetic with business interests can offer a more credible endorsement.

This leads to the prediction that inviting an investigation by a truly independent consumer advocacy group – even in the absence of a finding of innocence – serves as a *moral signal* of a company's good intentions and potential innocence, mitigating some of the ongoing concerns. In a series of studies examining independent investigations and whether they affect public opinion, Uhlmann, Heinze, and Diermeier found that a company that had committed a transgression (in this case,

58 Richard G. Peters, Vincent T. Covello and David B. McCallum, "The determinants of trust and credibility in environmental risk communication: An empirical study," *Risk Analysis*, 17, no. 1 (1997): 43–54.

59 Oscar Ybarra, "Naive causal understanding of valenced behaviors and its implications for social information processing," *Psychological Bulletin*, 128, no. 3 (2002): 421–441.

60 Daniel T. Gilbert and Randall E. Osborne "Thinking backward: Some curable and incurable consequences of cognitive busyness," *Journal of Personality and Social Psychology*, 57, no. 6 (1989): 940–949.

61 Roy F. Baumeister, Ellen Bratslavsky, Cartrin Finkenauer and Kathleen D. Vohs, "Bad is stronger than good," *Review of General Psychology*, 5, no. 4 (2001): 323–370; and Paul Rozin, and Edward B. Royzman, "Negativity bias, negativity dominance, and contagion," *Personality and Social Psychology Review*, 5, no. 4 (2001): 296–320.

62 Leda Cosmides, "The logic of social exchange: Has natural selection shaped how humans reason? Studies with the Wason selection task," *Cognition*, 31, no. 3 (1989): 187–276; and Roos Vonk, "The slime effect: Suspicion and dislike of likeable behaviors towards superiors," *Journal of Personality and Social Psychology*, 74 no. 4 (1998) 849–864.

63 Debora L. Spar, "Hitting the wall: Nike and international labor practices," Harvard Business School Case 9-700-047 (Cambridge, MA: Harvard Business School).

using an unhealthy food additive) was perceived more favorably when it invited an independent advocacy group to investigate the charges, compared with when there was no investigation or when the company announced it would undergo an internal investigation.[64]

As described previously, existing dispositions of respondents may affect their response on a given issue. That is, customers may vary both in their baseline attitudes toward companies and in their response to investigations by an independent advocacy group. In a second study, Uhlmann et al. investigated the role of political orientation as one such condition.[65] Because political liberals are both more skeptical of corporations and more sympathetic with the causes advanced by consumer advocacy groups than conservatives, individuals that hold liberal values were thought to respond more negatively to the company in the absence of an independent investigation, but more positively in its presence. Indeed, the study found that liberals expressed more negative evaluations of the company than did conservatives when an accused company did not invite an independent advocacy group to investigate the accusations. However, this completely reversed when the company invited an independent investigation by a consumer advocacy group, such that liberals evaluated the company significantly more *positively* than conservatives in the independent investigation condition. Surprisingly, liberals in the independent investigation provided the most positive evaluations of the company. Notably, this pattern of results was observed even though the advocacy group (simply described as "People for Consumers") was not overtly political.

In a second approach, the study design experimentally manipulated liberal versus conservative values using an implicit priming procedure,[66] specifically a goal contagion approach. Research on goal contagion indicates that merely reading about a person who holds a certain goal causes participants to implicitly adopt similar goals and values.[67] To implicitly prime liberal versus conservative orientations, Uhlmann et al. used supporting gun control (liberal prime) and gun rights (conservative prime). Both are clearly identified with liberal versus conservative political leanings and not directly related to unhealthy food additives.[68] Consistent with expectations, the participants implicitly primed with the liberal value (relative to the conservative value) evaluated the company less favorably in the absence of the independent investigation, but more favorably in its presence. In other words, when a company accused of using an unhealthy food additive invited an independent investigation by a consumer advocacy group, participants implicitly primed with liberal values evaluated the company more positively than participants primed with conservative

64 Eric L. Uhlmann, Justin E. Heinze, and Daniel Diermeier, "Strange bed fellows: Stakeholder outreach and the role of ideology in customer perceptions" (Unpublished manuscript, 2009).

65 *Ibid.*

66 Henk Aarts, Peter M. Gollwitzer, and Ran R. Hassin, "Goal contagion: Perceiving is for pursuing," *Journal of Personality and Social Psychology*, 87, no. 1 (2004): 23–37.

67 *Ibid.*

68 Eric L. Uhlmann, Justin E. Heinze, and Daniel Diermeier, "Strange bed fellows: Stakeholder outreach and the role of ideology in customer perceptions" (Unpublished manuscript, 2009).

values. Indeed, participants in the independent investigation condition primed with liberal values were the only group that perceived the company favorably overall. The priming approach is particularly important in the context of the need to change opinions because it indicates how the implicit context that shapes opinions may respond to certain communication approaches.

As yet unknown are the attributions that underlie conservatives' comparatively less positive responses to an investigation conducted by a consumer advocacy group. Conservatives may perceive such groups as biased against legitimate business interests and therefore less trustworthy than liberals do. Alternatively, conservatives may simply perceive advocacy groups as less capable of carrying out a competent investigation. These attributions point to different actions that an advocacy group might take to increase its credibility with politically conservative consumers. A deficit in trust would suggest highlighting shared values, such as a desire to enforce the rule of law in public safety contexts. A perceived deficit in competence would suggest highlighting the qualifications of the group members conducting the investigation.

In summary, the studies by Uhlmann et al. showed some empirical support for inviting unlikely allies to enhance credibility.[69] Inviting an independent investigation by a consumer advocacy group, even in the absence of a finding of innocence, appears to have served as an informative signal of the company's good intentions. Moreover, the effects of an independent investigation were stronger among participants who either endorsed liberal values or were implicitly primed with such values. In both studies, evaluations of a company accused of using an unhealthy food additive were most positive among comparatively liberal participants in the independent investigation condition. This occurred even though the advocacy group was not obviously political in nature.

Of related interest are reactions to government investigations. Given evidence that political conservatives both place less trust in the government and perceive government agencies as less competent, we would expect conservatives to respond less positively than liberals to a company that invites a government investigation.[70]

Finally, in some cases companies can utilize a pre-established reputation. Prior findings indicate that a company with a past record of pro-social acts can draw on this "moral bank account" to help it weather a crisis.[71] Past reputation seems especially likely to moderate the effects of an *internal* investigation. A company with a bad reputation that conducts an internal investigation and declares itself innocent may

69 Eric L. Uhlmann, Justin E. Heinze, and Daniel Diermeier, "Strange bed fellows: Stakeholder outreach and the role of ideology in customer perceptions," (Unpublished manuscript, 2009).

70 A. L. Comrey and J. A. Newmeyer, "Measurement of radicalism-conservatism," *Journal of Social Psychology*, 67, no. 2 (1965): 357–369, and Fred N. Kerlinger (1984). *Liberalism and Conservatism: The Nature and Structure of Social Attitudes* (Hillsdale, NJ: Lawrence Erlbaum Associates, 1984).

71 Niraj Dawar and Madan M. Pillutla, "Impact of product-harm crise on brand equity: The moderating role of consumer expectations," *Journal of Marketing Research*, 37, no. 2 (2000): 215–226; Eric L. Uhlmann, George E. Newman, Victoria L. Brescoll, Adam Galinsky, and Daniel Diermeier, "The sounds of silence: Effects of an engaged, defensive, and no comment response to a crisis on corporate reputation" (Unpublished manuscript).

provoke moral outrage and even more negative evaluations than a poorly regarded company that conducts no investigation at all.[72]

Another remaining question is how moral judgments are updated as an issue unfolds and the results of relevant investigations become public knowledge. Although a company that is initially presumed guilty and later cleared may benefit when it comes to people's deliberative, logical evaluations, bias against the company may persist at an implicit, intuitive level. When it comes to automatic associations (e.g., between social targets and the concept "bad"), people are unable to correct for negative first impressions based on information that is later proved completely false.[73] This further suggests the importance of communication speed, well-known from the crisis management literature.[74]

In sum, the experimental approach discussed in this section can be used to (1) understand the mechanisms that drive opinion formation on controversial products and technologies, and (2) test communication strategies to counteract current attitudes, even if these attitudes are shaped by preexisting context variables such as political orientation.

CONCLUSION

In just a few years, nanotechnology has moved from a promising to a controversial technology. Losing the trust of the public will likely lead to a less favorable regulatory environment, as well as limit customer acceptance in the marketplace. In addition to traditional public regulation, attempts to create private regulation through private politics channels are likely. These regulatory trends will significantly be influenced by public attitudes toward nanotechnology. Current research suggests that the public is largely ignorant of the technology but nevertheless holds increasingly firm attitudes about it. Moreover, these attitudes are more likely to be shaped by affect and psychological mechanisms than scientific arguments. Recent research shows that the very same mechanisms that can undercut trust in a product or technology can be used to enhance it. Particularly effective is the use of credible third parties. Even just the announcement of investigation (before results are known) can help companies to quickly restore public trust. This approach is particularly effective for the segment of the public that holds a political liberal value orientation, who are typically less trusting of corporations. Although the findings are preliminary and

[72] Jonathan Haidt, "The emotional dog and its rational tail: A social intuitionist approach to moral judgment," *Psychological Review*, 108, no. 4 (2001): 814–834; Cass R. Sunstein "Moral heuristics," *Behavioral and Brain Sciences*, 28, no. 4 (2005): 531–542.

[73] Aiden P. Gregg, Beate Seibt and Mahzarin R. Banaji, "Easier done than undone: Asymmetry in the malleability of implicit preferences," *Journal of Personality and Social Psychology*, 90, no. 1 (2006): 1–20.

[74] Daniel Diermeier, *Reputation Rules: Strategies for Building Your Company's Most Valuable Asset* (New York, NY: McGraw-Hill, 2011); and Steven Fink, *Crisis Management: Planning for the Inevitable*. (Lincoln, NE: iUniverse, Inc, 1986).

partial, they do point toward a different approach to understanding public attitudes toward nanotechnology and other emerging technologies.

This chapter has focused predominantly on describing private politics mechanisms in the context of emerging technologies such as nanotech. One of the striking features of private politics is that it can regulate global commerce as effectively as traditional public regulation. If ice cream companies universally shun milk that was produced using synthetic bovine growth hormones, the practical effect is (nearly) as complete as if its use had been prohibited by law. By definition, however, private regulation is not legitimized by public institutions such as elections, due process, or other fundamental attributes of democratic processes. At best, it involves some very general constitutional principles, such as freedom of speech and assembly. Yet, as just public politics it may have profound welfare consequences through the *de facto* regulation of commerce. Moreover, whether and to what extent regulation will occur may depend on seemingly irrelevant attributes, such as seemingly irrelevant triggers of media interest or the availability of credible third parties. From this perspective, private politics may appear to be a highly problematic, even dangerous form of regulation – a task better left to elected governments. But such a perspective would be naive. Modern political economy has amply demonstrated that regulation is not simply the implementation of optimal economic policies, but the consequence of competition among political interest groups in public arenas.[75] Factors such as media interest, coalition strength, external events (e.g., a terrorist attack) creating policy windows, etc. all have a profound impact on which policies are adopted. In addition, the reach of public regulatory intervention is dramatically limited by a global system of governance still dominated by nation states. In other words, activists that are bothered by the labor conditions in China have few better alternatives than to target Walmart and its global supply chain. This also implies that some companies (e.g., highly visible brands) may be more affected by private politics than other, more generic, and less well-known companies. In other words, private politics may be more constraining on some companies than others, but again, this is true for public regulation as well: German companies need to comply with a different set of labor standards than U.S. companies.

In other words, both private and public politics are forms of political competition, yet the arenas and forms of competition differ. This suggests that rather than dismissing one form of competition on *a priori* grounds, it may be more fruitful to compare and evaluate the normative properties of regulatory outcomes. This is a fruitful future endeavor that would highly benefit from the close interaction between legal scholars and social scientists.

75 David P. Baron, *Business and Its Environment, 7th Edition*. (Upper Saddle River, NJ: Prentice Hall).

4

How Scientific Evidence Links Attitudes to Behaviors

James N. Druckman and Toby Bolsen

Nanotechnology has the potential to revolutionize applications across a dizzying array of fields, including medicine, energy, cosmetics, computing, agriculture, and aerospace. Although many of these applications have become publically available, even more have yet to hit the marketplace. The ultimate plight of these technologies depends, in large part, on public acceptance and usage. New technologies will not find commercial acceptance or overcome regulatory hurdles if they are not embraced or at least tolerated by customers.

A growing body of work explores the determinants of attitudes or opinions about nanotechnology (e.g., Cobb & Macoubrie, 2004; Lee et al., 2005; Scheufele & Lewenstein, 2005; Lee & Scheufele, 2006). Yet the bulk of this work overlooks two important dynamics. First, public opinion analysts often strictly distinguish the role of factual information (e.g., knowing a nanometer is a billionth of a meter) from the impact of alternative processes such as framing (e.g., being told that nanotechnology has implications for energy costs). This is unfortunate because much of the information citizens receive melds frames and facts, as when an energy frame provides facts about cost savings. How does adding factual content to a frame influence public reactions? Second, extant work rarely explores the relationship between nanotechnology opinions and willingness to actually use nanotechnology – despite the well-documented disconnect between attitudes and behaviors, more generally. When do nanotechnology attitudes (e.g., support for investment and usage) predict behaviors (e.g., willingness to personally use)?

We address these questions by offering a psychological theory of opinion formation and behavior and test our expectations with an experiment. We find that adding factual content (e.g., a specific citation to a scientific study) to framed arguments has no effect on attitudinal support for a nanotechnology application. However, adding such information significantly strengthens the impact of the frame on behavioral intentions. Moreover, it heightens the connection between attitudes and behaviors by making respondents more certain of their attitudes. In short, adding factual evidence to frames (1) does not affect attitudes in ways that differ from analogous frames without facts, but it does (2) strengthen the effect of the frames on behavioral intentions, and (3) increase the correlation between attitudinal support and behavioral intention because individuals become more certain of their attitudes. These results have important implications for understanding public reactions to nanotechnology; it is critical to distinguish attitudinal support from behavioral intentions, and moreover, facts have differential effects on attitudes and behaviors.

NANOTECHNOLOGY ATTITUDES AND BEHAVIORS

Over the last several decades, scholars have developed a field of study that explores how citizens perceive the risks and benefits associated with new products (e.g., Currall et al., 2006). It is within this domain that most work on nanotechnology attitudes situates itself (e.g., Cobb & Macoubrie, 2004; Macoubrie, 2006). A long-standing theme of this literature is the need to inform the public about facts surrounding new technologies; that is, to make citizens scientifically literate (e.g., Miller, 1998; Bauer et al., 2007). New factual information presumably facilitates accurate assessment of risks and benefits and generates "support for science and technology" (Gaskell et al., 1999, p. 386; Nisbet & Goidel, 2007, p. 421; Miller, 1998; Sturgis & Allum, 2006). More recent work questions the scientific literacy approach, instead emphasizing how other factors shape emergent technology opinions, including values, trust in science, and the framing of the technologies. These factors seem to matter more than basic factual knowledge because people often possess little knowledge about the technologies and have scant motivation to learn more. Scheufele and Lewenstein (2005, p. 660) explain that "developing an in-depth understanding would require *significant* efforts on the part of ordinary citizens [and] the pay-offs . . . may simply not be enough" (emphasis in original; also see Lee et al., 2005; Scheufele, 2006; Kahan et al., 2007, 2008). Consequently, people form their opinions in a less deliberate manner that does not involve careful integration of factual information. Instead, they rely on shortcuts or heuristics that require less of them when forming opinions.

Most of these heuristic factors involve information that lacks clear factual content, with perhaps the most notable example being influence from framed communications. In their study of nanotechnology attitudes, Scheufele and Lewenstein (2005, p. 660) explain, "opinions will be influenced by factors *other* than [factual] information, such as . . . the way mass media frame issues . . . " A framing effect occurs when, in the course of describing a new technology, a speaker's emphasis on a subset of potentially relevant considerations causes individuals to focus on those considerations when constructing their opinions, which may in turn lead to a change in overall support (Druckman, 2001, pp. 226–231). For example, a news article on nanotechnology emphasizing consequences for human health may cause readers to focus on health risks and become less supportive, whereas an article focusing on consumer good production may lead readers to attend to those benefits and become more supportive. While numerous studies show that alternative frames can significantly shape nanotechnology opinions (e.g., Cobb, 2005; Scheufele, 2006; Kahan et al., 2008; Nisbet & Mooney, 2007), virtually all of this work employs frames that include no explicit factual content.[1]

For us, a fact is something that verifiably exists and has some objective reality (Merriam-Webster Online Dictionary). Facts come in a wide variety of forms and, on most issues, are ever-present (e.g., Shapiro & Block-Elkon, 2008). We (narrowly) focus on facts in the guise of "scientific *evidence*" that report a verified observation (e.g., an experimental outcome). For example, the statement "A recent study reported that material akin to that found in many nanotechnology applications was present in some rivers of Britain" constitutes a fact because it reports the confirmed result of a study. Facts differ from value judgments that contain subjective elements, often about prioritizing distinct considerations (e.g., Fairbanks, 1994). For example, the *claim* that "the most important implication of nanotechnology concerns its impact on the environment" contains no verifiable content and, as such, amounts to a value judgment.[2]

As mentioned, frames often do not include factual content – at least in the sense of reference to a confirmed scientific study – and thus are analogous to value judgments/claims insofar as they prioritize a consideration (which may but need not be a value) (e.g., Nelson et al., 1997; Berinsky & Kinder, 2006). Here are two examples of nanotechnology application frames that lack specific factual content: the first highlights a consideration – energy costs and availability – generally viewed as pro-nanotechnology (because nanotechnology reduces costs), whereas the second emphasizes a con-nanotechnology – health risks – consideration (because of the uncertain health consequences).

- Energy/costs availability (pro-nanotechnology): "Most agree that the most important implication of carbon nanotubes (CNTs) concerns how they will affect energy cost and availability."
- Potential health risks (con-nanotechnology): "Most agree that the most important implication of CNTs concerns their unknown long-run implications for human health."

[1] One exception is Cobb (2005), who finds that factually oriented frames have larger effects than those that lack facts.

[2] Our focus on the relative impact of facts as scientific evidence follows a long-standing concern of risk analysts. Fischhoff (1995, p. 139) explains, "Risk analysts have fought hard to create a clear distinction between the facts and values of risk management." That said, we recognize that not all accept the fact-value distinctions – those readers can view our work as instead focusing on "evidence" and "claims."

Analogous arguments that contain scientific evidence (i.e., what we are calling a fact) might cite a specific study:

- Energy/costs availability (pro-nanotechnology): "A recent study on cost and availability showed that CNTs will double the efficiency of solar cells in the coming years."
- Potential health risks (con-nanotechnology): "A recent study on health showed that mice injected with large quantities of CNTs reacted in the same way as they do when injected with asbestos."

These latter two statements are, in essence, frames with facts because they emphasize the relevant considerations of energy costs and health risks, respectively (by citing the studies in these areas). Nisbet and Scheufele (2009, p. 5) explain, "Framing is an unavoidable reality of the science communication process. Indeed, it is a mistake to believe there can be 'unframed' information." In other words, the evidentiary statements are a type of "fact frame" as compared with the first two examples, which are "factless frames" (which, as mentioned, are common in most studies; c.f., Cobb, 2005).

How will adding factual content – specifically a reference to a scientific study – influence the attitudinal impact of a frame? Chong and Druckman's (2007a) theory of framing suggests that, when it comes to attitudes (e.g., general support for nanotechnology), only motivated and able individuals scrutinize a frame's content such that the inclusion of facts enhance its effect. As explained, we expect no such motivation or ability in the case of nanotechnology, and thus we expect that facts do not significantly affect opinions, beyond the effects of a frame absent factual content.[3] Frames that contain factual content do not have a significantly greater impact on attitudes than frames without factual information (hypothesis 1). This prediction echoes Lakoff's (2004, p. 17) statement that "People think in frames . . . To be accepted, the truth must fit people's frames. If the facts do not fit a frame, the frame stays and the facts bounce off" (also see Eagly & Chaiken, 1993, p. 327; Fazio, 2000, p. 14; Kunda, 2001, p. 16). We test this hypothesis in two ways: (1) by comparing whether a frame containing factual content supportive of (opposed to) a new technology has a greater effect on opinions than analogous supportive (opposing) frames that lack factual content, and (2) by exploring whether a supportive (opposing) frame with a fact overpowers a competing opposing (supportive) frame that lacks factual content.

When it comes to *behavior* (i.e., willingness to use the technology), however, we suspect that adding scientific evidence may matter. To see why, first note that, in many cases, attitudes do not correlate with related (intended) behaviors – as Wicker (1969, p. 65) famously stated, "it is considerably more likely that attitudes

3 Similarly, Petty and Wegener (1999, p. 42) explain that when motivation and/or ability are low, individuals examine "less information . . . or examine . . . information less carefully."

will be unrelated or only slightly related to overt behaviors" (for a review see Miller & Peterson, 2004; Ajzen & Fishbein, 2005). Forty years of subsequent research, following Wicker's statement, identifies various factors that enhance the attitude–behavior connection. One such factor is attitude strength: "empirical research has shown that attitude strength – no matter how it is assessed – tends to moderate the attitude–behavior relation as expected. That is, strongly held attitudes generally predict behavior better than weakly held attitudes" (Fishbein & Ajzen, 2010, p. 261). Although there exist various conceptualizations of attitude strength (e.g., Miller & Peterson, 2004; Visser et al., 2006), the one relevant here is *certainty of or confidence in* one's attitude. Individuals who have confidence in their attitudes act on those attitudes; in contrast, individuals who lack confidence are "hesitant to use their attitudes to guide behavior" (Visser et al., 2006, p. 40–41; also see Krosnick & Smith, 1994, p. 284; Cooke & Sheeran, 2004; Druckman, 2004; Glasman & Albarracín, 2006).

Attitude strength tends to grow when individuals think about their attitudes or have attitude-relevant experiences (e.g., Krosnick & Smith, 1994; Visser et al., 2006; Glasman & Albarracín, 2006, p. 782). It also "is determined at least in part by the volume and perceived reliability of attitude-supportive information stored in memory... when an attitude is supported by a sufficiently large base of *reliable* information, people will feel confident that their attitude is valid" (emphasis added, Visser et al., 2006, p. 38–39; also see Berger, 1992). Adding factual content to a frame likely enhances the perceived dependability of the information and thus increases certainty and, subsequently, the attitude–behavior link.[4] We predict that frames with factual content – citing scientific evidence – will thus (1) increase attitude certainty (hypothesis 2a), (2) increase the link between attitude and behavior (hypothesis 2b), and, as a result, (3) have a greater effect on behaviors (e.g., frames lacking facts will not influence behaviors because people will not be willing to act per se on their attitudes, even though those attitudes were affected by frames) (hypothesis 2c).

Psychologically, our argument suggests that individuals form their attitudes based, in part, on the recently received frame. Individuals lack sufficient motivation and ability to downgrade frames that lack reliable information, and thus frames with or without facts have analogous attitudinal effects: individuals use them similarly as a basis for attitude formation.[5] However, the addition of facts makes individuals more certain or confident about the attitude they form based on the frame (because the facts offer more reliable/specific evidence). This coheres with the finding that

[4] Few framing studies, in general, explore behavior (as opposed to attitudes) (however, see, e.g., Vishwanath, 2009; Bolsen, 2010).

[5] Increased motivation and ability can itself influence attitude strength; however, we focus here on how reliable information does so, even in the absence of motivation and ability.

adding quantitative evidence to a statement typically does not enhance its persuasiveness (O'Keefe, 1998, p. 72; 2002b, pp. 229–230) but may constitute "explicit supporting argumentation [that] directly enhances belief in the relevant . . . argument" (O'Keefe, 2002a, p. 71; also see O'Keefe 1998, 2002b, pp. 186–187).

EXPERIMENTAL PARTICIPANTS, PROCEDURE, AND DESIGN

To investigate our hypotheses, we conducted an experiment that focused on a nanotechnology application: carbon nanotubes (CNTs).[6] CNTs are tiny graphite with chemical properties that, among other applications, facilitate the conversion of sunlight into electricity. Although CNTs came to prominence in the early 1990s, the mass public knows little of them, with 49% reporting that they have heard nothing about them (Peter D. Hart Research Associates, Inc., 2008). Our specific experiment took place in the context of an exit poll on Election Day in 2008. We opted for this approach for two reasons. First, it allowed us to include a heterogeneous sample of respondents. Second, and more importantly, it enabled us to provide perspective to this relatively unfamiliar technology by situating it within a context. Specifically, we explained that CNTs are likely to receive considerable attention during the next President's term (which coheres nicely with the attention energy received during the campaign). Although in some sense unusual, we believe this enhances experimental realism, compared with confronting respondents with a novel technology with no context whatsoever.[7]

We implemented the survey experiment by assembling 20 teams of student pollsters. We then randomly selected polling locations throughout the northern part of Cook County, Illinois. Each polling team spent a randomly determined 2- to 3-hour daytime period at their polling place. A pollster asked every third voter to complete a self-administered questionnaire in exchange for $5. Our sample ended up consisting of 621 individuals; their demographic profile appears in Table 4.1. The table shows that the respondents come from fairly diverse backgrounds; although, as would be expected in northern Cook County, the sample is skewed toward liberal and educated individuals.

The Election Day survey provided respondents with a description of CNT technology:

> One of the most pressing issues facing the nation – as has been clear from the election – concerns the limitations to our energy supply (e.g., with regard to coal,

[6] The study also included an experiment focusing on genetically modified food. We found no evidence of spill-over effects from the two experiments. For details on the genetically modified food study, see Druckman and Bolsen (n.d.).

[7] Perhaps the main disadvantage of our approach is that exit poll surveys need to be short, thereby constraining the number of items we could include.

TABLE 4.1. *Profile of sample*

Variable	Scale (Overall distribution)	Average (SD)
Political Ideology (Conservativeness)	1 (very liberal) = 17% (107) (total N = 616) 2 = 26% (156) 3 = 18% (111) 4 (moderate) = 20% (124) 5 = 9% (57) 6 = 6% (36) 7 (very conservative) = 4% (25)	3.12 (1.64)
Ethnicity (Minority Status)	White = 69% (409) (total N = 595) African Americans = 15% (87) Asian Americans = 5% (31) Hispanic =2% (13) Other = 4% (23) Prefer not to answer = 5% (32)	n/a
Sex (Female)	Male = 42% (251) (total N = 592) Female = 58% (341)	n/a
Age	1 (18–24) = 27% (160) (total N = 595) 2 (25–34) = 15% (89) 3 (35–44) = 14% (82) 4 (45–54) = 15% (90) 5 (55–64) = 13% (79) 6 (65–74) = 10% (57) 7 (75 +) = 6% (38)	3.27 (1.93)
Education	1 (less than high school) = 1% (5) (total N = 595) 2 (high school) = 9% (53) 3 (some college) = 30% (179) 4 (year college degree) = 27% (163) 5 (advanced degree) = 33% (195)	3.82 (1.01)
Newspaper Reading	1 (never) = 5% (31) (total N = 619) 2 = 10% (64) 3 = 10% (60) 4 (a few times a week) = 18% (114) 5 = 13% (79) 6 = 11% (70) 7 (everyday) = 33% (201)	4.87 (1.93)

SD, standard deviation.

> oil, and natural gas). One approach to addressing this issue is to rely more on carbon nanotubes, or CNTs. CNTs are tiny graphite with distinct chemical properties. They efficiently convert sunlight into electricity and thus serve as an alternative to coal, oil, and natural gas. The uncertain long-term effects of CNTs are the subject of continued study and debate.

Respondents then were randomly assigned to one of nine conditions (used to test our hypotheses) that offered distinct descriptions of CNTs (beyond what they read in the preceding description). Specifically, we used the four bulleted statements provided previously, allowing us to have pro (i.e., energy costs/availability) and con (i.e., potential health risks) factless frames and pro and

TABLE 4.2. *Experimental conditions*

	No fact frame	Pro fact frame	Con fact frame
No Factless Frame	(*Condition* 1) (N = 69)	(2) (N = 69)	(3) (N = 72)
Pro Factless Frame	(4) (N = 71)	(5) (N = 68)	(6) (N = 67)
Con Factless Frame	(7) (N = 70)	(8) (N = 67)	(9) (N = 68)

con fact frames. As mentioned, the fact frame statements contain verified scientific evidence.[8]

Table 4.2 presents the particular conditions (with the Ns appearing in the cells). Our first condition served as a baseline (frameless/fact-free) control; these respondents read only the brief background description and then answered our dependent variable questions (that we discuss momentarily). In conditions 4 and 7, respondents – after reading the brief descriptions – received the pro frame (without fact) or the con frame (without fact) (e.g., see the previously presented bulleted statements). These conditions mimic many framing experiments that expose participants to one frame or another (without factual content), with the expectation of the frames pushing opinions in distinct directions. Conditions 2 and 3 matched conditions 4 and 7; however, instead of the frame (without fact) statement, respondents received the factual (frame) statement. If facts have an additional effect on attitudes (counter to our prediction) or behavior (consistent with our predictions), then the effects from conditions 2 and 3 (facts alone) should significantly exceed those found in conditions 4 and 7 (frames sans facts), respectively.

The other conditions combine multiple statements. Conditions 5 and 9 offer respondents both frames without facts and the factual evidence frames.[9] Conditions 6 and 8 introduce facts that contradict the concomitant framed (without fact) statement; for example, the pro-frame-con fact condition (6) read "Most agree the most important implication . . . concerns . . . energy costs . . . A recent study, unrelated to energy costs, showed that mice . . . "[10] These two conditions directly pit the relative power of contrasting frames without facts against framed facts, allowing us to assess

[8] We pre-tested these and other statements (N = 34) with participants who did not take part in the main study. We used the pre-test to ensure that individuals viewed the statements as pointing in the direction we assumed (i.e., pro or con nanotechnology) and as containing facts or not (i.e., we asked pre-test participants to evaluate the extent to which distinct statements contained verifiable statements with an objective reality). Further details on this and other pre-test assessments are available from the authors. Also note that for the factless statements, we included a consensus endorsement to ensure its credibility (O'Keefe, 2002b, p. 150).

[9] In all cases, the frame (without fact) appeared first.

[10] We pre-tested the exact wordings of all conditions to ensure adequate flow.

whether frames that provide verifiable evidence overpower analogous arguments that lack factual evidence.

After reading the given CNT description, participants responded to our main dependent variables. Our attitudinal question asked participants to rate on a 7-point scale the extent to which they, generally, oppose or support "using CNTs," with higher scores indicating increased support (e.g., 1 = oppose strongly, 4 = not sure, 7 = support strongly). Next came our measure of attitude strength or certainty, in which we asked respondents to rate how strongly they felt about their attitude on a 7-point scale, with higher scores indicating increased certainty.[11] For our behavior variable, we followed others by focusing on a behavioral intention, which indicates the "person's readiness to perform a behavior ... [it] is a person's estimate of the likelihood or perceived probability of performing a given behavior" (Fishbein & Ajzen, 2010, p. 39; also see Sheeran, 2002; Ajzen & Fishbein, 2005, p. 188).[12] We asked respondents to rate how likely they would be to use CNTs (e.g., personally), with higher scores indicating increased likelihood (e.g., 1 = definitely not use, 4 = not sure, 7 = definitely use).

RESULTS

We begin by presenting, in Figure 4.1, the distributions of each dependent variable: attitudinal support for CNTs, attitude certainty, and likelihood of using CNTs (i.e., behavior).[13] When it comes to attitudes and behavior, nearly 40% opted for the mid-point of 4, which was labeled "not sure" – this undoubtedly reflects lack of knowledge and general ambivalence. The attitude certainty score distribution reveals a more varied range, although the modal response also is a 4. Perhaps the most relevant aspect of the figure is that the attitude line drops below the behavior line when it comes to the low scores (i.e., 1, 2) but exceeds it on the higher scores (e.g., 6, 7). In other words, people are more willing to offer attitudinal support than commit to actually using CNTs; this is reflected in a significant difference in the respective scores of 4.63 (standard deviation [SD] = 1.56; 619) and 4.14 (SD = 1.62; 616) ($t_{605} = 7.75$, $p \leq .01$ for a one-tailed test). (The average certainty score is 4.34 [1.80; 619].)

[11] Our particular measure of certainty differs from that of others who ask about "certainty" or "confidence." Our measure is more general and may envelope related attitude strength features, such as importance (see Visser et al., 2006, pp. 20, 51 on how importance and certainty generate similar effects, particularly regarding attitude-behavior connections; however, also see Visser et al., 2003).

[12] Ajzen and Fishbein (2005, p. 188) explain that "intentions to perform a behavior, rather than attitude, is the closest cognitive antecedent of actual behavioral performance ... This implies that we should be able to predict specific behaviors with considerable accuracy from intentions to engage in the behaviors under consideration."

[13] For the purposes of the figures, we rounded the scores of the few respondents who chose mid-points on the scales (e.g., 2.5). Also, for presentational purposes, we treat the dependent variables as interval levels throughout; however, our results are robust to treating them as ordinal.

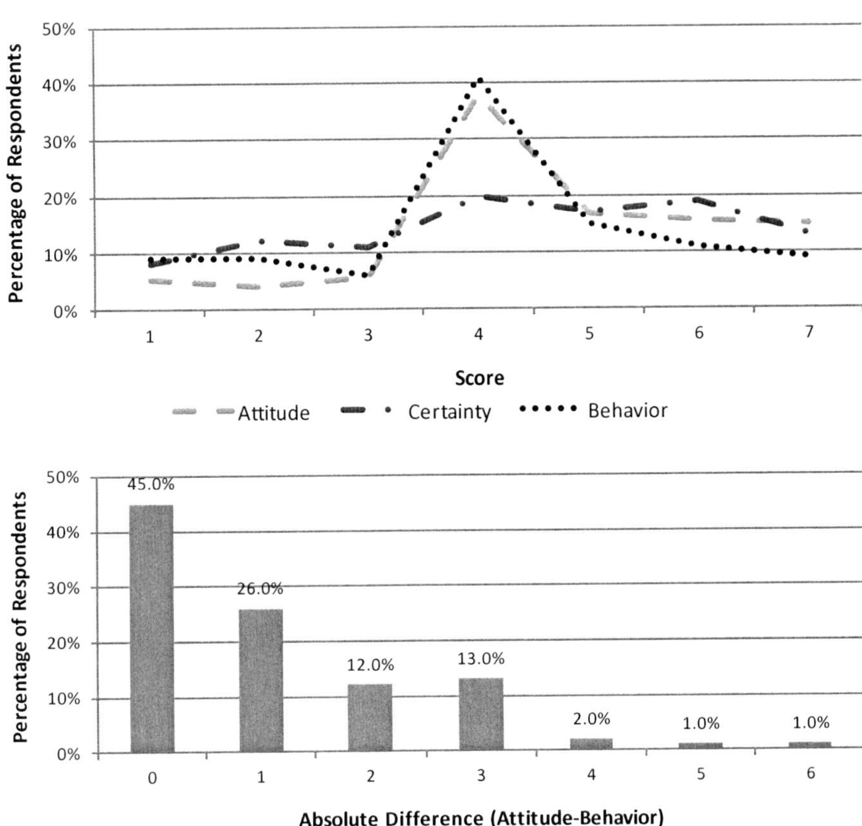

FIGURE 4.1. Distributions of CNT attitude, certainty, and behavior.

What this means is that, as expected, there exists some disconnect between attitudes and behaviors; to explore the range of this disjuncture, we take the absolute difference between each respondent's attitude and behavior scores. Figure 4.2 presents the distribution of those scores – for example, 45% of respondents registered exactly the same attitude and behavior scores, whereas only 1% provided responses to the two questions at each end of the 7-point continuum. The average difference is 1.06 (SD = 1.26; 616).[14] (Because these are absolute differences, the figure does not provide insight into which score – behavior or attitudes – was greater, but as mentioned, on average, attitude scores are higher.) Although the attitude–behavior differences are not extreme, they are nonetheless plainly evident. The question is whether the difference declines for those who express more certainty in their attitudes as driven by exposure to factual information.

We now turn to testing our hypotheses. We focus on the mean values of the dependent variables, by condition. We do this for simplicity's sake; the results are

[14] The correlation between attitude and behavior is .51.

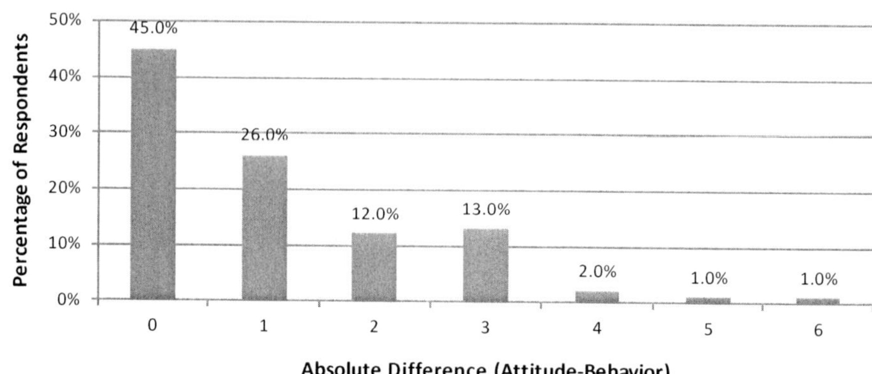

FIGURE 4.2. Distribution of attitude–behavior differences.

robust to multivariate analyses that include demographic controls.[15] Specifically, for each of our dependent variables, we report the percentage shift in the variable for each given condition relative to the control group (where respondents received no frames or facts).[16] The precise means and SDs for each dependent variable by condition appear in the Appendix.

In Figure 4.3, we plot the results for attitudinal support. This and all other subsequent figures use the abbreviations of "Eg" for energy, "Ht" for health, "Fr" for frame, and "Ft" for fact; they also label the conditions consistent with numbers in Table 4.2. Reading from left to right, we report results for the pro (energy) conditions, followed by the con (health) conditions, and then the mixed pro-con conditions.

The attitudinal results are stark. First, in every case, the pro factless frames, fact frames, and factless frame-fact frame combinations generate significantly more support (than the control group), whereas the con conditions do the reverse. Second and more importantly, adding facts does not significantly (e.g., at the .10 level) increase the impact of the frames. Although there is marginal evidence of a slightly larger effect from the fact frames (conditions 2 and 3), compared with the factless frames (conditions 4 and 7), the differences are nowhere near significant. For example, the CNT health risk factless frame (condition 7) alone versus the fact frame alone condition (condition 3) produced the largest difference between these conditions (-15.5% versus -18.8%) and the difference is far from significant ($t_{140} = .73$, $p \geq$

[15] We confirmed that random assignment to experimental conditions was successful in terms of analogous distributions of respondents in each condition. This ensures that mean differences across conditions are not spuriously due to confounding variables (at least those that we measured). Also, our survey included other measures shown to affect nanotechnology opinions, such as trust in science, general science knowledge, and certain values. Inclusion of these measures in multivariate analyses does not alter the results we report here. Also, the impact of these variables is of marginal interest, given the not perfectly representative nature of our sample; nonetheless, for details on the impact of such controls, see Druckman and Bolsen (2011).

[16] See Chong and Druckman (2007b) on using a control group as the appropriate point of comparison.

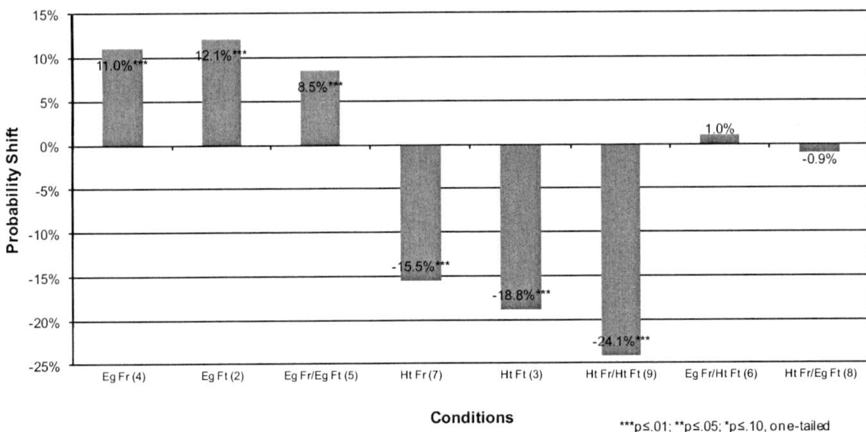

FIGURE 4.3. Attitudes toward CNTs.

.20 for a one-tailed test). Additionally, opposing fact frames do not overpower frames without facts – the mixed conditions (6 and 8) never produce significant effects (at anywhere near the .10 level), further supporting the finding that adding facts does little. Instead, the frames cancel each other out regardless of factual content.[17]

In sum, we find support for hypothesis 1: frames – with or without facts – substantially affect *opinions*, but adding reference to a factual scientific study does not enhance the effect. To be clear, the fact frames have effects. The fact frame alone statements (conditions 2 and 3) significantly move opinions and successfully counteract the factless frames (conditions 6 and 8). What our results suggest is that receiving factual information does not appear to have a greater impact on attitudinal support than exposure to analogous statements without factual content.[18]

When we turn to attitude certainty and behavior, we see a very different story. Figure 4.4 shows that, consistent with hypothesis 2a, adding factual content to the frames significantly increases the certainty with which individuals hold their attitudes, relative to the control groups (and the analogous factless frame groups). This is evident in every case, and interestingly, although not significantly different, the

[17] Two other dynamics are worth noting. First, although the most substantial effect occurs for the con-factless frame and fact-frame combination condition (condition 9), this likely reflects the mix of both statements rather than just the additional fact. Indeed, the effects from this combination condition are larger than the fact-frame alone condition (condition 3), as well as the factless-frame alone condition (condition 7). The con health factless frame-fact frame condition (condition 9) is significantly greater than the factless frame condition (condition 7) ($t_{136} = 1.96, p \leq .05$ for a one-tailed test) and marginally significantly greater than the fact frame condition (condition 3) ($t_{138} = 1.22, p \leq .12$ for a one-tailed test). Second, the negative conditions uniformly displayed larger effects than the positive conditions, perhaps echoing the well-known negativity bias (Rodriguez, 2007, pp. 478, 493).

[18] As mentioned, Cobb (2005) reports, in contrast to our results, that fact frames tend to have greater effects on attitudes. His design differs from ours, however, insofar as he does not strictly compare fact frames with factless frames along the same dimensions of consideration.

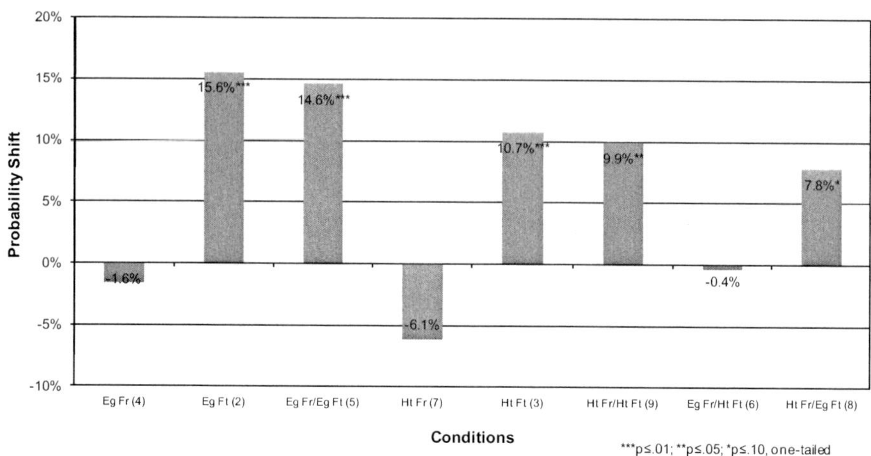

FIGURE 4.4. Attitude certainty.

largest effects occurred when the fact frame was not echoed by a consistent factless frame (i.e., compare conditions 2 and 3 with conditions 5 and 9, respectively). However, when the fact frame is challenged by a factless frame in the other direction, the results are mixed. When the con health fact frame is countered by the pro factless energy frame, there is no impact on certainty (condition 6), yet there is a marginal effect of the pro energy fact frame when it is challenged by the con factless health frame (condition 8). These latter results – of two-sided information vitiating the fact frame effect – are consistent with Glasman and Albarracin's (2006, p. 782) point that "*one-sided attitude-related information* can also increase attitude confidence [certainty] because univalent attitudes create less doubt than more complex ones" (emphasis in original).

We see the same pattern of results when we explore behavior – willingness to use CNTs – in Figure 4.5. Again, we see significant effects on behavior *only* in the conditions where fact frames appeared (i.e., conditions 2, 3, 5, & 9). The CNT pro-factless frame by itself (condition 4) increases willingness to use CNTs by 5.6%, and the con-factless health frame alone (condition 7) decreases willingness to use CNTs by 2.4%, but these differences are not significantly different from the control group. By contrast, exposure to a fact frame, alone or in combination with a factless frame, significantly increases intentions to use CNTs in the pro conditions (13.3% and 12.2% in conditions 2 and 5, respectively), and significantly decreases intentions to use CNTs in the con conditions (− 11.9% and − 9.6% in conditions 3 and 9, respectively). In the case of behavior, unlike certainty though, both mixed conditions (i.e., 6, 8) display no significant results. Thus it appears as if unidirectional fact frames move behavior, but any other mix (i.e., factless frames, or fact frames challenged by opposing factless frames) do not. This coheres with hypothesis 2c that the factual content is

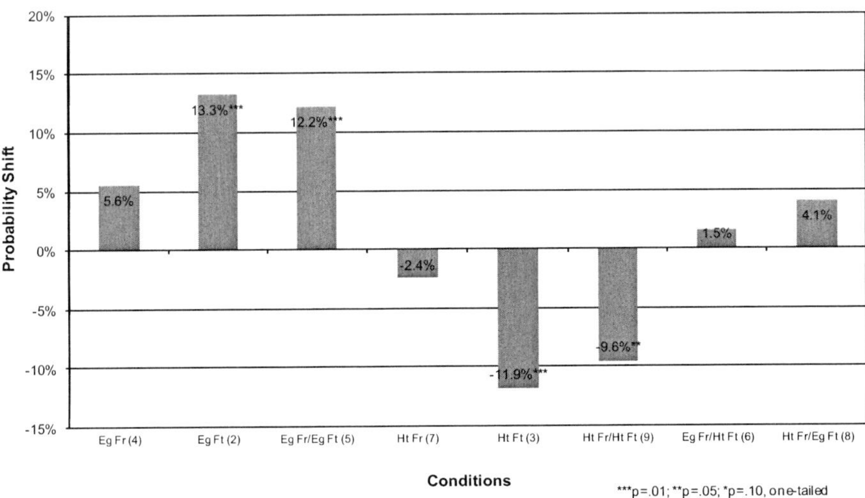

FIGURE 4.5. Behavior toward CNTs.

necessary to affect behavior (and, apparently, this content needs to be unchallenged).

Finally, Figure 4.6 displays the relative percentage effect of the given condition on the absolute difference between attitudes and behaviors. Negative scores show that there is a closer attitude–behavior link than that which appears in the control group. The results echo those in Figures 4.4 and 4.5, suggesting that the Figure 4.5 result showing behavioral effects (from the fact frames) reflects an increased link

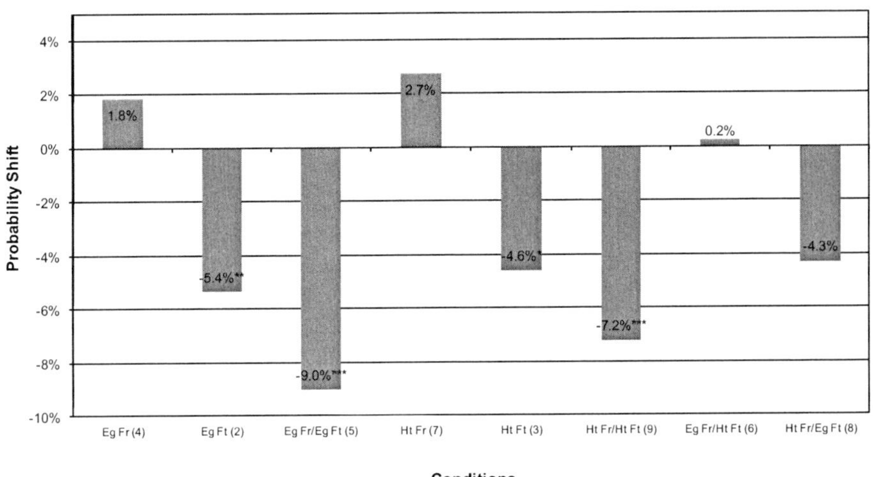

FIGURE 4.6. Attitude–behavior differences.

TABLE 4.3. *Determinants of attitude–behavior link*

Dependent variable: Absolute attitude–behavior difference (0 to 6)		
Experimental condition	Model 1	Model 2
Energy Frame	.11	.09
(Pro Frame) (4)	(.21)	(.20)
Energy Fact	–.32*	–.14
(Pro Fact) (2)	(.21)	(.21)
Energy Frame/Energy Fact	–.54***	–.38**
(Pro Frame/Pro Fact) (5)	(.22)	(.21)
Health Frame	.16	.09
(Con Frame) (7)	(.21)	(.21)
Health Fact	–.28*	–.15
(Con Fact) (3)	(.21)	(.20)
Health Frame/Health Fact	–.43**	–.32*
(Con Frame/Con Fact) (9)	(.21)	(.21)
Energy Frame/Health Fact	.02	.01
(Pro Frame/Con Fact) (6)	(.22)	(.21)
Health Frame/Energy Fact	–.26	–.17
(Con Frame/Pro Fact) (8)	(.22)	(.21)
Attitude Certainty		–.19***
		(.03)
Constant	1.23***	2.00***
	(.15)	(.18)
R^2	.04	
Number of Observations	616	

Note: Entries are OLS coefficients with standard errors in parentheses. ***$p = .01$; **$p = .05$; *$p = .10$ for one-tailed tests.

between attitudes and behaviors. As hypothesis 2b suggests, the presence of a fact frame increases the link between attitude and behavior.[19]

Taken together, the results show that adding factual content to frames has *no* effect on attitudes, but does significantly increase the certainty with which attitudes are held, generate an effect on behaviors, and heighten the link between attitudes and behaviors. Facts, such as a reference to a scientific study, matter even if they do not have a direct attitudinal effect.

A final question is whether the results reflect a meditational process such that the increased attitude–behavior linkage stems from a higher degree of certainty; that is, does willingness to act on one's attitudes stem from increased certainty with which those attitudes are held (which in turn, as we have shown, stems from the presence of more certain factual information)? We test this with two regressions that appear in Table 4.3 (see Baron & Kenney, 1986). The dependent variable

[19] The largest effects are again in the factless frame–fact frame combination conditions (i.e., conditions 5 and 9), but again, these differences are not statistically significant and likely result from the dynamics reviewed in footnote 17.

for both equations is the absolute difference between attitudes and behaviors (see Figures 4.2 and 4.6). The first column focuses on the experimental conditions as independent variables and matches what Figure 4.6 shows: only the presence of factual information significantly links attitudes to behavior. The second column adds one independent variable: attitude certainty (which we know increases from the presence of factual knowledge). That certainty is highly significant and the conditions become insignificant or less significant is suggestive of the meditational view that the fact frames increase certainty, which in turn heightens the attitude–behavior link. It is this increased link that finally leads to the direct fact frame impact on behaviors.[20]

CONCLUSION

The question of whether factual information influences the public's reactions toward new technologies is central to debates about public perceptions of new innovations (e.g., Lee et al., 2005; Scheufele & Lewenstein, 2005; Kahan et al., 2007, 2008). Although most acknowledge that facts matter under some conditions for some people (see, e.g., Cobb, 2005), extant work has not pinpointed how these differences work over distinct types of public responses. We presented a theory and evidence that shows that adding facts to frames does *not* impact attitudinal support but *does* affect behavioral willingness to use the technology. Moreover, it influences behavior by (1) increasing attitudinal certainty, which in turn (2) heightens the link between attitudes and behaviors, and then (3) leads to increased behavioral effects. Notably, however, the impact of fact frames only occurs when they go unchallenged even by non-factual frames. In other words, one can mute the impact of the fact frames by countering them even with opposing factless frames.

More work is needed on distinct technologies, with more varied populations, in different settings. In so doing, it is critical that analyses draw a distinction between attitudes and behavior and consider the intervening role of attitude strength (e.g., certainty). Indeed, it would be a mistake to assume that technologies that receive support necessarily will be used, or that certain arguments that lack attitudinal effects will not influence usage. In other words, support does not automatically translate into usage; efforts to increase support need to explore more than basic attitudinal variables. As nanotechnology continues to expand, it becomes increasingly important to understand public reactions and how individuals treat distinct types of information. Only then can predictions be made about how varied nanotechnology applications will fare once they enter the public domain.

20 When we regress behavior on the conditions but then add the attitude–behavior difference variable, we find that the latter is highly significant. However, it does not render the experimental condition main effects insignificant and thus is not wholly mediating the condition effects.

APPENDIX

Scores By Condition

	No fact	Pro fact	Con fact
No Frame	(*Condition* 1) Attitude = 4.82 (SD: 1.01; n = 68) Certainty = 4.04 (SD: 1.75; n = 68) Behavior = 4.06 (SD: 1.76; n = 68) Difference = 1.23 (SD: 1.23; n = 68)	(2) Attitude = 5.54 (SD: 1.32; n = 69) Certainty = 4.97 (SD: 1.65; n = 69) Behavior = 4.86 (SD: 1.34; n = 69) Difference = 0.91 (SD: 1.07; n = 69)	(3) Attitude = 3.69 (SD: 1.61; n = 72) Certainty = 4.68 (SD: 1.56; n = 72) Behavior = 3.35 (SD: 1.44; n = 72) Difference = 0.95 (SD: 1.27; n = 72)
Pro Frame	(4) Attitude = 5.48 (SD: 1.22; n = 71) Certainty = 3.94 (SD: 1.76; n = 71) Behavior = 4.39 (SD: 1.57; n = 71) Difference = 1.34 (SD: 1.57; n = 71)	(5) Attitude = 5.32 (SD: 1.29; n = 68) Certainty = 4.91 (SD: 1.61; n = 68) Behavior = 4.79 (SD: 1.21; n = 67) Difference = 0.69 (SD: 0.97; n = 67)	(6) Attitude = 4.88 (SD: 1.48; n = 66) Certainty = 4.02 (SD: 1.90; n = 66) Behavior = 4.15 (SD: 1.68; n = 66) Difference = 1.24 (SD: 1.38; n = 66)
Con Frame	(7) Attitude = 3.89 (SD: 1.61; n = 70) Certainty = 3.67 (SD: 2.04; n = 70) Behavior = 3.91 (SD: 1.52; n = 69) Difference = 1.39 (SD: 1.27; n = 69)	(8) Attitude = 4.76 (SD: 1.14; n = 67) Certainty = 4.51 (SD: 1.71; n = 67) Behavior = 4.30 (SD: 1.77; n = 66) Difference = 0.97 (SD: 1.32; n = 66)	(9) Attitude = 3.37 (SD: 1.50; n = 68) Certainty = 4.63 (SD: 1.79; n = 68) Behavior = 3.49 (SD: 1.57; n = 68) Difference = 0.79 (SD: 1.03; n = 68)

SD = standard deviation.

REFERENCES

Ajzen, Icek & Martin Fishbein. (2005). "The influence of attitudes on behaviors." In Dolores Albarracin, Blair T. Johnson, & Mark P. Zanna (Eds.). *The handbook of attitudes*. London: Lawrence Erlbaum Associates.

Baron, Reuben M. & David A. Kenny. (1986). The moderator-mediator variable distinction in social psychology research: Conceptual, strategic, and statistical considerations. *Journal of Personality and Social Psychology*, 51(6):1173–1182.

Bauer, Martin W., Nick Allum, & Steve Miller. (2007). What can we learn from 25 years of PUS survey research? *Public Understanding of Science*, 16:79–95.

Berger, Ida E. (1992). The nature of attitude accessibility and attitude confidence: A triangulated experiment. *Journal of Consumer Psychology*, 1:103–123.

Berinsky, Adam J., & Donald R. Kinder. (2006). Making sense of issues through media frames: Understanding the Kosovo crisis. *The Journal of Politics*, 68:640–656.

Bolsen, Toby. (2010). A light bulb goes on: Values, attitudes, social norms, and personal energy consumption. Unpublished manuscript. Evanston, IL: Northwestern University.
Chong, Dennis & James N. Druckman. (2007a). A theory of framing and opinion formation in competitive elite environments. *Journal of Communication*, 57(1):99–118.
Chong, Dennnis & James.N. Druckman (2007b). Framing public opinion in competitive democracies. *American Political Science Review*, 101(4):637–655.
Cobb, Michael D. (2005). Framing effects on public opinion about nanotechnology. *Science Communication*, 27:221–239.
Cobb, Michael D. & Jane Macoubrie. (2004). Public perceptions about nanotechnology. *Journal of Nanoparticle Research*, 6:395–405.
Cooke, Richard & Paschal Sheeran. (2004). Moderation of cognition-intention and cognition behavior relations: A meta-analysis of properties of variables from the theory of planned behavior. *British Journal of Social Psychology*, 43(2):159–186.
Currall, Steven C., Eden B. King, Neal Lane, Juan Madera, & Stacey Turner. (2006). What drives public acceptance of nanotechnology? *Nature Nanotechnology*, 1:153–155.
Druckman, James N. (2004). Political preference formation: Competition, deliberation, and the (ir)relevance of framing effects. *American Political Science Review*, 98(4):671–686.
Druckman, James N. (2001). The implications of framing effects for citizen competence. *Political Behavior*, 23 (September): 225–256.
Druckman, James N. & Toby Bolsen. (2011). Framing, motivated reasoning and opinions about emergent technologies. *Journal of Communication*, 61: 659–688.
Eagly, Alice H., & Shelly Chaiken (1993). *The psychology of attitudes*. Fort Worth, TX: Harcourt Brace Jovanovich College Publishers.
Fairbanks, A. Harris (1994). *Fact, value, policy: Reading and writing arguments*. New York: McGraw-Hill.
Fazio, Russel H. (2000). Accessible attitudes as tools for object appraisal. In Gregory R. Maio & James M. Olson (Eds.), *Why we evaluate* (pp. 1–36). Mahwah, NJ: Erlbaum.
Fischhoff, Baruch. (1995). Risk perception and communication unplugged. *Risk Analysis*, 15:137–145.
Fishbein, Martin & Icek Ajzen. (2010). *Predicting and changing behavior: The reasoned action approach*. New York: Psychology Press.
Gaskell, George, Martin W. Bauer, John Durant, & Nicholas C. Allum. (1999). Worlds apart? *Science*, 285:384–387.
Glasman, Laura R. & Dolores Albarracín. (2006). Forming attitudes that predict future behavior: A meta-analysis of the attitude behavior relation. *Psychological Bulletin*, 132(5):778–822.
Kahan, Dan M., Donald Braman, Paul Slovic, John Gastil, & Geoffrey L. Cohen. (2007). Affect, values, and nanotechnology risk perceptions. GWU Legal Studies Research Paper No. 261. Washington, DC: George Washington University.
Kahan, Dan M., Donald Braman, Paul Slovic, John Gastil, Geoffrey L. Cohen, & Douglas Kysar. (2008). Cultural cognition and nanotechnology risk perceptions. Unpublished paper. New Haven, CT: Yale University.
Krosnick, Jon A., & Wendy R. Smith. (1994). Attitude strength. In Vilayanaur S. Ramachandran (Ed.), *Encyclopedia of human behavior*. San Diego, CA: Academic Press.
Kunda, Ziva. (2001). *Social cognition*. Cambridge, MA: The MIT Press.
Lakoff, George (2004). *Don't think of an elephant?* White River Junction, VT: Chelsea Green Publishing.
Lee, Chul-joo & Dietram A. Scheufele. (2006). The influence of knowledge and deference toward scientific authority: A media effects model for public attitudes toward nanotechnology. *Journalism & Mass Communication Quarterly*, 83(4):819–834.

Lee, Chul-joo, Dietram A. Scheufele, & Bruce V. Lewenstein. (2005). Public attitudes toward emerging technologies. *Science Communication*, 27:240–267.

Macoubrie, Jane. (2006). Nanotechnology. *Public Understanding of Science*, 15:221–241.

Miller, Joanne M. & David A.M. Peterson. (2004). Theoretical and empirical implications of attitude strength. *The Journal of Politics*, 66:847–867.

Miller, Jon D. (1998). The measurement of civic scientific literacy. *Public Understanding of Science*, 7:203–223.

Nelson, Thomas E., Zoe M. Oxley, & Rosalee A. Clawson (1997). Toward a psychology of framing effects. *Political Behavior*, 19 (3):221–46.

Nisbet, Matthew C. & Robert K. Goidel. (2007). Understanding citizen perceptions of science controversy. *Public Understanding of Science*, 16:421–440.

Nisbet, Matthew C. & Chris Mooney. (2007). Framing science. *Science*, 316:56.

Nisbet, Matthew C. & Dietram A. Scheufele. (2009). What's next for science communication? Promising directions and lingering distractions. *American Journal of Botany*, 96:1–12.

O'Keefe, Daniel J. (1998). Justification explicitness and persuasive effect. *Argumentation and advocacy*, 35:61–75.

O'Keefe, Daniel J. (2002a). The persuasive effects of variation in standpoint articulation. In F.H. van Eemeren (Ed.), *Advances in pragma-dialectics* (pp. 65–82). Amsterdam: Sic Sat.

O'Keefe, Daniel J. (2002b). *Persuasion*, 2nd ed. Thousand Oaks, CA: Sage.

Peter D. Hart Research Associates, Inc. (2008). Awareness of and attitudes toward nanotechnology and synthetic biology. http://www.pewtrusts.org/.

Petty, Richard E. & Duane T. Wegener. (1999). The elaboration likelihood model: Current status and controversies. In *Dual process theories in social psychology*, Richard E. Petty, Duane T. Wegener, Chaiken, Shelly, & Yaacov Trope (Eds.), New York: Guilford Press.

Rodriguez, Lulu. (2007). The impact of risk communication on the acceptance of irradiated food. *Science Communication*, 28:476–500.

Shapiro, Robert Y. & Yaeli Block-Elkon. (2008). Do the facts speak for themselves? *Critical Review*, 20:115–139.

Sheeran, Paschal. (2002). Intention-behavior relations: A conceptual and empirical review. In Wolfgang Stroebe & Miles Hewstone (Eds.), *European review of social psychology* (Vol. 12, pp. 1–36). Chichester, UK: Wiley.

Scheufele, Dietram A. (2006). Five lessons in nano outreach. *Materials Today*, 9(5):64.

Scheufele, Dietram A. & Bruce V. Lewenstein. (2005). The public and nanotechnology. *Journal of Nanoparticle Research*, 7:659–667.

Sturgis, Patrick & Nick Allum. (2006). *A literature review of research conducted on public interest, knowledge, and attitudes to biomedical science*. Report prepared for The Welcome Trust.

Vishwanath, Arun. (2009). From belief-importance to intention: The impact of framing on technology adoption. *Communication Monographs*, 76(2):177–206.

Visser, Penny S., George Y. Bizer, & Jon A. Krosnick. (2006). Exploring the latent structure of strength-related attitude attributes. *Advances in Experimental Social Psychology*, 38:1–67.

Visser, Penny S., Jon A. Krosnick, & Joseph P. Simmons. (2003). Distinguishing the cognitive and behavioral consequences of attitude importance and certainty. *Journal of Experimental Social Psychology*, 39(March):118–41.

Wicker, Allan W. (1969). Attitudes versus actions: The relationship of verbal and overt behavioral responses to attitude objects. *Journal of Social Issues*, 25(4):41–78.

PART III

Meeting the Nanotechnology Challenge by Creating New Legal Institutions

5

Toward Risk-Based, Adaptive Regulatory Definitions

David A. Dana

Nanomaterials containing nanoparticles and nanoparticles themselves are now a focus of regulatory attention both in the United States and in various jurisdictions throughout the world. One of the motivations for developing regulation is the body of scientific studies suggesting that certain nanomaterials *could* pose environmental, health, or safety risks, but these studies are relatively few in number and involve only a relatively small number of nanomaterials in particular contexts. The studies may indicate that certain nanomaterials pose possible risks warranting at least some form of supervision by regulators, but they do not provide a generalized basis for presuming possible risk from all very small – or nanoscale – materials. The central challenge of developing a regulatory definition for nanomaterials is to be broad enough that it encompasses those materials that plausibly may exhibit the risk-creating properties that have led to the calls for regulation of nanomaterials in the first place *without* sweeping in many materials that plausibly cannot be expected to display such properties.

An overly broad definition for regulatory purposes is undesirable because it adds to the regulatory compliance costs of industry without producing corresponding environmental, health, or safety benefits. Moreover, an overly broad definition may result in an information overload on the part of regulators, which may delay regulators' ability to evaluate data and to develop substantive regulatory measures to reduce environmental, health, and safety risk. To borrow from Cass Sunstein, overregulation may lead to under- or ineffective regulation.[1]

The challenge of developing a regulatory definition that is broad enough to capture materials that pose possible risks but not so broad as to include many other materials is made more difficult by the fact that whether a given material displays properties that warrant regulatory concern is something that probably cannot be

[1] *See* Cass R. Sunstein, *Paradoxes of the Regulatory State*, 57 U. CHI. L. REV. 401, 413 (1990).

known (if it is knowable) without intensive case-by-case study of the material and its behavior in different environments. But the development of a regulatory framework, and hence regulatory definitions, cannot await the completion of such study on every material; indeed, one of the purposes of establishing a regulatory framework is to determine which materials should be studied before they are put into use and how much and in what way they should be studied. Thus a regulatory definition of nanomaterials and nanoparticles necessarily has to be based on criteria that screen for likely possible risk or absence of possible risk posed by the material. Because screening criteria presumably would be and should be shaped with an eye toward ensuring a margin of safety for human health and the environment, the criteria almost certainly will include some materials that in fact do not pose any possible risk. But, by the same token, even the most expansive definition may leave out some materials that may display properties that suggest possible risk to human health or the environment.

The size of one or more of the dimensions of a material or particles within a material has been the defining characteristics used not only in the scientific literature, but it also has been the (what I would call in my terminology) screening criteria employed in all regulatory definitions of nanomaterials to date.[2] However, how size (and what size) should be used as a screening criterion is debatable, as is the understanding of the number or kinds of dimensions that must meet the size criteria. Moreover, there are a number of other screening criteria that warrant attention as possible means of avoiding an overly broad regulatory definition of nanomaterials. These screening criteria, which this chapter addresses, include the following:

(1) Whether the material was intentionally produced or engineered
(2) Whether the material has a long history of production and use
(3) Whether the material is intended by its manufacturer for use in a mass production product and whether the material is intended for application to human skin, or inhalation or ingestion by human beings
(4) Whether the material has observable physical characteristics other than size that suggest either greater or lesser possible risk than would be indicated by size alone

[2] By regulatory definition, I mean a definition proposed or adopted by a government body as part of a mandatory or voluntary regulatory initiative. Definitions adopted by industry and professional standards organizations such as the International Organization for Standardization tend to be similar to the proposed or adopted regulatory definitions to date, except that they more often omit intentionality or engineered component in the definition. It is important to distinguish between scientific definitions, which are simply the conventional definitions used by scientists; regulatory definitions, which are definitions used by governments for policy purposes; and science-based regulatory definitions, which are regulatory definitions that are adopted for policy reasons but are informed by the best available science. It would seem uncontroversial that a desirable regulatory definition would not necessarily track the scientific definitions used by scientists as a matter of convention, but would take account of available science and therefore be science-based.

Achieving flexibility is another challenge inherent in the task of defining nanomaterials for regulatory purposes. Any regulatory definition of nanomaterials – whether it relies on the single criterion of size or a mix of size and other criteria – should allow for flexibility, out of recognition of the inherent limits in any screening criteria approach to defining which materials warrant inclusion in a regulatory framework. One way of achieving flexibility – and thereby tempering any over-inclusion or under-inclusion created by regulatory definitions based on screening criteria – would be to empower a regulatory agency (in the US context, presumably the Environmental Protection Agency [EPA]) to add or exclude particular materials from the scope of nanomaterials regulation, upon a showing by the agency of a reasonable basis for concluding that the material does or does not pose a possible risk of the sort that justifies its inclusion in the regulatory framework for nanomaterials. As has been done in a number of other regulatory contexts, citizens and regulated entities could be allowed to petition the EPA to include a material or exclude a material, and the agency could be required to respond to such petitions within a reasonable time. Although an allowance for petitioning carries with it the risk that scarce agency resources will be absorbed by petitions instead of potentially more important (in terms of health and the environment) tasks, allowance for petitioning fosters the generation of more data and serves the important values of public participation and transparency.[3]

In addition to developing screening criteria that are reasonably well-tailored to capture those materials that may pose a risk to human health or the environment, and including flexibility to address the over- and under-inclusion inherent in the use of any screening criteria, there is the challenge of achieving adaptability or reasonable dynamism in the regulatory definition itself. Nanotechnology has been, and presumably will continue to be, a rapidly developing field. The number and variety of nanomaterials is ever increasing, and screening criteria that may be suitable for the existing generation of materials may be unsuitable for the next generation. Moreover, even if nanomaterials themselves do not change much in a given time period, scientific understanding of them and tools for evaluating them may dramatically change. The process of making formal regulations, including regulatory definitions, however, is not usually a highly dynamic one. And, in part, for good reason: a certain degree of stability or "stickiness" in regulatory definitions is desirable because one of the purposes of regulatory definitions is to allow regulators and regulated entities to engage in planning, and planning is impeded by uncertainty in the defined scope of the regulatory framework. Thus the regulatory regime requires a balance of dynamism with stability and should build in measures to promote meaningful and periodic – but not constant – revisiting of the regulatory definition of nanomaterials.

3 *See generally* Jennifer Kuzma et al., *Evaluating Oversight Systems for Emerging Technology: A Case Study of Genetically Engineered Organisms*. 36 J. Law & Med. Ethics 36, 546 (2009) (discussing the link between components of the system of regulatory oversight and public confidence regarding emerging technologies).

THE MOTIVATIONS BEHIND DEFINING NANOMATERIALS AND REGULATORY DEFINITIONS TO DATE

The principal motivation behind the calls for regulatory frameworks for nanomaterials – and hence the need for a regulatory definition of nanomaterials – relates to the possibility that their small size may result in behavior that could pose a risk to human health or the environment. As the report of the Joint Research Center of the European Union (EU) describes, there seem to be two distinct concerns. One concern is that very small materials may not behave differently or display novel behaviors as compared with the same materials in "bulk" or "coarse" form, but the materials in very small form may be able to permeate barriers in the human body or other natural systems that were not designed to protect against such small materials, and these materials thus may enter into areas (e.g., the human brain) where they could cause harm.[4] This concern does not appear to be inherently limited to materials that are 100 nanometers or less, and could, depending on the context or environment in which the material would be introduced, be implicated by larger materials.[5] The second concern is that at very small sizes, the laws of physics apply to particles differently, and hence very small particles can display novel properties that are not found in bulk or coarse versions of the same elements or chemical compositions. Although novel properties can be good and indeed explain why investments are made to create nanoparticles and nanomaterials, what may be a good or benign property in some contexts could be risky in others; in addition, materials that have some desirable, selected-for novel properties could have some undesirable, not-understood, not-selected-for other novel properties. A recent review of the literature, however, suggests that novel properties usually characterize only particles that have at least one dimension of a size of 30 nanometers or less.[6]

Although a 100-nanometer upper threshold for regulated nanoparticles or materials containing nanoparticles does not perfectly track these two concerns motivating calls for nanomaterials regulation, it has been used in all but one of the regulatory definitions proposed or adopted so far.[7] (The single exception is a UK definition

[4] *See, e.g.*, Ben Harder, *Particles Enter the Nervous System Via the Nose – Conduit to the Brain*. Sci. News, Jan. 24, 2004. According to Dr. Denison of Environmental Defense, the "surprising results" in these studies of nanoparticles include that "[t]hey can cross from the lung, when inhaled, directly into our blood." *Environmental and Safety Impacts of Nanotechnology: What Research is Needed?: Hearing Before the H. Comm. on Science*, 109th Cong. 1 (2005) (statement of Richard A. Denison, PhD, Senior Scientist, Environmental Defense).

[5] European Union, Joint Research Centre, *Considerations on a Definition of Nanomaterial for Regulatory Purposes*, at 4.2.2, *available at* http://www.jrc.ec.europa.eu. (hereafter "JRC Report").

[6] M. Auffan et al., *Toward a Definition of Inorganic Nanoparticles From an Environmental, Health and Safety Perspective*. Nature Nanotechnology, 4, 634 (2009), available at www.nature.com/nnano/journal/v4/full/nnano.2009.242html.

[7] The single exception is the definition employed in the voluntary stewardship program of the UK's Department of Environment, Food & Rural Affairs, *see* www.defra.gov.uk. This regulatory definition is notable in requiring that at least two dimensions fall below the size threshold.

that employs 200 nanometers as an upper threshold). Also, with the same exception, the regulatory definitions to date have only required that one dimension of the material fall below the size threshold.[8] The Office of Pesticide Programs of the EPA recently stated that it is using as a working definition of nanoparticles those particles "that have at least one dimension that measures between approximately 1 and 100 nanometers."[9] Both the Cosmetics Regulation of the EU and proposed EU regulation for novel foods employ a similar definition, according to which nanomaterials are materials with "one or more dimensions of the order of 100 nm"[10] or "one or more external dimensions, or an internal structure, on the scale from 1 to 100 nm."[11]

Proposed and adopted regulatory definitions of nanomaterials generally require that the materials have been intentionally produced at the nanoscale or engineered to be nanoscale or to contain nanoscale particles. An exception to this pattern is the Danish Ministry of Environment definition, which includes no reference to the concepts of intentionality/engineered/manufactured, although even that definition suggests that nanomaterials must be "produced" or "made" as opposed to being naturally occurring.[12] What precisely is meant by intentionally produced at the nanoscale or engineered to be nanoscale has not been extensively addressed by regulatory authorities to date.[13]

SCREENING CRITERIA AND OTHER COMPONENTS OF A DEFINITION

Size

Size clearly is the principal screening criteria to be used for identifying a set of materials as posing enough possible risk to be included with a nanomaterials regulatory framework. The problem with the usual size formula, less than 100 nanometers on one dimension, is two-fold. First, it may not capture some materials that are larger but implicate the concerns motivating calls for nanomaterials regulation. Second, it may include some materials that have one nanoscale dimension but that may not implicate the concerns that motivate the calls for the regulation of nanotechnology. To date, proposed and adopted regulatory definitions take note of these concerns

[8] However, a Nanotechnology Panel of the American Chemistry Council, an industry group composed of leading corporations, proposed in February 2007 that "the presence of at least two [nano] dimensions" should be "necessary to define an engineered nanomaterial."

[9] *See* http//nanotech.law.bc.com/2010/05/articles/united-states/federal/ppdc-discusses-nanotechno.

[10] Commission proposal for a regulation on novel foods and amending Regulation (EC) No. 258/97 – 14.1.2008.

[11] Regulation (EC) No. 1223/2009.

[12] JRC Report, at 3.3.3.

[13] *See infra*. EPA defined "engineered" for purposes of its Nanoscale Materials Stewardship Program as "purposefully produced" or "purposefully designed to be a nanoscale material," but that definition does not resolve all possible ambiguities in the term. *See* http://www.epa.gov/oppt/nano/nmsp-conceptpper.pdf.

largely by using the qualifier "approximately" to describe the size range for materials that would fall under a regulatory framework. But "approximately" does not provide the notice and precision that regulated entities need to operate efficiently.

One solution to the upper threshold issue would be to increase the upper threshold in a regulatory definition of nanomaterials from 100 nanometers (perhaps to 300 nanometers or 1,000 nanometers[14]) but limit that increase to cases in which one of the other screening criteria discussed late in this chapter argues in favor of inclusion of the material in the nanomaterials regulatory framework. For example, one could postulate a general regulatory definition of nanomaterials as having a 100-nanometer upper threshold, but provide that where the manufacturer of a larger material intended or had engineered the material to have novel properties due to size or to display novel behavior associated with nanoscale materials, then the material would be treated as a nanomaterial for purposes of the regulatory framework. One disadvantage of this approach, as suggested below, would be the inherent ambiguity in defining such an intent and the difficulty of establishing its presence or absence.

A perhaps more promising approach would be to employ a higher upper threshold for nanomaterials for those materials for which the manufacturer anticipates mass exposure to the human system, and where, for that reason, the downside of omitting possibly risky materials from the regulatory framework may be particularly great in terms of human health. Such products might include food, drugs, cosmetics, and perhaps even pesticides, to the extent that they become incorporated into foods.[15] As indicated in the figure below, a relatively constrained space for regulation of materials between 100 nanometers and 1,000 nanometers could be created by limiting regulation to the intersection of that size range and screening criteria both for intentional engineering for novel properties and widespread, direct human exposure.

An alternative approach would be to maintain a 100-nanometer threshold in all contexts but allow the EPA to use rule making to add larger materials to the nanomaterials regulatory framework in cases in which the agency concludes the materials may have novel properties or display behavior associated with nanoscale materials. As suggested above, citizen petitions to the EPA to include a given material or kind of materials also might be part of the regime. One task under this approach would be to specify what the EPA's burden would be in seeking to add materials larger than 100 nanometers to the regulatory framework for nanomaterials. Such specification could be important in order to avoid *de facto* delegation to the courts

[14] The JRC Report suggests an upper limit of 1,000 nm. The National Organics Standards Board Materials Committee, convened under the authority of the U.S. Department of Agriculture, in a recent statement (February 25, 2010), has suggested an upper limit of 300 nm.

[15] The United States' regulatory regime generally follows this principle: regulatory review is much more oriented toward pre–market-release demonstrations of safety in the context of drugs and pesticides than it is the context of industrial chemicals. *See* Wendy E. Wagner, *The Precautionary Principle and Chemical Regulation in the U.S.* 6 Human and Ecological Risk Assessment 459, 464 (2000).

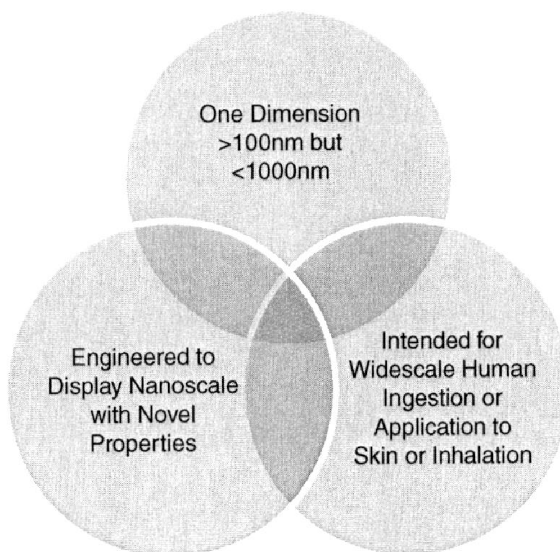

Hybrid, multi-criteria approach to upper threshold materials.

of the question of the scope of the EPA's discretion in adding larger materials to the nanomaterials category. Another, related question would be whether the EPA would have the same or different levels of flexibility or discretion in adding material greater than 100 nanometers to the scope of regulated nanomaterials than it would in declining a petition to add such a material.

A similar process could be employed by the EPA, with or without prompting by petitioners, to exclude from nanomaterials regulation those materials that have one dimension at the nanoscale but not two and that do not implicate the concerns motivating nanomaterials regulation. Again, an important question would be how much would a petitioner and/or EPA be required to show regarding the material in order to have it excluded from the scope of nanomaterials regulation. If too high a burden would be borne by a petitioner, in terms of testing and data development, then the exemption petition process might not reduce net compliance costs, which would be one of its purposes of allowing for exclusions via petition in the first place.

A Long History of Production and Use

One common approach in environmental regulation is to differentiate between new substances – those created after the date a new regulation was adopted – and old or existing ones that were created before the date of enactment. The old/new distinction, which pervades such major environmental statutes as the Clean Air Act, usually does not exempt older or existing substances from regulation but provides for relatively less stringent regulation for them. The new/old framework also can be used to explain the decision not to require any testing or lesser testing under such statutes as the Food and Drug Act and the Toxic Substances Control Act (TSCA) for a substance if that substance is considered sufficiently similar to an old or existing and approved substance as opposed to being a new substance that would require new testing and new regulatory approval.[16]

Indeed, both the Food and Drug Administration and the EPA at one point invoked this new/old notion to explain why nanomaterials might not require testing, that is, to the extent that nanomaterials contained the same chemical elements as drugs or chemicals that had been approved in bulk or coarse form, the nanomaterials might be regarded as part of an old or existing drug or chemical and hence would not trigger the requirements for new drugs or new chemicals. This treatment of nanomaterials has been controversial, in part because the concern about nanomaterials is that they may have novel properties that are not shared with their bulk or coarse counterparts. Moreover, EPA has suggested it may take a more aggressive approach toward nanomaterials under TSCA using its new use and other authorities, and pending legislation in Congress would specifically allow the EPA to designate a chemical as "new" on grounds other than molecular identity, such as, presumably, size.[17]

The new/old distinction can be useful in fashioning a regulatory definition for nanomaterials in the sense that it gives some precedential grounding for carving out an exception to the regulatory definition for nanomaterials for those materials that were in production and use long before the last 20 years and the emergence of nanotechnology as a distinct field. For these historically produced and long-used materials, there is no reason – and indeed no suggestion by anyone in the literature – that such materials pose possible environmental, health, or safety risk.

These historical materials include carbon black and a variety of materials used in food production, including the production of homogenized milk and mayonnaise. Although some or all of these materials might be excluded by a definition of nanomaterials that requires that nanomaterials have been "engineered," as the JRC Report suggests,[18] that is not obviously the case, so an explicit exclusion for materials produced prior to a plausible date (e.g., 1980 or 1990) might be preferable.

Intentionality/Engineered

That nanomaterials for regulatory purposes be intentionally produced or engineered at the nanoscale is important for several reasons. First, because an entity is unlikely to intentionally produce something at the nanoscale unless the material is expected to have novel properties, intentionally produced or engineered materials are likely to display novel properties. It is precisely such materials implicating the

[16] *See* J. Clarence Davies, *Oversight of Next Generation Nanotechnology* (April 18, 2008), available at www.nanotechproject.org/publications.

[17] *See* Control of Nanoscale Materials under the Toxic Substances Control Act, *available at* http://www.epa.gov/oppt/nano; Safe Chemicals Act of 2010, sec. 4(1)©.

[18] JRC Report, at 4.2.6.

concerns about unusual particle behavior that motivate the calls for the development of a regulatory framework for nanomaterials. Materials that are produced at a nanoscale inadvertently or by accident are less likely to be characterized by novel properties. Second, because very small, nano-like materials are not easy to detect unless one is trying to image and track them, a company that unintentionally produces nanoscale materials might not realize as much.

That said, there are difficulties in tying a regulatory definition to a concept of "intentionality" or "engineered," because it can be hard to know what is precisely meant by the concept, at least in the absence of a clear definition. Does intentional production include production in which the manufacturer reasonably should have known it was creating a nanoscale material but for whatever reason did not know? Does intentional production, for example, include the production of a nanoscale material that is an incidental byproduct of the production of another non-nanoscale material if the manufacturer is in fact aware of the byproduct and its nanoscale dimensions? Does intentional or engineered production mean that the manufacturer intended that a material have novel properties associated with nanoscale as opposed to bulk or coarse counterparts? And if a concept of novel properties is implicated or implicit in the intentional production or engineered component of a definition, how are novel properties to be defined? As one commentator has noted:

> While the "novel properties" concept rests at the center of much industry interest in nanotechnology, it also presents material characterization and regulatory problems. What exactly are these "novel properties"? How are they defined? Are they consistent from one type of nanomaterial to the next? Do they vary in intensity under certain circumstances, and are they measurable and capable of standardization? If not, how are scientists, regulators, and attorneys going to handle this aspect of the definition of nanotechnology when it comes to material characterization of projects and/or regulations?[19]

The preceding discussion is not meant to suggest that the concept of intentional production or engineered as part of a regulatory definition be abandoned. Rather, our suggestion is that care be paid to elaborating what is meant and not meant to be included within the intentional production or engineered concept at the time of the formulation of the regulatory definition in order to avoid possible disputes in the future.

Scope and Intensity of Intended Human Exposure

There is an intuitive argument for a broader or more expansive regulatory framework for nanomaterials in the context of their use in products or processes that by definition will entail large-scale, intimate exposure to human beings, as would be the case with

[19] John C. Monica, Jr., NANOTECHNOLOGY LAW s 1.3.

nanomaterials in foods, food packaging, drugs, and cosmetics. By contrast, when a material is not being produced for use in a mass market product and/or is intended only for use in an arena of relatively limited and controlled human exposure, there may be an argument for the application of a *de minimis* risk-based exclusion from an otherwise applicable regulatory definition of nanomaterials. A nanomaterial that is being produced in very tiny amounts for use in the construction of equipment for outer space, for example, could fall in such a *de minimis* exception.

The difficulties of fashioning an acceptable *de minimis* exception, however, are several. For one thing, a material that is initially intended not for mass marketing or human consumption could be redirected to such uses at a later date; moreover, materials can come into close human contact through the process of disposal and subsequent absorption into the environment (e.g., via leaching into a drinking water supply). Moreover, it is not immediately obvious what metric could be used for a *de minimis* exception in the nanomaterials context: in the EU's Regulation on the Registration, Evaluation, Authorisation and Restriction of Chemical Substances (REACH), in the context of bulk industrial chemicals, there is an implicit exclusion from registration requirements for any chemicals for which less than a ton is produced or imported annually in the EU.[20] But mass (or volume) is not easily translatable into the nano-world of very tiny, very light particles.

Physical Characteristics Other Than Size

It is widely acknowledged that certain physical characteristics of nanomaterials – such as surface area, active site density, or reactivity – may be more predictive of whether the materials will display novel properties than size.[21] Ideally, then, one might want to use these characteristics as screening criteria instead of size or along with size, but the understanding of these characteristics is not yet well-developed, and there are not widely accepted methods or metrics for measuring and comparing these characteristics. In the near term, therefore, the best that can be done is to assemble some kind of regulatory working group to actively assess the developing literature regarding these characteristics, with an eye to identifying what would be required to be done (in research terms) to make it possible to incorporate these non-size, physical characteristics into a workable regulatory definition of nanomaterials.

Distinguishing among Nanomaterials

Although some attention now is being paid to the important issue of how to differentiate nanomaterials from other (not nano) materials for purposes of regulation, there

[20] Despite its one ton per year threshold, the European Commission since at least December 2006 has expressed the view that REACH encompasses materials produced at the nano-scale that do not meet that threshold. See Lynn L. Bergeson, *REACH and Nano*, May 23, 2007, available at http://nanotech.lawbc.com/2007/05/article/international/reach-and-nano.

[21] *See, e.g.*, JRC Report, at 4.3.

has not been any attention paid to how to differentiate one particular nanomaterial or nanoparticle from another nanomaterial or nanoparticle for purposes of regulation. In a regulatory framework, there will presumably be some sort of requirement to register each distinct nanomaterial or nanoparticle.[22] In order to know how to go about such registration, regulated entities will need to know when it is permissible to group different materials or particles as the same for regulatory purposes and when that is impermissible. In the nanotechnology context, this is a challenging task because the usual means of differentiating materials – chemical composition, molecular identity – will not necessarily capture relevant differences. Indeed, two nanomaterials that have the same chemical composition and size but a different physical configuration and/or coating may exhibit different behaviors.[23] In order to define one nanomaterial as different from another, therefore, a better understanding of novel behaviors and what drives them will need to be developed.

Regulatory Definition as Adaptive Management

The whole enterprise of regulating nanotechnology – and hence the included enterprise of defining nanomaterials for regulatory purposes – ideally would be an exercise in "adaptive management," understood generally to mean management that continually adapts to take account of new information and new insights. Adaptive management in this context – as in most regulatory contexts – must grapple with the truth that regulated entities need some stability to operate, and stability means some periods of relative non-adaptation, as well as the truth that regulators, perpetually overworked and overburdened and at least at some remove from developments in science and industry, may not engage in even periodic adaptation unless institutional structures are in place to encourage them to do so.[24]

One such institutional means would be an agency commitment to issue a review of its regulatory definition no less than once every 5 years, in which the EPA would be required to explain why it was or was not changing the current regulatory definition at a minimum of 5-year intervals. The process of putting out such a review for notice and comment would help focus debate on changes in nanotechnology that might justify changes in the regulatory definition of nanomaterials. Another institutional means would be the creation of an advisory board to inform the EPA regarding relevant changes in the nanotechnology industry and composed of industry, academic, and

[22] For example, although the European Commissions' recent report suggests that a dossier must be prepared for each "composition" that is a nanomaterial under REACH, it does not offer any guidance regarding how a manufacturer could determine whether two similar materials are the same composition of nanomaterial for this purpose or rather different nanomaterials requiring the completion of separate dossiers. *See* ECHA, *IUCLID 5 Guidance and Support Nanomaterials* in IUCLID 5.2 (June 10 v 1.0), at 5.

[23] *See, e.g.*, Byoung-Kye Kim et al., *The Effect of Metal Cluster Coatings on Carbon Nanotubes*. Nanotechnology 17, 496 (2006).

[24] On regulatory inertia, see David E. Adelman, *Adaptive federalism: The case against reallocating environmental regulatory authority*. 92 Minn. L. Rev. 1796, 1826 (2008).

non-governmental organization representatives. One challenge for such an advisory board – and for the EPA generally – would be to address confidential business information concerns that might discourage industry from sharing with the EPA information regarding its investments in emerging forms of nanotechnology, for fear that doing so might result in the loss of protection for confidential business information.[25]

CONCLUSION

Nanomaterials cannot be defined without reference to size, but a size-based definition is likely to be under- and over-inclusive for regulatory purposes. The more we understand about nanomaterials and their distinctive behaviors, the more we will and should define them around their distinctive behaviors directly and the risks those may pose. Nanomaterials, more generally, require a dynamic, fluid definition that accounts for their rapid development and the fact that they can be distinguished from one another on a range of dimensions and not just the traditionally employed dimension of chemical identity or the size dimension that typically has dominated regulatory definitions of nanomaterials to date. The challenge of defining nanomaterials thus embodies the broader challenge of making regulation work in an age of fast-paced, even frenetic technological change.

[25] *See* Sunstein, *supra*, at 420 (noting that "Government is rarely in a good position to know what sorts of innovations are likely to be forthcoming."). Confidential business information is a challenge for the regulation of emerging technologies, and one that so far has not received due attention in the academic literature. In forthcoming work I hope to explore possible solutions to the dilemma of developing regulation in the context of confidential information concerns. There are two principal problems embedded in the problem of confidential information: (1) the fear of business entities that they will lose the legal protection under (primarily) state law when they submit confidential business information to the government, and (2) the fear of business entities that their competitors will be able to use their disclosures to government to develop competing products. The first concern could be addressed with a federal statute that preserves state confidential information status notwithstanding disclosure to federal agencies. The second concern is more difficult to address, as it is essentially a practical one and not a legal one. To be effective and achieve public trust, the federal government in the US context would need to reveal the bases for its regulatory responses, including information it received from businesses, and by doing so, the possibility of leakage of information from one business to its competitors becomes almost impossible to avoid. However, there may be ways for government to share information with the public and other governments that minimize the risks of such leakage, such as the use of redaction. Another possibility would be to substitute general public access and review to underlying submissions by businesses to certified representatives of the public, such as specially designated nongovernmental organizations.

6

The Missing Market Instrument

Environmental Assurance Bonds and Nanotechnology Regulation

Douglas A. Kysar

On January 30, 2009, US President Barack Obama issued a memorandum to the heads of executive departments and agencies expressing an intention to study and revise the manner in which the White House Office of Management and Budget conducts regulatory impact review, including economic cost–benefit analysis (CBA) of proposed rules. Opened to public comment after pressure from non-governmental organizations,[1] the review process revealed a deep split in civil society regarding the desirability of regulatory CBA as a tool for evaluating proposed policies.[2] Numerous commentators focused their suggestions on incremental methodological improvements to CBA, expressing unequivocal support for the evaluation of policies based on their predicted overall impacts for human well-being. Others, however, raised serious practical and ethical objections to the use of CBA. They offered instead a vision of policy making much more pluralistic in its conception of value and

[1] *See* RENA STEINZOR, CTR. FOR PROGRESSIVE REFORM, RE: PLANS TO REWRITE EXECUTIVE ORDER ON OMB REGULATORY REVIEW (2009), http://www.progressiveregulation.org/articles/PreliminaryCommentsonNewEO-Orszag.pdf.

[2] The public comments are available at GENERAL SERVICES ADMINISTRATION, PUBLIC COMMENTS ON OMB RECOMMENDATIONS FOR A NEW EXECUTIVE ORDER ON REGULATORY REVIEW (2009), http://www.reginfo.gov/public/jsp/EO/fedRegReview/publicComments.jsp. It bears noting that CBA is typically thought of as an ex post check on regulatory policies, the content of which has been determined according to other criteria such as health-based statutory requirements or qualitative balancing. Nevertheless, as I have argued elsewhere, CBA has begun to creep into the front end of regulatory decision making, becoming much closer to an ex ante determinant of the content of policies. *See* DOUGLAS A. KYSAR, *Fish Tales*, in ALTERNATIVE APPROACHES TO REGULATORY IMPACT ANALYSIS: A DIALOGUE BETWEEN ADVOCATES AND SKEPTICS OF COST-BENEFIT ANALYSIS (Winston Harrington, Lisa Heinzerling, & Richard Morgenstern, eds., 2009).

This chapters draws from an earlier article, "Ecologic: Nanotechnology, Environmental Assurance Bonding, and Symmetric Humility," which appeared in Volume 28, Issue 1 of the UCLA Journal of Environmental Law and Policy. Both projects benefited greatly from research assistance provided by Benjamin Ewing and Tafari Lumumba. For helpful comments and suggestions, I thank David Dana, Joseph Guth, Timothy Malloy, Sean Hecht, and the participants of the UCLA 2009 Working Conference on Nanotechnology Regulatory Policy. All misjudgments, errors, and omissions are my own.

much more pragmatic in its assumptions regarding the availability and certitude of empirical knowledge regarding policy effects. Although these commentators tended not to invoke the principle by name, their recommendations followed a course that internationally has come to be associated with the Precautionary Principle (PP), one that counsels erring on the side of safety when scientific uncertainty exists over the potential consequences of an action.

In a recent book,[3] I defended the conceptual coherence and normative desirability of policy approaches, such as those associated with the PP, that reject the idea that environmental, health, and safety law can be adequately addressed from an assumed viewpoint of objectivity. The danger, I argue, is that the attempt to render environmental, health, and safety regulation fully determinable through empirical assessment and formalized decision-making models – an attempt found most influentially in the methodology of CBA, but associated more generally with the economic regulatory reform project of the last three decades – obscures the relation of agency and responsibility that the political community bears to its decisions. Even robust institutional actors such as nation states confront forces that lie beyond complete prediction and control, including the operations of complex natural systems, the actions of foreign nations and other non-subjects that depend on and impact shared resources, and the future needs and circumstances of unborn generations that are a necessary but unknowable feature of any policy decision involving intergenerational consequences. I argue that, within such a decision-making context, the political community must always in a nontrivial sense stand outside of its tools of policy assessment, maintaining a degree of self-awareness and self-criticality regarding the manner in which its agency is exercised. The PP encourages such conscientiousness by reminding the political community, as it stands poised on the verge of a policy choice with potentially serious or irreversible environmental consequences, that its actions *matter*, that they belong uniquely to the community and will form a part of its narrative history and identity, helping to underwrite its standing in the community of communities that includes other nations, other generations, and other forms of life. Such considerations, in contrast, hold no clear or secure place within the logic of CBA, tending as it does to deny the political community a view from within itself and instead to ask the community, in essence, to regulate from nowhere.

This chapter seeks to make a more modest, but also more grounded contribution: it argues that the turn toward market-based policy instruments in environmental, health, and safety law has focused unduly on the use of pollution taxes and tradable permits and that a third market-based instrument, the *environmental assurance bond*, offers features that should commend it to proponents both of CBA and the PP. Especially in the context of a nascent field such as nanoscale science and engineering, where available information regarding potential consequences is highly incomplete

[3] Douglas A. Kysar, Regulating From Nowhere: Environmental Law and the Search for Objectivity (New Haven, CT: Yale University Press, 2010).

and uncertain, the environmental assurance bond is a normatively attractive policy tool because it displays the virtue of *symmetric humility*.[4] Promoters of CBA support analytical requirements for regulators that presuppose simplicity, predictability, and manipulability in the environment. In essence, they support something like central planning for the environment, even though they would abhor such planning in the economy. Regulatory reformers do so because they believe that economic incentives are sufficiently powerful – and private interactions sufficiently reliable – to promote overall human well-being with greater success than fallible and corruptible government agencies. Hence, in their view, regulators should be required to overcome a substantial burden of proof before interfering with the dynamism and complexity of the market. Conversely, PP proponents recommend precautionary and protective regulation because they appreciate the fragility and interconnectedness of ecological systems. Hence they would place a substantial burden of proof on private actors who seek to introduce new substances or technologies, alter existing land uses, or otherwise interfere with the dynamism and complexity of the environment. Like the asymmetric humility of their opponents, however, supporters of the PP arguably downplay the severity and significance of these same traits when it comes to socio-legal systems, ignoring problems associated with regulation such as unintended consequences, compensating behaviors, and agency capture.

The environmental assurance-bonding approach tries to steer a middle course between these extremes of asymmetric humility. Unlike typical cost-benefit approaches, environmental assurance-bonding acknowledges uncertainty regarding the value, resilience, and replaceability of biophysical systems by assessing serious ex ante financial responsibility for possible causation of environmental harm. At the same time – and in contrast to strict interpretations of the PP – environmental assurance bonding acknowledges the strength and dynamism of socio-legal systems such as markets by allowing private actors to proceed with potentially beneficial activities despite the existence of a credible risk of harm. Indeed, environmental assurance bonding actively marshals the decentralized decision-making power of markets as a force for the development of knowledge regarding uncertain substances and activities. As such, the policy approach reflects a high degree of what might be called *ecological rationality*, approaching ill-posed regulatory problems with a pragmatic combination of respect for the power of markets and human technology and caution before the complexities of nature.[5]

The chapter is organized as follows. Section I draws on complexity theory to describe the regulatory landscape, both as it pertains to biophysical systems such as

4 In this respect, I follow Albert Lin, who also has argued that environmental assurance bonding offers an attractive policy approach for the burgeoning field of nanoscale science and engineering. *See* Albert C. Lin, *Size Matters: Regulating Nanotechnology*, 31 HARV. ENVTL. L. REV. 349 (2007).

5 As noted in Section II, cognitive psychologists have coined the term *ecological rationality* to refer to choice and judgment heuristics that are well-adapted to real-world decision-making environments in which optimific approaches, such as CBA or other formal axiomatic systems, may founder.

wetlands and socio-legal systems such as product markets. As Section I describes, differences in ontological outlook tend to drive differences in scientific agenda: whereas classically oriented scientists hope to achieve *convergence* at the nanoscale by fusing nanotechnology, biotechnology, information technology, and cognitive science into a single, unified, and comprehensive scientific field, ecologists, conservation biologists, and other observers of complex adaptive systems emphasize the ineliminable phenomenon of *emergence*, whereby certain system properties appear at the macroscale in a manner that simply cannot be predicted or explained through an examination of constituent system components alone. Section II argues that the former approach tends to instill in adherents technological optimism and a conviction that human ingenuity and progress generally can overcome any impediments and scarcities posed by the natural world. The latter approach, in contrast, tends to counsel humility and caution in the face of inevitable – and often unpleasant – ecological surprise. Section II further uses the teachings of decision theory and cognitive psychology to reveal complementary inadequacies in the policy-making approaches that are epitomized by CBA and the PP. Finally, in light of these complementary inadequacies, Section III argues that participants in the risk regulation debate should offer their support for policy tools, such as environmental assurance bonds, that give due respect to the most critical aspects of both CBA and the PP.

I. UNCERTAINTY AND COMPLEXITY IN THE ENVIRONMENT

Managing the risks of a nascent field such as nanoscale science and engineering is a perplexing task, characterized by great uncertainty and seemingly unavoidable trade-offs. The same properties that make nanomaterials attractive as industrial inputs – namely, their increased reactivity and often dramatically altered optical, electrical, and magnetic behavior compared with macroscale counterparts – also make their toxicity and environmental fate difficult to predict and assess. For instance, given their miniscule size, nanomaterials may penetrate cells more easily than larger materials, a feature that makes them attractive as potential drug delivery devices, but that also raises concerns about possible adverse health effects. Similarly, although scientists expect to achieve a host of breakthroughs in electrical and mechanical engineering through the use of highly conductive carbon nanotubes that are as strong as steel but that remain remarkably light and flexible, regulators increasingly are expressing concern that such tubes also seem to share many of the physical and toxicological characteristics of asbestos fibers. Because an important feature of nanoparticles is their comparatively large surface area to mass ratio, some scientists also believe that they may be significantly more toxic per unit of mass than larger particles of the same chemical. Indeed, some scientists maintain that the nanoscale itself may entail toxic characteristics, irrespective of the particular chemical makeup of any nanomaterial that is confronted by a human subject.

Although the number of studies addressing potential adverse health and environmental effects of nanomaterials has increased significantly in recent years as governments have begun to direct a larger share of public research expenditures to such questions, the area remains riddled with uncertainty. Stark though it may be, this epistemic vacuum does not necessarily distinguish nanotechnology from other subjects of environmental, health, and safety regulation. Indeed, a long-recognized hallmark feature of such regulation has been the informational and cognitive limitations that face any regulator's ability to identify, understand, and predict the consequences of risk-creating activities, including the act of regulation itself. Accordingly, a critical challenge for risk regulators is to ensure that their decision-making models are appropriately suited to the nature and degree of uncertainty faced, whether the models concern the assessment of ecological or human health hazards, the calculation of economic costs, or some more ambitious integration of the two.

Biophysical Systems

As J.B. Ruhl has observed, advances in ecological science have made a "mess" of thinking about environmental law and policy.[6] The romantic notion that nature can be preserved in a stable equilibrium untouched by human influence has long since been discredited, not merely by improved theoretical understanding of the inherent dynamism and disorder of ecosystems, but also by increasing awareness of the fundamental interconnectedness between ecosystems and *other* complex adaptive systems, including especially those that are associated with human activity. To take only the most vivid example, greenhouse gases emitted through fossil fuel combustion, deforestation, and other human activities have contributed to climatic changes that are occurring on a planetary scale, with potential consequences for all life forms in all areas of the globe. Moreover, as demonstrated by the fact that existing anthropogenic greenhouse gas emissions will continue to affect the atmosphere for decades or even centuries beyond the present one, the desire simply to "let nature be" no longer generates meaningful guidance for environmental policy making. Instead, as Ruhl recently put it, "[t]he reality is that there simply is no way to 'preserve' nature without in some sense managing it somewhere with some human-defined purpose."[7]

In response to these developments, the concept of *ecosystem management* has arisen with a goal of "integrat[ing] scientific knowledge of ecological relationships within a complex sociopolitical and values framework toward the general goal of protecting native ecosystem integrity over the long term."[8] As conservation biologists

[6] J.B. Ruhl, *Thinking of Environmental Law as a Complex Adaptive System: How to Clean up the Environment by Making a Mess of Environmental Law*, 34 HOUS. L. REV. 933, 954 (1997).

[7] J.B. Ruhl, *The Myth of What Is Inevitable Under Ecosystem Management: A Response to Pardy*, 21 PACE ENVTL. L. REV. 315, 321 (2004).

[8] R. Edward Grumbine, *What Is Ecosystem Management?* 8 CONSERVATION BIOLOGY 27, 31 (1994). Ecosystem management relates closely to C.S. Holling's notion of "adaptive management," from which the newer field derives its basic management principle of continuous monitoring and adjustment. *See* ADAPTIVE ENVIRONMENTAL ASSESSMENT AND MANAGEMENT (C.S. Holling, ed., Chichester, NY: Wiley, 1978). *See also* KAI N. LEE, COMPASS AND GYROSCOPE: INTEGRATING SCIENCE AND POLITICS FOR THE ENVIRONMENT (Washington, DC: Island Press, 1993; p. 53) (describing adaptive

and others have emphasized, the long-run integrity of ecosystems is important not merely because non-human life forms within those systems may have some intrinsic value by virtue of their existence alone, but also because humanity depends in numerous ways on the *ecosystem services* that are provided by well-functioning ecosystems and the shifting web of life forms that comprise them.[9] Conversely, ecosystem functioning is affected in a multitude of ways by the behavior of humans, whose macroscale policies and microscale decisions contribute to a state of irrevocable interdependence between social and ecological systems. Accordingly, proponents of the ecosystem management paradigm view their task as one of identifying, monitoring, and sustaining evolutionary and ecological processes, recognizing that those processes occur within a complex of multiple, interconnected systems, including political, economic, and other socio-legal systems that help to determine the human impact on ecosystems.

Lurking behind the ecosystem management approach is an ontology informed by the teachings of complexity theory. In pithy terms, complexity theory suggests that researchers and regulators should expect the unexpected whenever they examine complex adaptive systems such as immune systems, coral reefs, the global climate, the world economy, or even something as seemingly mundane and uncomplicated as a dripping faucet.[10] Complexity theory should be deliberately contrasted with the reductionist focus of the Newtonian tradition in science, which attempts to understand the world by breaking it down into smaller and smaller components for isolated study. Although clearly fruitful for a variety of tasks, a central tenet of complexity theory is that "the reductionist methodology will never lead to a fully predictive theory of any complex system."[11] For instance, researchers may be able to identify the dose-response curve that characterizes the acute toxicity effects of a given nanomaterial on a given species within the splendor of a controlled laboratory environment, but at the same time they may miss entirely the effects of the substance on the species in its broader ecological context.

Complex adaptive systems differ in a number of significant ways from systems that are composed of linear, independently operating components. First, complexity theory presupposes that micro-level interactions between numerous forces or agents within a system give rise to patterns of behavior that are only detectable when the system is viewed at the macro-level, in its entirety. The ant or termite colony provides a vivid example, as it exhibits extraordinary features such as temperature regulation and geomagnetic orientation that simply cannot be predicted or accounted for by

management as an application of "the concept of experimentation to the design and implementation of natural-resource and environmental policies").

[9] *See* Nature's Services: Societal Dependence on Natural Ecosystems (Gretchen Daily ed., Washington, DC: Island Press, 1997).

[10] *See* Ruhl, *supra* note 6, at 936.

[11] *Id.* at 937.

examining the behavior of individual colony members alone.[12] Second, complex adaptive systems often exhibit nonlinear relationships and behaviors, such that they do not display mathematical proportionality in the tidy manner assumed by classical science and mathematics. This is not to suggest that the systems are indeterminate, but rather that their rules of operation give rise to stunningly complex and difficult-to-predict interactions. Extremely minor, even immeasurable variations in conditions between two otherwise identically situated systems – such as the presence in one system of the proverbial flapping of a butterfly's wings – can give rise to dramatic differences in outcome between the two systems only a few evolutionary steps later. The resulting "chaos" is not randomness per se, but rather "order masquerading as randomness,"[13] a state of being that, although deterministic, nevertheless remains irreducibly uncertain.

Third, in addition to sensitivity to minor variations in conditions, complex systems also are characterized by feedback and feedforward loops, in which system components influence other components that, in turn, cause their own effects on the original, as well as many other, components within the system. Cause and effect pathways, in other words, are not terminal and unidirectional. Instead, the components of a system are interconnected through numerous multidirectional paths of relation and dependence. This state of interconnection often leads to multiplier effects and other self-reinforcing tendencies that render a system's condition at any given time path-dependent and, therefore, not easily reversed or altered. For example, if researchers discover that release of nanoparticles into a habitat destroys zooplankton, which leads to proliferation of algae and in turn promotes the expansion of a particular species that feeds on the algae, it will be impossible for even the most skilled ecosystem manager to restore the original "equilibrium" that once characterized the habitat. Instead, the system will only be able to continue adapting in some manner or another from its present, path-dependent state.

Finally, an important consequence of these various features of complex adaptive systems is that normal or Gaussian probability theory may be highly misleading when used to predict or describe their behavior. As Daniel Farber has discussed, "[c]omplex systems . . . are often characterized by a different kind of statistical distribution called a 'power law.'"[14] Systems that are subject to power laws display a number of peculiar features. Most notably, they typically have *fat tails*, in which large or even extreme events appear with a regularity that would be unthinkable from the perspective of normal probability assumptions. Accordingly, systems governed by power laws are not adequately described by conventional statistical concepts such as the mean or the mode. Indeed, by focusing only on average outcomes in the conventional manner,

12 *See* J. Scott Turner, The Extended Organism: The Physiology of Animal-Built Structures (Cambridge, MA: Harvard University Press, 2000).

13 James Gleick, Chaos: Making a New Science (New York, NY: Viking, 1987; p. 22).

14 Daniel A. Farber, *Probabilities Behaving Badly: Complexity Theory and Environmental Uncertainty*, 37 U.C. Davis L. Rev. 145, 146–47 (2003).

analysts of complex adaptive systems risk ignoring important – even potentially catastrophic – aspects of the system's behavior.

Socio-Legal Systems

The process of Darwinian evolution has long provided the leading metaphorical explanation for the operation of economic markets. Naturally, then, as our vision of biophysical systems and evolutionary processes sharpens to include complexity and dynamism as foundational characteristics, so too might our understanding of market operations evolve to embrace such characteristics. Recently, a number of theorists have begun to mine the field of complexity theory for insight into economics in precisely this manner.[15] Their findings include nonlinear discontinuities in price dynamics, sensitivity over time to minor variations in conditions, powerful feedback loops that contribute to bubbles and other inertial economic events, and many other hallmark features of complex adaptive systems. Mathematician Benoit Mandlebrot, an important intellectual figure in the development of fractal geometry and complexity theory, expects these initial findings to lead in time to nothing short of a revolution in the theory of economics and finance. He argues that, at bottom, "[t]he geometry that describes the shape of coastlines and the patterns of galaxies also elucidates how stock prices soar and plummet."[16]

It is too early to tell whether Mandlebrot's vision of a revolutionized economic theory will come to fruition, although the global economic collapse of 2008–2009 has certainly strengthened the case for inclusion of greater systemic analysis of market behavior and greater levels of humility regarding the power of positivistic financial modeling. Even before those events, however, one already could identify traces of complexity theory in much of prevailing thought about markets and regulation. An important theme of the risk reform debate, for instance, has been repeated emphasis on the possibility of unintended consequences from regulation.[17] Just as ecosystems are believed to be characterized by pronounced and often unpredictable changes due to minor perturbations, markets are said to exhibit substitution effects,[18]

[15] *See, e.g.*, Benoit B. Mandelbrot & Richard L. Hudson, The (Mis)behavior of Markets: A Fractal View of Risk, Ruin, and Return (New York, NY: Basic Books, 2004); Edgar E. Peters, Chaos and Order in the Capital Markets: A New View of Cycles, Prices, and Market Volatility (New York, NY: Wiley, 1996).

[16] Benoit B. Mandelbrot, *A Multifractal Walk Down Wall Street*, 280 Sci. Am. 70 (1999).

[17] For a critical overview, see Mark Kelman, *On Democracy-Bashing: A Skeptical Look at the Theoretical and "Empirical" Practice of the Public Choice Movement*, 74 Va. L. Rev. 199 (1988).

[18] *See* Samuel J. Rascoff & Richard L. Revesz, *The Biases of Risk Tradeoff Analysis: Towards Parity in Environmental and Health-And-Safety Regulation*, 69 U. Chi. L. Rev. 1763, 1775 (2002) ("Sometimes a regulation will bring about a risk tradeoff when it effects a shift from one product or process to another, which in turn gives rise to risks of its own.").

compensating behaviors,[19] and a host of other unanticipated results that flow from government regulatory interventions. For instance, in one classic example, economist Sam Peltzman argues that highway safety regulations such as mandatory seatbelt laws may lead drivers to reduce their own level of caution, generating an accident rate that is higher overall than without the regulation.[20] Similarly, Kip Viscusi contends that child-proof container requirements for medicines may give parents a false sense of security, prompting them to leave drugs within reach of children and leading ultimately to more children at risk than before the requirements were imposed.[21]

Compensating behaviors are but one way in which government risk regulations are thought to entail subtle, but significant secondary effects. Other claimed risk tradeoffs[22] of environmental, health, and safety regulation include direct or iatrogenic effects, such as the possibility that "cleaning up Superfund sites, or removing asbestos from buildings, may put workers at risk of exposure and occupational injury"[23]; and health–health tradeoffs, such as the increased mortality and morbidity that is said to flow merely from the act of expending money on regulatory compliance.[24] In light of these various tradeoffs, scholars have advocated risk–risk analysis as a mechanism for focusing decision makers on *all* of the effects that may be expected to come from adopting a particular environmental, health, or safety standard. Such comprehensive risk analysis is thought to be desirable because the adaptive behaviors and activities of market participants evade casual prediction; accordingly, failure to rigorously cast about in search of unintended consequences before acting may lead regulators to govern ineffectively or, indeed, to cause harm where they intend good.

To date, critics of risk regulation have successfully highlighted the notion that government actions within market environments may cause unanticipated effects that work at cross purposes with the goal of government action. Less well appreciated, however, is the fact that regulations also can entail unintended consequences that

[19] *See* Peter A. Veytsman, *Drug Testing Student Athletes and Fourth Amendment Privacy: The Legal Aftermath of* Veronica v. Action, 73 TEMP. L. REV. 295, 325 (2000) (referring to "the theory of compensating behavior, in which people's responses to government regulations are often contrary to the intended effect of the regulation").

[20] *See* Sam Peltzman, *The Regulation of Auto Safety*, in AUTO SAFETY REGULATION: THE CURE OR THE PROBLEM? (Henry G. Manne & Roger LeRoy Miller, Eds., Glen Ridge, NJ: T. Horton, 1976; pp. 8–9).

[21] *See* W. KIP VISCUSI, FATAL TRADEOFFS: PUBLIC AND PRIVATE RESPONSIBILITIES FOR RISK (New York, NY: Oxford University Press, 1992; pp. 234–242).

[22] John D. Graham & Jonathan Baert Wiener, *Confronting Risk Tradeoffs*, in RISK VERSUS RISK: TRADEOFFS IN PROTECTING HEALTH AND THE ENVIRONMENT (John D. Graham & Jonathan Baert Wiener, Eds., Cambridge, MA: Harvard University Press, 1995; p. 1).

[23] Jonathan Baert Wiener, *Managing the Iatrogenic Risks of Risk Management*, 9 RISK: HEALTH, SAFETY, & ENVT. 39, 40 (1998).

[24] *See* Randall Lutter & John F. Morrall III, *Health-Health Analysis: A New Way to Evaluate Health and Safety Regulation*, 8 J. RISK & UNCERTAINTY 1, 44 (1994) ("Health-health analysis seeks to quantify the expected declines in health and safety that may be ascribed to the costs of complying with a regulation.").

are beneficial. Researchers studying climate change mitigation policies, for instance, have calculated that the ancillary benefits of greenhouse gas mitigation – such as the incidental reduction of other harmful air pollutants – may be comparable in magnitude to the direct benefits of climate change policies.[25] As Samuel Rascoff and Richard Revesz have argued, similar "ancillary benefits have been observed across a broad range of contexts."[26] Because the debate over regulatory reform has tended to ignore this reality, however, "[t]he resulting legal and scholarly conclusions about the desirability of regulation [have been] consistently distorted."[27]

The overlooked phenomenon of ancillary benefits suggests that the interaction between government regulation and markets is more complex than even members of the unintended consequences school tend to appreciate. To complicate matters still further, once analysts decide to include substitution effects or other endogenous behavioral responses to regulation, then it is not a large theoretical step to admit that endogenous shifts may also occur with respect to preferences. Contrary to the standard assumption of many schools of policy analysis, markets and other socio-legal systems are not characterized by linear, unidirectional relationships between public values and the law, on the one hand, and the law and its subjects, on the other. Rather, the system of relationships among these forces exhibits feedback loops, oscillations, and other characteristic traits of complex adaptive systems, including a state of reciprocal influence between the law and public values. Thus, just as legal policies may affect behavior in complex and unanticipated ways, so too may policies alter the beliefs and attitudes of individuals, including perhaps the very beliefs and attitudes that initially justify a policy choice. As Cass Sunstein has noted, these "preference-shaping effects of legal rules cast doubt on the idea that . . . regulation should attempt to satisfy or follow some aggregation of private preferences. . . . When preferences are a function of legal rules, the rules cannot be justified by reference to the preferences."[28]

Unintended consequences, ancillary benefits, and endogenous preferences all reflect an important truism identified nearly one half century ago by two economists in a classic article entitled "The General Theory of the Second Best."[29] In this article, the theorists demonstrated that alleviation of one distortion among many in a given

[25] *See* Douglas A. Kysar, *Some Realism About Environmental Skepticism: The Implications of Bjorn Lomborg's* The Skeptical Environmentalist *for Environmental Law and Policy*, 30 ECOLOGY L. Q. 223, 263–64 (2003).

[26] Rascoff & Revesz, *supra* note 18, at 1766.

[27] *Id.*

[28] Cass R. Sunstein, *Endogenous Preferences, Environmental Law*, 22 J. LEGAL STUD. 217, 234–35 (1993). Still further complications arise from the fact that government rules, regulations, and requirements may themselves interact and behave as a complex adaptive system, a point that J. B. Ruhl has urged in several articles. *See, e.g.*, J.B. Ruhl, *Complexity Theory as a Paradigm for the Dynamical Law-and-Society System: A Wake-Up Call for Legal Reductionism and the Modern Administrative State*, 45 DUKE L. J. 849 (1996).

[29] See R.G. Lipsey & Kelvin Lancaster, *The General Theory of the Second Best*, 24 REV. ECON. STUD. 11 (1956).

market may not necessarily lead to an overall increase in the efficiency of the market. For instance, at any given time, a particular microeconomic inefficiency may be serving to counteract the effects of another inefficiency such that, if the former were eliminated, society might become worse off in the aggregate, not better. Stated more precisely, "if one or more members of a set of optimal conditions cannot be fulfilled, there is no general reason to believe that fulfilling (or more closely approximating) more of the remaining conditions will bring [society] closer to the optimum than fulfilling fewer of the remaining conditions."[30] The macroeconomic efficiency problem, in that sense, is ill-posed: Many of its determining variables and rules of interrelationship are simply unknown, such that the impact that one or more microeconomic adjustments will have on the system as a whole remains shrouded in deep uncertainty.

Although not expressly premised on complexity theory, the General Theory of the Second Best shares much of that theory's pre-analytic vision. The theory notes at its heart that the factors determining a macroeconomic equilibrium are so numerous, multifaceted, and interdependent that one simply cannot know whether a microeconomic efficiency improvement will lead, on net, to an improvement at the macroeconomic scale, unless one assumes – contrary to all available evidence – that the microeconomic inefficiency under investigation is the only such inefficiency in the entire system. Participants in the risk regulation debate exhibit some sensitivity to this complexity by examining policy proposals with an awareness that market inefficiencies *other than* the target of the proposal may exist and may impact the outcomes of government intervention. For instance, analysts forego the unrealistic assumption that users of child-proof medicine containers are perfectly rational, and instead investigate empirically supported cognitive tendencies that lead them to predict a counterintuitive, and counterproductive, parental response. Similarly, rather than assume an absence of additional pollution externalities when evaluating the costs and benefits of climate change policies, analysts instead examine the actual evidence and discover that a host of harmful air pollution effects currently exist that serendipitously would be alleviated by greenhouse gas emissions reductions. In both cases, by attempting to model the welfare consequences of regulation in a highly interactive – and imperfect – world, the policy analyst demonstrates at least partial awareness of the complexity of socio-legal systems.

II. UNCERTAINTY AND COMPLEXITY IN THE MIND

In addition to the external environments that risk regulators aim to influence, such individuals also must grapple with problems of uncertainty and complexity within the mind itself: even well-behaved, well-understood systems will confound the

30 Richard S. Markovits, *Second Best Theory and Law and Economics: An Introduction*, 73 CHI.-KENT L. REV. 3, 3 (1998).

regulator whose judgment is influenced by psychological tendencies that conflict with the realization of a regulatory goal. Within cognitive psychology, a theoretical debate has raged for the last two decades over whether and when heuristic decision-making approaches provide superior results to more analytically formalized procedures. Psychologists participating in what has been called the *heuristics* research tradition claim that individuals often are wise to ignore available, relevant information and to eschew explicit attempts to calculate an optimal result in their personal judgment and decision making.[31] According to these theorists, relying instead on heuristic techniques that exploit informational cues and other features of the decision-making environment can conserve scarce computational effort while achieving a performance level that approaches the results of deliberate optimization techniques. Moreover, they argue that, in many instances, heuristics provide the only ecologically rational manner in which to solve problems given that many, if not most, real world problems are not posed in a manner that permits the identification of an optimal solution, let alone its attainment.[32]

In contrast to these psychologists, the *heuristics and biases* research program pioneered by Daniel Kahneman and Amos Tversky[33] has become associated with the view that individual decision-making heuristics frequently are unreliable, and that "corrective" measures such as debiasing efforts or legal interventions are necessary in order to better approximate the ideal of expected utility maximization.[34] Although at times overblown, the contrast between these two viewpoints is nevertheless instructive for the present chapter because it parallels in many ways the debate that has taken place between proponents of CBA and supporters of the PP within environmental law and policy. Moreover, in recent years, participants in theoretical debates over the PP and risk regulation have begun to turn to cognitive psychology and behavioral decision theory for insight and support of their policy recommendations.[35] To these theorists, psychological findings offer the potential not only to produce more reliable predictions of behavior among individuals and other actors that the law is attempting to influence, but also to provide guidance for shaping the content and

[31] *See* Gerd Gigerenzer & Peter Todd, Simple Heuristics That Make Us Smart (New York, NY: Oxford University Press, 1999; pp. 25–26) (describing decision-making heuristics as "useful, even indispensable cognitive processes for solving problems that cannot be handled by logic and probability theory . . . ").

[32] *See id.* at vii (arguing that simple cognitive heuristics persist because "they are ecologically rational, that is, adapted to the structure of the information in the environment in which they are used to make decisions").

[33] *See* Daniel Kahneman & Amos Tversky, *Judgment Under Uncertainty: Heuristics and Biases*, 185 Sci. 1124 (1974) (identifying decision-making heuristics as "principles which reduce the complex tasks of assessing probabilities and predicting values to simpler judgmental operations" and which "are quite useful, but sometimes . . . lead to severe and systematic errors").

[34] *See* Christine Jolls & Cass R. Sunstein, *Debiasing Through Law*, 35 J. Legal Stud. 199 (2006).

[35] *See, e.g.*, David A. Dana, *A Behavioral Economic Defense of the Precautionary Principle*, 97 Nw. U. L. Rev. 1315 (2003); Cass R. Sunstein, *Cognition and Cost-Benefit Analysis*, 29 J. Legal. Stud. 1059 (2000).

structure of legal rules themselves, so that they may better resonate with what we know about the human mind.

Rationality in Individual Choice[36]

Within the social sciences, one tends to encounter both optimality-based and heuristic-based models of how the human mind accesses and processes information. The former category of models, associated prominently with rational choice theory, encompass fully specified analytic systems in which the processes of decision making are given by formal rules of logic and computation that can be described with mathematical precision, replicated over multiple trials, and extended across diverse tasks. Optimality-based approaches seek to identify the solution to a problem that is singularly optimal according to a desired criterion, such as expected utility or wealth maximization. Optimization models can be prescriptive, in the sense that they aim to identify the solution that individuals or other decision makers should adopt for a given problem, or they can be simply descriptive, in the sense that they aim to predict the choices that decision makers will adopt for a given problem. Descriptive models may be further subdivided according to whether they purport to describe the actual processes that decision makers utilize in order to solve problems, or whether they instead merely aim to predict the outcomes of decisions, while remaining agnostic on the particular cognitive processes that individuals employ in order to produce such outcomes.

Psychologists in contrast seek to model and understand directly the cognitive processes that individuals use to make decisions. Such researchers differ, however, in the extent to which they believe that heuristic-based models supplant, as opposed to merely supplement, optimization models. The heuristics and biases research program, for instance, has used experimentally observed departures from rational choice theory to glean insights about the mental processes that individuals utilize when evaluating options and making decisions. Thus the optimality-based approach of rational choice theory remains an integral component of the heuristics and biases research program. The heuristics program, on the other hand, seeks to understand decision making from the "bottom up," by identifying and modeling the actual cognitive processes that individuals are believed to use for given decision-making tasks without regard to any basic underlying model of rational choice.

One important reason that researchers in the heuristics program seek to build a new decision-making model from the bottom up stems from their belief that optimization models offer limited applicability to many real-world problems. Specifically, in two different manners, decision-making problems may be intractable in the sense that no optimal solution can be identified by any presently available

36 This section draws on Douglas A. Kysar et al., *Are Heuristics a Problem or a Solution?*, in Heuristics and the Law (Christoph Engel & Gerd Gigerenzer eds., Cambridge, MA: MIT Press, 2005; pp. 103–140).

optimization model, let alone actually attained. First, many goals when specified mathematically take the form of ill-posed problems; that is, problems that cannot in principle be solved. In this category fall those problems with unknown, vague, or incalculable criteria, and those problems for which an adequate weighting function among criteria cannot be specified. Second, many of the remaining problems that are well posed are nevertheless computationally intractable. In this category fall those problems that are formally *NP-hard* – that is, intrinsically harder than the category of problems that can be solved in nondeterministic polynomial time – and those problems that are otherwise practically insoluble given the limits of currently available information technology.

According to researchers in the heuristics tradition, the fact that many problems cannot be solved with traditional optimization-based techniques has both descriptive and prescriptive implications. Descriptively, it raises a further challenge – in addition to the challenge presented by the behavioral findings of the heuristics and biases research program – to the notion that individual judgment and decision making can best be predicted by a model of expected utility maximization. The fact that humans face many problems that do not admit of optimal solutions has made it adaptively desirable over time that humans *not* seek to replicate optimization-based systems in their cognition, at least not universally. Similarly, in competitive environments, it often is desirable for human subjects to exhibit some degree of "irreducible uncertainty" in their behavior in order to evade precise anticipation by their opponents.[37] It is not surprising, therefore, that rational choice theory has proven unable to accommodate a wide range of stable individual behaviors: such behaviors have evolved in response to decision-making environments that often do not themselves conform to the presuppositions of rational choice theory.

Prescriptively, the existence of ill-posed and computationally intractable problems also disrupts the claim of optimization-based regimes to comprehensive application. Due to the existence of these types of problems, the limit of the solution frontier for a decision-making task in many cases will not be given by rational choice theory or any other available optimization system. Thus, unless one arbitrarily excludes relevant variables or otherwise "edits" the problem in order to yield an optimum solution, some normative benchmark other than conventional rational choice ideals will be necessary in these cases in order to assess the usefulness of decision-making techniques. Along these lines, researchers from the heuristics program argue that decision-making heuristics generally perform quite well if evaluated according to the criterion of ecological rationality; that is, the fitness of the heuristics for the environment in which they are being deployed, as judged by their relative success at achieving intended aims compared with other realistically possible decision-making strategies. Indeed, heuristics researchers argue that a variety of cognitive processes

[37] Paul W. Glimcher, Decisions, Uncertainty, and the Brain: The Science of Neuroeconomics (Cambridge, MA: MIT Press, 2004).

identified in the literature as biases or illusions appear remarkably well-adapted when viewed within the richer ecological context that shaped their development, rather than against a rational choice benchmark that is artificially divorced from many of the constraints that characterize real world decision making.[38]

Rationality in Social Choice

The two dominant paradigms for environmental decision making – CBA and the PP – nicely parallel the two conceptions of rational decision making that compete for acceptance within cognitive psychology. In both debates, a sharp contrast has been drawn between decision-making techniques that aim, on the one hand, to pursue optimal outcomes through the application of formal analytical systems and, on the other hand, to achieve realistically satisfactory outcomes through less formalized, more incremental decision-making processes. The former "synoptic paradigm"[39] is reflected both in the expected utility maximization model of rational choice theory and in the applied welfare economic technique of regulatory CBA. Similarly, the latter paradigm of "muddling through"[40] is reflected both in the ecological rationality view of decision-making heuristics championed by Gigerenzer and others, and in the centuries-old emphasis on foresight and anticipatory care that grounds the PP.

Legal academic treatment of CBA and the PP has likewise tended to parallel the theoretical debate that has taken place within psychology. A few prominent hold-outs aside, most scholars writing in the areas of environmental, health, and safety regulation today support the view that CBA is a desirable societal decision-making tool that outperforms any other available framework. Moreover, these thinkers often cite evidence from the heuristics and biases literature in support of their claim that CBA serves to discipline and improve collective judgment. Accepting the common interpretation of the heuristics and biases literature that human cognition is prone to systematic error, they argue that CBA helps to overcome such errors by forcing comprehensive, empirical evaluation of policy proposals, including the hazards that a proposal is designed to address, the proposal's expected behavioral and environmental consequences, and the financial expenditures and foregone opportunities that the proposal's enactment will entail.

The debate over CBA and the PP would benefit greatly from a broader reading of the psychological literature. Just as supporters of the PP seem to give insufficient regard to the possibility that public demand for regulation may be ill-informed or irrational, proponents of CBA fail to confront the possibility that their maximizing exercise may in some instances fail the test of ecological rationality. As the lessons of the heuristics research program suggest, the aspiration to optimize that lies at the

[38] *See* Gerd Gigerenzer, *Fast and Frugal Heuristics: The Tools of Bounded Rationality*, in HANDBOOK OF JUDGMENT AND DECISION MAKING (D. Koehler & N. Harvey, Eds., 2004; tbl. 4.1).

[39] Colin S. Diver, *Policy-Making Paradigms in Administrative Law*, 95 HARV. L. REV. 393, 400 (1981).

[40] Charles Lindblom, *The Science of "Muddling Through,"* 19 PUB. ADMIN. REV. 79 (1959).

heart of CBA may make little practical sense when applied to a world of complexity. If the teachings of complexity theory are sound, then environmental, health, and safety dilemmas will, almost by definition, present ill-posed problems that contain "nasty surprises"[41] and other intractable features. In such contexts, the deliberate attempt to optimize may not represent simply an imperfect but useful aid to decision making, as CBA defenders often assert. Rather, it may represent a solution concept that is fundamentally ill-suited to the problem tasks at hand. Because of this misfit, we cannot confidently expect that the errors of CBA will cluster around an "optimal" result – indeed, for ill-posed problems the very notion of an optimum eludes meaningful description. Instead, we must anticipate that the errors of CBA are capable of deviating substantially and unpredictably from decision paths that are easily recognized as desirable, if not necessarily optimal, through less formalistic decision procedures.

To give one pressing example, future generations may regard with marvel our present day attempts to meticulously calculate the costs and benefits of anthropogenic climate change. Such studies often lead to a conclusion that the economic benefits of continued fossil fuel consumption more than outweigh the physical, agricultural, and ecological costs that would be averted by restricting emissions, at least in the near term. Accordingly, the optimal greenhouse gas reduction policy under CBA is typically a rather limited one that should not commence for several decades. The important lesson from complexity theory, again, is that the apparent CBA consensus on climate change may not merely be wrong; it may be wildly wrong. Moreover, it may be wrong as a matter of consequentialist-utilitarian evaluation, the very domain in which CBA proponents proclaim their decision-making framework to be most adept. Truly rational regulatory decision making requires some understanding of when it is not optimal to optimize. CBA itself cannot generate such wisdom, for no well-formulated analytical system can be expected to derive its own demise. Instead, what is required in every case is an independent judgment – one that is crafted in light of evolving but always incomplete knowledge and that is offered in service of reasoned but always re-appraisable moral and political commitments.

This argument from complexity should be distinguished from the long-standing complaints of scholars that CBA and other formalistic aspects of the regulatory rule-making process can lead to a situation of "paralysis by analysis."[42] This traditional objection to CBA – that its enormous informational demands bog down the policy-making process to such a degree that, when viewed in light of administrative time and resource constraints, CBA becomes pragmatically irrational – might be thought of as mirroring the category of informationally and computationally daunting problems that the heuristics research paradigm has identified as inappropriate for resolution through optimization procedures. A second, more fundamental objection to CBA,

[41] Farber, *supra* note 14, at 146.

[42] Thomas O. McGarity, *A Cost-Benefit State*, 50 Admin. L. Rev. 7, 50 (1998).

however, is that its subject matter often takes the form of ill-posed problems – that is, problems whose imperviousness to resolution is not driven by a lack of information or computational capacity, but by features inherent to the problems themselves. Because complex adaptive systems contain irreducible levels of uncertainty that cannot be assumed to be of minor significance, such systems by their nature are likely to present ill-posed problems. In such cases, the heuristics research program advises the adoption of decision-making principles that are far more pragmatic – and more often overtly normative – than the optimization standard of CBA.

As proponents of CBA would be quick to point out, however, the non-optimizing approach of the PP (and related policy approaches, e.g., best availability technology requirements or safe minimum environmental standards) does not come without cost. Most notably, the PP is ill-designed to consider and manage the risks of regulation itself, including the risk that cautious regulation may entail significant opportunity costs. Although one can mount a variety of defenses for this apparent asymmetry, they are fragile defenses that depend at bottom on a wider degree of agreement regarding the need for a fundamental value shift away from economic growth and allocative efficiency toward human flourishing and environmental sustainability as the basic desiderata of social choice. Moreover, even if one accepts the contention of PP proponents that environmental, health, and safety decision making is characterized by deep and abiding uncertainty, it is still far from clear that extreme conservatism is appropriate as a general response to uncertainty. After all, John Rawls – whose difference principle for distributive equity focused attention on the least well-off member of society, much as the PP aims to focus attention on the worst-case outcome threatened by environmentally uncertain activities – argued that exclusive focus on the worst case would not be appropriate for determining "how a doctor should treat his patients."[43] Proponents of the safe minimum standards approach within environmental economics also tend to hedge their positions, arguing that fidelity to safe minimum standards should yield when the costs of precaution become "immoderate"[44] or "unacceptably large."[45] Within the legal literature, Farber similarly allows for departure from his strong "environmental baseline" approach to policy making "when costs would clearly overwhelm any potential benefits" from precautionary regulation.[46]

Although critics sometimes argue that these various safety valves suggest a latent efficiency criterion within the precautionary approach, there is an important distinction that prevents the PP from collapsing entirely into CBA, even granting the

43 John Rawls, *Some Reasons for the Maximin Criterion*, 64 AM. ECON. REV. 141, 142 (1974).

44 S.V. CIRIACY-WANTRUP, RESOURCE CONSERVATION: ECONOMICS AND POLICIES (1st ed., Berkeley, CA: University of California Press, 1952; p. 252).

45 R.C. Bishop, *Endangered Species and Uncertainty: The Economics of a Safe Minimum Standard*, 60 J. AM. AGRIC. ECON. 10, 13 (1978).

46 Daniel A. Farber, *Building Bridges Over Troubled Waters: Eco-pragmatism and the Environmental Prospect*, 87 MINN. L. REV. 851, 879 (2003).

addition of some form of cost sensitivity: the PP's understanding of cost is much broader than the notion presupposed by CBA. As Richard Bishop wrote in a seminal article on the safe minimum standards approach, the determination of "[h]ow much [cost] is 'unacceptably large' must necessarily involve more than economic analysis, because endangered species involve issues of intergenerational equity."[47] Similarly, advocates of the PP typically contemplate an open, pluralistic process for making determinations about when and how to apply the principle, suggesting that the decision to relax its dictates might be premised on a wide range of appropriate reasons.[48] The problem, though, is that PP proponents fail to provide adequate substantive guidance regarding how these various safety valves should be implemented. Given that society is to avoid serious or irreversible harm unless the costs of doing so become "intolerable," how is the notion of intolerability to be understood and operationalized? The PP raises this question and rightly emphasizes that its resolution is far more complicated and value-laden than the CBA procedure would indicate. To date, however, the PP has failed to provide a compelling resolution of its own and has instead tended to turn to a richer substantive framework such as the sustainability paradigm, or simply to equate sound policy making with the results of an idealized democratic decision-making process. In either case, as even its proponents acknowledge, "implementation of the [PP] in a consistent and broadly acceptable manner has been fraught with philosophical, legal, political, and scientific problems."[49]

III. THE PROMISE OF ENVIRONMENTAL ASSURANCE BONDING

An agreeable compromise between the extremes of CBA and the PP may be found in the form of environmental assurance bonding, a policy tool that has been remarkably understudied in the academic and policy literatures, despite the vast increase in attention paid to market-based regulatory instruments over the past three decades. As explained in this Section, the environmental assurance-bonding approach acknowledges the uncertainty and complexity of biophysical systems by attaching serious financial consequence to the causation of environmental harm, including even those worst-case harms that can be perceived to be theoretically plausible, though not presently estimable. The approach also, however, acknowledges the strength and dynamism of socio-legal systems by allowing market actors to proceed with potentially beneficial activities despite the existence of a credible risk of harm. Indeed, the assurance-bonding device actively marshals the decentralized decision-making

47 Bishop, *supra* note 45, at 10.

48 *See, e.g.*, The Wingspread Statement on the Precautionary Principle, available at http://www.sehn.org/state.html#w ("The process of applying the Precautionary Principle must be open, informed and democratic and must include potentially affected parties.").

49 Katherine Barrett & Carolyn Raffensperger, *Precautionary Science*, in PROTECTING PUBLIC HEALTH AND THE ENVIRONMENT: IMPLEMENTING THE PRECAUTIONARY PRINCIPLE (Carolyn Raffensberger & Joel A. Tickner, Eds., Washington, DC: Island Press, 1999; p. 106) [hereinafter *Protecting Public Health and the Environment*].

power of markets as a force for the development of knowledge regarding uncertain substances and activities. As such, the policy tool reflects a high degree of ecological rationality, approaching ill-posed regulatory problems with an aggressive combination of respect for the power of markets, incentives, and technology and caution before the complexities of nature.

Symmetric Humility

Before addressing more concrete aspects of the environmental assurance bonding device, it is helpful to observe at the theoretical level that CBA and the PP suffer from complementary blind spots – blind spots that should be recognized as such by partisans in the debate, even from within their respective theoretical frameworks. For instance, CBA begins with an assumption that government regulatory efforts are especially likely to lead to unintended consequences, lost opportunities, interest group distortions, and a variety of other harmful perturbations of the various complex systems that comprise the regulated market. In order to guard against such harms, proponents of CBA urge a decision-making framework that aspires to comprehensive rationality. They believe that requiring regulatory choices to be premised on an explicit and exhaustive accounting of the choices' costs and benefits will force government officials to more reliably promote the public interest than under less formalized decision-making procedures.

The limitation of CBA, however, is that it fails to appreciate the parallel manner in which human perturbations of the environment are likely to lead to unintended, unpredictable, and potentially harmful outcomes. Decision makers faced with such complex and uncertain problems must resort to a more pragmatic and incremental approach to policy making, one that includes criteria for guiding action in the absence of a demonstrable optima and that affords flexibility in the face of constantly evolving information regarding the need for and the consequences of regulatory action. CBA instead tends to presume static, linear, well-behaved biophysical systems that regulators can model and manage with precision. In essence, proponents of CBA accept the teachings of complexity theory with respect to socio-legal systems, but not biophysical systems, a critical shortcoming that casts doubt on the belief that CBA is the most ecologically rational approach to environmental, health, and safety decision making. Importantly, one need not suspend the strictly consequentialist-utilitarian philosophical premises of CBA in order to reach this conclusion. Rather, the ecological irrationality critique strikes against CBA on the methodology's own terms. It accuses CBA, in essence, of being insufficiently empirical.

The PP, on the other hand, is premised on the bedrock assumption that biophysical systems are complex, uncertain, and easily perturbed. Indeed, much of the confusion in the literature regarding the merits of the PP stems from a failure to acknowledge that environmental decision making often must proceed on the basis of dauntingly little understanding regarding the objects of regulation. When critics of the PP purport to identify harmful consequences of behaving according to the principle's dictates, they generally assume a stable and relatively complete state of knowledge. Proponents of the PP, on the other hand, regard environmental decision making as an inherently uncertain, evolving, and dynamic process, and they therefore seek to offer a decision-making principle that is *procedurally* rational. By providing that "[p]reventive action should be taken in advance of scientific proof of causality," and that "the proponent of an activity, rather than the public, should bear the burden of proof of safety,"[50] the PP incorporates a default assumption of harm and surprise from human alteration of biophysical systems and promotes a structure for revising the assumption in light of improved knowledge and changed circumstances. Thus, rather than insist on quantification as a predicate to decision making, proponents of precaution ask that environmental, health, and safety regulation instead become infused with a "culture of humility about the sufficiency and accuracy of existing knowledge,"[51] such that the burden of uncertainty regarding industrial substances, technologies, and processes is distributed in a manner that is believed to be more equitable, more conducive to the development of vital risk information, and, ultimately, more socially desirable.

The PP, however, also has a blind spot. When read to require affirmative action to guard against all environmental, health, and safety risks that meet some threshold of scientific credibility and significance, the PP quickly threatens to become an unrealistic and unworkable device. As proponents of CBA have emphasized, any attempt to guard against environmental, health, and safety risks – including risks that pose catastrophic or irreversible consequences – inevitably will entail a series of ripple effects in the market that may themselves cause harm. The fact that the empirical literature documenting such ripple effects is fairly weak to date[52] does not mean that the effects should be excluded wholesale from consideration. Such an exclusion would represent the very kind of reaction to uncertainty that the PP generally aims to avoid. Properly understood, therefore, the PP can only offer a starting point for societal discussion, a default assumption of extreme conservatism that is to be pondered, contested, and overcome through rules of procedure and substance about which the PP has little to say.

Table 6.1 reflects these complementary blind spots of CBA and the PP, showing that each methodology exhibits a measure of respect for complexity in only one domain as between biophysical and socio-legal systems. Table 6.2 then suggests that the complementary blind spots of CBA and the PP can be expected to cause the respective methodologies to err in predictable directions in the face of uncertainty.

[50] Carolyn Raffensperger & Joel Tickner, *Introduction: To Foresee and to Forestall*, in PROTECTING PUBLIC HEALTH AND THE ENVIRONMENT, *supra* note 49, at 1, 8–9.

[51] Andy Stirling, *The Precautionary Principle in Science and Technology*, in REINTERPRETING THE PRECAUTIONARY PRINCIPLE (Tim O'Riordan, James Cameron & Andrew Jordan, Eds., London, UK: Cameron May, 2001; pp. 61, 66).

[52] *See* Kelman, *supra* note 17 (providing an early but still powerful critique).

TABLE 6.1. *Complementary blind spots*

	Respect for biophysical complexity	Respect for socio-legal Complexity
CBA	No	Yes
PP	Yes	No

For instance, given the dearth of information regarding the environmental, health, and safety risks of many applications of nanotechnology, such as the free release of nanoparticles into ecosystems, regulators following either decision-making paradigm tend to display bias with respect to the type of error that they incur. By generally presuming that biophysical systems are well-understood, resilient, and replaceable, CBA tends to favor Type I errors, in which regulators permit the release of nanoparticles that turn out to be harmful, rather than entertain the opportunity cost of prohibiting an activity that might be beneficial. In contrast, the PP, through its asymmetric precautionary trigger, tends to favor Type II errors, apparently content to lament what beneficial opportunities might have been rather than actively permit ecological harm from potentially risky substances or activities.

Assuming that deep scientific uncertainty will continue to attend much of risk regulation, the question then becomes how to accommodate such uncertainty within the regulatory framework. The CBA approach seems to assume that uncertainty is simply addressed *out there*, through institutions and procedures that lie beyond the reach of the policy decision under inspection. This approach comports with the general permissiveness adopted in market liberal societies toward private action. Following the harm principle articulated by John Stuart Mill, such societies tend to place the burden on government regulators to persuasively demonstrate the reality and severity of an action's harmful effects before it may be curtailed. A basic aim of the PP approach to environmental law and policy is precisely to upset this long-standing allocation of the burden of proof, particularly in areas that are thought to be characterized both by scientific uncertainty and by the potential for serious or irreversible harmful effects. At present, nanoscale science and engineering appears to be just such an area. Thus a strict interpretation of the PP would counsel blocking wide deployment of nanoparticles and other fruits of nanoscale science and

TABLE 6.2. *Predictable errors*

	Substance or activity harmful	Substance or activity harmless
CBA	Type I error	Benefit allowed
PP	Cost avoided	Type II error

engineering, at least until their safety and efficacy had been demonstrated to the satisfaction of regulators.[53] Such a conservative stance may be undesirable for the reasons just described: nanoscale science and engineering research promises potentially dramatic benefits, in addition to risks, including benefits that may themselves take the form of improvements to environmental sustainability and human health.

What is needed, then, is some mechanism for exhibiting symmetric humility – that is, awareness of and respect for the problems of uncertainty and complexity as they characterize *both* biophysical and socio-legal systems. Environmental assurance bonding offers promise in this respect.

Environmental Assurance Bonding

Under an environmental assurance bonding scheme, before commencing an activity with uncertain but potentially serious adverse effects, regulated firms would be required to post a bond "equal to the current best estimate of the largest potential future environmental damages."[54] The bond would be returned to the firm "*if and when* the agent could demonstrate that the suspected worst-case damages had not occurred or would be less than originally assessed."[55] If damage did occur, the bond funds would be available to rehabilitate the affected environment or to compensate injured parties. As one can see, such an approach "combines the 'polluter pays' principle with the 'precautionary' principle, providing for internalization of costs where harm is possible but damages are uncertain."[56] In essence, the bonds work to shift the burden of proof off regulators and onto the promoters of potentially harmful actions, just as supporters of the PP have long advocated.[57] However, unlike a strict interpretation of the PP – which might ban a proposed activity, substance, or technology until its promoters had successfully demonstrated the absence of risk – the

53 *See* Gregory Mandel, *Nanotechnology Governance*, 59 Ala. L. Rev. 1323, 1325–26 (2008) (describing calls for a nanotechnology moratorium).

54 Robert Costanza et al., An Introduction to Ecological Economics (Boca Raton, FL: St. Lucie Press, 1997; p. 211).

55 *Id.* (emphasis in original).

56 Dana Clark & David Downes, What Price Biodiversity? Economic Incentive and Biodiversity Conservation in the United States (Center for International Environmental Law, 1995) (citing Robert Costanza & Laura Cornwell, *The 4P Approach to Dealing With Scientific Uncertainty*, 34 Environment 12, 12 [1992]).

57 *See* Michael Common, Sustainability and Policy: Limits to Economics (Cambridge, MA: Cambridge University Press, 1995; pp. 215–16). The degree to which the burden of proof actually is shifted would depend on details of the environmental assurance-bonding system. For instance, what threshold of scientific plausibility for a worst-case scenario would the agency need to demonstrate during the initial stage of establishing the bond requirement? Which actor, according to what standard of proof, would need to show that a posted bond could be returned or reduced as information develops suggesting that the threat was less severe than initially feared? Regardless of how these details are worked out, the assurance bonding approach still would represent a lower burden of proof for regulators than the conventional risk-assessment/CBA approach.

environmental assurance bonding approach allows private action to proceed, albeit under the revised incentive structure created by the bond posting requirement.

A variety of policy design considerations would need to be addressed. For instance, environmental assurance bonds might be used either to guarantee performance of an environmental standard, such as reclamation of a former mining or logging site to a specified set of conditions, or to guarantee payment of a predetermined amount of money, such as a level of damages estimated to be necessary to compensate third parties for harm that might be imposed by an uncertain activity. In addition, the financial instrument actually used to satisfy a bonding requirement could take one of several forms: (1) collateral bonds such as cash deposits, certificates of deposit, letters of credit, or security pledges; (2) so-called "self bonds," which consist of legally binding promissory obligations from regulated entities that pass certain tests of financial soundness; or (3) surety bonds, which constitute a guarantee from a third party to either perform the defaulted obligation or pay funds to the regulating agency. The surety bond approach is likely to be the most attractive, both because it tends to be associated with lower costs for regulated firms[58] and because it offers the prospect of marshalling the information-generating and risk-evaluating capacities of surety companies in service of environmental policy goals. Surety companies would price bonding services based not only on the creditworthiness and compliance history of the regulated firm, but also on the estimated likelihood and severity of harm occurring. This would create a strong incentive for firms to reduce the uncertainty surrounding their proposed activities, either by investing in the advancement of scientific knowledge or by switching to less dangerous alternative activities. Thus, in the competition for capital, those projects, products, or technologies posing less severe potential environmental impacts would obtain a cost advantage over alternatives.

From the perspective of regulated firms, environmental assurance bonds may provide a more equitable policy tool than alternatives such as environmental taxes or auctioned pollution permits. Because taxes and auctioned permits impose a nonrefundable fee applied at the time of use, they presuppose an accurate prediction of the long-term costs of the regulated activity. When regulators lack such an accurate prediction, currently imposed environmental fees run the risk of over-deterring private activity. The environmental assurance bond, on the other hand, explicitly allows for uncertainty by requiring a pledge of funds to cover the worst-case scenario, but allowing periodic refund of such funds as uncertainty dissipates. Under the environmental assurance bonding approach, so long as accounting and tax treatment of pledged amounts is properly aligned, "the efficiency advantages of economic incentives can be reaped without unduly penalizing current economic agents for the cost of unknown future damages."[59]

[58] *See* D.F. Ferreira & S.B. Suslick, *Identifying Potential Impacts of Bonding Instruments on Offshore Oil Projects*, 27 RESOURCES POL'Y 43, 43 (2001).

[59] *Id.* at 51.

The most difficult analytical and practical aspect of environmental assurance bonding is the determination of what precise amount of financial assurance must be pledged. The existing economic literature tends to assume that the role of environmental assurance bonding is simply to guarantee performance according to some prescribed environmental, health, or safety standard.[60] Thus commentators see the chief benefit of bonding requirements to be one of mitigating the risk of default, rather than serving more general environmental policy goals.[61] Likewise, commentators tend to believe that well-known damage valuations are a necessary prerequisite for environmental assurance bonding schemes to be effective.[62] Such discussions implicitly assume that regulators operate in a well-characterized policy space, wherein thorough empirical understanding of hazards can enable regulators to determine the "optimal" level of precaution. An alternative viewpoint would regard the generation of empirical understanding to be part and parcel of the policy-making process itself, such that a partial aim of the bonding requirement would be to shift society closer to an epistemic position in which it even makes sense to talk of "optimal" levels of precaution. From this perspective, bond-posting requirements would not be set at an "optimal" level, but at a level commensurate with the worst-case harm scenario that is threatened by a proposed activity and that meets some threshold standard of plausibility. This approach would require the development of new analytical tools for imagining and characterizing uncertain threats, tools that proponents of precautionary environmentalism regard as long overdue.

This discussion should not be read to suggest that the environmental assurance-bonding approach is free of limitations. To begin with, actual historical experience with the policy instrument in the context of mining reclamation has generated decidedly mixed results. In 1977, the United States Congress passed the Surface Coal Mining and Reclamation Act in light of the large number of mining sites that lay abandoned and unreclaimed across the country. The Act establishes performance requirements for the reclamation of completed mining sites and requires mining permit holders to either achieve the requirements or pay an amount necessary for public entities to achieve them. In addition, permit holders are required before the commencement of operations to submit a reclamation plan and post a reclamation bond in order to ensure compliance with the reclamation requirements. Despite the apparent theoretical advantages of bonding as an incentive device for environmental compliance, use of the device in the mining sector has repeatedly disappointed,

[60] *See id.* at 50 ("Setting the appropriate bond requirement (amount) may be one of the greatest predicaments within a bonding system. If bonds are set too low, the system may not provide the desired incentive effect. On the other hand, setting bonds too high may discourage investment in the sector.").

[61] David Gerard, *The Law and Economics of Reclamation Bonds*, 26 RESOURCES POL'Y 189, 195 (2000) ("The underlying motivation [for bonding systems] is the high default risk on the side of the agent.").

[62] *See* Jason F. Shogren, Joesph A. Herriges & Ramu Govindasamy, *Limits to Environmental Bonds*, 8 ECOLOGICAL ECON. 109 (1993).

chiefly due to the unwillingness of regulators to demand bond amounts at levels adequate to ensure coverage of actual reclamation costs.[63] Colorado's Summitville Mine, for instance, required more than $150 million in reclamation costs due to water contamination from the use of cyanide leaching at the site, yet the financial assurance bond posted for the mine had been only approximately $5 million. The Summitville subsidiary and its parent company filed for bankruptcy, abandoning the site to the state.[64] Experiments with environmental assurance bonding in other regulatory areas confirm that the problem of understated bond amounts is significant. In Indonesia, for instance, the government required the posting of restoration bonds in order for firms to obtain logging concessions, yet the per hectare bond fee was set at only a fraction of actual reforestation costs, thus leading to widespread forfeiture of posted bonds rather than actual environmental performance.[65]

Additionally, the uncertainty, complexity, and long latency periods likely to be at issue for many environmental, health, and safety risks – including those that might eventually be identified in relation to nanotechnology – create a practical impediment to the implementation of an environmental assurance-bonding system, given that cause–effect relationships are likely to be especially difficult to predict and quantify. As David Gerard notes, "[s]urety providers may respond to [such] uncertainty by requiring a higher percentage of the bond amount as a premium, requiring substantial collateral, or simply refusing to underwrite the bond."[66] Of course, this limitation may actually be a policy strength, in that a further option for the surety provider would be to require the regulated entity to better develop scientific understanding of the environmental, health, or safety threat at issue. Developing private information regarding the likelihood of the regulator's worst-case scenario thus would become a task with economic benefit to the firm, rather than an exercise that firms arguably have positive incentives *not* to pursue under current law.[67] Proponents of the PP might also argue that, in the event that a proposed activity is deemed to be non-coverable by the financial industry, then society should be relieved that the activity will not proceed. After all, the point of the environmental assurance-bonding requirement is to incentivize ex ante consideration of potential ex post harms, whenever those harms might possibly occur. If surety providers are unwilling

[63] *See, e.g.*, Gerard, *supra* note 61, at 194 (noting that a General Accounting Office study in 1986 determined that of 556 hard-rock mining operations in 10 states on Bureau of Land Management lands, only one operator had been required to furnish a bond).

[64] *See* Roger Flynn & Jeffrey C. Parsons, *Ensuring Long-Term Protection of Water Quality at Colorado Mine Sites*, 30-JUNE, COLO. LAW. 83 (2001).

[65] *See* DAVID O'CONNOR, MANAGING THE ENVIRONMENT WITH RAPID INDUSTRIALISATION: LESSONS FROM THE EAST ASIAN EXPERIENCE (Paris, France: Renouf Publ'g Co. Ltd., 1994; p. 130).

[66] Gerard, *supra* note 61, at 191 n.6.

[67] *See* Wendy E. Wagner, *Commons Ignorance: The Failure of Environmental Law to Produce Needed Information on Health and the Environment*, 53 DUKE L.J. 1619 (2004); Mary Lyndon, *Tort Law and Technology*, 12 YALE J. ON REG. 137 (1995).

to offer bonding services at a price that industry will bear, then powerful evidence exists that the potential harms are significant in relation to potential benefits.

A final concern stems from the possibility that bonding requirements might impose liquidity constraints on firms that, in turn, slow investment and innovation. Liquidity constraint problems are alleviated in part through the use of third-party surety firms.[68] Alternatively, if firms are required to post collateral bonds directly, then posted funds could be made interest-bearing and fully refundable such that, even while in escrow, they might be used to collateralize loans for other investments. Again, this approach would have the advantage of creating incentives for private actors to develop better knowledge regarding the likelihood and severity of worst-case risk scenarios, because that information would be necessary to properly estimate the value of the collateral bond in the secondary market. More generally, however, the threat posed by environmental assurance bonding schemes to capital availability is one that, at least for promoters of the PP, should not necessarily disqualify such schemes from consideration. Markets only work to optimize under a given set of constraints; for too long in the eyes of PP proponents, industrialized nations have failed to fully include environmental externalities within the set of constraints governing private economic behavior. By institutionalizing a stance of symmetric humility, long-term economic and development equilibriums will be shifted toward a "softer," more environmentally sensitive path. In that sense, a retraction of capital availability under an environmental assurance-bonding regime would simply represent the transformation of a growth economy to a sustainable economy.

CONCLUSION

Physicist Richard Feynman famously presaged the field of nanotechnology by observing that "there's plenty of room at the bottom."[69] The teachings of complexity theory suggest that there also is ample room at the top, where our reductionist habit of subdividing scientific investigation and knowledge into separate, narrowly delineated subject areas has left a gap of awareness and comprehension regarding complex adaptive systems. Moreover, just as scientists expect to achieve interdisciplinary convergence at the nanoscale – fusing biology, physics, chemistry, and information technology into a single atomic science – so too must policy analysts seek convergence at the macroscale, integrating moral philosophy, economics, psychology, and legal knowledge into a unified, pragmatic framework for societal risk decision making. CBA and the PP represent complementary attempts to manage such a convergence, focusing on the threats posed to human well-being when regulators display insufficient respect for the uncertainty and complexity of, respectively, markets and ecosystems. Despite – or perhaps because of – these deliberate focal points,

[68] *See* Gerard, *supra* note 61, at 191.

[69] Richard P. Feynman, *There's Plenty of Room at the Bottom*, Eng. & Sci., Feb. 1960, at 22.

each decision-making paradigm is flawed by a failure to recognize the challenges posed by uncertainty and complexity in the alternative sphere of concern. In order to fully address the issues that threaten our environmental future, policy makers must therefore begin to embrace an ethic of symmetric humility. One concrete method for doing so is through greater use of environmental assurance bonding.

7

Conditional Liability Relief as an Incentive for Precautionary Study

David A. Dana

Ignorance may be bliss, but it is not often good policy. That may be especially true with respect to existing and forthcoming products that embody the relatively new, still poorly understood technology called "nanotechnology." Nanotechnology products offer the promise of highly beneficial uses, but also pose uncertain risks of adverse health and environmental effects. For products embodying nanotechnology, there is a powerful normative case for adherence to what I will call "the precautionary-study principle." The principle requires that the possible risks from these products would be explored (if in all likelihood not really understood) before their release to the marketplace. It also would require that possible risks are thereafter continually studied. Continual study after the release of products into the market is important because it allows adverse effects to be isolated and understood using improvements in the background science and real-world observations and reports from consumers and others who have been exposed to the products.

A central question, therefore, is how to shift the nanotechnology status quo toward greater adherence to a precautionary-study principle. To that end, this chapter proposes a federal legislative regime of limited protections from tort liability for nanotechnology product manufacturers who engage in pre-market and post-market research and monitoring regarding possible adverse health and environmental effects from their products. The central argument is: less liability may mean more precaution and hence is a good thing.

There is no consensus regarding whether nanotechnology and nanotechnology products should be approached within the framework of the precautionary principle. Some commentators – including representatives of industry – have argued that there is an insufficient basis for the regulation of risks from nanotechnology and have emphasized the need to secure the potentially vast commercial benefits of nanotechnology.[1] These commentators have argued, in effect, against

[1] This has been the principal basis for industry arguments against regulation at this time. See Gary Marchant et al., *Nanotechnology Regulation: The United States Approach*, in New Global Frontiers

a precautionary approach to nanotechnology. In sharp contrast, some commentators and nongovernmental organizations (NGOs) have called for a moratorium on the release of nanotechnology products until product manufacturers can affirmatively demonstrate their safety.[2] In effect, these commentators have called for the application of a strong form of the precautionary principle to nanotechnology products. In this strong form of the precautionary principle, which might be called the precautionary-certification principle, new technologies may not be deployed in the marketplace unless and until the manufacturer first certifies that they are risk-free or "safe."

These two positions are both too extreme. There are sound theoretical reasons to believe that, absent some commitment to precautionary action, insufficient attention will be paid to the downsides from nanotechnology products. For social welfare as well as pragmatic political reasons, however, the precautionary focus with regard to nanotechnology products should be consistent with a less demanding, more flexible precautionary-study principle. The credible risk posed by most nanotechnology products is not qualitatively great enough – and our scientific abilities to fully evaluate the risks in a reasonable time frame are too limited – to justify a blanket moratorium approach.

Given the marked gaps in research regarding the environmental, health, and safety risk posed by nanotechnology products that are detailed in Part II, what is justifiable is greater realization of a precautionary-study principle with respect to nanotechnology products. There are many obstacles to achieving that greater realization. First, current laws and regulations in the United States (as well as other nations) do not provide a clear basis for requiring precautionary study on the part of nanotechnology product manufacturers. Nor has there been abundant public funding for research regarding nanotechnology's health and environmental risks. Moreover, even if there were a political consensus in support of new mandatory testing requirements and dramatically increased public funding, voluntary testing and monitoring by manufacturers would be an important component of any comprehensive precautionary-study approach. Industry actors have special access to knowledge about emerging technology and product development and products and can change and adapt quickly to follow a commercial marketplace that may move too fast for legislators and regulators and regulatory institutions to understand and react to on their own with mandatory testing requirements.

IN REGULATION: THE AGE OF NANOTECHNOLOGY (Graeme Hodge, ed., Cheltenham, UK: Edward Elgar, 2007; pp. 201–2).

[2] *See id.*; see also, NanoAction, *Principles for the Oversight of Nanotechnologies and Nanomaterials* (2008), http://nanoaction.org/nanoaction/doc/nano-02-18-08.pdf; Friends of the Earth, *Nanomaterials, Sunscreens, and Cosmetics: Small Ingredients Big Risks* (2006), http://www.foeeurope.org/activities/nanotechnology/nanocosmetics.pdf. One very highly regarded organization, the United Kingdom's Royal Society, has, although not endorsing the general moratorium approach, argued for mandatory regulatory reviews for safety of nanoparticles in products before their release into the marketplace. *See* ROYAL SOCIETY, *supra* note 1 at 84.

A key variable in considering liability's role as an incentive or deterrent to testing is the manufacturer's subjective assessment of the probability that any injuries from its product would be detected by the injured parties and successfully attributed to the product absent research by the manufacturer itself on the adverse effects of the product. Another key variable is the legal standard for tort liability and, specifically, how the applicable standard falls on a spectrum from the imposition of liability on manufacturers only for known risks on the one hand to the imposition of liability even for risks the manufacturer could not have reasonably foreseen on the other. The lower the perceived probability of detection without manufacturer research and the more the applicable liability standard veers toward requiring actual knowledge of risks on the part of the manufacturer, the more likely it is that the *ex ante* threat of liability will lead a manufacturer to choose *not* to conduct research into possible adverse effects, either before the product is marketed or once it is on the market. Consideration of these two variables in the nanotechnology context would tend to suggest that liability considerations indeed may be discouraging research into possible adverse effects of nanotechnology products under development and already on the market.

The closest precedent for the regime of limited liability relief that I propose is the regime of federal preemption of state torts that is afforded manufacturers of certain medical devices approved by the U.S. Food and Drug Administration (FDA) under federal law. FDA preemption of common law tort claims, however, is controversial, to say the least. In order to avoid the disadvantages and problems of the FDA preemption regime, any regime of liability relief for nanotechnology manufacturers who voluntarily engage in testing needs a number of components that would help ensure political accountability, scientific integrity, transparency, and a reasonable pool of compensation for injured people. The scope of preemption of state tort law claims would have to be specified by federal statute, not agency promulgation or interpretation. Any such preemption should not include claims based on allegations that a manufacturer violated a tort duty by acting or failing to act in response to actual knowledge of adverse health or environmental effects. And there must be vigorous government oversight of both voluntary pre-market and post-market testing and monitoring, and the public must have reasonable access to the key information provided to the regulators. Finally, in order to prevent drastic denials of compensation while encouraging voluntary study, all companies would be required to maintain liability insurance, and companies that engaged in pre- and post-market testing would receive insurance subsidies in one form or another.[3]

[3] There has been a call for liability protection for the nanotechnology industry, but that call has focused on the industry's desirability to avoid litigation and bankruptcies and has not outlined additional research and/or disclosure responsibilities that would be imposed on industry in return for liability protection. *See* George J. Mannina, Jr., *Nanotechnology: Don't Delay Liability Risk Assessments and Solutions*, 21 WASHINGTON LEGAL FOUND 37 (2006), *available at* http://www.wlf.org/upload/120806lbmannina.pdf. That the fear of liability or liability avoidance may contribute to an

In voluntary regimes generally, getting initial participation may be difficult due to uncertainties of costs and benefits of participation. As explained below, moreover, there would be strong incentives for some manufacturers to join a voluntary testing regime only once a number of other manufacturers of similar products have joined. Because the recruitment of initial or early participants may be difficult and would be very helpful in ultimately achieving broad participation in a voluntary testing regime, special incentives for early joiners may be warranted.

There are many possible objections to the proposed *quid pro quo* voluntary regime, one important one is how can regulators competently oversee the regime given the informational asymmetries between industry and the regulators regarding developments in technology and products containing nanotechnology. In a purely voluntary regime without a *quid pro quo* for industry participation, regulators have little leverage to demand that industry make key information readily available to them; the *quid pro quo* of liability relief would allow regulators to plausibly demand specific industry commitments of active cooperation and disclosure. That the tests and monitoring procedures and results would be made available to the broader public – including the scientific and public health communities – would provide an important safeguard against the danger of industry participants' obtaining relief in return for insufficient efforts on their part.

Another objection is why liability relief would or should be limited to nanotechnology, as opposed to any new (or existing but untested) technology or substance that poses unknown risks. My answer is largely pragmatic: the issue of nanotechnology risks and regulation is now a subject of public discussion and analysis, and nanotechnology products could be a good place to start to explore the merits of regimes of liability relief as a *quid pro quo* for voluntary testing. Were such a regime actually implemented, we could assess how well or not well it worked to advance overall public welfare and perhaps then move beyond nanotechnology. Indeed, the category of regulation I am exploring here – liability relief as a *quid pro quo* for voluntary pre- and post-market testing and monitoring – may well end up making even more sense in contexts outside nanotechnology.

FRAMING THE NANOTECHNOLOGY PROBLEM

What exactly is the nanotechnology "problem" regarding human health and environmental risks? This part argues that the essence of the problem is what we do not know. Any comprehensive response to the informational deficit regarding

absence of testing or monitoring on the part of companies has been a theme of commentary regarding conventional chemicals, including toxin or possible toxins. See Wendy E. Wagner, *Choosing Ignorance in the Manufacture of Toxic Products*, 82 CORNELL L. REVIEW 773, 820–21 (1997) ("the manufacturing community appears to believe that safety research regarding latent harms invites, rather than wards off, litigation. Defense lawyers tout the effectiveness of long-term product effects as a defense to litigation, and this advice appears to be followed. . . . ").

nanotechnology, this part argues, should include not just mandatory testing and public funding, but also a voluntary testing and monitoring component.

THE INFORMATION DEFICIT

Relatively little is understood about the health, safety, and environmental risks posed by the manufacture, use, and disposal of products containing nanotechnology. The lack of adequate research and hence adequate understanding of the risks is a theme of every major report regarding nanotechnology. Academic commentators, NGOs, scientific societies, legislators, and major industry players agree that too little research has or is being done – and, indeed, that too little is or likely will soon be known about these risks.[4]

In considering what needs to be known to understand nanotechnology and nanotechnology products better, it is useful to categorize the kinds of information that are not known and must be acquired or developed. One could develop a number of different lists of categories, but I suggest these three : (1) information regarding risk assessment and monitoring metrics, criteria, and methods uniquely suited for or tailored to nanotechnology; (2) information regarding the behavior and associated risks of different categories of nanotechnology and the significance of different pathways for the different categories of nanotechnology; and (3) information regarding risks associated with particular products that include nanotechnology.

The first category of information – information regarding nanotechnology risk assessment metrics, techniques, and methods – is the kind of information that is needed for assessing the risks associated with different types of nanotechnology and different nanotechnology products. Thus the incompleteness in category 1 information is a constraint on the acquisition and development of category 2 and 3 information. Not surprisingly, therefore, many scientists have focused on the pressing need for investment in the development of what I am calling category 1 information. For example, a group of prominent nanotechnology scientists writing in *Nature* in 2006 set forth a multi-decade agenda regarding what methods must be developed for nanotechnology to be responsibly commercialized. This agenda underscores how much critical category 1 information is not yet in place for assessment of risks, how big the task is for the development of the necessary methods, and how unlikely it

[4] On the general topic of possible risks posed by nanotechnology and the uncertainties surrounding those risks, *see generally* Jo Anne Shatkin, Nanotechnology: Health and Environmental Risks (Boca Raton, FL: CRC Press, 2008); U.S. Environmental Protection Agency, Nanotechnology White Paper 1 (2007), *available at* http://www.epa.gov/osa/pdfs/nanotech/epa-nanotechnology-whitepaper-0207.pdf; National Research Council, Review of the Federal Strategy for Nanotechnology-Related Environmental, Health, and Safety Research, 26 (2008), *available at* http://www.nap.edu/catalog/12559.html; Royal Society, *supra* note 1; *The National Nanotechnology Initiative Amendments Act of 2008: Hearing on H.R. 5940 Before the House Committee on Science and Technology* 110th Congress 37–38 (2008) (statement of Andrew D. Maynard, Chief Science Advisor, Project on Emerging Nanotechnologies, Woodrow Wilson International Center for Scholars).

is that this task will be substantially completed before hundreds or thousands of new nanotechnology products are prepared for and introduced into the commercial marketplace. According to the *Nature* agenda, key research goals should be:

- "Develop and validate methods to evaluate the toxicity of engineered nanomaterials, within the next 5–15 years."
- "Develop models for predicting the potential impact of engineered nanomaterials on the environment and human health, within the next 10 years."
- "Develop robust systems for evaluating the health and environmental impact of engineered nanomaterials over their entire life within the next 5 years."[5]

Similar calls have been made by representatives of public interest NGOs as well as entities affiliated with industry. The Environmental Defense Fund has argued that "[e]ven before the research that will allow hazards and exposures to be quantified, a number of more fundamental needs must be addressed" because "[w]e currently lack a good understanding of which specific properties will determine or are otherwise relevant to nanomaterials' risk potential." And "[m]any of the methods, protocols and tools needed to characterize nanomaterials, or to detect and measure their presence in a variety of settings (e.g., workplace environment, human body, environmental media) are still in a very early stage of development."[6] Lux Consulting, a private sector firm that advises nanotechnology companies, has likewise concluded that there is a great need for "frameworks . . . for evaluating" nanotechnology materials and that greater "understanding [of] the basic science of nanoparticle EHS factors" is needed for "safe nanotech developments."[7]

The second category of information – information about certain categories of nanotechnology and certain pathways into the human body (such as facial skin) or environment for these categories of nanotechnology – has been the subject of sporadic studies and now some significant, but still relatively nascent, research programs. For example, a number of studies have been completed on both carbon

5 *See* Andrew D. Maynard et al., Safe handling of nanotechnology, 444 Nature 267–69 (2006). *See also* National Research Council, *supra* note 9, at 97 (concluding that "[a] robust national strategic plan is needed for nanotechnology-related environmental, health, and safety research that. . . . should focus on research to support risk assessment and management, should include value-of-information considerations, and should identify . . . Specific research needs for the future in such topics as potential exposures to engineered nanomaterials, toxicity, toxicokinetics, environmental fate, and standardization of testing.").

6 *See* Richard Denison, Environmental Defense, A Proposal to Increase Federal Funding of Nanotechnology Risk Research By $100 Million, April 2005 ("Even before the research that will allow hazards and exposures to be quantified, a number of more fundamental needs must be addressed. We currently lack a good understanding of which specific properties will determine or are otherwise relevant to nanomaterials' risk potential. Many of the methods, protocols and tools needed to *characterize* nanomaterials, or to detect and measure their presence in a variety of settings (e.g., workplace environment, human body, environmental media) are still in a very early stage of development.").

7 Statement of Matthew M. Nordan, Lux Consulting, Nanotech Commercialization Has Advanced, but Government Action to Address Risk Has Not, Sept. 21, 2006.

nanotubes and titanium dioxide.[8] The completed studies so far often suggest inconsistent results or conclusions regarding the safety of categories of nanotechnology, and hence simply underscore the need for more research.[9]

Moreover, even if there were more and better category 2 information, we would need research at the level of particular nanotechnology products. For one thing, because there is an incomplete public inventory of nano-components in current products (not to mention products under development), we do not have reliable knowledge regarding the full range of categories of nanotechnology that are or soon will be embodied in commercial processes and products. And even if we had such an inventory, what we think is likely and certainly possible about nanotechnology is that the same categories of nanotechnology may behave differently with minor differences in production and formulation. And the distinctive differences in the environment (human and otherwise) in which particular products are used and disposed of may mean that there are significantly different risks from products that contain exactly or almost exactly the same nanotechnology.

How much information, then, has been assembled regarding health and environmental risks from particular nanotechnology production processes and products in commercial use? We really do not know, because we do not know how much testing has been completed by private industry. What is clear is that almost no public information exists regarding product-specific risks from nanotechnology products.

Government regulation in the United States and elsewhere has very largely not required pre- or post-market testing of products containing nanotechnology. There have been and are initiatives on the part of government agencies – and notably the federal Environmental Protection Agency – to encourage companies to voluntarily provide regulators with the information they possess regarding their products. But, relatively little of the content of those submissions has been made public, and what has been made public suggests a selective response by industry to the call for voluntary disclosure to regulators.

[8] One problem is that the studies have so heavily focused on carbon and ignored "broad classes of other materials already on the market" in products. *See* Robert F. Service, *Priorities Needed for Nano-Risk Research and Development*, 314 SCIENCE October 6, 2006, at 45. There has also been a marked inattention to possible effects on the non-human environment and the possible second-order effects on human beings. *See, e.g.*, Lloyd's Emerging Risks Team Report, RISKS: Nanotechnology Recent Developments, Risks, and Opportunities (2007), at 3 (explaining that "[i]t is unclear whether nanoparticles can cause chronic health impacts" and "[t]here is still too little research into the potential negative impacts of this technology on the environment"); ROYAL SOCIETY, *supra* note 1, at 45 (surveying the absence of studies on ecotoxicology of nanoparticles).

[9] *See, e.g.*, Statement of Matthew M. Nordan, Lux Consulting, Nanotech Commercialization Has Advanced, but Government Action to Address Risk Has Not, Sept. 21, 2006 (noting inconsistent results regarding nanoparticle toxicity to date, as "[f]or instance, while Günter Oberdörster at Rochester University found that smaller particles of titanium dioxide (TiO_2) are more harmful than large ones, David Warheit at DuPont found no relationship between size and toxicity; he also found that nanoparticles of silica (SiO_2) and zinc oxide (ZnO) are *less* harmful than larger ones.").

We do know that some companies clearly are doing testing on nanotechnology products. Most notably, DuPont, in conjunction with Environmental Defense, has developed and publicized a testing protocol and reported on the cases of a few nanotechnology products it has considered for development.[10] But the DuPont initiative is so notable in part because we have no idea what so many major companies, not to mention smaller companies, are or are not doing.

One possible response to the insufficiencies in our risk assessment methods and metrics for nanotechnology, in our understanding of risks from categories of nanotechnology, and in our knowledge about product-specific risks would be a moratorium on the release of new nanotechnology products – or even the continued marketing of those already on the market – pending the development of better assessment methods and better actual assessments. Indeed, in 2007, a broad range of NGOs called for such a moratorium as part of Principles for the Oversight of Nanotechnologies and Nanomaterials. That group endorsed a precautionary-principle regime which "would include prohibiting the marketing of untested or unsafe uses of nanomaterials and requiring product manufacturers and distributors to bear the burden of proof" or, more pithily, "Simply put, 'no health and safety data, no market.'"[11]

A broad-based moratorium, of course, would deny the public of some nanotechnology products that may have great utility to consumers and to the public at large. The very large economic value of current and projected nanotechnology products suggests that there is a great deal of consumer and other public utility at stake. Some nanotechnology products may have important medical applications. In any case, there appears to be insufficient political support for a general moratorium either in the United States or elsewhere. But the information deficit regarding nanotechnology – in particular, the deficit in what I have called category 1 and 2 information – does or should have implications for one's view of how a non-moratorium approach to nanotechnology products should be conceived. Specifically, these deficits suggest that any conclusions drawn from pre–market-release testing regarding safety must be tentative and should be openly acknowledged as such and that a substantial emphasis must be placed on post–market-release testing, monitoring, and disclosure.

Where (as with nanotechnology) there are theoretical reasons for believing that there may be adverse human or environmental effects from a kind of technology embodied in a product and there is an acknowledged informational deficit regarding the risk assessment methods for that technology, pre–market-release testing can reveal only so much. Open acknowledgment of that fact – and open embrace of a relatively undemanding or truly realistic stated goal for pre-market testing – is therefore appropriate. A very demanding stated goal regarding what pre-market testing must

10 *See* Environmental Defense Fund and DuPont, Nano Risk Framework 11 (2007) *available at* http://www.edf.org/documents/6496_Nano%20Risk%20Framework.pdf.

11 *See* Principles Declaration, *available at* http://www.icta.org/nanoaction/page.cfm?id=223.

or should show can have two possible, perverse consequences. If adherence to the goal is taken very seriously, then testing will be very expensive and prolonged and, even so, may often be deemed inadequate to make the necessary showing for commercial release. A too-demanding pre-market testing standard thus can become the equivalent of adoption of a moratorium. On the other hand, if there is a demanding standard but products are readily deemed to have met the standard notwithstanding the limits in what pre-market testing can reveal, there may be a tendency on the part of regulators, companies, and other stakeholders not to advocate for and/or engage in post-market monitoring and testing. Indeed, under the FDA registration system for new drugs, which does purportedly employ a very demanding standard for showings of safety based on pre-market testing, there reportedly has been an absence of adequate post-market monitoring, reporting, testing, and disclosure, notwithstanding FDA's legal authority to require companies to engage in such post-market measures.

The limits in information regarding risk assessment and substantive information regarding different categories of nanotechnology and different pathways – what I call category 1 and 2 information – counsels in favor of post-market measures in two senses. First, to the extent that risk assessment and evaluation methods are improving over time, post-market assessments allow products to be evaluated using better risk assessment methods than were available at the time the product was under development and was released into the marketplace. Second, because pre-market testing is not entirely reliable in detecting adverse effects, the only means to detect such effects and prompt further study of them sometimes may be by means of direct observation of workers, consumers, and others who have used or come into contact with nanotechnology products. The same argument has been forcefully made even in the context of conventional (not nanotechnology) drugs that have been subject to the pre-market FDA testing and approval process involving human clinical trials.[12]

Post–market-release testing is also important for another reason: hundreds of nanotechnology products are currently on the market that, as far as we know, never underwent pre-market testing or underwent testing that may have suggested potential adverse effects. For this set of products, post-market monitoring and testing may be the only feasible means for assessing risks of environmental, health, and safety adverse effects.

A nanotechnology product regime should include substantial, but realistically tentative, pre-market testing coupled with post-market monitoring and testing under conditions of transparency that allow for public accountability. There are three possible components of such a regime: mandatory product testing requirements,

[12] *See* Taylor, *supra* note [6], at 23–24 ("Even the large-scale clinical trials used to assess drug safety and efficacy, which may involve hundreds or even thousands of subjects, are not capable of detecting every low-incidence adverse effect that could occur and be of great public heath significance when the drug is administered over long periods to millions of people."); *see also* U.S. Government Accounting Office, Drug Safety Improvement Needed in FDA's Postmarket Decision-making and Oversight Process, 13 (2006) *available at* http://www.gao.gov/new.items/d06402.pdf.

public funding for testing, and voluntary commitments on the part of companies to engage in testing and monitoring. These means are in no way exclusive, and all three may be needed in combination.

THREE COMPONENTS OF A PRECAUTIONARY-STUDY APPROACH TO NANOTECHNOLOGY

Mandatory Testing and Monitoring Requirements

One approach to achieving pre- and post-market testing of products, clearly, is mandatory pre- and post-market release testing. It is at least arguable that current laws in the United States would not support such testing requirements. As Wendy Wagner and others have argued, U.S. laws tend to be very precautionary with respect to a limited range of items (such as certain new drugs) and almost entirely non-precautionary with respect to everything else.[13] As Terry Davies has suggested, a new law may be needed as a framework for mandatory pre- and post-market testing of nanotechnology products.[14] It remains to be seen whether interest group politics are such that we will see either the use of existing authorities to mandate more testing or the passage of a new mandatory testing law.[15]

Even if a new law were enacted, there are reasons to suppose that it might be under-inclusive or inadequate unless mandatory testing were supplemented by voluntary testing. Nanotechnology is a dynamic arena in which the kinds of nanoparticles and uses for them, as identified by industry, may be expected to change quickly over time. Mandatory testing rules will have to include definitions of the scope of substances or products to be tested and the substance of the testing. These rules could readily become obsolete as the commercial marketplace evolves in different directions that regulators do not understand or understand well.[16] Moreover, even if regulators

[13] *See* Wendy E. Wagner, *The Precautionary Principle and Chemical Regulation in the U.S.*, 6 Human and Ecological Risk Assessment 459, 464 (2000) (characterizing U.S. chemical regulation as "at best, a schizophrenic regulatory program that acts on a certain group of new chemical in a precautionary way, but otherwise proceeds in a way that is essentially unprecautionary: regulator intervention is typically correlated directly, rather than inversely, with the available scientific knowledge regarding product safety.").

[14] *See* Davies, *supra* note 1, at 18.

[15] It is also unclear whether the EU's chemical regulation "REACH" will translate into mandatory testing requirements, *see* Diana Bowman & Geert van Calster, *Reflecting on REACH: Global Implications of the European Union's Chemicals Regulation*, 4 Nanotechnology L. Bus. 375 (2007) (discussing whether a mass condition for testing will exclude nanotechnology products). *See also* John S. Applegate, Synthesizing TSCA and REACH: Practical Principles for Chemical Regulation Reform, 49–50, *available at* http://ssrn.com/abstract=1183942 ("Having created a demand for information, a regulatory system needs to supply it. As we have seen, REACH – with the advantage of thirty additional years of experience with chemical regulation in Europe and the US – is more urgently focused on information needs than TSCA was.").

[16] *See* Taylor, *supra* note [6], at 23 ("Companies that are developing new technologies and product applications always know more about them earlier in the process" than federal regulators).

can keep apace of changes in technology and commercial interest in emerging technology, it is inherently hard to change mandatory government rules quickly. Such rules can be expected to evoke opposition from at least some industry actors, and that opposition may well be enough, coupled with the well-known phenomena of legislative and regulatory inertia, to prevent rapid adoption of new rules. Even if new rules are authorized for implementation, implementation takes time.

Mandatory rules, moreover, almost always require voluntary compliance to be truly effective. In particular, regulators are not well-positioned to enforce mandatory post–market-release reporting and disclosure requirements, as they lack direct contact with distributors, vendors, consumers, and others who may be the best source of such information. Thus, even in an ostensibly mandatory regulatory regime, voluntary efforts – cooperation and collaboration by industry – are important and hence so are the strength of the incentives for industry to engage in such voluntary efforts.

Public Funding

The public certainly could fund pre- and post-market testing of products containing nanotechnology components that would help reveal their heath, environmental, and safety effects. There has indeed been a call for increased federal funding of this kind, at least on behalf of smaller start-ups in the nanotechnology industry.[17] Public funding, however, is unlikely to adequately fill the information deficits discussed previously.

First, the competition for federal research funds is intense. Research regarding the environmental, health, and safety implications of nanotechnology – research directed at what may be a real health and environmental problem, but is not known to be such – has and likely will continue to have difficulty attracting funding when legislators and regulators must make hard choices regarding where to allocate funds. There are simply too many known problems or ailments or crises that could make use of funding. Nanotechnology safety implications is not an issue that has a singularly motivated and hence powerful interest group behind it, as (for example) does autism research, and also does not have (yet anyway) a powerful, visceral hook for press coverage and popular mobilization.

Second, public funding, by definition, cannot address many questions of product safety without substantial information from and active cooperation of companies that

[17] *See* Prepared Statement of Mathew M. Nordan, Lux Research, Nanotech Environmental, Health, and Safety (EHS) Risks: Action Need, Nov. 17, 2005, at 39 (arguing that because "[s]tart-ups . . . have much shorter time horizons [than large corporations], and thus have financial incentives to bury or disregard EHS issues" and "Start-ups are generally the earliest commercial developers of new nanoparticles and also the parties least likely to be able to afford expensive toxicology studies," then the "only way . . . for nanotech commercialization to proceed rapidly while ensuring that toxicology studies are performed is for governments to supply the funds."), Hearing before the Committee on science, House of Representatives, Environmental and Safety Impacts of Nanotechnology: What Research is Needed? Nov. 17, 2005, serial No. 109–34.

are developing or have developed products containing nanotechnology. Whether research is funded by companies or by the public, companies must be willing to make disclosures that may be sensitive for trade secrets/business competition reasons and that may lead others to question the safety of the products and whether they have created or will create harm. The promise of funding alone may well not be enough motivation, as the discussion of liability concerns in Part III suggests.

Finally, as a normative matter, it would seem inappropriate for the federal government to fund product-specific safety testing (category 3 information). Such testing would seem to be rightly regarded as part of the costs of the production of the product. Production costs – like profits from production – presumptively rest with the producer in a market economy. In a standard model of allocative efficiency, product-specific subsidies would result in the overproduction of new nanotechnology products, particularly ones that may entail especially costly testing. Moreover, any proposal to subsidize testing for smaller companies or start-ups who cannot readily afford testing costs is likely to skew the marketplace for nanotechnology product development in favor of such companies. As a historic matter – for example in the FDA drug-approval context – product-specific testing has not been publically funded for either small or large entities, and the drug industry has included collaborations between start-ups and larger companies, perhaps partly as a result. The federal government, however, could conduct or facilitate some of the actual testing with company funding, in which case smaller companies could, collectively, perhaps take advantage of economies of scale they otherwise could not achieve.[18]

Voluntary Testing

As explained, mandatory testing requirements and public funding together are unlikely to result in comprehensive product-specific research that tracks and keeps pace with developments within the nanotechnology industry. Voluntary testing and monitoring, at a minimum, is needed to fill in important holes in what any mandatory requirements cover in theory or (given highly imperfect information and limited resources on the part of regulators) in practice. More specifically, what is needed is voluntary testing and monitoring, coupled with affirmative cooperation by industry with regulators, including cooperation in public disclosure of testing results. How then can voluntary testing with government oversight and genuine public disclosure be assured, or at least encouraged?

One conventional answer has been that the threat of common law tort liability will encourage companies to engage in voluntary testing in order to minimize harm to

[18] As Lux Research has advocated, there is a clearly a role for public funding of category one – framework and methods – research, as well as a role in supporting basic research that might be considered part of category two. Such research has sufficiently wide applicability to be regarded as a public good or quasi-public good, and there is substantial precedent for public funding of public goods or quasi-public goods that have significant benefits for industry.

consumers and the environment and hence to minimize their potential tort liability. The threat of liability, it has been supposed, will lead companies to cut off production of dangerous products or recall ones already on the market and will prompt full disclosure of the risks associated with products brought to or left on the market. The view that liability (or the possibility of liability) will encourage companies to invest in assessing risks from nanotechnology products appears to be shared both by those who oppose mandatory testing requirements as unduly intrusive or necessary and those who support tough mandatory testing and certification requirements.

The idea that the threat of liability will encourage voluntary testing and disclosure, however, presupposes two things that are not always true in all contexts and almost certainly not true in the context of nanotechnology products. First, this argument assumes a robust standard for liability whereby alleged tort feasors are held liable even when they did not actually have knowledge of a potential hazard or risk or adverse effects and could have gained such knowledge only with great difficulty, if at all. Second, this argument seems to assume that the harms that would form the basis of the tort claims would be apparent to the victims and that the connections between those harms and their causes could be readily drawn by the victims and accepted by courts. But as discussed next, the American tort system largely employs a standard of liability in which the absence of actual knowledge of a risk or hazard or adverse effect is extremely helpful in avoiding liability, inasmuch as plaintiffs must show that the defendant either knew or reasonably should have known of the risk or effect. Moreover, with respect to many kinds of products, the harms may not become apparent for many years and may not even occur to victims as related to particular products and indeed may be very hard for even the most determined plaintiffs to establish as having been caused by particular products.

Nanotechnology products, if they do have harmful effects, likely would fall in this category of products for which adverse effects are hard to isolate and connect to the production, use, or disposal of the products. Consider, for example, the possibility that nanoparticles in skin creams may have adverse effects. Because most consumers do not even know which creams contain nanoparticles and which do not, almost no one would ever retain records regarding which nanotechnology-containing cosmetics he or she used over time. Indeed, almost no one would retain records of the cosmetics he or she used at all. Moreover, if nanoparticles in skin creams indeed can permeate skin barriers and affect internal systems in the body, there might be any number of adverse effects from them. Many of these adverse effects might relate to conditions or ailments that might have a range of other causes, from genetics to diet to smoking.[19] And these ailments or conditions might

[19] *See* Margaret A. Berger, *Eliminating General Causation: Notes Towards a New Theory of Justice and Toxic Torts*, 97 COLUM. L. REV. 2117, 2121–22 (1997) (arguing that in toxic torts, generally "in most instances, the adverse health effects for which plaintiffs seek compensation are also found in others who have not been exposed to the substance or product in question. Because this 'background' rate exists, it is impossible to tell whether any individual plaintiff's injury is attributable to the product. . . .").

surface decades after the use of the product ended. Asbestos-based liability has dominated the American tort system in large part because asbestos exposure creates an easily identifiable, signature disease, asbestosis, but there is no *a priori* reason to suppose that nanoparticles in products would similarly result in signature diseases or conditions.

Moreover, the very defining attribute of nanoparticles – their incredibly small size – may mean that it will continue to be very hard to detect their presence in the environment.[20] As a result, it is and may well continue to be extremely hard to isolate nanoparticle pathways in the environment and prove that nanoparticles via these pathways caused human health effects or other harms that might be the basis for liability. The closest analogy would be endocrine disrupting chemicals, which may have some toxic effects but are pervasive in small quantities in the environment. Although much has been made of the possibility of tort liability related to endocrine disrupters, that liability in fact has not been imposed, perhaps because of the difficulty of establishing particular concentrations and particular pathways into the human body (or given the particularity of private tort, the particular human bodies of plaintiffs).[21] The possibility of environmental tort liability based on nanoparticle exposure may be even more uncertain, given nanoparticles' small size and elusive nature, even assuming *arguendo* that nanoparticles in fact can and will cause human health or other harms.

MODELING MANUFACTURER DECISION MAKING

This section develops a model that illustrates how the threat of liability may lead nanotechnology producers not to test products and how limits on liability might produce more testing.

One way to think about the decisions of nanotechnology companies under the current tort system is to imagine how a particular nanotechnology product manufacturer ("the company") might evaluate the decision of whether to invest in researching any adverse health effects of a product while it is under development and after its introduction to the market. Imagine that the product is a cosmetic such a wrinkle cream, that it contains a form of nanotechnology for which there is almost no or no existing research, and that it is not, to the company's knowledge, a known component of any other product under development or on the market.

[20] *See* Gregory Mandel, *Nanotechnology Governance*, 59 ALA. L. REV. 1323, 1345 (2008) (overviewing the risks from nanotechnology and noting that "[e]xacerbating the challenge of nanotechnology risks is that there currently is very limited capability to detect or measure nanoparticles. . . . ").

[21] For a review of the current state of the litigation and the defense bar's positions, see generally Bruce J. Berger & Michael L. Junk, *Endocrine Disrupters: The Potential Cloud of Manufacturer Toxic Tort Liability*, 74 DEF. COUNSEL J., 106 (2007). On the difficulties of prevailing in environmental tort actions, see generally Troyen A. Brennan, *Environmental Torts*, 46 VAND. L. REV., 1 (1993); *see* Berger, *supra* note 24, at 2138.

Assumptions

This model assumes that any assessment of the product's possible adverse effects would take significant time and that any reasonably reliable conclusions regarding what can be gleaned about adverse effects cannot be made until the assessment is complete.

The model also assumes that the company believes it has some reasonably reliable sense regarding how long the product, absent safety issues, would have a "run" on the market before it likely will be considered stale or obsolete and the company would introduce a new, differently composed product to take its place.

In addition, the company believes it has some reasonably reliable sense of how well the product will sell at different times during this run. That a company would have such beliefs would seem essential for the company to even consider making an investment in product development and marketing at all.[22]

The model contains three distinct time periods, which contain two distinct decision points for the company. At T0, the product is under development. T0 is the company's first decision point, because any pre-market testing for the product would have to begin then, so as to produce results by the time the product is scheduled for market release (T1). Period 1 is the time between T0 and T1.

At T1, the time of the product's release into the marketplace, the company has its second decision point. At that time, the company must decide whether to undertake post–market-release testing of the product, the results of which would not be available until T2. By T2, the product would have been on the market some time but still would have a significant amount of time left in its anticipated market run. Period 2 is the time between T1 and T2.

After T2, the company has no further decision points. Unless pulled from the market at T2, the product will remain on the market until it has finished its anticipated market run and is obsolete. T3 is the time at which the product has had its full anticipated market run: the company will introduce a next-generation product at that time to take its place. Period 3 is the time between T2 and T3.

Variables: Damages (D) and Standard of Liability (S)

The company realizes that if the product causes adverse health effects and those health effects are linked to the product, the company might incur substantial liability based on sales of the products during periods 2 and 3. As a baseline for estimating its liability exposure, the company might estimate the damages (in monetary terms) that consumers would incur as a result of the product, assuming very adverse effects for a significant fraction of consumers of the product. They might also include an estimate of environmental damages as a result of the manufacture and disposal of the product during those two periods. D is the damages attributable to the product.

[22] Somewhat unrealistically, in the interest of simplicity, the model will assume that the company does not update or change its projections of how long the product will have a run in the market and how well it will sell once the product enters the marketplace.

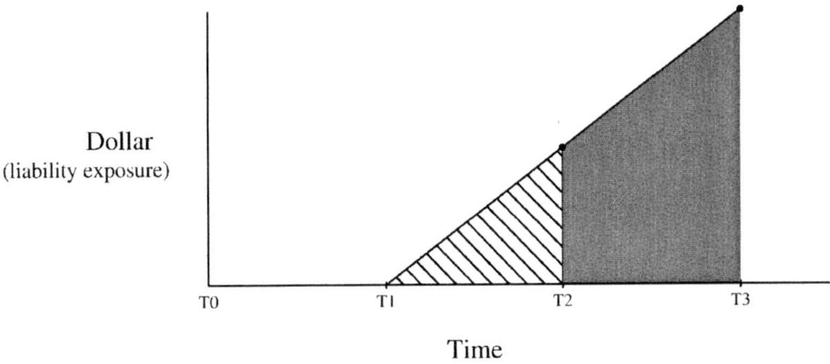

FIGURE 7.1. Damages estimates on the part of the company are depicted. Time is the variable on the x-axis above. The variables on the y-axis are total damages incurred up until time T. D_{T_2} represents total damages incurred during period 2. D_{T_3} represents total damages incurred during both periods 2 and 3. The upward slope of the line on the figure reflects the fact that as time passes, more people purchase and use the product, and as more people purchase and use the product, the number of potentially harmed people increases. As that number increases, total damages increases. For products with rapid growth in sales over time, we would expect a sharper upward slope than for products that maintain more or less even sales over time.

Actual damages – even damages clearly attributable to a product – do not necessarily translate into a liability to pay damages under tort law. There are several different liability standards for manufacturer liability, ranging in effect from liability only for sale and distribution of products known to be harmful to negligence to genuine strict liability. Depending on the applicable standard, a manufacturer might always or sometimes or virtually never be held liable for damages attributable to its product. S signifies the applicable standard for liability.

The two relevant causes of action in tort law for producers of a nanotechnology cosmetic would be a cause of action for defective product design and a cause of action for failure to warn of risks associated with the product. With respect to both such causes of action, three key points in time according to both the case law and commentary are (1) the time the product first enters the market, (2) the time the product is sold to the particular plaintiff, and (3) the time at trial. A central debate in tort law has concerned the question of when, if ever, should a manufacturer be held liable for product risks that the manufacturer did not know about and perhaps could not even have known about at the time of the sale of the product to the plaintiff(s). Arguments rooted in efficiency and fairness have been invoked to support and defend against manufacturer liability for failing to warn of, or otherwise address, unknown risks.

One position that some courts and commentators have sometimes articulated is that a manufacturer is or should be liable for harms that at trial can be shown to have been caused by the product even if the manufacturer did not know or could not have reasonably foreseen that the product would cause such harm when the product was first manufactured and released to the market or when it was sold to the particular plaintiff. This approach is sometimes described as hindsight liability or genuine strict liability, and it effectively removes any defense based on the absence of or limit in scientific evidence regarding causation prior to the time of trial.[23]

At the other side of the spectrum from genuine strict liability is liability that requires a showing of actual knowledge on the part of the manufacturer of the harmful effects of the product at the time when the product was sold to the particular plaintiff. Although actual knowledge has indeed been alleged in many of the best-known mass products liability cases, it is not clear that any court has completely embraced an actual knowledge requirement in products liability cases. The state tort statutes in some states establish a strong form of the so-called "state of the art" defense; such statutes could be read to mean that scientific information or evidence developed after a product is introduced into the market cannot be used against the manufacturer in establishing liability. However, these statutes presumably were drafted with mechanical devices in mind (e.g., lawnmowers that turn out to malfunction) and have not been construed to mean that a manufacturer has absolutely no obligation to ignore developments in scientific evidence regarding drugs, chemicals, or similar products after the product first enters the market, even if the market was tested to the highest industry standards prior to it being first introduced into the market.

The Restatement (Third) of Torts articulates what is probably the standard that most courts in the United States now endorse. Under this reasonable foreseeability or "should have known" standard, manufacturers can be held liable if they should have known of the harm the product could create when they sold it to the plaintiff without an appropriate warning. Lack of actual knowledge is not a defense, but neither can the plaintiff simply hold the manufacturers liable for risks and harms that the manufacturer could not have known when the products were sold to the plaintiffs.[24] The Restatement approach is very similar to that followed in European and Japanese law.[25]

[23] *See* Beshada v. Johns-Manville Products Corp., 447 A.2d 539, 548 (N.J. 1982) (apparently embracing hindsight liability in the asbestos context). *See also* Omri Ben Shahar, Should Products Liability Be based on Hindsight?, 14 J. L. Econ, and Org. 325 (1998) (reviewing the state of the law and then modeling corporate research incentives under hindsight liability).

[24] *See* Restatement (Third) of Torts: Products Liability § 2(c) (1998). Under this standard, lack of actual knowledge is not a defense, but neither can the plaintiff simply hold the manufacturers liable for risks and harms that the manufacturer could not have known when the products were sold to the plaintiffs. With respect to product testing, the Restatement provides that "a seller bears responsibility to perform reasonable testing prior to marketing a product and to discover risk and risk avoidance measures such testing would reveal. A seller is charged with knowledge of what reasonable testing would reveal." Restatement (Third) Sec. 2 comment m. As Mark Geistfeld has explained, because proving what a reasonable research program would reveal is an "extraordinarily demanding" standard, the Restatement (Third) standard "effectively immunizes" the manufacturer even from liability for many knowable risks. Mark A. Geistfeld, Principles of Products Liability (New York: Foundation Press, 2006, pp. 152–53).

[25] The Restatement approach is very similar to that followed in European and Japanese law. *See* Jane Stapleton, Product Liability (Boston, MA: Butterworths, 1994; pp. 50–51). The central legal development limiting liability in Europe was the EEC Directive (1985/374/EEC). See id at 49.

The reasonable foreseeability/should have known standard is, of course, a kind of negligence standard. Indeed, citing the Restatement and similar authorities, some commentators have concluded that American products liability torts, although still sometimes labeled a strict liability domain, are squarely within the domain of negligence.[26] And like all negligence standards, the reasonable foreseeability/should have known standard used for products is flexible and imprecise and subject to much more or much less defendant-friendly interpretations and applications. Indeed, there probably are few cases in which one could not plausibly argue opposite positions under this standard – that a manufacturer reasonably could not have foreseen an unknown product risk, or that a manufacturer reasonably should have foreseen the risk and engaged in more testing and product re-design or warned consumers of the risk. Everything depends on the conception of "reasonableness" one employs.

For the company facing potential liability, it might be logical for them to think of standard of liability as a spectrum variable, with proof of actual knowledge required on one end, a range of possible formulations of "should have known" in the middle, and hindsight/genuine strict liability at the other end. S has a value of 1 at the farthest right/hindsight liability end of the spectrum, which means that the company will be legally responsible for 100 percent of the damages its products cause. At the "actual knowledge required" end of the spectrum, S has a value of 0, which means that the company will not be legally responsible for any damages its products cause, at least assuming the company will not market or continue to market the product without warning once its has actual knowledge of harm. The magnitude of S increases from left to right as "should have known" is applied as imposing an increasingly demanding duty on the manufacturer to find out about possible risks and mitigate or avoid them and/or warn of them. In the middle of the spectrum, where $S = 0.5$, there is a 50% possibility that the court would conclude that the manufacturer should have known, which in expected value terms, means that, *ex ante*, the manufacturer's expected costs would be 50% of the damages its products actually cause.

For the company, there could be two relevant Ss. S_{T2} is the standard of liability applicable to period 2 consumers who sue after the company finishes its post-market testing and pulls the product at T2. S_{T3} is the standard of liability applied to period 2 and 3 consumers at T3, after independent research shows that the product, which by then will have finished its market run, is harmful. Under current tort law, the applicable standard of liability is formally the same whether the manufacturer removes the product voluntarily based on its own testing and monitoring before the end of the product's anticipated market run or whether the product completes its market run and then independent non-company research ties the product to injuries of consumers and others (at or after T3).

[26] *See* Geistfeld, *supra* note at 248 ("Despite the 'strict liability' rhetoric . . . this has overwhelmingly remained the majority view: the liability of manufacturers for design conditions . . . is . . . fault-based."); G. Schwartz, *The Beginning and the Possible End of the Rise of Modern American Tort Law*, 26 Georgia L. Rev. 601, 625–27 (1992).

L_{T2}, the total liability for the company at T2, would thus be $(D_{T2})(S_{T2})$, again assuming that the company finds adverse effects and pulls the product from the market. L_{T3}, the total liability for the company at T3 or after, would be (D_{T3}) (S_{T3}), assuming that non-company research at T3 or later has shown that the product caused adverse effects during periods 2 and 3. One might generally assume that L_{T3} will be greater than L_{T2} because more consumers are exposed as of T3 than as of T2. If neither the company nor entities outside the company detect and establish the link between the product and injuries to consumers and others, however, there will be no liability whatever for the company at either T2 or T3 or after.

Probability of Detection/Attribution (P) and Research Costs (R)

The model assumes that the company believes that, absent its own independent research into the possible links between the product and adverse effects, there is a zero possibility that the product will be linked to adverse effects prior to the end of period 3. For products whose potential adverse effects, if any, likely would not be obvious for years and would even then not be obviously linked to the product but instead could well be attributed to other causes or unknown causes, this would be a reasonable belief.

The company believes that there is some probability that, absent any research or monitoring for adverse effects on its part, the product could be linked to adverse effects by T3 or at some time thereafter. We will call that probability P_{T3}. The company's estimate of the magnitude of P_{T3} (and the actual P_{T3}) would depend on a number of factors. One of these would be any ingredient or component disclosure and labeling requirements, if any, for the product: the less those requirements are, the less likely it is that a link between adverse effects and product use could be drawn.

A second and crucial factor would be the extent of non-company investment in research that could shed light on the effects of nanotechnology generally, nanotechnology in cosmetics, and nanotechnology of similar or the same composition as that found in the company's products. Public and academic research investments might have the biggest influence on the estimate, because the products of such research investments would be most likely to be widely disseminated and could be used as a basis for ultimately assessing – or at least raising the question of – the effects of the company's product. Because nanotechnology research anywhere in the world might affect P_{T3}, public and academic investments levels throughout the world, and not just in the company's home country, would be relevant. The relevance of other companies' research would depend in substantial part on how likely it is that it would be shared with the public.

The legal standard for proof for admission of scientific evidence regarding causation of harm would also be relevant. The more demanding the standard for the admissibility of such evidence is, the more difficult it would be for plaintiffs at T3 or later to locate and/or generate evidence that would allow them to survive summary judgment in a tort lawsuit against the company. If, for example, the courts limit their vision of reliable and hence admissible evidence of causation of human harm to peer-reviewed, human-subject clinical or epidemiological studies, then the company's estimate of P_{T3} may be quite low, even if there is or is likely to be significant public investment in animal studies and other laboratory explorations of the possible toxic dimensions of nanotechnology. The overall attitude of the United States courts at the state and federal level in the last few decades has veered toward restrictiveness regarding what kinds of causation evidence is sufficiently reliable to warrant admission, so one relevant question for the company would be the likelihood that that trend would continue.

As noted, there are two possible research efforts the company could undertake – one during pre-market period 1, culminating at T1, and one during post-market period 2, culminating at T2. We will call the direct cost of the period 1 research efforts R1 and the direct costs of the period 2 research efforts R2.[27]

The company recognizes that there is some probability that the pre-market, period 1 research effort would detect adverse health effects, in which case the company would cancel the planned release of the product into the marketplace. We will call that probability P_{T1}. The company also realizes that there is some probability that the post-market research efforts would detect adverse health effects, in which case the product would be pulled from the marketplace at T2. We will call that probability P_{T2}.

One question is whether the company would assume that P_{T2} is greater when pre-market testing has been done and adverse effects are not found than when no pre-market testing has been done. On the one hand, one might suppose that the finding of no adverse effects in pre-market research would or could give rise to a greater confidence level that the product in fact is not harmful and hence a greater confidence that post-market research will not identify harmful effects. On the other hand, one might suppose that the more familiarity the company has with the behavior of the nanotechnology component of the product, the more effective it could be in structuring a post–market-release testing program that could find any adverse effects from the product. For example, if pre-market testing showed that certain nanoparticles tend to follow certain pathways, that would help the company know where to look, in the post–market-release period, for potentially problematic accumulations in consumers and the environment. These two effects – one tending

27 Specific pre-market testing could include a range of laboratory toxicity testing, and post-market testing could include follow-up surveys of distributors and consumers as well as longer term toxicity testing, such as longer term study of use or exposure of the product on an animal test group. For the purpose of the analysis here, the same reasoning would apply whether the company was choosing whether to adopt a given single pre- or post-market effort or whether they were making the marginal decision whether to undertake one more or one additional pre- or post-market effort.

to suggest a lower P_{T_2}, the other suggesting a higher P_{T_2}, as a result of pre-market testing having been done – might well cancel out.[28]

COMPARING THE EXPECTED COSTS OF THE FOUR OPTIONS

The first question for the company, presumably, would be what are the expected liability costs if the company does nothing – that is, invests in neither the pre-market, period 1 research effort or the post-market, period 2 research effort? If the company does nothing, it faces a possible liability of L_{T_3}, but it will be burdened with L_{T_3} only if independent, non-company research identifies adverse effects and links them to the company's product. Thus the expected liability costs if the company does nothing are $(P_{T_3})(L_{T_3})$. For the company, therefore, the relevant questions boil down to the following:

- Would conducting the pre-market research effort in period 1 result in lower expected costs than $(P_{T_3})(L_{T_3})$?
- Would conducting the post-market research effort in period 2 result in lower expected costs than $(P_{T_3})(L_{T_3})$?
- Would conducting both research efforts result in lower expected costs than $(P_{T_3})(L_{T_3})$?
- If doing nothing (forgoing both research efforts) is not the expected cost-minimizing choice, then which choice is: conducting only the pre-market research effort in period 1, conducting only the post-market research effort in period 2, or conducting both?

Period 1, Pre-Market Investment

If the company invests in research during period 1 and finds that the product is harmful, then the product will not be marketed and hence total liability will be zero, but the company will bear the direct research cost of R1. However, there presumably will be a relatively low expected probability of finding that the product is harmful by the end of the pre-marketing research: P_{T_1} is presumably well below 0.5. If no harm is found, then the company could bear liability if independent research links the product to harmful effects by T3 or later. Thus the expected costs of doing the pre-market research project is $R1 + (1 - P_{T_1})(P_{T_3})(L_{T_3})$. Undertaking the pre-market research is worthwhile if $R1 + (1 - P_{T_1})(P_{T_3})(L_{T_3}) < (P_{T_3})(L_{T_3})$.

[28] The model also assumes that the company's estimate of P_{T_2} and P_{T_3} are unconnected or independent variables. In the absence of a public disclosure requirement on the part of the company, that may be a reasonable assumption. However, if the company were required to disclose the research it conducted in period 1 or 2, then even if the company's conclusion were that the product is safe, the release of the research would increase the information available about the product and in that way might guide independent research and result in a higher P_{T_3}.

Period 2, Post-Market Investment

Now let us assume that the company chooses to skip the pre-market research investment. If the product does go to market, then the research during period 2 could detect harm and result in the product being removed from the market at the end of period 2, that is, at T2. The potential benefit for the company under this scenario is avoidance of the additional liability that otherwise might be imposed as a result of exposures that would take place during period 3. If the period 2 research detects harmful effects, and the company pulls the product, then the company will be liable only for L_{T_2}. If the research is conducted but does not detect harmful effects but independent research then links the product to adverse effects after the product has run its market course, then the company will be liable for L_{T_3}. Hence the company's total expected costs if it conducts only the period 2, post-market research are: $R2 + (P_{T_2})(L_{T_2}) + (1 - P_{T_2})(P_{T_3})(L_{T_3})$. It would make sense for the company to proceed with the period 2 research if $R2 + (P_{T_2})(L_{T_2}) + (1 - P_{T_2})(P_{T_3})(L_{T_3}) < (P_{T_3})(L_{T_3})$.

Combining Pre- and Post-Market Research

Another option for the company is to commit to undertake both pre-market, period 1, and (assuming the product goes to market after pre-market testing) post-market, period 2 research. The cost of pre-market research itself – R1 – remains the same whether or not post-market research is to be undertaken. If harm is detected and the product is never released to market, there will be (by definition) no post-market costs. If no harm is detected during the pre-market research and the product is released to the market, there is the possibility that post-market research will detect harm and the product then will be pulled from the market. There is also the possibility that, if post-market testing does not detect harm and the product remains on the market, independent research will later detect harm. Either way, the company bears R2, the direct cost of post-market testing. Thus the expected costs of the pre- and post-market research option are $R1 + (1 - P_{T_1})\,[R2 + (P_{T_2})(L_{T_2}) + (1 - P_{T_2})(P_{T_3})(L_{T_3})]$.

Comparing the Research Options

We now have cost estimates for the three research options and the do-nothing option. These are:

- Committing to the pre- and post-market research options ("the pre- and post-research option"): $R1 + (1 - P_{T_1})\,[R2 + (P_{T_2})(L_{T_2}) + (1 - P_{T_2})(P_{T_3})(L_{T_3})]$
- Committing to pre-market research only ("the pre-market–only option"): $R1 + (1 - P_{T_1})(P_{T_3})(L_{T_3})$
- Committing to post-market research only ("the post-market–only option"): $R2 + (P_{T_2})(L_{T_2}) + (1 - P_{T_2})(P_{T_3})(L_{T_3})$
- Doing nothing: $(P_{T_3})(L_{T_3})$.

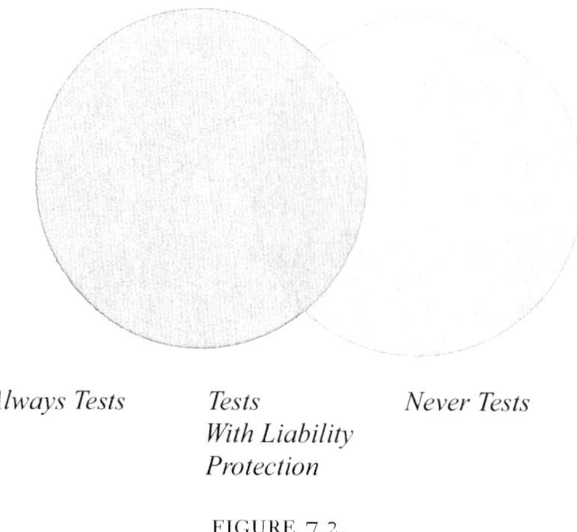

FIGURE 7.2.

For the company, absent the possibility of incurring LT2 liability as a result of its own testing and monitoring and the adverse effects they reveal, it would always be worthwhile to engage in post-market testing and monitoring if the condition is met that $R2 + (1 - P_{T2})(P_{T3})(L_{T3}) < (P_{T3})(L_{T3})$. That universe of cases is represented by the left side of Figure 7.2. There is a universe of cases for which the avoidance of possible LT2 liability makes it worthwhile to avoid post-market testing and instead do nothing, which meet the condition that $R2 + (P_{T2})(L_{T2}) + (1 - P_{T2})(P_{T3})(L_{T3}) > (P_{T3})(L_{T3})$. The right side of Figure 7.2 represents those cases. There is an intersection area in the middle consisting of cases that meet the two previous conditions and for which it is also true that $(P_{T2})(L_{T2}) > (P_{T3})(L_{T3}) - (R2 + (1 - P_{T2})(P_{T3})(L_{T3}))$. This is the universe of cases for which liability avoidance will lead a company to avoid post-market testing and monitoring that they otherwise would have undertaken.

How big is this intersection area? The answer, of course, all depends on the values we assign to the relevant variables. What we can say is that less testing or no testing may be a liability-minimizing option precisely in some cases when – on a social welfare basis – we would ardently want such testing to happen. Testing would be most attractive from a social perspective in those cases in which the testing would be highly effective at detecting any adverse effects from the product, such testing would be inexpensive, and the damages ultimately suffered by consumers and others would be huge if such testing does not occur and the product remains on the market without proper warnings. As described below, the company might well choose not to engage in testing in a subset of these cases – those in which the company perceives a very low perceived probability of detection of the product's adverse effects on the basis of independent, non-company research.

The easiest way to see how liability minimization can deter testing is to imagine an extreme case in which post-market testing would be extremely effective at detecting any adverse effects and would be extremely cheap to do. In such a case, there might be a 99% perceived probability that adverse effects (if there are any) would be detected by the company in post-market testing, and such testing would cost almost nothing, perhaps a few thousand dollars. It would be reasonable in such a case to round P_{T_2} up to 1 and round R2 down to 0. In terms of the intersection condition described above $[(P_{T_2})(L_{T_2}) > (P_{T_3})(L_{T_3}) - (R2 + (1 - P_{T_2})(P_{T_3})(L_{T_3})]$, that would mean that $(P_{T_2})(L_{T_2})$ now equals (L_{T_2}) and that $(1 - P_{T_2})(P_{T_3})(L_{T_3})$ becomes zero. The company therefore will prefer doing nothing to engaging in highly effective, cheap post-market testing if the liability the company would expect to incur as a result of post-market testing (L2) would be more than the liability the company would expect to bear if it does not test and keeps the product on the market without a warning $[(P_{T_3})(L_{T_3})]$. The relevant question then is: when would L_{T_2} ever be greater than $(P_{T_3})(L_{T_3})$?

One answer (but not necessarily the only one) is where the damages that will be incurred by consumers and others in period 3 are just enormous relative to the damages incurred in period 2 but the independent probability of detection at T3 (P_{T_3}) verges on zero. Where P_{T_3} is of a similar magnitude to P_{T_2}, the possibility of a huge L_{T_3} should make the company decide to engage in post-market testing. But it might be a liability-minimizing strategy for the company to avoid post-market testing even when confronted with a relatively huge L_{T_3} if P_{T_3} is very small. For example, imagine that L_{T_2} is 3 million, L_{T_3} is 400 million, and P_{T_3} is just 0.007. Recall that P_{T_2} is effectively 1 and R2 is effectively zero. The expected costs for the company of doing nothing and not engaging in post-market testing would be (400,000,000)(0.07) or $2.8 million, which is $200,000 less than L_{T_2}. In other words, doing nothing would save the company $200,000 in expected liability in a case in which post-market testing could yield great social benefits for minimal social costs.

DECREASING THE LIKELIHOOD OF LIABILITY-DRIVEN AVOIDANCE OF POST-MARKET TESTING

Let us assume that the scenario just described or similar ones is likely enough to warrant attention. The question then is how can any of the relevant variables be manipulated to make it less likely that companies will avoid post-market testing that they otherwise might have undertaken were it not for the threat of liability resulting from post-market testing? In the language of the previous discussion, that question boils down to: how can we make it more likely that $(L_{T_3})(P_{T_3})$ will be greater than (L_{T_2})? There are essentially three possible manipulations of the relevant variables – increasing P_{T_3}, increasing L_{T_3}, and decreasing L_{T_2}. The discussion that follows focuses on decreasing L_{T_2}, which is the most realistic policy option.

P_{T_3} – the independent detection variable – is a key variable in terms of creating an incentive for the company to engage in post-market testing. Any increase in P_{T_3} translates into an increase in the cost of doing nothing – $(P_{T_3})(L_{T_3})$ – and makes it more likely that post-market testing will be a cheaper option than doing nothing.

Any given increase in P_{T3}, moreover, also makes the pre- and post-testing option less expensive relative to all the other options. Increasing P_{T3}, therefore, might result in shifts not just from the do-nothing option to post-market testing, but also shifts from just-pre-market testing or just-post-market testing to both pre- and post-market testing.[29] That may be a good thing, at least from the vantage of the precautionary study principle, which would seem to call for both pre- and post- market testing.

It is not obvious, however, that increasing P_{T3} is feasible. The best means of increasing P_{T3} probably would be an increased expenditure in public research. As already discussed, there has not been political support for substantial public funding to date. It is also not clear how much of an expenditure in such research would be needed to lead to significant changes in estimates of P_{T3}. Moreover, as already discussed, there are probably inherent limitations in public funding as a means to fill the product-specific or category 3 information deficit and hence inherent limitations in the extent to which increases in public funding can boost P_{T3}.

One possible way to increase L_{T3} and hence the cost of doing nothing would be to alter the standard for liability applicable at time T3 and later. For example, if the standard of liability at T2 and T3 initially were a middle-of-the road "should have known" standard (e.g., $S = 0.5$), then a change to a genuine strict liability/hindsight standard at T3 and after would increase the magnitude of L_{T3} relative to L_{T2} by 100%. That change, in turn, could be enough to make post-market testing a liability-minimizing strategy when, before, doing nothing was the liability-minimizing strategy.

There is no tradition, however, of states and states common law imposing different standards of liability depending on whether adverse effects were detected by company research or were, instead, detected by independent, non-company research. One could imagine a federal law that purports to force the states to adopt a stricter standard of liability (genuine strict liability that is) when the adverse effects were detected by independent, non-company research after the product had been on the market a long time and completed its market run (T3). But there would be deep federalism, fairness, and chilling-investment concerns about, and strong political opposition to, any federal law that would require states to shift from a negligence standard to a genuine strict liability standard.

As discussed next, there are plausible federal law changes that could result in the reduction or elimination of L_{T2}. A reduction or elimination in L_{T2} would reduce the attractiveness of the do-nothing option relative to the post-market testing options. It thereby would alleviate the problem of liability avoidance leading companies to forego post-market testing.

[29] Assuming non-zero probabilities of detection of adverse effects for both pre- and post-market testing (i.e., a non-zero P_{T1} and a non-zero P_{T2}), the pre- and post-market approach is the strategy that minimizes the possibility of the company ultimately bearing the cost represented by (P_{T3}) (L_{T3}). Any increase in P_{T3} and hence $(P_{T3})(L_{T3})$, therefore, increases the expected costs of the pre- and post-market option the least and thus makes that option relatively less expensive than it previously was with respect to the other options.

However, reducing or eliminating L_{T_2} could have perverse effects. L_{T_2} liability is a component of the post-market testing option but not a component of the pre-market only research option, so reducing L_{T_2} will decrease the cost of the post-market testing option relative to the pre-market testing option. Moreover, L_{T_2} is a more heavily discounted component of the pre- and post-market research option than it is of the post-market testing only option.[30] As a result, any given reduction in L_{T_2} translates into a bigger cost reduction for the post-market testing than it does for the pre- and post-research option and hence decreases the cost of the post-market only testing option relative to the pre- and post-research options.[31]

The elimination of L_{T_2} liability may result in no change – the lowest-cost option before may be the same after. It is also possible that liability elimination would reduce the costs of the post-market only option and thus shift companies from doing nothing to post-market testing only. However, it is also the case that the reduction in the cost of the post-market only option may cause shifts from the pre-market only option or the pre- and post-market option to the post-market only research option.

From a public policy perspective, these two possible shifts – the shift from pre-market only research to post-market only research and the shift from pre- and post-market research to post-market only research – are problematic. It is not always true that pre-market testing is preferable to post-market testing, but pre-market testing is essential because such testing, if it does indeed detect harmful affects, can avoid putting any consumers or other human populations at risk. By definition, post-market testing entails putting human beings at risk. And (as already suggested) one certainly might not want to encourage shifts from a clearly higher research investment, greater precaution option (pre- and post-market testing) to a clearly lesser research investment, lesser precaution option (post-market only research).

These problematic shifts could be avoided by making L_{T_2} liability relief contingent on the company completing both pre- and post-market research. Conditioning liability relief on pre- as well as post-market testing raises the cost of obtaining the relief for companies and thus presents a difficult tradeoff, from a policy-making perspective. On the one hand, conditioning liability relief avoids the creation of an incentive for companies to abandon pre-market research they otherwise would have undertaken. On the one hand, conditioning liability relief may mean that some companies that would have shifted away from a do-nothing approach will instead continue to follow that approach and do nothing.

30 L_{T_2} is discounted by P_{T_2} in the formula for the post-market only option. L_{T_2} is discounted by (1 – PT1)(P2) in the formula for the pre- and post-market research option.

31 For a similar argument developed in the context of proposals to immunize companies from penalties from compliance violations discovered during internal audits, *see* David A. Dana, *The Perverse Incentives of Audit Immunity*, 81 Iowa L. Rev. 969, 982–88 (1996).

WHICH PRODUCTS WILL BE THE SUBJECT OF VOLUNTARY TESTING?

So far, we have spoken of a single nanotechnology product. However, a company may have many products that contain nanotechnology and that might be candidates for a regime of voluntary testing in return for liability relief. All else being equal, we might expect a company to choose those products with the greatest possibility of liability exposure – those it expects to sell the most or that it suspects may have some dangerous aspect – for enrollment in the regime of voluntary testing. In this way, the voluntary regime may focus attention on the products that pose the greatest perceived risks to public health. Mandatory testing requirements could also focus on such products, but in the context of the possible or planned imposition of mandatory testing requirements, the company would not necessarily have an incentive to share with regulators or the public its views (and the information behind its views) regarding which products pose the greatest possible risks to the public and hence most warrant testing and monitoring.

Products Containing Identical or Substantially Identical Materials or Technology

In the previous discussion of choosing options, we have assumed that there is simply one company making a decision regarding whether and how to invest in research regarding possible adverse effects. For that reason, it was assumed that the only research that can produce L_{T_2} liability is the period 2 research of that single company. But there may be many settings where several companies are producing substantially identical products or, more specifically, products that contain substantially identical materials or technology that may pose risks. For example, imagine that two companies – company A and company B – produce sunscreens containing precisely or virtually the same kind of nanomaterials in the same configuration. Pre- or post-market testing by company A could have an effect on company B whether or not company B chooses to engage in its own research. If company A detects harm as a result of its post-market research and recalls the product (or adds a warning), regulatory, market, and liability pressure may well force company B to take parallel action with respect to its product.

Let us first consider the case in which there is no liability (L_{T_2}) relief for a company that voluntarily tests its product and pulls the product if harm is detected. In that sort of regime, company B has a free-riding–related incentive not to engage in post-market research regarding its product. If company A finds that the product is harmful in post-market testing and both company A and company B therefore must pull their products from the market, company B is (all else being equal) better off than if it had undertaken the safety research: both company A and B will bear costs in terms of lost sales and perhaps liability awards, but at least company B will have avoided R2, the direct costs of research.

Now consider the case in which liability relief is available for any company that conducts post-market testing (in our model, period 2 testing) and finds harmful effects and removes the product from the marketplace. Any incentive company B might have had to free ride on company A's research now would be countered – and perhaps more than offset – by its incentive to obtain liability relief by engaging in testing. It might well be economically rational, therefore, for company B to agree to participate in a research-for-liability-relief program if company A has already agreed to participate and thus increased the likelihood of detection of harmful effects, but refuse to participate if company A has already refused to participate. Another possible incentive for company B to agree to participate in a program after company A has already agreed is that there might be savings from pooling research funds or merging research efforts with company A.

One implication of this analysis is that securing the initial participants in any research-for-liability-relief program is particularly important for – and may be particularly challenging – any such program. The first participant does not have as strong an incentive to join, all else being equal, as the second or third participant. In order to give all potential participants equally strong incentives to participate, the extent of liability arguably should be tiered, with greater relief going to early-to-agree companies and lesser relief to the later-to-agree companies.

Producers of Products Containing the Same General Category of Potentially Risky Materials or Technology

Large clusters of products may contain similar materials or technologies, and research regarding one or more of these products thus might help inform and focus research regarding the other programs in the cluster. For example, drug A may alter mood disorders through the same theorized chemistry as drug B but may have different active ingredients. The discovery of a correlation between use of drug A and heart attacks would not prove that such a correlation exists between use of drug B and heart attacks, but the discovery almost certainly would provide an impetus to study heart health within the pool of people using drug B. In the nanotechnology context, we believe that the same basic type of nanotechnology may behave differently in different product formulations. But research regarding any nanotechnology product may shed some light on nanotechnology generally and hence all nanotechnology products, and certainly research on any nanotechnology product containing a particular element (e.g., silver or carbon) may shed some light on the range of nanotechnology products containing that element.

In terms of the previous model, one way to understand the effect of some company's research on others is in terms of the variable P_{T3}, the probability that a product will be established as having harmful effects as a result of non-company research once the product has finished its market run (T3). We can imagine a company A and a company B that produce the same general category of nanotechnology.

The research completed by company A, if made public, would add to the body of scientific evidence and understanding and, in that sense, would be equivalent to additional academic or public research. That additional contribution to public knowledge would presumably increase (if minimally) the likelihood that any adverse effects from company B's product will be identified by the time that product has finished its market run at T3. Company A's additional contribution to public knowledge, in other words, would boost company B's estimate of P_{T_3} and hence boost the expected cost of the do-nothing option. If we imagine not just one company engaging in research but 100 companies engaging in research, we can imagine that that research would significantly boost company no. 101's estimate of P_{T_3} that that company will use in choosing whether to continue to do nothing or instead commence research and follow the lead of companies no. 1–100.

One possible implication of this analysis, like the analysis regarding substantially identical products, is that broad voluntary engagement in research efforts within an industry could itself result in more, even broader engagement in research in the industry – at least if the results of all the research were accessible to the public. If the goal is to significantly increase voluntary research regarding products that contain a general category of technology that is poorly understood and potentially risky, an important hurdle is to secure a research commitment from a good number of the companies in the industry. Special incentives for early committers can produce the dividend of voluntary engagement in research by companies that will then follow suit in part because of their perception that the research that will be produced by the early committers, on net, will increase the likelihood that adverse effects could one day be tied to their products.

FDA PREEMPTION AS A MODEL

Liability relief as a *quid pro quo* for voluntary testing is a policy or legal reform that could, in theory, be adopted at the state, federal, or international level. Because at least initial state or international adoption seems less likely than federal adoption, this section focuses on how such a federal regime could and should be structured. But first, it is worth explaining the difficulties with a state-based or international approach.

The basic political economy of state legislatures and courts would work against the adoption of any liability relief reform in the context of nanotechnology products. State courts, applying existing state common law, perhaps could reduce liability for companies that engage in voluntary pre- and post-market testing of products. More readily, state legislatures could adopt such liability relief by statute. But states are unlikely to adopt such measures and, even if they did, are not well-equipped to ensure that the appropriate kind of testing and monitoring actually was undertaken. For an individual state, a reduction in liability means (presumably) a reduction in resources available to its injured citizens. Liability relief is thus an in-state cost.

The manufacturers (and perhaps even distributors) of nanotechnology products sold or consumed within a state in many cases would be based outside the state and indeed might be based outside the United States altogether. And there is likely to be skepticism that liability relief in any particular state would lead to significantly more testing of the products developed and manufactured in that state, given that those products presumably would be marketed not just in that state, but also throughout the country and perhaps the world.

Even if states were open to adopting liability relief, they would not be well-positioned to implement it. States do not have the staff and other resources to oversee pre- and post-market voluntary testing and monitoring (let alone to undertake such testing with company funds). There are no state drug agencies akin to the FDA; there is no state institute of health comparable to the National Institutes of Health. The building blocks for meaningful oversight and administration are found at the federal, not state, level. And knowing that, even state officials and politicians who see the case for liability relief are likely to look to the federal government for any liability reforms tied to oversight of testing.

At the international level, any proposed legal reform that confronts the basic limitations is the deep difficulty of bridging national differences and sovereignty concerns to form binding and enforceable accords. Tort liability, in particular, has long been regarded as a domestic/national prerogative and is not the subject of even significant "soft" international law. There are also no international oversight agencies as such akin to the FDA. One might imagine international coordination once the United States, Japan, and the European Union adopted some kind of liability program, but action at the nation state level almost certainly would have to come first.[32]

It would thus seem that any liability relief-for-testing regime would have to be, vis-à-vis and within the United States, a federal regime established by federal statute. Tort liability is, of course, a traditional domain of the states. Congress has interfered with state prerogatives vis-à-vis tort, despite federalism concerns, in two situations. The first is where some good or activity deemed essential to national welfare is arguably not being produced or might not be produced because of liability threats (e.g., nuclear power, certain types of aircraft). The second is where a thorough regime of mandatory federal testing administered by and approval given by the FDA has (arguably) ensured that a product reflects a considered federal judgment regarding the balance of benefits and costs. An implicit rationale for FDA preemption may be

[32] Another consideration of institutional design is how a regime of voluntary testing for U.S. liability relief would dovetail with international law. Under the World Trade Organization's evolving jurisprudence, a U.S. statute providing liability relief in return for testing probably would pass muster as long as the stated purpose of encouraging testing would be the protection of U.S. consumers and others from effects realized in the United States from the use and disposal of imported products, as opposed to protection of foreign workers and others from adverse effects from the manufacture of the products outside the United States. There might, therefore, be some limits on the testing that could be asked of foreign companies vis-à-vis worker exposures and safety.

that if companies are to be willing to take on the costs and the burdens of a thorough approval process, including testing, they need to or at least should be able to set aside concerns about state tort liability that might require even more testing, even more limits on releases of product, and even more product warnings. Liability relief from state tort law for voluntary testing of nanotechnology products under federal oversight would be similar to liability relief from state tort law for mandatory testing and approval by the FDA: in both cases, testing with oversight would translate into some reduction in liability.

FDA preemption of common law tort law, however, has been and remains extremely controversial. A regime of liability relief for voluntary testing of nanotechnology products, depending on the design of the regime, could be subject to the same kinds of objections. To be tenable and succeed, therefore, a liability relief for voluntary testing and monitoring regime should have the component discussed in the following sections.

Genuine Statutory (Rather Than Agency) Preemption

One of the most controversial aspects of FDA preemption of state tort actions is that federal statutes, in plain language, do not clearly call for such preemption of tort actions at all. As a result, commentators – as well as some of the Justices – have criticized FDA preemption of common law suits as a joint creation of the courts and federal bureaucrats, instead of Congress.[33]

Preemption doctrine makes congressional intent the touchstone of when state law, including common law, is preempted. This is appropriate because, in a federal system in which state prerogatives necessitate respect, preemption should be regarded as an exceptional or unusual action and hence one that has courts should recognize only with clear direction from the only federal branch of government explicitly authorized to make federal law, Congress. Thus, to be fully legitimate, any regime of voluntary testing for liability must be built on specific language in federal statutes providing when and to what extent state common law claims are preempted.

Preemption Limited to Torts Based on Failures to Test or Monitor

Another source of controversy regarding FDA preemption of state tort case has been that it has been extended (or industry has sought to extend it, but not yet succeeded, as in *Wyeth v. Levine*) to risk or dangers of which the manufacturer/defendant allegedly had clear knowledge. Defendants have argued, with some success, that they were not required to warn of risks they comprehended as long as the warning they did issue had been approved by FDA. Critics of preemption in this context argue that federal

33 For example, Justice Ginsburg criticized the Court's finding of preemption of state common law suits under the Medical Device Act (MDA) as "not mandated by Congress" and "at odds with the MDA's central purpose: to protect consumer safety."

regulators sometimes do not understand or receive the necessary data or are unduly pressured to accept incomplete warning. To the extent this is so, federal preemption rewards companies for sitting on "bad" information and knowingly endangering the public without warning.

These same concerns all counsel in favor of circumscribing tort preemption as a *quid pro quo* for voluntary testing and monitoring to state tort claims predicated on allegations that the manufacturer failed to conduct adequate testing or monitoring and hence did not apprehend the risk from its products and make decisions based on knowledge of those risks. Companies that sat on "bad information," failed to disclose it as required, or misled the relevant agencies or public in the disclosure that was made would not be rewarded with liability relief. (If relief took the form of insurance premium subsidies, *see infra*, those subsidies could be recovered by the government if company misconduct later came to light.) Moreover, because a voluntary regime would not mandate any particular labels or warning labels for products, companies could not argue that they had every reason to think they need not have or should not have included any warning based on "bad information" in addition to those required by federal regulators.

Government Oversight and Transparency

In the FDA drug and device approval context, there have been strong claims made that there has been too little vigorous agency oversight of private research, and too little transparency, and hence too little oversight by the general public of failures of regulators.[34] The litany of charges includes that large companies pressure scientists to reach favorable results; scientists fail to disclose all conflicts or private finding sources; there is an inadequate accounting by regulators and lack of public information regarding studies that are abandoned, suspended, or left open indefinitely because preliminary results would not be helpful to the sponsoring company; and the public lack access to the data in studies submitted to regulators. Inadequate funding of FDA and other oversight bodies is another theme of the critics. Along with the criticisms have come many proposals, including more government research with public funding, a public registry for all initiated studies with updates, public access to the data supporting or underlying private study results relied on by regulators, and thorough disclosure of conflicts requirements for scientists and so on.[35]

34 Two powerful indictments of regulatory oversights are David Michaels, Doubt Is Their Product: How Industry's Assault on Science Threatens Your Health (Oxford, UK: Oxford University Press, 2008); Marcia Angell, The Truth About the Drug Companies: How They Deceive Us and What To Do About It (New York: Random House, 2004).

35 Two excellent sources regarding criticisms of the current regime and reform proposals are Thomas O. McGarity & Wendy Wagner, Bending Science: How Special Interests Corrupt Public Health Research (Cambridge, MA: Harvard University Press, 2008), especially chapters 10–12; and Christopher H. Schroeder & Rena Steinzor, eds., Rescuing Science From Politics (Durham, NC: Carolina Academic Press, 2006), especially pp. 281–298.

All of the concerns about oversight and public access and all the possible reforms that have been invoked vis-à-vis the FDA mandatory approval process would have relevance to a voluntary regime of testing and monitoring as a *quid pro quo* for liability relief. These oversight and transparency concerns would need to be addressed for a voluntary regime to gain widespread legitimacy. One particularly thorny issue concerns confidential business information: nanotechnology product developers and producers have and probably will continue to insist that such information is embedded in much of their testing data and reports and that such data and reports therefore cannot be disclosed to the public. Specific guidelines and review mechanisms, however, must be used to ensure that "confidential business information" is not invoked expansively to curtail all meaningful public access. Even with respect to core confidential business information, there must be creative means to ensure the substance of public accountability, such as release of detailed summaries by regulators and designated NGO (or other designated third-party inspectors) access to and review of the data.

Subsidized Insurance as an Alternative Liability-Relief Mechanism

FDA preemption – or any tort preemption – is also controversial because it can leave some injured persons without any compensation. One of the essential roles of the tort law is compensation, after all. The same concern would apply to injured persons whose suits would be preempted or partially preempted by any nanotechnology liability relief regime based on voluntary testing. One can of course argue that a regime of liability relief does not necessarily result in anyone being denied compensation because, in the absence of liability relief, companies might not have tested their products, and the information regarding adverse effects would not have come to light. However, in any particular case, it will be impossible to know whether the information regarding adverse effects and their causes would have come to light even in the absence of the promise of liability relief. Moreover, from the *ex post* perspective of an injured person and his family, what truly matters is not *ex ante* incentives and considerations of institutional design, but just the current moment and whether compensation is available now for very real injuries.

From the perspective of honoring the compensation mission of the tort system, the best way to provide liability relief would not be limits on liability *per se*, but rather subsidies for liability insurance. The federal government already provides or subsidizes insurance directly or re-insurance guarantees in some contexts[36] and could also subsidize part of the cost of private insurance premiums for companies that opt into a pre- and post-market testing regime for nanotechnology products. Insurance

[36] *See* Terrorism Risk Insurance Act of 2002, Public Law No. 107–297, 106 Stat. 2322 (requiring insurers not to exclude terrorism-related claims and providing for the government to act as an excess insurer of terrorism-related claims); Price-Anderson Act, 42 USC § 2210, as amended by the Energy Policy Act of 2005 (requiring nuclear power provider to carry an insurance and providing for federal payment of insurance claims in excess of the private insurance mandated by the statute).

subsidies could be as powerful an incentive for companies as direct liability relief, while avoiding the problem of the uncompensated injured. And insurance subsidies could be combined with partial tort preemption in a blended regime that would mean reduced, but not eliminated, compensation for injured persons.

There are, however, several problems with an insurance subsidy approach. First, there is a significant history of (in the view of many) industry capture of government insurance or insurance subsidy programs. Second, government insurance subsidies are, like direct funding of research, a government expenditure that must compete with a great many other possible claims on government resources. It is true, however, that the magnitude of insurance subsidies may be hard to calculate, and they are partly to be paid, if at all, in the future, so they are not particularly visible in the budgeting process. But that opaqueness, although making them more politically viable, also makes insurance subsidies more susceptible to interest group manipulation.

The value of insurance subsidies as a means to incentivize participation in a testing regime would be enhanced if the subsidies were tied to a requirement that all producers of nanotechnology products carry adequate liability insurance that does not exclude nanotechnology-related claims.[37] With a mandatory insurance requirement, small start-up companies that might be somewhat insensitive to long-term liability risks would have an incentive to test generally to keep private insurance premiums down (to the extent that insurers would give them credit for testing) and an incentive to test products to qualify for government insurance subsidies.[38] Indeed, the availability of subsidies might help counter arguments by such companies that they lack the cash for testing and insurance and therefore will be driven out of business if additional costs are foisted on them.

It is true, nonetheless, that the liability relief regime outlined here might be of greater advantage to larger, more liability-sensitive and perhaps better-funded companies than small start-ups with potentially limited lives as legal entities. It is also true that the adoption of mandatory insurance requirements with liability relief or subsidies for voluntary testing might change the patterns of organization among producers of nanotechnology products. We might observe fewer stand-alone start-ups and more collaborations and (in terms of product development) earlier collaborations between start-ups and larger companies. But such a shift in industries that produce nanotechnology products might be a good thing, reflecting the fact that the

37 *See* Robin Wilson, *Nanotechnology: The Challenge of Regulating Known Unknowns*, 34 J. L., MED. AND ETHICS 704, 711 (2006) (advocating that nanotechnology developers who receive federal funds be required to carry commercial liability insurance); Maksim Rakhlin, *Regulating Nanotechnology: A private-Public Insurance Solution*, DUKE L. & TECH. REV. (2008) (iBrief) (advocating mandatory insurance coverage for nanotechnology producers with government guarantees of liabilities over coverage caps, modeled after the insurance regime for nuclear power producers under the Price-Anderson Act and the Energy Policy Act of 2005).

38 Compare Davies, *supra* note 1, at 22 ("A major disadvantage of voluntary programs is that they may leave out the people who most need to be included. In the case of NT, small firms making risky products and large firms with small consciences are not likely to volunteer to do health testing or to give EPA information that might indicate significant risk.").

production and marketing of potentially very risky products (as with FDA-approved prescription drugs) may require the extensive participation, if not dominance, of relatively large corporate entities.

Features Unique to a Voluntary Regime

The goal of obtaining significant participation by industry makes it essential that there be some early participants who can in effect draw in later participants. Greater liability relief could be offered to early participants as an inducement, perhaps in the form of greater insurance subsidies than those that would be made available to later participants. Another inducement for early participants might be their ability to advertise to consumers and others that they have opted into and met the guidelines of a safety regime, whereas (if that were true) their competitors had not yet done so. As Wendy Wagner has suggested (although not in the nanotechnology context), legal authorization and protection for companies to make such claims might offer enough of a competitive advantage to encourage testing that they otherwise might have foregone.[39] Whether companies would regard the ability to make such claims as advantageous is unknown, but if they do, that ability, coupled with special liability relief incentives based on early entry into the voluntary testing regime, might be enough to energize an initial round of participation that could set the ground for broad industry participation.

CONCLUSION

This chapter offers a model of why nanotechnology companies might forego safety testing and monitoring in order to avoid liability and suggests a regime of liability relief as a *quid pro quo* for voluntary pre- and post-market testing and monitoring. Nanotechnology products fit the conceptual space in which such a voluntary regime might be helpful – a space in which the company developing the product rationally may foresee some liability risk in the absence of company research into environmental, health, and safety effects, but also rationally may perceive that such research itself could create liability that the company otherwise would have avoided.

[39] *See* Wendy E. Wagner, *Using Competition-Based Regulation to Bridge the Toxics Data Gap*, 83 Ind. L. J. 629, 631 (2008). In the consumer products realm of the nanotechnology product market, making such a claim could offer substantial competitive advantage as a practical matter if it were accompanied by an effective labeling regime that required all products containing nanotechnology to contain some kind of statement of that fact. However, if that were done, Wagner's point might be even more applicable in the nanotechnology context than in the context of industrial chemicals that are the focus of the Toxic Substances Control Act, because the primary consumers of such chemicals are businesses rather than retail, individual consumers.

8

Transnational New Governance and the International Coordination of Nanotechnology Oversight

Gary E. Marchant, Kenneth W. Abbott, Douglas J. Sylvester, Lyn M. Gulley

Two critical questions for the regulatory oversight of nanotechnology are (1) at what level of government should regulation take place, and (2) what form should regulation take? These questions are intrinsically linked. Regarding the first question, it is widely assumed that national governments are the appropriate locus of authority for regulating technologies, including nanotechnology. In this view, sub-national, international, and private measures should all be relegated, at most, to subservient and tentative roles. Regarding the second question, because national governments are presumptively the appropriate regulators, often it is assumed that the traditional tools of governmental oversight – command-and-control regulations – are appropriate for addressing the risks of new technologies.

Despite this mainstream wisdom, we and others have argued that *international coordination* of national regulation would provide important benefits.[1] International coordination promises to avoid many of the pitfalls experienced by prior technologies as a result of inconsistent national regulation. In addition, an international approach

[1] Kenneth W. Abbott, Douglas J. Sylvester, and Gary E. Marchant, *Transnational Regulation: Reality or Romanticism?*, in INTERNATIONAL HANDBOOK ON REGULATING NANOTECHNOLOGIES, eds. Graeme Hodge, Diana Bowman and Andrew Maynard (2010); Gary E. Marchant, Douglas J. Sylvester, Kenneth W. Abbott, Tara Lynn Danforth, *International Harmonization of Regulation of Nanomedicine*, STUDIES IN ETHICS, LAW & TECHNOLOGY 3(3): Article 6 (2009); Linda Breggin, et al., Securing the Promise of Nanotechnologies: Towards Transatlantic Regulatory Cooperation, Envtl. Law Inst. & London School of Economics (Sept. 2009), available at http://www.chathamhouse.org.uk/files/14692_r0909_nanotechnologies.pdf (last visited April 2, 2010); Vladimir Murashov & John Howard, *The US Must Help Set International Standards for Nanotechnology*, 3 NATURE NANOTECHNOLOGY 635 (2008); Diana M. Bowman & Graeme A. Hodge, *A Small Matter of Regulation: An International Review of Nanotechnology Regulation*, 8 COLUMBIA SCI. TECH. L. REV. 1 (2007); Environmental Law Institute, *Symposium on Nanotechnology Governance: Environmental Management from an International Perspective* (2006); J. Pelley & M. Saner, International Approaches to the Regulatory Governance of Nanotechnology, Ottawa: Carleton University

Research for this work was supported by Department of Energy Genomes to Life ELSI grant #DE-FG02-07ER64475. The views expressed in this chapter do not represent the views of the Department of Energy or the U.S. Government.

to regulation may create incentives for inter-state cooperation in trade, environmental protection, labor, and the numerous other fields that nanotechnology will necessarily implicate.

We focus here on a third advantage of international coordination: it offers an opportunity for states to develop and promote new regulatory approaches that are both more flexible and responsive than command-and-control and better attuned to promoting the benefits of nanotechnology, as well as controlling its risks. In particular, we argue that at the international level – or more appropriately, the transnational level – an approach that one of us has called *transnational new governance*[2] is particularly suitable to addressing the challenges nanotechnology currently poses. Under that approach, regulatory authority is distributed among public, private, and public-private actors and institutions, and regulation takes the form of public and private "soft law," as well as legally binding rules. Indeed, although there may be a place for treaties or other formal international agreements and institutions (*international old governance*) in dealing with scientific and technological innovations,[3] the extensive time and resources required for their negotiation, and the political difficulties inherent in inter-state negotiating processes, make such formal harmonization unlikely, at least in the near term.[4]

At the domestic level, moreover, while environmental, health, and safety regulation typically involves publicly adopted "hard law" that establishes command-and-control requirements (*domestic old governance*), the current complexity of nanotechnology – including its toxicological uncertainties and the heterogeneity of nanomaterials – make this approach challenging, if not impossible.[5] In these circumstances, international coordination of national responses (including the tentative national measures already beginning to emerge) can do more than minimize costly inconsistencies: it can also help to promote mutually reinforcing forms of *domestic new governance*.

In this chapter, we consider a number of measures that could help minimize costly divergences in national regulation while promoting responsive regulatory measures. As we urge the adoption of new governance approaches at both the national

Regulatory Governance Initiative (2009), available at http://www.carleton.ca/regulation/publications/Nanotechnology_Regulation_Paper_April2009.pdf (last visited April 2, 2010); Gary E. Marchant & Douglas Sylvester, *Transnational Models for Regulation of Nanotechnology*, 34 J. Law, Medicine & Ethics 714 (2006).

2 Kenneth W. Abbott & Duncan Snidal, *Strengthening International Regulation Through Transnational New Governance: Overcoming the Orchestration Deficit*, 42 Vand. J. Transnat'l L. 501 (2009).

3 Kenneth W. Abbott, *An International Framework Agreement on Scientific and Technological Innovation and Regulation*, forthcoming in The Growing Gap Between Emerging Technologies and Legal-Ethical Oversight: The Pacing Problem, ed. Gary E. Marchant et al. (2011).

4 Breggin et al., *supra* note 1.

5 Gary E. Marchant, Douglas S. Sylvester & Kenneth W. Abbott, *Risk Management Principles for Nanotechnology*, 2 NanoEthics 43 (2008).

and international levels, our recommendations open the door to synchronizing the oversight of nanotechnology on a global basis – both horizontally, as between states, and vertically, as between the national and international levels.

In the remainder of this chapter, we explore the benefits, challenges, and opportunities of international coordination, focusing on the role new governance mechanisms can play in horizontal and vertical coordination. Section I of this chapter makes the case for international coordination. We first suggest that the travails of prior technologies, especially genetically modified foods, illustrate the disruptions and inefficiencies that can result from disparate national regulations; we then identify some positive advantages of coordination. Section II provides a realistic assessment of the current state of national nanotechnology regulation – which is already starting to diverge, albeit modestly. We also identify certain impediments to international coordination, arguing that inter-state competition, vastly different regulatory approaches, and other factors make deep, legally binding international harmonization unlikely. Building on this assessment, Section III offers some tentative thoughts about current and proposed transnational new governance initiatives that could achieve a significant level of international coordination while also encouraging more flexible and responsive regulatory oversight.

I. THE CASE FOR INTERNATIONAL COORDINATION

The benefits of international regulatory coordination for the successful introduction and dissemination of new technologies are most clearly demonstrated by the difficulties faced by prior technologies for which international coordination was lacking. The best example is also the most current: the experience of genetically modified (GM) foods. We first summarize the lessons of that experience, highlighting the ways in which the lack of coordination impeded development of the technology, then consider the affirmative benefits of coordination.

A. *The Lessons of GM Foods*

There is no better argument for regulatory coordination than the story of GM foods; that story clearly illustrates the problems that can develop when nations go their own ways in regulating products traded internationally. The disparate regulatory standards of the European Union (EU), United States, and other importing and exporting nations have created a remarkable array of problems. These include restrictions on trade in products approved in one country but not another, recalls and embargoes imposed because a product not authorized in an importing country is found (even in very small quantities) to have contaminated a product exported from a nation with less restrictive regulations, disincentives for food-exporting nations to grow potentially beneficial GM crops because of the potential repercussions for trade, legal proceedings in the World Trade Organization (WTO), and distortions of national action on technical issues such as GM food-labeling tolerances.[6]

Most emblematic of these disruptions and conflicts is the U.S.-EU dispute before the WTO. In 2003, the United States, Canada, and Argentina initiated WTO proceedings against the EU and six of its member states for unduly delaying approval of GM foods and crops. The complainants argued that the EU restrictions would "harm worldwide agricultural exports, impede the development of advanced agricultural biotechnology, and increase negative public perceptions of GM foods."[7] The United States contended that EU regulatory delays were costing U.S. corn producers approximately $300 million per year.[8] These effects resulted from inconsistencies in the regulations applied to GM foods by the complainants and the respondents: the United States and other exporting countries treated GM foods much the same as non-GM products; the EU and its members applied more stringent *sui generis* restrictions on GM foods.[9] The WTO held in favor of the complainants, ruling that the EU had failed to provide a timely process for regulatory approvals.[10] Yet the dispute still lingers today, as several EU member states have refused to approve GM foods and crops.

In addition, after the EU amended its regulations in 2004 to impose labeling and traceability requirements on GM food and feed inconsistent with the standards in the United States – a major supplier to the EU of soybean products for animal feed – U.S. soy exports to the EU plummeted. The American Soybean Association reported a drop in exports of 65% (from $2.5 billion to $874 million per year) after the new regulations went into effect.[11] This caused major losses not only to U.S. producers, but also to the EU animal feed industry, which lost its main supply source. The European Commission noted that animal feed in the EU became 50% more expensive than in the United States because of the trade barrier and

[6] *See, e.g.*, USDA Advisory Committee on Biotechnology and 21st Century Agriculture, *Global Traceability and Labeling Requirements for Agricultural Biotechnology Derived Products: Impacts and Implications for the United States* (Feb. 8, 2005), available at http://www.usda.gov/documents/tlpaperv37final.pdf (last visited April 4, 2010); Mark Mansour & Sarah Key, *From Farm to Fork: The Impact on Global Commerce of the New European Union Biotechnology Regulatory Scheme*, 38 INT'L LAWYER 55 (2004); Rick Weiss, *Food War Claims Its Casualties: High-Tech Crop Fight Victimizes Farmers*, WASH. POST, Sept. 12, 1999, at A1; J. Howard Beales, *Modification and Consumer Information: Modern Biotechnology and the Regulation of Information*, 55 FOOD & DRUG LAW J. 105 (2000).

[7] Debra M. Strauss & Melanie C. Strauss, *Globalization and National Sovereignty: Controlling the International Food Supply in the Age of Biotechnology*, 15 J. LEG. STUD. BUS. 75, 80 (2009).

[8] Charles E. Hanrahan, Agricultural Biotechnology: The US-EU Dispute (CRS Rep. RS21556), at 1 (March 10, 2006).

[9] Strauss & Strauss, *supra* note 7, at 80–82.

[10] World Trade Organization, "European Communities: Measures Affecting the Approval and Marketing of Biotech Products," WT/DS291/R, WT/DS292/R, WT/DS293/R, 2006, http://www.wto.org/english/tratop_e/dispu_e/cases_e/ds291_e.htm (last visited December 14, 2009).

[11] American Soybean Association, "ASA Calls EU Traceability and Labeling Review a Whitewash," May 10, 2006, press release, http://www.soygrowers.com/newsroom/releases/2006_releases/r051006b.htm (last visited February 26, 2010).

warned that the failure to resolve the regulatory divergence could result in "dramatic consequences" for member states.[12] The EU Agriculture Directorate called it a "crisis" for European livestock growers, which could, in a worst-case scenario, result in a mass slaughter of livestock.[13] As a recent study of the EU-U.S. GM foods dispute observed,

> The transatlantic GMO dispute has brought into conflict two longtime allies, economically interdependent democracies with a long record of bilateral and multilateral cooperation in both economics and security. Yet the dispute has developed into one of the most bitter and intractable transatlantic and global conflicts, resisting efforts at resolution in bilateral networks and multilateral regimes alike, and resulting in a bitterly contested legal battle before the WTO.[14]

Numerous other disruptions have been caused by inconsistent national regulations and approval procedures for GM foods. Many countries restricted rice imports from the United States after an unapproved GM variety known as Liberty Link was found in certain U.S. rice shipments in 2006, resulting in the loss of hundreds of millions of dollars by U.S. farmers and seed companies.[15] Liberty Link was subsequently approved by the United States, but not by many of its trading partners, so the problem lingered for several years. The EU imposed costly testing and certification requirements for all Chinese rice products after finding a form of GM rice (known as Bt 63) in certain rice shipments from China.[16] The EU, Japan, and Brazil severely restricted imports of Canadian flax in 2009–2010, after certain shipments were found to contain trace amounts of a GM variety not approved in those jurisdictions, causing economic distress to Canadian flax farmers and their customers.[17]

In sum, GM foods provide a sober illustration of the disruption and conflict that can arise from divergent national regulation of inherently global technologies. Once the national regulatory paths for GM foods began to diverge, especially as between the United States and EU, national pride and path dependency ensured

[12] *EC Warns EU of Serious Consequences if Crop, Food Approval Process Suspended*, BIOTECH WATCH (BNA), Dec. 16, 2009.

[13] EurActiv, "'Crisis looming' as EU Blocks GM-Soy Imports," October 23, 2009, http://www.euractiv.com/en/cap/crisis-looming-eu-blocks-gm-soy-imports/article-186681 (last visited December 16, 2009); Amos Tversky, *Europe's Anti-GM Stance to Presage Animal Feed Shortage?*, 110 NATURE BIOTECHNOLOGY 1065 (2007).

[14] MARK A. POLLACK & GREGORY C. SHAFFER, WHEN COOPERATION FAILS: THE INTERNATIONAL LAW AND POLITICS OF GENETICALLY MODIFIED FOODS 2 (Oxford, UK: Oxford University Press, 2009).

[15] Marc Gunther, *Attack of the Mutant Rice*, FORTUNE, July 9, 2007, at 74, 77.

[16] European Union, Commission Decision 2008/289/EC of 3 April 2008 on emergency measures regarding the unauthorised genetically modified organism 'Bt 63' in rice products, available at http://gmo-crl.jrc.ec.europa.eu/doc/Bt63_2008_289_EC.pdf (last visited February 26, 2010).

[17] *Canadian Flax Output to Drop as GM Issue Continues*, TMCnews, Jan. 5, 2010, available at http://www.tmcnet.com/usubmit/2010/01/05/4558777.htm; Rod Nickel, *Canada Flax Not Shipping to EU, Key Port to Close*, Reuters UK, Dec. 9, 2009, available at http://ca.reuters.com/article/domesticnews/idCATRE5B84JP20091209 (last visited April 4, 2010).

that the gaps continued to widen. Many of the resulting differences remain unresolved and are likely to remain irresolvable for the foreseeable future. It is essential that nanotechnology and other innovative technologies avoid going down the same unfortunate pathway.

B. *Benefits of International Coordination*

While the GM foods experience illustrates the perils of uncoordinated national regulation, one can identify important affirmative benefits from coordinating regulatory oversight of nanotechnology.[18] First and perhaps foremost, of course, coordination – in the sense of limiting divergent regulations – would limit disruptions to international trade in nanotechnology products, along with the resulting economic losses and political tensions.

Second, coordination would create substantial efficiencies for researchers, manufacturers, and distributors of nanotechnology products in international commerce. For scientists and engineers who increasingly undertake joint research and development projects that span national borders, coordination would reduce the costs and legal risks of collaboration.[19] For companies that produce and distribute nanotechnology products, coordination would facilitate qualification for access to markets across the entire product life cycle, from product design and labeling requirements to product testing protocols and regulatory submission dossiers. For facilities that produce nanotechnology products, which for a given manufacturer may be located in several countries, coordination of environmental and occupational safety and health requirements would facilitate the adoption of uniform environmental, health, and safety programs, including internal company compliance, product stewardship, worker training, and reporting programs.

Third, coordination would help provide equivalent levels of protection to workers, consumers, and other groups in different jurisdictions, both with respect to products produced domestically and to those sold across borders. On the production side, moreover, providing equivalent protections might constrain the emergence of a "race to the bottom" – with states potentially competing to develop and attract nanotechnology investments by relaxing safety rules – and of "risk havens" – jurisdictions that sacrifice public health and safety for the short-term benefits of increased investment or tax revenues, often creating negative externalities for other countries by exporting locally produced products.[20]

[18] *See generally* Abbott et al., *supra* note 1; Marchant et al. *supra* note 1; Breggin et al., *supra* note 1, at 7.

[19] *See generally* Douglas J. Sylvester & Diana Megan Bowman, *English Garden or Tangled Grounds? Navigating the Nanotechnology Patent Landscape*, in BIOMEDICAL NANOTECHNOLOGY: METHODS IN MOLECULAR BIOLOGY-PATENT LANDSCAPES (John M. Walker, ed.) (forthcoming 2010) (draft available at http://papers.ssrn.com/sol3/papers.cfm?abstract_id=1535650) (identifying that pending nanotechnology patents increasingly include multinational inventors and institutions).

[20] *See e.g.*, Gareth Porter, *Trade Competition and Pollution Standards: "Race to the Bottom" or "Stuck at the Bottom"*, 8 J. ENV. & DEV. 133 (1999) (arguing that international coordination and setting of minimum standards is necessary to increase incentives in developing countries to raise environmental and

Fourth, coordination would produce *economies of scale* benefits for regulators. It would facilitate the sharing of resources and expertise among national regulators and provide opportunities for learning from the experiences of others – rather than leaving it to each jurisdiction independently to evaluate the risks of nanotechnology products and decide on appropriate regulatory responses. Beyond reducing the burden on regulators, information sharing and learning should significantly increase the quality of national regulation, disseminate regulatory knowledge and good regulatory practices to developing countries and other states with limited capacity, and allow regulators to prepare for and respond more effectively to international externalities caused by the use of new technologies elsewhere.[21]

Finally, as the previous point suggests, international regulatory coordination would almost inevitably be based on widely agreed-upon substantive principles, not merely on a mechanical notion of reducing divergences among national measures. As a result, coordination procedures could help steer national regulators toward superior forms of regulation.[22] Perhaps most significantly, coordination procedures could promote efficient and responsive forms of regulation, including the decentralized, participatory and responsive techniques associated with new governance.[23]

For all of these reasons, many scholars and governments have recognized the benefits of international coordination of nanotechnology regulation[24] – although relatively little coordination has in fact taken place. In Section II of this chapter, we consider some of the practical impediments that limit the potential for coordination in the real world, especially through the traditional mechanisms of international law.

II. THE REALISTIC PROSPECTS FOR INTERNATIONAL COORDINATION

International coordination of nanotechnology regulation faces major impediments. First, international harmonization around common standards is not always ideal, notwithstanding the benefits of coordination described in the previous section. There are some significant arguments in favor of at least partially divergent national standards, such as the need to account for different social, political, and legal structures and the benefits that might accrue from experimentation with different approaches in different jurisdictions.[25]

A second problem is that some divergent national regulations have already begun to appear.[26] The United States, the EU, and other jurisdictions have faced growing

other standards). But see David M. Konisky, *Regulatory Competition and Environmental Enforcement: Is There a Race to the Bottom?*, 51 Am. J. of Pol. Sci. 853 (2007) (questioning, in domestic context, whether state environmental policy is driven by asymmetric responses to policies of competing states).

21 Abbott, *supra* note 3, at 4–5.

22 *Id.* at 5–6.

23 *Id.*

24 *See supra* note 1.

25 Breggin et al., *supra* note 1, at 7; Marchant et al., *supra* note 1.

26 *See e.g.*, Breggin et al., *supra* note 1, at 47–56.

pressure to address the perceived risks of nanotechnology, from nongovernmental organizations (NGOs), legislators, journalists, scientists, scholars, and even some industry representatives.[27] In response, those jurisdictions are tentatively adopting regulatory measures.[28] As of yet, however, the new measures have not reached a level that would render coordination practically impossible.

We have recently created a searchable, online database[29] of worldwide nanotechnology regulations, and that database clearly shows the beginnings of a trend toward greater regulation of nanotechnology – regulation entirely devoid of international coordination considerations. For example, the U.S. Environmental Protection Agency (EPA) has proposed a Significant New Use Rule (SNUR) under the Toxic Substances Control Act (TSCA) that would require manufacturers of multi-walled and single-walled carbon nanotubes to notify the agency of each new product before it is commercialized.[30] EPA has also publicly stated that it is developing proposed rules under TSCA section 8(a) to require data reporting on nanomaterials and under TSCA section 4 to require testing of certain nanoscale materials.[31] In the EU, regulators have taken advantage of a pending revision of the regulatory frameworks for novel foods and cosmetics to insert specific labeling requirements for nanotechnology.[32] Europe is also moving toward regulating certain nanomaterials under its new REACH program.[33] The Australian government has recently started down its own unique regulatory path by proposing a regulatory notification and assessment scheme for industrial nanomaterials.[34]

27 Kevin Reinert, Larry Andrews & Russell Keenan, *Nanotechnology Nexus – Intersection of Research, Science, Technology, and Regulation*, 12 HUMAN ECOL. RISK ASSESSMENT 811 (2006); Robert Lee & P.D. Jose, *Self-interest, Self-restraint and Corporate Responsibility for Nanotechnologies: Emerging Dilemmas for Modern Managers*, 20 TECH. ANALYSIS & STRATEGIC MANAGEMENT 113 (2008); Andrew D. Maynard, *Safe Handling of Nanotechnology*, 44 NATURE 267 (2006).

28 In addition to addressing risk, regulation can enhance public confidence in nanotechnology. Douglas J. Sylvester, Kenneth W, Abbott & Gary E. Marchant, *Not Again! Public Perception, Regulation, and Nanotechnology*, 3 REGULATION & GOVERNANCE 165 (2009).

29 The Nanotech Regulatory Document Archive, available at http://nanotech.law.asu.edu/.

30 EPA, Proposed Significant New Use Rules on Certain Chemical Substances, 74 Fed. Reg. 57,430 (2009).

31 EPA, Control of Nanoscale Materials Under the Toxic Substances Control Act (undated), available at http://www.epa.gov/oppt/nano/#existingmaterials (last visited April 5, 2010).

32 Position of the European Parliament adopted at first reading on 25 March 2009 with a view to the adoption of Regulation (EC) No . . . /2009 of the European Parliament and of the Council on novel foods, amending Regulation (EC) No 1331/2008 and repealing Regulation (EC) No 258/97, available at http://www.europarl.europa.eu/sides/getDoc.do?pubRef=-//EP//TEXT ± TA ± P6-TA-2009–0171 ± 0 ± DOC ± XML ± V0//EN&language=EN (last visited April 5, 2010); *New European Nanotechnology Decree Requires Labelling of Nanoparticles in Cosmetics*, NANOWERK NEWS, Nov. 27, 2009, available at http://www.nanowerk.com/news/newsid=13723.php (last visited April 5, 2010).

33 Diana M. Bowman & Geert Van Calster, *Does REACH Go Too Far?*, 2 NATURE NANOTECHNOLOGY 525 (2007).

34 Australian Government, National Industrial Chemicals Notification and Assessment Scheme, Proposals for Regulatory Reform of Industrial Nanomaterials – Public Discussion Draft (Nov. 2009), available at http://www.nicnas.gov.au/Current_Issues/Nanotechnology/Consultation%20Papers/NICNAS_Nano_PUBLIC_DISCUSSION_PAPER_PDF.pdf (last visited April 5, 2010).

To be sure, most current regulatory actions are narrowly focused requirements applicable only to specific classes of products. For example, the EPA SNUR will address only carbon nanotubes and will impose only notice and certain exposure reduction actions, whereas the EU labeling measures are limited to food and cosmetics. What is more, these measures are not general, *sui generis* approaches to the regulation of nanotechnology; they are incremental actions, tailored to and limited by existing or revised regulatory frameworks, such as the U.S. TSCA statute and the EU novel foods program.

A major reason for the tentative nature of national responses is the difficulty of formulating *any* form of nanotechnology regulation at this time. The technology is developing very rapidly; its forms and applications are enormously heterogeneous; it can potentially alter the fundamental properties of substances. Indeed, because of its protean character, nanotechnology has yet to be defined in a legally feasible way. There also remain major uncertainties and data gaps regarding the risks of diverse nanomaterials. All of these features create difficult hurdles for traditional approaches to regulation.[35]

From the perspective of international coordination, these difficulties bring both good and bad news. On the positive side, they have kept national regulations narrow, incremental, and limited in number, making it easier to move toward a coordinated response. On the negative side, however, the same difficulties have led governments to embed their early regulations within existing statutory frameworks, which are legally, politically, and culturally specific. As a result, the first steps toward national regulation are already moving down divergent regulatory pathways, which are inherently difficult to bridge and may not reflect the most desirable approaches.

The difficulties of regulation pose especially high hurdles for formal, international old governance approaches to coordination, such as the negotiation of a substantive treaty for nanotechnology or other new technologies.[36] We have already identified some general problems with a formal legal approach: negotiations are time-consuming and require both substantial resources and serious political commitment. Neither resources nor commitment appear to be available today, as states face many more pressing issues – from climate change, to reshaping the global financial architecture, to nuclear proliferation – as well as stringent financial constraints. Because future amendments to a treaty would face similar transactions costs, international old governance would be relatively inflexible and unresponsive to changes in knowledge and other circumstances.[37] In addition, treaties face well-known problems of compliance and enforcement.

35 Marchant et al., *supra* note 5, at 43–44; Marcia C. Powell, Martin P.A. Griffin & Stephanie Tai, *Bottom-Up Risk Regulation? How Nanotechnology Risk Knowledge Gaps Challenge Federal and State Environmental Agencies*, 42 ENVT'L MANAGEMENT 426, 433 (2008); Lee & Jose, *supra* note 28, at 117.

36 Breggin, *supra* note 1, at xiii.

37 As discussed further below, one type of treaty, the framework convention, is designed to address these difficulties.

The current difficulties in formulating any type of nanotechnology regulation add a serious substantive hurdle. Simply put, an effective treaty requires strong substantive content, well-tuned to the nature of the underlying problems.[38] Under present circumstances, identifying appropriate substantive terms, let alone reaching international agreement on them, seems virtually impossible. Although the case for international coordination remains strong, then, unless some tragic nanotechnology crisis emerges to trigger regulatory change,[39] the traditional machinery of international law will be an inadequate tool of coordination.

III. TRANSNATIONAL NEW GOVERNANCE AND NANOTECHNOLOGY OVERSIGHT

A variety of new governance mechanisms specifically focused on nanotechnology oversight are currently being developed, partly in response to the limitations of international old governance. Many of these are domestic in origin, yet most are expressly intended to be applied transnationally, or replicated in other countries. We first discuss the benefits and limitations of this approach in general and then describe some significant specific initiatives.

A. *The Advantages and Limitations of New Governance Approaches*

Old governance is state-centric, concentrating regulatory authority in legislative and regulatory organs (domestic legislatures and agencies; international organizations and treaty bodies); it relies on top-down legal mandates (statutes and regulations; treaties). In new governance, in contrast, regulatory authority is decentralized across a range of public, private, and public-private actors and institutions, drawing on the expertise and regulatory capacities of diverse societal actors.[40]

One manifestation of transnational new governance is the rise of so-called "transgovernmental" institutions, in which national regulators, legislators, prosecutors, and even judges – rather than "states" as such – collaborate more or less informally to exchange information, provide assistance, adopt common norms, and cooperate on implementation.[41] More broadly, public agencies encourage firms, industry associations, and professional groups to regulate themselves and encourage civil society groups to participate in public and private regulatory arrangements. Public agencies also collaborate directly with firms, industry and professional groups, NGOs, and

38 *See* Kenneth W. Abbott & Duncan Snidal, *Pathways to International Cooperation*, in THE IMPACT OF INTERNATIONAL LAW ON INTERNATIONAL COOPERATION (E. Benvenisti & M. Hirsch, eds., Cambridge, MA: Cambridge University Press, 2004), at 50–84.

39 *See* Walter Mattli & Ngaire Woods, *In Whose Benefit? Explaining Regulatory Change in Global Politics*, in THE POLITICS OF GLOBAL REGULATION (Walter Mattli & Ngaire Woods, eds., Princeton University Press, 2009), at 22–26.

40 Abbott & Snidal, *supra* note 2, at 520–21, 524–25.

41 ANNE-MARIE SLAUGHTER, A NEW WORLD ORDER (Princeton, NJ: Princeton University Press, 2004).

other stakeholders to set and implement regulatory standards. Clearly, these mechanisms entail a modified, more nuanced role for government. New governance approaches also rely on "soft law," such as hortatory or voluntary norms, principles, and codes of conduct, in part because both transgovernmental groupings and private actors lack authority to adopt binding "hard law."[42]

As the limitations and costs of top-down regulation become apparent, domestic and transnational new governance approaches are flourishing at all levels of government and society. They are now prominent in a wide variety of fields, including worker rights, human rights, and environmental protection[43]; financial regulation[44]; sovereign debt restructuring[45]; and, as discussed further below, the responsible oversight and development of technologies.

The growing popularity of new governance approaches is due to the important benefits they provide. Soft law norms can often be adopted and revised relatively quickly, without many of the formalities required for more traditional regulation. Moreover, while traditional regulation is reactive, responding to problems after they have arisen, new governance arrangements can more easily be proactive and anticipatory. Similarly, by encouraging diverse public, private, and public-private initiatives, new governance stimulates experimentation, potentially leading to the emergence of superior forms of regulation.

In addition, new governance approaches are participatory in nature, bringing multiple stakeholders into the design and implementation of regulation. This allows regulators to draw on the expertise and other capacities of private actors, reduces demands on the state in an era of tight budgets, and helps build political support and buy-in. Even more significantly, decentralization and collaboration encourage researchers, firms, and other actors to take responsibility for ensuring the safety of their processes and products, instead of simply relying on government to specify the applicable requirements. By encouraging researchers and firms to exercise stewardship over their processes and products, new governance reinforces the ethos of corporate responsibility.

New governance can also address scientific, technological, and economic activities in ways not possible with traditional regulation. For one thing, centralized command-and-control regulation inevitably tends toward one-size-fits-all prescriptions; new governance facilitates fine-tuning to particular situations.[46] In addition,

[42] Abbott & Snidal, *supra* note [2], at 529–32.

[43] *Id.*

[44] *E.g.*, the Basel Committee on Banking Supervision; see Slaughter, *supra* note 42, at 42–43; Beth A. Simmons, *The International Politics of Harmonization: The Case of Capital Market Regulation*, 55 INT'L ORG. 589 (2001).

[45] Eric Helleiner, *Filling a Hole in Global Financial Governance? The Politics of Regulating Sovereign Debt Restructuring*, in Mattli & Woods, *supra* note 40, at 89, 111–116.

[46] *See, e.g.*, Andrew D. Maynard, *Oversight of Engineered Nanomaterials in the Workplace*, 37 J. LAW MED ETHICS 651, 657 (2009) ("it appears on balance that the current state of the science supports non-regulatory ad hoc approaches that are responsive to specific circumstances").

command-and-control regulation typically requires clear, verifiable metrics to assess and enforce performance. This often limits the scope of regulation to those activities that can be measured; in addition, precise regulatory "floors" may become performance "ceilings," as firms have little incentive to go beyond specific regulatory requirements. Decentralized, collaborative, soft law arrangements, in contrast, can internalize responsibility within firms and other target actors through techniques such as management systems and reporting, thereby encouraging continuous improvement. For example, under the EU Eco-Management and Audit System (EMAS), firms agree to conduct environmental reviews and audits, establish environmental management systems based on International Organization for Standardization (ISO) standards, and issue public performance reports, all with a view to continuous improvement, in exchange for market and reputational benefits and potentially more direct public incentives.[47]

At the same time, of course, new governance techniques have significant limitations. Most obviously, soft law norms are not enforceable in the same way as mandatory requirements. Where actors face strong incentives to avoid (or evade) regulatory constraints, skeptics argue that soft law and self-regulation may be too weak to restrain powerful actors. Indeed, they may be counterproductive, essentially "whitewashing" continuing behavior. Firms may also be able to "capture" private and public-private institutions, turning regulation to their own purposes.

Other limitations have appeared in practice. In some areas, soft law has proven to be no easier to adopt or more flexible than traditional regulation; the U.S. EPA's recent Nanoscale Materials Stewardship Program (NMSP)[48] for example, took several years to develop – to the frustration of many stakeholders.[49] In addition, some voluntary programs have produced very limited participation.[50] For example, a disappointingly small (29) number of firms volunteered to participate in the NMSP.[51] There are significant disincentives for participation in such a program, including the risks of disclosing proprietary information to competitors, alerting the agency that the firm may be a regulatory target in the future, and attracting unwanted media and activist attention.

A final limitation of new governance approaches is that they may provide a lesser degree of legitimacy than traditional regulation. An important function of regulation

[47] http://ec.europa.eu/environment/emas/about/summary_en.htm; http://ec.europa.eu/environment/emas/pdf/com_2008_402_draft.pdf.

[48] EPA, Nanoscale Materials Stewardship Program: Interim Report (Jan. 2009), available at http://www.epa.gov/oppt/nano/nmsp-interim-report-final.pdf (last visited April 5, 2010).

[49] Steffen Foss Hansen & Joel A. Tickner, *The Challenges of Adopting Voluntary Health, Safety and Environmental Measures for Manufactured Nanomaterials: Lessons From the Past for More Effective Adoption in the Future*, 4 NANOTECH. L & BUS. 341, 353–54 (2007).

[50] *See e.g.*, Balbus et al., 2007; Steffen Foss Hansen & Joel A. Tickner, *The Challenges of Adopting Voluntary Health, Safety and Environmental Measures for Manufactured Nanomaterials: Lessons From the Past for More Effective Adoption in the Future*, 4 NANOTECH. L & BUS. 341, 353–54 (2007).

[51] Hansen & Tickner, *supra* note 50, at 352–53.

is to assure the public that its interests are being protected through impartial and effective oversight. This role is usually best fulfilled by government. For nanotechnology specifically, opinion polls show that the public has much greater confidence in government supervision than in programs operated by industry or other private actors.[52] To some extent, however, the legitimacy problem can be addressed by varied forms of governmental involvement. New governance theory, after all, does not imply that government should retreat completely from its regulatory responsibility; rather, public agencies should initiate private and collaborative regulatory schemes when they can improve outcomes, "orchestrate" and support the resulting regulatory network, and stand ready to intervene with mandatory regulation where necessary.[53] In this as in other matters, the concrete design of specific institutions and programs is crucial.

B. *New Governance Programs and Proposals for Nanotechnology*

In the past few years, the nano-landscape has seen many new governance principles and applications put into practice. Although the approaches vary in terms of both the institutions undertaking them and the issues they seek to address, these initiatives are all "attempts at voluntary governance of nanotechnology in a situation characterised by uncertain risks."[54] They include a variety of public, transgovernmental, and private institutions, as well as public-private partnerships, which implement new governance principles such as collaboration, decentralization, flexibility, and transnationalism.

In this section, we provide brief summaries of the leading institutional examples, highlighting areas in which they consciously or unconsciously reflect new governance principles.

1. Private Sector/Civil Society: DuPont-EDF Nano Risk Framework[55]

One of the earliest private codes of conduct is the Nano Risk Framework (NRF), produced through the collaboration of one of the world's largest private companies, DuPont, and a leading environmental NGO, Environmental Defense Fund (EDF). Launched in 2007 after 2 years of negotiation and stakeholder input, the NRF seeks "to define a systematic and disciplined process for identifying, managing, and reducing potential environmental, health, and safety risks of engineered

[52] Jane Macoubrie, Woodrow Wilson Center, *Informed Public Perceptions of Nanotechnology and Trust in Government* (2005), available at http://www.wilsoncenter.org/news/docs/macoubriereport.pdf (last visited April 5, 2010).

[53] Abbott & Snidal, *supra* note 2, at 521–23.

[54] http://www.observatorynano.eu/project/document/1576/ (last visited April 18, 2010).

[55] DuPont and Environmental Defense, Nano Risk Framework (June 2007), available at http://www.edf.org/documents/6496_Nano%20Risk%20Framework.pdf (last visited April 18, 2010).

nanomaterials across all stages of a product's 'lifecycle'..."[56] The Framework provides guidance to firms and other institutions working with nanomaterials to achieve "responsible development of nanotechnology products.[57] Based on an admittedly limited precautionary approach that urges manufacturers to adopt "reasonable worst-case assumptions,"[58] the NRF calls for firms to adopt six distinct steps (or, better described, practices) that will increase knowledge about nanotechnology risks and safety. These best practices focus on internal structure, testing, transparency, and decision making, with short-term emphasis on information gathering and data sharing. The NRF itself is intended to act as a responsible code of conduct for any firm anywhere – as evidenced by the facts that it may be downloaded in English, Spanish, French, and Mandarin, and that DuPont has included five case studies from its own internal review of nanomaterials that other companies may use as templates for implementation.[59]

Despite much media and professional attention and the backing of one of the world's largest chemical companies and most influential environmental NGOs, however, it is unclear how broadly the NRF has been adopted by other companies and entities, although the ISO is reportedly using the NRF as a framework for developing its own risk-management standard for nanotechnology. At the same time, the NRF has been heavily criticized by some other NGOs for "usurping the role" of traditional government regulation.[60]

2. Public/Private: Responsible NanoCode

The Responsible NanoCode is a voluntary code of conduct for companies handling nanomaterials, launched in 2008. It was developed by a coalition of four diverse organizations – the Royal Society, Insight Investment, the Nanotechnology Industries Association, and the Nanotechnology Knowledge Transfer Network (a project of the UK Department of Trade and Industry) – with input from a range of businesses and other stakeholders. The objective of this initiative is "to establish a consensus of good practice in the research, production, retail and disposal of products using nanotechnologies."[61] Thus, in addition to adopting a code of principles, the sponsor organizations compiled examples of good practice, illustrating ways in which firms may demonstrate compliance with the principles. Although initially launched in the United Kingdom, the Responsible NanoCode, like the DuPont-EDF NRF, was

56 *Id.* at 12.
57 *Id.* at 7.
58 *Id.* at 8.
59 http://nanoriskframework.org/page.cfm?tagID=1326 (last visited April 18, 2010).
60 Civil Society-Labor Coalition Rejects Fundamentally Flawed DuPont-ED Proposed Framework, April 12, 2007, available at http://www.etcgroup.org/upload/publication/610/01/coalition_letter_april07.pdf (last visited April 19, 2010).
61 Responsible NanoCode, available at http://www.nanotechia.org/content/activities2/responsible-nano-code/ (last visited April 12, 2010).

conceived as a transnational normative framework, expressly intended "to be international in scope."[62] The code is currently being promoted throughout Europe, as well as in North America and Asia.

3. Non-Governmental: Standard-Setting Bodies

Several transnational standard-setting bodies have begun promulgating consensus standards on nanotechnology, led by the ISO. The ISO is not an inter-governmental organization, but rather an NGO whose members are the most representative standard-setting bodies in each country; many of these are private bodies funded primarily by industry. ISO originally promulgated technical standards for mechanical products, but it has since expanded its work into many new fields; perhaps best known are its standards for management systems designed to ensure product quality (ISO 9000 series) and environmental management (ISO 14000 series).

In 2005, ISO established Technical Committee (TC) 229 to develop global standards for nanotechnology. TC 229 has published several international standards. One specifies terminology and definitions,[63] akin to traditional ISO outputs; another addresses environmental, health, and safety (EHS) management in occupational settings,[64] more akin to the 9000 and 14000 series. The EHS standard provides detailed recommendations for managing occupational and environmental risks in the production, handling, use, and disposal of a broad range of manufactured nanomaterials.

ISO standards are essentially voluntary and are intended for use throughout the world. In spite of their voluntary character, some are incorporated into law by national and sub-national governments, and others become practical requirements by virtue of market demand. Other standard-setting organizations such as ASTM International have also published relevant standards with an international focus, including standards on risk management of nanomaterials.[65]

4. Private Sector Firm Codes: BASF

Some individual companies, such as the chemical manufacturer BASF, have developed voluntary codes of conduct for their nanotechnology activities. The BASF

62 *Id.*

63 ISO/TS 27687:2008 Nanotechnologies – Terminology and Definitions for Nano-Objects – Nanoparticle, Nanofibre and Nanoplate (2008), available at http://www.iso.org/iso/iso_catalogue/catalogue_tc/catalogue_detail.htm?csnumber=44278 (last visited April 12, 2010).

64 ISO, ISO/TR 12885:2008, Nanotechnologies – Health and Safety Practices in Occupational Settings Relevant to Nanotechnologies (2008), available at http://www.iso.org/iso/iso_catalogue/catalogue_tc/catalogue_detail.htm?csnumber=52093 (last visited April 12, 2010).

65 ASTM E2535 – 07 Standard Guide for Handling Unbound Engineered Nanoscale Particles in Occupational Settings, available at http://www.astm.org/Standards/E2535.htm (last visited April 12, 2010).

code of conduct, based on the German Republic's "Principles" of nanotechnology governance, includes four core principles, relating to (1) production, (2) risk management, (3) product safety, and (4) dialogue.[66] BASF views these principles as the foundation for a range of activities to ensure the responsible development of nanotechnology.[67] For example, to back up its claim of responsible development, BASF (like DuPont) espouses a precautionary approach, stating that "BASF only markets products if their safety and environmental impact can be *guaranteed* on the basis of all available scientific information and technology."[68] In addition to this strong statement of public assurance, BASF's code mandates that it "immediately . . . disclose new findings to the authorities and the public."[69] In this way, the BASF code demonstrates a strong commitment to a different form of public-private governance: creating private sector transparency and accountability to the public at large through internal commitments, rather than legislation or external pressure. Finally, also like DuPont, BASF has released some internal findings on the toxicity of single- and multi-walled carbon nanotubes: reports that have been praised both for BASF's use of Organisation for Economic Co-operation and Development (OECD) testing protocols and for the degree of transparency and public information they create.[70]

5. Industry Standards: Responsible Care

In addition to actions by individual firms, entire industries can set standards through their trade associations; standards adopted by transnational industries are typically applied internationally. A leading example is the Responsible Care program, which consists of a series of principles and codes of conduct for the responsible production, handling, and use of chemicals, implemented through performance metrics and independent third-party certification. Responsible Care was first developed in Canada, but has since been adopted by the national chemistry trade associations in more than 50 additional countries; the program is now coordinated globally through the International Council of Chemical Associations.[71] The chemical industry asserts that its member companies are developing nanotechnology applications in

66 http://www.basf.com/group/corporate/en/sustainability/dialogue/in-dialogue-with-politics/nanotechnology/implementation (last visited April 12, 2010).

67 *Id.*

68 *Id.* (emphasis added).

69 *Id.*

70 Sheona A.K. Peters & Rob J. Aitken, Inhalation Toxicity of Multi-wall Carbon Nanotubes in Rats Exposed for Three Months, A SAFENANO Commentary, available at http://www.basf.com/group/corporate/en/function/conversions:/publish/content/sustainability/dialogue/in-dialogue-with-politics/nanotechnology/knowledge/images/SAFENANO_Contribution_of_BASF.pdf (last visited April 21, 2010).

71 Jean Belanger et al., Responsible Care: History & Development (April 22, 1009), available at http://msep.mcmaster.ca/epp/publications/RC_Final_IUPAC_2009-April-23.pdf (last visited April 23, 2010).

accordance with the Responsible Care principles and requirements for responsible stewardship.[72]

Within the Responsible Care program, certain individual companies (e.g., Bayer,[73] Evonik[74]) and specific industry groups (e.g., CEFIC,[75] ICCA[76]) have engaged in long-term and short-term strategies to, among other goals, "promote the implementation of harmonized, global standards for Risk Assessment to ensure workplace and consumer safety and health. . . ."[77] Bayer, one of the leaders in Responsible Care, has explicitly declared that its main strategies for the responsible manufacturing of nanotechnology products include promoting "global coordination of safety research, regulatory, and standard setting activities"[78] and engaging in "continued efforts to appeal to global authorities to provide support for the development of both nanotechnology and related health and safety research."[79]

6. Private Sector, For-Profit Certification: CENARIOS®

Another recent entrant in the world of new governance approaches to nanotechnology is the CENARIOS® certification system. This private certification scheme, offered by a joint venture of two private Swiss entities,[80] offers, according to its materials, the "World's First Certifiable Risk Management and Monitoring System for Nanotechnologies."[81] As part of its package, CENARIOS® offers two main products to nanotechnology manufacturers. First, CENARIOS® offers a series of "modules" that firms "can employ [to] identify, analyse and assess potential risks and

72 *See, e.g.*, American Chemistry Council, Nanotechnology Panel (undated), available at http://www.americanchemistry.com/s_acc/sec_statistics.asp?CID=654&DID=2564 (last visited April 23, 2010) ("the panel promotes the responsible development of nanoscale materials in accordance with Responsible Care®").

73 Bayer, Nanomaterial Stewardship, available at http://baycareonline.com/nano_stewardship.asp (last visited April 23, 2010).

74 Evonik, responsible Handling of Nanomaterials at Evonik, available at http://nano.evonik.com/sites/dc/Downloadcenter/Evonik/Microsite/Nanotechnology/en/Nano%20Guideline_e.pdf (last visited April 23, 2010) (noting that "we produce and market nanomaterials only if the latest available research shows they can be manufactured and applied in a safe and environmentally compatible manner.").

75 The European Chemical Industry Council (Cefic) Position: Nanomaterials and Nanotechnologies, available at http://www.cefic.be/en/Nanomaterials.html (last visited April 23, 2010).

76 International Council of Chemical Associations, available at http://www.icca-chem.org/ (last visited April 23, 2010) (The *ICCA* represents the global chemical industry and highlights its economic, social and environmental contributions to society).

77 CEFIC Strategy for Nanomaterials and Nanotechnologies (February 2009), available at http://www.cefic.be/en/Nanomaterials.html (last visited April 23, 2010).

78 Bayer, *supra* note 78.

79 *Id.*

80 The two participants are "The Innovation Society" and "TUV SUD".

81 CENARIOS® – Managing Nano Risks, available at http://www.innovationsgesellschaft.ch/images/publikationen/Factsheet_CENARIOS_english_arial2.pdf (last visited April 23, 2010).

opportunities in products and processes."[82] Second, CENARIOS® offers a certification program, backed by a well-known certification authority (TUV SUD), which is also one of the program co-sponsors. The certification program attempts to ensure that participants use "best practices." As with most of the other transnational initiatives we have discussed, the CENARIOS® approach is focused primarily on internal risk assessment, identification, and reduction programs aimed at guaranteeing "responsible" development of nanotechnology. Any company from any nation in the world that is interested in the program may participate.

7. Trans-Governmental: OECD Working Groups

The OECD has established two working groups to promote the harmonization of nanotechnology oversight. The Working Party on Manufactured Nanomaterials (WPMN) was established in 2006 to consider the environmental, health, and safety (EHS) implications of nanotechnologies, with an emphasis on testing and assessment methods.[83] The Working Party on Nanotechnology (WPN) was established in 2007 to give advice on emerging policy-relevant issues concerning the responsible development and use of nanotechnology.[84] Both groups have undertaken a number of projects involving expert government representatives from participating nations – essentially transgovernmental processes – intended to promote communication and facilitate coordination of national policies. These include the creation of a database of EHS research projects to facilitate research and information exchange and a coordinated program on safety testing of nanomaterials.

8. Other Proposals

A number of additional mechanisms reflecting the principles of new governance have been proposed for nanotechnology. For example, Marchant et al. have proposed a government-run, voluntary certification scheme for nanotechnology products that have been appropriately safety tested.[85] Howard and Murashov have proposed a partnership involving industry, government, workers, and academics to generate risk data and risk control approaches for occupational exposures to nanotechnology.[86]

[82] *Id.*

[83] OECD, Safety of Manufactured Nanomaterials, available at http://www.oecd.org/department/0,3355,en_2649_37015404_1_1_1_1_1,00.html (last visited April 23, 2010).

[84] OECD, Working Party on Nanotechnology, available at http://www.oecd.org/document/36/0,3343,en_2649_34269_38829732_1_1_1_1,00.html (last visited April 23, 2010).

[85] Gary E. Marchant, Douglas J. Sylvester & Kenneth W. Abbott, *A New Soft Law Approach to Nanotechnology Oversight: A Voluntary Product Certification Scheme*, 28 UCLA J. Environmental Law, 123 (2010).

[86] John Howard & Vladimir Murashov, *National Nanotechnology Partnership to Protect Workers*, 11 J. Nanoparticle Res. 1673 (2009).

Dana has proposed specific forms of liability protection and relief for companies that voluntarily test their nanotechnology products.[87] And Abbott et al. have proposed an international framework convention as a hybrid hard law–soft law mechanism for coordinating nanotechnology governance.[88]

C. *The Path Forward*

The programs just discussed are innovative and ambitious. They are not mutually exclusive; indeed, most are complementary. Yet despite their considerable potential and some significant progress with respect to specific firms and products, their overall impact to date is quite limited in comparison to the size of the overall nanotechnology endeavor.

Given the difficulties of moving to hard law regulation in the near future, at either the domestic or the international level, the most sensible strategy at present is to reinforce, replicate, and expand these soft law initiatives. Most are already intended to be applied transnationally and so can immediately begin to align regulatory approaches in different jurisdictions. In addition, these initiatives reflect the flexible, responsive principles of new governance, the most desirable current approach to the rapidly evolving challenges of nanotechnology. If nothing else, they constitute important regulatory experiments of the sort favored by new governance; it is important that they be given time and scope to operate so that others can learn from their results.

A strategy of supporting existing private and transgovernmental initiatives in the immediate future fits with a longer-term regulatory strategy that we have discussed elsewhere.[89] In their seminal work on responsive regulation, Ayres and Braithwaite present two "pyramids" to illustrate their flexible approach to regulation.[90] The first is an "enforcement pyramid," which represents the spectrum of sanctions that can be imposed for violations of mandatory regulations; if regulators use the threat of tough sanctions (at the peak of the pyramid) effectively, they can keep most of their actual enforcement activity much closer to the base of the pyramid (making it much less costly; e.g., by issuing warnings). The second pyramid expands the same concept to include complete regulatory strategies: voluntary, private mechanisms such as self-regulation form the base; supervised self-regulation, multi-stakeholder regulation and other modestly more intrusive methods form the middle; and command-and-control regulation forms the peak. Again, regulators can use the threat of tough

87 David A. Dana, *When Less Liability May Mean More Precaution: The Case of Nanotechnology*, 28 UCLA Journal of Environmental Law & Policy, 153 (2010).

88 Kenneth W. Abbott, Gary E. Marchant & J. Sylvester, *A Framework Convention for Nanotechnology?*, 38 Environmental Law Reporter, 10507 (2008).

89 Marchant et al., *supra* note 5, at 50–58.

90 Ian Ayres & John Braithwaite, Responsive Regulation: Transcending the Deregulation Debate (1992).

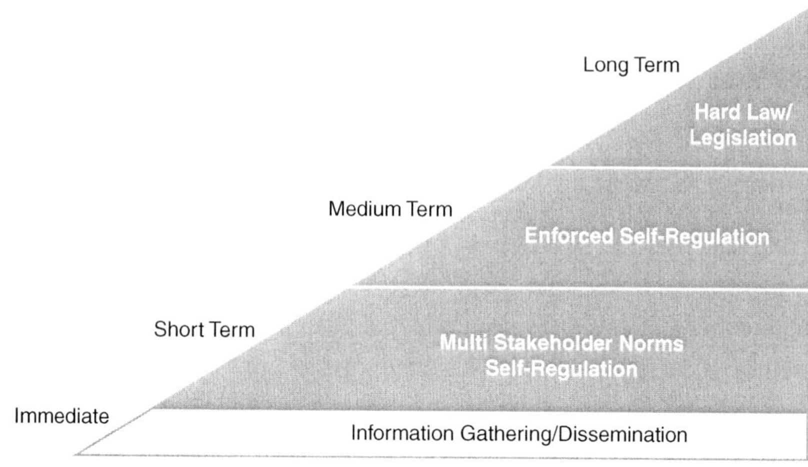

FIGURE 8.1. Graduated regulatory pyramid.

mandatory regulation to persuade actors to adopt softer mechanisms that are relatively effective at a much lower cost. The precise regulatory approach can be fine-tuned to particular industries and other circumstances.

We apply a dynamic version of the regulatory strategy pyramid, illustrated in Figure 8.1.[91] In the short term, where uncertainty prevails regarding so many aspects of nanotechnology risks and benefits, we suggest a focus on self-regulation and multi-stakeholder regulation. Such programs are speedy to create, as well as flexible and responsive to new information and other changing circumstances; in addition, they draw on the superior expertise and other capacities of business, concerned NGOs, and other stakeholders. The initiatives discussed previously fit comfortably into this approach; of special interest are programs such as the DuPont-EDF Nano Risk Framework and the Responsible NanoCode, which represent unusual and potentially fruitful experiments in multi-stakeholder regulation. As Figure 8.1 shows, we also suggest that in the short term, all types of regulatory approaches should focus on the generation of better information; in this regard, many of the existing initiatives could be improved. In addition to focusing more clearly on generating information, the implementation of voluntary self-regulatory and multi-stakeholder programs should be expanded, both domestically and transnationally. To achieve this, we recommend more visible moral and material support by leaders in government, industry, the media, and the NGO community.

Over time, as more information and experience accumulates, private voluntary initiatives may prove to be satisfactory for many issues, products, and industries. For others, however, it may prove necessary to move higher up the pyramid to

[91] Marchant et al., *supra* note 5, at 54.

more intrusive forms of regulation. Eventually, it may be necessary to adopt formal command-and-control regulation for certain issues, products, or industries. But our dynamic pyramid remains cumulative over time: all regulatory options remain available over time, and all may well be used for particular issues, products, and industries. Such an incremental, graduated response provides a realistic future pathway for nanotechnology oversight.

Because some governments have already begun to adopt formal regulations, it is important to establish as soon as possible some mechanism of coordination at the governmental level. Because most national measures remain narrow and tentative, however, this coordination mechanism may – and as we have argued, must – fall lower on the pyramid than traditional international hard law.

A workable first step would be to develop a transgovernmental mechanism in which national regulatory officials, and perhaps legislators as well, meet regularly (at least annually), with the explicit objective of promoting coordination of nanotechnology regulation on a prospective basis. Such a transgovernmental dialogue would provide an informal, flexible forum in which expert regulators can share information and best practices; seek to harmonize regulatory principles, standards, and procedures; and identify and resolve regulatory inconsistencies.[92] Transgovernmental fora are well suited to these tasks: they "provide a structure that is less threatening to democratic governance than private transnational action and less costly than inter-state negotiations, yet they can lay a firm foundation for harmonized national regulation and even, if appropriate, for international regulation."[93]

A relatively successful example in a cognate field is the International Conference on Harmonisation of Technical Requirements for Registration of Pharmaceuticals for Human Use (ICH), which consists of national regulators from the United States, EU, and Japan – as well as representatives from the pharmaceutical sector from each jurisdiction – who meet regularly to discuss pharmaceutical regulatory issues with a view to coordination.[94] A similar institution established for medical devices, the Global Harmonization Task Force (GHTF), provides for regular dialogue among regulators and industry representatives from participating countries "to achieve greater uniformity between national medical device regulatory systems."[95]

92 Kenneth W. Abbott, Douglas J. Sylvester and Gary E. Marchant, *Transnational Regulation: Reality or Romanticism?*, in: INTERNATIONAL HANDBOOK ON REGULATING NANOTECHNOLOGIES (eds. Graeme Hodge, Diana Bowman and Andrew Maynard). Cheltenham, U.K: Edward Elgar Publishing, (2010)

93 *Id.*

94 International Conference on Harmonization (ICH) (undated). Welcome to the Official Web Site for the ICH, available at http://www.ich.org/cache/compo/276-254–1.html (last visited April 23, 2010). See also Gary E. Marchant, Douglas J. Sylvester, Kenneth W. Abbott, Tara Lynn Danforth, *International Harmonization of Regulation of Nanomedicine*, STUDIES IN ETHICS, LAW & TECHNOLOGY, 3(3): Article 6, at 10–11 (2009).

95 Global Harmonization Task Force (GHTF) (undated). Welcome to the Global Harmonization Task Force Website, available at http://www.ghtf.org/ (last visited April 23, 2010). See also Marchant et al., *supra* note 94, at 11.

With their direct industry participation, the ICH and GHTF go beyond pure transgovernmental dialogue to reflect the new governance principle of private participation in regulation. Private participation provides an especially important benefit in areas of rapid technological development, giving regulators access to the latest information and knowledge regarding technical innovations (subject to confidentiality concerns) and the practical impact of different regulatory approaches. However, industry participation in these fora without offsetting input from civil society groups raises a red flag in terms of democratic legitimacy and possible barriers to public-interest regulation.

Another example is the OECD Working Group on Harmonisation of Regulatory Oversight in Biotechnology, established in 1995 to promote harmonization of national regulatory systems for biotechnology products.[96] Although these efforts have been relatively unsuccessful – as demonstrated by the continuing GM foods controversy discussed previously – the Working Group has succeeded in preparing a series of consensus documents that have helped to promote consistent practices across participating nations on issues such as risk assessment and identification of products.[97]

In the field of nanotechnology, there have already been some initial attempts at transgovernmental dialogue on which further efforts could build. The two OECD working groups discussed above include as part of their mission the coordination of certain aspects of risk assessment and management; this mission could be expanded to expressly cover the coordination of broader areas of national regulation. Important groundwork has also been laid by The International Dialogue on Responsible Research and Development of Nanotechnology, a forum initially sponsored by the Meridian Institute, which has brought together regulators from almost 50 nations every 2 years (2004, 2006, 2008) to discuss nanotechnology regulation.[98] If the International Dialogue met more frequently and on an established schedule, and was supported by a permanent "secretariat" structure that could advance agreed goals between meetings, this would be an excellent first step toward coordination through transgovernmental dialogue.

Yet another model for transnational dialogue is the International Conference on Chemicals Management (ICCM). The ICCM is an international gathering of government and private experts that convened initially in 2006 in Dubai to

[96] Organisation for Economic Development and Co-ordination, Report of the Working Group on Harmonisation of Regulatory Oversight in Biotechnology, C(2000)86/ADD2, May 25, 2000, available at http://www.olis.oecd.org/olis/2000doc.nsf/LinkTo/NT00000DDA/$FILE/10078081.PDF (last visited April 23, 2010).

[97] *See* OECD, Documents on Harmonisation of Regulatory Oversight in Biotechnology, available at http://www.oecd.org/documentprint/0,3455,en_2649_34387_1891281_1_1_1_1,00.html (last visited April 23, 2010).

[98] Meridian Institute, *Report on the International Dialogue on Responsible Research and Development of Nanotechnology* (2004); see also http://cordis.europa.eu/nanotechnology/src/intldialogue.htm (last visited April 23, 2010).

create the Strategic Approach to International Chemicals Management (SAICM), a policy framework for the global promotion of chemical safety.[99] SAICM is being implemented through a Global Plan of Action. At the second session of ICCM in May 2009, the conference agreed to put on the agenda for its third session, scheduled for 2012, the issue of adding nanotechnology to the Global Plan of Action.[100] The ICCM may therefore become another semi-official, public-private, transnational body deliberating on the global oversight of nanotechnology.

A second step toward short-term international coordination, one that would support both public and private regulatory approaches, might be the formation of an international scientific advisory body. This entity might be modeled on the Intergovernmental Panel on Climate Change or the International Whaling Commission Scientific Committee, both of which work with the relevant scientific communities to provide authoritative consensus statements on the current status and scientific understandings of particular sets of issues. A body that could provide authoritative scientific assessments of what is known (and not known) about the EHS impacts of specific nanotechnology materials, applications, and processes would provide invaluable input into private and public regulation; indeed, the intellectual impact of such assessments alone might well lead to more consistent national regulations.

In the medium and long terms, more formal, top-down regulation may well be required for particular products, industries, and processes. However, these would not necessarily displace existing new governance approaches, such as voluntary codes of conduct and industry standards, in areas where those remain satisfactory. In addition, top-down regulation need not move all the way to precise, command-and-control prescriptions; in the medium term, as Figure 8.1 suggests, regulation might consist of public certification systems like the EMAS, mandatory reporting requirements, or supervised requirements for self-assessment or self-regulation, established at the national level. In some areas, of course, evidence might emerge that makes stringent EHS regulation, at the top of the pyramid, necessary.

As national regulation moves toward more formal measures, so too must the mechanisms for international coordination. As we have argued elsewhere, a particularly suitable mechanism, one that allows international institutions and norms to evolve in step with the emerging need for coordination, is the framework convention.[101] A framework convention (FC) is a legally binding treaty. Unlike a full substantive agreement, however, the FC initially establishes only certain basic governing principles (which could include a preference for efficient and effective forms of regulation, including new governance approaches); procedures for reporting, scientific analysis,

[99] *See* Strategic Approach to International Chemicals Management, Introducing SAICM, available at http://www.saicm.org/index.php?menuid=2&pageid=256 (last visited April 25, 2010).

[100] ICCM, Report of the International Conference on Chemicals Management on the Work of Its Second Session, May 11–15, 2009, available at http://www.saicm.org/documents/iccm/ICCM2/ICCM2%20Report/ICCM2%2015%20FINAL%20REPORT%20E.pdf (last visited April 25, 2010).

[101] Abbott et al., *supra* note 94.

and other forms of information gathering and assessment; a process for considering more specific substantive requirements in the future; and appropriate supporting institutions such as a secretariat and an annual meeting of the parties, which could promote appropriate forms of new governance regulation to participating states.[102]

A key advantage of the FC is that it facilitates formal international engagement without requiring an initial consensus on substantive provisions or obligations. As such, it represents a relatively risk-free opportunity for nations to participate without having to commit to specific requirements, whose impact and costs may not yet be known. It is therefore easier to negotiate than a substantive agreement; if states were willing, a relatively simple FC for nanotechnology could even be negotiated in the immediate future. Over time, as the science matures and the need for substantive action in particular areas becomes clear, protocols that establish specific substantive requirements can be separately adopted. The framework convention-protocol approach has been used with success in a number of other areas of international concern, including climate change, ozone depletion, and tobacco control.[103]

CONCLUSION

There are strong arguments for coordinating national regulatory responses to nanotechnology, notwithstanding the practical difficulties and limitations of both national regulation and international coordination. The objective of a coordinated approach, intended to avoid the disruptions that have hampered other technologies such as GM foods, can best be achieved by a parallel approach that integrates the locus of regulatory oversight with the form of oversight. Initially, national responses will necessarily consist primarily of soft law measures such as codes of conduct and self-regulation. Many of these initiatives are amenable to a transnational approach because they do not involve legislation or regulation of any one jurisdiction. The international response to such measures, then, should focus on information sharing and dialogue, including within transgovernmental fora. As national regulation begins to harden in particular areas, in response to growing information and experience, the international response should likewise migrate to more formal action, perhaps in the form of a framework convention.

[102] *Id.* at 10514.

[103] *Id.* at 10510–15; Allyn L. Taylor, *An International Regulatory Strategy for Global Tobacco Control*, 21 Yale J. Int'l L. 257 (1996).

9

Labeling the Little Things

Jonathan H. Adler

The nanotechnology revolution is already underway. More than 1,000 consumer products sold in the United States use nanotechnology or contain nanoscale particles.[1] These products range from computer chips and stain-resistant pants to window coatings and sunscreens. By 2007, the global market for nanotech goods was almost $150 billion,[2] up from an estimated $30 billion in 2005.[3] By 2015, the global market for nanotech products is likely to be in the trillions.[4]

Some manufacturers have been happy to disclose their use of nanotechnology or have signed on to voluntary labeling guidelines. Others have adopted nanotech techniques or incorporated nanoscale particles into their products without any meaningful public disclosure. Relatively few products containing nanomaterials reveal this fact on the product label. In some cases, manufacturers' own public relations officials are unaware of whether their products include nanoscale materials.[5]

The use of nanotechnology in consumer products has many potential benefits, but it may also pose unforeseen risks. Nanoscale particles have the potential to act differently than larger size particles of the same substance. This is their benefit, and it is also their curse. Perhaps ironically, what makes nanomaterials useful and attractive to manufacturers – "their small size, chemical composition, surface structure, solubility, shape, and aggregative tendencies" – may also make them more dangerous.[6] Due to their unique characteristics, nanotech particles may pose unique threats to

1 *See* The Project on Emerging Nanotechnologies, Inventory of Consumer Products, *available at* http://www.nanotechproject.org/inventories/consumer/.

2 David Rajeski, *The Molecular Economy*, ENVIRONMENTAL FORUM (Jan/Feb 2010), at 38.

3 J. Clarence Davies, *EPA and Nanotechnology: Oversight for the 21st Century*, Woodrow Wilson International Center for Scholars, Project on Emerging Technologies, May 2007, at 13.

4 *Id.* (citing estimate of $2.6 trillion market for goods with nano components by 2014).

5 *See* "No-Nano Sunscreens?" Consumer Reports Health, December 2008, *available at* http://www.consumerreports.org/health/healthy-living/beauty-personal-care/skincare/no-nano-sunscreens-12-08/overview/no-nano-sunscreens-ov.htm.

6 *See* Albert C. Lin, *Size Matters; Regulating Nanotechnology*, 31 HARV. ENVTL. L. REV. 349, 358 (2007).

public health or the environment. Although people have been exposed to naturally occurring nanoscale particles for centuries, human-created nanoparticles may be more persistent and have different properties or protective coatings.[7]

There is as yet no definitive evidence that nanoscale materials used in consumer products pose a threat to human health. Studies have demonstrated the potential for nanoscale materials to cause harm, but these threats have yet to materialize outside the laboratory setting. In 2007 it was still possible to claim "[t]here have been no known cases of people or the environment being harmed by nanomaterials."[8] Several dozen people in Germany reported respiratory problems connected with a cleaning product called "Magic Nano."[9] Yet subsequent investigation revealed that the only thing "nano" about this product was the name, and it did not contain any nanoscale materials.[10]

Some consumer and environmentalist groups are concerned that nanomaterials are proliferating without much discussion or public awareness. These groups have urged governments to adopt regulatory controls on the use of nanotechnology in consumer products. Some propose mandatory labeling for consumer products containing nanoscale particles, whether a generic nanotech label to indicate the presence of nanoscale particles or a more detailed disclosure. A labeling requirement would make it more likely that consumers are aware when they expose themselves to the fruits of nanotechnology. Right now, consumers are unaware that they may be purchasing and using products containing nanoscale particles on a regular basis. Mandatory labels would not reduce the threat posed by the use or disposal of any particular product, but could empower concerned consumers to limit their exposure. Product labels can help consumers manage their exposure to risky or unproven products without unduly inhibiting consumer preferences generally.

Mandatory labels have their benefits, but they also have their costs – and not just to product manufacturers and sellers. Labeling requirements may increase marketplace efficiency and consumer autonomy. On the other hand, label requirements could frustrate market responses to changes in scientific understanding or consumer preferences, impose unnecessary costs on manufacturers, and fail to address marketplace inefficiencies. In the United States, mandatory labeling requirements also raise potential First Amendment concerns. Before adopting a mandatory labeling requirement, policy makers should consider whether mandatory labels are necessary, or whether voluntary labeling regimes may be superior, with or without government assistance.

[7] *Id.* at 356–57.

[8] Davies, *supra* at 14; *see also* Lin, *supra* at 360 (noting the lack of reports of scientist or worker injury or illness attributed to exposure to nanoparticles).

[9] Lin, *supra* at 360.

[10] Davies, *supra* at 14. There is a plausible claim that workers exposed to nanoparticles at production facilities may have been hurt, or even killed, but causation has not been established. *See* Tracy D. Hester, *Quiet So Far: A Muted Response to Allegations of the First Human Fatalities Linked to Nanoparticles*, 40 Envtl. L. Rep. 10007, 10007 (2010).

THE PUSH FOR LABELS

Environmentalist and consumer groups as well as regulatory analysts and academics have called for the adoption of nanotechnology labels. Some groups have asked the FDA to require nanotech warning labels on cosmetics that contain nanoscale particles.[11] Others have called for the adoption of stringent labeling requirements across a wider range of consumer products.[12] Friends of the Earth (FOE) warned in a report that "[i]n the absence of mandatory product labeling, public debate, or laws to ensure their safety, products created using nanotechnology have entered the food chain."[13] FOE advocates a moratorium on the use of nanotechnology in consumer products until nanotechnology-specific regulatory laws are adopted, including a mandatory labeling requirement.[14] Specifically, FOE advocates that "[a]ll manufactured nano ingredients must be clearly indicated on product labels to allow members of the public to make an informed choice about product use."[15] The Natural Resources Defense Council has likewise endorsed a label requirement.[16]

Regulatory analysts have also proposed labels for nanotechnology. J. Clarence Davies proposes a basic labeling regime for both nanomaterials and nanoproducts (products that contain nanomaterials).[17] Nanotech labels would be required to disclose the existence of nanoparticles in consumer products and a telephone number or e-mail address where consumers could report adverse effects. Davies also proposes that a government agency should have the power to ban, recall, or otherwise regulate nanoproducts and nanomaterials believed to be responsible for reported adverse effects.[18]

An alternative labeling regime loosely modeled on California's Proposition 65 would involve the development of a set of safety tests for products containing nanomaterials and a requirement that manufacturers disclose the presence of nanomaterials in products that had not been subject to the required tests.[19] This label would have to disclose both the presence of nanomaterials and the lack of safety testing. In effect, the label would warn consumers that they are purchasing and using a nano-based product at their own risk. One problem with this sort of approach, Davies notes,

[11] *See* NANOTECHNOLOGY: A REPORT OF THE U.S. FOOD AND DRUG ADMINISTRATION NANOTECHNOLOGY TASK FORCE 34 (2007).

[12] *See generally* http://nanoaction.org.

[13] *Out of the Laboratory and On to Our Plates: Nanotechnology in Food and Agriculture*, Friends of the Earth, March 2008, at 2, *available at* http://www.foeeurope.org/activities/nanotechnology/Documents/Nano_food_report.pdf.

[14] *Id.* at 3.

[15] *Id.*

[16] *See* Jennifer Sass, *Nanotechnology's Invisible Threat: Small Science, Big Consequences*, Natural Resources Defense Council, May 2007, at 9, *available at* http://www.nrdc.org/health/science/nano/nano.pdf.

[17] Davies, *supra* at 34.

[18] *Id.* at 34–35.

[19] *Id.* at 35.

is that "at present, it is not clear that the science is adequate to promulgate testing requirements."[20] Too little is known about nanoscale materials to design a particularly reliable or informative testing protocol. As a consequence, this approach would effectively require warning labels on virtually all products containing nanoscale materials, at least for the immediate future.

A third labeling regime suggested by Professor Albert C. Lin proposes to require all manufacturers of products containing nanoscale particles to disclose the particular nanomaterials contained in a product on its label and "to provide a brief comparison of the nanomaterial with the bulk version of the material."[21] Such a labeling requirement, according to Lin, would "convey information that consumers can use to make rational decisions."[22] Yet he also acknowledges that, even with an extensive labeling requirement, "consumers will not be able to make fully informed decisions because of the uncertainty surrounding the effects of exposure to nanomaterials."[23] What they will be able to do, however, is make an active choice regarding whether they prefer to purchase or avoid those products identified as containing nanomaterials and, by extension, whether they wish to expose themselves to any as yet unidentified risks some nanomaterials may pose. Like Davies' second proposal, Lin's recommendation would result in de facto warning labels for nanotechnology products.

Labeling proposals have not gotten far in the United States thus far. Although several consumer and environmentalist organizations have urged federal agencies to adopt formal labeling or disclosure requirements, no such requirements have been adopted. In some cases, federal agencies lack statutory authority to impose a labeling requirement. In others, federal agencies have determined that a label requirement is not yet justified under current law.

A large proportion of nanotech products currently on the market fall under the jurisdiction of the Consumer Product Safety Commission (CPSC). At present, however, the CPSC does not have clear authority to require manufacturers to disclose the presence of nanomaterials in their products.[24] The Environmental Protection Agency (EPA), on the other hand, might be able to impose labeling rules for some nanotech products under existing laws, but only in selected product areas. For instance, the EPA might be able to regulate some nanomaterials as "chemical substances" under the Toxic Substances Control Act (TSCA), though it must first find that the product or substance "presents or will present an unreasonable risk of injury to health or the environment"[25] and might have to designate and regulate distinct

[20] *Id.*

[21] Lin, *supra* at 393. Lin would also require manufacturers to make similar disclosures to their employees. *Id.*

[22] *Id.* at 395.

[23] *Id.*

[24] David Rejeski, Comments on CPSC FY2010 Agenda and Priorities, Woodrow Wilson International Center for Scholars Project on Emerging Nanotechnologies, Aug. 18, 2009.

[25] 15U.S.C. § 2605(a).

types of nanomaterials separately.[26] If nanotech pesticides are registered with the EPA, they would have to display a government-approved label under the Federal Insecticide, Fungicide, and Rodenticide Act (FIFRA), but this label would not necessarily have to disclose the presence of nanomaterials.[27]

The U.S. Food and Drug Administration (FDA) has broader authority over drugs, cosmetics, and some food products. The FDA has explicitly considered whether to pursue labeling requirements under any of its existing authorities. In 2007, the FDA's Nanotechnology Task Force concluded that a general nanotechnology labeling requirement cannot be justified scientifically based on current knowledge. Instead, the FDA concluded, the need for any product disclosure about the presence of nanoscale materials should be evaluated on a case-by-case basis once there is evidence that a particular nanoscale particle may present a particular type of threat.[28]

According to the FDA, "the use of nanotechnology does not mean that a product's safety or effectiveness is necessarily increased, decreased, or affected in any way."[29] Use or inclusion of nanotechnology, by itself, does not provide an adequate basis for mandatory technology. If, however, the FDA were to conclude that the inclusion of nanoscale materials in a given product was a "material fact" for a category of products, it would require a disclosure label for that product.[30] But the FDA has yet to make any such determination. The FDA's task force concluded:

> Because the current science does not support a finding that classes of products with nanoscale materials necessarily present greater safety concerns than classes of products without nanoscale materials, the Task Force does not believe there is a basis for saying that, as a general matter, a product containing nanoscale materials must be labeled as such.[31]

The Task Force also recommended that producers consult with the agency before making voluntary nanotech claims about their products, "because claims regarding the use of nanoscale materials might be misleading and, therefore, misbrand a product."[32]

Although the FDA does not believe that comprehensive labeling of nano-containing products is required, cosmetics manufacturers may be required to include information about the inclusion of nanoscale materials in their products nonetheless. Under the FDA's current regulations, all ingredients used in cosmetic products

[26] *See* Davies, *supra* at 22–23. *See also* American Bar Association, Section of Environment, Energy, and Resources, *Regulation of Nanoscale Materials under the Toxic Substances Control Act*, June 2006.

[27] Davies, *supra* at 34.

[28] *See* Nanotechnology: A Report of the U.S. Food and Drug Administration Nanotechnology Task Force (2007).

[29] *Id.* at 34.

[30] *Id.* at 35.

[31] *Id.*

[32] *Id.*

must be "adequately substantiated for safety."[33] If the safety of all ingredients cannot be substantiated, the product must bear a warning on the label disclosing that the product's safety "has not been determined," or it will be considered "misbranded" under the federal Food, Drug, and Cosmetics Act.[34] Insofar as nanoscale materials may not behave or perform like larger scale materials within a product, cosmetic manufacturers may not be able to rely on prior studies substantiating the safety of earlier product formulations and might be required to label their products in order to comply with existing law.[35]

Though labeling has yet to advance in the United States, label proponents have found more fertile ground overseas. In 2008, the European Commission proposed specifically including nanotechnology under the EU's Novel Foods law.[36] In November 2009, the European Union also adopted new regulations to require the labeling of cosmetics that contain nanoscale materials. Specifically, the new rules require including the word "nano" in cosmetic product ingredient listings.[37] Although US and EU officials have begun efforts to coordinate, if not harmonize, some regulation of chemicals and food products, such efforts have yet to encompass nanotechnology.[38]

LOOKING AT LABELS

Government-mandated product labels are usually adopted for one or more of several purposes, such as reducing potential information asymmetries between producers and consumers, ensuring fair competition among producers, reducing potential threats to public health and safety, or altering consumer behavior in line with a broader social objective.[39] Economic arguments for labels typically boil down to either (1) the market fails to provide consumers with sufficient information to make purchasing decisions that align with their preferences, or (2) individual purchasing decisions have a different effect on social welfare than on the welfare of individual consumers.[40] Measures designed to address the former problem seek to enhance economic efficiency by providing consumers with greater information on which to base their decisions. The aim "is not so much to *alter* consumption behavior

[33] 21 C.F.R. §740.10.

[34] 21 C.F.R. §740.10.

[35] *See* John C. Monica, Jr., *FDA Labeling of Cosmetics Containing Nanoscale Materials*, 5 NANOTECHNOLOGY L. & BUS. 63 (2008).

[36] *See* Robert Falkner, et al., *Consumer Labeling of Nanomaterials in the EU and U.S.: Convergence or Divergence?* Chatham House Briefing Paper, October 2009, at 7.

[37] John Pendergrass, et al., *Consumer Labeling of Nanomaterials in the European Union and the United States*, 40 ENVTL. L. REP. 10117, 10117 (2010).

[38] Falkner, et al., *supra* at 11.

[39] Elise Golan, et al., *Economics of Food Labeling*, 24 J. CONSUMER POL'Y 117, 118 (2001).

[40] *Id.* at 136.

but to increase *informed* consumption."[41] The assumption here is not that there is imperfect information – there is always imperfect information – but that there is an information asymmetry between producers and consumers that reduces economic efficiency. Measures designed to address the latter problem, on the other hand, do seek to use information disclosure to alter consumer behavior to advance social welfare. Empirical studies of labeling rules suggest that such disclosures are more effective at addressing potential information asymmetries than environmental or other spillover effects.[42]

Information disclosure can increase marketplace efficiency by overcoming the problem of asymmetric information.[43] Put in the simplest terms, producers know more about the characteristics of the products they sell than do consumers. As a consequence, consumers may have a more difficult time identifying and acquiring utility-maximizing products. Requiring producers to disclose certain information on a product label can reduce the information asymmetry and facilitate consumer choices that are more closely aligned with consumer preferences.[44] Labeling may enhance economic efficiency by making it easier for consumers to make welfare-maximizing decisions.[45]

Product labeling is a particularly effective way to address potential asymmetric information problems, as labels provide information when a purchase is made.[46] This can make labels superior to government or industry-sponsored education campaigns. Ippolito and Mathios found that "government and general sources of information appear to be effective at reaching some subgroups of the population, but not all groups."[47] Labels, however, have the potential to reach all consumers of a given product – provided that they are sufficiently clear and contain useful and relevant information easily understood by consumers.

The value of the information conveyed by a label depends on the degree to which consumers are able to identify relative product characteristics. Some product

41 *Id.* at 137. *See also* WESLEY MAGAT & W. KIP VISCUSI, INFORMATIONAL APPROACHES TO REGULATION (1992).

42 Golan, et al., *supra* at 119 (reporting mandatory labels "are best suited to alleviating problems of asymmetric information and are rarely effective in redressing environmental or other spillovers associated with food production and consumption.").

43 The classic discussion of the problem of information asymmetry as a source of market failure is George A. Akerloff, *The Market for "Lemons": Quality Uncertainty and the Market Mechanism*, 84 Q. J. ECON. 488 (1970). *See also*, Sanford J. Grossman & Joseph E. Stiglitz, On the Impossibility of Informationally Efficient Markets, 70 AMER. ECON. REV . 393 (1980).

44 *See, e.g.*, Mario F. Teisl and Brian Roe, *The Economics of Labeling: An Overview of Issues for Health and Environmental Disclosure*, 27 AGRIC. & RES. ECON. REV. 140, 141 (1998).

45 Golan, et al., *supra*, at 127 ("Labeling decisions may enhance economic efficiency by helping consumers target expenditures toward products they most want.").

46 *See* Pauline M. Ippolito & Alan D. Mathios, *The Regulation of Science-Based Claims in Advertising*, 12 J. CONSUMER POL'Y 413, 419 (1990) (noting that health information provided by producers, as in advertising, "is likely to be linked directly to product choices, making it simpler to incorporate . . . into behavior").

47 *Id.* at 421–22.

attributes, *search attributes*, are easy for a consumer to identify and assess before making a purchase.[48] For this sort of product attribute, labeling requirements add little value.[49] For example, a consumer can assess the size, shape, and color of a product quite easily and inexpensively before making purchase. So requiring the disclosure of such information on the label would add nothing.

Some attributes are just as easy to assess, but can only be evaluated after a purchase is made. A consumer must actually experience a product to evaluate such *experience attributes*, such as taste or quality. Insofar as such product characteristics can be measured and assessed relatively objectively, labeling experience attributes may be valuable to consumers, particularly if the product at issue is not the sort that is relatively inexpensive and purchased repeatedly. Whether a labeling requirement for experience attributes is justified depends in part on the cost of the good and whether it is likely to be the subject of a repeat purchase.[50] For some experience characteristics, such as food content, labels can be particularly valuable insofar as they help consumers avoid harm, such as by indicating the presence of allergens or other ingredients that could cause health problems for some consumers. In such contexts, labeling allows consumers with particular sensitivities to avoid products that could cause harm without constraining choices for other consumers.

The potential value of labeling is greatest with *credence attributes* – those attributes like the nutritional content of food or how a product was made, that "cannot be easily verified even after purchase and use but whose value effects utility."[51] A good example is organic food. Some consumers prefer food products that were produced in a particular way. It does not matter whether this preference is driven by health or ideological concerns. A consumer does not know whether a given good meets their desired standard unless the producer or a seller discloses the relevant information (and even then there is a risk of deception or puffery).

Insofar as labeling requirements ensure that certain types of consumer-relevant information is presented in an easy-to-digest and standardized fashion, they could further enhance consumer welfare. Consumers are most likely to read and respond to product labels that are "clear and concise."[52] When labels are ambiguous or unclear, on the other hand, consumers may not pay them much attention at all.[53] Standardization of product labels can also facilitate their use by consumers.[54]

48 For a discussion of different types of good attributes, see Golan, et al., *supra* at 127–28.

49 *See* Paul H. Rubin, *The Economics of Regulating Deception*, 10 CATO J. 667, 673 (1991).

50 *See Id.* at 673. Rubin notes that for some experience goods, advertising can serve as a powerful indicator of product quality, lessening the value of potential government intervention. *Id.* at 673–74.

51 Teisl and Roe, *supra* at 141.

52 Golan, et al., *supra*, at 139.

53 Lars Noah, *The Imperative to Warn: Disentangling the 'Right to Know' from the 'Need to Know' About Consumer Product Hazards*, 11 YALE J. ON REG. 293, 365 (1994) ("ambiguous warnings will undermine consumer confidence in the reliability of truly important label information").

54 Teisl and Roe, *supra* at 144 ("standardizing the presentation of information can reduce the cognitive costs of information processing.").

Labeling is a particularly useful approach to product regulation when there is no consensus about the desirability of a given product's attribute and the effects of a product's consumption are borne primarily by the purchaser or user. Whereas a ban deprives all consumers of the opportunity to purchase a given good or service, a label "allows consumers to match their individual preferences with their individual purchases."[55] This is even true when product ingredients or characteristics may cause a health threat, as with allergens in foods. As previously noted, ingredient labeling enables those with a particular allergy to avoid those products that could pose a threat to them without appreciably narrowing product choices available to other consumers.[56] This is also true when individuals have ethical, spiritual, or ideological preferences about the sorts of products they purchase or consume. Labels enable them to satisfy their preferences without foreclosing others from making different consumption choices. As Beales, Craswell, and Salop explain:

> Remedies which simply adjust the information available to consumers still leave consumers free to make their own choices, thus introducing less rigidity into the market. Such remedies leave the market free to respond as consumer preferences and production technologies change over time. For the same reason, information remedies pose less risk of serious harm if the regulator turns out to have been mistaken.[57]

Nanotechnology labels could divide markets in interesting ways, as it is not clear whether consumers would view nanotech labels in a positive or negative fashion. As Davies notes, "A peculiarity of labeling nanoproducts is that for some people the nano label would be a plus and for others it would be a negative.... For most other types of labels this kind of ambiguity does not exist."[58] Nanotech labels could serve a signaling function and suggest other product attributes that are potentially desirable (or not). Disclosing that a product contains nanomaterials may indicate that a product is "new" or cutting-edge, whereas as a "nanotech-free" label may indicate a producer's commitment to sustainability or other environmental values.[59]

There are also non-economic arguments for a mandatory labeling requirement. According to some, labeling promotes "personal liberty and democratic deliberation."[60] Specifically, "a labeling requirement for nanomaterials would enable consumers to decide whether to purchase conventional products, whose risks

55 Golan, et al., *supra*, at 145.

56 Howard Beales, Richard Craswell, and Steven C. Salop, *The Efficient Regulation of Consumer Information*, 24 J.L. & Econ. 491, 513 (1981) ("information remedies allow consumers to protect themselves according to personal preferences rather than place on regulators the difficult task of compromising diverse preferences with a common standard.").

57 *Id.* at 513.

58 Davies, *supra* at 34.

59 The claim here is not that there is something "unsustainable" about nanotechnology, but that refusal to use nanotechnology may be seen by some as environmentally preferable as is the refusal to use biotechnology.

60 Lin, *supra* at 393.

may be better known, or 'new and improved' products containing nanomaterials, whose health effects are uncertain."[61] From this perspective, consumers have a "right to know" that they are being exposed to potential (albeit unproven) risks.[62] According to Lin, mandatory labels would also "raise public awareness of the growing presence of nanotechnology and stimulate dialogue on the future role of nanotechnology in society."[63] This connection between mandatory product labels and democratic governance could raise constitutional problems, however, insofar as producers are compelled to present what amounts to a political message, or politically relevant symbol, on their products. As discussed below, the First Amendment may protect producers against regulatory measures that would require them to stigmatize their own products without a sufficiently substantial government justification.

An additional problem with relying on a generic "right to know" as the basis for a labeling requirement is that it could encompass just about anything.[64] Consumers have a wide range of preferences that may influence their purchasing decisions. For many consumers, price and quality are primary. Others care about how a product choice influences their self-image or reinforces their ethical, spiritual, or religious values. Consumers care not just about the products they purchase, but also about those who make the products and how the products are made.[65] Just as a consumer may want to know about the use of a given technology, another consumer may care about whether a product was tested on animals, made in a country without unions or limitations on child labor, or perhaps even by a company that shares the consumers' ideological preferences. An op-ed by Whole Foods' CEO John Mackey critical of the Obama Administration's health care reform proposals prompted a boycott of the company.[66] Labeling for one of these characteristics could justify labeling for them all, and yet not everything can be on a product label.

A regulatory requirement that a manufacturer disclose some product facts, but not others, is not a neutral act. For some consumers, the mere fact that the government has required companies to disclose particular information or place a warning or consumer advisory on a product package contains the implicit message that the government has determined that *this* specific information is important. This is particularly likely in the case of a warning or a specific disclosure about the presence of nanoscale materials, as opposed to the inclusion of such information in a preexisting list of ingredients. Why does the government think the lack of testing for nanoscale

[61] *Id.*

[62] *Id.* at 395.

[63] *Id.* at 394.

[64] J. Howard Beales, *Modification and Consumer Information: Modern Biotechnology and the Regulation of Information*, 55 Food & Drug L.J. 105, 109 (2000) ("It is impossible to list all the things that might matter to everyone.").

[65] *See generally*, Douglas A. Kysar, *Preferences for Processes: The Process/Product Distinction and the Regulation of Consumer Choice*, 118 Harv. L. Rev. 525 (2004).

[66] *See* Amos Tversky, *The Conscience of a Capitalist*, Wall St. J., Oct. 3, 2009.

ingredients is more relevant or important to highlight than the lack of testing of other ingredients?

If, as recent polls indicate, most Americans know relatively little about nanotechnology, the adoption of a mandatory label for consumer products that contain nanoscale materials could stigmatize those products with a portion of the market. Some consumers who would have bought such products without a second thought may be discouraged were they to see a nano-specific warning, particularly if it in any way suggested that nanoscale particles were particularly unsafe. This could not only have effects on producers of products containing nanoscale materials, but it could also have effects on consumers as well. In some cases, products containing nanoscale materials may be superior, or even safer, than conventional alternatives. As a consequence, a warning label that stigmatizes nano-containing products could discourage the use of products that could be more beneficial to consumers.

The existence of labels or disclosure may alter consumer preferences. Indeed, for some labeling advocates, that would appear to be the point. If all consumer products containing nanoscale materials were required to disclose this information and were perhaps also required to highlight the relative lack of scientific information about the potential risks posed by such materials, some consumers might alter their consumption patterns because they are now concerned about a product characteristic about which they had been previously unaware. This may or may not enhance consumer welfare. If nanotechnology labels are viewed as warnings, rather than simple disclosures, they may discourage consumers from purchasing more welfare-enhancing products. Although some environmental and consumer organizations have gone after sunscreen producers for failing to disclose the use of nanoscale materials, an analysis by the Environmental Working Group found that "nanotech-based sunscreens may be among the safest and most effective on the market."[67]

The disclosure of information can also influence producer behavior. Indeed, that is part of the point as well. Some information-based regulatory tools are explicitly designed to "shame" companies to change their behavior.[68] If producers are required to disclose potentially undesirable aspects of their products, they may alter their production methods or product content to more closely match consumer preferences. So, for instance, if a substantial portion of consumers are reluctant to purchase certain types of products if they contain nanoscale materials, even if those products are "superior" or more effective in some other way, producers that currently incorporate nanotechnology into their product design may make changes in product design in response to a disclosure requirement. Information can be quite powerful. When

67 Barnaby J. Feder, *Nanoparticles in Your Sunscreen: Too Hot to Handle?* N.Y. TIMES, Aug. 13, 2007.

68 *See, e.g.*, Davies, *supra* at 34 (discussing value of "public shame" to "discourage bad behavior" in context of mandatory disclosure laws).

food companies were allowed to begin making modest health claims on their labels, this altered both consumer purchasing patterns and the relative supply of products.

Labels seek to improve market efficiency by increasing information in the hands of consumers when they make decisions. Yet just as there can be too little information, there can also be too much. It is wrong to assume that more information is always better for consumers or always enhances market efficiency. Information is not free.[69] It is costly to acquire, disclose, and evaluate.[70] The more information on a label, the more information a consumer must process or the more time a consumer must take to identify that information most important to her given her preferences. As Professor Lars Noah notes, too many labels or product warnings "may dilute the impact of truly important cautionary information."[71] If there is too much information on the label, a consumer may not read it at all.[72] Further, a "required disclosure necessarily displaces other information" that the producer or seller would rather convey to the consumer and that the consumer may actually find to be more valuable.[73]

When embodied in a statute or an administrative rule, labeling requirements can cause "excess inertia" or "lock-in" within a product market, slowing the rate at which information flows respond to changes in consumer preferences, scientific knowledge, or market conditions.[74] In the case of nutritional labeling, for example, expert medical opinion about whether consumers should seek or avoid particular substances (e.g., types of cholesterol, sources of fat, etc.) has changed over time. If labeling requirements are imposed through a legislative or administrative process, there is a risk that the requirements will not keep pace with such changes. Government standards, whether embodied in statute or regulation, "may be less flexible than industry standards, and may reduce innovation."[75] As Ippolito and Mathios note:

> Excessive disclosure requirements, standardized language, rules that do not react to new information in a timely fashion, and sharp limits on who can make such claims, all have the potential to limit firms' incentives to compete by improving and promoting better products.[76]

A complicating factor in any discussion of a labeling regime is that what precisely constitutes nanotechnology is still open to dispute. A nanometer is one-billionth of

[69] Beales, Craswell, and Salop, *supra* at 500 ("Information is costly, and perfect information is neither feasible nor desirable").

[70] *Id.* at 503 ("Information is costly to produce and disseminate.").

[71] Noah, *supra* at 374–75; *see also* Golan et al., *supra*, at 143 ("Costs of additional labeling also include the extent to which it dilutes the effectiveness of the information already included on the product label.").

[72] Golan et al., *supra*, at 139 ("A large number of warnings or a large list of detailed product information may cause many consumers to disregard the label completely.").

[73] Beales, Craswell & Salop, *supra* at 528.

[74] Teisl and Roe, *supra* at 142.

[75] Golan et al., *supra*, at 164.

[76] Ippolito and Mathios, *supra* at 440.

a meter, and most analysts refer to nanoscale particles or materials as those between 1 and 100 nanometers in diameter or length. Nonetheless, analysts and regulatory agencies are uncertain about how to define the field. The FDA, for example, does not believe it should adopt "formal, fixed definitions for regulatory purposes" until scientists understand more about the effects of and risks posed by such particles.[77] As a consequence, adopting a meaningful labeling standard, particularly one that is not appreciably over- or under-inclusive, would be quite difficult. The FDA Nanotechnology Task Force further concluded:

> The available information does not suggest that all materials with nanoscale dimensions will be hazardous. Furthermore, if all nanoscale materials are compared to all non-nanoscale materials, whether larger or smaller, it is not apparent that the nanoscale materials as a group would have more inherent hazard.[78]

CONSTITUTIONAL CONCERNS

Whatever its other merits, a mandatory labeling requirement could raise constitutional concerns in the United States. Product labels are commercial speech subject to First Amendment protection, albeit significantly less protection than most core political speech. In 1976 the U.S. Supreme Court first held that commercial speech is eligible for protection under the First Amendment, even if it does no more than propose a commercial transaction.[79] As the Court has explained, "A commercial advertisement is constitutionally protected not so much because it pertains to the seller's business as because it furthers the societal interest in the free flow of commercial information."[80] The Court has repeatedly reaffirmed the constitutional protection of commercial speech over the past several decades. In 2001, for example, the Court stated clearly that "The fact that the speech is in aid of a commercial purpose does not deprive respondent of all First Amendment protection."[81]

The First Amendment applies both when the government seeks to restrict speech as well as when it seeks to compel speech.[82] As a consequence, the First Amendment can prevent the government from requiring corporations from communicating messages with which they disagree, even in the commercial context. In *Pacific Gas & Electric Company v. Public Utilities Commission of California*, for instance, the Court struck down a requirement that a public utility enclose a message in its billing statements to which it objected.[83] Laws that compel speech, even by commercial

77 NANOTECHNOLOGY: A REPORT OF THE U.S. FOOD AND DRUG ADMINISTRATION NANOTECHNOLOGY TASK FORCE 6–7 (2007).

78 *Id.* at 11.

79 Virginia Board of Pharmacy v. Virginia Citizens Consumer Council, Inc., 425 U.S. 748 (1976).

80 First National Bank v. Belotti, 435 U.S. 765, 783 (1978) (internal quotation omitted).

81 United States v. United Foods, Inc., 533 U.S. 405, 410 (2001).

82 *Id.* ("Just as the First Amendment may prevent the government from prohibiting speech, the Amendment may prevent the government from compelling individuals to express certain views.").

83 475 U.S. 1 (1986).

actors, "pose the inherent risk that the Government seeks not to advance a legitimate regulatory goal, but to suppress unpopular ideas or information or manipulate the public debate through coercion rather than persuasion."[84]

Although commercial speech receives constitutional protection, government regulation of commercial speech is subject to a less-demanding level of scrutiny than other types of speech. In *Central Hudson Gas & Electric Corp. v. Public Service Commission*, the Supreme Court established a four-part test for government restrictions on commercial speech. First, the speech must concern lawful activity and not be misleading to qualify for protection. If the speech qualifies, courts next consider whether the government has asserted a "substantial" governmental interest, such as preventing consumer deception or protecting public health. If so, courts proceed to consider whether the regulation "directly advances" the government's asserted interest and whether or not it is "more extensive than is necessary to serve that interest."[85] The government bears the burden of establishing that its regulation meets these requirements.[86]

When the speech in question is actually or potentially misleading, courts have given government agencies wide latitude to impose curative labeling or disclosure requirements. In *Zauderer v. Office of Disciplinary Counsel*, for example, the Court upheld a requirement that attorneys who advertise that they will take cases on a contingency-fee basis must also disclose that clients could be liable for court costs.[87] Under *Zauderer*, a requirement that the purveyor of a good or service disclose factual information will be upheld so long as the requirement is not unduly burdensome and the requirement is "reasonably related to the State's interest in preventing deception of consumers."[88] In the government's view, promoting contingency-fee services without disclosing a client's potential liability was inherently misleading, as potential clients would not be aware that a contingency fee could still cost them out of pocket. As the Court held more recently, the "essential features of the rule at issue in *Zauderer*" were that the disclosure requirement was "intended to combat the problem of inherently misleading commercial advertisements" and only entailed "an accurate statement" about the nature of what was being advertised that did not prevent those regulated from "conveying any additional information" about the services they provide.[89] Although courts purport to impose a less stringent

84 Turner Broadcasting System, Inc. v. FCC, 512 U.S. 622, 641 (1994).

85 447 U.S. 566 (1980). It should be noted that although the Court continues to apply the *Central Hudson* test, several justices on the Court have signaled their disagreement with it. *See* 44 Liquormart, Inc. v. Rhode Island, 517 U.S. 484 (1996); *see also* United States v. United Foods, 533 U.S. 405, 409-10 (2001) (noting "criticism" of *Central Hudson* test by multiple justices); Thompson v. Western States Medical Center, 535 U.S. 357, 367–68 (2002) (same).

86 *Central Hudson*, 447 U.S. at 570.

87 Zauderer v. Office of Disciplinary Counsel of Supreme Court of Ohio, 471 U.S. 626 (1985).

88 *Id.* at 651; *see also* Milavetz, Gallop & Milavetz, P.A. v. United States, __ U.S. __ (2010) (slip op. at 20).

89 *Id.*

test in such instances, their approach is consonant with *Central Hudson* as only non-fraudulent speech is protected, preventing consumer deception is clearly a substantial government interest, and disclosure requirements are almost necessarily more narrowly tailored to prevent potential deception or miscommunication than bans or limitations on commercial messages.

When speech is potentially misleading, a requirement of curative counter-speech is preferable to a limitation on speech. In short, when possible, the remedy for potentially misleading speech should be yet more speech. On this basis, requirements that producers or vendors qualify claims about products in advertisements and labels are more permissible than limitations on label or ad claims. This does not mean that affirmative labeling requirements are always permissible, however, as a recent fight over the labeling of products using biotechnology shows.

In 1994, Vermont adopted a law mandating disclosure labels for milk and milk products offered for retail sale if the dairy cows from which the milk was taken had been injected with recombinant bovine somatotropin (aka rBST or rBGH).[90] Bovine somatotropin (BST) is a naturally occurring growth hormone that affects the amount of milk dairy cows produce. rBST is produced in a lab through recombinant DNA techniques. Injected into dairy cows, rBST increases milk production. According to the FDA, the use of rBST affects the dairy cows, but has no effect on the chemical composition of the milk produced and raises no human health or safety concerns.[91] Use of rBST on dairy cows results in no measurable increase in milk BST levels, although it does increase the incidence of mastitis in cows. The FDA went even further to declare that any suggestion that milk from non–rBST-treated cows was preferable for health or safety reasons would be "false and misleading."[92] Lacking any definitive scientific basis for claiming that the labeling law protected human health or safety, Vermont justified its law on the grounds that the public had a "right to know" whether given milk products had come from cows treated with rBST. Vermont consumers, the state argued, would benefit from knowing which milk products came from cows treated with BST and the consequent ability of altering their buying habits accordingly.

Dairy manufacturers successfully challenged Vermont's labeling requirement in federal court.[93] In *International Dairy Foods Association v. Amestoy*, the U.S. Court of Appeals for the Second Circuit found that Vermont's labeling requirement violated dairy manufacturers' First Amendment rights. Applying the *Central Hudson* analysis, the Court found that Vermont did not have a substantial interest in compelling dairy manufacturers to adopt mandatory rBST labels. Vermont cited no evidence that milk

90 6 V.S.A. § 254 (1995) provided: "If rBST has been used in the production of milk or a milk product for retail sale in this state, the retail milk or milk product shall be labeled as such."

91 Interim Guidance on the Voluntary Labeling of Milk and Milk Products From Cows That Have Not Been Treated With Recombinant Bovine Somatotropin, 59 Fed. Reg. 6279, 6280 (Feb. 10, 2004).

92 *Id.*

93 International Dairy Foods Association v. Amestoy, 92 F.3d 67 (1995).

from rBST-treated cows posed any risk to public health and did not claim that health or safety concerns motivated adoption of the labeling requirement. Indeed, as the court noted, it was "undisputed that the dairy products derived from herds treated with rBST are indistinguishable from products derived from untreated herds."[94] Rather, Vermont adopted the standard due to "strong consumer interest and the public's 'right to know.'"[95] This, the court held, was insufficient.

The Second Circuit pointedly rejected the argument that consumer interest or an alleged "right to know" about how a product was made constituted a sufficiently substantial government interest to justify compelling commercial speech.[96] In the court's words, "consumer curiosity alone is not a strong enough state interest to sustain the compulsion of even an accurate, factual statement."[97] Although the court accepted that some consumers may wish to know which milk products came from rBST-treated or rBST-free cows, in the absence of some health or safety-related concern, this interest was not sufficient to impose a requirement on producers.[98]

There is a virtually infinite array of characteristics about any given product or the process through which it was made that may interest consumers. Thus, if consumer interest alone were sufficient to authorize a labeling requirement, the court observed, "there is no end to the information that states could require manufacturers to disclose about their production methods."[99] A consumer interest standard would empower governments to force producers to stigmatize their own products. Yet the court reported that it could find no case in which a federal court had upheld a regulation "requiring a product's manufacturers to publish the functional equivalent of a warning about a production method that has no discernible impact on a final product."[100] If the First Amendment freedom to speak includes a "concomitant freedom not to speak publicly"[101] – and if the Amendment's protection extends to commercial speech – then the court found that an undifferentiated consumer interest would not be enough.

Does this mean that a mandatory labeling requirement for nanomaterial content would run afoul of the First Amendment? Not necessarily. The Second Circuit's *Amestoy* decision rested on the court's finding that there was no public health or safety justification for the mandated disclosure. The FDA and others had reviewed extensive evidence concerning milk from rBST-treated cows and found the milk to be indistinguishable from milk from untreated cows. Had there been a difference, and had there been a plausible argument that the difference could have a health effect, the labeling requirement would likely have been upheld.

[94] *Id.* at 69.

[95] *See* International Dairy Foods Association v. Amestoy, 898 F.Supp. 246, 249 (D. Vt. 1995).

[96] *See Amestoy*, 92 F.3d at 73 n.1 ("mere consumer concern is not, in itself, a substantial interest.").

[97] *Id.* at 74.

[98] *Id.*

[99] *Id.*

[100] *Id.* at 73.

[101] Harper & Row Publishers v. Nation Enterprise, 471 U.S. 539, 559 (1985).

Whereas milk from rBST-treated cows was no different from other milk, products containing nanoscale materials are physically different from other products. In addition, those differences could have health or safety consequences. Because nanoscale particles often behave differently than larger particles of the same substance, the switch from larger material to nanoscale material in a product could alter the product's effects.

Where there is scientific evidence that the inclusion of nanoscale materials poses a health or safety risk, it should be relatively easy to impose a product or material-specific labeling requirement without violating constitutional norms. Where health and safety risks are hypothesized, but not demonstrated, a labeling rule might be more vulnerable to challenge. In neither *Amestoy* nor other cases have courts addressed whether government agencies may adopt a "precautionary" approach to disclosure and mandate a label on the basis of potential but unverified risks. The question with such labels is whether the government has a greater interest in allowing consumers to pursue their subjective risk preferences than with their product preferences generally.

Courts have also upheld disclosure or compelled speech requirements where the speech or message was part of a broader regulatory scheme of which the compelled disclosure or communication was merely one element of the broader scheme.[102] On this basis, the Supreme Court has upheld compelled contributions to agricultural marketing programs,[103] and lower courts have upheld labeling requirements designed to facilitate compliance with other state regulations. In *Sorrell v. National Electrical Manufacturers Association*, for example, the U.S. Court of Appeals for the Second Circuit upheld a state labeling requirement for light bulbs containing mercury.[104] This law, the court held, facilitated the state's efforts to reduce mercury pollution and to ensure the proper disposal and recycling of mercury-containing products. In accordance with these precedents, a nanomaterial content labeling requirement that is part of, and facilitates the administration or enforcement of, a broader regulatory initiative program would be more insulated against First Amendment challenge. So, for instance, were the FDA to require cosmetics manufacturers to disclose nanomaterial content that has not been subject to safety testing, such a requirement might be justified as part of the agency's broader regulation and disclosure rules for cosmetics.

Where labels are permissible, not any mandatory label will do, however. There would have to be a sufficiently close relationship between the government's interest, such as a specific health or safety threat, and the label. Therefore, a requirement that manufacturers disclose specific types of nanoparticles believed to pose a potential risk would be easier to defend than a generic "contains nanoscale particles" label

[102] *See* Glickman v. Wileman Brothers & Elliott, Inc., 521 U.S. 457 (1997) (upholding compelled assessments on tree fruit growers to support advertising as part of larger regulatory marketing scheme).

[103] *Id.*

[104] National Elec. Mfrs. Ass'n v. Sorrell, 272 F.3d 104 (2nd Cir. 2001).

applied across a wide range of products, irrespective of the types of nanomaterial content. Although any labeling requirement would be subject to First Amendment scrutiny, a label rule tied to a particular health or safety concern would be more likely to withstand legal challenge.

THE PROMISE OF VOLUNTARY LABELING

Government regulation is not the only impetus for product labels. Manufacturers have substantial economic incentives to provide consumers with information about their products, particularly information that serves to differentiate one maker's products from another's. Firms use labels to attract customers, differentiate their products from those of their competitors, and promote the presence of potentially desirable product characteristics.[105] Indeed, in competitive markets, producers have an incentive to disclose any information that is likely to make their product more desirable to consumers, at least so long as the cost of providing the information is less than its value to consumers.[106]

At the same time, consumers have a strong incentive to search out products that satisfy their preferences. If a preference is strongly held, consumers are likely to invest time and effort to satisfy that preference. As Beales, Craswell, and Salop note, "Increases in the efficiency of purchase decisions made are equivalent to increases in real income."[107] When consumers do not seek out such information, this is because the cost of obtaining the information is greater than the value of the information to the consumer, indicating that the information is costly to obtain (as with a credence attribute) or the preference is not particularly strong.

In competitive markets, firms have an incentive to provide consumers with positive information about their products, and failure to disclose information that consumers desire can be costly. In a competitive marketplace, rational consumers may assume that firms highlight the positive attributes of their products. The failure to disclose something positive creates a negative inference.[108] As Golan et al. note, "competitive disclosure," also referred to as "unfolding," often "results in explicit claims for all positive aspects of products and allows consumers to make appropriate inferences about foods without claims."[109] As Ippolito and Mathios report, "in cases where an issue is important to consumers and there is adequate competition among producers of goods with varied levels of characteristics, competition will generate the desirable information."[110]

[105] Golan et al., *supra*, at 119.
[106] Beales, Craswell, & Salop, *supra* at 502.
[107] *Id.*
[108] Golan et al., *supra*, at 128.
[109] *Id.* at 129; *see also* Ippolito and Mathios, *supra* at 427 ("If consumers value the characteristic and if firms have a credible means of disclosing the characteristic, economic theory predicts that firms with superior products would have an incentive to highlight that fact voluntarily.").
[110] Ippolito and Mathios, *supra* at 428.

If all products in a given market share a negative characteristic, however, competitive disclosure will only occur if producers of potential substitutes draw attention to these product attributes.[111] This situation is likely to occur with product categories in which there is a certain degree of uniformity or a basic characteristic that all must share. It is unlikely that any egg producer is going to advertise or voluntarily disclose the cholesterol content of eggs.[112] When products differ within a given category, comparative marketing is common. So if only some products in a given category contain nanoscale ingredients, and this information is relevant to consumers, manufacturers have adequate incentive to disclose this information, on the product label or otherwise.

The ability to make positive health claims about their products has provided food producers with an incentive to improve the healthfulness of their products.[113] By extension, if the presence or lack of nanoscale materials is desirable, and producers are allowed or required to disclose this information, they will have a greater incentive to alter their product designs in accord with consumer preferences.[114] Even for those product lines in which nanoscale ingredients are common, such as sunscreens, they are not universal, and there is ample market space for a competing firm to promote itself as a "nano-free" alternative.

Consider the development of kosher foods. Religiously observant Jews demand food that is prepared in accordance with Kosher laws. In response to this demand, many food producers submit their products to evaluation by a Rabbinical council so that it can be certified as kosher and be eligible for a voluntary label. Even though the demand for kosher foods is only a small part of the market, many large corporations participate in this process.

Producers are more likely to under-provide information about the consequences and risks associated with nanomaterials than with the presence or use of nanotechnology. This may be because some of the potential risks and characteristics of nanotech materials may have public good properties.[115] Product-specific information, such as whether nanoscale particles were used and what their specific benefits are in a particular product, is more likely to be provided. As a consequence, mandatory disclosure or labeling requirements are "most likely to be appropriate when information affects an entire product class without differentiating the brands

[111] Golan, et al., *supra*, at 129.

[112] Though, it should be noted, where a given product category shares a negative characteristic, this creates an incentive for other firms to create a competing substitute that does not have this negative feature and promote this attribute, as has occurred with egg substitutes.

[113] Ippolito and Mathios, *supra* at 419.

[114] Beales, *supra* at 111 ("If there are enough consumers willing to pay to avoid a particular process, or obtain a process they prefer, manufacturers have every incentive to provide those products.").

[115] Beales, Craswell & Salop, *supra* at 503 (discussing how producers are likely to under-provide information that has public good properties); *id.* at 504 "When information benefits all sellers equally" there is less incentive for sellers to disclose).

within that class."[116] It is unclear whether this is the case with nanotechnology, however.

If a substantial minority of consumers desires information about the nanomaterial content of consumer products, it is likely that more firms will begin to label their products accordingly. Firms making products containing nanoscale materials might not so label their products, but firms that make competing nano-free products will have ample incentive to differentiate their products in this fashion to attract those consumers for whom this is a plus. In this way, voluntary nano-content labeling could develop along a path followed by organic labels. A non-trivial portion of consumers had a preference for organic products, prompting many producers to identify their products as organic. This drew consumers away from conventional products toward those with the desired characteristics. Over time, the organic share of the market grew. Federal agencies facilitated this process not by mandating labels, but rather by issuing labeling guidelines to ensure that label terms would be commonly understood. The promulgation of such definitions may have actually enhanced the value of organic labels, as it may have buttressed consumer confidence by making such labels more trustworthy and reliable. Federal agencies, or private third-party organizations, could play a similar role to facilitate voluntary nanotech labeling. There are already a handful of third-party entities offering or promoting nano-related certification and private labeling.

In many contexts, the best first step for the government to take is to remove or reduce barriers to greater private provision of information. Restraints on information disclosure inhibit competition in addition to limiting consumer choice.[117] Insofar as the FDA or other agencies are discouraging firms from making claims about nanotechnology, it may be inhibiting welfare-maximizing disclosures.

Some fear that the absence of an official labeling requirement, or government standards defining what label terms mean, will undermine consumer confidence.[118] This is a reasonable concern. If consumers lack confidence in a label and cannot be sure it provides accurate or relevant information, then they are unlikely to pay it much heed. This is true whether the label is mandatory or voluntary. The adoption of regulatory definitions and standards by regulatory agencies can address this concern by clarifying what relevant terms mean. Standardizing terminology in this way can give consumers greater confidence in labels and other disclosures without inhibiting market efficiency or consumer choice.

[116] *Id.* at 527.

[117] *Id.* at 514.

[118] *See, e.g.*, Kenneth W. Abbott, Gary E. Marchant, & Douglas J. Sylvester, A Framework Convention for Nanotechnology? 36 Envtl. L. Rep. 10931, 10932 (2006) ("an official process is needed to provide assurances of safety and regulatory capacity so that the public can have confidence in this new technology, which will not occur with informal or voluntary controls.").

CONCLUSION

Consumers do not know much about nanotechnology,[119] nor much about the nanomaterial content of the products they buy. At present, it is also not clear that consumers care. The primary purpose of a mandatory labeling requirement is to increase market efficiency by making it easier for consumers to identify those products that match their preferences. But in the case of nanotechnology, do consumers even have preferences to match?

The purpose of a labeling requirement cannot be to give consumers "perfect" information or to prevent them from relying on "incomplete" information. Consumers never have perfect information. The question is thus whether labeling regulations will enhance marketplace efficiency over what is likely to emerge in the alternative.[120] Absent evidence that there is an existing market failure to justify intervention, many analysts would argue that regulators should leave well enough alone.[121] This is particularly true in an area like nanotechnology in which it is not clear what a labeling regime would require.

A generic "contains nanomaterials" label would not be particularly informative to consumers. Although some nanoscale particles may pose new or unique risks, others will not. Although the small size of nanoscale particles is part of what may make them dangerous, small size itself is not indicative of a health or safety threat. A labeling regime that suggests that any and all products containing nanoscale materials pose the same degree of risk would likely mislead more than inform. Yet scientific understanding of nanotechnology is not sufficient for a more detailed labeling regime – at least not yet.

One possible approach to disclosure is that embodied in the FDA's regulation of cosmetics. As discussed previously, cosmetic manufacturers are required to disclose the presence of ingredients the safety of which they cannot assure. Insofar as some nanoscale materials have not been tested or used long enough to indicate whether they have potentially deleterious effects, cosmetic makers may be required to disclose this information with their ingredients. This sort of mandatory disclosure would provide a degree of accurate and worthwhile information – the lack of scientific knowledge about an ingredient that may or may not be dangerous – without imposing a blanket and uninformative label requirement.

[119] *See generally*, Peter D. Hart Research Associates, *Awareness of and Attitudes Toward Nanotechnology and Synthetic Biology: A Report of Findings*, Sept. 16, 2008.

[120] Howard Beales, Richard Craswell, and Steven C. Salop, *The Efficient Regulation of Consumer Information*, 24 J.L. & ECON. 491, 501 (1981) ("the real issue is when the government can or ought to intervene in the information market to improve the market's performance.").

[121] Beales, Craswell & Salop, *supra* at 512 ("intervention must be limited to those instances in which information imperfections demonstrably lead to significant consumer injury and which can be corrected in a cost-effective manner – without creating serious distortions or side effects which lead to even greater injury.").

The absence of mandatory labels would not necessarily leave consumers without information. When a group of consumers have a strong preference for products with particular characteristics, producers have an incentive to cater to that group's preferences. Several organizations have begun to develop labels or labeling guidelines, and little stops other consumer or industry organizations from following suit. If the public, or a substantial minority, begins to care about the use or presence of nanomaterials in consumer products, producers will have an incentive to identify those products that match strongly held consumer preferences. There will also be market opportunities for firms that seek to augment consumer awareness of nanotechnology and market products accordingly. So even if consumer curiosity provides an inadequate legal or policy basis for mandating a disclosure or warning label, it is more than ample reason for producers to disclose information that consumers desire.[122]

[122] Frederick H. Degnan, *The Food Label and the Right-to-Know*, 52 FOOD & DRUG L.J. 49, 59 (1997).

10

Public Nuisance

A Potential Common Law Response to Nanotechnology's Uncertain Harms

Albert C. Lin

We live in a chemical soup. On a daily basis, each of us is exposed to hundreds of chemicals, the vast majority of which have been subject to little or no testing to determine whether they are toxic to humans or the environment.[1] Many of these chemicals will turn out to be harmless, but others will have detrimental or even devastating effects that will become apparent only with the passage of time. By introducing thousands of new substances whose health and environmental effects are poorly understood, if at all, nanotechnology will only add to the complexity of this chemical soup.

The problem of toxic ignorance is widely recognized, yet legislatures, regulatory agencies, courts, and the chemical industry have done relatively little to address the problem. Without analyzing the risks posed by chemicals before they become widely distributed, it is difficult to determine the precautions that should be taken or the scope of any health and environmental problems that may result. Experiences in which we have discovered the hazards of chemical substances belatedly – ranging from asbestos to benzene to polychlorinated biphenyls (PCBs) – illustrate the potentially broad and serious consequences of toxic ignorance.[2]

[1] *See* Marla Cone, *Chemicals Get the Safe Treatment*, L.A. TIMES, Sept. 14, 2008, at A1 (reporting that tests of umbilical cords show that a newborn's body contains nearly 300 chemical compounds); Douglas Fischer, *Study Ties Pollution to Cancer*, OAKLAND TRIB., May 14, 2007, at 1 (reporting that "[w]omen face daily and widespread exposure to hundreds of chemicals linked to breast cancer"); Douglas Fischer, *The Great Experiment*, OAKLAND TRIB., Mar. 10, 2005, http://www.insidebayarea.com/bodyburden/ci_2600903 (stating that "[t]housands of chemicals are found in everyday consumer products" and that "EPA has full toxicity data for about 25 percent [of them]").

[2] *See* David Gee & Morris Greenberg, *Asbestos: From 'Magic' to Malevolent Mineral, in* THE PRECAUTIONARY PRINCIPLE IN THE 20TH CENTURY 49 (Poul Harremoës et al., eds., London, UK: Earthscan Publication, 2002) (describing the toxic effects of asbestos exposure); Peter F. Infante, *Benzene: A Historical Perspective on the American and European Occupational Setting, in* THE PRECAUTIONARY PRINCIPLE IN THE 20TH CENTURY, *supra*, at 35 (describing poisonous and carcinogenic effects of use of benzene as solvent); Janna G. Koppe & Jane Keys, *PCBs and the Precautionary*

Uncertainty is a constant companion in scientists' efforts to understand the phenomena occurring around us, and the field of toxicology is no exception to that principle.[3] Rarely do we know as much as we would like to know about cause-and-effect relationships. Yet the level of toxic ignorance that surrounds us is not the inevitable result of the limits of scientific inquiry. Rather, it is the consequence of deliberate decisions by the chemical industry and by those who incorporate chemicals into their manufacturing processes to avoid testing that would identify at least some of the likely harms.

A regulatory mandate to conduct comprehensive testing is one possible response to the problem, but such an approach would meet formidable political resistance. It might also require significant resources and drive useful substances from the market. This chapter discusses how public nuisance litigation might be applied in the absence of such a mandate to attack the toxic ignorance problem presented by untested substances, including engineered nanomaterials. After a brief discussion of our ignorance of the possible hazards posed by nanotechnology, this chapter explains how a public nuisance action might be used to compel manufacturers, processors, and importers to perform safety testing on nanomaterials. In light of various historical limitations on the scope of public nuisance doctrine, such an action could prompt the desired testing without imposing overly onerous liability on nanotechnology companies.

I. THE PROBLEM OF TOXIC IGNORANCE

A. *Background*

According to some estimates, chemical exposure is responsible for tens of thousands of deaths per year in the United States.[4] Nonetheless, we have surprisingly little

Principle, *in* The Precautionary Principle in the 20th Century, *supra*, at 64 (describing toxic effects of PCBs, a class of organic compounds widely used as insulators in electrical equipment).

3 *See* Albert C. Lin, *The Unifying Role of Harm in Environmental Law*, 2006 Wis. L. Rev. 897, 968–69 (discussing uncertainty associated with toxic exposure); Comm. on Improving Risk Analysis Approaches Used by the U.S. EPA, Nat'l Research Council, Science and Decisions 4 (2009) [hereinafter Nat'l Research Council, Science and Decisions], *available at* http://www.nap.edu/openbook.php?record_id=12209 (describing uncertainty as "an inherent property of scientific data").

4 *See* Christine H. Kim, *Piercing the Veil of Toxic Ignorance: Judicial Creation of Scientific Research*, 15 N.Y.U. Envtl. L.J. 540, 542 (2007) (reporting an estimated 33,900 annual United States cancer deaths from occupational and environmental exposure to pollutants); David Pimentel et al., *Ecology of Increasing Disease: Population Growth and Environmental Degradation*, 48 BioScience 817, 817 (1998) (noting estimate of 30,000 cancer-related deaths per year in the United States attributable to chemical exposure and calculating that "40% of world deaths can be attributed to various environmental factors, especially organic and chemical pollutants"); *see also* Comm. on Developmental Toxicology, Nat'l Research Council, Scientific Frontiers in Developmental Toxicology and Risk Assessment 1 (2000), *available at* http://books.nap.edu/openbook.php?record_id=9871 (estimating that 3% of approximately 120,000 birth defects in the United States per year are attributable to exposure to toxic chemicals and physical agents).

information about the health and environmental effects of the thousands of chemicals that we use on a daily basis.[5] A 1998 Environmental Protection Agency (EPA) study of toxicity data on high production volume (HPV) chemicals – those 3,000 or so chemicals imported or produced in the United States in a volume of more than 1 million pounds per year – found no toxicity information publicly available for nearly half of the chemicals identified.[6] For only a handful of these chemicals – 7% – was a full set of basic toxicity information available.[7] Although voluntary efforts in the last decade have sought to collect or generate more information on the potential toxic effects of HPV chemicals, significant information gaps remain.[8] Toxicity data are even more lacking for the 80,000 or so non-HPV chemicals found in commerce today.[9]

Expert panels and government agencies have decried the lack of toxicity testing,[10] and even the chemical industry has acknowledged the wide information gap.[11] With the rapid development and commercialization of nanotechnology, the information

[5] *See* John S. Applegate, *Bridging the Data Gap: Balancing the Supply and Demand for Chemical Information*, 86 TEX. L. REV. 1365, 1381–83 (2008) (discussing lack of information); Wendy E. Wagner, *Commons Ignorance: The Failure of Environmental Law to Produce Needed Information on Health and the Environment*, 53 DUKE L.J. 1619, 1625–30 (2004) (describing lack of monitoring information, toxicity testing, and theoretical understanding regarding how hazardous substances affect human health and environment).

[6] OFFICE OF POLLUTION PREVENTION & TOXICS, ENVTL. PROTECTION AGENCY, CHEMICAL HAZARD DATA AVAILABILITY STUDY 2 (1998) [hereinafter EPA, CHEMICAL HAZARD DATA], *available at* http://www.epa.gov/HPV/pubs/general/hazchem.pdf; *see also* ENVTL. HEALTH PROGRAM, ENVTL. DEF. FUND, TOXIC IGNORANCE 7, 15 (1997), *available at* http://www.edf.org/documents/243_toxicignorance.pdf (reporting, based on sample of 100 HPV chemicals, that "even the most basic toxicity testing results cannot be found in the public record for nearly 75% of the top-volume chemicals in commercial use"). An earlier study by the National Research Council of the National Academy of Sciences found similar information gaps. *See* NAT'L RESEARCH COUNCIL, NAT'L ACAD. OF SCIS., TOXICITY TESTING 12 fig. 2 (1984), *available at* http://books.nap.edu/openbook.php?record_id=317 (finding "minimal" toxicity information available for only twenty-two percent of high volume chemicals).

[7] *See* EPA, CHEMICAL HAZARD DATA, *supra* note 6, at 2.

[8] *See* Albert C. Lin, *Deciphering the Chemical Soup: Using Public Nuisance to Compel Chemical Testing*, 85 NOTRE DAME L. REV. 955, 970–71 (2010).

[9] *See* CTRS. FOR OCCUPATIONAL & ENVTL. HEALTH, UNIV. OF CAL., GREEN CHEMISTRY 1 (2008), *available at* http://coeh.berkeley.edu/docs/news/green_chem_brief.pdf ("[H]ealth and environmental effects of the great majority [of such chemicals] . . . are largely unknown."); U.S. GOV'T ACCOUNTABILITY OFFICE, CHEMICAL REGULATION 1–2 (2005), *available at* http://www.gao.gov/new.items/d05458.pdf (stating there are more than 82,000 chemicals listed in EPA's Toxic Substances Control Act [TSCA] inventory); Applegate, *supra* note 5, at 1383 (contending that studies finding data gap for chemical testing likely understate extent of problem because studies focus on HPV chemicals, for which presumably greatest amount of data exists).

[10] *See* Wendy Wagner, *Using Competition-Based Regulation to Bridge the Toxics Data Gap*, 83 IND. L.J. 629, 636 & n.40 (2008) (listing studies that recommend more toxicity testing).

[11] *See* EPA, CHEMICAL HAZARD DATA, *supra* note 6, at 4 (discussing analysis by Chemical Manufacturers Association concluding that 47% of chemicals studied had full screening information data); *cf. Hearing Before the S. Comm. on Env't & Pub. Works*, 109th Cong. 2 (2006), *available at* http://epw.senate.gov/109th/Wilson_Testimony.pdf (testimony of Michael P. Wilson, PhD, MPH, Univ. of Cal., Berkeley) (describing inability of manufacturers and other businesses to identify and

gap threatens to expand into an information chasm.[12] Through nanoscale science and engineering, researchers are creating substances with new physical and chemical properties. The enhanced mechanical, electrical, optical, catalytic, and/or biological properties of these substances have led to their use in various consumer products, including cosmetics, sunscreens, stain-resistant clothing, paints, food storage containers, and electronics, and a much wider array of applications is on the way.[13] Yet many of the very properties that make these substances useful for certain products and processes – their small size, chemical composition, surface structure, solubility, shape, and aggregative tendencies – also may make them harmful when they enter the human body or the environment.[14] Nanomaterials that are inhaled, ingested, or absorbed through the skin, for example, may enter the bloodstream and penetrate the blood–brain barrier and possibly could interfere with DNA processes.[15] Despite such concerns, relatively little is known about the health and ecological effects of nanomaterial exposure. Research efforts regarding such effects, the processes that govern environmental fate and transport of nanomaterials, and the likelihood of exposure are just getting underway.[16] The toxic ignorance problem is especially acute with respect to engineered nanomaterials because these substances vary widely in shape, size, and surface coatings.[17]

B. *Incentives Not to Test*

The toxic ignorance problem is the unsurprising result of rational decisions by chemical manufacturers not to conduct extensive testing.[18] Our legal system generally assumes that chemicals are "innocent until proven guilty"; we restrict chemical manufacture and distribution only if and when harm is demonstrated.[19] To make

replace hazardous chemicals); Mark Schapiro, *Toxic Inaction: Why Poisonous, Unregulated Chemicals End Up in Our Blood*, HARPER'S MAG., Oct. 2007, at 78, 80–81 (reporting chemical industry representative's praise of ineffective toxic regulatory statute).

12 *See* Jeffrey Rudd, *Regulating the Impacts of Engineered Nanoparticles Under TSCA: Shifting Authority from Industry to Government*, 33 COLUM. J. ENVTL. L. 215, 229 (2008) (expressing concerns regarding prioritization of "commercialization of nanoparticles over EPA's ability to assess and regulate the risks that nanoparticles pose to public health and the environment"). *See generally* Albert C. Lin, *Size Matters: Regulating Nanotechnology*, 31 HARV. ENVTL. L. REV. 349 (2007) (arguing that existing regulatory authority is inadequate to handle developments in nanotechnology and proposing a more adequate legislative framework).

13 *See* Lin, *supra* note 12, at 353–54.

14 *See id.* at 358.

15 *See* PRESIDENT'S CANCER PANEL, REDUCING ENVIRONMENTAL CANCER RISK: WHAT WE CAN DO NOW 40 (2010).

16 *See* EPA, Nanomaterial Research Strategy 11–36 (2009).

17 *See* Lin, *supra* note 12, at 357–58.

18 *See* Wagner, *supra* note 5, at 1622–25.

19 *See* Carl F. Cranor, *Do You Want to Bet Your Children's Health on Post-Market Harm Principles? An Argument for a Trespass or Permission Model for Regulating Toxicants*, 19 VILL. ENVTL. L.J. 251, 252

matters worse, the system largely excuses manufacturers from having to produce toxicity information, and as described further below, even gives manufacturers incentives not to test. In theory, government agencies, consumer organizations, and others can step in and perform toxicological research on their own. These actors, however, rarely have the resources to do so.[20] In addition, they may not be able to access the information needed to conduct safety testing because of trade secret claims by manufacturers.[21] Consequently, society relies heavily on chemical manufacturers to do the testing themselves.[22]

Manufacturers have the greatest familiarity with their products and the most opportunities to learn about them, can channel the results of safety testing back into product design to avoid injuries, and can spread the costs of testing among customers.[23] Various factors discourage manufacturers from generating toxicity information, however. First, thorough toxicity testing can be expensive, and manufacturers cannot easily profit from investments in producing toxicity data.[24] In ordinary product development research, companies transform knowledge from that research into private gain through the development and sale of marketable products.[25] By contrast, it is much more difficult for private entities to capture the value of information generated from toxicity research.[26] Indeed, from a company's perspective, investment in such research is risky if not unwise.[27] It is impossible for studies to establish that a substance poses no risks at all, whereas results suggesting a potential hazard could trigger

(2008). *See generally* Lin, *supra* note 3 (contending that environmental law has generally responded to demonstrated harm).

20 *See* John S. Applegate, *The Perils of Unreasonable Risk: Information, Regulatory Policy, and Toxic Substances Control*, 91 COLUM. L. REV. 261, 298–99 (1991) ("Toxicology information is too expensive for workers and consumers [or even unions and consumer organizations] to generate."); *id.* at 306–07 (concluding that "[t]here will never be enough money in a federal or state budget to fill the existing data gaps on a chemical-by-chemical basis," given the number of substances for which testing would be required); Wendy E. Wagner, *Choosing Ignorance in the Manufacture of Toxic Products*, 82 CORNELL L. REV. 773, 789 (1997).

21 *See* Wagner, *supra* note 20, at 798; Wagner, *supra* note 5, at 1645, 1699–1705. See generally Thomas O. McGarity & Sidney A. Shapiro, *The Trade Secret Status of Health and Safety Testing Information: Reforming Agency Disclosure Policies*, 93 HARV. L. REV. 837 (1980) (arguing for broad disclosure of health and safety data, notwithstanding trade secret claims).

22 *See* Applegate, *supra* note 20, at 299.

23 *See* Wagner, *supra* note 20, at 798–802.

24 *See* Mary L. Lyndon, *Information Economics and Chemical Toxicity: Designing Laws to Produce and Use Data*, 87 MICH. L. REV. 1795, 1813 (1989) (noting benefits from toxicological research, including health information and identification of externalities, "may not be recovered by individual firms, or their impact may not be easily identifiable as the results of one company's research"); Wagner, *supra* note 5, at 1634–35 (noting high out-of-pocket costs associated with safety research); *see also* Jennifer H. Arlen, *Compensation Systems and Efficient Deterrence*, 52 MD. L. REV. 1093, 1121 (1993) ("Manufacturers do not benefit from proving that their product is free from a risk – if indeed it is – if consumers do not expect the product to be risky in the first place.").

25 *See* Wagner, *supra* note 5, at 1631.

26 *See* Lyndon, *supra* note 24, at 1813; Wagner, *supra* note 5, at 1631–32.

27 *See* Lyndon, *supra* note 24, at 1813; Wagner, *supra* note 5, at 1631–32.

negative publicity as well as an obligation to do additional, more costly testing.[28] Moreover, because of the long-term and latent effects frequently involved in toxic exposure, chemical toxicity is not readily visible to consumers.[29] This gives manufacturers little economic incentive to undertake research that might only identify and document toxic effects.[30] In the resultant market, untested chemicals – which will appear to the consumer to pose no detrimental risks – possess an advantage over chemicals having some indication of potential toxicity.[31] Although it is theoretically possible for a manufacturer to gain a commercial advantage by marketing a tested product as "safe," the ease of making such claims and the difficulty of verifying them often lead consumers to discount them.[32]

C. *Tort Law Exacerbates the Ignorance Problem*

1. The Duty to Test

In theory, liability rules promote toxicity research by giving manufacturers an incentive to ensure that their products are reasonably safe. Indeed, tort law imposes on manufacturers an unequivocal duty to test their products for dangers associated with their use.[33] This duty includes the duty to test for toxic risks associated with the use of chemical products.[34] As the *Third Restatement of Torts* notes:

> Of course, a seller bears responsibility to perform reasonable testing prior to marketing a product and to discover risks and risk-avoidance measures that such testing would reveal. A seller is charged with knowledge of what reasonable testing would reveal. If testing is not undertaken, or is performed in an inadequate manner, and this failure results in a defect that causes harm, the seller is subject to liability for harm caused by such defect.[35]

[28] *See* Wagner, *supra* note 5, at 1635–36.

[29] *See* Albert C. Lin, *Beyond Tort: Compensating Victims of Environmental Toxic Injury*, 78 S. CAL. L. REV. 1439, 1446 (2005).

[30] *See* Applegate, *supra* note 20, at 299; Lyndon, *supra* note 24, at 1813–14; Alan Schwartz, *Products Liability, Corporate Structure, and Bankruptcy: Toxic Substances and the Remote Risk Relationship*, 14 J. LEGAL STUD. 689, 700–01, 710 (1985); Wagner, *supra* note 5, at 1631–32. Moreover, corporate managers face short-term profit motivations that further disfavor testing. *See* Margaret A. Berger, *Eliminating General Causation: Notes Towards a New Theory of Justice and Toxic Torts*, 97 COLUM. L. REV. 2117, 2138–39 (1997); Wagner, *supra* note 20, at 785.

[31] *See* Lyndon, *supra* note 24, at 1814.

[32] *See id.* at 1816 ("Even when privately produced information is of high quality, the commercial context diminishes its credibility and, thus, its value."); Wagner, *supra* note 10, at 635.

[33] *See* AMERICAN LAW OF PRODUCTS LIABILITY § 11:1 (John D. Hodson & Charles J. Nagy, Jr. eds., 3d rev. ed. 2005) (explaining that duty to test and inspect products is an aspect of manufacturer's duty of reasonable care); Wagner, *supra* note 20, at 803–04 (describing duty "to resolve at least basic preventable scientific uncertainties prior to marketing a product").

[34] *See* 72A C.J.S. *Products Liability* § 112 (2004) (stating that "manufacturer of a chemical, a dangerous product, is under a duty to exercise a high degree of care," which "includes the duty to inspect or test the chemical product").

[35] RESTATEMENT (THIRD) OF TORTS: PRODUCTS LIABILITY § 2 (1998).

Numerous cases recognize the existence of a duty to test for hazards.[36] In light of this duty, manufacturers are presumed to have the knowledge of an expert in the field and to be aware of reasonably foreseeable dangers.[37] Under certain circumstances, a manufacturer may have a continuing duty to test for hazards after the sale of a product.[38] And in some jurisdictions, manufacturers who conduct "state of the art" testing for toxic hazards may gain a complete defense to liability.[39]

2. Difficulties in Enforcing the Duty to Test

The duty to test for toxic hazards, however, is enforceable only if a plaintiff is injured and brings a cause of action against the manufacturer in strict liability, negligence, negligent failure to warn, or the like.[40] Under existing law, the failure to test for toxic hazards cannot, by itself, serve as the basis for an independent cause of action.[41]

36 *See* Messer v. Amway Corp., 106 F. App'x 678, 686 (10th Cir. 2004) (recognizing duty to test under Kansas law); George v. Celotex Corp., 914 F.2d 26, 28 (2d Cir. 1990) ("[A] manufacturer has a duty to test fully and inspect its products to uncover all dangers that are scientifically discoverable."); Dartez v. Fibreboard Corp., 765 F.2d 456, 461 (5th Cir. 1985) (holding, in products liability action, that asbestos manufacturers had "duty to fully test their products to uncover all scientifically discoverable dangers before the products are sold"); Borel v. Fibreboard Paper Prods. Corp., 493 F.2d 1076, 1090 (5th Cir. 1973); Kociemba v. G.D. Searle & Co., 707 F. Supp. 1517, 1527 (D. Minn. 1989) ("[A] manufacturer has a duty to inspect and test its products."); Elam v. Lincoln Elec. Co., 841 N.E.2d 1037, 1043–45 (Ill. App. Ct. 2005) (upholding finding that defendants breached duty to investigate health hazards associated with welding); Owens-Corning Fiberglas Corp. v. Malone, 916 S.W.2d 551, 562 (Tex. App. 1996), *aff'd* 972 S.W.2d 35 (Tex. 1998) (same); *see also* American Law of Products Liability, *supra* note 33, § 11:8 (noting manufacturer must conduct reasonable testing to demonstrate product's safety under conditions matching product's expected use).

37 *See George*, 914 F.2d at 28–29 (holding asbestos manufacturer could be charged with knowledge of adverse health effects based on what it "reasonably should have known had it either conducted its own tests or been in contact with others in the industry . . . that were testing"); *Borel*, 493 F.2d at 1089; Valentine v. Baxter Healthcare Corp., 81 Cal. Rptr. 2d 252, 269 (Dist. Ct. App. 1999) (charging manufacturer "with the best scientific and medical knowledge, and with knowledge of substantial dangers involved in [product's] reasonably foreseeable use"); *Owens-Corning*, 916 S.W.2d at 562 (charging asbestos manufacturer with knowledge of discoverable dangers, including dangers known at time by other manufacturers).

38 *See Kociemba*, 707 F. Supp. at 1528 (holding that continuing duty to test exists where manufacturer has knowledge of problem with product, product is subject to continued sale or advertising, and where there was pre-existing duty to warn of dangers associated with product).

39 *See* Wagner, *supra* note 20, at 794–95 (noting that "[s]tate-of-the-art testing generally consists of 'all of the available knowledge of a subject at a given time,'" including scientific, medical, engineering, and any other knowledge (quoting Lohrmann v. Pittsburgh Corning Corp., 782 F.2d 1156, 1164 (4th Cir. 1986))).

40 *See Kociemba*, 707 F. Supp. at 1527.

41 *See* Burton v. R.J. Reynolds Tobacco Co., 397 F.3d 906, 919–20 (10th Cir. 2005) (noting plaintiff must show failure to test and that such failure caused harm); *Kociemba*, 707 F. Supp. at 1528; *Valentine*, 81 Cal. Rptr. 2d at 265 (rejecting plaintiff's argument for independent duty to test); Vassallo v. Baxter Healthcare Corp., 696 N.E.2d 909, 921 (Mass. 1998) ("[E]vidence of failure adequately to test a product is relevant to claims of design, manufacturing, or warning defects, but does not furnish a separate, independent basis for liability."); Viguers v. Philip Morris USA, Inc., 837 A.2d 534, 541 (Pa. Super. Ct. 2003); Burley v. Kytec Innovative Sports Equip., Inc., 737 N.W.2d 397, 408 & n.6 (S.D. 2007) (noting plaintiff must show failure to test and that such failure caused harm).

For many product liability cases, this is not a significant problem: plaintiffs injured by a defective tool or appliance typically will have little difficulty in identifying their injury and the manufacturer responsible for that injury. Plaintiffs in toxic tort cases, however, face numerous obstacles to bringing successful claims. These obstacles could be especially problematic with respect to engineered nanomaterials, where small amounts of a substance may be at issue and where exposure may be undetectable or difficult to prove.

For plaintiffs, proof of causation could pose the greatest challenge of all. Toxic tort plaintiffs must prove both general causation – that a substance is capable of causing the injury at issue – and specific causation – that exposure to the substance in fact caused the plaintiffs' injury.[42] Because of the extensive research required, the probabilistic nature of research results, and the uncertainty often associated with those results, plaintiffs are rarely in a position to prove either general or specific causation.[43] The manufacturer is often the only party with the knowledge and resources to do the necessary testing, but has little reason to generate the very evidence that plaintiffs might use against it.[44] For manufacturers, ignorance about potential detrimental effects often represents a "willful, strategic choice."[45] Compounding the difficulties of potential plaintiffs, certain claims may be available only to product users and not to others exposed to toxins incidentally.[46] Ultimately, placing the burden of proof

[42] *See* Lin, *supra* note 29, at 1446–47. As Mark Geistfeld points out, a plaintiff can avoid some of the difficulties involving causation in products liability cases by alleging that a defendant manufacturer is liable for failing to warn that a product *might be* carcinogenic. *See* Mark Geistfeld, *Scientific Uncertainty and Causation in Tort Law*, 54 VAND. L. REV. 1011, 1018 (2001). Such warnings, even where toxicity data are inconclusive, "allow the user or consumer to avoid the risk warned against by making an informed decision not to purchase or use the product at all and hence not to encounter the risk." *Id.* at 1019 (quoting RESTATEMENT [THIRD] OF TORTS: PRODUCTS LIABILITY § 2 cmt. m. [1998]); *cf.* RESTATEMENT (THIRD) OF TORTS: PRODUCTS LIABILITY § 2 cmt. m (noting seller of product must perform reasonable testing but is not liable for unforeseeable risks).

[43] *See* Lin, *supra* note 29, at 1446–47. There are a few decisions in favor of toxic tort plaintiffs notwithstanding weak evidence on causation. *See* Wagner, *supra* note 20, at 828–32. Although these decisions have sometimes been cited as examples of the inability of judges and juries to handle complex scientific issues, Wendy Wagner instead characterizes these cases as examples of judge or jury nullification in which defendants are being held responsible for failing to conduct basic safety testing and thereby depriving plaintiffs of critical causation evidence. *See id.*

[44] *See* Lyndon, *supra* note 24, at 1817; Wagner, *supra* note 10, at 636 ("When virtually no toxicity information is available on a chemical product, the manufacturer has little to fear from tort liability.").

[45] Wagner, *supra* note 5, at 1638–39 (citing examples of Dalkon Shield, high-absorbency tampons, Bendectin, DES, breast implants, and tobacco); *see also* Wagner, *supra* note 20, at 775 (remarking that "it would be surprising if manufacturers ever conducted voluntary research on the long-term hazards of their products," in light of incentives generated by common law not to conduct toxicity research).

[46] *See* RESTATEMENT (SECOND) OF TORTS § 402A caveat (1965) (expressing "no opinion" as to whether strict liability for defective products extends "to harm to persons other than users or consumers"); *id.* cmt. o (noting courts have generally denied recovery to casual bystanders and others who are neither users nor consumers). *But see* DAVID G. OWEN, PRODUCTS LIABILITY LAW 266–67 (2005) (noting recent cases "have almost unanimously allowed foreseeable bystanders . . . to recover for their injuries caused by defective products").

of causation on toxic tort plaintiffs discourages manufacturers from producing toxicity information, encourages manufacturers to hinder third-party efforts to develop such information, and renders effective enforcement of the duty to test impossible. And as discussed elsewhere, the existing regulatory regime actually discourages manufacturers from performing the necessary tests.[47]

II. ARTICULATING AN ENFORCEABLE DUTY TO TEST IN PUBLIC NUISANCE DOCTRINE

To address the problem of inadequate toxicity testing, I propose the recognition of a new type of public nuisance for the failure to test engineered nanomaterials and other chemical substances. This cause of action would be enforceable against manufacturers, processors, or importers of such substances. In contrast to conventional toxic tort litigation, however, no showing of physical injury would be required. Rather, the failure to test itself constitutes a public nuisance because that failure puts the public health at risk and because the resultant lack of information undermines the ability of governments and individuals to protect public health. This section explains the legal foundation for this cause of action.

A. *Public Nuisance Doctrine*

Originating in common law criminal prosecutions by the king to address encroachments on the royal domain, public nuisance is more commonly a source of civil tort liability today.[48] The quasi-criminal nature of the tort of public nuisance nevertheless is reflected in one commentator's remark that "the sovereign's suit against a nuisance is not a tort action, but an exercise of the police power."[49] This power is a broad one, with public nuisance encompassing any "unreasonable interference with a right common to the general public."[50]

Public nuisance includes a wide variety of conduct ranging from actions harmful to public health to behavior deemed damaging to public morals.[51] Plaintiffs have asserted public nuisance claims successfully in response to various environmental problems, including dust, smoke, noise, odors, and releases of hazardous

47 *See* Lin, *supra* note 8, at 970.

48 *See* Donald G. Gifford, *Public Nuisance as a Mass Products Liability Tort*, 71 U. Cin. L. Rev. 741, 790–809 (2003) (providing a historical account of the development of public nuisance doctrine).

49 *See* Louise A. Halper, *Public Nuisance and Public Plaintiffs: Rediscovering the Common Law* (Part I), 16 Envtl. L. Rep. 10,292, 10,292 (1986).

50 Restatement (Second) of Torts § 821B(1) & cmt. a (1979).

51 *See* William L. Prosser, *Private Action for Public Nuisance*, 52 Va. L. Rev. 997, 999 (1966) (describing public nuisance as "a species of catch-all low-grade criminal offense, consisting of an interference with the rights of the community at large, which may include anything from the blocking of a highway to a gaming-house or indecent exposure").

chemicals.[52] Attempts to apply public nuisance theory in recent environmental litigation include actions against automobile manufacturers and operators of coal-fired power plants to reduce greenhouse gas emissions, as well as actions against lead paint companies to recoup the cost of lead abatement.[53] Given the breadth of conduct that might fall within its scope, it is not surprising that efforts to apply public nuisance doctrine in mass products liability cases against handgun manufacturers and tobacco companies have fueled criticism of the doctrine as lacking meaningful boundaries.[54]

So what exactly must be proven to demonstrate a public nuisance? Confusion has sometimes surrounded the definition of public nuisance, and the contours of the doctrine vary by state.[55] The term "public nuisance" sometimes refers to conduct that creates an unreasonable interference with a public right and at other times refers to the resulting harm or damages suffered by the public at large.[56] Notwithstanding such discrepancies, the basic elements of a public nuisance claim can be distilled into the following elements: (1) an unreasonable and substantial interference (2) with a public right (3) where the defendant has control of the instrumentality causing the nuisance.[57] Courts and commentators are divided over the role of fault, with some

[52] Restatement (Second) of Torts § 821B cmt. b (1979); Denise E. Antolini & Clifford L. Rechtschaffen, *Common Law Remedies: A Refresher*, 38 Envtl. L. Rep. 10,114, 10,120–21 (2008) (listing examples of circumstances in which environmental harms have been found to be public nuisances). In contrast to private nuisance, public nuisance does not require proof of interference with use and enjoyment of land. *See* Restatement (Second) of Torts § 821B cmt. h (1979); Antolini & Rechtschaffen, *supra*, at 10,120.

[53] *See* Matthew F. Pawa, *Global Warming: The Ultimate Public Nuisance*, *in* Creative Common Law Strategies for Protecting The Environment 107 (Clifford Rechtschaffen & Denise Antolini eds., 2007) [hereinafter Creative Common Law Strategies]; Katie J. Zoglin, *Getting the Lead Out: The Potential of Public Nuisance in Lead-Based Paint Litigation*, *in* Creative Common Law Strategies, *supra*, at 339. District courts have dismissed the climate change public nuisance claims on political question grounds. *See* California v. Gen. Motors Corp., No. C06–05755, 2007 WL 2726871, at *16 (N.D. Cal. Sept. 17, 2007); Connecticut v. Am. Elec. Power Co., 406 F. Supp. 2d 265, 274 (S.D.N.Y. 2005), *vacated* 582 F.3d 309 (2d Cir. 2009), rev'd, 131 S. Ct. 2527 (2011).

[54] *See, e.g.*, Gifford, *supra* note 48, at 834 (contending that public nuisance should not be a means of recovering damages from product manufacturers).

[55] *See* Robert Abrams & Val Washington, *The Misunderstood Law of Public Nuisance: A Comparison with Private Nuisance Twenty Years After* Boomer, 54 Alb. L. Rev. 359, 359 (1990); Gifford, *supra* note 48, at 774–75 (noting public nuisance's lack of meaningful definition and discernible boundaries).

[56] *See* Gifford, *supra* note 48, at 779–80 (discussing courts' different understandings of the term).

[57] *See* Dan B. Dobbs, The Law of Torts 1334 (2000) (defining public nuisance as "a substantial and unreasonable interference with a right held in common by the general public, in use of public facilities, in health, safety, and convenience"); Abrams & Washington, *supra* note 55, at 374–75; Gifford, *supra* note 48, at 813–30 (outlining "fundamental principles" governing public nuisance).

Although some definitions of public nuisance, including that found in the *Second Restatement of Torts*, do not explicitly demand that the defendant be in control of the instrumentality causing the nuisance, *see* Restatement (Second) of Torts § 821B (1979), a majority of courts have continued to look for this traditional element. *See, e.g.*, Camden County Bd. of Chosen Freeholders v. Beretta, U.S.A. Corp., 273 F.3d 536, 539 (3d Cir. 2001) (discussing public nuisance under New Jersey law); State v. Lead Indus. Ass'n, 951 A.2d 428, 446 (R.I. 2008); Gifford, *supra* note 48, at 820–21 n.394 (citing cases); Victor E. Schwartz & Phil Goldberg, *The Law of Public Nuisance: Maintaining Rational Boundaries on a Rational Tort*, 45 Washburn L.J. 541, 567–68 (2006) (discussing cases). *But cf. In re*

requiring that the defendant's conduct be intentional, unreasonable, violative of a statute, or otherwise tortious; and others holding that liability for public nuisance is strict.[58]

In addition, public nuisance claims traditionally have been subject to two important limitations. First, only public authorities could bring such claims, a feature that reflected the doctrine's common law roots in criminal proceedings.[59] Second, public authorities generally could obtain only injunctive relief when bringing a civil public nuisance action.[60] Modern precedents have relaxed these limitations to some degree. Private plaintiffs may bring public nuisance claims if they have suffered a "special injury" – an injury different in kind from the public's general injury.[61] And some courts allow public authorities to recover damages in public nuisance actions under the theory that the state is acting as a "quasi-sovereign" in a *parens patriae* action.[62] The following paragraphs consider the basic elements of public nuisance in further detail.

Public nuisance encompasses "interference with public rights."[63] What exactly is a "public right" for purposes of public nuisance doctrine? The *Second Restatement of*

Lead Paint Litig., 924 A.2d 484, 510–11 (N.J. 2007) (Zazzali, C.J., dissenting) (citing cases that reject control requirement).

58 *Compare, e.g.*, City of Cincinnati v. Beretta U.S.A. Corp., 768 N.E.2d 1136, 1143 n.4 (Ohio 2002) (requiring negligence, intent, or unlawful activity), RESTATEMENT (SECOND) OF TORTS § 821B cmt. e (1979) ("[T]he defendant is held liable for a public nuisance if his interference with the public right was intentional or was unintentional and otherwise actionable under the principles controlling liability for negligent or reckless conduct or for abnormally dangerous activities."), *and* Gifford, *supra* note 48, at 828–30 (contending failure to require fault "invites the court and jury to find a public nuisance without guidance and standards"), *with* New York v. Shore Realty Corp., 759 F.2d 1032, 1051 (2d Cir. 1985) (rejecting landowner's claim that other parties were responsible for chemical contamination on property and explaining that one can be "liable for maintenance of a *public* nuisance irrespective of negligence or fault"), Abrams & Washington, *supra* note 55, at 368 ("[T]he application of fault principles is certainly erroneous; the standard of liability in a public nuisance action is strict."), *and* Halper, *supra* note 49, at 10,294.

59 *See* Gifford, *supra* note 48, at 814.

60 *See* Abrams & Washington, *supra* note 55, at 379; Gifford, *supra* note 48, at 814 ("The core concept behind public nuisance is the right of public authorities to end defendant's conduct that harms the public, through remedies of either injunctive relief or criminal prosecution."); *see also In re Lead Paint Litig.*, 924 A.2d at 498–99 (contending that public plaintiff asserting public nuisance claim is limited to remedies of abatement and recovery of costs of abatement, in contrast to private plaintiff, who can sue for damages caused by public nuisance if he can demonstrate special injury). Gifford further notes that "[h]istorically, the recovery of damages has been an ancillary and unusual remedy when a public nuisance was found to exist." Gifford, *supra* note 48, at 814. *But see* 58 AM. JUR. 2D *Nuisance* § 31 (2002) ("Both private and public nuisances are actionable either for their abatement or for damages, or both.").

61 *See* RESTATEMENT (SECOND) OF TORTS § 821C (1979); DOBBS, *supra* note 57, at 1335; Gifford, *supra* note 48, at 814. *See generally* Denise E. Antolini, *Modernizing Public Nuisance: Solving the Paradox of the Special Injury Rule*, 28 ECOLOGY L.Q. 755 (2001) (suggesting an "actual community injury" standard to revitalize public nuisance as a broad remedy).

62 *See* Antolini & Rechtschaffen, *supra* note 52, at 10,120; Gifford, *supra* note 52, at 784.

63 *See* Antolini & Rechtschaffen, *supra* note 52, at 10,120 ("The interference need not be related to land, but can be much broader, affecting virtually any public resource or place."). Public nuisance thus stands in direct contrast to private nuisance, which requires interference with the enjoyment of private property. *See* DOBBS, *supra* note 57, at 1335; Abrams & Washington, *supra* note 55, at 364.

Torts describes a public right as "one common to all members of the general public" and "collective in nature."[64] Such a right can be distinguished from the "individual right that everyone has not to be assaulted or defamed or defrauded or negligently injured." [65] In other words, for a public right to be violated, there must be more than an aggregation of private rights violations.[66] A public nuisance involves an act "that could hurt any member of the public, not just a plaintiff situated in circumstances unique to an individual or subsection of the general public."[67] Public rights thus include common law rights in health, safety, and comfort – such as the right to unobstructed highways and waterways and the right to unpolluted air and water – as well as rights identified by statute.[68] Attempting to distill the various situations in which public nuisance doctrine has been applied, the Wisconsin Supreme Court has suggested that public nuisance involves interference "with the use of a public place or with the activities of an entire community."[69] Although the public rights that fall within the protection of public nuisance doctrine are broad in scope, they are not limitless. Contrasting public right with the broader concept of "public interest," Donald Gifford contends that "while it is in the public interest to promote the health and well-being of citizens generally, there is no common law public right to a certain standard of medical care or housing."[70] These concerns, Gifford suggests,

[64] Restatement (Second) of Torts § 821B cmt. g (1979).

[65] *Id.*

[66] *See* State v. Lead Indus. Ass'n, 951 A.2d 428, 448 (R.I. 2008); Gifford, *supra* note 48, at 817. *But cf.* Restatement (Second) of Torts § 821B cmt. g (1979) (noting that "no public right as such need be involved" in those states where public nuisance is defined to include interference with "any considerable number of persons").

[67] Adams v. City of W. Hartford, No. HHDCV064027110, 2008 WL 4253413, at *6–7 (Conn. Super. Ct. Aug. 28, 2008) (holding that a child injured in public school could not assert public nuisance claim); Gifford, *supra* note 48, at 818 (questioning whether injuries suffered in private home could be subject to public nuisance claim).

[68] *See Lead Indus. Ass'n*, 951 A.2d at 453 (describing public right); Dobbs, *supra* note 57, at 1335; Gifford, *supra* note 48, at 815 (describing fact patterns constituting public nuisance under common law). California, for example, defines a nuisance as:

> Anything which is injurious to health, including, but not limited to, the illegal sale of controlled substances, or is indecent or offensive to the senses, or an obstruction to the free use of property, so as to interfere with the comfortable enjoyment of life or property, or unlawfully obstructs the free passage or use, in the customary manner, of any navigable lake, or river, bay, stream, canal, or basin, or any public park, square, street, or highway. . . .

Cal. Civ. Code § 3479 (West 1997). Public nuisance is defined as "[a nuisance] which affects at the same time an entire community or neighborhood, or any considerable number of persons, although the extent of the annoyance or damage inflicted upon individuals may be unequal." *Id.* § 3480.

[69] Gifford, *supra* note 48, at 815 (quoting Physicians Plus Ins. Corp. v. Midwest Mut. Ins. Co., 646 N.W.2d 777, 788 (Wis. 2002)).

[70] Gifford, *supra* note 48, at 815. *But cf.* James L. Huffman, *Beware of Greens in Praise of the Common Law*, 58 Case W. Res. L. Rev. 813, 826–27 (2008) (suggesting that "the concept of public rights . . . is more than elusive of definition" and that "'public rights' is just another term for public interest").

do not involve interference with use of a public place or with activities of an entire community.[71]

The interference with public rights must be substantial (i.e., significant) and unreasonable in order to be a public nuisance.[72] Significance requires that the harm complained of be more than trivial, although the mere threat of substantial harm will suffice.[73] The requirements of significance and unreasonableness essentially overlap, as section 821B of the *Second Restatement of Torts* suggests. Section 821B lists various circumstances that may sustain a finding that interference with a public right is unreasonable:

(1) Whether the conduct involves a significant interference with the public health, the public safety, the public peace, the public comfort or the public convenience
(2) Whether the conduct is proscribed by a statute, ordinance, or administrative regulation
(3) Whether the conduct is of a continuing nature or has produced a permanent or long-lasting effect, and, as the actor knows or has reason to know, has a significant effect upon the public right.[74]

Reasonability turns on the significance of the interference, as in the first and third *Restatement* examples, or on a prior legislative or administrative judgment of unreasonability akin to per se negligence, as in the second example.[75] Note, moreover, that this inquiry into "reasonability" is not concerned with whether the actor's conduct was negligent, but rather focuses on the resulting interference with public rights. Consistent with this view, Donald Gifford has suggested that courts should consider the following factors in determining whether interference is unreasonable: "(i) the number of people susceptible, (ii) the degree of risk of harm occurring, (iii) the duration of the risk of harm occurring, and (iv) the severity of the harm that may occur."[76] In contrast to private nuisance, where the reasonableness inquiry calls for a weighing of the gravity of the harm to the plaintiff against the utility of the defendant's conduct,[77] public nuisance involves no such balancing of the utilities.[78]

71 Gifford, *supra* note 48, at 815. In contrast, Gifford concedes that persons sickened by exposure to secondhand smoke in public places – a situation analogous to exposure to untested chemicals – could conceivably demonstrate interference with a public right. *Id.* at 817.

72 *See* Abrams & Washington, *supra* note 55, at 374.

73 *Id.*

74 Restatement (Second) of Torts § 821B (1979); *see also* Dobbs, *supra* note 57, at 1334 (defining public nuisance as "a substantial and unreasonable interference with a right held in common by the general public, in use of public facilities, in health, safety, and convenience").

75 *See* Restatement (Second) of Torts § 821B cmt. e.

76 Gifford, *supra* note 48, at 816.

77 *See* Restatement (Second) of Torts § 826 (1979).

78 *See* Abrams & Washington, *supra* note 55, at 376–78 (arguing that commentary suggesting that balancing of utilities test should apply to public nuisance claims is impractical and contrary to precedent); *see also* Georgia v. Tenn. Copper Co., 206 U.S. 230, 238–39 (1907) (rejecting balancing of

Many courts also require as an element of public nuisance that the defendant have control of the instrumentality causing the nuisance. This element is rooted in the historical use of public nuisance by the state to enjoin conduct injuring the public health, safety, or welfare.[79] A defendant who no longer exercises possession or control, the reasoning goes, is not in position to abate a nuisance.[80] The requirement of control has proven fatal to most attempts to apply public nuisance doctrine against product manufacturers, including makers of handguns and lead paint.[81] In the handgun cases, states alleged that handgun manufacturers created a public nuisance by making handguns readily available and sought compensation for expenses incurred in responding to handgun violence.[82] In the lead paint litigation, states sought damages from paint manufacturers as well as abatement of lead paint in residences.[83] A number of courts have rejected public nuisance claims in these contexts on the ground that the respective manufacturers were no longer in control of the instrumentality causing the nuisance and thus had no ability to abate the nuisance.[84]

Some jurisdictions confronted with public nuisance claims against product manufacturers interpret the control element more loosely, however.[85] Rather than requiring control, these courts hold that a defendant manufacturer's acts or omissions

utilities in granting injunction to State of Georgia against air pollution generated by defendant based on finding of public nuisance).

79 *See* Gifford, *supra* note 48, at 819–20.

80 *See, e.g.*, State v. Lead Indus. Ass'n, 951 A.2d 428, 449 (R.I. 2008) ("The party in control of the instrumentality causing the alleged nuisance is best positioned to abate it and, therefore, is legally responsible.").

81 The issue of control is sometimes subsumed within a requirement of causation. *See, e.g.*, City of Chi. v. Beretta U.S.A. Corp., 821 N.E.2d 1099, 1132 (Ill. 2004) (characterizing control as "a relevant factor in both the proximate cause inquiry and in the ability of the court to fashion appropriate injunctive relief").

82 *See, e.g.*, Camden County Bd. of Chosen Freeholders v. Beretta, U.S.A. Corp., 273 F.3d 536, 538–39 (3d Cir. 2001) ("The County alleges that the manufacturers' conduct . . . imposed inordinate financial burdens on the County's fisc."); *City of Chi.*, 821 N.E.2d at 1107–09 (describing the City's complaint, including assertions that the dealers' practices had caused a large underground market for illegal firearms).

83 *In re* Lead Paint Litig., 924 A.2d 484, 486–87 (N.J. 2007); *Lead Indus. Ass'n*, 951 A.2d at 440.

84 *See, e.g.*, City of Phila. v. Beretta U.S.A. Corp., 277 F.3d 415, 422 (3d Cir. 2002) (deciding under Pennsylvania law that gun manufacturers were not liable because of lack of control); *Camden County*, 273 F.3d at 541–42 (affirming dismissal of public nuisance claim against gun manufacturers under New Jersey law); *In re Lead Paint Litig.*, 924 A.2d at 501 (rejecting public nuisance claims against lead paint manufacturers because such theory would "eliminate entirely the concept of control of the nuisance"); *Lead Indus. Ass'n*, 951 A.2d at 455 (holding that public nuisance claims against lead paint manufacturers should have been dismissed); *see also* Gifford, *supra* note 48, at 822 (contending that in such cases, "[t]he harm or injurious condition allegedly created by the public nuisance clearly is not within the control of the defendants").

85 *See* Ileto v. Glock Inc., 349 F.3d 1191, 1212 (9th Cir. 2003); City of Cincinnati v. Beretta U.S.A. Corp., 768 N.E.2d 1136, 1143 (Ohio 2002) (rejecting gun manufacturer's contention that lack of control of firearms at moment of harm barred liability under public nuisance); Northridge Co. v. W.R. Grace & Co., 556 N.W.2d 345, 351–52 (Wis. Ct. App. 1996) (holding asbestos manufacturers liable under public nuisance theory).

need only be a substantial factor with respect to the harm suffered in order for the defendant to be liable under public nuisance.[86] Such decisions recognize that a manufacturer should be held responsible for the consequences of its actions, even if those consequences are somewhat removed from the manufacturer.[87]

Finally, as noted above, courts are divided over whether fault is necessary to demonstrate a public nuisance.[88] Requiring such a showing is inconsistent with the common law examples of nuisance, which concern themselves primarily with redressing the interference with a public right, rather than with judging the moral culpability of a defendant's conduct.[89] As one commentator has contended, "[t]he public should not be made to suffer an unreasonable interference with its rights merely because the entity responsible for the interference is acting nonnegligently and without bad intent."[90]

B. *Applying Public Nuisance Doctrine to the Failure to Test*

Do the "rights common to the general public" and subject to protection against interference through a public nuisance action extend to a right not to be exposed to untested or inadequately tested engineered nanomaterials? In other words, can public nuisance doctrine encompass a company's failure to test the nanomaterials it manufactures or incorporates into its products before releasing them into the stream of commerce? Even though application of public nuisance in such situations would represent an extension beyond common law precedents, consideration of the scope, purpose, and origins of the public nuisance doctrine suggests an affirmative answer.

As discussed previously, public nuisance essentially involves interference with public rights. The public rights that a state may protect via public nuisance include the collective interests of its citizens in the quality of the state's environment, a point illustrated by *Georgia v. Tennessee Copper Co.*,[91] one of the Supreme Court's leading decisions on public nuisance. In that case, Georgia sought to enjoin out-of-state copper companies from discharging pollutants that were allegedly damaging forests and crops within the state of Georgia.[92] Noting that the case involved "a suit by a State for an injury to it in its capacity of *quasi*-sovereign," the Court observed that "[i]n that capacity the State has an interest independent of and behind the titles of its citizens, in all the earth and air within its domain. It has the last word as to whether

[86] *See Ileto*, 349 F.3d at 1212; *City of Cincinnati*, 768 N.E.2d at 1143.

[87] *See Ileto*, 349 F.3d at 1212–13; *City of Cincinnati*, 768 N.E.2d at 1143.

[88] *See supra* note 58 and accompanying text.

[89] *See, e.g.*, Commonwealth v. Barnes & Tucker Co., 319 A.2d 871, 883, 885 (Pa. 1974) (finding that acid mine drainage discharging from mine constituted public nuisance and explaining that "[t]he absence of facts supporting concepts of negligence, foreseeability or unlawful conduct is not in the least fatal to a finding of the existence of a common law public nuisance").

[90] Abrams & Washington, *supra* note 55, at 370.

[91] 206 U.S. 230 (1907).

[92] *Id.* at 236.

its mountains shall be stripped of their forests and its inhabitants shall breathe pure air."[93] *Tennessee Copper* is instructive on at least two important points. First, the decision underscores that the state's police power is the basis for public nuisance actions brought by a public entity. Public nuisance thus is quite distinct from private nuisance in its origins as well as in the scope of interests it seeks to protect.[94] Acting as *parens patriae*, the state may bring public nuisance actions to protect the health and welfare of its citizens.[95] Second, *Tennessee Copper* affirms the breadth of the power that the state can effectuate through public nuisance actions. Rejecting the defendants' argument that the harm to the state had to be balanced against the economic benefit of the copper smelting operations, the Court characterized the state's quasi-sovereign authority in these matters as virtually absolute:

> Whether Georgia by insisting upon this claim is doing more harm than good to her own citizens is for her to determine. The possible disaster to those outside the State must be accepted as a consequence of her standing upon her extreme rights.[96]

Admittedly, the failure to undertake testing to determine health and safety risks differs from the palpable harm of *Tennessee Copper* and familiar examples of interferences with public health or comfort – smoke, noise, and the like – that constituted public nuisances under the common law. The modern understanding of "interference with public rights," however, is broader than the limited conception of nuisance as a tangible harm or annoyance.[97] First, public nuisance has not been confined to situations where plaintiffs have suffered tangible injury. Interference with the public peace, as by loud noises, and interference with public morals, as in cases of

[93] *Id.* at 237. *See also* Missouri v. Illinois, 180 U.S. 208, 241 (1901) ("[I]f the health and comfort of the inhabitants of a State are threatened, the State is the proper party to represent and defend them.").

[94] *Cf.* People *ex rel.* Gallo v. Acuna, 929 P.2d 596, 603 (Cal. 1997) ("Unlike the private nuisance – tied to and designed to vindicate individual ownership interests in *land* – the "common" or *public* nuisance emerged from distinctly different historical origins. The public nuisance doctrine is aimed at the protection and redress of *community* interests and, at least in theory, embodies a kind of collective ideal of civil life which the courts have vindicated by equitable remedies since the beginning of the 16th century.").

[95] *See* Alfred L. Snapp & Son, Inc. v. P.R. *ex rel.* Barez, 458 U.S. 592, 600–07 (1982) (noting that *parens patriae*, literally meaning "parent of the country," refers to authority of the state to litigate to defend quasi-sovereign interests, including health and well-being of its residents).

[96] *Tennessee Copper*, 206 U.S. at 239. The Court recently reaffirmed these principles in *Massachusetts v. EPA*, a successful challenge by several states to EPA's refusal to regulate greenhouse gas emissions from new motor vehicles under Section 202 of the Clean Air Act. *Massachusetts v. EPA*, 127 S. Ct. 1438 (2007). Discussing whether the states had standing to sue, the Court cited *Tennessee Copper* for the proposition that states have standing "to litigate as *parens patriae* to protect quasi-sovereign interests – *i.e.*, public or governmental interests that concern the state as a whole." *Id.* at 1455 n.17. Although the Supreme Court has declined to set out an exhaustive definition of quasi-sovereign interests, it has made clear that "a State has a quasi-sovereign interest in the health and well-being – both physical and economic – of its residents in general." *Snapp & Son, Inc.*, 458 U.S. at 607.

[97] *See* Prosser, *supra* note 51, at 997 (noting that "[*n*]*uisance* is a French word which means nothing more than harm").

prostitution, were recognized as public nuisances by the common law.[98] Indeed, the *Second Restatement of Torts* identifies five broad categories of public rights subject to protection through a public nuisance action: "the public health, the public safety, the public peace, the public comfort or the public convenience."[99] Not surprisingly, the mere risk of harm has long been sufficient to establish a public nuisance,[100] as demonstrated by common law cases involving the keeping of diseased animals, the maintenance of a pond breeding malarial mosquitoes, and the storage of explosives in the midst of a city.[101] A state's quasi-sovereign interests "in the well-being of its populace"[102] readily extend beyond these situations and include protection against potential injury from exposure to untested nanomaterials.[103]

Untested nanomaterials do present a somewhat more complicated situation than the above-noted examples of public nuisance with respect to the uncertainty surrounding potential hazards. More specifically, although we have a sound basis for suspecting that some engineered nanomaterials may pose a significant threat to public health, there is almost no way of knowing whether they actually do so without testing – testing that the manufacturer is in the best position to perform. Absent testing, nanotechnology companies are imposing uncertain risks on consumers and on the public at large. Although the law typically has not recognized such uncertainty as harm per se,[104] the public right to unpolluted air and water, which undoubtedly includes a right to protect the public against exposure to substances known to be harmful, also should encompass a right to protect the public against exposure to untested substances. Such exposure is problematic not only because of its potential to interfere with the public health and the environment, but also because it runs afoul of principles of personal autonomy and valid consent.[105] These principles,

[98] *See* Restatement (Second) of Torts § 821B cmt. b (1979); *e.g.*, Price v. State, 600 N.E.2d 103 (Ind. Ct. App. 1992) (discussing common law prohibition on noise); City of N.Y. *ex rel.* People v. Taliaferrow, 544 N.Y.S.2d 273, 275–76 (Sup. Ct. 1989) (discussing prostitution as a public nuisance).

[99] Restatement (Second) of Torts § 821B(2)(a) (1979).

[100] *See* Mugler v. Kansas, 123 U.S. 623, 673 (1887) ("[Courts of equity] can not only prevent nuisances that are threatened, and before irreparable mischief ensues, but arrest or abate those in progress, and, by perpetual injunction, protect the public against them in the future. . . ."); Abrams & Washington, *supra* note 55, at 374 ("[T]he harm need not even be actual if the threat of harm is great enough.").

[101] Restatement (Second) of Torts § 821B cmt. b (1979).

[102] Alfred L. Snapp & Son, Inc. v. P.R. *ex rel.* Barez, 458 U.S. 592, 602 (1982).

[103] *Cf.* Allan Kanner, *The Public Trust Doctrine,* Parens Patriae, *and the Attorney General as the Guardian of the State's Natural Resources*, 16 Duke Envtl. L. & Pol'y F. 57, 109 (2005) (listing examples of threats to public health, safety, and welfare where courts have recognized states' authority to sue as *parens patriae*).

[104] *See* Lin, *supra* note 3, at 975 (explaining that concept of harm reflects community's normative judgments regarding significant setbacks to one's interests); *see also* Claire Finkelstein, *Is Risk a Harm?*, 151 U. Pa. L. Rev. 963, 970–73 (2003) (contending that persons subjected to risks, even if no physical harm comes to pass, have nevertheless suffered harm); Glen O. Robinson, *Probabilistic Causation and Compensation for Tortious Risk*, 14 J. Legal Stud. 779, 783 (1985) (proposing liability based on creation of risk of injury).

[105] *See* E. Donald Elliott, *The Future of Toxic Torts: Of Chemophobia, Risk as a Compensable Injury and Hybrid Compensation Systems*, 25 Hous. L. Rev. 781, 789 (1988) (contending that "[t]he violation

which are implicated by matters involving "the integrity of [an] individual's own projects and self-conception," particularly "the use made of one's own body,"[106] are denigrated whenever the public is exposed to untested chemicals.[107] Even absent proof of physical harm or causation, such exposure deprives the public of its ability to choose whether or not to be exposed to an untested product.[108]

Application of public nuisance in these circumstances would be consistent with the origins of public nuisance doctrine in the state's police power.[109] The police power, commonly described as the power to protect public health, safety, morals, and general welfare,[110] comprehends the authority to enact legislation to prevent environmental pollution and to abate public nuisances.[111] This power is the "least limitable" of all state powers and may be exercised broadly as long as its exercise is not arbitrary.[112] Although states generally have not taken a precautionary approach

of a person's bodily autonomy . . . that occurs when one is assaulted with a potentially hazardous chemical[] is . . . an injury that the law should recognize and compensate"); Clifford Rechtschaffen, *Advancing Environmental Justice Norms*, 37 U.C. DAVIS L. REV. 95, 112–13 (2003); *see also* Margaret A. Berger & Aaron D. Twerski, *Uncertainty and Informed Choice: Unmasking* Daubert, 104 MICH. L. REV. 257, 258, 259 (2005) (arguing for right of patients to informed choice about a drug's risks and for enforceability of such right without having to prove that drug caused plaintiffs' harms).

[106] Peter H. Schuck, *Rethinking Informed Consent*, 103 YALE L.J. 899, 924 (1994).

[107] *See* Berger & Twerski, *supra* note 105, at 273 ("[T]he denial of the right to choose not to expose oneself to an uncertain risk violates a very basic human right of autonomous decision making. . . . "); *cf.* Cranor, *supra* note 19, at 283 ("Under post-market laws the American citizenry are, in effect, human guinea pigs for the commercial creations of American industry."). The importance of bodily autonomy is reflected in its protection through individual torts such as assault and battery. *Cf. id.* at 300–01 ("Morally, citizens should regard invasion of their bodies without permission by humanly created substances as a trespass.").

[108] *Cf.* Berger & Twerski, *supra* note 105, at 274 ("If indeed there is a right to informed choice, conditioning the right on proof that the harm was actually brought about by the defendant's conduct makes no sense whatsoever. If an uncertain risk of harm should have been communicated to the plaintiff so that the plaintiff could assess whether she wished to play this game of russian roulette, to then say that the plaintiff is not entitled to recovery because she cannot prove that the harm was actually caused by the suspect drug, renders the right to informed choice illusory.").

[109] *See* Abrams & Washington, *supra* note 55, at 362 ("[A]uthority for an action in public nuisance derived from what is now known as the sovereign's police power and not from tort law."); Halper, *supra* note 49, at 10,296.

[110] *See, e.g.*, Bacon v. Walker, 204 U.S. 311, 317 (1907) (noting that police power "embraces regulations designed to promote the public convenience or the general prosperity, as well as regulations designed to promote the public health, the public morals, or the public safety"); Lawton v. Steele, 152 U.S. 133, 136 (1894) (explaining that police power encompasses "everything essential to the public safety, health, and morals . . . ").

[111] *See* Huron Portland Cement Co. v. City of Detroit, 362 U.S. 440, 442 (1960) ("Legislation designed to free from pollution the very air that people breathe clearly falls within the exercise of even the most traditional concept of what is compendiously known as the police power."); *Lawton*, 152 U.S. at 136; Exxon Mobil Corp. v. EPA, 217 F.3d 1246, 1255 (9th Cir. 2000) ("Air pollution prevention falls under the broad police powers of the states, which include the power to protect the health of citizens in the state. Environmental regulation traditionally has been a matter of state authority.").

[112] Hadacheck v. Sebastian, 239 U.S. 394, 410 (1915); Halper, *supra* note 49, at 10,296; Donna Jalbert Patalano, *Police Power and the Public Trust: Prescriptive Zoning Through the Conflation of Two Ancient Doctrines*, 28 B.C. ENVTL. AFF. L. REV. 683, 708–09 (2001) (noting "elastic" nature of police

to chemical regulation by requiring proof of safety as a condition of manufacture or distribution,[113] there is no doubt that the police power extends to the authority to regulate – and even prohibit – untested substances that may be harmful to public health or that may pollute the environment.[114] This understanding of the police power supports a recognition that exposure to untested substances constitutes an actionable interference with public rights.

In order to constitute a public nuisance, an interference with public rights generally must be substantial and unreasonable.[115] At first glance, the requirement of substantiality may appear to be a serious obstacle to asserting a public nuisance claim for the failure to test engineered nanomaterials. By virtue of the very failure to test, substantial physical harm usually cannot be shown.[116] However, a showing of substantial harm is not strictly required where the state seeks only injunctive relief, as opposed to damages.[117] In order to obtain an injunction against a public nuisance, harm need only be threatened and need not actually have been sustained at all.[118] Moreover, the responsibility of chemical manufacturers in perpetuating the condition of toxic ignorance argues in favor of a shift in the burden of proving substantiality (or the lack thereof) to chemical manufacturers.[119]

The third element of a public nuisance action, the requirement that the defendant have control of the instrumentality causing the nuisance, is easily satisfied when the nuisance involves a failure to test. After all, the manufacturer is responsible for introducing a substance into the stream of commerce and has complete control over whether testing is done. This situation is thus distinguishable from the efforts to apply public nuisance doctrine in handgun and lead paint litigation, where the instrumentalities causing the nuisance long ago left the manufacturers' control and

power and stating that it "creates protections for the public when individual interests need to yield to general social interests because of social, economic, and political conditions").

113 *See generally* Lin, *supra* note 3, at 910–11 (observing that existing regulatory schemes primarily involve regulation of demonstrated risks).

114 In *Village of Euclid v. Ambler Realty Co.*, the Supreme Court upheld the power of local authorities to adopt zoning ordinances governing industrial facilities even though such ordinances might exclude facilities that are "neither offensive nor dangerous." 272 U.S. 365, 388 (1926). By analogy, the police power extends not only to demonstrably harmful chemicals, but also to chemicals whose effects are currently unknown and that ultimately may pose no health or environmental risks.

115 *See supra* Part II.A.

116 Three of the four factors suggested by Donald Gifford as relevant to determining the significance of interference with a public right, *see supra* text accompanying note 76 – the degree of harm, its duration, and its severity – will be difficult to demonstrate because of the lack of safety testing.

117 *See* Restatement (Second) of Torts § 821B cmt. i (1979) ("[F]or damages to be awarded significant harm must have been actually incurred, while for an injunction harm need only be threatened and need not actually have been sustained at all."); *cf.* People v. McDonald, 137 Cal. App. 4th 521, 538 (2006) (citing *Second Restatement of Torts* for proposition that "[a] public nuisance may be prosecuted criminally although it has not yet resulted in any significant harm, or indeed any harm to anyone").

118 *See* Restatement (Second) of Torts § 821B cmt. i (1979).

119 *Cf.* Wagner, *supra* note 5, at 1742 (advocating "that at least part of the burden of resolving . . . uncertainty falls to the actors whose products and activities create the uncertainty in the first place").

arguably became subject to superseding causes.[120] A company that releases untested substances into the marketplace is analogous to a factory that releases smoke and dust to the detriment of its neighbors and is liable therefore under nuisance theory. Moreover, although a few courts suggest that public nuisance "has historically been tied to conduct on one's own land or property as it affects the rights of the general public,"[121] such a view takes an overly narrow approach to public nuisance doctrine even under common law precedents.[122] Obstructions of public roads and waterways could readily occur without any land ownership by the defendant; indeed, the "catch-all criminal offense" of public nuisance came to encompass such diverse circumstances as diversion of water from a mill, unlicensed stage plays, and indecent exposure.[123] The common element in these situations was not the presence of a real property interest; rather, control of the obstruction or source of the nuisance sufficed. Such control is readily present when a manufacturer has failed to test the safety of its products.

Finally, applying public nuisance to the failure to test nanomaterials also raises the issue of whether a manufacturer must be at fault in order to be held liable. As noted previously, some jurisdictions require intent, negligence, or a violation of law as an element of public nuisance.[124] Such a requirement would be readily met in failure to test cases. By definition, a failure to test involves negligent conduct by a chemical manufacturer: the failure to conduct reasonable health and safety testing.

[120] *See, e.g.*, State v. Lead Indus. Ass'n, 951 A.2d 428, 455 (R.I. 2008); *In re* Lead Paint Litig., 924 A.2d 484, 501 (N.J. 2007). In some of these cases, courts have rejected public nuisance claims out of a concern that such suits could be used to circumvent products liability law pertaining to defective products. *E.g.*, *Lead Indus. Ass'n*, 951 A.2d at 456; *In re Lead Paint*, 924 A.2d at 503. With respect to untested chemicals, however, the allegation is not so much that the chemicals are defective, as that manufacturers have failed to test for defects in the first instance.

[121] *See, e.g.*, *In re Lead Paint*, 924 A.2d at 495; *see also Lead Indus. Ass'n*, 951 A.2d at 452 ("[T]o date, the actions for [public] nuisance in this jurisdiction have been related to *land*."); Gifford, *supra* note 48, at 832 (contending that "a finding of public nuisance historically involved the use of land"). Gifford suggests that confining public nuisance claims to cases involving land makes sense in light of the availability of claims of negligence, strict liability for abnormally dangerous activities, and strict products liability for personal injuries resulting from conduct not involving the use of land. *See id.* at 833. Public nuisance law, however, incorporates an element of fault and thus cannot be strictly separated from the law of negligence or strict liability. *See supra* note 58 and accompanying text. In addition, the availability of one cause of action in specific factual circumstances does not necessarily preclude the availability of another. Public nuisance's requirement of interference with a *public right* reduces any concern that the tort might swallow up other torts and apply to "any unreasonable harm that might result from human interaction." Gifford, *supra* note 48, at 833.

[122] *See* 58 Am. Jur. 2d *Nuisances* § 31, at 592 (2002) ("[A]n action for public nuisance may lie even though neither the plaintiff nor the defendant acts in the exercise of private property rights."); W. Page Keeton et al., Prosser and Keeton on Torts § 86, at 617–18 (5th ed., St. Paul, MN: West Pub. Co., 1984) (distinguishing narrow civil action of private nuisance, "narrowly restricted to the invasion of interests in the use or enjoyment of land," from the "entirely separate" criminal action of public nuisance, "extending to virtually any form of annoyance or inconvenience interfering with common public rights").

[123] Keeton et al., *supra* note 122, § 86, at 617–18.

[124] *See supra* note 58.

C. An Alternative Public Nuisance Theory Centered on the Right to Information

Public nuisance theory also can be applied to the problem of untested nanomaterials under an understanding of "public right" that focuses on harms to personal autonomy. Under this approach, the public right that is interfered with is a procedural right, the right to information, rather than the substantive right against exposure to untested substances. This sort of interference represents a significant departure from the common law examples of public nuisance, but it still falls within public nuisance's broad definition. Although the public right to information regarding environmental hazards is a fairly modern concept, it is one that has received growing recognition in recent years.[125]

The adoption of various statutes promoting the dissemination of information about chemical hazards to the public reflects the development of this right. At the federal level, the Emergency Planning and Community Right-to-Know Act[126] (EPCRA) requires facilities to report annually their releases of chemicals that have been listed as toxic by Congress.[127] As required by statute, EPA gathers the data in the Toxics Release Inventory and makes it available to the public.[128] The Safe Drinking Water Act[129] requires community water systems to send each customer an annual report on the level of contaminants in the drinking water purveyed by the system and to notify customers of certain violations of the act.[130] In the workplace, the Occupational Safety and Health Act[131] requires that employees be "apprised of all hazards to which they are exposed, relevant symptoms and appropriate emergency treatment, and proper conditions and precautions of safe use or exposure."[132] In the consumer marketplace, federal statutes and regulations mandate ingredient and nutrition labeling on processed foods, as well as risk labels on pharmaceuticals.[133] And at the state level, a number of similar measures have been enacted, the most

[125] *Cf.* Gary E.R. Hook & George W. Lucier, *The Right to Know Is for Everyone*, 108 Envtl. Health Persp. A160, A160 (2000) (editorial) (noting origins of right to know and arguing that "[i]n a free and open society, the concept of 'right to know' seems fundamental").

[126] *See* 42 U.S.C. §§ 11,001–11,050 (2006).

[127] *See id.* § 11,023. EPCRA also requires facilities to provide information to state and local emergency planning groups regarding the quantities of certain hazardous chemicals on site. *See id.* §§ 11,002(c), 11,022. The public can obtain much of this information upon request. *See id.* § 11,021(c)(2) (public request for material safety data sheets); *id.* § 11,022(e)(3) (public request for emergency and hazardous chemical inventory forms); *id.* § 11,044(a) (public availability of plans, data sheets, forms, and notices).

[128] *See id.* § 11,023(j).

[129] Pub. L. No. 95-523, 88 Stat. 1660 (1974) (codified as amended at 42 U.S.C. §§ 300f–300j–26 [2006]).

[130] *See* 42 U.S.C. §§ 300g-3(c)(1), (4).

[131] Pub. L. No. 91-596, 84 Stat. 1590 (1970) (codified as amended at 29 U.S.C. §§ 651–78 [2006]).

[132] *See* 29 U.S.C. § 655(b)(7); 29 C.F.R. § 1910.1200 (2009) (OSHA hazard communication regulation).

[133] *See, e.g.*, Nutrition Labeling and Education Act of 1990, Pub. L. No. 101–535, 104 Stat. 2353 (codified as amended primarily at 21 U.S.C. § 343 (2006)); 21 C.F.R. § 201.57 (2008) (labeling requirements for prescription drugs).

well known of which is California's Proposition 65.[134] Passed by popular initiative, this statute requires businesses to warn consumers of products that contain listed carcinogens or reproductive toxins.[135] Many of the above statutes contain provisions authorizing citizen enforcement for failure to disclose the required information.[136]

Furthermore, a right of access to environmental information, including toxicity data, is arguably an emerging principle of international law. Principle 10 of the 1992 Rio Declaration on Environment and Development discusses this point:

> Environmental issues are best handled with the participation of all concerned citizens, at the relevant level. At the national level, each individual shall have appropriate access to information concerning the environment that is held by public authorities, *including information on hazardous materials and activities in their communities*, and the opportunity to participate in decision-making processes. States shall facilitate and encourage public awareness and participation by making information widely available.[137]

Although Principle 10 hardly establishes an enforceable right to such information, it does reflect a recognition of the importance of "information on hazardous materials" to human well-being and the role of governments in developing and disseminating that information.

The "right-to-know" laws discussed previously, as well as Principle 10, share a common rationale of promoting individual autonomy by facilitating the ability of individuals to make choices about the risks to which they are exposed.[138] The right to know and the right not to be exposed to untested substances thus are two sides

[134] *See* John D. Echeverria & Julie B. Kaplan, *Poisonous Procedural "Reform": In Defense of Environmental Right-to-Know*, 12 *Kan. J.L. & Pub. Pol'y* 579, 585 (2003).

[135] Cal. Health & Safety Code § 25249.6 ("No person in the course of doing business shall knowingly and intentionally expose any individual to a chemical known to the state to cause cancer or reproductive toxicity without first giving clear and reasonable warning. . . . ").

[136] *See* 42 U.S.C. § 11,046(a)(1) (authority under EPCRA to bring citizen suits against facility owner or operator for failure to submit information); Cal. Health & Safety Code § 25249.7(d) (authorizing suits "by any person in the public interest" for Proposition 65 violations if certain conditions met).

[137] U.N. Conference on Environment & Development, June 3–14, 1992, Rio Declaration on Environment and Development, princ. 10, U.N. Doc. A/CONF.151/5/Rev. 1. (June 14, 1992) (emphasis added).

[138] *See* Kathryn E. Durham-Hammer, *Left to Wonder: Reevaluating, Reforming, and Implementing the Emergency Planning and Community Right-to-Know Act of 1986*, 29 Colum. J. Envtl. L. 323, 333 (2004) (describing "creat[ion of] a statutory right-to-know that affords community members an opportunity to make informed decisions about how to respond to environmental risks in their neighborhoods" as one of the primary objectives of EPCRA); Echeverria & Kaplan, *supra* note 134, at 590; McGarity & Shapiro, *supra* note 21, at 844 ("Members of the public have a legitimate interest in knowing the full health effects of products which receive agency approval so that they can decide for themselves whether to use them."); Clifford Rechtschaffen, *The Warning Game: Evaluating Warnings Under California's Proposition 65*, 23 Ecology L.Q. 303, 314 (1996). In practice, mandatory information disclosure requirements have prompted companies to reduce their emissions or reformulate their products voluntarily. *See* Bradley C. Karkkainen, *Information as Environmental Regulation: TRI and Performance Benchmarking, Precursor to a New Paradigm?*, 89 Geo. L.J. 257, 287 (2001); Rechtschaffen, *supra*, at 341–47.

of the same coin, both safeguarding individual autonomy. The development and disclosure of risk information enable individuals to protect their self-interests and to defend themselves and their families from external threats.[139] Information disclosure is also critical to democratic decision making, as only an informed citizenry can participate effectively in the political process and make considered judgments.[140] Ultimately, information disclosure requirements reflect a public desire to hold manufacturers responsible for the effects of their products and suggest the existence of an enforceable public right to be informed.[141] Although this right touches both individual and collective interests, it should be considered a *public* right because the injury – the lack of information – is shared equally by all members of the public and is supportive of the public right to an unpolluted environment. Moreover, access to accurate information, like access to unobstructed highways, is essential to healthy open markets.

D. *Litigating Public Nuisance for Failure to Test*

A public nuisance cause of action to enforce manufacturers' and importers' duty to test is attractive for a number of reasons. First, it would make the duty to test a meaningful obligation. A cause of action as delineated in this chapter would be available upon the introduction of an untested nanomaterial into the stream of commerce. No physical injury would be required, nor would causation – a formidable barrier to the filing of toxic tort claims, let alone their successful prosecution – be at issue. Second, such a cause of action would enable a measured public response to a public problem.[142] Because individual members of the public would suffer from virtually the same injury, potential private plaintiffs would not be able to assert the special injury necessary to sue. Rather, only public entities would be able to bring failure-to-test claims under a public nuisance theory.[143] This limitation on the pool

[139] *See* Echeverria & Kaplan, *supra* note 134, at 590; Timothy William Lambert et al., *Ethical Perspectives for Public and Environmental Health: Fostering Autonomy and the Right to Know*, 111 ENVTL. HEALTH PERSP. 133, 135 (2003) ("Fostering understanding enables people to think and care for themselves and also to help in the preventive action by assisting other people to stay out of harm's way. . . . ").

[140] *See* Echeverria & Kaplan, *supra* note 134, at 590; Rechtschaffen, *supra* note 138, at 313–15 (noting contentions that right-to-know laws promote economic efficiency and democratic decision making).

[141] *Cf.* Wagner, *supra* note 20, at 808–09 ("The legislative history undergirding at least some of the right-to-know laws also supports an inference that the public expects manufacturers to bear responsibility for generating and providing basic information on potentially toxic products and by-products."). The right of citizens to know of the hazards posed by chemicals in the environment around them is analogous to the right of a patient to informed consent under medical malpractice law. *See* Berger & Twerski, *supra* note 105, at 270–73 (discussing informed consent paradigm).

[142] *See* Antolini & Rechtschaffen, *supra* note 52, at 10,119 (noting that public nuisance "offers a community-oriented remedy").

[143] *Cf.* Sara Zdeb, Note, *From* Georgia v. Tennessee Copper *to* Massachusetts v. EPA: Parens Patriae *Standing for State Global-Warming Plaintiffs*, 96 GEO. L.J. 1059, 1077 (2008) (describing purpose of *parens patriae* doctrine as "to allow states to vindicate public rights and guard against injuries that might be too widely-shared to support standing for any particular individual").

of potential plaintiffs would ameliorate concerns that manufacturers would be inundated by lawsuits. And because of limited public resources, state attorneys general would need to be selective in deciding what cases to pursue and which companies to name as defendants.[144] Third, the relief granted would directly redress the problem. Although damages are sometimes recoverable in public nuisance actions, the most common remedy is injunctive relief.[145] This general rule would hold true for failure-to-test claims as well. Injunctive relief would be preferable to damages because of the difficulty of determining the economic value of the information not developed. In addition, to the extent that damages might in theory compensate for tangible injuries, it is improbable that plaintiffs would be able to demonstrate injuries caused by exposure to as-yet untested substances. Ultimately, injunctions ordering companies to perform testing in order to manufacture or distribute a chemical within a state would be a particularly appropriate remedy, and courts could tailor compliance deadlines to account for individual circumstances, such as the continued distribution of useful or important chemicals for a period of time adequate to allow for testing.

CONCLUSION

Public nuisance actions offer a potentially powerful tool to goad chemical manufacturers into performing safety testing that they already should be doing under fundamental principles of tort law and responsible corporate behavior. The range of substances possibly subject to such actions is quite broad, but public officials would almost certainly focus their limited resources on a narrow subset of the thousands of chemicals found in commerce. In setting their priorities for investigation and subsequent litigation, officials likely would consider factors relating to both risk and exposure. On the risk side, these factors could include anecdotal accounts of adverse effects, statistical clusters of symptoms or illness, known or suspected hazards in similar chemicals, or studies suggesting positive correlations between chemical exposure and illness, even if those correlations fall short of statistical significance. On the exposure side, factors worth considering might include widespread distribution or use of a chemical; intended use or foreseeable misuse of a chemical product; likely exposure among children, pregnant women, and other vulnerable populations; and the tendency of a chemical to disperse in the environment. None of this is to suggest that any of these factors is necessary in order to bring a failure to test claim; rather, these factors are among those that may be relevant to the choice of chemicals to target for public nuisance actions.

[144] *See* Calvin Massey, *State Standing After* Massachusetts v. EPA, 61 *Fla. L. Rev.* 249, 274 (2009) (contending political processes and limited resources constrain ability of state attorneys general to litigate public rights).

[145] *See supra* note 60 and accompanying text.

Ultimately, a statutory mandate to develop risk assessments for all chemicals in commerce could serve as a more comprehensive response to the widespread failure of manufacturers, processors, and distributors to conduct adequate testing. Whether such a mandate will be enacted in the near future, however, is uncertain, given the opposition it would likely encounter from the chemical industry.[146] Public nuisance actions for failure to test can help to address the toxicity gap in the meantime and lay the foundation for a broader statutory mandate.[147] Such actions can be brought immediately, without any legislative action, and can be brought by one or more states, consistent with their significant role in U.S. environmental policy.[148] The bringing of failure-to-test actions, and the possibility that such actions may be brought, will force nanotechnology companies to take seriously their obligations to ensure that the substances that they introduce into commerce and the environment are reasonably safe.

146 Senator Frank Lautenberg recently introduced a bill that would require manufacturers to develop and submit a minimum data set for each chemical they produce. *See* Safe Chemicals Act of 2010, S. 3209, 111th Cong. § 5 (2010).

147 *See* Kirsten H. Engel, *Harmonizing Regulatory and Litigation Approaches to Climate Change Mitigation: Incorporating Tradable Emissions Offsets Into Common Law Remedies*, 155 U. PA. L. REV. 1563, 1572–77 (2007) (describing potential for state-initiated public nuisance litigation to trigger federal regulatory response in context of climate change).

148 *See generally* David E. Adelman & Kirsten H. Engel, *Adaptive Federalism: The Case Against Reallocating Environmental Regulatory Authority*, 92 MINN. L. REV. 1796, 1796 (2008) ("The current system of environmental federalism is thus a dynamic one of overlapping federal and state jurisdiction."); William W. Buzbee, *Contextual Environmental Federalism*, 14 N.Y.U. ENVTL. L.J. 108, 108 (2005) (contending that "overlap, cooperative federalism structures, and redundant enforcement mechanisms ... [within] the American system of environmental federalism reduce the risk of regulatory underkill that can result from failures to address environmental ills, as well as failures adequately to fund, implement and enforce written laws and regulations"); Alexandra B. Klass, *State Innovation and Preemption: Lessons From State Climate Change Efforts*, 41 LOY. L.A. L. REV. 1653, 1656 (2008) ("[S]tate common law and regulatory efforts to control GHG emissions illustrate today's almost complete linkage between the common law of torts and the regulatory state in areas of public health, safety, and environmental protection.").

11

Enlarging the Regulation of Shrinking Cosmetics and Sunscreens

Robin Fretwell Wilson

Although one is hard-pressed to name an industry that has not jumped on the nanotechnology bandwagon, the makers of cosmetics and sunscreens have capitalized on nanotechnology more aggressively than any other.[1] Already by 2006, 5% of all cosmetic products contained nanoparticles (NPs),[2] whereas more than 300 sunscreens contained nano-sized zinc oxide or titanium dioxide.[3]

The appeal of using NPs in sunscreens and cosmetics rather than their conventional counterparts (called here super-sized particles, or SSPs) comes from their small size. Unlike SSPs, NPs in sunscreens can provide ultraviolet (UV) protection while remaining transparent, avoiding the pasty white appearance of conventional sunscreens.[4] With cosmetics, NPs hold the promise to provide deep, targeted delivery of moisturizers to the living layers of skin.[5] Makers of nano-cosmetics and

[1] Andrew D. Maynard, Nanotechnology: A Research Strategy for Addressing Risk 13 (Project on Emerging Nanotechnologies, Woodrow Wilson International Center for Scholars 2006); Jessica K. Fender, *The FDA and Nano: Big Problems with Tiny Technology*, 83 Chi.-Kent L. Rev. 1063, 1074 (2008) (cosmetics "make up more than 15% of the nanotechnology-product market").

[2] *Nanotechnology in Cosmetics* at 2 (April 24, 2009), *available at* http://www.observatorynano.eu/project/filesystem/files/Cosmetics%20report-April%2009.pdf [*hereinafter* Nanotechnology in Cosmetics].

[3] *See* Cathy Garber & Michael Berger, *Nanoparticles and sunscreen safety*, at 1, http://www.nanowerk.com/spotlight/spotid=714.php (August 3, 2006). More than two thirds of titanium dioxide sunscreens use engineered NPs, as do one third of zinc oxide sunscreens. *See* Katherine A. Van Tassel & Rose H. Goldman, *The Growing Consumer Exposure to Nanotechnology in Everyday Products: Regulating Innovative Technologies in Light of Lessons from the Past*, *available at* http://works.bepress.com/cgi/viewcontent.cgi?article=1000&context=k_vantassel&sei-redir=1#search=The+Growing+Consumer+Exposure+to+Nanotechnology+in+Everyday+Products:+Regulating+Innovative+Technologies+in+Light+of+Lessons+from+the+Past [forthcoming in 44(1) Connecticut Law Review (2011)] [*hereinafter* Growing Consumer Exposure].

[4] Michael Dore, *Nanotechnology: Evaluate the Product Liability Risks*, 198 N.J. L.J. 1, 1 (December 14, 2009) [*hereinafter* Product Liability Risks].

[5] *Nanotechnology in Cosmetics* at 3.

nano-sunscreens not only acknowledge that NPs will penetrate the skin more deeply, but tout their health effects as well.[6]

With any new or powerful technology, there is the potential for bad along with the potential for good. Federal regulators, like the Environmental Protection Agency (EPA), large reinsurers, nongovernmental organizations (NGOs), scientific organizations, toxicologists, and other scientists widely recognize that "[w]hile nanotechnology looms large with commercial promise and potential benefit, an equally large issue is the evaluation of potential effects on human and environmental health."[7] Indeed, "[t]he very characteristics that make nanotechnology potentially spectacular also present its potential risks."[8]

This possibility for harm has been largely ignored by the federal agency with oversight responsibility for both cosmetics and sunscreens, the US Food and Drug Administration (FDA). Unlike the FDA's robust regulation of drugs, which requires drug makers to secure approval for marketing by showing safety and efficacy through human clinical trials, cosmetics can be marketed without such proof. Although sunscreen manufacturers are required to demonstrate safety before marketing because sunscreens are considered a drug, the FDA accepts proof that sunscreens using SSPs are safe – without inquiring further into the safety of nano-ingre-dients.

A raft of studies have now examined whether NPs penetrate or harm damaged or intact skin. These studies show that NPs have different toxicity than SSPs because of their small size and high reactivity and sometimes exert drug-like effects on the body. This emerging body of evidence calls into question the wisdom of leaving nano-sunscreens and nano-cosmetics largely unregulated. The weight of the evidence suggests that, at a minimum, questions about safety need to be asked – and answered. To date, however, no manufacturer has been required to make any significant showing of safety.

This chapter shows that concerns over the safety of nano-cosmetics and nano-sunscreens have moved rapidly from the realm of speculation to grounds for real concern, and as a consequence, this regulatory void is no longer tenable or responsible. Section I demonstrates that many cosmetics and sunscreens use NPs. Section II explains the legal regulation of nano-cosmetics and nano-sunscreens, highlighting both Congress' choice in the Food, Drug, and Cosmetic Act (FDCA), enacted in 1938, to subject cosmetics to far less scrutiny than drugs *and* the FDA's 1999 policy stance that nano-sunscreens pose no more risk than their larger counterparts.

[6] *See* Section I *infra*.

[7] Michael P. Holsapple & Lois D. Lehman-McKeeman, *Forum Series: Research Strategies for Safety Evaluation of Nanomaterials*, 82(2) TOXICOLOGICAL SCIENCES, 315 (2005) [*hereinafter* Research Strategies]. *See also* Section III.

[8] Gregory Mandel, *Nanotechnology Governance*, 59 ALA. L. REV. 1323, 1341 (2008) [*hereinafter* Nanotechnology Governance].

Section III presents studies over the past decade that have shown that NPs, far from acting like SSPs, penetrate the protective outer layers of the skin to reach living tissues. There, NPs can cause oxidative stress, damaging cellular DNA. NPs also trigger structural changes and even programmed cell death in many cells they reach. In light of this evidence of biological impacts, Section IV calls on Congress and the FDA to revisit the laissez-faire regulation of nano-cosmetics and nano-sunscreens to better ensure the public's safety.

I. SHRINKING COSMETICS AND SUNSCREENS

NPs are popping up in personal care products of every variety – from cleansers, exfoliants, makeup removers, toners, and moisturizers to acne spot treatments, anti-wrinkle and anti-aging products, bronzers and self-tanning gels, cellulite creams, toothpastes, and even spray-on condoms.[9] Some of the most recognizable names in the industry offer these products – Banana Boat, Burt's Bees, Chanel, Coppertone, Dior, L'Oréal, Lancôme, and Neiman Marcus, among others.[10]

Companies exploiting NPs boast that the products "are small enough to easily penetrate the skin's natural surface barrier, but large enough so the body will not counterproductively absorb them prior to full effectiveness."[11] Having "travel[led] deep and directly into the skin," these NPs provide a "'supply' depot" so that "the skin can take what it needs, whenever it needs it" by drawing the "tiny crystals directly into the cell nucleus."[12]

The makers not only acknowledge that NPs will penetrate the skin, but tout their health effects as well. Some, like JamieO Skincare, assert that NPs stimulate "collagen and elastin production . . . [and] prevent free radical damage,"[13] whereas other products claim to stimulate "fibroblast activity" to "rejuvenate lips."[14] Nanoseal-Hairna Essence, a hair-loss prevention product, "transmit[s] . . . [a] cell activation

9 *See* Appendix.

10 *See* Appendix.

11 Kara Vita, http://www.karavita.com/aboutourproducts/lyphazometechnology.aspx (relying on "14 years of research and development" that show "such superior benefits"). *See also* Nano Anti Aging Cream, http://www.nanotechproject.org/inventories/consumer/browse/products/nano_anti_aging_cream/ ("using the newest nano technology and transdermal delivery"); Rewind Time, at http://www.nanotechproject.org/inventories/consumer/browse/products/rewind_time/ (utilizing NPs "to ensure the active ingredients penetrate the skin's surface and travel deep into the lower level of skin called the dermis"); Crystal Radiance, at http://www.nanotechproject.org/inventories/consumer/browse/products/crystal_radiance/ (same); Indulgence, http://www.nanotechproject.org/inventories/consumer/browse/products/indulgence/ (releasing "marine extracts and a nine percent concentration of transdermal and essential oils over time").

12 JUVENA (International) AG, http://web.archive.org/web/20071212035044/http:/www.cosmetic-business.com/en/showartikel.php?art_id=1122.

13 JamieO Skincare, http://www.businesswire.com/portal/site/google/index.jsp?ndmViewId=news_view&newsId=20070221005160&newsLang=en.

14 DERMAdoctor®, http://www.nanotechproject.org/inventories/consumer/browse/products/5093/.

substance to stimulate hair root and inactive cell [sic],"[15] whereas St. Herbs Nano Breast Cream "expands the cellular substructure and promotes development of the lobules and alveoli of the breasts."[16] And in perhaps the most intimate and bizarre application of NPs, a spray-on foam condom using nanosilver integrates "conception control, antibiosis and lubrication into a whole."[17] Many of these products "are especially formulated to be used on damaged skin" and exploit "penetration enhancers."[18]

Of the four classes of nanomaterials recognized by the National Toxicology Program – fullerenes, nanotubes, metal oxides, and quantum dots–only the latter does not appear to have any utility for cosmetics or sunscreens.[19] Fullerenes are currently used in men's shaving creams, face creams, and eye creams.[20] One cosmetic maker, NaturalNano, is exploring the use of naturally occurring nanotubes.[21] Metal oxides, like titanium dioxide and zinc oxide, appear in sunscreens, whereas other metal oxides, like aluminum oxide and iron oxide, are used in lipsticks, makeup foundation, and eye shadow.[22] Nanosilver appears in such products as cosmetics,[23] exfoliating washes,[24] body soap,[25] and hair loss treatments.[26]

15 Nanoseal-Hairna essence [*hereinafter* Nanoseal-Hairna], http://www.nanotechproject.org/inventories/consumer/browse/products/5294/.

16 St. Herb Nano Breast Cream, http://www.nanotechproject.org/inventories/consumer/browse/products/nano_breast_cream/.

17 Blue Cross Bio-Medical, http://www.bluecrossgroup-china.com/products/p_l_02.htm.

18 *Growing Consumer Exposure* at 25.

19 NTP Nanotechnology Safety Initiative, *National Toxicology Program Fact Sheet, available at* http://ntp.niehs.nih.gov/ntp/Factsheets/NanoColor06SRCH.pdf; *Quantum Dot Skin Penetration Study*, NANOTECHNOLOGY LAW REPORT, *available at* http://www.nanolawreport.com/2008/10/articles/quantum-dot-skin-penetration-study/ (October 15, 2008) (indicating quantum dots are not being used in cosmetics or sunscreens).

20 Joint ANEC/BEUC position, *Nanotechnology: Small Is Beautiful But Is It Safe?, available at* http://www.anec.org/attachments/ANEC-PT-2009-Nano-002final.pdf (2009); Sircuit White Out, http://www.nanotechproject.org/inventories/consumer/browse/products/sircuit_white_out/; Bethany Halford, *Fullerene for the Face: Cosmetics Containing C_{60} Nanoparticles Are Entering the Market, Even If Their Safety Is Unclear*, 83(13) SCIENCE & TECHNOLOGY 47 (2006).

21 Simon Pitman, *NaturalNano teams up on nano cosmetics research*, Cosmetics design.com, Oct. 10, 2007, http://www.cosmeticsdesign.com/Formulation-Science/NaturalNano-teams-up-on-nano-cosmetics-research (describing research on "naturally occurring nanotubes, which have a unique hollow-tube structure that allows chemicals, additives or other materials to be placed inside the tubes, creating a slow or controlled release of the materials").

22 Allusion Alumina Powders, http://www.nanotechproject.org/inventories/consumer/browse/products/alusion_alumina_powders/ (makeup foundation and eye shadow); Damon C. Sacco et al., *Artifacts Caused by Cosmetics in MR Imaging of the Head*, 148 AMERICAN JOURNAL OF ROENTGENOLOGY 1001, 1003 (1987) ("[T]he pigment used to give makeup a black color contains Fe_3O_4; other pigments used in makeup are Fe_2O_3 (red) and $FeO\text{-}H_2O$ (yellow).").

23 *Nanotechnology in Cosmetics* at 9.

24 Nano Cyclic Cleanser PINK, http://www.nanotechproject.org/inventories/consumer/browse/products/nano_cyclic_cleanser_pink/.

25 Cosil Nano Beauty Soap, http://www.nanotechproject.org/inventories/consumer/browse/products/cosil_nano_beauty_soap/.

26 *Nanoseal-Hairna*.

The NPs used in cosmetics vary in size from 15 nanometers (nm) up to several micrometers (μm, or several thousand nm),[27] whereas NPs in sunscreens typically range from 15 to 500 nm.[28] The FDA permits concentrations in sunscreens of titanium dioxide and zinc oxide up to 25%.[29] NPs in both cosmetics and sunscreens "have a tendency to form very tightly bound 'aggregates'"[30] which range from clusters of 600 to 700 nm in size to "very large agglomerates of over 2μm [or 2000 nm]."[31] Surface modifications affect the formation of such clusters.[32]

Until the last five years, no one paid much attention to the risks of using nano-cosmetics and nano-sunscreens, including the FDA. "[C]onventional thought [assumed] that the skin barrier is impervious to materials and that abrasion or mechanical stressors would be required for nanomaterial penetration."[33] Although a

27 *Nanotechnology in Cosmetics* at 3; The Royal Society, *Nanoscience and Nanotechnologies: Opportunities and Uncertainties* at 10, 43 (July 2004) [*hereinafter* Royal Society Nanoscience] (describing cosmetic pigments over 100 nm in size). One micrometer equals 1000 nanometers.

28 Anna Wokovich et al., *Particle Size Determination of Sunscreens Formulated With Various Forms of Titanium Dioxide*, 35(10) DRUG DEVELOPMENT AND INDUSTRIAL PHARMACY 1188 (2009) [*hereinafter* Particle Size Determination]; Graham Aldous & Paul Kent, *Titanium Dioxide and Zinc Oxide Nanoparticles in Sunscreen Formulations: A Study of the Post Production Particle Size Distribution of Particles in a Range of Commercial Emulsion Variants*, *available at* http://www.hamiltonlabs.com.au/webdata/resources/files/Hamilton_Sunscreen_Nanoparticles_Paper.pdf (unpublished paper) [*hereinafter* Sunscreen Formulations].

29 *Sunscreen Drug Products for Over-the-Counter Human Use*; Final Monograph, 64 Fed. Reg. 27666, §352.10(p) and (r) (May 21, 1999), *available at* http://frwebgate3.access.gpo.gov/cgi-bin/PDFgate.cgi?WAISdocID=UlvF5W/1/2/0&WAISaction=retrieve [*hereinafter* Sunscreen Monograph].

30 *Sunscreen Formulations* (noting that NPs form aggregates due to chemical forces between particles, which "require large amounts of energy to disrupt;" aggregates in turn may cluster to form "less strongly bound 'agglomerates'").

31 *Particle Size Determination* at 1180. *See also id.* at 1180, 1183 (finding in a FDA Center for Drug Evaluation and Research study of three finished sunscreen formulations to "determine whether the formulation process caused a change in the size distributions," that NPs in finished products were "the same as . . . in the powder form"); *Sunscreen Formulations* (finding that true particle size of agglomerates in various sunscreen emulsions ranged from 127 to 5570 nm); Jeanne E. Skebo et al., *Assessment of Metal Nanoparticle Agglomeration, Uptake, and Interaction Using High-Illuminating System*, 26 INTERNATIONAL JOURNAL OF TOXICOLOGY 135, 137 (2007) (studying natural agglomeration of silver, aluminum, and manganese nanometals, which ranged in size from 25 to 130 nm, and finding agglomerates of 200 nm to 16 μm or 16,000 nm); Francis Quinn, *Nanotechnologies in Cosmetics*, Presentation from L'Oréal held at the IRGC Workshop "Appropriate Risk Governance Options for Nanotechnologies in Food and Cosmetics," at 32, 28 April 2008, Geneva (stating, as a L'Oréal representative, that clusters generally ranged "between 300 nm and 10000 nm depending on the manufacturer").

32 Ludwig K. Limbach et al., *Oxide Nanoparticle Uptake in Human Lung Fibroblasts: Effects of Particle Size, Agglomeration, and Diffusion at Low Concentrations*, 39 ENVIRON. SCI. TECHNOL. 9370, 9372, 9374–5 (2005).

33 Jessica P. Ryman-Rasmussen et al., *Penetration of Intact Skin by Quantum Dots with Diverse Physiochemical Properties*, 91 TOXICOLOGICAL SCIENCES 159, 164 (2006). Reviewing this study, Nohynek and colleagues emphasized the "significant penetration of [NPs] (diameters: spherical 4.6 nm, ellipsoid 6 × 12 nm) into the epidermis and, for cations, also into the dermis." Although these findings suggest that "very small [NPs] may have a capacity for passive penetration into intact skin, the relevance of pig skin and of the alkaline pHs used to defining likely human exposure is not clear. Accordingly, these data require confirmation in humans using in-use conditions." Gerhard J. Nohynek et al., *Grey Goo*

primary function of the skin is to "act as a barrier," the skin is also "the largest organ of the body" and so "serves as a primary [exposure] route."[34] Indeed, the skin "is one of the principal portals of entry by which environmental toxicants or nanomaterials can enter into the body."[35] As Section III.B explains, a "potentially important uptake route [for NPs] is through dermal exposure."[36]

The FDA paid scant attention to NPs applied directly to the skin for a variety of technical reasons, as the next section explains. This section shows that Congress did not empower the FDA to regulate cosmetics meaningfully like the FDA does with drugs. Adding to this vacuum, the FDA reached a policy judgment about the safety of NPs based on a nearly non-existent empirical record: specifically, the FDA maintained that NPs do not pose different risks than their larger counterparts.

This assumption is now widely recognized as disproven. The world's oldest scientific academy,[37] the Royal Society, concluded that "[i]t is clear that nanoparticles have different properties to the same chemical at a larger scale, and the implications of these different properties for long-term toxicity to the skin require rigorous investigation on a case-by-case basis."[38] Toxicologists, large reinsurers, and NGOs have all also recognized that NPs act differently than SSPs.[39] Indeed, scientists widely acknowledge that nanomaterials have different toxicity than SSPs because of their

on the Skin? Nanotechnology, Cosmetic and Sunscreen Safety, 37 Critical Reviews in Toxicology 251, 261 (2007) (discussing the safety of nanotechnology used in cosmetics and sunscreens). As noted in Section I, quantum dots do not appear to be used in nano-cosmetics or nano-sunscreens.

34 *Research Strategies* at 13.

35 *Id.* at 12.

36 Günter Oberdörster et al., *Nanotoxicology: An Emerging Discipline Evolving From Studies of Ultrafine Particles*, 113 Environmental Health Perspectives 823, 834 (2005) [*hereinafter* An Emerging Discipline].

37 *Royal Society Nanoscience* at 10, 43; The Royal Society, *What is the Royal Society?*, http://royalsociety.org/about-us/.

38 Royal Soc'y & Royal Acad. of Eng'g, *Nanoscience and Nanotechnologies: Opportunities and Uncertainties* 43 (2004), *available at* http://www.nanotec.org.uk/report/chapter5.pdf.

39 *Research Strategies* at 16 ("[N]anomaterials exhibit unique properties that clearly distinguish them from their bulk counterparts."); Tian Xia et al., *Comparison of the Abilities of Ambient and Manufactured Nanoparticles To Induce Cellular Toxicity According to an Oxidative Stress Paradigm*, 6(8) Nano Letters 1794 (2006) [*hereinafter* Comparison of Abilities] ("Nanomaterial properties differ from those bulk materials of the same composition, allowing them to execute novel activities."); *An Emerging Discipline* at 824 ("Not only may adverse effects be induced, but interactions of NPs with cells and subcellular structures and their biokinetics are likely to be very different from those of larger-sized particles."); Annabelle Hett et al., Nanotechnology: Small Matter, Many Unknowns 7 (Swiss RE 2004) ("In contrast to larger microparticles, nanoparticles have almost unrestricted access to the human body."); International Risk Governance Council (IRGC), Policy Brief: Appropriate Risk Governance Strategies for Nanotechnology Applications in Food and Cosmetics 19 (International Risk Governance Council 2009) ("The properties of [titanium dioxide] vary as a function of size."); K. Donaldson et al., *Nanotoxicology*, 61 Occup. Environ. Med. 727, 728 (2004) ("Very small particles and structures could have a range of effects that are not seen with conventional particles. For instance, they may not be detected by the normal phagocytic defences, allowing them to gain access to the blood or the nervous system. Very small particles are smaller than some molecules and could act like haptens to modify protein structures, either altering their function or rendering them antigenic, raising the potential for autoimmune effects.").

small size and high reactivity.[40] Silver provides a good example. In bulk form, silver has many inert forms that are safe for use,[41] but on the nano-scale, silver is "a rather potent biocide."[42] This demonstrates that an accurate gauge of risk "cannot be derived from knowledge about the toxicity of similar material at a macroscale."[43]

Other federal regulators, including the EPA and the US National Institute for Occupational Safety and Health, as well as officials with the FDA, also now acknowledge the different behavior of NPs.[44] Despite this widespread, shared appreciation, the FDA's policy positions on nano-sunscreens and nano-cosmetics remain entrenched, as the next section shows.

II. THE CORE CONUNDRUM: REGULATING WITH INCOMPLETE INFORMATION

A. *Regulators Always Act in Contexts of Greater or Lesser Information*

New technologies often create "information voids" about risks to the environment or human health.[45] As scientific knowledge fills that void, "the level of uncertainty . . . progresses from ignorance (where scientists *don't know* what they don't know) to indeterminacy (where scientists *know* what they don't know but can plan the scientific experiments necessary to find out) to, finally, a tipping

40 Xiaoyong Deng et al., *Nanosized Zinc Oxide Particles Induce Neural Stem Cell Apoptosis*, 20 NANOTECHNOLOGY 1 (Feb. 2009) [*hereinafter* Nanosized Zinc].

41 Pål Strandbakken & Harald Throne-Holst, *"Nobody Told Me I was a Nano-Consumer:" How Nanotechnologies Might Challenge the Notion of Consumer Rights*, 32 J. CONSUM. POLICY 393, 397–98 (2009) [*hereinafter* Nano-Consumer].

42 *Id.* at 398.

43 *Nanotechnology Governance* at 1341. *See also Product Liability Risks* at 2 (observing that "traditional 'route of the administration' factors involved in traditional risk assessments are open to question since nano materials may enter and potentially impact the body in ways in which non-nano materials cannot").

44 JEFF MORRIS ET AL., NANOTECHNOLOGY WHITE PAPER 78 (US Environmental Protection Agency Science Policy Council 2007), *available at* http://www.epa.gov/osa/pdfs/nanotech/epa-nanotechnology-whitepaper-0207.pdf ("[I]t is generally believed that nanoparticles can have toxicological properties that differ from their bulk material."); CHRISTINE M. BRANCHE ET AL., CURRENT INTELLIGENCE BULLETIN 60: INTERIM GUIDANCE FOR MEDICAL SCREENING AND HAZARD SURVEILLANCE FOR WORKERS POTENTIALLY EXPOSED TO ENGINEERED NANOPARTICLES 1 (National Institute for Occupational Safety and Health 2009), *available at* http://www.cdc.gov/niosh/docs/2009-116/ (2009) ("[Nano]materials often exhibit unique properties beyond those expected at the chemical or bulk level that affect their physical, chemical, and biological behavior."); Nakissa Sadrieh & Parvaneh Espandiari, *Nanotechnology and the FDA: What Are the Scientific and Regulatory Considerations for Products Containing Nanomaterials?*, 3 NANOTECH. L. & BUS. 339, 347 (2006) [*hereinafter* Nanotechnology and the FDA] (paper by the Associate Director for Research Policy and Implementation for the Office of Pharmaceutical Science at FDA's Center for Drug Evaluation and Research (CDER) and a toxicologist with CDER) ("As particle size gets smaller, there may be size-specific effects. These effects may impact safety if the smaller materials are more reactive.").

45 *Growing Consumer Exposure* at 36.

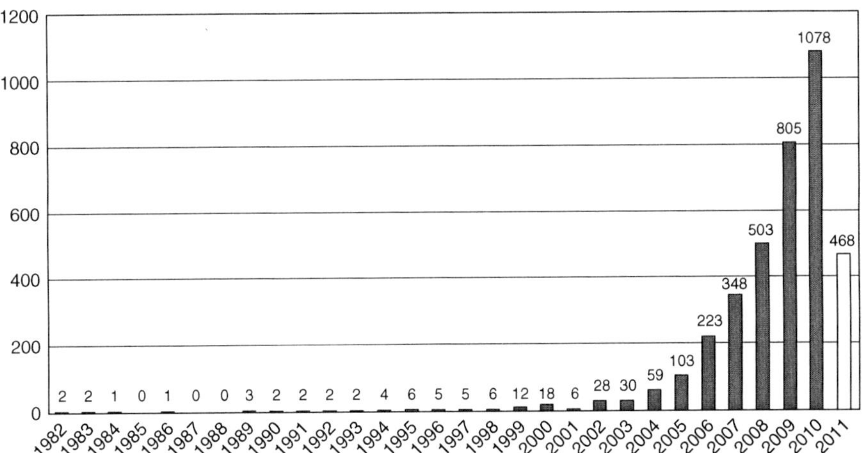

FIGURE 11.1. Number of NP toxicity studies by year.

point . . . when classic probability analysis can be applied to predict, or quantify, risk levels."[46]

Studies of NP safety have followed this trajectory. In 1999, the FDA stated that NPs in sunscreens are not sufficiently different from SSPs to be a new ingredient – in effect stating that NPs pose no more risk than SSPs.[47] As Figure 11.1 shows, PubMed at that time contained only 55 studies examining the toxicity of NPs,[48] only one of which focused principally on the skin.[49] Thus, the FDA drew its conclusion on a razor-thin empirical record. In 2007, with considerably more evidence available to it, the FDA's Nanotechnology Taskforce (NTF) again concluded that NPs pose no "greater safety concerns" than SSPs,[50] a policy judgment that it sticks by today.[51]

As Figure 11.1 illustrates, while the FDA's policy judgment that NPs act no differently than SSPs has become entrenched, scientific research on nanotoxicity has exploded. Nanotoxicity studies increased slowly from a pair of studies in 1982 to hundreds by 2005, reaching a record 1,078 articles in 2010. As this area of scientific inquiry ballooned, researchers began to focus explicitly on the skin (Figure 11.2). Today, policymakers have the benefit of more than 3,700 nanotoxicity studies, with more than 150 focusing on the skin.[52]

[46] *Id.*

[47] *Sunscreen Monograph* at 27671. Later FDA documents explicitly state that NPs pose no more safety concerns than SSPs. *See* Sections II.A. and II.B.2 (discussing the 2007 Nanotechnology Taskforce Report and the FDA's 2010 Frequently Asked Questions about nanotechnology).

[48] *See* Figure 11.1 (summing studies before 1999).

[49] *See* Figures 11.1 and 11.2.

[50] FDA, *Nanotechnology, Frequently Asked Questions* [*hereinafter* Nanotech FAQ], *available at* http://www.sit-or.com/index.php?option=com_content&view=article&id=7&Itemid=15.

[51] *See* Section II.B.2.

[52] To measure the increase in attention to the toxicity of nanomaterials, we searched PubMed, the US National Library of Medicine's electronic database, on May 17, 2011, for papers that included

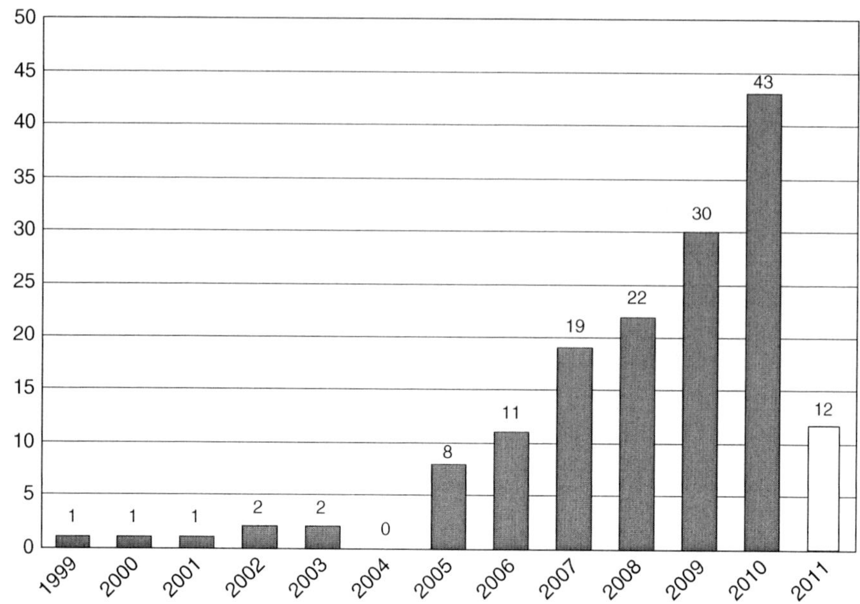

FIGURE 11.2. NP toxicity studies involving skin by year.

As the next sub-section explains, the FDA has been "complacent to a degree not justified by current scientific understanding."[53]

B. *An Industry That Receives a Regulatory Pass and Not a Hard Look*

Two pivotal judgments have created a regulatory void for nano-cosmetics and nano-sunscreens. First, long before the advent of nanotechnology, Congress decided in the FDCA[54] to give the makers of cosmetics a virtual free pass to market cosmetics without proof of safety.[55] Second, the FDA took the position in 1999, a position it maintains to this day despite substantial evidence to the contrary, that NPs in sunscreens act no differently than SSPs.[56]

the terms "toxicity" or "toxicology" *and* the terms "nanomaterial*" or "nanoparticle*," where the * indicates a universal character [search field: ((toxicity) OR toxicology) AND ((nanomaterial*) OR nanoparticle*)]. This search captures both "nanomaterial" and "nanomaterials." Figure 11.1 presents those results. To produce Figure 11.2, we performed the same search with the additional term "AND skin." Yearly tallies were taken by selecting the "Limits" tab and filtering the search from January 1st to December 31st for each individual year.

53 *Nanotechnology Governance* at 1368.

54 Food, Drug, and Cosmetic Act, Pub. L. No. 75-717, 52 Stat. 1040 (1930) (codified as amended at 21 U.S.C. §§ 331–397 (2000)).

55 *Id.*

56 *Sunscreen Monograph.*

Although the FDA has failed to address adequately the adverse effects of nanomaterials on human and environmental health, governmental entities and private organizations in the European Union

1. Cosmetics

As FDA Associate Commissioner for Science Norris Alderson has noted, the FDA has "only limited authority for potentially high risk nano-products[, like] cosmetics."[57] Originally passed in 1938, the FDCA gives the FDA the authority to regulate drugs, medical devices, cosmetics, food, and dietary supplements[58] – each of which has a "distinct regulatory pathway[] and thereby [receives] distinct FDA scrutiny."[59] The scope of the FDA's authority depends on the product's intended use as described by its maker.[60] Thus, the "FDA only regulates to 'claims by a sponsor.'"[61]

A cosmetic is any article "intended to be rubbed, poured, sprinkled, or sprayed on, introduced into, or otherwise applied to the human body or any part thereof for cleansing, beautifying, promoting attractiveness, or altering the appearance."[62] The FDA has no pre-market approval authority over cosmetics, as it does with drugs.[63] Although "numerous bills have been introduced to require premarket testing of cosmetics" since the FDCA's passage in 1938, "none have passed."[64]

Instead, federal law requires that cosmetics not be adulterated or misbranded.[65] To avoid misbranding, a cosmetic ingredient must be "adequately substantiated for

have explored regulatory responses to the threats posed by nanomaterials. For example, the Environment Committee in the European Parliament recently moved in June 2010 to ban silver NPs and certain carbons after testimony and research from various European groups indicated that these materials were sufficiently dangerous to be deemed unfit for European markets. *See* Royal Society of Chemistry, *EU ministers call for nanomaterial ban, available at* http://www.rsc.org/chemistryworld/News/2010/June/14061001.asp (last visited May 18, 2011). The European Parliament subsequently abandoned the attempt to ban silver NPs. *See RoHS Recast: Nanomaterials Escape Explicit Regulation*, Nanotechnology Industries Association, Jan. 7, 2011, http://www.nanotechia.org/global-news/rohs-recast–nanomaterials-escape-explicit-regulation.

57 Norris E. Alderson, Associate Commissioner for Science, US Food and Drug Administration, FDA Regulation of Nanotechnology Products, Mar. 30, 2004, at 8 (on file with author) [*hereinafter* FDA Regulation Slides].

58 Brianna (MacDonald) Sandoval, *Perspectives on FDA's Regulation of Nanotechnology: Emerging Challenges and Potential Solutions*, 8 Comprehensive Reviews in Food Science and Food Safety 375, 381 (2009) [*hereinafter* Perspectives on FDA].

59 Brian Wilhelmi, *Nanosilver: A Test for Nanotech Regulation*, 63 Food & Drug L.J. 89, 103 (2008).

60 FDA, *Is it a Cosmetic, a Drug, or Both? (Or is it Soap?)* (July 8, 2002), http://www.fda.gov/Cosmetics/GuidanceComplianceRegulatoryInformation/ucm074201.htm (last visited May 18, 2011) [*hereinafter* FDA Factsheet] (noting that intended use can be established by labeling or advertisement, consumer perception, or the use of certain ingredients with a well-known function).

61 *FDA Regulation Slides* at slide 8.

62 21 U.S.C. § 321(i) (2010).

63 *FDA Factsheet*; Nicole Abramowitz, *The Dangers of Chasing Youth: Regulating the Use of Nanoparticles in Anti-Aging Products*, 2008 U. Ill. J.L. Tech. & Pol'y 199, 210 (2008) [*hereinafter* Chasing Youth].

64 Jacqueline A. Greff, *Regulation of Cosmetics That are Also Drugs*, 51 Food and Drug Law Journal 243, 244 (1996) [*hereinafter* Regulation of Cosmetics].

65 21 U.S.C. §§ 331, 361, 362 (2010); *Chasing Youth* at 210 ("Therefore, the FDA's authority over anti-aging products classified as 'cosmetics' is essentially limited to prosecution after sale for violations of its prohibition on the introduction into interstate commerce of 'adulterated' and 'misbranded' cosmetics.").

safety" before marketing *or* bear a warning label[66] – requirements that are enforced in a "self-policing manner."[67] Manufacturers are ill-equipped to act on this duty because the FDA has declined to issue guidance on exactly what is meant by "adequately substantiated."[68]

Under the Fair Packaging and Labeling Act,[69] cosmetics manufacturers must list all ingredients on the product label. Most ingredients used in cosmetics are found on a list created by the FDA Commissioner or in certain accepted compendia created by the Cosmetic, Toiletry, and Fragrance Association (CTFA).[70] Although these lists contain numerous SSPs, no separate listings exist for NPs.[71]

To avoid adulteration, a material must not contain "any poisonous or deleterious substance which may render it injurious to users,"[72] including "specifically listed 'adulterated' materials."[73] Crucially, "the FDA has not specifically classified any nanoparticles used in . . . cosmetics as 'adulterated.'"[74]

Together, the misbranding and adulteration prohibitions "have generated only limited enforcement activity."[75] This is not surprising because "[c]osmetics are the only major FDA-regulated product group that does not have its own center."[76]

In addition to lacking pre-market approval, the FDA lacks the authority to force a recall of cosmetic products.[77] The FDA relies on a number of voluntary programs for its oversight,[78] but "it remains unclear . . . how many companies will participate in [voluntary programs], and it is not evident that there is enough incentive for

66 21 C.F.R. § 740.10(a) (2011) ("Each ingredient used in a cosmetic product and each finished cosmetic product shall be adequately substantiated for safety prior to marketing. Any such ingredient or product whose safety is not adequately substantiated prior to marketing is misbranded unless it contains the following conspicuous statement on the principal display panel: *Warning* – The safety of this product has not been determined.").

67 Tim Little, Sanford Lewis & Pamela Lundquist, Beneath the Skin: Hidden Liabilities, Market Risk and Drivers of Change in the Cosmetics and Personal Care Industry 8 (Investor Environmental Health Network 2007) [*hereinafter* Beneath the Skin].

68 *Id.*

69 15 U.S.C. §§ 1451–1461 (2010).

70 21 C.F.R. § 701.3(c) (2011).

71 John C. Monica, Jr., *FDA Labeling of Cosmetics Containing Nanoscale Materials*, 5 Nanotech. L. & Bus. 63, 71 (2008) [*hereinafter* FDA Labeling].

72 21 U.S.C. § 361 (2010).

73 *Chasing Youth* at 209.

74 *Id.*

75 *Regulation of Cosmetics* at 245; P.J. Orvetti, *FDA Cafeteria Serves Drinks With Label Lies*, *NBC Washington*, http://www.nbcwashington.com/news/local-beat/Drunk-on-Lies-at-FDA-98065024.html (July 9, 2009) (reporting that on a recent trip to FDA headquarters, a lawyer for the Center for Science in the Public Interest found three beverages making illegal claims on their labels in the FDA cafeteria).

76 *Regulation of Cosmetics* at 248.

77 FDA, *FDA Authority Over Cosmetics*, http://www.fda.gov/Cosmetics/GuidanceComplianceRegulatoryInformation/ucm074162.htm (2005) ("FDA is not authorized to require recalls of cosmetics . . . and may request a product recall if the firm is not willing to remove dangerous products from the market.").

78 *Perspectives on FDA* at 384. In 1976, the CTFA created the Cosmetic Ingredient Review (CIR) to conduct and publish independent, scientific reviews on the safety of cosmetics ingredients. The

such firms to do so, especially if participation may lead to more stringent oversight."[79]

Cosmetics trigger the same rigorous scrutiny as drugs if the manufacturer claims they will produce drug-like effects.[80] However, "sunscreen ingredients may also be used in some products for nontherapeutic, nonphysiologic uses (for example, as a color additive or to protect the color of the product). To avoid consumer misunderstanding, if a cosmetic product contains a sunscreen ingredient and uses the term sunscreen or similar sun protection terminology anywhere in its labeling, the term must be qualified by describing the cosmetic benefit provided by the sunscreen ingredient."[81] Thus, manufacturers avoid "more onerous classifications by simply controlling marketing claims."[82]

In its 2007 NTF report, the FDA acknowledged just how empty its regulatory arsenal is.[83] Noting FDA's "limited" authority to regulate the cosmetics field effectively without pre-market safety data and post-market adverse event reports, the NTF bluntly recognized "the [FDA] may have a comparatively difficult burden in assembling the necessary data to support a product removal action under these authorities (whether the product contains nanosized or other materials)."[84] Adding to this regulatory void, the FDA "may be unaware that nanotechnology is being employed"[85] because so much depends on the manufacturers' own disclosures.

"[i]ndustry uses the CIR's findings, but is not bound specifically to follow them." *Regulation of Cosmetics* at 246. The utility of the CIR is further limited because it has assessed "only 11 percent . . . [o]f the 10,500 normal size ingredients used in cosmetic products." *Growing Consumer Exposure* at 25.

More recently, the CTFA has developed a Consumer Commitment Code whereby cosmetics companies promise to make all safety data available to FDA at its request. *Perspectives on FDA* at 384. Finally, the FDA's Voluntary Cosmetic Registration Program provides a mechanism for post-market reporting of adverse reactions. *Id.*

79 Evan S. Michelson & David Rejeski, Falling Through the Cracks? Public Perception, Risk, and the Oversight of Emerging Nanotechnologies 5 (Project on Emerging Nanotechnologies, Woodrow Wilson International Center for Scholars 2006) [*hereinafter* Falling Through the Cracks].

80 *Regulation of Cosmetics* at 243. "The tension between the FDCA's definitions of 'drugs' and 'cosmetics' has been important to the evolution of cosmetic law in the last fifty years, with the focus being avoidance of drug regulation." *Id.* at 244–45.

81 FDA, *Ingredients Prohibited and Restricted by FDA Regulations* (May 30, 2000), http://www.fda.gov/Cosmetics/ProductandIngredientSafety/SelectedCosmeticIngredients/ucm127406.htm (last visited May 18, 2011). *See also* 21 C.F.R. § 700.35(a) (2011).

82 *Beneath the Skin* at 8.

83 FDA, *Press Release, FDA Nanotechnology Report Outlines Scientific, Regulatory Challenges* (July 25, 2007), http://www.fda.gov/NewsEvents/Newsroom/PressAnnouncements/2007/ucm108954.htm. Formed in 2006, the NTF was charged with "determining regulatory approaches that encourage the continued development of innovative, safe, and effective FDA-regulated products that use nanotechnology materials." FDA, Nanotechnology Task Force, Fact Sheet, http://www.fda.gov/ScienceResearch/SpecialTopics/Nanotechnology/NanotechnologyTaskForce/default.htm.

84 Nanotechnology: A Report of the US Food and Drug Administration Nanotechnology Task Force 15, 30 (U.S. Food and Drug Administration 2007) [*hereinafter* FDA Nanotechnology Report].

85 *FDA Regulation Slides* at slide 8.

In short, as a host of commentators have noted, "it is not much of an exaggeration to say that cosmetics in the United States are essentially unregulated."[86] As the next section explains, nano-sunscreens also fall through a regulatory crack.

2. Sunscreens

Nano-sunscreens also escape robust oversight. Typically, if a product uses the term "sunscreen" on its label, it will be subject to regulation as a drug.[87] At some point, therefore, the bulk ingredients in the product would have been shown to be safe.[88]

Some sunscreens are "marketed under over-the-counter [] monographs" which "outline the active ingredients the FDA has found to be safe and effective."[89] If "the active ingredients that are used in sunscreens . . . are manufactured according to published monographs . . . [which] do not specify particle size[,] . . . a manufacturer can formulate a sunscreen using particles of titanium dioxide and zinc oxide that may or may not be in the nanosize range."[90]

This is possible because in 1999 the FDA chose in its Sunscreen Monograph not to classify NPs as "new ingredients."[91] The FDA explained that it "does not consider micronized titanium dioxide to be a new ingredient but considers it a specific grade of the titanium dioxide originally reviewed by the FDA.[92]

Since 1999, the FDA has repeatedly reiterated its stance that NPs pose no unique safety concerns. In 2004, the Associate Commissioner for Science indicated that "[e]xisting pharmatox [pharmacotoxicity] tests are probably adequate for most nanoproducts."[93] In 2007, the NTF concluded that "current science does not support a finding that classes of products with nanoscale materials necessarily present greater safety concerns than [those] without nanoscale materials."[94] In its Frequently Asked Questions about nanotechnology, dated June 28, 2010, the FDA stated that it "is currently not aware of any safety concerns . . . [though the agency] is planning additional studies to examine the effects of select nanoparticles on skin penetration."[95]

[86] J. Clarence Davies, Managing the Effects of Nanotechnology 13 (Project on Emerging Nanotechnologies, Woodrow Wilson International Center for Scholars 2006) [*hereinafter* Managing the Effects]. *See also Chasing Youth* at 209–10 ("Therefore, cosmetic companies are free to use nanoparticles in their products without much interference from the FDA. . . . The FDA's current system is inadequate to protect consumers from nanoparticles in anti-aging products.").

[87] 21 C.F.R. § 700.35(a) (2011).

[88] *See* Section II.B.3.

[89] *Nanotechnology and the FDA* at 342.

[90] *Id.*

[91] *Sunscreen Monograph* at 27671.

[92] *Id.*

[93] *FDA Regulation Slides* at slide 8.

[94] *FDA Nanotechnology Report* at 35.

[95] *Nanotech FAQ*. The FDA also believes that its "[e]xisting requirements may be adequate for most nanotechnology products that we will regulate." *Id.*

In short, nano-sunscreens are marketed after an approval process that is "based not on measured outcomes showing that the product... is safe. Instead, it is based at least in part on assumptions about what makes one compound 'like' another."[96]

3. Robust Regulation of Drugs

In contrast, drugs receive robust oversight for safety and efficacy. Under federal law, a drug includes "articles intended for use in the diagnosis, cure, mitigation, treatment, or prevention of disease in man or other animals" and "articles (other than food) intended to affect the structure or any function of the body of man or other animals."[97] Drugs must be approved by the FDA before marketing.[98] Manufacturers must demonstrate both the safety and efficacy of the drug and provide labeling information, information on the chemical parts and structure of the drug, samples, and information on any patents covering the drug.[99]

Manufacturers show safety and efficacy through clinical trials.[100] A prerequisite to approval, clinical trials may also be performed after approval to provide additional data on safety or efficacy, new uses for a drug, or effectiveness of widespread usage.[101] Post-approval clinical trials often "facilitate FDA's post-approval monitoring of an approved drug."[102]

Because many problems do not appear until a drug reaches a large and diverse pool of users, drugs are subject to extensive post-market surveillance. Manufacturers must review reports of adverse drug experiences linked to their drugs

96 James Yeagle, *Nanotechnology and the FDA*, 12(6) Virginia Journal of Law & Technology 49 (2007).

97 21 U.S.C. § 321(g)(1) (2010).

98 *FDA Factsheet*.

99 21 U.S.C. § 355 (2010). Drug manufacturers are also required to register their drug products with the FDA and adhere to strict good manufacturing practices. *Id.*

100 A Phase 1 clinical trial seeks to determine dosing, show how a drug is metabolized and excreted, identify acute side effects, and, if possible, to gain early evidence of effectiveness. The results of the Phase 1 clinical trial are ultimately used to design a well-controlled, scientifically valid Phase 2 clinical trial, which uses "control" groups of participants who do not receive the drug under investigation. Phase 2 clinical trials seek to obtain preliminary data on drug effectiveness for patients with the disease or condition, as well as the common short-term side effects and risks. Phase 2 clinical trials use a relatively small number of patients, usually several hundred.

Phase 3 clinical trials consist of expanded controlled and uncontrolled clinical trials. Phase 3 clinical trials seek to gather additional information about effectiveness and safety in order to evaluate the overall benefit-risk relationship of a drug or therapy. Usually encompassing several hundred to several thousand participants, Phase 3 clinical trials provide the basis for extrapolating results to the general population and transmitting that information through the drug's labeling. FDA Center for Drug Evaluation and Research Handbook 8–9 (US Food and Drug Administration 1998), *available at* http://www.fda.gov/downloads/AboutFDA/CentersOffices/CDER/UCM198415.pdf.

101 A Practical Guide to Food and Drug Law and Regulation 111 (Kenneth R. Pina & Wayne L. Pines eds., Food and Drug Law Institute 1998).

102 *Id.*

"promptly ... regardless of the source from which such reports are obtained."[103] Serious and unexpected events – those that are "fatal, life-threatening, or permanently disabling" or not predicted by the labeling – must be reported to the FDA within 15 working days.[104] All other adverse reactions must be reported quarterly for three years, after which they must be reported annually.[105]

When drugs pose unforeseen hazards, the FDA has the authority to act directly. The FDA can withdraw a drug's New Drug Application (NDA) and therefore the drug from the market.[106] This may occur if the drug is unsafe for the approved use or "if new clinical evidence shows that the drug is not safe under approved conditions, or if the drug is not effective."[107] Although withdrawal of the NDA usually requires notice and the opportunity for a hearing, "[i]f the drug in question presents an 'imminent hazard,' ... [then] the Secretary of Health and Human Services can summarily suspend approval" of the NDA in advance of an expedited hearing.[108]

III. MOUNTING EVIDENCE OF RISK

A. *An Evolving Appreciation*

More than 2000 studies have examined the toxicity of NPs in living systems, both human and animal, leading a number of scientists to raise alarm bells about possible risks. This section highlights the conclusions that scientists have drawn from that body of research before detailing those very technical studies in Section III.C.

For example, in a 2006 review of nano-toxicity, Nel and colleagues observed that "some studies suggest that [nanomaterials] are not inherently benign and that they affect biological behaviors at the cellular, subcellular, and protein levels ... some nanoparticles readily travel throughout the body, deposit in target organs, penetrate cell membranes, lodge in mitochondria, and may trigger injurious responses."[109] Colvin and colleagues likewise believe that "nanoparticles can be taken up by

[103] *Id.* at 110.

[104] *Id.*

[105] *Id.* at 111.

[106] *Id.*

[107] *Id.*

[108] *Id.*

[109] Andre Nel et al., *Toxic Potential of Materials at the Nanolevel*, 311 SCIENCE 622 (2006) (discussing potential hazards of nanomaterials). *See also* Paul JA Borm et al., *The potential risks of nanomaterials: a review carried out for ECETOC*, 3(11) PARTICLE AND FIBER TOXICOLOGY at 23, *available at* http://www.particleandfibretoxicology.com/content/pdf/1743-8977-3-11.pdf (2006) ("Non-soluble nanoparticles can stay for years in the lungs, GI-tract or brain; they are less well taken up by professional macrophages of the defence system but interact with cells of the epithelium, the interstitial tissue and vascular cells allowing pro-inflammatory reactions of these cells which usually do not see any particles. In addition, nanoparticles can bind to proteins or translocate into the circulation and reach secondary target organs like liver, spleen, kidneys, heart and brain; rates and fractions are still under debate and depend particularly on the chemical and surface properties of nanoparticles.").

cells . . . [p]ossible impacts of nanomaterial uptake include: direct toxicity to cells, alteration of protein conformation, structural interference in cell division, persistence within the cell, [and] the ability to transport other associated materials into cells such as contaminants or scavenged genetic material."[110]

Scientists have also done literature reviews of the more than 150 studies of skin absorption and toxicity, many of which are detailed in Section III.C. These reviews now conclude that NPs used in nano-cosmetics and nano-sunscreens can sometimes penetrate the skin's protective layer to reach living cells and cause cell death.[111] Reviewing more than 25 studies from 1988 to 2001, Kreilgaard concluded that "very small titanium dioxide particles (e.g. 5–20 nm) penetrate into the skin and can interact with the immune system."[112] In 2004, Hoet and colleagues reported that "[l]iposomes with an average diameter of 272 nm can reach into the viable epidermis and some are found in the dermis[, with s]maller sized liposomes of 116 and 71 nm [] found in higher concentration[s]."[113] In 2005, Holsapple and colleagues concluded that "[l]arger particles of zinc oxide and titanium dioxide used in topical skin-care products are able to penetrate the stratum corneum barrier of rabbit skin . . . and this should also apply to manufactured nanomaterials."[114] Oberdörster and colleagues went further, saying that "NPs, once in the dermis, will localize to regional lymph nodes"[115] and may "conceivabl[y]" be taken up by sensory skin nerves along which they can translocate since such "[n]euronal transport . . . is well established for herpes virus."[116]

[110] Mark R. Wiesner & Vicki L. Colvin, *Environmental Implications of Emerging Nanotechnologies*, 41, 47–48, in ENVIRONMENTALISM & THE TECHNOLOGIES OF TOMORROW: SHAPING THE NEXT INDUSTRIAL REVOLUTION 47 (Robert Olson & David Rejeski eds., Island Press 2005) [*hereinafter* Environmental Implications]. Protein conformation can be problematic. For example, prion diseases like Kuru disease and Mad Cow disease result from conformational changes to normal proteins that corrupt each other in an autocatalytic process, like dominos falling. The corrupted proteins compromise neural cell activities. Centers for Disease Control, *Prion Diseases*, http://www.cdc.gov/ncidod/dvrd/prions/index.htm (last visited October 5, 2010).

[111] A number of studies examine the toxicity of carbon nanotubes, quantum dots, and other NPs to skin cells or other tissues and are summarized in two appendices contained at http://law.wlu.edu/faculty/facultydocuments/wilsonr/AppNPSkin.pdf and http://law.wlu.edu/faculty/facultydocuments/wilsonr/AppGNT.pdf. Because neither carbon nanotubes nor quantum dots appear to be used in nano-cosmetics or nano-sunscreens, this chapter's recommendations do not rest on those findings.

[112] Peter H.M. Hoet et al., *Nanoparticles – Known and Unknown Health Risks*, 2(12) J. OF NANOBIOTECHNOLOGY 9 (2004) [*hereinafter* Known and Unknown] (summarizing Kreilgaard's conclusions).

[113] *Id.* Although "[o]nly limited literature on nanoparticles penetrating the skin is available, but some conclusions can already be drawn. Firstly, penetration of the skin barrier is size dependent, nano-sized particles are more likely to enter more deeply into the skin than larger ones. Secondly, different types of particles are found in the deeper layers of the skin and at present it is impossible to predict the behaviour of a particle in the skin." *Id.* at 9–10.

[114] *Research Strategies* at 14.

[115] *An Emerging Discipline* at 834 (citing quantum dot study).

[116] *Id.* at 834–35. In 2007, Baroli and colleagues cited studies finding that "only small (<600 Da) [dalton] lipophilic molecules can easily penetrate the skin passively." Biancamaria Baroli et al., *Penetration of Metallic Nanoparticles in Human Full-Thickness Skin*, 127 JOURNAL OF INVESTIGATIVE DERMATOLOGY 1701, 1702 (2007) [*hereinafter* Penetration of Metallic].

A growing number of toxicologists also warn that damaged skin is particularly at risk. For example, Kezic and Neilsen concluded that a "compromised skin barrier will not only increase absorption, but will also allow for penetration of larger compounds which normally would not be able to penetrate intact skin."[117]

This risk profile has filtered into professional assessments of risk. In 2006, the German Federal Institute of Risk Assessment convened 100 experts from academia, industry, NGOs and public authorities to assess the nano-toxicity of selected nanomaterials.[118] Forty-one percent rated fullerenes and anti-aging creams as having "medium toxic potential," which was "the highest potential risk of all the materials assessed."[119]

This growing appreciation of the unique properties and risks of NPs calls into question the FDA's decade-old conclusion that NPs in sunscreens act no differently than SSPs. Because "[t]he ability for nanomaterials to traverse the skin is a primary determinant of their dermatotoxic potential,"[120] a quick primer on the skin is useful, to which this chapter now turns.

B. *The Nature of Skin*

The adult human skin is "roughly 1.5 m^2 in area"[121] and consists of a number of layers that can act as barriers.[122] Substances may pass through the skin intercellularly between cells, transcellularly through cells, or transappendageally through hair follicles, sweat glands, or sebaceous glands,[123] which serve as shunt routes.[124]

As Figure 11.3 shows, the outermost layer of the epidermis, known as the stratum corneum (SC) or horny layer, is composed mainly of dead keratinocyte cells that are heavy in lipids. These form "a dense and compact . . . 'brick and mortar' structure."[125] Beneath the SC lies the stratum lucidum, a "thin, clear layer of dead skin cells

[117] Sanja Kezic & J. B. Nielsen, *Absorption of Chemicals Through Compromised Skin*, 82(6) International Archives of Occupational and Environmental Health, 677, 684 May 2009 [*hereinafter* Absorption of Chemicals]. "Mechanical damage caused by scrubbing, skin friction or abrasion will result in partial or complete removal of the SC" and not surprisingly, leads to increased "percutaneous penetration." *Id.* at 683. *See also* Adnan Nasir, *Dermatologic Toxicity of Nanoengineered Materials*, 144(2) Arch. Dermatol. 253 (2008) (reporting that "[p]articles smaller than 7000 nm penetrate skin damaged by diseases such as atopic dermatitis, contact dermatitis, acne, and seborrheic dermatitis. Shaving, sunburn, [or] cuts . . . can further increase cutaneous permeability").

[118] Antje Grobe & Alexander Jaeger, Risk Governance of Nanotechnology Applications in Food and Cosmetics 28 (International Risk Governance Council 2008), *available at* http://www.irgc.org/IMG/pdf/IRGC_Report_FINAL_For_Web.pdf.

[119] *Id.*

[120] *Research Strategies* at 13.

[121] *Known and Unknown* at 2.

[122] *Absorption of Chemicals* at 677.

[123] Frank C. Lu, Basic Toxicology: Fundamentals, Target Organs, and Risk Assessment 14 (Hemisphere Publishing Corporation 1985) [*hereinafter* Basic Toxicology]; *Research Strategies* at 14.

[124] *Absorption of Chemicals* at 677.

[125] *Id.*

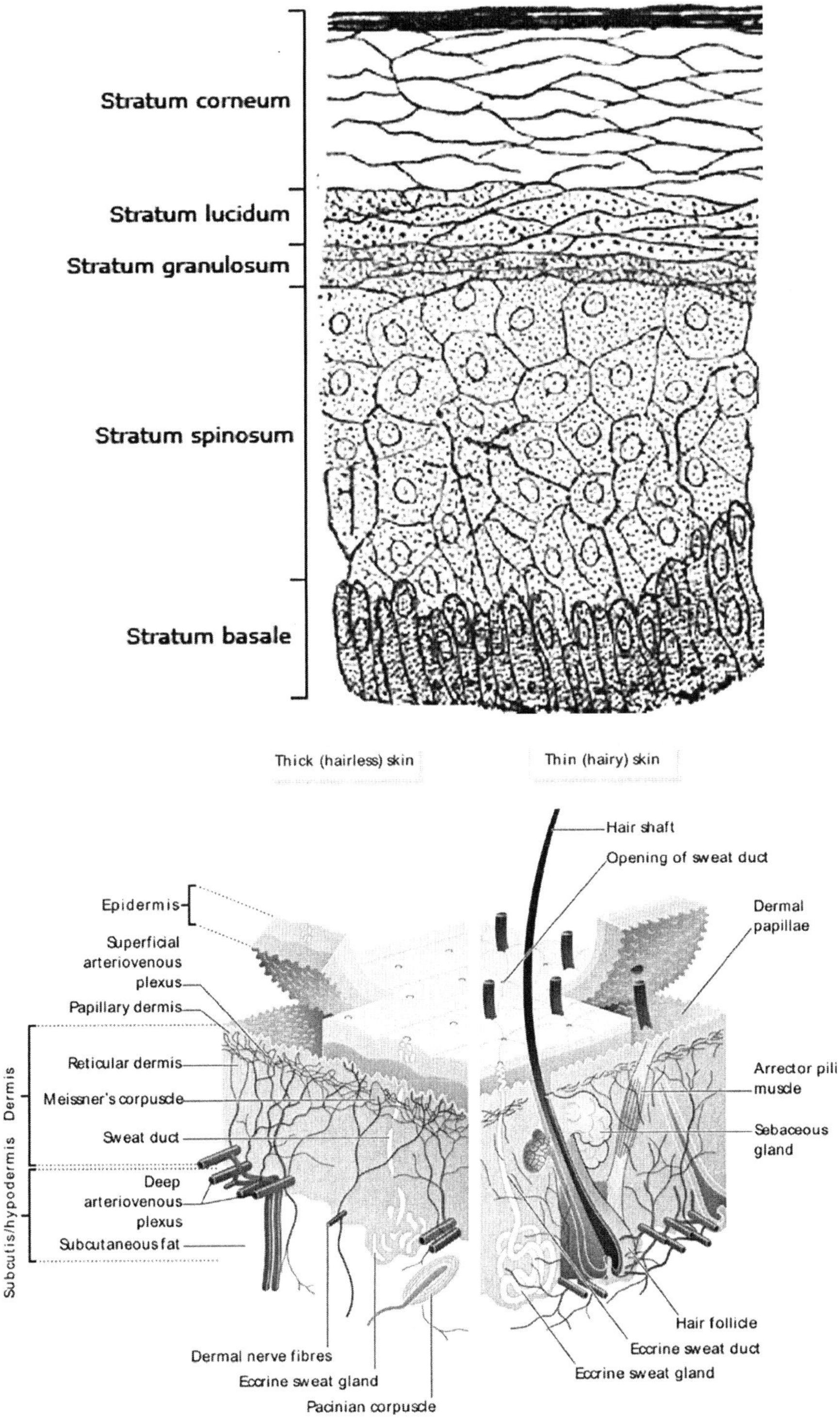

Stratum corneum
Stratum lucidum
Stratum granulosum
Stratum spinosum
Stratum basale

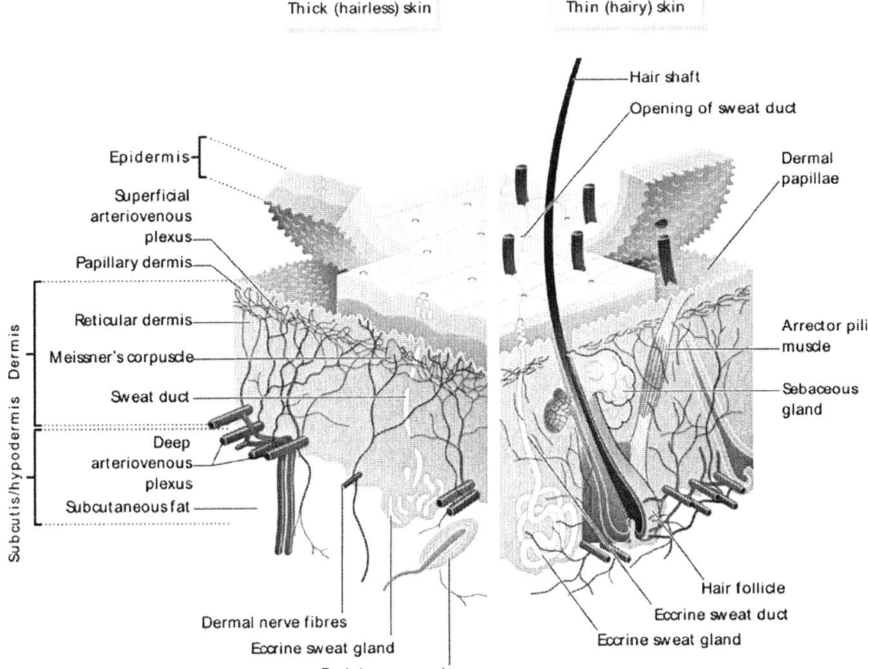

FIGURE 11.3. The skin.

in the epidermis."[126] Underneath this layer lies the stratum granulosum, stratum spinosum, and stratum basale, all of which contain living cells.[127] Beyond all these layers, collectively known as the epidermis, lies the dermis, which contains "a rich supply of blood and tissue macrophages, lymph vessels, dendritic cells, and five different types of sensory nerve endings."[128]

With intercellular penetration, lipids – the mortar between the cells – control the rate of "penetration of chemicals across the skin."[129] The lipids form overlapping sheets, which can provide "pathways for molecular transport into and through the [SC]. These channels follow a winding but continuous path from the surface of the skin into the epidermis."[130] The gap between layers measures only 0.5 to 1.0 nm, although it can "enlarge into bigger clefts when filled with topically applied materials."[131] "[N]onpolar substances [can] dissolve in and diffuse through the lipid matrix" to reach lower layers of the skin,[132] whereas ionic compounds and water-soluble molecules have much greater difficulty passing through the SC.[133] In a process known as percutaneous absorption, the slow diffusion through the SC is "followed by rapid diffusion through the viable epidermis and papillary dermis into the microcirculation of the skin."[134] "[A]n additional factor that influences toxicity via the percutaneous route is the blood flow at the site of exposure."[135]

The skin also provides a site for deposit where NPs could potentially cause harm.[136] In the parts of the epidermis without a blood supply, "particles could potentially lodge and not be susceptible to removal by phagocytosis,"[137] a cellular process for removing pathogens and other cell debris.[138]

[126] Laurie Swezey, *The Layers of the Skin*, http://www.woundeducators.net/profiles/blogs/the-layers-of-the-skin (last visited May 26, 2011).

[127] *Id.* The stratum granulosum is "the highest layer in the epidermis where living cells are found." Stratum Granulosum, WEBSTER'S ONLINE DICTIONARY, http://www.websters-dictionary-online.com/definitions/stratum%20granulosum?cx=partner-pub-0939450753529744%3Avoqd01-tdlq&cof=FORID%3A9&ie=UTF-8&q=stratum%20granulosum&sa=Search#906 (last visited May 18, 2011).

[128] *An Emerging Discipline* at 834.

[129] *Absorption of Chemicals* at 677.

[130] Sally S. Tinkle et al., *Skin as a Route of Exposure and Sensitization in Chronic Beryllium Disease*, 111 ENVIRONMENTAL HEALTH PERSPECTIVES 1202, 1207 (2003) [*hereinafter* Beryllium Study].

[131] Mei-Heng Tan et al., A *Pilot Study on the Percutaneous Absorption of Microfine Titanium Dioxide From Sunscreens*, 37 AUSTRALIAN JOURNAL OF DERMATOLOGY 185, 186 (1996) [*hereinafter* Pilot Study].

[132] *Basic Toxicology* at 14.

[133] *Known and Unknown* at 2.

[134] *Pilot Study* at 186.

[135] STANLEY E. MANAHAN, TOXICOLOGICAL CHEMISTRY: A GUIDE TO TOXIC SUBSTANCES IN CHEMISTRY 49 (Lewis Publishers, Inc. 1989) [*hereinafter* Toxicological Chemistry Guide].

[136] *Research Strategies* at 13–14.

[137] *Id.* at 13.

[138] Phagocytosis is "the engulfing and usually the destruction of particulate matter by phagocytes that serves as an important bodily defense mechanism against infection by microorganisms and against

Importantly, some people, like children, have skin that is more susceptible to penetration, as sunscreen companies themselves acknowledge.[139] Similarly, certain portions of the skin are more vulnerable because they are thinner,[140] as is skin "damaged by eczema, severe sunburn, or acne."[141] In psoriatic skin, the outer protective barrier is damaged as well.[142] Broken skin also "represents a readily available portal of entry even for larger [500–700 nm] particles."[143] Abrasion or removal of the SC "causes a marked increase in the percutaneous absorption,"[144] as does "laceration . . . irritation . . . inflammation[,] and higher degrees of skin hydration."[145]

As the next section shows, "processes driving nanoparticles into skin may be different from those governing" SSPs.[146]

C. *Studies Showing Significant Risk*

Risk assessments seek to answer two questions: (1) what happens to the entire body after topical administration (systemic effects), and (2) what happens to the skin itself after topical exposure (cutaneous hazard).[147] In other words, are NPs safely scavenged by the processes that normally remove foreign substances in the body or do they instead travel elsewhere, and do NPs kill living cells?

Risk assessments may be done *in vivo* on human volunteers or animals or *in vitro* with sections of skin or individual cells.[148] Importantly, toxicologists believe that the existing "methods . . . that have been the cornerstones of traditional approaches to safety assessment . . . can also be applied to . . . studies characterizing nanomaterial safety."[149]

Scientists widely believe that the degree of toxicity will depend on the precise nature of a given NP, "including the size/shape/aspect ratio, hardness/deformability, composition, surface area and surface chemistry, types of coatings/modifications,

occlusion of mucous surfaces or tissues by foreign particles and tissue debris." Phagocytosis, Dictionary.com, MERRIAM-WEBSTER'S MEDICAL DICTIONARY. Merriam-Webster, Inc., http://dictionary.reference.com/browse/phagocytosis (last visited May 18, 2011).

139 Laroche-Posay, http://www.laroche-posay.com/home/specific-treatments/Children-s-skin-and-the-sun-t78.aspx (last visited May 18, 2011 July 28, 2010) ("[C]hildren's skin is 'thinner.'").

140 "[T]he thinnest skin is found on the eyelids and in the post-auricular region [in front of the ear]." WebMD, *Skin Grafts, Split-Thickness*, http://emedicine.medscape.com/article/876290-overview.

141 *Chasing Youth* at 207.

142 Environmental Working Group, *EWG's 2009 Sunscreen Investigation*, http://www.ewg.org/nanotechnology-sunscreens (last visited May 24, 2011) [*hereinafter* EWG Report].

143 *An Emerging Discipline* at 834.

144 *Basic Toxicology* at 14.

145 *Toxicological Chemistry Guide* at 50–51.

146 *Research Strategies* at 13–14.

147 *Id. at* 14.

148 There are two key methods for assessing skin absorption and toxicity of NPs: (1) "*in vitro* cell cultures, flow-through diffusion cells, or perfused skin model systems," and (2) "[i]n vivo studies conducted in rat or preferably pig skin (since it is anatomically, physiologically, and biochemically similar to man)." *Id.*

149 *Id.* at 16. *See also Known and Unknown* at 12 ("The tests currently used to test the safety of materials should be applicable to identify hazardous nanoparticles.").

and stability," all of which likely will influence the mode of action for observed effects.[150] This sub-section summarizes the contemporary understanding emerging from a diverse range of studies.

1. NPs in Cosmetics

Nano-cosmetic ingredients can penetrate healthy skin cells, unlike their SSP counterparts, as well as intact and damaged skin.[151] The growing evidence of penetration is summarized below, followed by the studies analyzing NP toxicity.

A. PENETRATION. One of the earliest studies to raise caution flags about dermal penetration tested skin exposure to beryllium oxide NPs, a NP which does not appear to be used in cosmetics or sunscreens.[152] Beryllium oxide NPs less than 1,000 nm in diameter penetrated into the dermis when applied with a rubbing action or after flexing.[153] Topical application of beryllium oxide particles also produced a cell-mediated immune response.[154] The authors speculated that the particles moved through intercellular pathways in the SC and, over time, could "continue to move into the skin" and eventually be absorbed by other cells.[155]

The concern raised by the beryllium study prompted later studies of ingredients that are used in cosmetics and sunscreens. These studies found reasons for concern. Rouse and colleagues topically applied a 3.5 nm[156] peptide sequence containing a fullerene, another cosmetic ingredient, to intact pig skin sections "because of its physiological and structural similarities to human skin."[157] The skin was flexed for 60 or 90 minutes to "mimic . . . conditions involved in consumer use."[158] After flexing,

[150] *Research Strategies* at 15 ("In the testing of nanomaterials, there needs to be an emphasis on the characterization of the materials themselves."). *See also Absorption of Chemicals* at 677 (suggesting that the extent of dermal absorption rests on "physico-chemical properties of the penetrant, exposure conditions and the state of the skin").

[151] Jillian G. Rouse et al., *Effects of Mechanical Flexion on the Penetration of Fullerene Amino Acid-Derivatized Peptide Nanoparticles through Skin*, 7(1) NANO LETTERS 155, 159 (2007) [*hereinafter* Effects of Mechanical Flexion].

[152] *Beryllium Study* at 1202; Part I *supra*.

[153] Other studies involving larger particles did not find any instances of dermal penetration. *Beryllium Study* at 1207.

[154] *Id.* at 1206. Cell-mediated immunity is "immunity independent of antibody but dependent on the recognition of antigen by T cells and their subsequent destruction of cells bearing the antigen or on the secretion by T cells of lymphokines that enhance the ability of phagocytes to eliminate the antigen." Cell-mediated immunity, Dictionary.com, DICTIONARY.COM UNABRIDGED, Random House, Inc., http://dictionary.reference.com/browse/cell-mediated immunity (last visited May 18, 2011).

[155] *Id.* at 1207. Other researchers have speculated that the lipid layers of the SC "form a pathway by which the particles can move into the skin and be phagocytized by the Langerhans cells." *Known and Unknown* at 9.

[156] *Effects of Mechanical Flexion* at 155, 157.

[157] *Id.* at 157.

[158] *Id.* at 158.

the NPs "penetrated the skin" at eight hours and "showed evidence of greater epidermal (60 minutes) and dermal (90 min) penetration."[159] By contrast, in non-flexed skin, "[t]he fullerenes were localized primarily in the epidermal layers."[160] At 24 hours, "[s]kin flexed for 90 min showed the greatest amount" of skin penetration.[161] The "fullerenes localized within intercellular spaces of the epidermis," suggesting "passive diffusion" between cells of the SC rather than through the cells themselves.[162] The authors predicted that NPs "could get absorbed by the capillaries of the papillary layer with the potential to localize elsewhere in the body . . . [a] potential risk[] for systemic toxicity," which would have "profound implications" for occupational exposure, as well as commercial use.[163]

Others have reported that rigid NPs "smaller than 10 nm . . . are able to passively penetrate the skin through the SC lipidic matrix and hair follicle orifices, reaching the deepest layers of the SC, the stratum granulosum, and hair follicles" and "[i]n some exceptional cases . . . the viable epidermis."[164] Baroli and colleagues applied iron oxide NP dispersions, like those used in cosmetics, to human full-thickness skin samples from healthy female donors to assess penetration and permeation.[165] The iron NPs ranged in size from roughly five to more than 80 nm.[166] They found that "nanoparticles were able to penetrate the hair follicle and [SC], occasionally reaching the viable epidermis" but did not "permeate the skin."[167] In rare cases, NP aggregates also appeared below the "SC-viable epidermis junction," which occurs at 30 to 100 μm or 30,000 to 100,000 nm.[168] The researchers attributed this penetration to the "extremely small dimensions" of NPs and the fact that the clusters they formed were "not rigidly fixed and may adapt to the penetration-pathway size."[169]

[159] *Id.* at 157–58.

[160] *Id.*

[161] *Id.* at 158.

[162] *Id.* Penetration of the NP through the skin depends on "the hydrophobic lipid entities that are present between the epidermal cells." *Id.* Commenting on the beryllium study, Rouse and colleagues suggested that "flexing [may] increase[] this penetration" and that this may occur because the "forces applied to the skin during flexing cause changes in the morphology and architectural lipid organization of the upper epidermal layers," triggering a "transient increase in the size of the intercellular spaces during mechanical stimulation. (Tinkle et al., 2003)." *Id.* at 159.

[163] *Id.* at 158.

[164] *Penetration of Metallic* at 1708. *But see* Mark A. Nelson et al., *Effects of Acute and Subchronic Exposure of Topical Applied Fullerene Extracts on the Mouse Skin*, 9(4) Toxicology and Industrial Health 623, 626 (1993) (investigating a single topical application of 1-nm fullerenes to mouse skin and finding "no effect on either DNA synthesis or ornithine decarboxylase activity" 72 hours after treatment, no "benign or malignant skin tumor formation" after 24 weeks, or no other pathological changes).

[165] *Penetration of Metallic* at 1701–2, 1704.

[166] Specifically, they ranged from 4.9 ± 1.3 nm up to 82.6 ± 63.9 nm. *Id.* at 1702–3.

[167] *Id.* at 1701. The "roundish aggregates" were found "less often in the uppermost strata of the viable epidermis," suggesting that the "junction between the SC and the viable epidermis may modulate further penetration." *Id.* at 1707–8.

[168] *Id.* at 1708. The hair infundibulum and furrows in the skin "also appeared to be privileged locations for [NP] penetration." *Id.*

[169] *Id.* at 1709.

In the researchers' words, the study "provides a major breakthrough in the study of skin absorption, which allows [the authors] to envisage potential toxicological risks."[170]

Using another cosmetic ingredient, nano-silver, Larese and colleagues evaluated the penetration *in vitro* of silver NPs ranging from 7.1 to 48.8 nm through full-thickness human abdominal skin obtained from donors after surgery.[171] After testing for skin integrity, the researchers separated the samples into intact and damaged skin.[172] They found that "silver can pass through intact human skin" after 24 hours but that five times greater penetration occurs through damaged skin.[173] Although the absorption of NPs through intact and damaged skin was "very low but detectable," silver NPs reached not only the SC, but also the "outermost surface of the epidermis."[174] The findings provide "experimental evidence for *in vitro* [NP] skin permeation, and . . . an appreciable increase in permeation using damaged skin."[175]

Some studies report skin penetration but no distinct pathway. In a study of uncoated 6 to 20 nm titanium dioxide NPs, Butz and colleagues exposed "porcine [pig] skin, healthy human skin from biopsies and explants, human foreskin transplanted to [severe combined immunodeficiency] mice, and psoriatic skin [to] a variety of [sunscreen] formulations" to visualize putative pathways of NPs in skin cross sections.[176] In healthy skin, titanium dioxide "was detected on top of the stratum corneum and in the topmost layers of the stratum corneum disjunctum"[177] and around the hair follicle "at a depth of almost 0.5 (mm) [millimeter]."[178] But with psoriatic skin, the researchers observed titanium dioxide "on top of the stratum corneum, but occasionally also at much greater depth in contact with vital keratinocytes [the predominate cell type in the epidermis]."[179] The authors concluded that "for the sake of safety, direct contact of skin cells with [titanium dioxide NPs]

[170] *Id.*

[171] Francesca Filon Larese et al., *Human Skin Penetration of Silver Nanoparticles Through Intact and Damaged Skin*, 255 TOXICOLOGY 33, 33–34 (2009).

[172] *Id.* at 34.

[173] *Id.* at 35. The silver passed through with a "median amount of 0.46 ng/cm^2 at 24 hours." *Id.*

[174] *Id.* at 33, 36.

[175] *Id.* at 36. Other studies have shown that elastic particles can readily gain access to the deeper layers of the SC. P. Loan Honeywell-Nguyen et al., *Quantitative Assessment of the Transport of Elastic and Rigid Vesicle Components and a Model Drug from these Vesicle Formulations into Human Skin In Vivo*, 123 J. INVEST. DERMATOL. 902 (2004) (assessing the distribution profiles of elastic and rigid vesicle material in human skin and finding that elastic vesicle material can enter the deeper layers of the SC and can reach the SC-viable epidermal juncture in 1 hour, whereas rigid vesicle material did not penetrate deep into the SC).

[176] TILMAN BUTZ ET AL., NANODERM: QUALITY OF SKIN AS A BARRIER TO ULTRA-FINE PARTICLES 45 (Nanoderm Project 2007) [*hereinafter* Nanoderm].

[177] *Id.*

[178] *Id.* at 31 (speculating that NPs "are introduced mechanically by stretching and compressing the follicle during application").

[179] *Id.* at 34.

should better be avoided, e.g. application of sunscreens into open wounds is not recommended."[180]

B. TOXICITY. In addition to studies of penetration, a number of studies have investigated whether NPs hasten cell death. Brunner and colleagues tested for cytotoxicity in human and rodent cells after exposure to zinc oxide, titanium dioxide, and iron oxide NPs like those used in cosmetics, for 3 to 6 days at concentrations of 0 to 30 parts per million (ppm).[181] Human cells exposed to uncoated iron oxide NPs were "highly sensitive," whereas rodent cells were "not greatly affected."[182] Indeed, the authors concluded that the iron oxide NPs "exhibited an astonishingly high toxicity" to human skin, eclipsing that of larger iron oxide particles.[183]

Hussain and colleagues studied the toxicity in rat liver cells[184] of two NPs that are used in nano-cosmetics, 15- and 100-nm silver NPs and 30- and 47-nm iron oxide (Fe_3O_4) NPs at varying concentrations.[185] Both sizes of silver NPs were "highly toxic" and "significantly increased" lactate dehydrogenase (LDH) leakage in cells,[186] although the 100-nm NPs showed higher toxicity at concentrations of 25 and 50 μg/ml.[187] Silver NPs also "significantly" decreased) mitochondrial function[188] and hastened "significant depletion of [glutathione][189] level[s], reduced mitochondrial

[180] *Id.* at 45.

[181] Tobias J. Brunner et al., *In vitro Cytotoxicity of Oxide Nanoparticles: Comparison to Asbestos, Silica, and the Effect of Particle Solubility*, 40(14) ENVIRON. SCI. TECHNOL. 4374 (2006) [*hereinafter* In vitro Cytotoxicity]. Cell toxicity included a measure of mean cell culture activity, which provides an "indicator for stress, toxic effects targeting metabolic pathways, and overall viability," as well as DNA content, which "gives information on the cell proliferation." *Id.*

[182] *Id.* at 4379.

[183] *Id.* ("Iron oxide nanoparticles exhibited an astonishingly high toxicity that could not be explained by purely chemical effects of dissolved iron ions and thus indicates a [NP-specific cytotoxicity not found in larger particles of iron oxide]."). *But see* Andrea Gojova et al., *Induction of Inflammation in Vascular Endothelial Cells by Metal Oxide Nanoparticles: Effect of Particle Composition*, 115(3) ENVIRONMENTAL HEALTH PERSPECTIVES 407 (2007) [*hereinafter* Induction of Inflammation] (finding that iron oxide NPs (Fe_2O_3) "did not lead to visible cell loss after 4 hr of incubation" with human aortic endothelial cells).

[184] The researchers chose rat liver cells because it "has been well characterized for its relevance to toxicity models." S.M. Hussain et al., *In Vitro Toxicity of Nanoparticles in BRL 3A Rat Liver Cells*, 19 TOXICOLOGY IN VITRO 975, 976 (2005) [*hereinafter* BRL 3A Rat Liver Cells].

[185] *Id.* at 975, 978. The researchers tested concentrations of 0, 10, 50, 100, and 250 μg/mL. *Id.*

[186] "Measurement of LDH release (leakage) is an important and frequently applied test for cellular membrane permeabilization (rupture) and severe irreversible cell damage." Andrey V. Kuznetsov & Erich Gnaiger, *Laboratory Protocol: Lactate Dehydrogenase Cytosolic Marker Enzyme* at 2 (2006), *available at* http://www.oroboros.at/fileadmin/user_upload/Protocols/MiPNet08.18_LDH.pdf.

[187] *BRL 3A Rat Liver Cells* at 975.

[188] Mitochondrial function is gauged by MTT Assays, which detect "living, but not dead cells and the signal generated is dependent on the degree of activation of the cells. This method can therefore be used to measure cytotoxicity, proliferation or activation." Tim Mossman, *Rapid Colorimetric Assay for Cellular Growth and Survival: Application to Proliferation and Cytotoxicity Assays*, 65 JOURNAL OF IMMUNOLOGICAL METHODS 55,155 (1983).

[189] Glutathione is an antioxidant defense. *See Anatase and Rutile* at 11. Antioxidants are "chemical compound[s] or substance[s] that inhibit[] oxidation. Certain vitamins, such as vitamin E, are antioxidants and may protect body cells from damage caused by the oxidative effects of free radicals."

membrane potential[190] and increase in reactive oxygen species (ROS) levels,[191] which suggested that cytotoxicity of [silver] (15, 100 nm) in liver cells is likely to be mediated through oxidative stress."[192] After microscopic evaluation, the authors found that the NPs "associate with cell membranes" and are sometimes "internalize[d]," which is "likely to have an effect on cellular function."[193]

Iron oxide NPs with surface coatings also cause cell death. Pisanic and colleagues exposed iron oxide anionic magnetic NPs (MNPs) of 5 to 12 nm in size to a rat pheochromocytoma cell line (PC12). PC12 is a cell line that researchers use to study nerve cell growth.[194] The researchers observed "Statistically significant reductions in PC12 cell viability after exposure to the particles. Almost all observed cell death within the first 48 [hours] following incubation with the particles and . . . increase[ed] as a function of . . . exposure concentration."[195] Significant cell detachment also correlated with exposure, confirming "previous reports that . . . intracellular Fe_2O_3 nanoparticle constructs can result in significant changes in cell behavior and viability."[196]

Pisanic and colleagues added nerve growth factor to exposed cells, which then produced "fewer neurites per cell" of dramatically shorter length, suggesting that NPs "reduce[d] the ability of neurites to develop intercellular contacts and thus physically interact with one another."[197] Because "historically Fe_2O_3 nanoparticles are considered to be well tolerated *in vivo*," the researchers urged that thefindings have "significant implications for *in vivo* [use of] . . . Fe_2O_3 MNPs in

Antioxidant, Dictionary.com, The American Heritage Science Dictionary, Houghton Mifflin, http://dictionary.reference.com/browse/antioxidant (last visited June 8, 2011).

[190] Mitochondrial membrane potential is "a key indicator of cellular viability, as it reflects the pumping of hydrogen ions across the inner membrane during the process of electron transport and oxidative phosphorylation, the driving force behind ATP production." B.M. Acton et al., *Alterations in mitochondrial membrane potential during preimplantation stages of mouse and human embryo development*, 10(1) Molecular Human Reproduction 23–32 (2004). ATP is a nucleotide that "contains high-energy phosphate bonds and is used to transport energy to cells for biochemical processes." ATP, Dictionary.com, The American Heritage Dictionary of the English Language, Fourth Edition, Houghton Mifflin Company, http://dictionary.reference.com/browse/ATP (last visited May 18, 2011).

[191] ROS contributes "to the microbicidal activity of phagocytes, regulation of signal transduction and gene expression, and the oxidative damage to nucleic acids; proteins; and lipids." Unified Medical Language System (MeSH) at the National Library of Medicine, 2010, http://ghr.nlm.nih.gov/glossary=reactiveoxygenspecies (last visited May 18, 2011).

[192] *BRL 3A Rat Liver Cells* at 975.

[193] *Id.*at 982.

[194] Thomas R. Pisanic II et al., *Nanotoxicity of Iron Oxide Nanoparticle Internalization in Growing Neurons*, 28 Biomaterials 2572, 2573 (2007).

[195] *Id.* at 2575.

[196] *Id.* at 2573, 2579. They speculated that "the observed cytotoxic effects are . . . possibly due to free radical generation" or "migration of the [anionic MNP] . . . to the proximal perinuclear region . . . imped[ing] transcriptional regulation and protein synthesis . . . resulting in loss of cell phenotype and possibly cell death." *Id.* at 2579.

[197] *Id.* at 2576.

general."[198] All of this, the authors believe, should be "a caveat . . . more study into the effects of cellular iron oxide internalization is both warranted and necessary."[199]

Nano-sized zinc oxide particles, which are frequently used in sunscreens, also provide pigment in cosmetics. Like the cosmetic ingredients just described, these particles can damage "human skin and the horny layer,"[200] as the next section explains.

2. NPs in Sunscreens

Two principle metal oxides are used in sunscreens: zinc oxide and titanium dioxide. A limited number of studies examining the risks of nano-zinc oxide and nano-titanium dioxide have had the benefit of human subjects. Instead, the overwhelming majority of studies to date have been in animals or *in vitro*.

A. HUMAN STUDIES. Two studies of human exposure examined in small groups of volunteers less than healthy skin or skin that was intentionally damaged, whereas a third presented a single case study of damaged skin.[201]

In the first study, researchers created damaged skin by inducing blisters on the lower arm of 15 healthy volunteers, age 22 to 54 years.[202] In the zinc-treated group, "zinc content was significantly increased in the epidermis . . . and the accumulated blister fluid."[203] With higher concentrations, topically applied zinc appeared to reach the dermis after 10 strippings.[204] "Zinc oxide did penetrate normal human skin" and "penetration was enhanced" after the skin was blistered.[205] This is problematic because "a local zinc oxide supply can influence cellular and biochemical reactions

198 *Id.* at 2573, 2579.

199 *Id.* at 2580.

200 Hisao Hidaka et al., *DNA Damage Photoinduced by Cosmetic Pigments and Sunscreen Agents under Solar Exposure and Artificial UV Illumination*, 55(5) JOURNAL OF OLEO SCIENCE 249, 249 (2006) [*hereinafter* DNA Damage].

201 Professor Berube correctly cautions that early studies from the 1980s highlighted the case histories of one or two persons to argue that soil particles can penetrate the skin. *See* David Berube, *Rhetorical gamesmanship in the nano debates over sunscreens and nanoparticles*, 10(1) JOURNAL OF NANOPARTICLE RESEARCH 23–37 (2008) [*hereinafter* Rhetorical Gamesmanship]. These small-scale studies have since been augmented by a burgeoning number of studies of toxicology and the skin. *See* Figure 11.2 in Section II (reporting 152 studies).

202 Magnus S. Agren, *Percutaneous Absorption of Zinc from Zinc Oxide Applied Topically to Intact Skin in Man*, 180 DERMATOLOGICA 36 (1990) [*hereinafter* Percutaneous Absorption of Zinc]. The researchers created the blisters with 10 tape strippings. *Id.* at 37.

203 *Id.*

204 *Id.* In the dermis the "mean zinc concentration" was 24 μg/g, contrasted with 15 μg/g for the control. *Id.*

205 *Id.* at 38.

both in the epidermis and in sub-epidermal tissues."[206] Because "dermal zinc levels were increased beneath zinc-treated skin," the researchers believed "that zinc can penetrate the whole epidermis."[207]

In a second, but weaker study, researchers recruited 13 patients scheduled for surgery on skin lesions to apply titanium dioxide to the surrounding skin for up to six weeks.[208] The researchers removed 4-mm punches of skin and compared them with cadaver hip sections, which likely would not have been exposed to sunscreen.[209] They found higher levels of titanium dioxide in the dermis of patients than in cadaver controls but the difference did not reach statistical significance because of one "outlier control specimen."[210] When the researchers excluded the outlier, "a statistically significant difference" emerged.[211] Emphasizing that the study was a pilot study, the authors concluded that "there [was] a need to follow up . . . and to demonstrate the safety and lack of toxicity from microfine titanium dioxide-containing sunscreen products."[212] This study is weaker than others because it excluded an outlier. Nonetheless, it is included here because the literature contains so few human studies.

A third case study examined the experience of a single 22-year-old man with lesions on his penis as a result of several venereal diseases, lesions he treated three times a day with a 13.5% titanium dioxide-containing ointment.[213] The ointment healed his herpes lesions but left brown pigmented spots on his penis.[214] Biopsied sections contained "numerous brown granules of various sizes in the dermis . . . concentrated in the upper part . . . rarely in macrophages,[215] and sometimes localized around capillaries" but not in the "epidermis or in granular structures."[216] Electron

[206] *Id.* Studies of super-sized zinc oxide also report the presence of zinc in the epidermis, dermis, and whole skin after topical application to 400 μm (or 400,000 nm) sections of "human abdominal skin obtained from surgery," although less than 2% of the applied dose was absorbed after 72 hours. F. Pirot et al., *In Vitro Study of Percutaneous Absorption, Cutaneous Bioavailability and Bioequivalence of Zinc and Copper from Five Topical Formulations*, 9 SKIN PHARMACOL. 259, 259–60 (1996).

[207] *Percutaneous Absorption of Zinc* at 38.

[208] *Pilot Study* at 185.

[209] *Id.* at 185–86.

[210] *Id.* at 186.

[211] *Id.*

[212] *Id.* at 187.

[213] Andre Dupre et al., *Titanium Dioxide Pigmentation: An Electron Probe Microanalysis Study*, 121 ARCH. DERMATOL. 656 (1985) [*hereinafter* Titanium Pigmentation].

[214] *Id.*

[215] A macrophage is "[a]ny of various large white blood cells that play an essential immunologic role in vertebrates and some lower organisms by eliminating cellular debris and particulate antigens, including bacteria, through phagocytosis. Macrophages develop from circulating monocytes that migrate from the blood into tissues throughout the body, especially the spleen, liver, lymph nodes, lungs, brain, and connective tissue. Macrophages also participate in the immune response by producing and responding to inflammatory cytokines." Macrophage, Dictionary.com, THE AMERICAN HERITAGE SCIENCE DICTIONARY, Houghton Mifflin Company, http://dictionary.reference.com/browse/macrophage (last visited May 18, 2011).

[216] *Titanium Pigmentation* at 656–58.

microscopy confirmed that "[t]he smallest particles were approximately 500 nm and the largest were 600 nm in diameter."[217] The researchers ultimately concluded that "it [was] highly probable that the titanium dioxide [cream]...was directly responsible for the dermal deposit" and that the patient's herpes lesions "allowed increased percutaneous penetration."[218]

B. ANIMAL STUDIES. A number of good studies in animals have also emerged. Perhaps most telling is one that appeared in 2009. Wu and colleagues investigated the potential toxicity and penetration of three different forms of uncoated titanium dioxide NPs – 4- and 10-nm anatase; 20-, 60-, and 90-nm rutile; and 21-nm 75% anatase/25% rutile (or mixed) powder[219] – applied *in vitro* and *in vivo* to pigs and hairless mice.[220] Ultimately, the titanium dioxide NPs "accumulated in the spleen, heart, and liver" of the mice after dermal exposure, with one NP passing through the blood–brain barrier; in pigs the NPs penetrated to a "deeper layer of the skin."[221]

Surprisingly, in the *in vitro* studies of pig skin, Wu and colleagues found no penetration after exposure.[222] However, the researchers saw very different results with live animals. After topically administering a 5% titanium dioxide solution to pigs' ears for 30 days, they detected titanium dioxide NPs not only in the SC, but also in the living tissues below – the stratum granulosum, stratum spinosum (or prickle cell layer), and the deepest layer of the epidermis, the basal cell layer.[223] Penetration was size-dependent.[224] As the authors noted, "[p]articles of smaller size have a higher penetration capacity and can reach deeper layers of the skin, and cause more severe pathological changes in the skin structures."[225]

The researchers also applied 5% solutions of titanium dioxide NPs[226] to the dorsal skin of hairless mice.[227] The mice treated with 10- and 25-nm titanium dioxide and

[217] *Id.* at 658. The particles "were free in the dermis among collagen fibers or localized within the cytoplasm of macrophages either free or within membrane-bound lysosomelike bodies." *Id.* A lysosome is "[a] cell organelle that is surrounded by a membrane, has an acidic interior, and contains hydrolytic enzymes that break down food molecules, especially proteins and other complex molecules. Lysosomes fuse with vacuoles to digest their contents. The digested material is then transported across the organelle's membrane for use in or transport out of the cell." Lysosome, Dictionary.com, THE AMERICAN HERITAGE SCIENCE DICTIONARY, Houghton Mifflin Company, http://dictionary.reference.com/browse/lysosome (last visited May 18, 2011).

[218] *Titanium Pigmentation* at 658.

[219] Rutile and anatase are different crystal phases of titanium dioxide. *Anatase and Rutile* at 3.

[220] Jianhong Wu et al., *Toxicity and Penetration of TiO_2 Nanoparticles in Hairless Mice and Porcine Skin After Subchronic Dermal Exposure*, 191 TOXICOLOGY LETTERS 1, 1–2 (2009) [*hereinafter* Toxicity and Penetration].

[221] *Id.* at 3–5.

[222] *Id.* at 3.

[223] *Id.*

[224] *Id.* at 3–4. Only the 4-nm titanium dioxide reached the basal cell layer. *Id.* at 3.

[225] *Id.* at 7.

[226] The study used 10-, 25-, 60-nm and normal-sized titanium dioxide and 21-nm mixed powder. *Id.* at 4.

[227] *Id.* at 2–3.

21-nm mixed powder experienced significant decreases in body weight, as well as enlarged livers and (with the exception of the 25-nm titanium dioxide-treated mice) spleens.[228] After 60 days of exposure, the titanium dioxide NPs "penetrate[d] through the skin, reach[ed] different tissues" – including "subcutaneous muscle, liver, heart, lungs and spleen" – and "induce[d] diverse pathological lesions in several major organs."[229]

In the liver, severe oxidative stress resulted from all NPs, whereas focal necrosis[230] followed exposure to the 25-nm and 60-nm titanium dioxide and liquefaction necrosis[231] followed exposure to the 10-nm titanium dioxide – "strongly suggest[ing] that titanium dioxide [NPs] may induce certain functional impairment."[232] In the spleen and lungs, all titanium dioxide NPs induced minor lesions.[233] All treated mice experienced harm to the kidney.[234] All NPs precipitated "excessive keratinization[235] [in the skin], and other pathological changes such as thinner dermis and an epidermis with wrinkles," with the 10-nm and 21-nm treated mice showing "more severe damage."[236] The skin samples also showed "oxidative stress by increased lipid peroxidation products and reduced collagen contents."[237]

The researchers believe "that the porcine [pig] skin *in vivo* model is more suitable for penetration studies than the *in vitro* model."[238] Although the SC of hairless mice is "less than half as thick" as human skin, the researchers believed that the findings were "nevertheless relevant . . . from a risk assessment standpoint . . . because they illustrate a wide range of phenomena and provide preliminary data to assess the

[228] *Id.* at 4–5.

[229] *Id.*

[230] Focal necrosis is the "occurrence of numerous, small, fairly well circumscribed, foci of necrosis." Focal Necrosis, Dictionary.com, The American Heritage Stedman's Medical Dictionary, Houghton Mifflin Company, http://dictionary.reference.com/browse/FOCAL NECROSIS (last visited May 18, 2011).

[231] Liquefactive necrosis is a necrosis "marked by a circumscribed lesion consisting of the fluid remains of necrotic tissue that was digested by enzymes." Liquefactive necrosis, Dictionary.com, The American Heritage Stedman's Medical Dictionary, Houghton Mifflin Company, http://dictionary.reference.com/browse/Liquefactive necrosis (last visited May 18, 2011).

[232] *Toxicity and Penetration* at 5–7.

[233] *Id.* at 6. The heart "was not significantly damaged by the accumulated titanium dioxide [NPs] except the 10 nm ones." *Id.* at 5–6. The researchers did not find titanium dioxide in the blood obtained from the mice 24 hours after the last treatment. From this the authors concluded that the titanium dioxide NPs "are most likely scavenged from blood circulation and mainly entrapped by liver, spleen and lungs for a long time." *Id.* at 7.

[234] *Id.* at 6.

[235] Keratinization is the "conversion of squamous epithelial cells into a horny material, such as nails." Keratinization, Dictionary.com, The American Heritage Stedman's Medical Dictionary, Houghton Mifflin Company, http://dictionary.reference.com/browse/keratinization (last visited May 18, 2011).

[236] *Toxicity and Penetration* at 5.

[237] *Id.* at 7.

[238] *Id.* (according the researchers's findings with the *in vitro* studies conducted by Lademann et al. (1999), Pflucker et al. (2002), Schulz et al. (2002), and Gamer et al. (2006), which found that "titanium dioxide [NPs were] only deposited on the outermost surface" of the SC).

potential health effects of [NPs] after long-term use, in particular if significant amounts of these microfine metallic oxides would be absorbed through the skin."[239]

Menzel and colleagues investigated the penetration depth and pathways of titanium dioxide NPs into the skin of live pigs at intervals up to 48 hours.[240] They found "penetration of [titanium dioxide] particles through the [SC] into the underlying stratum granulosum via intercellular space . . . [into deeper] vital skin layers."[241] The authors caution that "sunscreens with physical UV filters have [the] potential to cause allergies"[242] and they urged the use of coatings in order to prevent damage to cell components.[243]

Other studies have explored the interaction of nano-sunscreens and sweat on the body and found that "UV-exposed skin may be a significant target for the photo-sensitized damage."[244] Because "in the production and application process of nano [titanium dioxide], protein nitration will happen on the skin, which can lead to some skin diseases[,] . . . more attention[ ] should be paid to the potential biological hazards of this nano material application."[245]

A small number of studies examine the worst-case scenario, namely exposure to the internal tissues of the body.[246] Takeda and colleagues subcutaneously administered titanium dioxide 25 to 70 nm in size to pregnant mice and found that it was "transferred to the offspring and affects the genital and cranial nerve systems of the

[239] *Id.*

[240] F. Menzel et al., *Investigations of Percutaneous Uptake of Ultrafine Titanium Dioxide Particles at the High Energy Ion Nanoprobe LIPSION*, 219–220 Nuclear Instruments and Methods in Physics Research Section B 82, 83 (2004) (using NPs 45–150 nm long and 17–35 nm wide).

[241] *Id.* at 82. Hair follicles did not appear to serve as important penetration pathways, however, because the researchers did not detect any titanium dioxide inside. *Id.*

[242] *Id.* at 86. "Accumulations of titanium dioxide particles in the skin can decrease the threshold for allergies of the immune system or cause allergic reactions directly." *Id.* at 82.

[243] *Id.* at 86.

[244] Naihao Lu et al., *Nano Titanium Dioxide Photocatalytic Protein Tyrosine Nitration: A Potential Hazard of Titanium Dioxide on Skin*, 370 Biochemical and Biophysical Research Communications 675 (2008).

[245] *Id.* at 679.

[246] Ken Takeda et al., *Nanoparticles Transferred From Pregnant Mice to Their Offspring Can Damage the Genital and Cranial Nerve Systems*, 55(1) Journal of Health Science 95, 97–98 (2009) ("[Titanium dioxide]-exposed group had significantly lower body weight (88% relative to control) and significantly higher weight of epidermis per body weight (117% relative to control) . . . aggregates of [titanium dioxide] nanoparticles (100–200 nm) were detected in Leydig cells, Sertoli cells, and spermatids in the testis at both 4 days and 6 weeks of age. . . . Testicular morphology in [titanium dioxide]-exposed mice was abnormal compared to that in control mice. In exposed mice, some seminiferous tubules appeared disorganized and disrupted. There were fewer mature sperm in the tubule lumen. The damaged tubules were scattered randomly throughout the testis. . . . These effects were dependent on the dose of [titanium dioxide] and were significantly higher in the titanium dioxide exposed mice than in control mice. . . . Nano-sized [titanium dioxide] particles were detected in cells in brains of 6-week-old mice exposed prenatally to [titanium dioxide]. . . . Numerous cells positive for caspase-3, a common enzymatic marker of apoptosis, were observed under light microscopy in the olfactory bulb of 6-week-old mice exposed prenatally to [titanium dioxide], and the number of caspase-3-positive mitral cells was significantly higher in exposed mice than in control mice.").

male offspring," causing "brain damage and reduced sperm production."[247] The researchers concluded that "prenatal exposure of mice to [nano-titanium dioxide] has a severe negative effect on fetal brain development and carries a risk of various nervous system disorders."[248]

Bai and colleagues investigated the toxicity on zebrafish embryos – "a good model vertebrate to assess the toxicity of nanoparticles" – 96 hours post-fertilization.[249] They found that the 30-nm zinc oxide – which aggregated to as much as 1,000 nm at certain concentrations[250] – killed the embryos, retarded the embryo hatching, reduced the body length of the larvae, and caused tail malformation.[251]

Liu and colleagues also evaluated the toxicity of 5-nm titanium dioxide NP by injecting them into the adominal cavity of mice daily over two weeks. They found that "nano-anatase [titanium dioxide] in higher dose[s] caused serious damage to the liver, kidney, and myocardium of mice and disturbed the balance of blood sugar and lipid in mice."[252]

Long and colleagues investigated the effect of nanomaterials in culture on brain microglia and found "a rapid and sustained . . . release of reactive oxygen species" and that "mouse microglia respond to [nanomaterial] with cellular and morphological expressions of free radical formation."[253] They concluded that "nanosize [titanium dioxide] could pose a risk to biological targets that are sensitive to oxidative stress damage (e.g., brain)."[254] Other researchers have explored the environmental effects of metal oxides and also report toxicity.[255]

247 *Id.* at 95.

248 *Id.* at 98.

249 Wei Bai et al., *Toxicity of Zinc Oxide Nanoparticles to Zebrafish Embryo: A Physiochemical Study of Toxicity Mechanism*, 12 J. NANOPART. RES. 1645, 1645–47 (2010) [*hereinafter* Zebrafish].

250 Particles aggregated in the suspension, with sizes "increase[ing] with increasing concentrations" up to 1002 nm. *Id.* at 1647.

251 *Id.* at 1648. "The hatching rates of embryos exposed to nano-[zinc oxide] decreased with the increasing concentrations of 1–10 mg/L" and "no embryo[s] hatched after exposure to nano-[zinc oxide] over the concentration range of 25 to 100 mg/L." *Id.* at 1648. The researchers speculated that the dissolved zinc and small zinc oxide aggregates penetrated the embryos through the chorion pore and that large aggregates broke up and "pass[ed] through the chorion" but that the "exact toxic mechanism is still unclear." *Id.* at 1652. The researchers did not perform any independent test of zinc oxide SSPs.

252 Huiting Liu et al., *Biochemical Toxicity of Nano-anatase Titanium Dioxide Particles in Mice*, 129 BIOL. TRACE ELEM. RES. 170 (2009).

253 Thomas C. Long et al., *Titanium Dioxide (P25) Produces Reactive Oxygen Species in Immortalized Brain Microglia (BV2): Implications for Nanoparticle Neurotoxicity*, 40(14) ENVIRONMENTAL SCIENCE & TECHNOLOGY 4346 (2006).

254 *Id.* (finding "[t]he biological response of BV2 microglia to noncytotoxic (2.5–120 ppm) concentrations of P25 was a rapid (<5 min) and sustained (120 min) release of reactive oxygen species").

255 *See* Xiaoshan Zhu et al., *Comparative Toxicity of Several Metal Oxide Nanoparticle Aqueous Suspensions to Zebrafish (Danio rerio) Early Developmental Stage*, 43 JOURNAL OF ENVIRONMENTAL SCIENCE AND HEALTH Part A 278, 278, 284 (2008) (releasing zinc oxide, titanium dioxide, and aluminum oxide (Al_2O_3) to aquatic environments of zebrafish embryos and larvae to determine "the developmental toxicities" and finding that nano-zinc oxide NPs and SSPs "delayed zebrafish embryo and larva development, decreased their survival and hatching rates, and caused tissue damage" whereas neither titanium dioxide nor Al_2O_3 NPs or SSPs showed such toxicity; and concluding that "some

C. IN VITRO STUDIES. A raft of studies have examined toxicity *in vitro*. Brunner and colleagues tested for cytotoxicity of 19- to 36-nm zinc oxide and 8 to 20-nm titanium dioxide in human and rodent cells.[256] "[I]n the case of [zinc oxide] virtually all MSTO [human mesothelioma] or 3T3 [rodent fibroblast] cells died after exposure to [zinc oxide] nanoparticle concentrations above 15 [parts per million]."[257] In rat cells, "reduced proliferation" followed exposure to zinc oxide, which was greater than that observed with asbestos, which the researchers used as a control.[258] Some changes appeared irreversible after six days.[259] Zinc oxide also "provoked rapid drop of cell functionality" at low concentrations.[260] In contrast, titanium dioxide was not found to be "exceedingly toxic up to 30 ppm."[261]

Jin and colleagues studied the effects of two different crystalline phases of titanium dioxide NPs, anatase and rutile, on the generation of ROS,[262] which can cause oxidative stress and damage to "proteins, lipids, and DNA."[263] The researchers exposed less than 25-nm anatase titanium dioxide particles, less than 5,000-nm rutile titanium dioxide particles, and less than 100-nm mixed titanium dioxide particles

nanoscale metal oxide particles might exert detrimental effects to the aquatic ecosystem health when they were released into the aquatic environment. And it also emphasizes the necessity of responsible use of nanoparticles in the process of commercial production, environmental application and safety disposal of manufactured nanomaterials"); Laura K. Adams et al., *Comparative Eco-Toxicity of Nanoscale Titanium, SiO_2, and Zinc Water Suspensions*, 40 WATER RESEARCH 3527, 3529 (2006) (testing "[t]he potential eco-toxicity of nanosized titanium dioxide (TiO_2), silicon dioxide (SiO_2), and zinc oxide (ZnO) water suspensions . . . using Gram-positive *Bacillus subtilis* and Gram-negative *Escherichia* coli," and finding that "[n]anosized [titanium dioxide], [silicon dioxide], and [zinc oxide] water suspensions exhibited antibacterial properties towards B. subtilis and to a lesser extent to E. coli. Overall, antibacterial effects increased from [silicon dioxide] to [titanium dioxide] to [zinc oxide]" and "[t]he presence of light was a significant factor . . . due to its role in promoting generation of" ROS).

256 *In vitro Cytotoxicity* at 4375. For zinc oxide, "[p]article size calculated from the specific surface area" was 19 nm and "[h]ydrodynamic particle size as measured by X-ray disk centrifugation" was 36 nm. *Id.* For titanium dioxide, specific surface area was 8 nm and hydrodynamic particle size was 20 nm. *Id.*

257 *Id.* at 4377.

258 *Id.* at 4378. The researchers used a form of asbestos called crocidolite. *Id.* at 4379. Although the researchers did not specify the particle size of the crocidolite, 100% of the crocidolite was greater than 200 nm. *Id.* at 4375.

259 *Id.* "The overall cell culture activity," measured by MTT conversion, was "drastically reduced for zinc oxide and asbestos." *Id.* at 4378.

260 *Id.* at 4379. "[A]s low as 3.75 ppm," a toxic effect likely came from "the release of Zn^{2+} ions before or after the uptake into the cell." *Id.*

261 *Id.*

262 Chan Jin et al., *Cellular Toxicity of Titanium Dioxide Nanoparticles in Anatase and Rutile Crystal Phase*, 141 BIOLOGICAL TRACE ELEMENT RESEARCH 3 (2010) [*hereinafter* Anatase and Rutile], *available at* http://www.springerlink.com/content/044k181x1113522j/fulltext.pdf. ROSs "disrupt the balance between oxidative pressure and antioxidant defense" causing oxidative stress, and "can also cause damage to protein, lipids, and DNA in cells." *Id.* at 4.

263 *Id.* Other studies have reported "anatase [titanium dioxide] NPs to be more biologically active than rutile [titanium dioxide] NPs in terms of cytotoxicity." *Id.* (citing Kazutaka Hirakawa et al., *Photo-Irradiated Titanium Dioxide Catalyzes Site Specific DNA Damage via Generation of Hydrogen Peroxide*, 38(5) FREE RADICAL RESEARCH 439 (2004) [*hereinafter* Photo-Irradiated]).

to immortalized human skin cells.[264] They found that "anatase [titanium dioxide] NPs allow spontaneous [ROS] generation, but rutile [titanium dioxide] NPs do not."[265]

The rutile NPs collected in the cytoplasm,[266] whereas anatase NPs were phagocytosed in small clusters, lodged inside the mitochondria, and present in the nucleus.[267] Cells exposed to anatase NPs showed "extensive disruption of mitochondrial cristae, which results in a vacuolar[268] cellular appearance;"[269] ROS were "not timely cleared by antioxidant defenses[270] and [thus could] lead[] to the disruption of the mitochondria."[271] The titanium dioxide NPs in the nucleus indicated not only "cytotoxicity but also genetic toxicity."[272]

Together, these impacts "may lead to the release of pro-apoptotic factors and programmed cell death."[273] The researchers concluded that "NPs in the anatase phase cause ultrastructural damage of cells through the generation of ROS by itself and mitochondria disruption."[274]

In a 2006 study, Jeng and Swanson found "dramatic changes" to mouse neuroblastoma cells after exposure to zinc oxide for 24 hours, especially at concentrations greater than 50 μg/mL: "The cells became irregular and shrank."[275] At 50 μg/mL, the cells exhibited evidence of apoptosis,[276] whereas at 100 μg/mL "they became

[264] *Anatase and Rutile* at 2–3.

[265] *Id.* at 1.

[266] Both "anatase and rutile [titanium dioxide] NPs [were] found in the cytoplasm and cytoplasmic vacuoles as a small cluster." *Anatase and Rutile* at 8.

[267] *Id.*

[268] A vacuole is a cellular organelle that "stores food reserves, pigments, defensive toxins, and waste products to be expelled or broken down." Vacuole, Dictionary.com, The American Heritage® Science Dictionary, Houghton Mifflin Company. http://dictionary.reference.com/browse/vacuole (last visited May 18, 2011).

[269] *Anatase and Rutile* at 7.

[270] *Id.* at 11. As the researchers explained, "under normal conditions in the mitochondria, ROS is generated at low frequency and easily neutralized by antioxidant defenses such as glutathione and antioxidant enzymes." *Id.*

[271] *Id.*

[272] *Id.*

[273] *Id.* The researchers suggest several steps in the chain of toxicity. Specifically, the "lodg[ing] in the mitochondria . . . could lead to the disruption of the mitochondrial electron transduction chain, which may induce additional O_2^- production. Then, together with the ROS generation by titanium dioxide itself, the mitochondria cristae are disrupted. It means that the mitochondrial membrane permeability transition pore has begun to open and apoptotic or necrotic signals are initiated." *Id.*

[274] *Id.* They note that rutile NPs did "not collect[] in the mitochondria" but cautioned that they may not have been detectable. *Id.*

[275] Hueiwang Anna Jeng & James Swanson, *Toxicity of Metal Oxide Nanoparticles in Mammalian Cells*, 41 Journal of Environmental Science and Health Part A 2699, 2704 (2006) [*hereinafter* Mammalian Cells].

[276] Apoptosis is "a genetically determined process of cell self-destruction that is marked by the fragmentation of nuclear DNA." Apoptosis, Dictionary.com, Merriam-Webster's Medical Dictionary, Merriam-Webster, Inc., http://dictionary.reference.com/browse/Apoptosis (last visited May 18, 2011).

necrotic."[277] In the band between 50 and 100 μg/mL, zinc oxide NPs "caused 15% to 50% of the cells to die."[278]

A 2007 study by Gojova and colleagues cultured human aortic endothelial cells in a range of concentrations of zinc oxide NPs for up to eight hours and assessed the impact.[279] The researchers found that "[a]t the two highest concentrations, [zinc oxide NPs] provoked considerable cell death at the end of the 4 hr incubation period.... At 50 μg/mL, cell loss after 4 hr [zinc oxide] incubation was approximately 50%; at 10 μg/mL, cell loss was approximately 20%."[280]

In 2007, Reddy and colleagues evaluated the toxicity of zinc oxide NPs on human T lymphocytes, which are crucial for protecting against pathogens.[281] They found that 13-nm zinc oxide NPs "caused a significant decrease in viability" at certain concentrations.[282] After exposure for 20 hours, 23% of the cells had died when exposed to five millimoles per liter (mM), and 57% died when exposed to 10 mM.[283] The researchers concluded that "cell cytotoxicity is limited to [zinc oxide] in the nanoscale size range as no significant effect of bulk [zinc oxide] powder was observed."[284]

Deng and colleagues exposed different sized zinc oxide particles ranging from 10 to 200 nm to mouse neural stem cells (NSCs) for 24 hours.[285] They found that doses above 24 ppm caused "almost all NSCs to become dead" – ranging from approximately an 82% reduction in cell viability for 10-nm NPs to approximately a 90% reduction with 200-nm NPs.[286] At 12 ppm, "a significant toxic effect was found,"[287] although the researchers observed "no toxic effects" below 6 ppm.[288]

Because it is possible that any toxic effects of titanium dioxide may result from the particular crystal structure rather than the small size, a 2009 study by Braydich-Stolle and colleagues sought to isolate the importance of size and crystal structure

[277] *Mammalian Cells* at 2704.

[278] *Id.* at 2705. At lower concentrations, no "distinct change in morphology of cells was observed" (10 μg/mL) and "cell viability was not affected" (<25 μg/mL). *Id.* at 2704–05.

[279] *Induction of Inflammation* at 403. The researchers concluded that the composition of the metal oxide, e.g., zinc, titanium, or another material, "is a major determinant of propensity to induce inflammation" but were unsure of "the mechanistic basis." *Id.* at 408.

[280] *Id.* at 407. In contrast, "[n]o cell loss was noted at the lower concentrations." *Id.*

[281] K.M. Reddy et al., *Selective Toxicity of Zinc Oxide Nanoparticles to Prokaryotic and Eukaryotic Systems*, 90 APPLIED PHYSICS LETTERS 213902, 213902–3 (2007).

[282] *Id.*

[283] *Id.*

[284] *Id.*

[285] *Nanosized Zinc* at 1–2.

[286] *Id.* at 4–5.

[287] The toxicity ranged from approximately 40% reduction in cell viability for 30 nm NPs to approximately a 50% reduction with 200 nm NPs. *Id.*

[288] *Id.* Deng speculated that "[zinc oxide NP] toxicity mainly comes from the dissolved Zn^{2+} in the culture medium or inside cells" and concluded that the toxicity of 10 to 200 nm zinc oxide NPs was dependent on dosage, not on particle size. *Id.* at 7.

to nanotoxicity.[289] Using a "mouse keratinocyte cell line as a model for dermal exposure," the researchers studied titanium dioxide particles of roughly the same size but of different crystal structures.[290] They concluded that "both size and crystal structure contribute to cytotoxicity . . . [but] that the mechanism of cell death varies based on crystal structure."[291] The "anatase [titanium dioxide] nanoparticles, regardless of size, induced cell necrosis[292] . . . [and] rutile [titanium dioxide] nanoparticles initiated apoptosis through formation of ROS."[293]

Looking at structural damage, the Braydich-Stolle team found that "the majority of [titanium dioxide NPs] were localizing in the lysosomes," but that some "localized, in the mitochondria indicating that mitochondrial function can be altered by the presence of [NPs] in a cell."[294] Regarding cell viability after 24 hours of exposure to titanium dioxide agglomerates,[295] the researchers found "significant cytotoxicity" induced by the different sized NPs but that the smallest agglomerate "induced significant toxicity at all concentrations indicating that there could be a possible size-dependent effect."[296] The researchers "saw a size and crystal structure dependent effect on [membrane] leakage and ROS formation,"[297] but also found that "100% rutile [titanium dioxide] produced the most ROS."[298]

Ultimately, the researchers concluded "that regardless of size or crystal structure, [titanium dioxide NPs] were able to be taken up by the cell and disrupt cell viability."[299] Anatase NPs generated high levels of membrane leakage but not ROS, making "necrosis [the] most likely . . . mechanism of cell death."[300] Rutile NPs displayed insignificant levels of membrane leakage but high levels of ROS formation, indicating "apoptosis [as] the likely mechanism of cell death."[301] Because

[289] Laura K. Braydich-Stolle et al., *Crystal Structure Mediates Mode of Cell Death in Titanium Dioxide Nanotoxicity*, 11 J. NANOPART. RES. 1361 (2009) [*hereinafter* Crystal Structure].

[290] *Id.* at 1361. Specifically, the researchers studied anatase, rutile, amorphous, and anatase/rutile.

[291] *Id.*

[292] Necrosis is the "death of cells or tissues from severe injury or disease, especially in a localized area of the body. Causes of necrosis include inadequate blood supply (as in infarcted tissue), bacterial infection, traumatic injury, and hyperthermia." Necrosis, Dictionary.com, THE AMERICAN HERITAGE SCIENCE DICTIONARY, Houghton Mifflin Company, http://dictionary.reference.com/browse/necrosis (last visited May 18, 2011).

[293] *Crystal Structure* at 1361.

[294] *Id.*

[295] The agglomerates were 1550 nm (Primary 50 nm), 1800 nm (Primary 10 nm), and 1800 nm (Primary 100 nm), at concentrations ≥ 10 μg/mL. *Id.* at 1368.

[296] *Id.* Crystal structure did impact membrane integrity more than size, however: "[T]he 1,800 nm titanium dioxide illustrated significant amounts of leakage at all concentrations, while all the other nanoparticles demonstrated significant leakage at ≥ 25 μg/mL." *Id.* at 1370.

[297] *Id.* at 1371.

[298] *Id.* at 1370.

[299] *Id.*

[300] *Id.* at 1372.

[301] *Id.*

antioxidants reversed toxicity in rutile titanium dioxide but not anatase, "the anatase structure [was] more toxic than the rutile."[302]

A separate study using human gene DNA fragments looked for "the mechanism of DNA damage catalyzed by photo-irradiated [titanium dioxide]."[303] Hirakawa and colleagues found "[p]hoto-irradiated [titanium dioxide] (anatase and rutile) caused DNA cleavage."[304] The researchers hypothesized that "photo-irradiated [titanium dioxide] caused not only DNA strand breakage but also base modification" through the formation of hydrogen peroxide rather than through a free hydroxyl radical.[305]

The list of studies goes on.[306] Dunford and colleagues studied titanium dioxide 20 to 50 nm in size and zinc oxide of unknown size and composition extracted from

[302] *Id.*

[303] *Photo-Irradiated* at 439.

[304] *Id.* Breaks occurred sometimes at the guanine residue and other times at the thymine residue. *Id.*

[305] *Id.* at 443–44. Others have found no oxidative stress or mitochondrial damage after exposure to a mixed anatase/rutile particle. Xia and colleagues exposed a phagocytic cell line representative of a lung target to several NPs including 80% anatase/20% rutile titanium dioxide of an average diameter between 175 and 364 nm. *Comparison of Abilities* at 1796. "Despite being the most active material under abiotic conditions, [titanium dioxide] did not generate ROS in cells," raising the question whether "differences in ROS production at a cellular level translate into different levels of biological injury." *Id.* at 1798. The researchers also found "[titanium dioxide] particles were taken up into lose-fitting (sic) phagosomes without noticeable mitochondrial damage." *Id.* at 1800. But, the authors cautioned, the "study did not address NP effects on other cell types . . . relevant to particle toxicity . . . such as . . . keratinocytes." *Id.* at 1806. Indeed, their preliminary data indicates "response differences due to differences in cellular uptake, subcellular localization, and engagement of biological pathways leading to ROS production." *Id.*

[306] A.B.G. Lansdown & A. Taylor, *Zinc and Titanium Oxides: Promising UV-Absorbers But What Influence Do They Have on the Intact Skin?*, 19 INTERNATIONAL JOURNAL OF COSMETIC SCIENCE 167, 172 (1997) (finding percutaneous absorption in a study of microfine titanium dioxide and zinc oxide dissolved in water, polyethylene glycol and castor oil on rabbit skin, with "uptake . . . influenced by the vehicle used," but that most particles remained on the surface of the skin and urging that the findings "provide provocative evidence that both titanium and zinc oxides do have the capacity to interact with components of the intact skin, which may have undesirable consequences in the long term"); Vlasta Brezova et al., *Reactive Oxygen Species Produced Upon Photoexcitation of Sunscreens Containing Titanium Dioxide (an EPR Study)*, 79 JOURNAL OF PHOTOCHEMISTRY AND PHOTOBIOLOGY B: BIOLOGY 121, 131–132 (2005) (irradiating sunscreens containing titanium dioxide and finding that the generation of reactive oxygen species depends upon their composition and that "[t]he continuous . . . irradiation of titanium dioxide powder, recommended for cosmetic application . . . resulted in the generation of oxygen-centered ROS (superoxide anion radical, hydroxyl and alkoxyl radicals)" and concluding that "[o]ur investigations indicate the formation of ROS in sunscreens"); Su Jin Kang et al., *Titanium Dioxide Nanoparticles Trigger p53-Mediated Damage Response in Peripheral Blood Lymphocytes*, 49 ENVIRONMENTAL AND MOLECULAR MUTAGENESIS 399, 399–400 (2008) (investigating the underlying mechanisms of titanium dioxide NP-induced cytotoxicity using titanium dioxide particles approximately 25 nm in size in peripheral blood lymphocytes, and finding "increased micronucleus formation and DNA breakage . . . [and] ROS"); Jia-Ran Gurr et al., *Ultrafine Titanium Dioxide Particles in the Absence of Photoactivation Can Induce Oxidative Damage to Human Bronchial Epithelial Cells*, 213 TOXICOLOGY 66, 71 (2005) (reporting that treatment of human bronchial epithelial cells with "10 and 20 nm [titanium dioxide] particles induced oxidative DNA damage, lipid peroxidation, micronuclei formation, and increased hydrogen peroxide and nitric oxide production in the absence of photocatalysis" and concluding that "intratracheal instillation of ultrafine particles may

various sunscreens in conditions that were more likely to mimic the real world, under simulated sunlight.[307] Using DNA plasmids and human fibroblast cells,[308] the researchers found that each titanium dioxide NP catalyzed photo-oxidation and that sunlight-illuminated titanium dioxide and zinc oxide NPs "catalyse[d] DNA damage both *in vitro* and in human cells."[309] The titanium dioxide caused DNA strand breaks and lesions.[310] The DNA breaks, the researchers concluded, were "due to direct attack by hydroxyl radicals," demonstrating that "sunscreen [titanium dioxide] and [zinc oxide] can catalyse oxidative damage to DNA *in vitro* and in cultured human fibroblasts."[311]

Others have also found that the "toxic response of [nano-titanium dioxide] increased substantially with UV illumination."[312] Sayes and colleagues exposed immortalized human lung epithelial cells and human dermal fibroblasts in culture to nano-titanium dioxide samples and measured viability at various times. Although titanium dioxide NPs showed a "relatively low toxicity compared to other [NPs like] fullerenes . . . different types of [nano-titanium dioxide also] exhibit[ed] different levels of toxicity. [Nano-titanium dioxide] anatase particles were the most cytotoxic to human cells in culture, while [nano-titanium dioxide] rutile particles were the least cytotoxic."[313] "[U]nder UV illumination, cell death increase[d] by 20% . . . for a fixed dose."[314] High concentrations of titanium dioxide NPs disrupted "the normal activity of cells in culture. Particle exposure caused . . . increase[s in]

cause oxidative stress," although results differed by the size of the particle and whether it was rutile or anatase).

307 Rosemary Dunford et al., *Chemical Oxidation and DNA Damage Catalysed by Inorganic Sunscreen Ingredients*, 418 FEBS Letters 87, 87–89 (1997) (testing 12 titanium dioxide samples, including one sample that also contained 1.95% zinc oxide, which was "the most active sample") [*hereinafter* Chemical Oxidation].

308 A fibroblast is a "connective-tissue cell of mesenchymal origin that secretes proteins and especially molecular collagen from which the extracellular fibrillar matrix of connective tissue forms." Fibroblast, Dictionary.com, Merriam-Webster's Medical Dictionary, Merriam-Webster, Inc., http://dictionary.reference.com/browse/fibroblast (last visited May 18, 2011).

309 *Chemical Oxidation* at 87.

310 Lesions occurred "at some, but not all, guanine residues." *Id.* at 89.

311 *Id.* at 88–89.

312 Christie M. Sayes, *Correlating Nanoscale Titania Structure With Toxicity: A Cytotoxicity and Inflammatory Response Study With Human Dermal Fibroblasts and Human Lung Epithelial Cells*, 92 Toxicological Sciences 174, 179 (2006) [*hereinafter* Nanoscale Titania]. *See also* T. Uchino et al., *Quantitative Determination of OH Radical Generation and Its Cytotoxicity Induced by Titanium Dioxide–UVA Treatment*, 16 Toxicology in Vitro 629 (2002) (analyzing the effect on Chinese hamster ovary cells of ultraviolet-A (UVA) irradiation with various titanium dioxide sunscreen samples, ranging from 15 nm to 400 nm, and finding that "[i]rradiation of the anatase form of [titanium dioxide] produced large numbers of OH radical[s]" that induce cytotoxicity "in a dose dependent manner . . . [and] rutile form . . . showed less OH radical generation"). *But see Nanoderm* at 45 (arguing that "[t]he relevance of these observations on the cellular level is still an open question because the exposure is rather low, if it exists at all").

313 *Nanoscale Titania* at 179.

314 *Id.*

LDH release, decrease[d] mitochondrial activity, and produced increased levels of IL-8 [an inflammatory mediator]."[315]

Hidaka and colleagues studied the effect *in vivo* of nano-sized zinc oxide particles extracted from four Japanese sunscreens on DNA plasmids under UV illumination and found that they generate free radicals causing "considerable damage to the DNA plasmids."[316] They concluded that "[t]he zinc oxide pigment used in cosmetics and as a sunscreen active agent in commercial formulations" damage "human skin and the horny layer."[317]

D. *Equivocal Studies*

The emerging literature on exposure of skin to NPs is by no means a monolithic whole. Some studies report no penetration beyond the SC. For example, a study of three different methods of topical application found titanium dioxide only in the outermost layer of the skin,[318] concluding that "neither surface characteristics, particle size nor shape of the [titanium dioxide NPs] result in any dermal absorption."[319] Kuo and colleagues in 2009 also found that zinc oxide NPs distribute within the SC, primarily in the uppermost layers with insignificant second harmonic generation[320] detected beyond that depth.[321] A study by Gamer and colleagues reached similar results.[322] Other studies investigating toxicity have found no cellular damage.[323]

315 *Id.* at 176, 182.

316 *DNA Damage* at 254.

317 *Id.* at 258, 249.

318 F. Pflucker et al., *The Human Stratum Corneum Layer: An Effective Barrier against Dermal Uptake of Different Forms of Topically Applied Micronised Titanium Dioxide*, 14 SKIN PHARMACOLOGY & APPLIED SKIN PHYSIOLOGY 92, 97 (2001) (studying exposure of three different sunscreens containing 20 and 100 nm titanium dioxide NPs to the forearm of a human volunteer and finding with light and electron microscopy that titanium dioxide "is solely deposited on the outermost surface of the stratum corneum and cannot be detected in deeper stratum corneum layers, the human epidermis and dermis," suggesting "the safe use of micro-fine titanium dioxide for topical application to humans").

319 *Id.* at 92.

320 Second harmonic generation is "a phenomenon that an input wave in a nonlinear material can generate a wave with twice the optical frequency." Encyclopedia of Laser Physics and Technology, http://www.rp-photonics.com/frequency_doubling.html (last visited May 18, 2011).

321 Tsung-Rong Kuo et al., *Chemical Enhancer Induced Changes in the Mechanisms of Transdermal Delivery of Zinc Oxide Nanoparticles*, 30 BIOMATERIALS 3002, 3006 (2009) (using imaging to assess the transdermal delivery of zinc oxide NPs approximately 10 nm in diameter "under the chemical enhancer conditions of oleic acid (OA), ethanol (EtOH) and oleic acid–ethanol (OA–EtOH)," and finding that "OA, EtOH and OA-EtOH were all capable of enhancing the transdermal delivery of [zinc oxide] NPs by increasing the intercellular lipid fluidity or extracting lipids from the SC").

322 A.O. Gamer et al., *The In Vitro Absorption of Microfine Zinc Oxide and Titanium Dioxide Through Porcine Skin*, 20 TOXICOLOGY IN VITRO 301, 306 (2006) (investigating "the in vitro absorption of microfine zinc oxide [with an average size of 80 nm] and titanium oxide [30–60 x 10 nm in size] in cosmetic formulations through porcine [pig] skin," and finding "that neither . . . zinc oxide . . . or titanium dioxide particles were able to penetrate porcine stratum corneum").

323 Elizabeth Theogaraj et al., *An Investigation of the Photo-Clastogenic Potential of Ultrafine Titanium Dioxide Particles*, 634 MUTATION RESEARCH 205 (2007) (investigating whether ultrafine titanium

Other studies find penetration deeper in the skin, but without a clear indication that the particles actually reached any living tissue.[324] For instance, a study of coated titanium dioxide applied to the outer layer of the skin and orifice of the human hair follicle concluded that presence deep in the follicle could not be interpreted as "penetration into living layers of the skin, since this part . . . is covered with a horny layer" too.[325]

Some studies are simply equivocal, with both positive and negative findings. For instance, Kang and colleagues found oxidative stress and other cell damage after exposure to titanium dioxide NPs without "significantly alter[ed] cell viability."[326]

Of course, negative findings simply demonstrate that NPs in cosmetics and sunscreens are not always harmful. Because size and crystal structure appear to be important factors,[327] negative findings in some studies should not be surprising. Furthermore, demonstration that *some* NPs are safe does not argue against testing to determine *which* NPs are safe and which are not. As one commentator noted with respect to another emerging technology more than a decade ago, the absence of evidence of harm is *not* evidence of the absence of harm.[328]

dioxide particles aggregated into clusters approximately 30–150 nm in size caused chromosomal breaks in the Chinese hamster ovary WBL cell line (CHO-WBL), and finding that "[n]one of the titanium dioxide particles tested induced any increase in chromosomal aberration frequencies either in the absence or presence of UV").

[324] Juergen Ladermann et al., *Penetration of Titanium Dioxide Microparticles in a Sunscreen Formulation into the Horny Layer and the Follicular Orifice*, 12 Skin Pharmacology & Applied Skin Physiology 247 (1999) (examining penetration into skin and hair follicles after 16 applications over 4 days of titanium dioxide microparticles of unspecified size, taken from sunscreens, showing that "[i]n isolated areas, a penetration of coated [titanium dioxide] into the open part of the follicle was observed . . . [in roughly] less than 1% of the applied total amount of sunscreens" and that "penetration of microparticles into viable skin tissue could not be detected"). This was true even after repeated application of the NPs. *Id.* at 250.

[325] *Id.* at 255.

[326] Jihee Lee Kang et al., *Comparison of the Biological Activity Between Ultrafine and Fine Titanium Dioxide Particles in RAW 264.7 Cells Associated With Oxidative Stress*, 71 Journal of Toxicology and Environmental Health, Part A 478 (2008) (evaluating "the biological activity of" 21 nm and 1000 nm titanium dioxide in a mouse peritoneal macrophage cell line for oxidative stress and finding that the 21 nm titanium dioxide "enhanced intracellular generation of [ROS, 2.4-fold more than the untreated control, and] to a greater extent than" the 1,000-nm titanium dioxide, and that ultrafine (< 100 nm in diameter) titanium dioxide exposure "significantly enhanced tumor necrosis factor (TNF)-α and macrophage inflammatory protein (MIP)-2 secretion in a concentration dependent manner" but that exposure to both 21 nm and 1000 nm titanium dioxide "did not significantly alter cell viability"). *See also* Sheree E. Cross et al., *Human Skin Penetration of Sunscreen Nanoparticles: In-Vitro Assessment of a Novel Micronized Zinc Oxide Formulation*, 20 Skin Pharmacol. Physiol. 148,148 (2007) (testing "human epidermal penetration of a [26 to 30 nm] novel, transparent, nanoparticulate zinc oxide sunscreen formulation" after 24 hours of exposure with electron microscopy and finding that "[l]ess than 0.03% of the applied zinc content penetrated the epidermis . . . [No particles could be detected in the lower stratum corneum or viable epidermis by electron microscopy").

[327] As Section III illustrated, nano-cosmetics exploiting fullerenes and iron oxides likely pose greater risk than nano-sunscreens using zinc and titanium. Although nano-zinc and nano-titanium dioxide both induce oxidative stress and other cell damage, zinc may be less reactive than titanium dioxide.

[328] Commission of Inquiry on the Blood System in Canada (Krever Commission), Final Report. Volume 1, Part III, 294 (1997) (noting that threats to Canada's blood supply from possible HIV contamination

3. The Weight of the Evidence

Clearly, "no one study should be interpreted as definitive."[329] Studies to date provide neither a perfect nor complete snapshot of risk. Although many of these studies use humans or live vertebrates, others rely on *in vitro* methods. Studies of cells, not whole organisms, cannot capture the effect of the body's many lines of defense.[330] The studies report a range of findings, which one would expect given the different study methods[331] and the different materials studied.

Although these studies do not all reach a conclusion that there is risk, they do follow a distinct trend. They show an impact on cell viability, proliferation, apoptosis, and differentiation. These impacts would give rise to little concern if the NPs did not penetrate to living tissues, but a significant number of studies now show that they do. Together, these toxicological studies of "adverse impacts on human health and environmental species" make the claim that NPs are "biosafe and biocompatible" controversial.[332]

Even those researchers who have found no penetration or toxicity in healthy skin agree that pockets of risk likely exist. A literature review by the consumer group Environmental Working Group faulted studies showing penetration of NPs in the skin of hairless mice, but conceded that "the available research . . . does not completely address the potential for penetration in damaged skin."[333]

Some argue that cell death would occur in the absence of these products, pointing out that humans lose 50,000,000 cells a second.[334] This claim essentially maintains that no one can say definitively that nano-cosmetics and nano-sunscreens will have health effects in humans. Although true, the observation does not negate the fact that policymakers now know enough to begin to ask the safety question – and therefore to require proof of safety before marketing. Put another way, the weight of the evidence suggests at a minimum that questions about safety need to be asked – and answered.

occurred because "[t]he Red Cross did not carry out risk-reduction measures assiduously. It did not appropriately weigh the competing concerns. Rather, it consistently used the absence of 'definitive proof' of a link between AIDS and blood transfusion as a justification for maintaining the status quo. Its employees or officials repeatedly expressed the view that the threat from AIDS to the blood supply was not sufficient to require a significant change in its donor-screening measures").

329 *Research Strategies* at 16.

330 Lianghao Ding et al., *Molecular Characterization of the Cytotoxic Mechanism of Multiwall Carbon Nanotubes and Nano-Onions on Human Skin Fibroblast*, 5(12) NANO LETTERS 2448, 2457–58 (2005).

331 As one toxicologist remarked, "changes to nanomaterials within an *in vitro* and *in vivo* testing environment should be expected. . . . [T]he specific composition of an *in vitro* and *in vivo* test system will likely play a huge role in how a nanomaterial interacts with a cell, or other biological target. . . . Depending on the experimental conditions used, the pH, and specific protein content of the environment, methods used to 'solubilize' nanomaterials, etc., what was 'tested' may often bear little resemblance to the material as it exists in the real world or in a different test system." Nigel J. Walker & John R. Bucher, *A 21st Century Paradigm for Evaluating the Health Hazards of Nanoscale Materials?*, 110(2) TOXICOLOGICAL SCIENCES 252 (2009), http://toxsci.oxfordjournals.org/cgi/content/full/110/2/251.

332 *Zebrafish* at 1645 (criticizing the claim by Berube).

333 *EWG Report*.

334 *Rhetorical Gamesmanship* at 30–1.

IV. REGULATING NANO-SUNSCREENS AND NANO-COSMETICS LIKE DRUGS

Nanotechnology poses "significant oversight challenges" because of "[t]he diversity of nanoproducts" and the speed at which NPs have moved into cosmetics and sunscreens.[335] Regulators straddle risks on each side: "jeopardizing public safety in a rush to technology on the one hand and strangling nanotechnology in the crib on the other."[336] A focused examination of the risk from dermal exposure suggests that public safety, long a given with SSPs, should now be rigorously evaluated when it comes to NPs. Only premarket testing can answer the question: is this nano-cosmetic or nano-sunscreen safe?

Reversing the US present course would involve two straight-forward policy moves. First, Congress should pass new legislation requiring the kinds of proof about safety of nano-cosmetics that Congress now requires for drugs.[337] Congress should also borrow from the regulation of drugs and require post-market surveillance. It is likely that most problems will not be detected until NPs reach a large number of users and are used over a long period of time. As two scientists noted recently, "[i]f nanomaterials behave anything like other foreign particles with respect to human health, their effects are likely cumulative and may not be apparent in individuals for decades."[338]

Second, the FDA should revisit the Sunscreen Monograph, correcting what scientists and other federal regulators now recognize is an unfounded and unwarranted assumption. Doing so would return the oversight of nano-sunscreens to the default rule used for new drugs: requiring proof of safety from each individual product.

Some may object that it is difficult to say conclusively whether the class of nano-cosmetics and nano-sunscreens are safe because properties vary from one NP to the next. The FDA grapples with this issue routinely. It assesses individual drugs for

[335] Jordan Paradise et al., *Developing Oversight Frameworks for Nanobiotechnology*, 9 MINN. J.L. SCI. & TECH. 399, 413 (2008).

[336] *Perspectives on FDA* at 378.

[337] The FDA's statutory authority to regulate nano-cosmetics is not obvious. It might label all nano-cosmetics as adulterated products, an approach suggested by the NTF. *FDA Nanotechnology Report* at 34 (recommending the FDA "[i]ssue guidance describing safety issues that manufacturers should consider to ensure that cosmetics made with nanoscale materials are not adulterated"). The FDA could also treat nano-cosmetics as products for which safety has not been adequately substantiated.

Neither regulatory fix would necessarily elicit proof of safety before marketing. *See* Section II *infra*. Moreover, "rulemaking takes time." Robin Fretwell Wilson, *Nanotechnology: The Challenge of Regulating Known Unknowns*, 34 JOURNAL OF LAW, MED. & ETHICS 704, 707 (2006) [*hereinafter* Known Unknowns] (quoting estimates by an official at the National Science Foundation that "regulations 'generally require about ten years from genesis to application'") (*quoting* O. Renn & M. C. Roco, Nanotechnology and the Need for Risk Governance (8) 2, JOURNAL OF NANOPARTICLE RESEARCH at 1, Table 3 (2006)). Although the FDA cannot easily require cosmetic manufacturers to test ingredients or products, Congress can.

[338] *Environmental Implications* at 48–49 (noting the near absence of papers concerning the toxicology of these new materials).

proof of safety on a daily basis. The question for regulators, therefore, is not whether the class is safe, but whether a *particular* product using a NP is safe.

Meaningful regulation likely will better protect the public while allowing further innovation. This approach would place the burden on manufacturers for pre-market testing, provide disclosure, and increase consumer confidence. As Professor Graeme Hodge (Director of Regulatory Studies of the Monash University Centre for Regulatory Studies) has said, "[i]t would be a tragedy if governments around the world waited until a nano-disaster occurred before thinking seriously about regulatory needs. This would most likely produce an over-reaction and severely restrict the ability of companies to innovate and grow."[339]

A. *Better Than Alternative Proposals*

Regulating nano-cosmetics and nano-sunscreens like drugs has a number of advantages over previous proposals. A number of consumer and environmental groups urge the recall of all products containing nanomaterials and a moratorium on further manufacturing of nanomaterials pending comprehensive scientific review of their safety.[340] Because the nanotechnology genie is already out of the bottle, a complete ban would likely be "politically and practically impossible."[341] Billions of dollars have already been expended on nanotechnology research, and a ban in the United States likely would drive nanotechnology research and development to other countries.[342]

At the other end of the spectrum, some assert that policymakers should continue to rely on voluntary programs of self-regulation. But "[v]oluntary efforts to gather information on the production of nanomaterials have been largely unsuccessful."[343] In 2006, a UK request for self-reports of "information on due production of nanomaterials" elicited "just 13 submissions in two years," whereas the EPA's 2008 voluntary disclosure program received 29 responses about a mere 123 different NPs.[344] EPA concluded "that approximately 90% of the different nanoscale materials that are

[339] *Is nanotechnology below the regulatory radar in Australia?*, INDUSTRY SEARCH, Jul. 20, 2006, http://www.industrysearch.com.au/Features/Is-nanotechnology-below-the-regulatory-radar-in-Australia-650.

[340] *See, e.g.*, *Friends of the Earth, Nanomaterials, Sunscreens, and Cosmetics: Small Ingredients Big Risks* 5 (May 2006) (advocating a "moratorium on the further commercial release of personal care products that contain engineered nanomaterials").

[341] Albert C. Lin, *Size Matters: Regulating Nanotechnology*, 31 HARV. ENVTL. L. REV. 349, 407 (2007) [*hereinafter* Size Matters].

[342] *Id*; *Perspectives on FDA* at 386; *Managing the Effects* at 23 ("Most knowledgeable observers believe that the benefits of [nanotechnology] will outweigh the adverse consequences, especially if steps are taken to minimize adverse effects.").

[343] Andrew Maynard & David Rejeski, *Too Small to Overlook*, 460 NATURE 174 (9 July 2009), *available at* http://www.nature.com/nature/journal/v460/n7252/full/460174a.html [*hereinafter* Too Small].

[344] *Id.*

likely to be commercially available were not reported."[345] Low reports should surprise no one – reporting requires "businesses to expend considerable resources in gathering information, with little direct benefit to themselves."[346]

In the middle, some urge the use of warning labels for products containing NPs.[347] This might take the form of labels noting that a product uses NPs or that the safety of NPs is unsubstantiated, or alternatively, the disclosure of nano-sized ingredients.[348] Although labeling may create better informed consumers, promoting economic efficiency,[349] labeling only works if (1) someone polices the use of labels, and (2) consumers weigh the benefits of new nano-products against the risks and health effects.[350]

Unlike "protected or mandatory label[s]"[351] for other products like champagne, no one polices the use of "nano" in product names or labels. "Nano" sometimes designates a product "where it does not seem very appropriate," whereas a "significant group of products . . . actually *do* use nanotechnologies but . . . this fact is not stated."[352] Not surprisingly, eight of 10 respondents in one study "were not aware of any nano-enabled products on the market," even though "more than 1,000 products . . . openly communicate that they contain nanotechnology."[353]

More troubling, labeling does little to impact consumer behavior.[354] The frequency of warning labels today has already hastened "risk fatigue."[355] Because "most Americans apply about 10 cosmetics or other personal care products containing

[345] "The progress made under the NMSP [Nanoscale Materials Stewardship Program] should be tempered against a number of considerations [including]: It appears that nearly two-thirds of the chemical substances from which commercially available nanoscale materials are based were not reported under the Basic Program. . . . The low rate of engagement in the In-Depth Program suggests that most companies are not inclined to voluntarily test their nanoscale materials." US Environmental Protection Agency, Nanoscale Materials Stewardship Program: Interim Report, Office of Pollution Prevention and Toxics at 27 (2009), *available at* http://www.epa.gov/oppt/nano/nmsp-interim-report-final.pdf.

[346] *Too Small* at 174.

[347] *Size Matters* at 391.

[348] *FDA Labeling* at 69 (summarizing the various labeling proposals). *See also* Victoria Farren, Note, *Removing the Wrinkle in Cosmetics and Drug Regulation: A Notice Rating System and Education Proposal for Anti-Aging Cosmeceuticals*, 16 Elder L.J. 375, 399 (2008) (proposing a labeling system with different color codes corresponding to the level of risk associated with a cosmetic containing nanomaterials).

[349] *Size Matters* at 393.

[350] *Id.* Labeling might also force industries to take greater care regarding the safety of their products. Certain companies may even adopt a "non-nano" label to gain a competitive advantage, like that for "organic" foods. *Falling Through the Cracks* at 5. It would also give manufacturers the ability to determine the content of supplied goods. *Managing the Effects* at 23.

[351] *Nano Consumer* at 398.

[352] *Id.* at 399.

[353] *Id.*

[354] *Managing the Effects* at 23.

[355] David M. Berube, *Regulating Nanoscience: A Proposal and a Response to J. Clarence Davies*, 3 Nanotech. L. & Bus. 485, 494 (2006) [*hereinafter* Regulating Nanoscience] (describing the phenomenon of "risk fatigue," diluting the effect of any one label).

over 126 distinct ingredients to their bodies daily,"[356] the sheer volume of warnings that consumers would have to process makes it extremely unlikely that any individual could rationally process the risks. Even if consumers could stomach additional labels, our developing understanding of health effects and how much risks differ from one NP to the next would make it difficult for consumers to effectively weigh risks.[357] Some consumers will ignore warnings, trusting that "'somebody' controls products before they appear on shelves."[358] Others may place undue emphasis on the label, believing that there is something "wrong" with all nanoproducts when in fact risks may be concentrated only in certain types of products.[359] Indeed, the FDA has rejected a blanket labeling approach as premature.[360]

Federal regulations already require such labels for products containing ingredients that are not adequately substantiated as safe. One review of products containing NPs already on the market found that none have such labels.[361]

Some advocate a liability regime in which the markets would allocate risk.[362] Obviously, our emerging understanding of risk makes it difficult for insurance companies to effectively allocate risk, although some do offer coverage for nanotechnology. Manufacturers may be motivated to benefit from risk allocation, creating a "second stream of information for the regulatory regimes from insurance companies and litigation."[363] Yet there are a number of problems with relying exclusively on such a system. Some manufacturers may carry no, or inadequate, liability insurance.[364] Commercial coverage may not be available through every carrier.[365] If insurers walk away, large companies in the nanobusiness may be able to pay claims, but start-up companies likely would not.[366] More fundamentally, lawsuits the vehicles for risk allocation: are unlikely to adequately encourage responsible behavior, both because of the potential for

[356] *Beneath the Skin* at 2; Investory Environmental Health Network, *available at* http://iehn.org/filesalt/IEHNCosmeticsReportFin.pdf.

[357] *Size Matters* at 395. *See also Regulating Nanoscience* at 494 ("A labeling regime provides data without information. While labeling a food item's dietary cholesterol and saturated fat and trans fat content makes sense because both are implicated in coronary heart disease, there will not be such a clear cut case with products containing nanoparticles.").

[358] *Nano-Consumer* at 397 (summarizing a focus group conducted in Oslo, Norway in 2008). As one participant explained, "We trust the authorities; if it is on sale at a pharmacy, we regard it as safe." Consumers in the United States may differ from these study participants. *Id.*

[359] *Perspectives on FDA* at 387.

[360] *FDA Nanotechnology Report* at 35.

[361] Environmental Working Group, *EWG Comments to the FDA on Nano-Scale Ingredients in Cosmetics*, http://www.ewg.org/node/21738 (last visited May 18, 2011).

[362] *See Regulating Nanoscience* at 497.

[363] *Id.* at 499. More information for insurers could lead to more manageable rates for manufacturers. *Id.* at 501.

[364] *Known Unknowns* at 711.

[365] *Id.* One insurance carrier has excluded harm from NPs in its standard Commercial General Liability policy. *Product Liability Risks* at 2 (discussing product liability concerns and safety risks associated with nanotechnology).

[366] *Known Unknowns* at 711.

long latency between exposure and harm and because so many nanoproducts will have been deployed worldwide,[367] frustrating the necessary showing of causation.

Closely related to a liability scheme is a bonding proposal, advanced by Professor Albert C. Lin. This proposal would require any manufacturer or distributor of products containing free nanomaterials to post a dated assurance bond to cover any damages that could arise from the company's products.[368] The EPA would set the value and term of the bond, subject to future adjustment as manufacturers and regulators accumulated short-term and long-term toxicity data, with options for a partial refund for manufacturers with no adverse events.[369] The bonding proposal's advantages over a pure tort liability scheme are that it provides a baseline of protection for consumers and encourages manufacturers to collect safety data themselves instead of relying on insurers to do the work for them.[370] Similar bonding schemes are currently used in the mining industry to ensure site reclamation.[371] Lin admits that one potentially negative effect of a bonding requirement is that it favors larger corporations that have greater access to capital than their smaller counterparts.[372]

V. CONCLUSION

Nano-cosmetics and nano-sunscreens have gone mainstream, reaching millions of consumers. Although manufacturers like L'Oréal, which ranks sixth among US patent holders of nanomaterials,[373] asserted as late as 2005 that "[n]obody in any lab has ever shown that [nanoparticles] penetrate[] into the living part of the skin,"[374] the scientific community openly recognizes that safety assessments are "urgently required."[375] Enough evidence of risk from dermal exposure has now accumulated to warrant the safety question: will this particular nano-sunscreen or nano-cosmetic reach living cells and cause harm? Requiring proof of safety and continual monitoring of these nano-products by the manufacturers who sell them to an unsuspecting public is nothing new and may avoid unnecessary harm to consumers.

367 *Known Unknowns* at 710.

368 *Size Matters* at 397–405.

369 *Id.* at 398.

370 *Id.* at 399.

371 *See id.* at 400–1 (mentioning the Surface Mining Control and Reclamation Act, which mandates the use of performance bonds to guarantee reclamation of coal mining sites).

372 *Id.* at 401–2.

373 Copley (posted by), *What Is It: Nanotechnology in Cosmetics* (Part One), Jun. 9, 2009, http://truthinaging.com/body/what-is-it-nanotechnology-in-cosmetics-part-one.

374 *Nano, Nano, On The Wall… L'Oréal and Others Are Betting Big on Products With Microparticles*, BUSINESS WEEK, 12 December 2005.

375 *Comparison of Abilities* at 1794.

ACKNOWLEDGMENT

Thanks to Julie Arrington, Kelsey Baughman,Will Bridges, George Davis, Merilys Huhn, Steve Mammerella, Joe Mercer, and Anna Katherine Moody for diligent research assistance and to Robert Best, Albert Carr, and David Dana for thoughtful comments. I greatly benefited from the opportunity to present this work at the Searle Center Research Round table on environmental, Health, and Safety Risks of Emerging Technologies, at Yeditepe University in Istanbul, Turkey, and at the Second World Congress of the International Academy of Nanomedicine in Antalya, Turkey.

APPENDIX: SUNSCREENS/COSMETICS/PERSONAL CARE PRODUCTS ON THE MARKET CONTAINING NPS[376]

		Sunscreens		
#	Name of product	Type of product	Maker	Country of origin
1	Advanced Protection SPF 30 Oil w/Clear Z COTE Zinc	Sunscreen SPF 30	Skin Rx Solutions	United States
2	All Day Suncare SPF 15	Sunscreen SPF 15	Kara Vita	United States
3	All Day Suncare SPF 30	Sunscreen SPF 30	Kara Vita	United States
4	Applied Therapeutics Sunscreens	Sunscreen	Applied Therapeutics	United States
5	Bebe/Enfant High Protection SPF 50	Sunscreen SPF 50	Mustela	United States
6	Blue Lizard BABY	Sunscreen (baby)	Crown Laboratories, Inc.	Australia
7	Blue Lizard Regular	Sunscreen	Crown Laboratories, Inc.	Australia
8	Blue Lizard Sensitive	Sunscreen (sensitive skin)	Crown Laboratories, Inc.	Australia
9	Chemical-Free Sunscreen SPF 15	Sunscreen SPF 15	Burt's Bees, Inc.	United States
10	Cotz SPF 58	Sunscreen SPF 58	Fallene	United States
11	Daily Sun Defense SPF 30	Sunscreen SPF 30	SkinCeuticals	United States
12	Dermatone SPF 20 Natural Formula	Sunscreen SPF 20	Dermatone Laboratories	United States
13	IS Clinical SPF 20 Moisturizing Treatment	Sunscreen/ moisturizer	Innovative Skincare	United States
14	Kids Tear Free SPF 30	Sunscreen (kids) SPF 30	Banana Boat	United States

(*continued*)

[376] The products included in this Appendix are adapted from products listed as of May 18, 2011, on Woodrow Wilson International Center for Scholars, *The Project on Emerging Nanotechnologies*, Consumer Products, at http://www.nanotechproject.org/inventories/consumer/browse/categories/ (last visited May 18, 2011) (PEN Website). For reasons explained below, this Appendix excludes certain products listed on the PEN Website.

Sunscreens				
#	Name of product	Type of product	Maker	Country of origin
15	Lips 'n Face Protection Crème and Sunblock Crème	Sunscreen (lips/face)	Dermatone Laboratories	United States
16	Lyphazome and Celazome Cosmetics and Sunscreens	Sunscreen	Dermazone Solutions	United States
17	Optisol Sun Defence	Sunscreen	Oxonica Ltd.	UK
18	Physical UV Defense SPF 30	Sunscreen SPF 30	SkinCeuticals	United States
19	Q-SunShade SPF 30+ Tinted Zinc Oxide Sunscreen with Z-COTE	Sunscreen (tinted) SPF 30+	International Cosmeceuticals, Inc.	United States
20	Rosacea Care Sunscreen "30"	Sunscreen (rosacea) SPF 30	Rosacea Care	United States
21	Solar Defense Crème and Organic Moisturizer	Sunscreen/ moisturizer	Image Skin Care	United States
22	Solar Rx SPF 30+ Nano-Zinc Oxide Sunblock	Sunscreen SPF 30+	Keys Soap	United States
23	Soltan Facial Sun Defence Cream – Optisol	Sunscreen	Boots and Oxonica Ltd.	UK
24	Spectra3 SPF 50	Sunscreen SPF 50	Coppertone	United States
25	SPF 20 Sunscreen Powder	Sunscreen (powder) SPF 20	Innovative Skincare	United States
26	Sport UV Defense SPF 45	Sunscreen SPF 45	SkinCeuticals	United States
27	SunDressed Self Tanner	Self-tanner	Kara Vita	United States
28	Sunscreen Plus Clear Zinc SPF30+	Sunscreen SPF 30+	Cancer Council Australia	Australia
29	SunSense SPF 30+ Sunscreen	Sunscreen	NuCelle Inc.	United States
30	SunVex Dailywear Lotions[377]	Sunscreen/ lotion	SunVex	United States
31	SunVex Sunscreens	Sunscreen	SunVex	United States
32	Ultimate UV Defense SPF 30	Sunscreen SPF 30	SkinCeuticals	United States
33	ZinClear Nano Zinc Oxide[378]		Advanced Nanotechnology Limited	Australia

[377] The PEN Website lists some products multiple times under the "Cosmetics," "Sunscreens," and "Personal Care" product inventories. Those products are listed only once in this Appendix. For example, SunVex Dailywear Lotion is listed on the PEN Website as a "Cosmetic" and a "Sunscreen," but is listed here only as a "Sunscreen."

[378] This is an ingredient for use in other products. http://web.archive.org/web/20071125115127/http://www.advancednanotechnology.com/zinclear.php.

Cosmetics[379]

#	Name of product	Type of product	Maker	Country of origin
1	Acnel Lotion N	Facial moisturizer	DERMAVI-DUALS U.S.A.	United States
2	Arbonne NutriMinC RE9 Products	Skin care product line	Arbonne International	United States
3	Arouge Deep NanoMoisture Care Set	Skin moisturizer line	Zenyaku Kogyo Co., Ltd.	Japan
4	Awake Nano Lotion White	Facial toner	KOSE Corporation	Japan
5	Bain de Terre Recovery Complex	Hair care products	Zotos International, Inc.	United States
6	Beautiful Face Series – Nano-in Deep Cleaning for make-up removal and exfoliation and Cleaning Gel	Facial cleanser	Nano-Infinity Nanotech Co., Ltd.	Taiwan
7	BIONOVA Cosmetics	Cosmetics product line	Barneys New York	United States
8	Bimene	Face cream	Telemolecular	United States
9	Calming Emulsion	Face cream	Chanel	France
10	Chantecaille Nano Gold Energizing Cream	Face cream	Chantecaille	France
11	Christian Dior DiorSkin Extreme Fit Extreme Wear Flawless Makeup SPF15 - # 011	Foundation makeup	Dior	France
12	Clearly It! Complexion Mist	Facial toner	Kara Vita	United States
13	Clearly It! Spot Treatment	Acne spot treatment	Kara Vita	United States
14	Clearly It! Acne Treatment Lotion	Acne treatment lotion	Kara Vita	United States
15	Coco Mademoiselle Fresh Moisture Mist	Fragrance	Chanel	France
16	CollagenFusion Botanical Skincare System	Skin care line	AmerElite Solutions	United States
17	Cosil Nano Beauty Soap	Soap	Natural Korea Company, Ltd.	Korea
18	Cosil Whitening Mask	Skin care mask	Natural Korea Company, Ltd.	Korea
19	Crystal Radiance	Facial exfoliant	JamieO Skincare	United States

(*continued*)

[379] This Appendix includes only 125 of the 141 products listed as "Cosmetics" on the PEN Website, omitting such products as hair styling tools and small electronic devices.

Cosmetics				
#	Name of product	Type of product	Maker	Country of origin
20	Cuticle Tender	Cuticle cream	Kara Vita	United States
21	D-Fense Antioxidant Moisturizer with SPF 17	Moisturizer	MOXIE for men	United States
22	Derma Swiss Nanosphere	Facial moisturizer	DermaSwiss	Switzerland/ United States
23	Diorskin Forever – Extreme Wear Flawless Makeup SPF 25	Foundation makeup	Dior	France
24	DiorSnow Pure UV Base SPF 50	Makeup base	Dior	France
25	DNA Skin Optimizer, SPF 20, Cream	Face cream	JUVENA (International) AG	Switzerland
26	DNA Skin Optimizer, SPF 20, Fluid	Face cream	JUVENA (International) AG	Switzerland
27	Doctor Gunderson's Raahj Nano Copper Facial Spray	Anti-aging facial spray	Freedom Plus Corporation	United States
28	Doctor Gunderson's Raahj Synergized DHEA Facial Spray	Anti-aging facial spray	Freedom Plus Corporation	United States
29	Dual Finished Pressed Compacts	Skin care/makeup line	Colorescience	United States
30	Eczemel Nano-Cream	Face cream	DERMAVI-DUALS U.S.A.	United States
31	EGF Complex Cocktail	Facial serum	BellaPelle	United States
32	Enlighten Me!	Facial clarifier	Kara Vita	United States
33	Eternalis Hydrating Face Mist	Facial moisturizer	Beyond Skin Science, LLC	United States
34	Eternalis Intense Day Treatment	Face cream	Beyond Skin Science, LLC	United States
35	Eternalis Night Cream	Face cream	Beyond Skin Science, LLC	United States
36	Eternalis Skin Purifying Cleanser	Facial cleanser	Beyond Skin Science, LLC	United States
37	Everyday Skin Penetrating Cream	Face cream	Kara Vita	United States
38	Eye Contour Nanolift	Eye cream	Euoko	Canada
39	Eye Tender	Eye cream	Kara Vita	United States
40	EyeWish! Bioserum	Eye serum	Kara Vita	United States
41	Face Brushes – After Glow Brush and Brush Colores	Skin care/makeup products	Colorescience	United States
42	Flash Bronzer Glow 'N Wear	Bronzer	Lancôme	France

Cosmetics				
#	Name of product	Type of product	Maker	Country of origin
43	Fresh As A Daisy Body Lotion	Body lotion	Kara Vita	United States
44	Glycol-X Treatment Cream	Skin cream	Kara Vita	United States
45	Glycol-X Treatment Lotion	Lotion	Kara Vita	United States
46	GreenYarn G-moist soft cloth mask	Facial mask	Greenyarn LLC	United States
47	Hand Tender	Lotion	Kara Vita	United States
48	HYDRA FLASH BRONZER Daily Face Moisturizer	Facial moisturizer	Lancôme	France
49	HYDRA ZEN CREAM	Face cream	Lancôme	France
50	Indulgence	Facial moisturizer	Kara Vita	United States
51	INNERMOST Cosmetics	Skin care product line	Enprani	Korea
52	Komenuka Bijin NSK A-10 Cream	Face cream	UNICO Enterprises	Japan/United States
53	Komenuka Bijin NSK C-10 Essence	Skin brightener	UNICO Enterprises	Japan/United States
54	Lancôme Renergie Flash Lifting	Anti-aging facial serum	Lancôme	France
55	Lancôme Renergie Microlift	Anti-aging face cream	Lancôme	France
56	Lancôme Renergie Microlift Eye	Eye cream	Lancôme	France
57	Lancôme Renergie Neck	Neck cream	Lancôme	France
58	Laser in a Bottle Products	Skin care	Dr Brandt	United States
59	LEOREX Cosmetics	Skin care product line	GlobalMed Technologies	UK
60	LifeWave NanoTechnology Skin Care System	Skin care system	LifeWave, LLC	United States
61	Lip Tender	Lip plumper/ moisturizer	Kara Vita	United States
62	Lipoduction Body Perfecting Complex	Cellulite cream	Osmotics Cosmeceuticals	United States
63	Lyphazome and Celazome Cosmetics and Sunscreens	Suncare and body lotions	Dermazone Solutions	United States
64	Nano Anti Aging Cream	Face cream	Soxton Enterprise	United States

(continued)

Cosmetics				
#	Name of product	Type of product	Maker	Country of origin
65	Nano Breast Cream	Breast cream	St. Herb Cosmetics International	Thailand
66	Nano Cosmetics	Cosmetics/skin care line	SongSing Nano Technology Co., Ltd.	Taiwan
67	Nano Cyclic Cleanser PINK	Facial cleanser	NanoCyclic, Inc.	United States
68	Nano Gold Energizing Cream	Face cream	Neiman Marcus	United States
69	Nano-C powder Cosmetics	Cosmetics line	Cell Rx	United States
70	Nano-in Hand and Nail Moisturizing Serum and Foot Moisturizing Serum	Hand and nail/foot crème	Nano-Infinity Nanotech Co., Ltd.	Taiwan
71	Nano-mascara	Mascara	Nano Concept	Norway
72	Nanoce Moisture Liquid Foundation	Liquid foundation makeup	Ishizawa Labs	Japan
73	Nanorama – Nano Gold Mask Pack	Facial mask	Lexon Nanotech, Inc.	United States
74	Nanoseal G.N.C.	Face cream	NanoPlasma Center Company, Ltd.	Korea
75	Nanoseal G.S.E.	Face/eye cream	NanoPlasma Center Company, Ltd.	Korea
76	Nanoseal-Hairna essence	Hair growth product	NanoPlasma Center Company, Ltd.	Korea
77	Nourish	Facial serum	BellaPelle	United States
78	NutraFirm Body Wash and Lotion	Body wash/lotion	RBC Life Sciences, Inc.	United States
79	Oleogel	Skin care gel	DERMAVI-DUALS U.S.A.	United States
80	Peroxel Gel	Skin care gel	DERMAVI-DUALS U.S.A.	United States
81	Platinum Silver Nanocolloid Cream	Facial moisturizer	DHC Skincare	Japan
82	Platinum Silver Nanocolloid Milky Essence	Anti-aging skin booster	DHC Skincare	Japan
83	POUTlandish Hyper Moisturizing Lip Paint	Lip color	DERMAdoctor	United States

Cosmetics				
#	Name of product	Type of product	Maker	Country of origin
84	Primordiale Nanolotion	Face cream	Lancôme	France
85	Primordiale Optimum Lip	Anti-aging lip base	Lancôme	France
86	Proxiphen-N (Prox-N) & Nano Shampoo	Shampoo	Prox-N	United States
87	Psorinel Lotion	Skin care lotion	DERMAVI-DUALS U.S.A.	United States
88	Pureology Nano Glaze	Hair care products	Pureology	United States
89	Pureology Nano Works Shine Luxe – Finishing Hair Polish	Hair care products	Pureology	United States
90	Pureology Nanowax	Hair care products	Pureology	United States
91	Q10 Skin Care Nano Lipobelle Coenzyme Q10	Skin cream	Tina Concept Co., Ltd.	China
92	Quan Zhou Hu Zheng Nano Technology Co., Ltd. Nano-gold Mask	Facial mask	Quan Zhou Hu Zheng Nano Technology Co., Ltd.	China
93	RevitaLift Double Lifting	Anti-aging face cream	L'Oréal	France
94	RevitaLift Intense Life Treatment Mask	Anti-aging facial mask	L'Oréal	France
95	Revite, NANOTECHNOLOGY Hair Growth Stimulating Shampoo	Shampoo	NANORMIN	
96	Rewind Time	Anti-aging face serum	JamieO Skincare	United States
97	Rutina nano-force moisturizer	Face cream	KOSE Corporation	Japan
98	Rutina nano-white	Skin brightener	KOSE Corporation	Japan
99	Serge Lutens Blusher	Blush	Barneys New York	United States
100	Shiseido "The Makeup" Dual Balancing Foundation SPF 17	Foundation makeup	Chantecaille	France
101	Sircuit White Out	Eye treatment	Sircuit Cosmeceuticals Inc.	United States

(*continued*)

Cosmetics				
#	Name of product	Type of product	Maker	Country of origin
102	Sircuit O.M.G. Serum	Skin care serum	Sircuit Cosmeceuticals Inc.	United States
103	Sircuit Sircuit Addict version 1.0	Firming antioxidant serum	Sircuit Cosmeceuticals Inc.	United States
104	Skin Caviar Ampoules	Anti-aging skin cream	Bergdorf Goodman	Switzerland
105	Soothing Moisturizing Lotion Nanoemulsion 10–9	Skin cream	G.M. Collin	France
106	StriVectin-NE NanoExfoliant For The Hands	Skin (hands) exfoliant	StriVectin	United States
107	Super "h" Serum	Skin booster serum	3Lab	United States
108	SUPER AQUA Cosmetics	Moisturizing skin care line	Enprani	Korea
109	Susie-K Nano Beauty Soap	Soap	Segae-I Pte Ltd.	Singapore
110	Susie-K Whitening Mask	Skin brightening mask	Segae-I Pte Ltd.	Singapore
111	The Skin Lightening Collection	Skin brightening product line	Porselene	United States
112	TIME RESPONSE Eye Renewal Crème	Eye cream	AmorePacific	Korea
113	TIME RESPONSE Intensive Skin Renewal Ampoule	Anti-aging skin cream	AmorePacific	Korea
114	TIME RESPONSE Skin Renewal Crème	Skin cream	AmorePacific	Korea
115	Turn The Tides Blemish Serum	Skin blemish serum	Colorescience	United States
116	Up Tight Firming Peptide Complex	Skin firming cream	Kara Vita	United States
117	Up Tight Firming Peptide Cream	Skin firming cream	Kara Vita	United States
118	VECTEANA Clear Wash	Facial cleanser	Faith Cosmetics Group	Japan
119	VECTEANA Nanomode Essence RC	Face cream	Faith Cosmetics Group	Japan
120	VECTEANA White Powder	Skin moisturizer	Faith Cosmetics Group	Japan

		Cosmetics		
#	Name of product	Type of product	Maker	Country of origin
121	Vital Essence with Arbutin	Face and eye serum	Chantecaille	France
122	WW Eye Cream	Eye cream	3Lab	United States
123	Zelens Fullerene C-60 Day Cream	Face cream	Zelens	UK
124	Zelens Fullerene C-60 Eye Cream	Eye cream	Zelens	UK
125	Zelens Fullerene C-60 Night Cream	Face cream	Zelens	UK

		Additional Nano Ingredients		
#	Ingredient	Type of product	Maker	Country of origin
1	Alusion Alumina Powders[380]		Advanced Nanotechnology Limited	Australia
2	Radical Sponge		Vitamin C60 BioResearch Corporation	Japan
3	UV Pearls		Sol-Gel Technologies	Israel

		Personal Care Products[381]		
#	Name of product	Type of product	Maker	Country of origin
1	Ag Nano Phytoncide Toothpaste	Toothpaste	SH Pharma Co Ltd	Korea
2	Agera Nano Eye Lift	Eye lift treatment	Agera Medical Formula	UK
3	Apagard Oral Care Toothpaste	Toothpaste	Sangi Co., Ltd.	Japan

(continued)

[380] Although listed under the "Cosmetics" product inventory on the PEN Website, Alusion and the Radical Sponge are not products, but ingredients that can be used in products. *See* http://www.alliedhightech.com/polishing/aluminaprods/ and http://www.nanotechproject.org/inventories/consumer/browse/products/5091/.

[381] Although the PEN Website had 267 products listed in its "Personal Care" product inventory category, this Appendix includes only 105. Those excluded here include hair styling tools, such as hair brushes, curling irons, straighteners, and blow dryers; razors; toothbrushes; pencils; clothing; towels; bidets; dietary supplements; home pregnancy tests; earplugs; hearing aids; makeup instruments; and joint braces/supporters.

Personal Care Products				
#	Name of product	Type of product	Maker	Country of origin
4	Body Volume Conditioner	Conditioner	COLURE True Color Care	United States
5	Body Volume Shampoo	Shampoo	COLURE True Color Care	United States
6	Curlwave Styling Creme	Hair styling product	COLURE True Color Care	United States
7	Cyclic Nano Silver Cleanser	Facial cleanser	NanoCyclic, Inc.	United States
8	Daejanggum Yellow Earth Phlogopite Soap	Soap	Claypia Co., Ltd.	Korea
9	Dentasil Gel	Mouth gel	Altermed a.s.	Czech Republic
10	Dentasil Mouthwash	Mouth wash	Altermed a.s.	Czech Republic
11	Diorskin Forever Compact	Foundation makeup	Dior	France
12	Energy Booster Serum	Hair care serum	ALFAPARF Milano	Italy
13	Equilibre Nano Silver Cleanser	Facial cleanser	EVELINE-CHARLES SALONS and SPAS	Canada
14	Exfoliant Gelscrub	Hair care scrub	ALFAPARF Milano	Italy
15	FirmHold Styling Gel	Hair styling product	COLURE True Color Care	United States
16	Flex-Power Joint & Muscle Pain Relief Cream	Joint & muscle cream	Flex-Power, Inc.	United States
17	Hair Power Nano-Tech Solutions Shampoo	Shampoo	ALFAPARF Milano	Italy
18	Happylogy Serum	Skin serum	Guerlain	France
19	Healing Volume daily Thickening Treatment	Hair treatment	L'anza	United States
20	Healing Volume Thickening Conditioner	Hair conditioner	L'anza	United States
21	Keratin Reinforcer	Hair strengthener	ALFAPARF Milano	Italy
22	L'anza Healing Volume Shampoo	Hair shampoo	L'anza	United States
23	La Science Anti Hair Loss Serum	Hair thickener	Lifestyle Aesthetics Ltd	UK
24	La Science Follicle Stimulating Shampoo	Hair shampoo	Lifestyle Aesthetics Ltd	UK
25	Life Ritual Firming Nano-Lotion with Collagen Activator	Lotion	Helena Rubinstein	United States

Personal Care Products				
#	Name of product	Type of product	Maker	Country of origin
26	Line Smoothing Complex Treatment Masks	Facial mask	Dr Lewinn's	United States
27	Lion Ban Powder Spray	Antiperspirant deodorant	Lion Corporation	Japan
28	Lissage Nano Silver Cleanser	Facial cleanser	EVELINE-CHARLES SALONS and SPAS	Canada
29	Marie Louise Vital Nanoemulsion	Skin serum	Marie Louise	United States
30	Milk Shake Permenant Colour (hair dye)	Hair dye	z.one conceptTM	Italy
31	Mosquito Repellent Spray	Bug spray	J International CityM Korea Co., Ltd.	Korea
32	Nanbabies Element 47 Moisturizing Spray	Antimicrobial	Nanbabies	United States
33	Nano Gold Firming Treatment	Skin firming treatment	Chantecaille	France
34	Nano hair extension	Hair extension	Baltic hair	Lithuania
35	Nano line: Bio Royal Nano	Skin treatment	Helen Pietrulla Kosmetika	Germany
36	Nano line: Hydrosoftcare Nano	Skin treatment	Helen Pietrulla Kosmetika	Germany
37	Nano line: Lipo Liquid HP Nano	Skin treatment	Helen Pietrulla Kosmetika	Germany
38	Nano line: Moisture Cream Activ Nano	Skin treatment	Helen Pietrulla Kosmetika	Germany
39	Nano Magic White Body	Skin brightener	Soxton Enterprise	United States
40	Nano Shampoo and Conditioner	Shampoo/ conditioner	Dr. Peter Proctor	United States
41	NanO Silver	Antibacterial	Nano Health Solutions	United States
42	Nano Silver 650 Beauty Soap	Soap	DongYang Nanotech Co. Ltd	Korea
43	Nano Silver Toothpaste	Toothpaste	Ace Silver Plus	Korea
44	Nano Silver Wet Wipes	Antibacterial wipes	Nanogist Co., Ltd.	Korea
45	Nano-in Body Freshness Control	Deodorant/ fragrance	Nano-Infinity Nanotech Co., Ltd.	Taiwan

(continued)

Personal Care Products				
#	Name of product	Type of product	Maker	Country of origin
46	Nano-in Foot Deodorant Powder/Spray	Deodorant	Nano-Infinity Nanotech Co., Ltd.	Taiwan
47	Nano-silver Aroma Soap	Soap	Summitek Inc.	Korea
48	Nano-silver Toothpaste	Toothpaste	Summitek Inc.	Korea
49	Nano-silver Women Antimicrobial Gel for External Use	Antimicrobial	Health & Health (Hong Kong) International Holdings Ltd.	China
50	Nanoceuticals Citrus Mint Shampoo	Shampoo	RBC Life Sciences, Inc.	United States
51	Nanogen Locking Mist	Hair loss treatment spray	Nanogen Products	UK
52	Nanogen Nanofibers	Hair loss treatment product	Nanogen Products	UK
53	Nanogen Nanogaine	Hair loss treatment product	Nanogen Products	UK
54	Nanogen Nanoguard	Hair loss root treatment	Nanogen Products	UK
55	Nanogen Nanoscalp	Hair loss scalp treatment	Nanogen Products	UK
56	Nanogen Nanothick	Hair loss thickening treatment	Nanogen Products	UK
57	Nanometer-Silver Foam Condom	Condom	Blue Cross Bio-Medical (Beijing) Co., Ltd.	China
58	Nanorama – Gold Toothpaste	Toothpaste	Lexon Nanotech, Inc.	United States
59	Nanorama – Nano Beauty Soap	Soap	Lexon Nanotech, Inc.	United States
60	Nanoseal Toothpaste	Toothpaste	NanoPlasma Center Company, Ltd.	Korea
61	NANOVER Wet Wipes	Antimicrobial wipes	GNS Nanogist	Korea
62	NANOVER Cleansing Soap	Soap	GNS Nanogist	Korea
63	NANOVER Hair Care	Shampoo	GNS Nanogist	Korea
64	NANOVER Mask Pack	Facial mask	GNS Nanogist	Korea
65	NANOVER Toothpaste	Toothpaste	GNS Nanogist	Korea
66	Nanowhitening	Whitening toothpaste	Swissdent	Switzerland
67	Natural Ingredients (Face Foam)	Liquid soap	Gaia Infonet Co., Ltd.	Korea

Personal Care Products				
#	Name of product	Type of product	Maker	Country of origin
68	Natural Ingredients (Body Foam)	Bath soap	Gaia Infonet Co., Ltd.	Korea
69	Oligo DX cellulite reducing gel	Cellulite reducing gel	DS Laboratories	United States
70	Oragan Nano Silver Toothpaste	Toothpaste	LK Trading Co., Ltd.	Korea
71	Perfect Mask	Facial mask	3Lab	United States
72	Precision Blanc Essentiel Nanolotion	Lotion	Chanel	France
73	Purelogicol Instant Lip Plumper	Lip plumper	PureLogicol International	UK
74	Pureology COLOURMAX	Hair care product	Pureology	United States
75	Pureology HoldFast	Hair styling product	Pureology	United States
76	Pureology Nanoworks Conditioner	Conditioner	Pureology	United States
77	Pureology Nanoworks Shampoo	Shampoo	Pureology	United States
78	Quan Zhou Hu Zheng Nano Technology Co., Ltd. Gold Nanoparticle soaps	Soaps	Quan Zhou Hu Zheng Nano Technology Co., Ltd.	China
79	Quan Zhou Hu Zheng Nano Technology Co., Ltd. Nano-silver Toothpaste	Toothpaste	Quan Zhou Hu Zheng Nano Technology Co., Ltd.	China
80	Richly Moisturize Conditioner	Conditioner	COLURE True Color Care	United States
81	Richly Moisturize Shampoo	Shampoo	COLURE True Color Care	United States
82	Shakti Resculpting Body Lotion	Body lotion	Tracie Martyn	UK
83	Shine Serum	Hair styling product	COLURE True Color Care	United States
84	Shuga Hair Products	Hair care products	Ariella, Inc.	United States
85	Silver Colloid for Antimicrobial in Exterior Medicine	Antimicrobial	Shanghai Huzheng Nano Technology Co., Ltd.	China
86	Spectral.DNC-L hair-growth treatment	Hair-growth treatment	DS Laboratories	United States

(continued)

Personal Care Products				
#	Name of product	Type of product	Maker	Country of origin
87	Spectral.RS hair-growth treatment	Hair-growth treatment	DS Laboratories	United States
88	St. Botanica Nano Breast Cream: Breast Massage Cream – Instant Breast Enhancement	Breast cream	St. Botanica Pueraria	India
89	St. Botanica Pueraria Nano Breast Serum – Instant Breast Enhancement and Firmness	Breast serum	St. Botanica Pueraria	India
90	Stainless Toothpaste	Toothpaste	Swissdent	Switzerland
91	Stherb Anti-Cellulite Nano cream	Cellulite cream	StHerbs	Thailand
92	StraightHair BlowDry Crème	Hair styling product	COLURE True Color Care	United States
93	Swissdent Nanowhitening Toothpaste	Toothpaste	Swissdent	Switzerland
94	System absolute series for skincare: Beauty Fluid	Skin treatment	Annemarie Börlind	Germany
95	System absolute series for skincare: Cleansing Milk	Skin treatment	Annemarie Börlind	Germany
96	System absolute series for skincare: Day Cream	Skin treatment	Annemarie Börlind	Germany
97	System absolute series for skincare: Night Cream	Skin treatment	Annemarie Börlind	Germany
98	Texture Creme	Hair styling product	COLURE True Color Care	United States
99	Theramed S.O.S. Sensitive toothpaste with Nanitactive	Toothpaste	Henkel KGaA	Germany
100	Toothpaste Gel	Toothpaste	Gaia Infonet Co., Ltd.	Korea
101	True Volume Thickening Shampoo with Expansion Technology, Basil and White Lupine	Thickening shampoo	Jack Black	United States
102	Ultim Reflex Advanced Cellulite Smoothing Emulsion	Cellulite cream	Phytomer	France
103	Vitamin Soap Nano Silver Skin Remedy – 60 + day supply	Soap	ByeBye Acne	United States
104	Viterol.A anti-ageing cream	Anti-aging cream	DS Laboratories	United States
105	Wella SP Silk Fiber	Hair wax	Wella	Germany

12

Accelerating Regulatory Review

John O. McGinnis

Technology is transforming the world more rapidly than ever before. Because of such technological acceleration, our polity faces the possibility of more beneficial and more dangerous events than at any time in human history. To address these coming dangers and benefits, particularly in the area of the environment and health, our regulatory structures must become more nimble and accurate in evaluating technological changes. Because sound regulation thrives on information, the key to regulatory reform is to create legal rules and institutions that will make use of technological advances in information creation, analysis and dispersion. Thus regulation in an era of technological acceleration contains within itself the dynamo of its own management, but only if the rules of social governance permit the information revolution to wash through our democratic and regulatory structures.

The rate of technological change has always been an important, albeit largely unrecognized, factor underlying the design of legal and social institutions. The Babylonians chiseled their laws onto diorite steles.[1] This method of legal production reflected a world of technological stasis. Laws did not need to be updated from generation to generation. Democracy itself can be seen as a reaction to the accelerating change of the scientific revolutions of the seventeenth and eighteenth centuries. More oligarchic ways of ruling simply did not generate the information needed to address the new social dilemmas raised by ongoing invention. Democracy, in contrast, unlocked information about the consequences of change by permitting a wide range of citizens to vote on the basis of their own private information.

The rise of the administrative state in the late nineteenth and early twentieth century coincided with the even faster change brought about by industrialization.[2]

[1] *See* Klaas R. Veenhof, "*In Accordance with the Words of the Stele:" Evidence for Old Assyrian Legislation*, 70 Chi.-Kent. L. Rev. 1717, 1720–1722 (1995).

[2] James M. Landis, The Administrative Process 33–35 (1938).

The dispersed sources of information provided by ordinary citizens were seen as inadequate in formulating regulatory responses to such change, and legislative implementation was too slow. For the first time, a few of the architects of the new legal and political order were aware that technological change was a cause of that new order's necessity.[3]

Thus the centrality of the rate of technological change to the structure of our regulatory regime is not new, but the need to take conscious account of its importance in every aspect of regulatory institutions is more urgent than ever before. Many theorists of technology expect exponential technological change: a citizen living to mid century can expect to experience at least 10 times as much change as those who lived through the last century. Society will need to accommodate change that rapidly and continuously transforms the social landscape.

As a result, society needs better decision making in regulatory institutions, both because it must address more changes at a faster pace and because some of these changes are more likely to be profoundly destabilizing. In this essay, I consider three problems in particular that accelerating technology creates for regulatory decisions. First, accelerating technology makes the future state of technology more present in any current regulatory decision. The technology of the future can appropriately change the timing and content of current regulatory decisions because of its large effect on the costs and benefits of regulation. Indeed, because technological change can be so important to the costs and benefits of regulation, government decisions to spur such technology need to be better integrated into those decisions. Second, because of technological acceleration, there are greater risks of catastrophes and cascading benefits in the future. Even small probabilities of such events need to be taken account of in current regulatory decisions. (Because there has been much discussion of catastrophe in the recent regulatory literature and little discussion of cascading benefits in this article, I will focus on the latter). Third, because of accelerating technology, generations to come – even the next generation – may be substantially wealthier than we are. This development raises issues of generational equity in a more acute form than ever before.

One of the main themes of this essay is that even as accelerating technology is making issues of regulation potentially more urgent and complicated, it is also increasing our ability to analyze the need for and consequences of regulation. For instance, technological change is creating better opportunities for accurate regulation by providing the resources for better empiricism and by creating the infrastructure for prediction markets to provide information about the likely consequences of regulation and technology. The key to making regulation work now is to embed the new technologies of information into the process of regulation making itself.

[3] *Id.* at 7. For an excellent discussion of the relation of technology and the administrative state, *see* John F. Duffy, *The FCC and Patent Regulation: Progressive Ideals, Jacksonian Realism, and the Technology of Regulation*, 71 Colo. L. Rev. 1071 (2001).

The new technology of information also allows us to address the greatest single problem of centralized regulation – its lack of access to dispersed information. Although the regulatory process through notice and comment of rule making has tried to acquire information from outside the government, these processes cannot systematically capture information about the likely consequences of regulation that is dispersed throughout society. In contrast, the regulatory regime in an age of accelerating technology can incorporate focused mechanisms of decentralized learning, like prediction markets and empirical testing of diverse regulatory solutions. The result can be regulation that is not only more accurate but is also seen to rest on more objective and less insular sources of information, providing more legitimacy.

Avoiding regulatory backlash will be essential in the age of accelerating technology, because the scope of regulation may need to be expanded to address the possibility of very large externalities from accelerating technology. Global warming may have been the first example of this phenomenon. The new technologies of energy production in the nineteenth and twentieth centuries created carbon emissions, with resulting changes in the climate. Nanotechnology, biotechnology, and other forms of accelerating technology have the capacity to create similar externalities.

Transforming the regulatory process into a mechanism of learning will be a slow and incremental process, but this essay offers some steps to facilitate the transition. Some proposals here focus on deploying mechanisms for decentralized information, such as creating units devoted to prediction markets and empirical testing within the regulatory review process in the Office of Management and Budget (OMB). The former would take advantage of the dispersed information afforded by prediction markets, and the latter would take advantage of the rise of empirical methods to conduct randomized experiments by deploying different regulations where empirical evaluations of such differences will help resolve disputed issues of regulatory policy. Another proposal is to create a formal technology assessment review as part of cost–benefit analysis, because the content and timing of regulation is dependent on changing technology. Regulatory review must be connected with government decisions about spurring technological changes that would have positive regulatory externalities. These changes in regulatory review should be embodied in new units devoted to prediction markets, experimentation, and technology. In a bureaucracy, function follows form.

I. TECHNOLOGICAL ACCELERATION

In this section, I describe separately three reasons to believe that technology is accelerating and that this acceleration will have substantial effects on social life. First, from the longest term perspective, epochal change has speeded up. The transition from hunter-gatherer society to agricultural society to the industrial age each took progressively less time to occur, and our transition to an information society is taking less time still. Second, from a technological perspective, computational power is increasing exponentially, and increasing computational power facilitates the growth of other society-changing technologies such as biotechnology and nanotechnology. Third, from a more personal or experiential perspective, technology now changes culture on yearly basis. The combination of these three perspectives makes a powerful case for the existence of the phenomenon of technological acceleration.

Some theorists of technology believe that such technological acceleration is likely to result in a technological "singularity" – an event or rapid series of events that will transform civilization as we know it and make it difficult to imagine, let alone predict, what the shape of human society will resemble after the singularity occurs.[4] I describe briefly the arguments for this possibility, but stress that it is not necessary to believe that such an event is likely in order to think that our social and political institutions need to adapt to technological acceleration.

We now consider the epochal, technological and experiential perspective on change. From the longest term perspective, it seems clear that technological change is accelerating, and with it the basic shape of human society and culture.[5] Anthropologists suggest that for a hundred thousand years, members of the human species were hunter gatherers.[6] About ten thousand years ago, humans made a thousand-year transition to agricultural society.[7] From 1750–1900, with the advent of the industrial revolution, the West transformed itself into a society that thrived on manufacturing.[8] Since 1950, the West has been rapidly entering the information age. Each of the completed epochs has been marked by a transition to sharply higher growth rates.[9] The period between each epoch has become substantially shorter. Thus there is reason to extrapolate to even more and faster transitions in the future.

The inventor and engineer Ray Kurzweil has dubbed this phenomenon of faster transitions "the law of accelerating returns."[10] Seeking to strengthen the case for exponential change, he has considered in a more granulated way important events of the last thousand years to show that the period between extraordinary advances, such as great scientific discoveries and technological inventions, has decreased.[11]

4 Vernor Vinge, a mathematician and science fiction writer, first put forward the idea of the singularity in a speech at a conference sponsored by NASA. *What Is the Singularity*, http://mindstalk.net/vinge/vinge-sing.html. *See also* Ray Kurzweil, The Singularity is Near: When Humans Transcend Biology (New York: Viking, 2005).

5 Robin Hanson, *The Economics of the Singularity*, 45 IEEE Spectrum 6 (June 2008), *available at* http://www.spectrum.ieee.org/jun08/6274.

6 Nicholas Wade, Before The Dawn: Rediscovering the Lost History of our Ancestors 7 (New York: Penguin Press, 2006).

7 *Id.* at 125.

8 *See* David Hounshell, From the American System to Mass Production 1800–1932: The Development of Manufacturing Technology in the United States, at 15–46 (Baltimore, MD: Johns Hopkins University Press, 1984).

9 Hanson, *supra* note 5.

10 Kurzweil, *supra* note 4, at 35–51.

11 *Id.* at 19.

He also looked back to the dawn of life to show that even evolution seems to make transitions to higher organisms ever faster.[12] Thus, even outside the great epochs of recorded human history as well as within them, the story of acceleration is similar.

The second perspective on accelerating change is provided by the technology of computation. The easiest way to grasp this perspective is to consider Moore's law. Moore's law, named after Gordon Moore, one of the founders of Intel, is the observation that the number of transistors that can be fitted onto a computer chip doubles every 18 months to 2 years.[13] This prediction, which has been approximately accurate for the last 40 years, means that almost every aspect of the digital world – from computational calculation power to computer memory – is growing in density at a similarly exponential rate.[14] Moore's law reflects the rapid rise of computers to become the fundamental engine of mankind in the late twentieth and early twenty-first century.[15]

The power of exponential growth is hard to overstate. As the economist Robert Lucas said, once you start thinking about exponential growth, it is hard to think about anything else.[16] The computational power in a cell phone today is a thousand times greater and a million times less expensive than all the computing power housed at MIT in 1965.[17] Projecting forward, the computing power of computers 30 years from now is likely to prove a million times more powerful than those today.[18]

To be sure, many people have long predicted the imminent death of Moore's law, but it has nevertheless continued. Intel – a company that has a substantial interest in accurately telling software makers what to expect – projects that Moore's law will continue at least until 2029.[19] Kurzweil shows that Moore's law is actually part of a more general exponential computation growth that has been gaining force for over a hundred years.[20] Integrated circuits replaced transistors, which previously replaced vacuum tubes, which in their time had replaced electromechanical methods of computation. Through all these changes in the mechanisms of computation, its power increased at an exponential rate.[21] This perspective suggests that other

12 *Id.* at 14–20.

13 *See* Moore's Law, Intel Corp., http://www.intel.com/research/silicon/mooreslaw.htm (discussing Moore's law, which predicts that the number of transistors on a silicon chip will roughly double every 18–24 months, thus increasing microprocessor speed on a regular basis).

14 *See* Dan Burke & Mark Lemley, *Policy Levers in Patent Law*, 89 VA. L. REV. 1575, 1620 n.147 (2003).

15 *Cf.* Henry Adams, *The Education of Henry Adams* 379–390 (1980) (discussing the Virgin as the symbol of the middle ages and the steam engine as that of the nineteenth century).

16 Robert E. Lucas, Jr., *On the Mechanics of Economic Development*, 22 J. OF MONETARY ECON. 3 (July 1988).

17 *See* Ray Kurzweil, *Making the World a Billion Times Better*, WASH. POST at B-4 (April 13, 2008).

18 *See* HANS MORAVEC, ROBOT: MERE MACHINE TO TRANSCENDENT MIND 7 (New York: Oxford University Press, 1999).

19 *No End in Sight for Moore's Law*, SOAWORLD MAGAZINE (May 1, 2008), *available at* http://java.sys-con.com/read/557154.htm.

20 KURZWEIL, *supra* note 4, at 67.

21 *Id.*

methods under research from carbon nanotechnology to optical computing to quantum computing are likely to continue exponential growth, even when silicon-based computing reaches its physical limits.[22]

Another way to confirm and to provide perspective on accelerating computing power is to see it in the context of the culture of improvement that has been ongoing for the last one thousand years.[23] Once invented, technologies from plows to mills to steam engines undergo continuous and often exponential improvement.[24] Given the many axes available for improvement of an invention, many minds can work simultaneously on different aspects.[25] Thus the combinatorial power of multiple linear improvements can generate exponential improvement.

The salient feature of exponential growth of computers is their tremendous range of application compared with previous improvements. Almost everything in the world can be improved by adding an independent source of computational power. That is why computational improvement has far greater social effect than improvements in technologies of old. Energy, medicine and communication are now being continually transformed by the increase in computational power.[26] Given the prospect for continued exponential technological acceleration, some computer scientists and theorists are positing a technological "singularity."[27] In physics, a singularity is a rip in the fabric of the universe, such as that caused by a black hole, beyond which it is difficult for outside observers to see. By analogy, a technological singularity is a rip in the fabric of civilization beyond which it is difficult for observers now to comprehend the tenor of human life. The most important marker of such a singularity is thought to be computational power equal to human intelligence. Once humanity designs such a computer, such computational power can design further computers of even superhuman intelligence. Because these computers, unlike humans, can share information and work ceaselessly, technological change will then occur even more rapidly. Theorists put the date for the singularity any time between 2025 and 2100.[28] Although this idea has been discussed by theorists of technology for over a decade, it has now become more mainstream. Google and NASA are funding the Singularity University that will be focused on preparing for this event.[29] Although it is not necessary to credit the

[22] For a good introduction to quantum computing, see GEORGE JOHNSON, A SHORTCUT THROUGH TIME: THE PATH TO THE QUANTUM COMPUTER (New York: Alfred A. Knopf, 2004).

[23] *See* ROBERT FRIEDEL, A CULTURE OF IMPROVEMENT: TECHNOLOGY AND THE WESTERN MILLENNIUM (Cambridge, MA: Cambridge University Press, 2007) (describing continuous improvements along many technological fronts as the essence of Western culture).

[24] *Id.*

[25] *See* Martin Weitzman, *Recombinant Growth*, 113 QUART. J. ECON. 331 (1998).

[26] *See* KURZWEIL, *supra* note 4, at 243–250 (energy); 206–226 (biotechnology).

[27] Vinge, *supra* note 4.

[28] *See* Max More and Ray Kurzweil on the Singularity, http://www.kurzweilai.net/articles/art0408.html?printable=1.

[29] See David Gelles, *NASA and Google to Back School for Futurists*, FINANCIAL TIMES (February 3, 2008), found at http://www.ft.com/cms/s/0/8b162dfc-f168–11dd-8790–0000779fd2ac.html.

likelihood of a technological singularity in the near future to be concerned about the effects of accelerating technology on social institutions, the singularity represents the most extreme form of accelerated change.

The final perspective on accelerating technology is the most experiential. Technology changes the whole tenor of life more rapidly than ever before. At its most basic level, technological products change faster.[30] A visit to an electronics store or even a grocery store reveals a whole new line of products within 2 years, whereas someone visiting a store between 1910 and 1920 – let alone 1810 and 1820 – would not have noticed much difference. Even cultural generations move faster. Facebook, for instance, has changed the way college students relate in a few years,[31] whereas the tenor of college life would not have seemed very different to students in 1920 and 1960. Our political life is changed by technology. Four years ago the rise of blogs played an important part in the presidential election as they knocked down a key story about the incumbent President.[32] That event changed the dynamics of the election, and the existence of blogs may have made the difference in the final result. The election of Barack Obama was in some measure a function of his ability to raise large sums of money through the internet.[33]

Although social and legal institutions have always been shaped by the level of technology and the rate of technological change, the exponential rate of this change across such a broad range of invention makes it imperative to harness this technology for better governance in general and regulation in particular.

II. REGULATORY CHANGE IN AN AGE OF ACCELERATING TECHNOLOGY

Accelerating technology has implications for regulatory policy generally, because it makes future technological change more relevant to current regulation. In a world of technological stasis, there would be no need to consider technological changes, because the costs and benefits of regulation would not be changed by technology over time. But as technology changes ever faster, the stream of costs and benefits can change radically, making future technology ever more central to current regulatory decisions. Thus modeling future technological change needs to be made a central and formal part of any cost–benefit analysis. Moreover, given the importance of

30 Ray Kurzweil, *The Law of Accelerating Returns*, March 7, 2001, http://www.kurzweilai.net/articles/art0134.html?printable=1.

31 Maria Tess Shier, *The Way Technology Changes How We Do What We Do*, Wiley Interscience, December 15, 2005, http://www3.interscience.wiley.com/cgi-bin/fulltext/112217008/PDFSTART. *See* Matthew Vanden Boogart, *Uncovering the Social Impacts of Facebook on a College Campus* (2006), http://krex.k-state.edu/dspace/bitstream/2097/181/1/MatthewVandenBoogart2006.pdf.

32 Mark Memmott, *Scoops and Skepticism: How the Story Unfolded*, USA Today, September 21, 2004, *available at* http://www.usatoday.com/news/politicselections/nation/president/2004-09-21-guard-scoops-skepticism_x.htm.

33 Matthew Mosk, *Obama Rewriting Rules for Raising Campaign Money Online*, Wash. Post, March 28, 2008, at A06.

technological change, any government regulatory regime must consider whether government elicitation of technological change may dominate direct regulation as a policy option. Thus subsidies and prizes for technologies should be considered as an integral part of the regulatory review process.

Second, accelerating technology makes it important to consider the huge benefits of possible outcomes as well as possible catastrophes, even if those outcomes are relatively improbable. Catastrophe has been analyzed in risk regulation,[34] but enormous transformative benefits have not been touched upon. For instance, it seems conceivable that accelerating technology could lead to continuous improvements in longevity, permitting some individuals today to have very long or almost indefinite life spans, if they could live long enough to catch the next wave of improvements. That prospect may mean that it is rational for individuals to undertake some risky courses of health treatment because of this prospect and for government to permit them to choose such risks. I call the possibility of such an event that positively transforms human life the Pascal regulatory effect after Blaise Pascal who argued that it may be rational to believe in God even if his existence is quite improbable given the huge benefits of doing so.

Third, accelerating technology accentuates the issue of intergenerational equity. If accelerating technology will make the next generations hugely better off, then there are arguments for transferring wealth from those generations to previous generations. Concretely, for instance, such considerations may suggest that social security's exactions on the younger generations are less unfair than they appear.

The danger is that taking such important issues into account in regulatory review increases the risks of the inevitable errors in centralized planning. The antidote is for regulation to be guided by more accurate, dispersed information than it is today. Thus, in this section, I also discuss how two important technologies of information need to be deployed in the regulatory review process – prediction markets and empiricism. Prediction markets help assess likely future outcomes and thus become an essential part of regulation as the prediction of future consequences become an integral part of current regulation. Empirical assessment is more backward looking, but it allows more disciplined testing of different regulatory regimes to help assess which ones should be made permanent for the future.

Thus a theme of this section is that accelerating technology itself provides the crucial tools with which to update the regulatory process. The task of modern regulatory review is to make optimal use of these tools. To be clear, for the foreseeable future, the technology-based methods will remain tools. Decisions will continue to be made by regulators assisted by new technologies, not by the new technologies themselves.

34 Most notably in Richard A. Posner's CATASTROPHE: RISK AND RESPONSE (NEW YORK: OXFORD UNIVERSITY PRESS, 2004).

A. *The Integration of Technology and Regulation*

Because of technological acceleration, future technology is more relevant to current decisions about regulation. First, it is relevant in the simple sense that the timing of regulation may change depending on the future technological landscape. For instance, if we could predict the development of carbon-eating plants 20 years out, we should be less interested in controlling current emissions.[35] Second, because of the relevance of technogical change, regulatory processes will need better tools, such as prediction markets, to chart technology's likely future course. Finally, the costs (and benefits) of regulation may crucially depend on government decisions about technology itself, including decisions to fund it directly or provide prizes for certain technological innovation. As a result, regulatory decisions need to be better integrated with decisions about how to spur technological change.

Accordingly, regulatory review should incorporate technological assessment, including recommendations for government programs to spur technology. Thus Section III will focus on translating the opportunities created by accelerating technology into new mandates and structures within OMB to integrate technological innovation with regulatory assessment.

1. The Timing of Regulation

I begin by considering the effect of technology on the timing of regulation. First, the decision whether to adopt a regulation now can depend on the predictions about the arc of technological change. Accelerating technology may create better mechanisms to take carbon out of the air than are currently available. Accordingly, it may be more effective to delay certain kinds of emission standards, because those kinds of emissions can be cleaned up at low cost in the relatively near future.

But although the possibility of technological innovation will sometimes favor less regulation, it will sometimes favor more regulation. Climate change provides again a good example. For instance, technological acceleration may ameliorate a central problem of regulating global emissions – the difficulty of creating effective regulation without participation of important nations around the globe.[36] If regulating emissions encourages even further innovation, the new technology may be sufficiently cheap to be used even by nations that did not participate in any regulatory regime. Thus the sensitivity of innovation to particular regulations may provide an important impetus for domestic regulatory regimes even in the absence of a global consensus.

It is clear that considering whether to postpone or accelerate a regulation in light of technological change is part of cost–benefit analysis and central to it in an age

[35] As suggested by Freeman Dyson, *A Question of Global Warming*, N.Y. Review of Books (June 12, 2008)

[36] *See* Richard Posner, note 34 at 157 (2004).

of accelerating technology. Nevertheless it might be questioned whether regulatory review's scope should be expanded to include these issues. If the shape of future technology is unknowable, it is a waste of money and a misdirection of OMB's mission to consider such matters.

But the future shape of technology can be estimated, even if it is uncertain. Technological assessment is just another aspect of regulation under uncertainty. There are tested methods to address uncertainty in regulation and new methods, spurred in part by accelerating technology on the horizon. Failure to take account of uncertainties in our regulatory regime would result in less beneficial decisions. First, some technological change can be predicted with relative certainty. Moore's law, discussed earlier in this essay, predicts expansion of computer capacities for the next two decades. As a result, scientists have sometimes postponed solving mathematical problems today that can be resolved much more rapidly within a few years. Some have argued that other processes, such as the improvement of solar panels, are also now approximating a glide path of predictability.[37] Second, even processes of improvement that cannot be predicted so accurately may be estimated within parameters. As Richard Posner has noted, most catastrophic risks are profoundly uncertain, and yet a failure to address these uncertain risks may well make us worse off.[38] For instance, even when we cannot fix the probability of catastrophic climate change with certainty we should consider that possibility in our regulatory assessments, if we can estimate the range of its risk. Similarly, we should consider the possibility of technological innovation if we can estimate the range of its likelihood. Finally, as discussed in section III, regulations can be designed to require periodic revisions that will take advantage of growing certainty about the future technological landscape.

2. Prediction Markets

Moreover, new technology provides us with new ways of estimating the likelihood of future technology in the regulatory context. The most important is provided by prediction markets. As Michael Abramowicz outlines in his superb book, *Predictocracy*, prediction markets are markets in which traders can buy shares that pay off if a specified event occurs, like a presidential victory or finding evidence of life on Mars.[39] As of August 4, 2011, for instance, on Intrade – an online gambling market – one can buy for 55 cents a share that will pay a dollar for a victory by the Democratic

[37] http://technocrat.net/d/2008/5/16/41454/ (cost of solar panels falling at rate of 6% every year).

[38] Posner, *supra* note 34, at 171–175.

[39] Michael Abramowicz, Predictocracy: Market Mechanisms for Private and Public Decisionmaking (2007). *See also* Robert W. Hahn, *Statement on Prediction Markets*, AEI-Brookings Joint Center for Regulatory Studies (May 2007), http://ssrn.com/abstract=984584.

presidential candidate in 2012 and for 44 cents a share that will pay a dollar for a victory by the Republican presidential candidate.[40]

It is important to note that the market not only predicts a Democratic victory in 2012, but also gives a rough likelihood of the victory. If the probability of a Democratic victory was much less than 55%, then presumably individuals would not have an incentive to bid so much, and if it were much higher, they presumably would have an incentive to bid more. The market also gives a rough probability of a judgment that is not likely to happen – a Republican victory.[41]

To be sure, the notion of gambling on events is not dependent on technological acceleration. Bookmakers made odds on the elections of medieval popes.[42] Gamblers' betting lines accurately predicted the winner of presidential elections in the United States in the last century.[43] But as a practical matter, the internet permits these markets to operate on a much larger scale and with far lower transaction costs than they could have in the past.[44]

Most importantly for improving information in public policy, new technology makes it possible to make markets in thousands of events, including conditional events.[45] A conditional event market permits people to bet on an event conditional on another event occurring. Before the 2008 election, on the market Intrade one could have bet on the economic growth rate conditional on Senator Obama being elected and conditional on Senator McCain being elected.[46] Of course, only one of these bets could have paid off, and the wagers will have to be returned to those who bet on the growth rate on the candidate who is not elected.[47] But in the run up to the election, such markets, if they drew sufficient money, could provide very useful comparative information about which President would be better for the nation on a variety of important axes of policy.

The greatest advantage of prediction markets over other sources of information is that they aggregate information from those who have incentives to get their predictions right. If you do not know anything about the subject in which shares are being sold, it is a bad idea to participate, because you are likely to lose out to those who

40 http://www.intrade.com/jsp/intrade/contractSearch/.

41 On the theory of prediction markets, see Justin Wolfers and Eric W. Zitzewitz, *Prediction Markets*, 18 J. Econ. Persp. 107 (Spring 2004); Robert W. Hahn and Paul C. Tetlock, *Using Information Markets to Improve Public Decision Making* (AEI-Brookings Joint Center for Regulatory Studies Working Paper 04–18, 2005).

42 Michael Ott, *Pope Gregory XIV*, The Catholic Encyclopedia vol. 7 (New York: Robert Appleton Company 1910), *available at* http://www.newadvent.org/cathen/07004a.htm.

43 Paul W. Rhode and Koleman S. Strumpf, *Historical Presidential Bidding Markets*, 18 J. Econ. Persp. 127, 127 (2004).

44 Wolfers and Zitzewitz, *supra* note 45, at 122–23.

45 *Id.*

46 http://www.intrade.com/jsp/intrade/contractSearch/. At the moment, however, these markets are not thick enough to yield real information.

47 The prospect also impedes the growth of conditional markets. But subsidization of markets by the government could remove this impediment.

do.[48] Moreover, like the stock market, a prediction market elicits information from those who would otherwise be unlikely to offer it to the public, because the market provides them a monetary incentive to act on their otherwise private information.[49] The argument is a Hayekian one: information about the world is dispersed among many people.[50] A key to sound governance is to sustain institutions that aggregate that information. Prediction markets are like markets generally: their prices pool that crucial dispersed information.

There is no reason that prediction markets cannot be made on the emergence of certain technologies.[51] These future technologies can be defined functionally, and then markets can be made when they occur. For instance, we could define a technology as one that removes carbon dioxide for a certain cost per amount of carbon dioxide removed. Prediction markets can make a market in the emergence of technology by a certain date conditional on a certain regulation being imposed. This kind of market can help evaluate how likely various regulations are to elicit beneficial technological change.[52]

Elsewhere I describe laws that needed to be changed to permit more and thicker prediction markets to arise spontaneously.[53] But given the substantial public benefits of predictions markets focused on the technical questions of our technological future, an administrative agency should be willing to subsidize such markets to get the maximum number of informed players. Such subsidies could certainly include paying for all the transaction costs of such a market. Particularly in technical areas, prediction markets may also need to exempt players from taxes to encourage greater participation. Such subsidies and tax exemptions can be justified by the benefits such a market provides to regulators. In such technical areas, the market may not always be thick enough to prevent manipulation by special interests and appropriate conflict of interest rules might be needed. For these reasons, I suggest in Section III that a unit be established in OMB to develop and deploy policy expertise in the creation of prediction markets across the regulatory agenda.

48 Hahn, *supra* note 39.

49 Cass R. Sunstein, *Group Judgments: Deliberation, Statistical Means, and Information Markets* (U. Chi. L. & Econ., Olin Working Paper No. 219, 2004), *available at* http://ssrn.com/abstract=578301.

50 Cass R. Sunstein, Infotopia: How Many Minds Produce Knowledge 118–121 (New York: Oxford University Press, 2006).

51 Michael Abramowicz has already suggested the use of prediction markets in administrative agencies. See Abramowicz, *supra* note 39 at 162–194. His focus is largely on the uses of such markets to predict whether regulation will reflect normative preferences. There is also a substantial need to predict the future shape of technology.

52 Conditional markets are not a panacea, however, because sometimes the conditions are correlated with other factors that are really cause the phenomenon to be predicted. Perhaps the impulse to have a certain kind of regulation is correlated with some kind of behavior that will encourage the technology even in the absence of the regulation. I discuss these complexities in John O. McGinnis, Accelerating Democracy (Princeton University Press) (forthcoming).

53 *See Id.*

3. Government Support for Technology as Alternative or Complement to Direct Regulation

Accelerating technology also requires that the decisions that the government makes more generally about laws that bear on technological innovation be connected to the regulatory process. If changing technology is important to regulatory decisions, then the government should consider whether certain programs to elicit appropriate technology may be the most cost-efficient way of solving a social problem either as a substitute for regulation or in conjunction with regulation.

It might be thought that the government should not be involved in establishing policy to encourage any particular technology as opposed to promoting general policies for encouraging innovation. If the government chooses the appropriate regulations, companies will have the incentives to invent technology so that other companies can comply with those regulations most cheaply. Regulation in this sense would be the invisible hand of technological progress. In these cases, the value of the technological innovation can be easily captured by those who invest in it.

But there are several problems with fully accepting this argument. First, a principal difficulty with regulatory solutions is that special interests may inhibit the creation of purely regulatory solutions. Programs with concentrated costs and diffuse benefits are hard to enact.[54] For instance, concentrated groups such as energy companies may successfully oppose regulations curbing global warming. In contrast, government spending to subsidize technology or to establish a technology prize to solve the problem that regulation addresses can be financed with general revenues. Programs with both diffuse benefits and costs are easier to enact. In a world of technological stasis, often the regulatory solution may be the only alternative. But in a world of technological acceleration, technological solutions may be not only feasible technologically but also the most feasible solutions politically.

A second reason to believe that even efficient regulation will not stimulate the optimal amount of innovation in technology is the international nature of many regulatory problems in the environmental and health areas. Again, climate change provides a salient example. If other nations, particularly developing nations, do not regulate emissions, companies operating in those nations will not have the right incentives to buy technology that reduce emissions, and technologists will not have the right incentives to produce it.[55] Even worse, because of the imperfect

54 *See* Einer R. Elhauge, *Does Interest Group Theory Justify More Intrusive Judicial Review?*, 101 YALE L.J. 31, 43 (1991) (suggesting that such a constellation of interest results in opposition to legislation that is in the public interest).

55 *See* Jonathan H. Adler, Eyes on a Climate Prize: Rewarding Energy Innovation to Achieve Climate Stabilization, 21-22 (Case Research Paper Series in Legal Studies, Working Paper No. 2010-15, 2010) available at http: papers.ssrn.com sol3 papers.cfm?abstract_id 1576699.

enforcement of property rights in much of the world, companies cannot be sure that other companies in foreign nations will use their inventions without payment. As a result, companies creating technology cannot be confident that they will capture the worldwide value of their innovation. Thus regulation within our own jurisdiction may not assure that all the social benefits of technology are internalized to produce the correct amount of innovation. In other words, creating cheap technological solutions to pollution will have global effects that mere domestic regulation may not replicate.

Thus it is possible that the best solution for solving a problem of externalities, such as climate change, will not be a purely regulatory one, but a scheme to elicit particular technology that reduces that kind of emissions in question. Put in another way, the best regulatory response will include a package of technological incentives. It is important to note that designing the appropropriate technological incentives is itself a nice question. For instance, when the government can observe the quality of research and development before the results are known, it may be prudent to subsidize the research.[56] When the government cannot easily observe the quality of the research, prizes may be superior.[57] Of course, determining how far the government can evaluate quality may itself be quite complicated. The need for such analysis supports the proposal in Section III to add a unit devoted to technological analysis in OMB's regulatory review process.

B. *Accounting for Elysian Benefits*

Another issue raised by accelerating technology is how to consider small probabilities of extremely, almost unimaginably, beneficial consequences. For instance, the possibility that medical discoveries may lead to much longer life spans raises hard issues for regulators. How is one to value such an outcome in a cost–benefit analysis, whatever its probability?

The extraordinary benefits of accelerating technology are the flip side of its potential catastrophes – a subject that has been extensively analyzed and will not be independently considered here.[58] Accelerating technology increases the possibilities of both kinds of outcomes. Indeed, the same technological advances may raise the prospect of both. Thus another question in regulatory review is how to compare the small probabilities of catastrophe and almost infinite beneficence that might arise from an accelerating series of technological breakthrough. Elysian benefits may sometimes be as relevant to regulatory calculation as doomsday scenarios.

[56] *See* William A. Master & Benoit Delbecq, Accelerating Innovation with Prize Rewards, found at http://technocrat.net/d/2008/5/16/41454/. See also Adler, *supra* note 55, at 32–39 (discussing relative advantages of prizes).

[57] Id.

[58] *See, e.g.*, Posner, *supra* note 34.

One might argue that we should weight catastrophic loss, such as destruction of the entire human species, more heavily than an equal probability of an extremely beneficial outcome, like a technological singularity that creates indefinite lives,[59] because the total catastrophe precludes the possibility of any future life and the potential progress life brings with it. But this argument seems too facile. For instance, beneficial discoveries may provide the resources or knowledge to help preclude catastrophes.

In particular, strong forms of artificial intelligence might have beneficial externalities in helping predict and avoid catastrophic events, as well as helping evaluate the hidden benefits and costs of other accelerating technologies.[60] Thus even a relatively small probability of creating strong artificial intelligence might justify a substantial government program of subsidization or prizes designed to stimulate its creation.

Radical life extension is another instance of an Elysian benefit of which regulation must take account. For instance, if indefinite life spans are a possibility, then individuals could well choose rationally to seek risky treatments so that they are more likely to be alive at a time when technology puts people then alive on the glide path by which they can reach such life spans. Indeed, this question presents a kind of secular version of Pascal's wager. Just as it may be rational to believe in God even if there is only a tiny probability of his existence, given the infinite benefits of such belief, it may be rational to take risks to live to a certain time in the future if by doing so one can enjoy what one regards as the almost infinite benefits of an indefinite life. Such an analysis would be relevant to the U.S. Food and Drug Administration's regulation of drugs. For instance, even if a drug is on balance harmful or at least largely ineffective, the possibility of its extending life even in rare cases for a substantial period becomes a substantial benefit in a period in which accelerating technology may lead to lives of infinite duration.

Once again, prediction markets are likely to help regulators to consider how much they should count these possibilities in their calculation. One advantage of prediction markets is that they not only provide evidence of whether an event is unlikely, but also of the probability that even an unlikely event will happen. Regulatory choices about the structure of our health care system bear on the pace of medical innovation and thus on the possibility of radical life extension.[61] Thus prediction markets about the likelihood of increases in longevity depending on the structure of the health care system will yield useful information, even if the probability of radical life extension is substantially less than 50%.

59 For discussion of the technological singularity, see *supra* notes 27–30 and accompanying text.

60 See John O. McGinnis, *Accelerating AI*, 104 N. W. L. Rev. 1253 (2009).

61 The theory behind radical life extension is that in an age in which medical advances occur with increasing rapidity, an individual merely has to live until medical advances permit him to surmount diseases that would otherwise kill him. If he continues to do this, he will have reached an "escape velocity" that will permit a life of indefinite length.

Richard Posner has objected to the utility of prediction markets about events that depend on scientific predictions on the grounds that these issues are the domain of scientists and that the man on the street can add little information.[62] But even if it were true that only experts could contribute first order scientific information, the bounds of expertise are contested and unclear in complex social problems whose solution sits at the intersection of many disciplines. A market could help mediate between disagreeing experts from different disciplines by assessing their relative confidence in their predictions. Moreover, even if a layman lacks substantial knowledge of a field, he may have enough information about the relative insularity and biases of experts to perform a useful mediating function. For instance, he may think that economists face a more competitive market and more scrutiny from colleagues than scientists on issues of public concern and so tend to favor their predictions about resource depletion.

Another concern is that prediction markets may have trouble accurately predicting low probability events because people tend to have a long-shot bias.[63] Most people are not good at discerning the difference between small and very small likelihoods.[64] But predictions for long shots can be seen through the prism of that bias and then discounted to an extent. Moreover, there is some evidence that information markets may still aid in correcting even greater biases people have in estimating the probability of long-shot events in the absence of markets.[65]

Indeed, prediction markets may help regulators not only directly in evaluating small probability events, but also indirectly by increasing public awareness of their relevance. These markets address a problem humans have in taking account of small probabilities. When the probability of an event is sufficiently small, it has been argued that individuals sometimes seem to dismiss the event from their calculations, and they may not give enough weight to events that are less likely than not to happen.[66] But prediction markets will dramatize the probabilities of various events by giving them a firm number and making individuals more aware of the comparisons of the likelihood of events likely to happen and those not likely to happen.

C. *Intergenerational Equity*

Another important effect of accelerating technology is to raise in a more acute form than ever before the problem of intergenerational equity. If accelerating technology likely makes the next generations much wealthier than those in this generation, it prompts questions of whether we need to take more account of intergenerational

62 See Posner, supra note 34, at 175–176.

63 See Erik Snowberg and Justin Wolfers, *Explaining the Long Shot Bias: Is it Risk Love or Misperceptions* 118 J. Pol. Econ. 723 (2010).

64 *Id.* at 743–744.

65 http://predictocracy.org/blog/?p=110 (comments of Michael Abramowicz)

66 *See* Posner, supra note 34, at 120–121 (2004).

redistribution in our policies.[67] Ever since there has been substantial economic growth, a potential issue of intergenerational equity has existed. But accelerating technology makes the issue far more pressing, because it increases the wealth gap between proximate generations, making redistribution thinkable.

One obvious area where such considerations are important is Social Security. Social security has been criticized as an intergenerational transfer from the young, who as a class have relatively few assets to the old who have relatively many assets. But to the degree that accelerating technology will very substantially increase the wealth of those starting out in the workforce today, this argument is much diminished.[68] But it is also relevant more generally to the question of who should bear the costs of regulation today. It is frequently said that we should not leave messes, like global warming, for our grandchildren to clean up. But if they are far wealthier they may be in a better position to pay the costs of cleanup.

Before considering each of these issues, it is important to distinguish intergenerational efficiency from intergenerational equity.[69] Intergenerational efficiency focuses on assuring that the public investments we make in such matters as a health, safety, or environmental protection are efficient ones for the long term. Intergenerational efficiency requires that we use a discount rate to assess the benefits (and costs) generated by our future regulations so that we can compare the effects of this regulation with the money that the regulation costs.

Intergenerational equity in contrast, focuses on treating people across the generation equally when we make our regulatory decisions. Of course, the concept of equity may well be more contested than the concept of efficiency, because there are many different views of the equity required within a generation, let alone among generations. This conceptual difficulty is relatively unaffected by the fact of accelerating technology, and thus I will not investigate here what is the appropriate standard for intergenerational equity. Instead, I will assume here a Rawlsian view that requires us to respect the difference principle and be concerned with policies that help the most disadvantaged so long as these policies do not offend a set of fundamental rights.[70] It seems to me that these policies can also be justified by an intergenerational appeal to the original position: individuals cannot choose the generation in which they will be born and thus would, according to the traditional Rawlsian analysis, want to give priority to the least advantaged among the generations.[71]

67 Andrew C. Kadak, *The Societal Fairness of Intergenerational Equity*, 2 PROC. INT. CONF. PROBABILISTIC SAFETY ASSESSMENT AND MANAGEMENT 1005–1010 (1998).

68 Even without accelerating technology, Neil H. Buchanan has noted that on relatively pessimistic assumptions of economic growth, subsequent generations are likely to be much better off. See Neil H. Buchanan, *What Do We Owe Future Generations?* 77 GEO. WASH L. REV. 1237, 1272 (2009).

69 *See* Louis Kaplow, *Discounting Dollars, Discounting Lives: Intergenerational Distributive Justice and Efficiency*, 71 CHI. L. REV. 79, 79 (2007).

70 *See* JOHN RAWLS, A THEORY OF JUSTICE (Oxford: Clarendon Press, 1971).

71 In my view, the maximin rule does not necessarily call for large-scale redistribution once one adds in a certain degree of social realism about the institutions work.

Indeed, in a world of accelerating technology, intergenerational issues of equity may become more pressing than intragenerational ones, at least those within a single nation, because there is evidence that technological innovation in contemporary society filters more and more rapidly down to the poor.[72] For instance, the almost universal adoption of cell phones has happened much faster than the adoption of televisions. Moreover, the intellectual property at the root of technology can be used simultaneously by everyone. For instance, discoveries in medicine may rapidly increase everyone's longevity. In contrast, the fruits of the real or personal property that was the basis of most wealth in the past cannot be as easily consumed jointly. A civilization with almost universal access to accelerating innovations might have a greater measure of effective equality, even within large income differentials.

To evaluate issues of intergenerational equity, we need to predict the income of future generations. Although economists have a variety of long-term predictions of economic growth, regulators should not just choose one. Instead, regulators should undertake decisions based on a range of forecasts weighted by their likelihood. That process will capture as well as we can the estimate of a future generation's income. Prediction markets provide once again the mechanism that can provide such information. Although individuals and institutions are already engaged in making these long-term economic predictions, regulatory authorities lack the capacity to choose among them and should therefore use prediction markets to discipline their choices. Prediction markets are also useful to predict the existence of future technologies that may illuminate how much better off future generations will be.

Of course, the growth rates that will lead to an increase in the well-being of future generations are dependent on regulatory and other governmental decisions. One political danger of considering intergenerational equity issues at all is that the politicians and the regulators who are accountable to them will have incentives to engage in more intergenerational redistribution than is justified in order to please current voters.[73] One constraint on this tendency may be the conditional prediction markets described previously. Markets can be made in rates of economic growth conditional on important regulatory and/or tax schemes and at least provide information about wealth-destroying redistribution.

One other complication can arise because of the greater wealth of subsequent generations. As generations get wealthier, their prices for enduring risks, like the

See Richard Epstein, *Rawls Remembered*, http://www.nationalreview.com/comment/comment-epstein112702.asp. For instance, redistributionist institutions are likely often to misfire, and those running them have little interest in directing in distributions to the least advantaged. Moreover, individuals have an interest in making their children (and other collateral relatives) somewhat better off than they are. Thus they will tend to favor policies that promote economic growth, even at some expense to their share of the resources.

72 See Kurzweil, *supra* note 4, at 469–470 .

73 Neil Buchanan makes the important related point that our generation should try to avoid the economic and political crises. Our self-interest and that of subsequent generations substantially converge in these matters. *See* Buchanan, *supra* note 68, at 1284–6.

risk of death from pollutants, rise. This is a well-known fact of insurance. A risk-averse person's utility rises less proportionately than his increases in wealth.[74] That is why the need for insurance rises as wealth rises. Regulation decreasing the risk of death provides a form of social insurance, and the need for that arises along with wealth as well.[75] Discounting costs that future generations will face, including their risks of death, is a matter of generational efficiency, not equity. But as a matter of generational equity, regulators must remember that their preferences will change and thus the amount that a future generation will demand for enduring a risk of death may rise.

Accelerating technology and the growth it will bring in its wake may make this issue more salient. Because of the possibility of life extension, one can imagine that the amount of money that a future generation may demand for risks of death may grow exponentially. Radical life extension offers the prospect of accelerating increases in life span until people live more or less indefinitely in some form. Thus by avoiding death in a particular year, one may get onto a glide path to a much longer or even indefinite life span. Thus the amount demanded for risk of death will also get larger because what a person gains through avoiding this risk is greater.

This consideration suggests that prediction markets in longevity and medical innovations will be particularly necessary to perform risk regulation in a sensible matter. Agencies may have to subsidize such markets because the opportunity cost of those who can make useful predictions will be high, given the increasing demand for life-extending technology to which they will be contributing.

D. *Empiricism*

A final area of integration of modern technology with regulatory review lies in the area of empiricism. As I have described elsewhere,[76] the ever-growing power of computers is creating a bonanza for empiricism – both in the ability to create data sets and to analyze those data sets to draw conclusions about the causes of social phenomenon. Such empiricism can be enormously helpful to the regulatory process. It permits sustained analysis of which, if any, regulation will best address a market failure.

Making use of such new tools is important in an age of technological acceleration. First, as described previously, the stakes of regulation may be greater. Second, because it is possible that the scope of regulation in general may become greater,

74 See Albert H. Mowbray et. al., Insurance: Its Theory and Practice in the United States 32–35 (6th ed., New York: McGraw-Hill, 1979) (explaining that risk-averse person's utility increases less than proportionately with increases in wealth, thereby making insurance attractive to such a person).

75 *Id.*

76 See John O. McGinnis, *Age of the Empirical*, 137 Pol'y Rev. 47 (2006), *available at* http://www.hoover.org/publications/policyreview/3402126.html.

it may be more difficult and yet more important to retain the public's confidence in the accuracy and impartiality of the regulatory process. A focus on showing in a more scientific manner that a regulation helps solve a problem better than the alternatives can help accuracy and demonstrate impartiality.

If empiricism is likely to provide a source for better and more rapid democratic decision making, then the regulatory regime should create structures to foster more and better empiricism. I discuss two kinds of structures here – decentralization and randomization. In Section III, I discuss what changes can be made to executive orders and within the structure of the Office of Information and Regulatory Affairs (OIRA), including establishing a unit focused on the benefits of learning through regulation.

1. Decentralization

Of all the governmental structures facilitating empiricism, the most important is decentralization. One of the most powerful investigative tools in social science is to compare how different laws work in different jurisdictions, whether states or nations.[77] Such careful comparisons make manifest the consequences of good and bad policies.[78] But that kind of investigation can work only if policies are permitted to differ among jurisdictions.

Of course, advancing empiricism is not the only consideration in reaching the proper tradeoff between centralization and decentralization in the polity. When one jurisdiction is able to cause substantial externalities to another, those externalities provide reason to create a more centralized government spanning the different jurisdictions to create policies to address the externalities.[79] In contrast, when policies in an area do not create substantial externalities, federalism has other advantages: decentralization creates a market for governance by allowing different jurisdictions to compete to attract people and investment.[80] It also permits the formulation of diverse policies that meet the diverse preferences of people.[81]

Thus the degree of centralization of government policy is a judgment call, depending on the substantiality of the externalities that more centralization could address

77 *See, e.g.*,Fred C. Zacharias, *Who Can Best Regulate the Regulators or Who Should Regulate the Regulators*, 65 FORD. L. REV. 429, 455 (1996) (against federal regulation of ethics because empirical tests of best practices will thrive best through permitting diversity).

78 *See, e.g.*, Jerome H. Reichman and Rochelle Cooper Dreyfuss, *Harmonization Without Consensus Critical Reflections on Drafting a Substantive Patent Treaty*, 57 DUKE L. J. 85, 129–129 (2006) (arguing against premature harmonization of patent systems to gain data about what works).

79 Henry N. Butler & Jonathan N. Macey, *Externalities and the Matching Principle: The Case for Reallocating Environmental Regulatory Authority*, 14 YALE J. ON REG. 23, 25 (1996) (arguing that regulatory authority should be allocated to areas affected by spillovers from one jurisdiction to another.)

80 *See* Richard A. Epstein, *Exit Rights Under Federalism*, 55 LAW & CONTEMP. PROBS. 147 (1992).

81 *See* Michael W. McConnell, *Federalism: Evaluating the Founders' Design*, 54 U. CHI. L. REV. 1484, 1494 (1987).

and the quantum of competition and satisfaction of diverse preferences that decentralization can permit. But the possibility of sustained empiricism adds a heavy weight on the decentralization side of the scale: decentralization facilitates the empirical investigation of the differing consequences of social policy. Thus, far from being a relic of the past, federalism's virtues are reinforced by modern technology, because our computer age makes federalism a more effective discovery machine. In Section III, I discuss the way the President can order agencies to consider the dynamic advantages of federalism and other forms of decentralization in the regulatory review process.

2. Randomizing Policy

Another way for empirical social science to assess the effects of social policy is to use natural experiments that take advantage of a random event that permits the direct measure of the effect of a given policy, such as increasing the number of police in an area. But the government can also create natural experiments through policy and thereby facilitate social learning. The most obvious way it can do so is through randomization – assigning different individuals or groups of individuals to different programs at random. Social scientists can then measure the different outcomes. The idea here has parallels in trial of a new medication. In order to ascertain whether a new drug is efficacious, a randomized trial is devised in which one group of patients is given a new drug and another is given a placebo or an old drug. The difference in outcomes can be measured and attributed to the difference in treatments.

The government has already engaged in some random social experiments. But these experiments have mostly centered on "individuals who are somehow disadvantaged."[82] Thus, for instance, a wide variety of studies have focused on how differences in job training or counseling in government programs affect employment.[83] Individuals were randomly assigned to different "treatments," such as receiving different training, and the results were measured. There is room for more such experiments. The nation still has a variety of public assistance programs, and the nature of the conditions required of recipients is still subject to debate.[84] The extent to which the prolongation of unemployment benefits results in longer unemployment is still controversial and could be assessed through social experiments.[85]

[82] David Greenberg, Mark Shroder, Matthew Onstott, *The Social Experiment Market*, 13 J. ECON. PERSPECTIVES 157, 159 (1999).

[83] *Id.* at 160.

[84] *See, e.g.*, Lee Anne Fennell, *Relative Burdens: Family Ties and the Safety Net*, 45 WM. & MY. L. REV. 1453, 1508 (2004) (discussing different conditions that encourage recipients of public assistance to control medical costs).

[85] As recognized by the President Obama's economic adviser, Larry Summers, see LAWRENCE H. SUMMERS, UNEMPLOYMENT IN THE CONCISE ENCYCLOPEDIA OF LIBERTY, http://www.econlib.org/library/Enc/Unemployment.html.

Sadly, however, the government has almost never conducted policies directed at testing policies affecting middle- or upper-class individuals or corporations or the structure of government itself. Policies to be tested that affect individuals would include how electricity charges that vary with time might improve usage patterns or how differing deductibles for health care coverage would affect medical usage and health outcomes.[86] Another area for testing would be the efficacy of private school vouchers as opposed to traditional public schools on individuals of varying income levels. It is one of the most important yet contentious issues in education today and can be assessed best through randomized testing.[87]

Randomization can also be applied to corporations and the government itself. For instance, there remains a substantial debate over whether the conditions the Federal Communications Commission (FCC) imposes on public broadcasters are effective at meeting their purported objectives.[88] The FCC could randomize some of the policy conditions to test their effectiveness in encouraging a diversity of voices and other public policy objectives. The amount of concentration in an industry that should trigger antitrust scrutiny of mergers remains controversial.[89] The antitrust enforcement agencies could apply different standards to different industries and evaluate the results. There is a wide variety of auctions that government can use for its contracts.[90] Procurement policy could at times be randomized to gain information about the advantages and disadvantages of different methods.

In the health and safety area as well, gains can derive from randomization. It is often disputed whether a particular regulation contributes to safety. Take Occupational Safety and Health Administration, for instance. An experiment in which certain regulations would be imposed on some factories and not on others offers the real prospect of determining whether those regulations are useful.

Of course, natural experiments are not always going to be worth the cost. Social phenomena often have complex interactions. Even if in Minneapolis it is discovered that pupils assigned to charter schools fare better than those assigned to public schools, it might turn out that it is something about charter schools in Minnesota that cannot be generalized throughout the United States. Nevertheless, even if most social phenomena have such thick and complex causation that interactions are important, such an experiment has value because it will change our prior beliefs

86 Greenberg et al., *supra* note 82, at 160.

87 For a discussion of latest issues in the school voucher debate, see Terrence Moe, *Beyond the Free Market: The Structure of School Choice*, 2008 B.Y.U. 557 (2008).

88 *See, e.g.*, Kimberley Christensen, *Campaign Finance and Electoral Reform*, 24 Buff. Pub Int. L. Rev. 131, 172 (2005–2006).

89 *See* Eleanor Fox, *Consumers, Beware Chicago*,84 Mich. L. Rev. 1714, 1716 (1986) (suggesting that an important question in antitrust law is what level of concentration has problematic effects.)

90 Harold J. Krent and Nicholas S. Zeppos, *Monitoring Governmental Disposition of Assets: Fashioning Regulatory Substitutes for Market Controls*, 52 Vand. L. Rev. 1703, 1720 (1999) (discussing debate over the nature of optimal auctions).

about how important a factor charter schools is likely to be in improving educational outputs. The salient question is whether this additional information is worth the costs, broadly assessed, of the experiments. For that reason, a unit within OMB should develop and deploy the expertise to help determine the extent to which regulation should be designed to promote such social learning.

In Section III I suggest new provisions for the executive order on regulatory review that would require regulations including social experiments where doing so would help generate data to resolve policy debates.

It might be objected that it is wrong to use individuals as the subjects of social experiments, as contemporary guinea pigs for the benefit of future generations. But in medicine, randomized trials of new pharmaceuticals are routinely undertaken. There as here, the justification is that we are not confident which course of action will provide more social benefits in the long run. Randomization of social policy should only be used when there is a genuine controversy over what social policy to follow, and those are the precise circumstances in which it is politically plausible that randomization may enjoy political support.

While there is no Supreme Court precedent on the subject of randomization, Henry Friendly, one of the greatest judges of the twentieth century, emphasized the public benefits of randomization in rejecting the only substantial legal challenge to embedding social experimentation within regulatory policy.[91] In that case New York State appeared to require family members in the households of public recipients to engage in training or working, but imposed these requirements in only certain districts, choosing them on a random basis. Judge Friendly responded to the equal protection challenge by noting the policy of social experimentation was wholly rational, given the importance of experiments to both medical and social policy.

III. ACCELERATING REGULATORY REVIEW

The analysis offered in the previous section suggests that the government's regulatory review process should be updated in a variety of ways to address the issues raised by accelerating technology and to make use of the information resources that the revolution in information technology is providing. The need to take into account technological acceleration is not unique to the government regulatory sector. Private companies must consider the effects of future technological change.

But the government may have more trouble integrating such predictions into its regulatory assessment. First, government is less skilled than business and science at integrating innovations into routines. Second, government bureaucrats are risk

[91] *See* Aguayo v. Richardson, 473 F. 2d 1090 (2d Cir. 1973) (Friendly, C.J.), This case is discussed extensively in Adam M. Samaha, *Randomization in Adjudication*, 51 Wm. & My. L. Rev. 1, 42–43 (2009).

averse in ways that will discourage this kind of innovation in particular. At least at first, modeling the effect of technological change will prove a novel and inexact art. Therefore, government regulators may be in danger of being subject to criticism for their analysis, giving them incentives to avoid this kind of assessment altogether because, unlike actors in the private sector, they cannot personally capture a substantial portion of the gains their innovative analysis makes possible.

Bureaucrats also may be risk averse because of concerns about their own function. Although technological change will certainly not always be a reason to postpone or forestall regulation, sometimes it will be. Moreover, technological assessment may show that some current functions of their bureaucracy are already obsolete. Given bureaucrats' interest in maintaining and expanding their jurisdiction and budgets, they are not likely to welcome the risks that come from generating information that may provide reasons to change the bureaucratic structures and mandates. Thus it will be important to create a new framework of regulatory review that emphasizes the salience of technology and provide both the additional resources and bureaucratic structures to pursue this objective. Only then is the process of regulatory review likely to overcome bureaucratic inertia and reflect the need to adapt to technological change. As discussed next, both revisions in the President's order on executive review and new legislation will be necessary to create that framework.

A. *Creating Technology Review and a Technology Office Within OIRA*

Currently, by order of the President, the OIRA reviews all major regulations and, to the extent permitted by law, evaluates whether their costs exceed their benefits. In my view, it is important for the President to amend OIRA's regulations expressly to take account of technological change.[92] Perhaps the most important recommendation would be to make technological review an explicit part of cost–benefit analysis. For reasons discussed previously, mapping current and future technological capabilities in an area is now a crucial part of cost–benefit analysis, but because of bureaucratic inertia, the analytic innovation necessary to address technological innovation may not be taken without express direction. Moreover, if such analysis is taken as part of the President's regulatory review of all important orders, agencies throughout the executive branch will take technological assessment more seriously.

In order to carry out technological assessment, OIRA will need to establish a technology unit within its office. Although technological assessment is necessary to carry out effective cost–benefit analysis, some of the skills needed for technological assessment are different from those needed to crunch numbers. In particular, the office would need to employ scientists as well as economists. Congressional legislation is needed to establish the requisite funding and staffing.

[92] Currently, there is a brief reference in OMB circular A-4 for the need for regulations to reflect "credible assessments of technology." See Circular A-4, Regulatory Analysis (September 17, 2003).

B. *Integrating Regulatory Review with Funding of Technology*

As discussed in Section II, the government needs to integrate its regulatory review with the funding of technology, because often the optimal approach to a problem will be regulation combined with additional technological incentives. Technological incentives require money in the form of subsidies or prizes. As a result, congressional appropriations will be required.

It would be wise for Congress to appropriate some money for this purpose generally and permit OIRA to determine how it should be spent. For the same reasons that it is more efficient for Congress to delegate decisions over the precise shape of regulations to agencies, it is efficient for Congress to delegate at least some of the funding decisions about technology. Nevertheless, for large sums of money to be given as subsidies or awarded as prizes, Congress will need to be involved to assure financial accountability and legitimacy. To assure prompt consideration of such issues, Congress could pass framework legislation that permits the President to submit requests for technology funding related to regulation through a special legislative track. On the receipt of such requests, the legislation would create fast-track procedures that assure that such requests will be voted on without the interposition of procedural delays, like those caused by the filibuster rule.

C. *Creating the Flexibility to Modify Rules to Reflect Technological Change*

Given the speed of technological change, it will be important to assure that the regulatory process itself has enough flexibility to take account of these changes. The ossification of the regulations has long been a concern of the administrative process, and thus many proposals to address that entrenched difficulty can be translated to address the opportunities afforded by accelerating technology.

Lynn Blais and Wendy Wagner have the most promising proposals to address regulatory ossification and by extension to create structures well designed to update regulations by reference to the acceleration in technology.[93] One proposal is for an agency to specify that regulations should change if certain technological advances arise.[94] As they suggest, building such revisions into regulations themselves will also be helpful for planning purposes for affected companies.

A second proposal permits a petition process to allow others to require the agency to take account of technological change.[95] Strangely, Blais and Wagner suggest that this petition process be permitted only when information arises that makes more stringent regulations appropriate. But there is no reason to impose a one-way ratchet on the petition process. As discussed previously, at times it may be cost-effective to

[93] Lynn E. Blais & Wendy E. Wagner, *Emerging Science, Adaptive Regulation, and the Problem of Rulemaking Ruts*, 86 Tex. L. Rev. 1701 (2008).

[94] *Id.* at 1731–2.

[95] *Id.* at 1734.

postpone (and thus by extension suspend regulations) if the new technology or the prospect of technology in the future permits us to address a problem in a cheaper way. But so long as the petition proposal is permitted to address both the need for more and the need for less regulation in light of technological change, the proposal is a sound one.

Third, they suggest that a science panel be convened to review the scientific basis of particular regulations on a periodic basis.[96] They worry, however, about the costs of such a proposal.[97] An even more important concern, in my view, is that it is hard to be sure *ex ante* in what areas such a review will be most useful. Thus another new mandate for OIRA would be to have the office of technological assessment conduct mini-reviews on an ongoing basis through the use of prediction markets and scientific analysis. The office could then choose to convene scientific panels only when new scientific or technological developments warrant. Such an office would also permit the government to make effective cost-benefit decisions about what areas are in most need of monitoring.

D. *Prediction Markets*

As discussed at length in Section II, prediction markets are central to predicting the arc of accelerating technology, along with many of the other issues that technological acceleration will make salient. OIRA needs to create within itself a unit devoted to prediction markets. Although such prediction markets will be useful in a variety of regulatory areas, the expertise required to have accurate predictions will be common to all of them, and thus a central clearing house for market information should be made part of OIRA. As described previously, some government prediction markets may be thin enough that conflict-of-interest regulations may need to be designed to prevent special interests from skewing the market.

E. *Revising Regulations to Reflect Need for Empirical Testing*

Accelerating technology is creating more resources for empirical testing. Because of the lower cost and greater effectiveness of empiricism, the government should be conscious to create regulations that provide where possible the greatest opportunities for empirical learning to resolve still disputed areas of social policy.

The most important opportunity, as discussed in Section II, is for the government to create randomized experiments. There I offered some specific examples where random experiments would be helpful. But the presidential order on regulatory review should be revised more generally to direct agencies to include such experiments whenever such experimentation will be useful to resolve disputed issues

96 *Id.* at 1737.
97 *Id.*

of policy. The complexity of the tradeoffs between the benefits provided by such experiments and their possible costs suggests that an office of empiricism should be established within OIRA.

Even in areas where there are not opportunities for randomized experiments, OMB should assure that all government data are transparent and accessible, because statistical investigations need data above all. Over the years, government has become more transparent; the Freedom of Information Act was landmark legislation in this regard.[98] But with the rise of empiricism, there are even greater reasons to make public everything government does (outside of sensitive national security matters, business trade secrets, and matters that trench on personal privacy). Thus government data should be posted automatically and in machine-readable form so that it can be easily used for empirical research. Agencies would do well to follow the lead of the U.S. Securities and Exchange Commission (SEC), which has begun an initiative both to tag electronically the data the SEC receives from companies and to make sure that its future data are displayed in the most readily usable form.[99]

As discussed previously, decentralization is useful to create the conditions for empirical learning. The federalism executive order thus should be revised to make clear that the opportunity for empiricism afforded by federalism should be taken into account before federal regulators decide to preempt state regulatory regimes.[100] Through all these changes in the process of regulatory review the government would better structure itself as an instrument of learning from the dispersed information available in the modern world and lessen its reliance on top-down decisionmaking.

CONCLUSION

To create the possibility of human flourishing, society's institutions of governance must respond to the rate of technological change. Because that rate of technological change today is accelerating, our own regulatory institutions must renew themselves to meet a new challenge.

Fortunately, at the heart of today's technological change are new ways of creating and analyzing information about social policy. The task of regulatory reform is thus, in no small measure, creating the legal regime that will best promote the integration of richer and more accurate forms of information into regulatory decision making.

In short, the regulatory review process must become a better mechanism for social learning from dispersed sources of information. This kind of improvement is all the more important because the tasks that regulatory review must consider are broader

[98] *See* 5 U.S.C. § 552 (1982), *amended by* Pub. L. No. 98–620, 98 Stat. 3335 (1984).
[99] *See* SEC Announcement, 2004-97, http://www.sec.gov/news/press/2004–97.htm.
[100] For the federalism executive order, see Exec. Order. 13, 132 (1999).

in scope and may be more urgent because of the high stakes of catastrophic risk and Elysian benefits. As a result, regulatory review needs to reduce the errors inherent in centralized planning. Using the information tools created by technology itself offers the best prospect of keeping our regulatory regime abreast of accelerating change.

13

The Ethical Issues in Nanotechnology

Persons and the Polity

Laurie Zoloth

In 1917, as a war marked by blindingly murderous technology wound down, a curious phenomena swept Britain: a belief in spiritualism and magic, which existed directly alongside a sincere faith in science. It was a time when electrical engineering was transforming the Victorian landscape, electrifying factories for evening shift work, and linking the Empire with new, rapid, forms of communication – the technology was both mesmerizing and terrifying, threatening a physical and social order of long stable relationships of production and creation. It was a time when the breadth of the global world was fully revealed, and the Empire became linked by instant communications. The premise was that beneath the new technology, the new industrial organization, and the mystery of electrification lay a life-world within an unblemished and innocent nature that must be uniquely protected. This was signified perhaps in its purest form by the fascination with the Cottingley Fairies, fairy figures "captured" on the new media of photography, when children in the household of one of Britain's first electrical engineers took photographs they claimed as real. What is important about the Cottingley fairies was that they were widely believed, evidence of the limits of science and of the public unease and uncertainty about the "wonders" of the future. After all, the fairies seemed, in the context of the times, as neither more nor less fantastic than the idea of electrical currents coursing through the air, or across wires traversing a many miles, or of photography itself, which created narratives that were both real (in science) and set piece constructions of a photographic framer (in the case of the fairies). The father of the children who reported the fairies was part of the effort to electrify the textile factories, transforming the darkness of the north English winter night into perpetual day.

Belief in things unseen made oddly consonant bedfellows with technology. The children's photographs were not only championed by Harry Houdini, three experts from the Kodak camera company, and others who also embraced industrialization, modernity, and progress and were skeptical about fakes, but also by Sir Arthur Conan Doyle and other spiritualists who had an interest in promoting the existence of a spiritualized world and contact with ghosts.[1] The girls' photographs were fully and widely believed to be authentic (which seems remarkable, given what looks to our eyes to be an obvious fake) because they had not *claimed* to see fairies, they had the *mechanical photographic proof* they had seen them. Of course, faked photographs, as was demonstrated in the pages of *Science* in 2007 with the faked stem cell cloning photos,[2] would become a constant feature of science hoaxes. In 1917, after a decade of scientific progress, an optimistic public was ready to believe in what the experts confirmed was true.

I begin this chapter on the ethical issues in nanotechnology and the environment in this manner for several reasons. First, because of the linguistic tension between the norms of scientific inquiry and the norms of the cost–benefit driven discourse that is at the core of much of the modern response to environmental catastrophe.

Second, because the story indicates a central error that was operative in the first industrial revolution, that a focus on short-term problems obscures long-term and more consequential ones. In that era, the public fears were that electricity might explode, or cause strange fires, when the real problems were rather more complex – the social realities that changed when shift-work into the night became a norm rather than an impossibility. They feared the loss of innocence or "naturalness" and missed seeing the need to insist on procedures for justice as the technology unfolded in ways that would create class inequities beyond those imagined in a more agrarian economy.

Third, because it represents the problem of the title: ethical issues in new technology are not only faced by persons, but by a larger polity, who are often at some remove from the direct effects. Thus, thinking about need and risk must be both larger yet more specific than is usually advanced. Both need and risk emerge from embodied persons, to be sure, but within complex communities of interest and position.

Lastly, the story illustrates a final point: the power of new technology to do work that was largely understood as bettering the world eventually overcame the predicable sequences of opposition, fear, and fantasy that queried it. Electricity, if it were to be suddenly introduced into our skeptical 2010 world, would be fiercely opposed, but that would be an error, overall, for without it, modernity and all of its salvations could hardly exist. It is likely that nanotechnology, a new way of manufacture and control of the natural world, will allow a similar set of advances. However, this narrative

[1] Bensley, D. Alan. Why Great Thinkers Sometimes Fail to Think Critically. *Skeptical Inquirer*, 30(4) (July/Aug 2006):47–52.

[2] Kolata, Gina. A Cloning Scandal Rocks a Pillar of Science Publishing. *The New York Times*, December 18, 2005. http://www.nytimes.com/2005/12/18/international/asia/18clone.html?_r=1&ref=hwang_woo_suk.

is not an argument for an uncomplicated acceptance of any new technology, for example, nanotechnology – the subject of the inquiry in this essay – because of its utilitarian appeal. Indeed nanotechnology, precisely because it presents so powerful a case, needs to be the subject of external reflection, serious moral concern, and equally powerful oversight. It is the argument of this essay that there are other ethical considerations as well, not only issues of negative rights and protection, but also of positive duties toward the future. This essay aims to outline some of the ethical questions that can be raised about the short- and long-term consequences of this new technology; explore how they will affect our debates on the effects of such technology on the person, polis, and place; and suggest some responses for normative guidelines as the science proceeds.

I. ALL NEW TECHNOLOGY PRESENTS SIGNIFICANT ETHICAL DILEMMAS

It is a logical commonplace to worry about moral and ethical issues whenever new technology is advanced. We are correct to ask whether the scientific advances and the technology that is derived from them will achieve the moral aims of societies – justice, individual human flourishing, and an increased sense of general social welfare. We live in a world that is haunted by the tragic specters of the late twentieth century, in which technology was turned to murderous uses, and in which scientific reassurances failed to prevent technological collapses that harmed thousands. We greet new science and technology in the context of a series of massive industrial disasters: Chernobyl, Three Mile Island, Bhopal, the Exxon-Valdez, and the latest and worst yet, the BP oil spill. Each such disaster, and each disclosure that the "most sophisticated" technology and most confident assurances have failed, deepens the generalized sense that the promises of technology are unstable and the dreams of the scientist are suspect. Medical research is haunted by another series of disasters: the Tuskegee syphilis trials,[3] the Oak Ridge radiation studies,[4] and most recently, the Jesse Gelsinger case, in which confident University of Pennsylvania scientists promised safe "gene therapy" to young clinical trial participants and withheld the full extent of risk, which led not only to the tragic death of Mr. Gelsinger,[5] but also, eventually, to the halting of human genetic modification trials for an extended period.[6] Despite the widespread use of genetically altered food and crops in the

3 The Tuskegee Syphilis Study Legacy Committee, "Final Report of the Tuskegee Syphilis Study Legacy Committee," Tuskegee University, http://www.tuskegee.edu/Global/story.asp?S=1141982.

4 Moss, William and Roger Eckhardt. The Human Plutonium Injection Experiments. *Los Alamos Science*, 23 (1995):177–233. www.fas.org/sgp/othergov/doe/lanl/pubs/00326640.pdf.

5 Stolberg, Sheryl G. Institute Restricted after Gene Therapy Death. *The New York Times*, May 25, 2000. http://www.nytimes.com/2000/05/25/us/institute-restricted-after-gene-therapy-death.html?ref=jesse_gelsinger.

6 Stolberg, Sheryl G. Trials Are Halted On Gene Therapy. *The New York Times*, October 4, 2002. http://www.nytimes.com/2002/10/04/us/trials-are-halted-on-a-gene-therapy.html?ref=jesse_gelsinger.

United States, there is a constant unease over the use of genetically modified organism (GMO) crops in Europe,[7] and even when a technology is proven safe – as in childhood vaccines – the public is willing to believe that it is not.[8]

Nanotechnology is built on the historical terrain of scientific mistrust/untrustworthiness. The fear that nanotechnology is dangerous is not unique, to be sure, but it is still the first question bioethicists raise when considering the range of other, more intricate moral issues. Risk versus benefit discussions are not the whole of ethics, but they are necessary, if not sufficient, conditions for reflection. Because nanotechnology emerges after a long series of remarkable advances in the latter twentieth and early twenty-first centuries, neither the safety issues nor other concerns that are raised by bioethicists when we are called to reflect on the ethical implications of nanotechnology are being raised for the first time. Let us turn to the classic responses to all new technology in bioethics literature.

Is It Safe? Health and Safety Issues Considered

First, bioethicists traditionally raise the issue of whether new technology, called into service to alleviate human illness, will in fact result in new risks to human health. This concern is not an inconsequential problem. Nanotechnology is useful because it creates and manipulates at the scale of DNA, intracellularly, and because of the ability of particles to pass through cellular walls and be taken into the cell nucleus using the processes and pathways of endocytosis. Cell signaling pathways used by the immune system, for example, will react in some way to the presence of nanoparticles, and more research will need to be done to find out how this reaction will affect the cellular function of the targeted cell and finally, the entire organism.[9] Unknown health risks were the rate-limiting step in the first bioethical discussions about genetic modification in 1975 at Asilomar. The response to fear of creating genetically altered *Escherichia coli* bacteria was to draft safety guidelines, including the call to do the research in Level 4 containment facilities and to establish a standing national oversight committee of scientists, public advocates, and bioethicists to review all genetic modification experiments.[10,11]

7 Dunmore, Charlie. EU Move to Break GM Deadlock Could Sow Discord. *Reuters News Service*, June 29, 2010. http://in.reuters.com/article/idINIndia-49750020100629\.

8 Harris, Gardiner. "Journal Retracts 1998 Paper Linking Autism to Vaccines." *The New York Times*, February 2, 2010. http://www.nytimes.com/2010/02/03/health/research/03lancet.html.

9 Kim, Eun-Young, et al. Gold Nanoparticle Oligonucleotide Complexes Impart Widespread Changes in Gene Expression in Primary Immune Cells. Division of Infectious Diseases, (unpublished) Feinberg School of Medicine, Northwestern University, Chicago.

10 Walters, LeRoy and Julie Gage Palmer. *The Ethics of Human Gene Therapy*. Oxford: Oxford University Press, 1996.

11 Tucker, Jonathan B. and Raymond A. Zilinskas. The Promise and Perils of Synthetic Biology. *The New Atlantis*, Spring 2006:25–45.

Health risks in nanotechnology are unknown and are difficult to test. Some researchers[12,13] have noted that any particle that is introduced into the cell will trigger changes in cell activity. Froines noted the similarities between carbon nanotubes and prions; Kim et al. noted the activation of pathways similar to that of asbestos. Thus the first questions that need to be raised about the immediate and long-term effects of newly created nanoparticles – whether they are designed for use within the human body or whether they are designed for use in the environment – involve how they are to be made, controlled, and then tracked after release. Where and how are they released during manufacture? Where do the particles go after they are used and excreted in the urine or waste of animal or human subjects and patients in the future? Do they aggregate and are their properties different when they do? How many generations of cell lines and animal models have been studied to determine how the long-term use of nanoparticles affects organisms? Although it is reassuring to be told that "nanoparticles already naturally occur" or that "humans have used nanoparticles since the medieval period to make stained glass windows,"[14] such an explanation is not fully adequate. Many past practices (using naturally occurring mercury to make watches iridescent or dyeing beaver pelts with lye to make hats) turned out to be harmful, and many naturally occurring substances affect our health negatively when manipulated or used in new ways or in mass scale. It is likely that some risk to health may be discovered, either for individual patients (as in the risk of radiation or chemotherapy) or for societies (as in the risks of electricity) and then, once more fully analyzed and openly publicized, the risks of use can be weighed against the benefits.

Will It Be Used for War? Dual Use of Technology

Bioethicists traditionally raised the problem of "dual use" of new technology, which means that any new biological intervention intended to cure disease could also be used for nefarious purposes. Nanotechnology, because of its size, is undetectable, raising fears that it could be used without the knowledge of citizens or subjects. Nanotechnology's applicability for use in detection of biological chemicals means that it could be used to detect neurotransmitters and, some fear,[15] alter neurotransmitters. Nanotechnology coupled with neuroscience is a potent intervention, because we know that minute alterations in the blood–brain chemistry can affect behaviors.

[12] Froines, John R. Nanotechnology – How to Define Risks and Control Them. (Presentation) www.cns.ucsb.edu/storage/conf/presentations/John%20Froines.pdf

[13] Kim, Eun-Young, et al. Gold Nanoparticle Oligonucleotide Complexes Impart Widespread Changes in Gene Expression in Primary Immune Cells. Chicago, IL: Division of Infectious Diseases, Feinberg School of Medicine, Northwestern University. (unpublished)

[14] Ratner, Mark A. and Daniel Ratner. *Nanotechnology: A Gentle Introduction to the Next Big Idea*. Upper Saddle River, NJ: Prentice Hall PTR, 2002.

[15] Wolpe, Paul Root. Treatment, Enhancement and the Ethics of Neurotherapeutics. *Brain and Cognition*, 50 (2002):378–395.

Nanotechnology's ease of use is a wonderful feature of its potential in the developing world, but on the other hand, its portability and invisibility give potential to nations and powers outside of the usual spectra of United Nations sanctions on warfare or weapons production. Nanotechnology linked to new biology, or synthetic biology, raises fears that it could be used to create de novo pathogens, to which specific populations could be particularly susceptible.

Even without the fears raised by intervention in human bodies, detection of substances by nano-chip technology, such as the "biobarcode,"[16] raises fears of surveillance without consent. To be sure, as Ratner and others have noted,[17,18] dual use is a feature of any new technology, starting with iron smelting. However, critical ethical questions can be raised about who controls the experiments and how limits are set on use for military purposes. There is a long history of moral discourse about these questions that emerged from the development of nuclear weapons, and drawing on this expertise will be critical for the considerations of dual use in nanotechnology.

What about Mistakes? Errors and Their Inevitable Place

Even with the most careful structures in place, errors in the use of new technology are inevitable.[19] All human activity is error-ridden and takes place across a constantly mutable knowledge base, accomplished within the flawed temporal and sensorial phenomena available to human-willed activity.[20] Errors become an ethical problem in new technology only when their existence and their probability is denied, or when no provision for their inevitability is created. We can say without a doubt that there will be some fundamental mistake in the further development of nanotechnology. This mistake may well occur in a way we cannot anticipate or regulate. Some mistakes will be avoidable, however, or will be minimized by transparent and accountable regulation. The question to raise is: what regulations or procedures need to be set in place to protect against errors we can anticipate? What regulations or procedures need to be set in place that might provide a shield against the consequences of errors beyond our imagination?

[16] Nam, J.M., C. S. Thaxton and C. A. Mirkin. "Nanoparticle-based bio-bar codes for the ultrasensitive detection of proteins." *Science*, 301(5641) (Sep 26, 2003):1884–6.

[17] Ratner, Mark A. and Daniel Ratner. *Nanotechnology: A Gentle Introduction to the Next Big Idea*. Upper Saddle River, NJ: Prentice Hall PTR, 2002.

[18] Institute of Medicine. *Globalization, Biosecurity, and the Future of the Life Sciences*. Washington, DC: National Academies Press, 2006.

[19] Rubin, Susan B. and Laurie Zoloth, eds. *Margin of Error: The Ethics of Mistakes in the Practice of Medicine*. Hagerstown, MD: University Publishing, 2000.

[20] Herresl, Edmund. Ideas Pertaining to a Pure Phenomenology and to a Phenomenological Philosophy: First Book General Introduction to a Pure Phenomenology. In *Edmund Herresl Collected Works Volume I: Phenomenology and the Foundations of Science*, translated by T. E. Klein and W. E. Pohl. New York: Springer Publishing Co., 1980.

The public fear of errors is heightened by the public impatience with scientific hubris. Critics looking for hubris need look no farther than the nanotech websites themselves, which proclaim the scientists "superstars" or make claims that nanoparticles will "revolutionize" or "transform" all of science. Although a certain level of enthusiasm for one's work is critical, hubris becomes an ethical issue when other sources of expertise are not taken seriously. Thus a part of oversight is the structuring of the questions of outsiders to the discipline. The creation of what is called a "hermeneutics of suspicion" when questionable texts are studied would be an important move forward in reading the texts of nanotechnology. Is it unrealistic to ask for certain virtues – such as humility, honesty, or courage in the face of failure – for scientists? Classically, such calls for virtue have been a part of academic research. Reflecting on the problem with hubris is the other side of the problem of error.

Can You Tamper with Nature? Synthetic versus "Natural" in Technology

A complaint made against nanotechnology, one raised with some frequency in bioethics, is the claim that nanotechnology represents the final assault of the synthetic and artificial against the natural world.[21,22,23] Nanotechnology is indeed a manipulation of the material world at the molecular level. However, the claim that this is a new or a different act cannot be fully justified. I have argued in the past[24] that the act of manipulation of the tangible world in which human primates live is one of the fundamental aspects of humanity itself. Manipulation of larger objects or ones very far away, as in reworking coastlines or sending probes to Mars, or manipulation of smaller objects, such as in the work of nanotechnology or synthetic biology, is largely a function of our increased ability to visualize the world with more power and specificity. It is a change in power and scale, but in intent or motive it is a quantitative not qualitative change. All interventions in the natural world disrupt the givenness of the present moment to suggest that human history is progressive and incremental, and iterative changes can be made that advance our understanding and credible use of the world. In fact, calls for a return to the natural light cycles were a part of the concern about electricity in our earlier example. But the "naturalness" of the world is an elusion phenomena, largely created in the twenty-first century in a fictive space. Even the sharpest critics of nanotechnology do not really advocate for a complete

[21] Bostrom, Nick. In Defence of Posthuman Dignity. *Bioethics*, 19(3) (2005):202–214.

[22] Levin, Yuval. Imagining the Future. *The New Atlantis*, Winter 2004:48–65.

[23] Kass, Leon R. Preventing a Brave New World. *The New Republic Online*, June 21, 2001. www.csus.edu/indiv/g/gaskilld/ethics/BanCloning.doc.

[24] Zoloth, Laurie. 'When You Plow the Field Your Torah Is with You': Genetic Modification and GM Food in the Jewish Tradition(s). In *Acceptable Genes? Religious Traditions and Genetically Modified Foods*, edited by Conrad Brunk and Harold Coward, 81–114. Albany, NY: SUNY Press, 2009.

return to a hunter and gatherer society, which is perhaps the last moment before the creation of the slash and burn agriculture that begins what we call civilization. Can any of the arguments that call nanotechnology unethical because it interferes with nature be properly defended? It may not be the case, but what can be found within this genre of argument is the deeper sense that organic processes may be irreversibly lost if they are undone, or that some complexities, not understood, may be destroyed in a synthetically designed world. Raising the question "what happens when this organic process is changed and what are the risks and benefits for individuals and our society?" is a more directed way to deal with the inchoate calls for naturalness that are a feature of much of the literature of opposition to nanotechnology.

Will It Be fair? Justice and Distribution in New Technology

In the previous sections, this essay reviewed the most common ethical issues raised about nanotechnology and made the larger claim that many of them are versions of risk assessment research. They are similar in kind and in many details to earlier arguments about genetic intervention, or electricity, or radiation research. However, asking about the possible harms of science and asking for care, humility, and oversight of science projects is only half of the ethical issue. The other set of ethical issues concerns our duties, responsibilities, and liberty interests when the science is useful, desired, and costly. Thus we are called to ask the ethical question of justice and fair distribution.[25,26] My opening example, which raised questions that were a serious part of the Industrial Revolution and noted how the issues of power and control and expertise are long-standing, is based on reflection on the classic questions of the Industrial Revolution: how will the change in industry create a more humane society? What will be the relationship between a free market and a democratic state? How will the workers participate in controlling the conditions of their daily lives?[27] Thus, when we turn our attention to the claims of nanotechnology, we are moved to ask: how will the change in industry create a more humane society? What will be the relationship between a free market and a democratic state? How will all citizens participate in controlling the conditions of their daily lives?

Such questions must be a part of research in the ethics of nanotechnology, especially because the efforts are supported by both an aggressive market economy, and in the public section, funding in a time of increased calls for justice within

[25] Zoloth, Laurie. Person, Polis, Risk, Need and Uncertainty: Justice and consent in emerging technology. In *Nanotechnology and the Weight of Justice: The Social Scale*, edited by Laurie Zoloth, Daniel Seltzer and Bryan Breau (not yet published) 2010.

[26] Traina, Cristie. Old Wine, Old Wineskins: Nanotechnology and Justice. In *Nanotechnology and the Weight of Justice: The Social Scale*, edited by Laurie Zoloth, Daniel Seltzer and Bryan Breau (not yet published) 2010.

[27] Zimmer, Carl. *Soul Made Flesh: The Discovery of the Brain*. New York: Free Press, 2004.

such venues. At Northwestern University, for example, we hold public Town Hall Meetings in which we ask scientists to discuss such questions as:

> What ethical choices do you think may be created by your research? How will your work benefit our town? How may it challenge us? What should a citizen of our town know in order to participate in these choices? What policies are needed to regulate your research? Who should oversee them?

Such questions were useful for addressing the ethical issues, widespread and significant, about the limits of power that new science and technology affords. Critics of new technology worry that it will deepen divisions that are already unjust or create a "digital divide" or a "genetic divide" that will potentiate the existing divisions created by colonial organization. As noted by Diamond,[28] technological advances created long-standing divisions in the pre-modern period. Will new technology make the world more unjust?[29] Or will it make it more "flat"?[30]

Responding to the Issues: An Argument Typology

My contention is that there are five types of arguments that are mounted in response to these ethical challenges. First is the medical-scientific one: basic science exploration is a part of the way that humans are constituted, and in particular, it is a human response to the existential situation of humanity. We are born into suffering, morbidity, and mortality, and science is simply our way of responding. Even if nothing comes of research, research itself is a human and a moral gesture, like art, that is a critical human response. To stop its direction would be impossible and wrong and would distort our very being. The second argument is that of therapeutic pragmatism: new technology, from electricity to nanotechnology, is ethically defensible because it has pragmatic application for human use. This instrumentality, often linked to utilitarian justifications, moves scientific advances from the lab to the clinic, regardless of larger social effects. Linked to this argument are the market-based drivers: new science and its associated technologies will allow market expansion, and denying this is a form of Ludditism and would retard the natural regulatory power of free markets. In this argument for the warrant for nanotechnology, a free-market call for technology is the best determinant of its value and will lead us to the best distribution scheme as well. There are theo-philosophical reasons to support new technology. Some have argued (including this author) that acts of research directed toward repairing a world theologically understood as broken are acts of impelled

[28] Diamond, Jared. *Guns, Germs and Steel: The Fates of Human Societies*. New York: W. W. Norton & Co., 1997.

[29] Robert, Jason S. Just Scenarios: Cultivating Anticipatory Assessment of Novel Technologies. In *Nanotechnology and the Weight of Justice: The Social Scale*, edited by Laurie Zoloth, Daniel Seltzer and Bryan Breau (not yet published) 2010.

[30] Friedman, Thomas. *The World is Flat: A Brief History of the Twenty-first Century*. New York: Farrar, Straus and Giroux, 2005.

responsibility.[31,32] Policy and political arguments are made to support technology as well: science is a part of the neoliberal project of modernity. Its veracities undermine authoritarian regimes and inspire personal and collective liberty. Further, science and technology are the way that the largest global challenges of climates and energy limitations can be overcome. In this way, say the supporters of nanotechnology, the catastrophes of the Industrial Revolution, such as pollution, or geopolitical realities brought into being because of the need for oil and natural gas, can be cured. They argue that nanotechnological fixes must be supported despite their cost because they could create new answers to older problems. Now that we are aware of the need for caution, goes this argument, and attentive to the reality of error, hubris, and injustice that plagued earlier technologies, we can create far better devices or products.

In academic circles, unlike the larger public discourse, the reality and necessity of science and technology is largely assumed. Here, the issue is *self* regulation: can scientists be organized to regulate science and the transition to new technology, or should this process be externally organized? This question becomes far more interesting when new technology such as nanotechnology suddenly and massively attracts the attention of the marketplace. Can scientists self-regulate, and if so, under what constraints? Can the market be an adequate control on harms to the polis? Private industry funds nanotechnology. Academic scientists are urged to "spin-off" companies that may choose to have ethical oversight, but may choose not to. As academic salaries are constricted, the idea of finding sources of income linked directly to one's hypotheses becomes logical. Yet, can a scientist whose income is profoundly affected by the market's perception of her work accurately assess the safety of the technology that she creates?

Premise 1: Publically Funded Science Must Be Publicly Regulated Science

Scientists have a unique insight into their work and the possibilities for ethical issues that it creates and should be involved in science regulation. Yet publicly regulated and funded science is in the best interest of states, polities, and persons because scientists alone cannot create complete regulatory strategies for oversight.

As the emerging biotech institutions were created in the early 2000s, several different methods of regulation of science emerged. These different models offer different ideas about how to regulate nanotechnology, which as a field has not created a robust self-governance oversight, nor does it fall under one coherent federal or international system for regulation. The earliest efforts in the regulation of science began with the recognition that nuclear research held considerable dangers

31 Dorff, Elliott N. and Louis E. Newman, eds. *Contemporary Jewish Theology: A Reader*. New York: Oxford University Press, 1999.

32 Zoloth, Laurie. 'When You Plow the Field Your Torah Is with You': Genetic Modification and GM Food in the Jewish Tradition(s). In *Acceptable Genes? Religious Traditions and Genetically Modified Foods*, edited by Conrad Brunk and Harold Coward, 81–114. Albany, NY: SUNY Press, 2009.

and that every single person involved in its use, if at all possible, was to come to a common understanding of its dangers. Physicists led the way first toward internal codes of ethical use and then to national and international demands for regulation. Nuclear technology is hardly subtle. Its creation requires vast and visible sums of money and large projects. The amount of resources needed is largely only available to states. Molecular biologists working with recombinant DNA in the early 1970s also recognized the importance of self-regulation, both to quell national public fears and to set internal standards in the hope of avoiding government interference that might create a permanent ban.[33] The initial recombinant DNA advisory committee began as a National Academies project and then became the Recombinant DNA Advisory Committee ("the RAC"), housed in the U.S. Department of Health and Human Services, which still meets to advise and approve all rDNA de novo research. Because much of genetic modification does not involve human subjects, it falls outside of traditional research codes, which were defined by the clinical terrain of their first use. Limits are set by the RAC, for example, on inheritable genetic modification.[34,35] But other technologies, such as stem cell research and synthetic biology, can also be done successfully at far smaller scales, and it was these scientists that met to define the ethical, technical, and political perimeters for their fields in the early 2000s (and, which I argue here, should be duplicated by nanotechnology scientists). Stem cell researchers and synthetic biology researchers work nearly exclusively at a few academic centers and have organized sturdy organizations with international codes, large public town hall meetings to discuss governance, and ongoing oversight for their products. Stem cell researchers were aware that traditional institutional review boards (IRBs) would not possess the specialized knowledge to set limits on research and thus called for the development of Embryonic Stem Cell Research Oversight (ESCRO) committees at each institution where the research is conducted. A national oversight committee, set in place by federal guidelines, has finally, in 2010, begun to explore federal regulatory ideas, but only later after new federal cells were approved, long after scientists using privately funded cell lines had established the need for self-regulation.

Synthetic biologists meet at international conferences and argue about how best to control unregulated and harmful uses of their technology, controlling scientific publication unless internal standards are met, controlling presentations at conferences, and finally, developing policies in which biotech companies that support new science advances (e.g., companies that provide DNA sequences) are supported

[33] Walters, LeRoy and Julie Gage Palmer. *The Ethics of Human Gene Therapy*. Oxford: Oxford University Press, 1996.

[34] Frankel, Mark S. and Audrey R. Chapman. Human Inheritable Genetic Modifications: Assessing Scientific, Ethical, Religious, and Policy Issues. AAAS, 2000. http://www.aaas.org/spp/sfrl/projects/germline/report.pdf.

[35] Cohen, Cynthia B. *Renewing the Stuff of Life: Stem Cells, Ethics, and Public Policy*. New York: Oxford University Press, 2007.

or avoided unless they comply with programs, such as the Blackwatch program, to search for deadly gene sequences. Blackwatch programs are an invention not of governments, but of scientists concerned with harmful "dual use" of synthetic biology.

Premise 2: All Risks Are Fundamentally Unknowable

We can study the social impacts of nanotechnology, in one sense, when we compare its emergence with other technological changes, as I have done with electricity. Yet anticipatory anxieties have their limits, as in the case described – one can raise concerns based on the present, but new technology both creates a future and is then created by the frames of knowledge that such a future allows. Technology such as nanotechnology raises risks that are fundamentally unknowable. New technology is not only the production of things or objects, it is also the creation of things as signs, in the semiotic sense, and as de nova relationships. Science is a cultural production as much as it is a technological one. It creates identity, power, and expectations for its practitioners and for its consumers. Risks are unknowable in the literal sense as well as the metaphysical, for even health risks may not be experienced for generations (a case in point is DES, (diethylstibesteriol), which raises the risk of cancer and other abnormalities in children born to women who took this drug to avoid miscarriages in pregnancy; another is asbestos, which was the main ingredient in materials intended to be fire retardant). In a sense, what is at stake is not only the extent of the risk, but also the nature of the need and the author of that need, for the choice of risk is largely a matter of justice and priorities. Thus what is at stake is how societies decide to take risks: whether this is driven privately (and its limits), whether this is a decision held within the sphere of the market, whether this is a decision made by experts alone, the nature of the data and the nature of the principles used to interpret the data, and (usually covert) theories of justice. The Industrial Revolution was case in point. Electricity made shift work possible, but it also shifted notions of "naturalness" and altered the family. The most profound effects were not physical. Despite a large and public debate about AC versus DC, threats of mass electrocutions, and a massive legal battle over the patents and the regulation, regulators missed the most significant social harms. Thus the true consideration of the Ethical, Legal, and Social implications committees (ELSI) if they considered electrification, would have little to do with risks of electrocution.

Premise 3: Risk in Nanotechnology Is Fundamentally Unknowable

Beyond the unknown that is a core part of all new technology, nanotechnology – and the science that enables it – carries special uncertainties. Nanotechnology is largely a method and not a commodity, a mutable world of both processes and things, but it shares one common theme: although much is known about the properties of things at larger scales, little is yet known about how properties understood as fixed will change at the nanoscale. Further, its most important and most direct applications may largely be biological and thus inherently stochastic, and in fact, when married to synthetic biology, one core purpose is to create small molecules, molecular "machines," that act directly within cell signaling pathways to alter the production of proteins. But altering proteins or changing forces at that scale creates new forces that may not be predictable. Many proteins unfold in long temporal periods and have uncertain effects. Many such effects will not be assessable for years, perhaps decades – delaying negative consequences, or, perhaps, revealing few negative effects at all.

Premise 4: Public Regulation Is Not without Other Problems, Especially Since Science Literacy in the General Public Remains Very Minimal, Yet Such Oversight Is Critical

Northwestern University has had considerable experience with town hall meetings, but nowhere is the general practice more developed than in Germany, where science forums are an established feature of political life. American public discourse about science has followed a predictable path in the first years of the twenty-first century. Several core arguments about research are repeatedly made, in many cases, as noted previously, no matter what the content of the scientific research entails. The questions raised in our town hall meetings in Chicago were similar to ones raised in Munich, that slopes are slippery and the future is thus dangerous, because once a technology is begun, there will be larger and more terrible uses for it; that the marketplace is inherently corrupting and that scientists are blinded to ethical norms because the profits are so high; that nature is both fixed and sacred and should not be altered; that suffering defines humanity, and the push to relieve suffering is just "one goal among many"[36]; or that our finitude leads humans to our aspirations and to happiness itself. It is argued that a principle of precaution (prohibiting) is the only way to protect us from the harms that new technology will create because (as in the first slippery slope argument) we humans are not able to stop ourselves from the evil we create. Since 1948 and the collapse of the narrative of progress and of German science, the public fears about the terrible uses of science must always be a part of the discourse. We are led, not only by what is named the "shadow of eugenics,"[37] but also by older concerns, to ask about technology we cannot fully understand. When nanotechnology promises to "combat the most threatening diseases" or to "overcome one of the most difficult obstacles to gene regulation: safe and effective

36 Kass, Leon R. *Toward a More Natural Science: Biology and Human Affairs*. New York: Free Press, 1985.

37 Jeungst, Eric T. The Ethics of Prediction: Genetic Risk and the Physician-Patient Relationship. *Genome Science & Technology*, 1(1) (1995):21–36.

delivery into cells" for therapeutic uses,[38] we then are moved to ask more ontological than ethical questions: is this permissible to engineer? May you make the world?

Many arguments that oppose any science are not rooted in legal or regulatory concerns, but are profoundly religious statements. They are statements of faith, of world view, not of moral arguments about consent or risk. As such, they will not – cannot – be entirely agreed upon in a pluralistic democracy. Like many faith claims in our world, they are eschatological in nature, for the problems then rest not with current nanotechnology (leisure suits or sunscreen) but with the imagined future (two classes of people). In other work,[39] I noted that some fears are rooted in the classic tropes of Greek philosophy: that the world is terrifyingly mutable and unfixed in its borders and caprices and species; that Pandora is trouble; that god-person boundary is at stake at all times; that to know is to make. Other fears about science are rooted in classic fears of modernity itself: that the ability to understand comes from disassembly and assembly and that we might not be able to put a disassembled world back correctly or that that such knowledge is power itself (alchemy) or that the human is really a sort of machine or that perhaps there is no "real" at all (deconstruction).

When the public raises the concern that nanoscience is a sort of knowledge that is synthetic and complains that what is lost to us is the pre-textual, natural past, wherein the "real" lies,[40] then we understand that a larger concern is raised, akin to the fears manifest in the Cottingly case. It is my hypothesis that many of the concerns that are called "ethical" ones are of this sort, a metatrophic synecdoche for anxieties far larger than this particular technology, an anxiety about what modernity takes as it gives, and a yearning for an easier, less machined world, or, as in the Cottingly case, a "darker" world. This trans-historic and trans-geographic turn to fundamentalism in an anxious time is apparent in many scientific (and indeed, many non-scientific) venues. It is repeated at moments of "threshold tension" when science takes large leaps forward.

Science is seeing *as* knowing, science is both a witness and a presence. Its narrative rests on the central ideas: that time and space can be quantified and measured, that the actual world both exists and can be understood – science is *phronesis*, that understanding is making – science is *techica*, that labor can be best done by machines, that we can anticipate the effect of our actions and prevent harm. Science also has a distributive principle, or rather, follows a predictable process of distribution when it is developed in a market-based economy. Scientists think the research is good, meaning that it is reasonable, exciting, useful, and controllable; activists and ethicists will think it is not, meaning it might be unsafe, surely is profitable, perhaps

38 AuraSense.com. http:///www.AuraSense.com.

39 Zoloth, Laurie. Ethical Issues in Synthetic Biology. In *The Ethics of Protocells – Moral and Social Implications of Creating Life in the Laboratory Second Life*: edited by Mark Bedau and Emily C. Parke. Cambridge, MA: MIT Press, 2009.

40 Berry, Wendell. *What Are People For?: Essays*. New York: North Point Press, 1990.

unfair (or at least insecure), and surely synthetic. But when the technology is created and marketed, ordinary people will buy polyester T's and plastic shoes because they are cheap and sturdy. Even the most exotic science will come to seem reasonable if it is useful and cheap – even if the risks are completely unknown (e.g., cell phone technology.)

Premise 5: Science Regulation Has Changed Because of the Context of Mistrust

"The time has past when a bunch of elite true-meaning experts could go into the next room and make conclusions. They have to be transparent. That is a change in culture."[41]

Transparency is now a standard of science. Regulations limit proprietary knowledge, call for public membership on committees, call for a higher level of assurance before technology is approved, and ask that moral issues be considered before projects are funded. However, insider knowledge is a part of all science as well, and the structure of nanoscience, with its complex and specialized knowledge base, can often be completely opaque to public scrutiny. How can such a contradiction be resolved?

Calling for a more moral science is still not adequate. For example, should all moral appeals be equally considered? Who decides "need" and "good" and "necessary loss"? When there is such an uneasy history of genius, magic, and technology, can the marketplace set the limits on the power that technology brings, or does the polity need a separate voice? When the polity can barely know what is truly real (as was the case in the first industrial revolution, as the example of photography of fairies proved), how can a proper tension be created to balance expertise with the mistrust of expertise?

Premise 6: We Need to Move beyond "Precaution " and "Utility" to "Social Fidelity"

There are two ways to think about the problem of nanoscience, nanotechnology, and the ethical duties of a polity. The first is the "Precautionary Principle," and the second, older standard is "Risk Benefit," which is based on the principle of Utility or public beneficence. I will suggest a third way, which I will call a "Principle of Fidelity." This is because there are serious flaws with how precautionary or risk analysis is structured and the principle on which they are based.

First, there are covert moral appeals you get with precaution: that natural is good; that nature is normative; that moral agency is linked to action, but not inaction; that the future can be known; that the world, thus and so, is good, and will continue in this

[41] Overbye, Dennis. In the Hunt for Planets, Who Owns the Data? *The New York Times*, June 14, 2010. http://www.nytimes.com/2010/06/15/science/space/15kepler.html.

good and normative manner, only if we do not interfere with it. These premises are problematic, and they not only understand the nature of moral activity incorrectly (inaction is just as powerful as action), but they also make the assumption that what we have come to know as "nature" is inevitable, which contains within it deeper assumptions about one's social location.

There are covert appeals with risk analysis as well: that risks can be known and quantified (when we know this is not fully true), that mistakes are not inevitable, that membership in affected groups is chosen and can be decided against, that markets are logical. These premises are problematic, especially in the case of nanotechnology. Nanotechnology is both larger and smaller in terms of risk. It may present a smaller risk because each use is entirely idiosyncratic – the alleles affected, the size and the manufacture shape vary per use. Thus harm may be particular. Yet it is a larger risk because unlike a particular cancer drug, entire societies are affected by each such choice, and larger because risk is then in several categories. The risk can be for bodies now, and for bodies and persons that will not exist until much later, my body now and later, my progeny's body, and hers, and so on. The risk can be to my river, or to my nation, or to other nation states and to the individual bodies within them. And each risk category exists if you proceed or desist from proceeding with nanotechnology.

A principle of social fidelity takes into account these issues, because a risk exists both for doing and not doing, and here we can reference the case of GMO corn, boycotts of corn, and famines that exist when seed of boycotted corn are not planted, or epidemics that emerge when vaccines are not given, and so on. As Pogge reminds us, it is an accident of history that we in the West, making the technology, are here and others are elsewhere, and this precondition of contingency creates duties.[42] In the face of these duties, our response cannot be to simply desist from technology. But it must proceed with some constraints, because of a principle of social fidelity to the neighbors with whom we share the world. A principle of social fidelity means several things. First it means that we have to treat testing as the first question of justice. Justice issues exist both for who gets the goods and who takes on the risk. Second, a principle of social fidelity suggests a contract or covenant between science and the polity who both takes the risk and reaps the benefits. For a justice theorist – to whom consent, and how the consent is obtained, is important – this contract or covenant must provide for a joint undertaking, a mutual agreement. Risks are correlative, and rights are correlative to duties, the duties which arise from situations that are not chosen. A principle of social fidelity as opposed to a principle of precaution suggests that there is a relationship between bioethics, health, and safety and the larger debates about global justice.

Social fidelity also demands a commitment to the entire range and scope of the project. This is true, by the way, for both action and inaction – the body that

[42] Pogge, Thomas W. *Global Justice (Metaphilosophy)*. Malden, MA: Blackwell Publishing, 2001.

regulates and decides and who profits from the decision is accountable to repair any harms that occur. Unlike precaution, which takes no responsibility for the negative consequences of inaction, a principle of social fidelity means that ill effects must be addressed and paid for, and this payment is a price of the decision. Unlike risk analysis, which assumes that failure was a risk "paid for," as it were, in advance by the acceptance of benefits, a principle of social fidelity would take into account the responsibility for repair for harm in addition to the fact that the technology might have already created compensatory benefits.

CONCLUSION AND NEXT STEPS

Social fidelity as a principle draws on several sources within the tradition of ethics. First, it recalls the optimism of Popperian science, avoiding mass "paradigm shifts" and proceeding with slow steps and careful assessment along the way. It draws from traditional sources for morality and ethics within religious traditions that see duties and responsibilities to fix a broken world and contain the sense of hope that a chosen telos can better the world that is given, yet incomplete and unfair. It will mean that bioethicists will need to continue to assess nanotechnology, without focusing on the tempting bottom of slippery slopes, or science fiction movies, but, rather, focusing on the science we are actually asked to reflect upon as we remind our colleagues in science of the primacy of justice in moral philosophy.

Such a set of guidelines has been suggested in the consideration of other science advances that promised much, but seemed worrisome. Guidelines for basic research established for inheritable genetic modification can be fruitfully modified for our case. Science can be ethically assessed before its use if these questions are answered adequately: are there reasons *in principle* why the act is impermissible? Are there reasons in principle that it is imperative? What purposes, techniques, or applications would be permissible and under what circumstances? What *contextual* factors should be taken into account, and do any of these prevent development of the research? What procedures, structures, involving what policies, should be used to decide on appropriate techniques and uses[43]?

There are profound ethical choices in all technologies, as societies and democratic institutions consider the changing world. Ethical reflection of this sort is a civic witness, for the polity cannot fully be experts to the events of the lab. It is naive to expect that the potent combination of human curiosity, an aesthetic sense of the beauty and integrity of knowledge, the drive for profits, and the genuine moral gesture of altruism that science represents will be halted without a serious cost. It should not be a choice we make, for an ethical argument can be made to develop

[43] Frankel, Mark S. and Audrey R. Chapman. Human Inheritable Genetic Modifications: Assessing Scientific, Ethical, Religious, and Policy Issues. AAAS, 2000. http://www.aaas.org/spp/sfrl/projects/germline/report.pdf.

a range of responses to nanotechnology: prohibited, permitted, or rewarded, and these moral assessments can be reflected upon at regular intervals as conditions demand. We have developed such conversations in the late twentieth and twenty-first century that mark our difference from the eighteenth and nineteenth century reactions to science. We can insist on public accountability, with ethical oversight at the national, international, and local institutional level, with members of the public, and published reports that set standards, regulate research, and review ongoing research once funded. These forms of response, so directed at individual risks, and so limited by the principle of autonomy to prevent unwanted harm, will have to be expanded to take into account collective risks as well and will need to be guided by the principle of fidelity, a broader claim than autonomy.

At the core of ethical oversight are two critical agencies, one individual, one collective. The first is the moral agency of each nanoscience and each technician. States cannot station moral police at every lab bench and board room. Moral agency must be taught, supported, and rewarded, and violations of standard in research need to be punished. The principle of fidelity can only really work well if it engages faithful agents, duty-bound to be "honest and stand up for all humanity" in the words of Sydney Brenner. The other critical agency is the individuals within the polity. Science and technology that we use are ours in the deepest sense. We partake of the trajectories of science and of dreams. Thus is it our responsibility to not only count the costs and promise to repair, but also to learn how the world is understood. We are possessed of a mutual duty toward the future of the environment we share, and it cannot be avoided.

PART IV

Where We Are Now – The Current Framework for Nanotechnology Regulation

14

An Overview of the Law of Nanotechnology

Fern P. O'Brian

I. INTRODUCTION

With the growing prevalence of nano-enabled materials reaching the marketplace in new products, the perceived need for regulation of such materials has correspondingly increased. There is significant debate, however, regarding the extent to which the government should regulate nanotechnology or nanotechnology-based products, and this uncertainty is reflected in the lack of comprehensive oversight of both the development and the sale of nano-enabled products and technologies. In the United States, regulatory agencies at both the state and national level have struggled to keep pace with the exploding market for nano-enabled products, from electronics to cosmetics, food, and other industrial uses. The European Union, on the other hand, has attempted to lead the way with a precautionary approach to nanotechnology in the marketplace. This chapter provides a general overview of current and proposed nanotechnology regulations, in both the United States and the European Union.

II. ENVIRONMENTAL PROTECTION AGENCY

Although there is no uniform and comprehensive regulation of nanomaterials in the United States, the U.S. Environmental Protection Agency (EPA) regulates nanomaterials in several ways: through the reporting requirements of the Nanoscale Materials Stewardship Program; through the Green Chemistry Initiative; through the complex regulatory scheme established by the Toxic Substances Control Act; and through potential new interpretations of the Federal Insecticide, Fungicide, and Rodenticide Act.

A. *Nanoscale Materials Stewardship Program*

In early 2008, EPA unveiled the Nanoscale Materials Stewardship Program (NMSP) with the stated goal of helping provide a firmer scientific foundation for regulatory

The author wishes to acknowledge the assistance of Barbara A. Lum, Associate, Thompson Hine LLP.

decisions by encouraging submission and development of information for nanoscale materials.[1] This program marked a tipping point of government interest in nanoscale materials. The NMSP comprised two sub-programs, the Basic Program and the In-Depth Program, both of which were voluntary information collection mechanisms to assemble existing data and information from manufacturers, importers, and processors of nanoscale materials.

Under the Basic Program, EPA invited manufacturers, importers, and processors of nanoscale materials to voluntarily report available information by July 29, 2008, on the engineered nanoscale materials they manufacture, import, process, or use.[2] EPA stated that it would evaluate the information submitted under the Basic Program through a process similar to that of a new chemical review.[3] By December 8, 2008, 29 companies or associations submitted information to EPA covering 123 nanoscale materials, and a further seven companies had outstanding commitments to the Basic Program.[4]

Under the In-Depth Program, EPA invited participants to work with the Agency and others on a plan for the development of data on representative nanoscale materials over a longer timeframe. By December 8, 2008, only four companies had agreed to participate in the In-Depth Program. In January 2009, the EPA Office of Pollution Prevention and Toxics issued its Interim Report on the NMSP, which outlined several next steps for the program, including initiating discussions with In-Depth participants and evaluating Basic Program submissions to identify characteristics of nanoscale materials that should be considered in risk assessment as well as approaches for risk management.[5] The program ended January 2010.[6]

B. *Green Chemistry Initiative*

Pursuant to the passage of the Pollution Prevention Act of 1990, the U.S. EPA's Office of Pollution Prevention and Toxics (OPPT) began exploring the idea of developing new or improving existing chemical products and processes to make them less hazardous to human health and the environment.[7] By 1993, the OPPT had launched the Green Chemistry Program, which provided unprecedented grants for research projects focusing on pollution prevention in the design and synthesis of greener solvents and safer chemicals.[8] Through the Green Chemistry Program, EPA has

[1] U.S. E.P.A., Nanoscale Materials Stewardship Program Interim Report (January 2009) (*available at* http://www.epa.gov/oppt/nano/nmsp-interim-report-final.pdf).

[2] *Id.*

[3] *Id.*

[4] *Id.*

[5] *Id.*

[6] *Id.*

[7] U.S. E.P.A., Green Chemistry Program at EPA, http://www.epa.gov/gcc/pubs/epa_gc.html.

[8] *Id.*; EPA Has Touted Twelve Principles of Green Chemistry: Prevention, Atom Economy, Less Hazardous Chemical Syntheses, Designing Safer Chemicals, Safer Solvents and Auxiliaries, Design for

collaborated with academia, industry, other government agencies, and nongovernmental organizations through completely voluntary, nonregulatory partnerships to promote the use and design of chemical products and processes in a way that reduces or eliminates the use or generation of hazardous substances.[9]

More recently, the OPPT has turned its attention toward research efforts focusing on green manufacturing. EPA believes that nanotechnology will have a significant impact on developing green and clean technologies with considerable environmental benefits and is therefore currently supporting research that will be used to inform EPA, industry, and academia about potentially greener approaches for nanomanufacturing.[10]

C. *Toxic Substances Control Act*

The Toxic Substances Control Act of 1976 (TSCA)[11] establishes a complex regulatory scheme that provides EPA with comprehensive authority to regulate virtually all chemical substances, excluding, among others, food, drugs, cosmetics, and pesticides.

Under TSCA, EPA may:[12]

Require testing of chemicals by manufacturers, importers, and processors where risks or exposures of concern are found.	Section 4
Require pre-manufacture notification (PMN) and approval for "new chemical substances" at least 90 days in advance of its production, import, or manufacture.	Section 5
Issue Significant New Use Rules (SNURs) when it identifies a "significant new use" that could result in exposures to, or releases of, an existing chemical substance of concern already on the TSCA inventory.	Section 5
Prohibit or limit manufacture, or restrict processing or distribution, if a chemical substance is found to present an unreasonable risk of injury to health or the environment.	Section 6
Maintain the TSCA Inventory, which contains more than 83,000 chemicals. As new chemicals are commercially manufactured or imported, they are placed on the list.	Section 8

Energy Efficiency, Use of Renewable Feedstocks, Reduce Derivatives, Catalysis, Design for Degradation, Real-time analysis for Pollution Prevention, and Inherently Safer Chemistry for Accident Prevention (*available at* http://www.epa.gov/gcc/pubs/principles.html).

9 http://www.epa.gov/gcc/pubs/epa_gc.html.

10 U.S. Environmental Protection Agency, Research Advancing Green Manufacturing of Nanotechnology Products, http://www.epa.gov/nanoscience/quickfinder/green.htm.

11 Toxic Substances Control Act of 1976, 15 U.S.C. §§ 2601–2692 (1976) (*available at* http://frwebgate.access.gpo.gov/cgi-bin/usc.cgi?ACTION=BROWSE&TITLE=15USCC53).

12 U.S. Environmental Protection Agency, Summary of the Toxic Substances Control Act, http://www.epa.gov/lawsregs/laws/tsca.html.

Require reporting and record keeping by persons who manufacture, import, process, and/or distribute chemical substances in commerce.	Section 8
Require that any person who manufactures (including imports), processes, or distributes in commerce a chemical substance or mixture and who obtains information that reasonably supports the conclusion that such substance or mixture presents a substantial risk of injury to health or the environment to immediately inform EPA, except where EPA has been adequately informed of such information.	Section 8(e)
Require those importing or exporting chemicals to comply with certification reporting and/or other requirements.	Sections 12(b) and 13

Further, EPA currently has broad authority under TSCA to require health and safety testing of new chemical substances or significant new uses of existing chemical substances when it believes that it has insufficient data or information necessary to evaluate the substance's safety.

The issue of nanoscale materials, however, has caused much debate regarding whether – because of their small size and sometimes unique properties – EPA should treat all nanoscale materials as "new" chemicals and whether the use of nanoscale materials constitutes a "significant new use" of an existing chemical substance, which also triggers TSCA's pre-manufacturing notice and approval requirements.[13] TSCA grandfathered in more than 60,000 industrial chemicals that were already in use in 1976, with no safety testing, and new chemicals have gone straight to the marketplace with little government oversight.[14] In the 34 years since TSCA was enacted, EPA has required testing for only 200 chemicals out of the more than 80,000 available for use in the United States, and has regulated only five.[15] Interest groups have questioned whether TSCA, as it is currently written, allows EPA to effectively regulate the use and development of nanomaterials, in light of the challenges posed by science's current lack of understanding of many aspects of nanotechnology.[16]

1. Recent EPA Regulation under Current Toxic Substances Control Act Regarding Nanotechnology

As EPA entered the uncharted waters of nanomaterial regulation, it encountered a variety of challenges in applying TSCA to such substances. Because all substances

13 John C. Monica, Jr. & John C. Monica, *Examples of Recent EPA Regulation of Nanoscale Materials Under the Toxic Substances Control Act*, 6 Nanotechnology Law & Business 388 (Fall 2009).

14 Bryan Walsh, *Regulation of Toxic Chemicals Faces Tightening*, Time, April 16, 2010, http://www.time.com/time/health/article/0,8599,1982489,00.html.

15 *Id.*

16 Richard Denison, Ph.D., Environmental Defense Fund, EPA Nano Authority under TSCA, Part 1: It All Depends on What "New" Means, http://blogs.edf.org/nanotechnology/2008/04/22/epa-nano-authority-under-tsca-part-1-it-all-depends-on-what-%E2%80%9Cnew%E2%80%9D-means/.

that meet the TSCA definition of chemical substance are subject to TSCA, EPA has recognized the importance of defining the extent to which nanoscale substances may be considered "new chemical substances" under TSCA and therefore subject to reporting under TSCA Section 5(a). In January 2008, EPA clarified its definition of "new" versus "existing" chemicals.[17] According to EPA's clarification, it did not consider nanoscale materials "new" substances just because of their diminutive size; rather they must have a distinct molecular identity that is not shared with any other chemical on TSCA's existing chemical substance inventory before they are considered "new."[18]

2. EPA's Focus on Carbon Nanotubes

As if to underscore its clarification, EPA, in October 2008, published a notice in the Federal Register regarding the TSCA Inventory status of carbon nanotubes (CNTs).[19] In it, EPA noted that "EPA generally considers CNTs to be chemical substances distinct from graphite or other allotropes of carbon listed on the TSCA inventory. Many CNTs may therefore be new chemicals under TSCA section 5." Manufacturers or importers of CNTs not on the TSCA Inventory are thus required to comply with TSCA reporting requirements, and EPA indicated that it anticipated focusing its efforts on monitoring industry compliance with TSCA section 5 reporting requirements for CNTs.

Around the same time as the EPA's October 2008 Federal Register notice, EPA issued its first consent order pertaining to nanomaterials. In September 2008, EPA entered into a consent order with Thomas Swan & Co., a leading manufacturer of CNTs based in the United Kingdom, which allowed Thomas Swan & Co. to supply small quantities of CNTs into the United States and required the company to issue a Notice of Commencement (NOC) of Manufacture or Import to EPA when it believes U.S. sales have reached commercial quantities.[20]

Under TSCA, EPA may negotiate a consent order with a manufacturer who submits a PMN to EPA if EPA determines that use, under certain specific conditions and with agreed precautions, would not pose an unreasonable risk to consumers, but that use under other conditions may pose such a risk. EPA's findings of a potentially unreasonable risk or substantial exposure may be based either on: (1) information about the chemical substance itself; (2) information about its close "analogs" showing

[17] U.S. E.P.A., TSCA Inventory Status of Nanoscale Substances – General Approach, January 23, 2008 (*available at* http://www.epa.gov/opptintr/nano/nmsp-inventorypaper2008.pdf).

[18] *Id.*

[19] U.S. E.P.A, Toxic Substances Control Act Inventory Status of Carbon Nanotubes, http://www.epa.gov/fedrgstr/EPA-TOX/2008/October/Day-31/t26026.htm.

[20] In the matter of Premanufacture Notice Number P-08–0177 – Consent Order and Determinations Supporting Consent Order, at 5 (*available at* http://www.nanolawreport.com/EPA%20Premanufacture%20Notice%20Number%20P-08–0177.pdf).

that it can pose problems; or (3) inadequacy of the information available to EPA.[21] Risk-based consent orders typically contain requirements regarding toxicity or environmental fate testing by a certain production volume, new chemical exposure limits, worker personal protective equipment, hazard communication, distribution, release to water, other disposal options, and record keeping.

In addition, EPA used the Swan consent order to require Thomas Swan & Co. to perform testing on the substance it had submitted for approval. The consent order prohibited the company from manufacturing or importing the PMN substance beyond limited production limits established in the order, unless Thomas Swan & Co. conducted a 90-day inhalation toxicity study on rats with a post-exposure observation period of up to 3 months.[22] EPA defined the protocol for the study, required submission of the results, and encouraged Thomas Swan & Co. to develop additional health effects testing in coordination with other multi-walled CNT manufacturers.[23]

3. SNURs Pertaining to Nanomaterials

As previously discussed, TSCA gives EPA authority to issue SNURs when it identifies a "significant new use" that could result in exposures to, or releases of, an existing chemical substance of concern already on the TSCA inventory. SNURs compel anyone who intends to manufacture, import, or process any of the subject nanomaterials for a significant new use to notify EPA at least 90 days before beginning to do so and thereby permits EPA to evaluate the intended use and issue an order that prohibits or limits the use. EPA has issued several SNURs pertaining to nanomaterials that have been challenged by the chemical industry.

On November 5, 2008, EPA published a Federal Register notice promulgating two final SNURs under TSCA Section 5(a)(1)(B) for certain siloxane-modified silica and alumina nanoparticles.[24] These were the first SNURs known to have been issued on nanomaterials. These substances were the subject of PMNs filed by an undisclosed company or companies in October 2005 for "additive, open, non-dispersive use."[25] As in the Swan CNT consent order, EPA indicated its concern with the health effects of similar analogous respirable, poorly soluble particulates, as well as the physical properties of the substances.[26] One of the "significant new uses" of these

[21] *Id.* EPA noted that it had determined the "probable" toxicity, human exposure, and environmental release of nanotubes based on currently available information.

[22] *Id.*

[23] *Id.*

[24] Significant New Use Rules on Certain Chemical Substances, 73 FED. REG. 65743 (Nov. 5, 2008) (*available at* http://edocket.access.gpo.gov/2008/pdf/E8–26409.pdf).

[25] Certain New Chemicals; Receipt and Status Information, 70 FED. REG. 46513 (Aug. 10, 2005) (*available at* http://edocket.access.gpo.gov/2005/pdf/05–15841.pdf).

[26] Proposed Significant New Use Rules on Certain Chemical Substances, 74 FED. REG. 57430–57436, at 65751 (November 6, 2009) (*available at* http://www.regulations.gov/search/Regs/home.html#documentDetail?R=0900006480a52a30).

substances being regulated under these SNURs, however, is not the use of the chemical substances as additives, but the use of the substances without appropriate personal protective equipment.[27]

EPA recommended that manufacturers of siloxane-modified silica and alumina nanoparticles implement and submit the results of a 90-day inhalation toxicity test, which would help characterize the human health effects of the two nanomaterials.[28] Although the test is not required, the fact that EPA has recommended this test in both of its initial forays into nanotechnology regulation may indicate that manufacturers can look forward to EPA requiring this test in future nanomaterial regulation.

On June 24, 2009, EPA issued two proposed SNURs for multi-walled and single-walled CNTs. These SNURs, however, supposedly affected "generic" single-walled and multi-walled CNTs, which EPA later clarified to mean that the SNURs only applied specifically to the Swan nanoparticles.[29] By August 21, the SNURs were withdrawn on procedural grounds,[30] after a notice of intent to submit adverse comments was filed on July 22, 2009, complaining that the SNUR did not "properly present the chemical identity of the substances" regulated by the SNUR, and EPA's promulgation of the regulations had not allowed for public comments.[31] EPA then proposed a new SNUR on February 3, 2010, only for multi-walled CNTs described in PMN P08–199, with comments due on or before March 5, 2010.[32] The comment period was re-opened July 28, 2010, upon new information.[33]

EPA published its final SNUR for single-walled and multi-walled CNTs on September 17, 2010.[34] The final rule became effective October 18, 2010.[35] Persons who intend to manufacture, import, or process either of these substances for a use that is designated as a significant new use by the final rule must notify EPA at least

[27] *Id.* at 65752.

[28] *Id.*

[29] Proposed Significant New Use Rules on Certain Chemical Substances, 74 Fed. Reg. 57430–57436 (November 6, 2009) (*available at* http://www.regulations.gov/search/Regs/home.html#documentDetail?R=0900006480a52a30).

[30] Certain Chemical Substances; Withdrawal of Significant New Use Rules, 74 Fed. Reg. 42177–42178 (August 21, 2009).

[31] Letter from James G. Votaw, WilmerHale, to U.S. E.P.A. Office of Pollution Prevention and Toxics (September 17, 2009) (*available at* http://www.regulations.gov/search/Regs/contentStreamer?objectId=0900006480a35183&disposition=attachment&contentType=pdf).

[32] Proposed Significant New Use Rules on Certain Chemical Substances, 74 Fed. Reg. 57430–57436 (November 6, 2009) (*available at* http://www.regulations.gov/search/Regs/home.html#documentDetail?R=0900006480a52a30).

[33] Proposed Significant New Use Rule for Multi-walled Carbon Nanotubes; Reopening of Comment Period, 75 Fed. Reg. 44198 (July 28, 2010) (*available at* http://edocket.access.gpo.gov/2010/2010–18543.htm).

[34] Multi-Walled Carbon Nanotubes and Single-Walled Carbon Nanotubes; Significant New Use Rules, Fed. Reg. 56880- 56889 (September 17, 2010) (*available at* http://edocket.access.gpo.gov/2010/pdf/2010-23321.pdf).

[35] *Id.*

90 days before commencing that activity.[36] EPA now requires extensive characterization data from the original manufacturer, including whether the graphene layers that make up the tubes are straight, bent, or buckled, and the shape of its hexagonal arrays.[37] The required notification provides EPA with the opportunity to evaluate the intended use and, if necessary, to prohibit or limit that activity before it occurs.

In response to public comments on the applicability of the SNURs for these chemicals, EPA included clarifying language indicating particular uses of the CNTs that are exempt from the provisions of the SNURs, including the use of CNTs (1) after they have been completely reacted (cured); (2) incorporated or embedded into a polymer matrix that itself has been reacted (cured); or (3) embedded in a permanent solid polymer form that is not intended to undergo further processing except for mechanical processing.[38] The SNURs also incorporate the initially proposed CNT SNUR regulations regarding the protection of any workers who come into contact with CNTs by requiring employees to wear gloves and full-body clothing that are impervious to CNTs, as well as respirators.[39] Purposeful or predictable releases of CNTs into water are banned.[40] Further, current and future manufacturers, importers, and processers are encouraged to conduct a 90-day inhalation study of their CNTs.[41] In its consent orders, EPA has offered to consider waiving the 90-day inhalation test if a consortium of companies commits to testing a representative sample of carbon materials.[42] Each 90-day inhalation test cost between $350,000 and $500,000, which can be prohibitively expensive for a small chemical manufacturer.[43] Any company that began to make, import, or process the multi- or single-walled CNTs after EPA proposed the SNURs in November 2009 must cease that activity and comply with the final rules.[44]

36 *Id.*

37 Pat Rizzuto, *EPA Issues Significant New Use Rules Covering Multi-, Single-Walled Nanotubes*, 34 CRR 903 (September 20, 2010), http://news.bna.com/chln/CHLNWB/split_display.adp?fedfid=17798084&vname=chenotallissues&fn=17798084&jd=17798084&lf=eml&emc=chln:chln:108.

38 Multi-Walled Carbon Nanotubes and Single-Walled Carbon Nanotubes; Significant New Use Rules, 75 Fed. Reg. 56880–56889 (September 17, 2010) (to be codified at 40 CFR 9 & 721) (*available at* http://www.gpo.gov/fdsys/pkg/FR-2010-09-17/html/2010–23321.htm).

39 *Id.*

40 *Id.*

41 Pat Rizzuto, *Carbon Materials Manufacturers Hope to Work Out Testing Agreement with EPA*, 34 CRR 925 (Sept. 20, 2010) (*available at* http://news.bna.com/chln/CHLNWB/split_display.adp?fedfid=17811756&vname=chenotallissues&fn=17811756&jd=a0c4f3j4q0&split=0).

42 *Id.*

43 *Id.*

44 Pat Rizzuto, *EPA Issues Significant New Use Rules Covering Multi-, Single-Walled Nanotubes*, 34 CRR 903 (September 20, 2010), http://news.bna.com/chln/CHLNWB/split_display.adp?fedfid=17798084&vname=chenotallissues&fn=17798084&jd=17798084&lf=eml&emc=chln:chln:108; Janice Valverde, *EPA Proposes Significant New Use Rules For Two Types of Carbon Nanotubes*, 33 CRR 1126 (November 16, 2009), http://news.bna.com/chln/CHLNWB/split_display.adp?fedfid=15750288&vname=chenotallissues&fn=15750288&jd=a0c1h7f7r0&split=0.

4. Legal Consequences of TSCA

Although TSCA has been criticized as "ineffective," it does lay out a variety of enforcement mechanisms. TSCA Section 15 makes it unlawful for any person to: (1) fail to comply with any rule promulgated or order issued under TSCA; (2) use for commercial purposes a chemical substance or mixture that such person knew or had reason to know was manufactured, processed, or distributed in commerce in violation of TSCA; (3) fail or refuse to establish or maintain records, submit reports, notices, or other information, or permit access to or copying of records, as required by this chapter or a rule thereunder; or (4) fail or refuse to permit entry or inspection as required by TSCA.[45]

Violation of these requirements can carry both civil and criminal penalties. On the civil side, violation of TSCA Section 15 can result in a fine "not to exceed $25,000 for each such violation," with each day counting as a separate violation.[46] Criminal penalties provide for a fine of not more than $25,000 for each day of violation, or imprisonment for not more than 1 year, or both for any person who is convicted of knowingly or willfully violating any provision of TSCA.[47]

TSCA also provides for "citizen civil actions" and "petitions" against any person, including the U.S. government, to restrain violations of TSCA or any rule or order issued under TSCA. This can include petitions to compel EPA to enforce testing, notification, manufacturing, and use restrictions.[48]

Finally, TSCA gives EPA authority to seek court orders for "specific enforcement" and "seizure," which includes the ability to enjoin the manufacture or processing of the substance and/or seizing the substance.[49] EPA may also conduct on-site inspections to verify compliance with TSCA requirements.[50]

Subject to some exceptions, states are preempted from imposing additional testing requirements or health requirements if EPA has prescribed a more stringent rule or order under TSCA that is applicable to a chemical substance or mixture and that is designed to protect against a risk of injury to health or the environment associated with such substance or mixture.[51] Upon application by a state, however, EPA may exempt the state's applicable rule from preemption if: (1) compliance with the requirement would not cause the manufacturing, processing, distribution in commerce, or use of the substance, mixture, or article to be in violation of TSCA; and (2) the state (A) provides a significantly higher degree of protection from such risk than the TSCA rule, and (B) is not unduly burden interstate commerce.[52]

45 40 C.F.R. § 720.120.
46 15 U.S.C. § 2615(a).
47 15 U.S.C. § 2615(b).
48 15 U.S.C. § 2619(a).
49 15 U.S.C. § 2616(a)-(b).
50 15 U.S.C. § 2610.
51 15 U.S.C. § 2617.
52 *Id.*

Thus, under TSCA, EPA sets minimum testing requirements or health requirements, which generally preempt state regulations.

5. Proposed New Rules under TSCA and Proposed Legislation to Change TSCA Itself

As the debate continues regarding how EPA should regulate nanoscale materials, EPA has indicated that it intends to develop a proposed new TSCA Section 8(a) rule to obtain information on the production, uses, and exposures of existing nanoscale materials.[53] EPA would ensure the collection of data by requiring mandatory data submission by manufacturers under TSCA Section 4.[54] The TSCA Interagency Testing Committee (ITC) has expressed interest in investigating: fullerenes, titanium oxide nanowires, titanium oxide nanoparticles, nano zinc oxide, nanosilver, silica, quartz, cerium oxide, indium tin oxide, dendrimers, single-walled carbon nanotubes, multi-walled carbon nanotubes, carbon nanofibers, Se and Cd quantum dots, nanoceramic particles, and nanoclays.[55] The fate of these proposals is unclear, in light of the sweeping changes proposed by subsequent legislation that seeks to completely overhaul TSCA itself.

New legislation has been proposed that would fundamentally change TSCA.[56] In 2010, H.R. 5820, Toxic Chemicals Safety Act of 2010[57] as introduced in the House Committee of Energy and Commerce, and its corresponding sister bill S. 3209, Safe Chemicals Act[58] as introduced in the Senate, proposed requiring the chemical industry to demonstrate that chemicals are safe, rather than EPA having to prove they are unsafe.[59] Both bills, however, failed to secure final approval before the end of the 111th Congress, and died in committee.

53 Sixty-Fourth Report of the TSCA Interagency Testing Committee to the Administrator of the Environmental Protection Agency; Receipt of Report and Request for Comments; Notice, 74 Fed. Reg. 38880 (August 4, 2009) (*available at* http://edocket.access.gpo.gov/2009/pdf/E9-18469.pdf).

54 *Id.*

55 *Id.*

56 Law360, Potential Dramatic Changes To US Chemicals Law, August 03, 2010, http://www.law360.com/articles/184807; Jessica Dye, Updated Chemical Safety Bill Unveiled in Senate, April 14, 2011, http://www.law360.com/articles/239110/updated-chemical-safety-bill-unveiled-in-senate.

57 Toxic Chemicals Safety Act of 2010, H.R. 5820, 111TH Cong. (2D SESS. 2010) (*available at* http://energycommerce.house.gov/Press_111/20100415/TCSA.Discussion.Draft.pdf).

58 Safe Chemicals Act, S. 3209, 111TH Cong. (2D SESS. 2010) (*available at* http://frwebgate.access.gpo.gov/cgi-bin/getdoc.cgi?dbname=111_cong_bills&docid=f:s3209is.txt.pdf).

59 Toxic Chemicals Safety Act of 2010, H.R. 5820, 111TH Cong. (2D SESS. 2010) (*available at* http://energycommerce.house.gov/Press_111/20100415/TCSA.Discussion.Draft.pdf). "(1) SAFETY STANDARD. – The Administrator shall apply, as a safety standard under this title, a standard takes into account aggregate and cumulative exposure to a chemical substance or mixture and that provides a reasonable certainty of no harm, including to vulnerable populations, and protects the public welfare from adverse effects, including effects on the environment.

"(2) BURDEN OF PROOF. – The manufacturers and processors of a chemical substance or mixture shall bear the burden of proving that the chemical substance or mixture meets the safety standard."

On April 14, 2011, Senator Frank Lautenberg introduced a revised version of the previously introduced chemical safety legislation, in an attempt to boost public health and environmental protections and reflect a more risk-based approach to chemical regulation.[60] The 2011 bill proposes to replace TSCA's "unreasonable risk" standard with a "reasonable certainty of that no harm will result to human health or the environment" standard for the intended use of chemicals.[61] The safety standard would consider aggregate exposures for the whole chemical life cycle.[62]

Under the proposed legislation, the EPA would receive new authority to regulate all industrial chemicals made, imported, or sold in the U.S., and the burden would be placed on manufacturers to prove their chemicals are safe before being permitted to enter or stay on the U.S. market.[63] The bill would require safety testing of each chemical and expedited risk management for chemicals of highest concern.[64] The legislation also calls for publication of all "significant information" submitted to the EPA pursuant to the legislation via a public, Internet-accessible database within 18 months of the bill's enactment.[65] As of the date of this publication, the bill has not yet been passed.

Passage of the proposed TSCA legislation would represent a major regulatory shift, and as a result, it has been hotly debated. The new safety standard proposed by the legislation evidences a willingness to adopt a protectionist standard, which has already been previously adopted by European nanomaterial legislation, including European Union (EU) Regulation on the Registration, Evaluation, Authorization and Restriction of Chemicals (REACH) and other EU regulations applicable to nanomaterials. The thrust of the new TSCA legislation appears directed at creating lists of "priority" nanomaterials subject to regulation, while simultaneously placing the burden of testing, reporting, and proving "a reasonable certainty of safety" on the manufacturer.

This controversy was aired during the July 29, 2010 hearing before the House Energy and Commerce Subcommittee on commerce, trade, and consumer protection. During the hearing, industry witnesses and Republican members challenged the bill's proposed increased regulatory burdens as unworkable and an impetus for driving jobs and innovation overseas.[66] Nongovernmental organization witnesses and most Democratic members, on the other hand, argued that the bill could actually create jobs and drive innovation by restoring public confidence in the chemical industry and promoting green chemistry.[67]

60 Safe Chemicals Act of 2011, S. 847, 112TH Cong. (1ST SESS. 2011) (available at http://lautenberg.senate.gov/assets/SafeChem.pdf).

61 *Id.*

62 *Id.*

63 *Id.*

64 *Id.*

65 *Id.*

66 Law360, Potential Dramatic Changes To US Chemicals Law, August 03, 2010, http://www.law360.com/articles/184807.

67 *Id.*

D. *Federal Insecticide, Fungicide, and Rodenticide Act*

The Federal Insecticide, Fungicide, and Rodenticide Act (FIFRA) provides the basis for regulation, sale, distribution, and use of pesticides in the United States.[68] FIFRA authorizes EPA to review and register pesticides for specified uses.[69] EPA also has the authority to suspend or cancel the registration of a pesticide if subsequent information shows that continued use would pose unreasonable risks.[70]

In early November 2009, EPA Scientific Advisory Panel (SAP) convened a meeting regarding the evaluation of the hazard and exposure associated with nanosilver and other nanometal pesticide products.[71] During this meeting, the SAP discussed the lack of studies definitively answering the question of whether agglomerated silver nanoparticles in the range of 100 to 1,000 nm pose different hazards than larger sized particles. The SAP concluded that it "strongly believed that in addition to current data requirements under FIFRA, additional assays which compared nanoscale and bulk materials would be most beneficial in addressing this question."[72]

Heeding this call for greater reporting and analysis under FIFRA, EPA is poised to announce its adoption of a policy that would require any pesticide registrant that is aware that some constituent of a registered pesticide product is nanosized (i.e., presumably that has particles or structures with a diameter less than 100 nanometers) to submit the information to EPA pursuant to FIFRA Section 6(a)(2).[73] Rather than issuing a new regulation, EPA has said that it will be announcing a new interpretation of FIFRA 6(a)(2) and existing regulations at 40 CFR part 159, which will apply not only to registered products, but also to "new" products that are submitted for registration under FIFRA.[74] Under the new policy, an active or inert ingredient would be considered "new" if it is a nanoscale material, even if the non-nanoscale form of that same active or inert ingredient is already in a registered product.[75] Thus nanosilver, for instance, would be considered a "new" product, and therefore subject to reporting requirements, even though silver is a registered pesticide.[76] Companies

[68] U.S. E.P.A., Regulating Pesticides, http://www.epa.gov/oppooool/regulating/laws.htm.

[69] *Id.*

[70] *Id.*

[71] Meeting Minutes, FIFRA Scientific Advisory Panel, Evaluation of the Hazard and Exposure Associated with Nanosilver and other Nanometal Pesticide Products (November 3–5, 2009) (*available at* http://www.epa.gov/scipoly/sap/meetings/2009/november/110309ameetingminutes.pdf).

[72] *Id.*

[73] U.S. E.P.A, EPA Pesticide Program Dialogue Committee Meeting (April 29, 2010); http://www.epa.gov/oppfead1/cb/ppdc/2010/april2010/transcript.pdf; presentation by William Jordan, Senior Policy Adviser, Office of Pesticide Programs, *Nanotechnology and Pesticides* (April 29, 2010), http://www.epa.gov/pesticides/ppdc/2010/april2010/session1-nanotec.pdf.

[74] U.S. E.P.A, EPA Pesticide Program Dialogue Committee Meeting (April 29, 2010); *available at* http://www.epa.gov/oppfead1/cb/ppdc/2010/april2010/transcript.pdf.

[75] Presentation by William Jordan, Senior Policy Adviser, Office of Pesticide Programs, *Nanotechnology and Pesticides* (April 29, 2010), *available at* http://www.epa.gov/pesticides/ppdc/2010/april2010/session1-nanotec.pdf.

[76] *Id.*

that are seeking to register products or that already have products in the marketplace will need to disclose to EPA the presence of a nanoscale material in their product, if they have not already done so.[77] Any person applying for registration of a product will continue to have to report as part of its application any information that would be reportable under 6(a)(2). This new interpretation of FIFRA will place the burden of reporting on the nanomaterials registrants – even if their non-nanoscale counterpart products have already been registered – who are responsible for proving the safety, or continued safety, of their products.

III. STATE AND LOCAL GREEN CHEMISTRY AND NANOPARTICLE INITIATIVES[78]

Several states have proposed or enacted legislation to reduce the use of toxic chemicals, prioritize harmful chemicals, and identify safer alternatives. None, however, are as comprehensive as California's Green Chemistry Initiative. The State of California is making great strides in creating a systematic, science-based process to evaluate chemicals of concern in products, including nanomaterials. On September 29, 2008, California Governor Arnold Schwarzenegger signed the California Green Chemistry Initiative into law, thus making California the first U.S. state to move toward a comprehensive chemicals policy, which includes the regulation of nanomaterials. The legislation gives the California Department of Toxic Substances Control (DTSC) authority to develop regulations that create a process for identifying and prioritizing chemicals of concern and to create methods for analyzing alternatives to existing hazardous chemicals.[79]

Pursuant to this authority, the DTSC released a final draft of proposed regulations, entitled "Safer Consumer Product Alternatives," on September 14, 2010.[80] The proposed regulation put forth a framework for DTSC to scientifically and systematically identify and prioritize chemicals and consumer products to develop a list of "Priority Products" and "Priority Chemicals" containing "Chemicals under Consideration."[81] Similar to the proposed TSCA legislation, the thrust of California's

77 U.S. E.P.A, EPA Pesticide Program Dialogue Committee Meeting (April 29, 2010), *available at* http://www.epa.gov/oppfead1/cb/ppdc/2010/april2010/transcript.pdf.

78 California's Green Chemistry Initiative, and other state Green Chemistry and nanoparticle legislation, although inspired by the same goals of reducing or eliminating the use of hazardous materials as the U.S. E.P.A.'s Green Chemistry Program, are separate, state-level initiatives.

79 Press Release, State of California Office of the Governor, Governor Schwarzenegger Signs Groundbreaking Legislation Implementing First-in-the-Nation Green Chemistry Program (September 29, 2008) (*available at* http://gov.ca.gov/press-release/10666).

80 California Department of Toxic Substances Control, Proposed Regulations: Safer Consumer Product Alternatives, http://www.dtsc.ca.gov/LawsRegsPolicies/SCPA.cfm.

81 SAFER CONSUMER PRODUCT ALTERNATIVES, CAL. CODE REGS. tit. 22, division 4.5, chapter 53 (proposed September 2010) (*available at* http://dtsc.ca.gov/LawsRegsPolicies/upload/SCPA-Regs_APA-format-9–07-10-rev-9–12.pdf).

Green Chemistry Initiative appeared directed at creating lists of "priority" nanomaterials subject to regulation. DTSC would create a list of chemicals that are toxic and can harm people or the environment based on a variety of factors, including chemical and physical properties; adverse public health impacts; adverse ecological impacts; adverse environmental impacts; the dispersive volume information, as it relates to the volume of a chemical placed into the stream of commerce in California; the potential for the public or the environment to be exposed to the chemical in commonly used products that contain the chemical; and the existence of data and other information relating to actual or potential public or environmental exposures to the chemical.[82] The proposed regulation applied to all chemicals that exhibit a hazard trait and are reasonably expected to be contained in products placed into the stream of commerce in California, unless the DTSC determined that the chemical: (1) is regulated by one or more federal and/or other California State regulatory program(s) that, in combination, address, for each life cycle segment, the same public health and environmental threats as the proposed regulation, and (2) there is no exposure pathway by which the chemical might pose a threat to public health or the environment in California during the useful life or the end of life of the chemical or any product containing the chemical.[83] If the DTSC did not determine that the proposed legislation applies to a chemical, a person may petition the DTSC to make such a determination upon proof by clear and convincing evidence.[84]

The DTSC indicated that the initial list would be drawn from databases maintained by the International Agency for Research on Cancer, the National Toxicology Program, and other authoritative bodies.[85] The DTSC would have required manufacturers of Priority Products to conduct Alternative Assessments to determine the availability of technologically and economically feasible alternative products[86] and allowed the DTSC a variety of regulatory responses, including requiring the manufacturer to publish information about the selected alternative, labeling requirements, and prohibiting Priority Product production, as well as other regulatory responses.[87]

Upon review and in response to public comments, the DTSC issued a significantly revised draft of its proposed regulations on November 16, 2010 that eliminated all references to nanotechnology; prioritized the evaluation of children's products, personal care products, and household cleaning products; and limited the application of the regulations to only manufacturers and retailers.[88] The DTSC's new proposed regulation, however, drew strong criticism from environmental and public health

[82] *Id.*

[83] *Id.*

[84] *Id.*

[85] *Id.*

[86] *Id.*

[87] *Id.*

[88] Safer Consumer Product Alternatives, Cal. Code Regs. tit. 22, division 4.5, chapter 53 (proposed November 2010)(*available at* http://www.dtsc.ca.gov/LawsRegsPolicies/upload/SCPA_Regs_15Day_Revisions_COURTESYCLEAN.pdf).

groups, scientists, and industry, and its implementation has been delayed indefinitely pending review by the Green Ribbon Science Panel, a panel established by the underlying Green Chemistry legislation to provide advice on scientific matters, chemical policy recommendations, and implementation strategies, in light of the substantive concerns raised by the regulations' opponents.[89]

These proposed regulations come on the heels of a DTSC Chemical Information Call-In program which began in late 2008. Under this program, the DTSC requested information pursuant to *Health and Safety Code*, Chapter 699, sections 57018–57020, regarding analytical test methods, fate and transport in the environment, and other relevant information from manufacturers of certain chemicals of concern.[90] On January 22, 2009, DTSC sent out its first formal information request letter to manufacturers who produce or import CNTs in California. A year later, the Department posted responses from 17 companies who received a formal information request letter regarding CNTs on the DTSC website. The Department also listed the companies who failed to respond by the January 22, 2010 due date on the DTSC website. DTSC issued follow-up letters to nine companies who failed to respond on February 16, 2010.[91]

According to the DTSC website, the Department is interested in and plans to contact manufacturers of other nano-enabled chemical classes, which include members of the methyl siloxanes (i.e., decamethylcyclopentasiloxane); members of the brominated flame retardants; nanometal oxides, such as nano titanium dioxide and nano zinc oxide; and nanometals, such as nanosilver, nano cerium oxide, quantum dots, and nano zerovalent iron.[92]

In addition to California, at least five other states, including Connecticut,[93] Maine,[94] Michigan,[95] Minnesota,[96] and Washington,[97] have enacted Green Chemistry legislation. Of these five state laws, four were enacted to ensure that children's products are free from hazardous chemicals and materials, and none are as comprehensive as the California Green Chemistry Initiative. In addition, legislators in

89 Linda S. Adams, Letter to Assembly Member Feuer, Dec. 23, 2010(*available at* http://www.dtsc.ca.gov/upload/GRSP-12-23-2010.pdf).

90 California Department of Toxic Substances Control, Chemical Information Call-In, *available at* http://www.dtsc.ca.gov/pollutionprevention/chemical_call_in.cfm.

91 California Department of Toxic Substances Control, Nanomaterials Information Call-In, *available at* http://www.dtsc.ca.gov/TechnologyDevelopment/Nanotechnology/nanocallin.cfm.

92 California Department of Toxic Substances Control, Chemical Information Call-In, http://www.dtsc.ca.gov/pollutionprevention/chemical_call_in.cfm.

93 An Act Concerning Child Product Safety, Public Act No. 08–106 (Conn. 2008) (*available at* http://www.cga.ct.gov/2008/ACT/PA/2008PA-00106-R00HB-05650-PA.htm).

94 Regulation of Chemical Use in Children's Products, Me. Rev. Stat. Ann., Title 38, chapter 16-D, §§ 1691–1699-B (2010) (*available at* http://www.maine.gov/dep/rwm/rules/pdf/ch880_final_adopted.pdf).

95 Promotion of Green Chemistry for Sustainable Economic Development and Protection of Public Health, Executive Directive No. 2006–6 (2006) (*available at* http://www.michigan.gov/gov/0,1607,7–168-36898_40426–153806–,00.html).

96 Toxic Free Kids Act of 2009, Minn. Stat. 116.9401 – 116.9407 (2009).

97 Children's Safe Product Act, RCW 70.240.010, *et. seq.* (2008).

Illinois,[98] New York,[99] and Oregon[100] have proposed similar child safety legislation addressing chemicals that pose a threat to children's health. Four more states, including Massachusetts, Michigan, Minnesota, and Vermont, have pending Green Chemistry legislation, which variously proposes prioritizing chemicals of high concern and creating advisory panels that would develop a comprehensive framework for promoting product designs that would reduce or eliminate risks to health or the environment through reduced use of hazardous substances.[101] Currently, no other state has proposed or enacted any Green Chemistry legislation that is nearly as comprehensive or far reaching as the DTSC's California Green Chemistry Initiative.

Two individual cities have taken it upon themselves to enact or explore local legislation specifically addressing the production and manufacture of nanoparticles. Effective December 15, 2006, the City of Berkeley, California, enacted the nation's first local ordinance regulating the production and use of manufactured nanoparticles.[102] The Berkeley Municipal Code's hazardous materials title requires manufacturers, researchers, and other businesses to identify their production or use of nanoparticles, disclose toxicity data, and provide plans for safe handling and disposal.[103] The ordinance applies to the production or use of all "manufactured nanoparticles" with "one axis below 100 nanometers in length," and therefore the

[98] Child-Safe Chemicals Act, HB 3792 (Ill. 2009) (*available at* http://www.ilga.gov/legislation/96/HB/PDF/09600HB3792lv.pdf); Child-Safe Chemicals Act, HB 2485 (Ill. 2009) (*available at* http://www.ilga.gov/legislation/96/HB/PDF/09600HB2485lv.pdf).

[99] An act to amend the environmental conservation law, in relation to regulation of toxic chemicals in children's products, Bill No.: A10089 (N.Y. 2010) (*available at* http://open.nysenate.gov/legislation/bill/A10089).

[100] Children's Safe Products Act of 2009, HB 2367 (Or. 2010) (*available at* http://www.oregontoxics.org/household/kids/HB_2367.pdf).

[101] An Act for a competitive economy through safer alternatives to toxic chemicals, S442 (Mass. 2009); An Act for a competitive economy through safer alternatives to toxic chemicals, H757 (Mass 2009); Michigan strategic fund act, HB-4817 (As Passed by House, May 19, 2009) (*available at* http://www.legislature.mi.gov/documents/2009–2010/billengrossed/House/pdf/2009-HEBH-4817.pdf); Michigan economic growth authority act, HB-4818 (as Passed by House, May 19, 2009) (*available at* http://www.legislature.mi.gov/documents/2009–2010/billengrossed/House/pdf/2009-HEBH-4818.pdf); Michigan strategic fund act, HB-4819 (as Passed by House, May 19, 2009) (*available at* http://www.legislature.mi.gov/documents/2009–2010/billengrossed/House/pdf/2009-HEBH-4819.pdf); a bill for an act relating to the environment; creating an advisory council on development and regulation of consumer products; establishing a comprehensive framework for consumer products that protect, support, and enhance human health, the environment, and economic development; providing appointments; proposing coding for new law in Minnesota Statutes, chapter 325F, S.B. 618 (MN 2009) (*available at* https://www.revisor.mn.gov/bin/showPDF.php); a bill for an act relating to the environment; requiring the Pollution Control Agency to annually report on regulating and nonregulating mechanisms and regulations to mitigate risk or prevent exposure to chemicals in children's products; requiring the agency to make annual recommendations to the legislature; proposing coding for new law in Minnesota Statutes, chapter 325F, H.B. 458 (Minn. 2009) (*available at* https://www.revisor.mn.gov/bin/bldbill.php?bill=H0458.1.html&session=ls86); An act relating to the regulation of toxic substances, H.484 (Vt. 2010) (*available at* http://www.leg.state.vt.us/docs/2010/bills/Intro/H-484.pdf).

[102] Berkeley Municipal Code, §§ 15.12.040, 15.12.050.

[103] *Id.*

ordinance may be construed to extend to commonly used materials that contain nanoparticles, not just engineered nanomaterials created for a specific purpose.[104] Although Berkeley's ordinance applies only within the City's limits,[105] it has been cited as a model for similar legislation by other localities and, possibly, state governments.

At least one other city has explored the development of a similar local ordinance. On January 8, 2007, the City Council of Cambridge, Massachusetts, adopted a resolution to examine Berkeley's municipal ordinance concerning hazardous substances and nanoparticles and develop a recommendation for a similar ordinance for Cambridge, Massachusetts.[106] No Cambridge ordinance has yet been suggested. The spectre of irregular nanoparticle regulation at the state and local levels remains a salient issue for legislators, lawyers, entrepreneurs, and consumers alike – especially as the fate of TSCA and the very definition of "nanomaterial" remain undefined.

IV. U.S. FOOD AND DRUG ADMINISTRATION

The U.S. Food and Drug Administration (FDA), an agency within the Department of Health and Human Services, is responsible for protecting the public health by assuring the safety, efficacy, and security of human and veterinary drugs, biological products, medical devices, our nation's food supply, cosmetics, and products that emit radiation, and by regulating the manufacture, marketing, and distribution of tobacco products. There is no specific mention of nanomaterials in the Food, Drug and Cosmetics Act, however, so any regulation of such materials by the FDA must be made on a case-by-case basis, often focusing on pre-market approval and extensive data requirements.

Historically, the FDA has approved many products with particulate materials in the nano-size range, including nanosilver particles, engineered calcium phosphate, nanoparticle dental restoratives, and a variety of cosmetics and sunscreens containing nano-sized ingredients.[107] More recently, however, the FDA has demonstrated its willingness to consider regulating nanomaterials. In August 2006, the FDA formed the Nanotechnology Task Force, which it charged with determining regulatory approaches that would encourage the continued development of innovative, safe, and effective FDA-regulated products that use nanotechnology materials, while also identifying and recommending ways to address any knowledge or policy gaps that exist so as to better enable the agency to evaluate possible adverse health

104 *Id.*

105 *Id.*

106 http://www.cambridgema.gov/cityclerk/PolicyOrder.cfm?item_id=16916.

107 Nakissa Sadrieh, PhD, *FDA Considerations For Regulation Of Nanomaterial Containing Products*, Office of Pharmaceutical Science, CDER, FDA (*available at* http://www.fda.gov/ohrms/dockets/ac/06/briefing/2006–4241B1–02-31-FDA-Nano%20Sadrieh%20nanotech%20presentation%20%282%29.pdf).

effects from such products.[108] The Task Force has only released one report, in July 2007, which addressed the scientific and regulatory needs regarding drugs, medical devices, cosmetics, food additives, and other products built on the nanoscale.[109] In particular, the report called for guidance to be issued to define particle size for pre-market authorization requirements and guidance requesting submission of information on whether and how the presence of nanoscale materials affects the manufacturing process for products.[110]

In August 2007, the FDA proposed a new rule for sunscreen products, with standards for formulating, testing, and labeling over-the-counter sunscreen drug products with ultraviolet A (UVA) and ultraviolet B (UVB) protection.[111] The proposal featured a four-star grading system for UVA protection, with 1 being the lowest and 4 being the highest degree of protection.[112] The ratings would be derived from two tests: one measuring the product's ability to reduce the amount of UVA radiation passing through it, and one measuring the product's ability to prevent tanning – a test almost identical to the SPF test used to assess UVB sunscreens.[113] Finally, the regulation would require sunscreen manufacturers to place a "Warnings" statement in the "Drug Facts" box of all sunscreen products.[114] More than 3 years later, on June 14, 2010, Senator Charles Schumer of New York called for the FDA to investigate reports suggesting a link between skin cancer and retinyl palmitate, a chemical found in many sunscreen products, and pressed the FDA for a timeline for new sunscreen regulations.[115] The proposed regulation has garnered more than 3,000 public comments,[116] but the final regulation has not yet been issued as of the date of this publication.

Most recently, on July 20, 2010, Rep. Janice Schakowsky of Illinois, with 22 co-sponsors, introduced H.R. 5786, the Safe Cosmetics Act of 2010. The act proposed to amend Chapter VI of the Federal Food, Drug & Cosmetic Act by adding specific nanomaterial labeling requirements for minerals and other particulate ingredients "if not less than 1 dimension is 100 nanometers or smaller for not less than 1 percent of 10

[108] Press Release, FDA Forms Internal Nanotechnology Task Force (August 9, 2006) http://www.fda.gov/NewsEvents/Newsroom/PressAnnouncements/2006/ucm108707.htm.

[109] FDA, Nanotechnology Task Force Report (2007) (*available at* http://www.fda.gov/ScienceResearch/SpecialTopics/Nanotechnology/NanotechnologyTaskForceReport2007/default.htm#regulatory).

[110] *Id.*

[111] Press Release, FDA Proposes New Rule for Sunscreen Products (August 23, 2007) (http://www.fda.gov/NewsEvents/Newsroom/PressAnnouncements/2007/ucm108970.htm).

[112] *Id.*

[113] *Id.*

[114] *Id.*

[115] Press Release, Schumer Reveals: Evidence Mounting that Suggests Possible Link Between Chemical Found in Most Sunscreens and Skin Cancer, FDA Has Been Studying Issue for Almost a Year; Schumer Calls on FDA to Make Results of Investigation Immediately Clear (June 14, 2010) *available at* http://schumer.senate.gov/new_website/record.cfm?id=325644.

[116] Catherine Saint Louis, *UVA Reform: It's Not PDQ*, N.Y. Times, June 23, 2010, *available at* http://www.nytimes.com/2010/06/24/fashion/24Skin.html.

the ingredient particles in the cosmetic."[117] Further, the act proposed a safety standard that required the cosmetics manufacturers, packager, or distributers to prove "*a reasonable certainty that no harm will result* from aggregate exposure to the cosmetic or ingredient, including impacts on vulnerable populations, taking into account possible harmful effects from low dose exposures to the cosmetic or ingredient or from additive effects, where such evidence exists . . . "[118] This standard is similar to the standard proposed in the Safe Chemicals Act of 2011, which also proposes to place the burden of testing, reporting, and proving "a reasonable certainty of safety" on the manufacturer[119] and evidences a worrying potential U.S. regulatory trend toward the protectionism already embraced in the EU. H.R. 5786 had been referred to the House Committee on Energy and Commerce and the House Committee on Education and Labor[120], but failed to secure final approval before the end of the 111th Congress, and died in committee.

V. OSHA AND NIOSH

The Occupational Safety and Health Act of 1970 created both National Institute for Occupational Safety and Health (NIOSH) and the Occupational Safety and Health Administration (OSHA). OSHA is in the U.S. Department of Labor and is responsible for developing and enforcing workplace safety and health regulations.[121] OSHA sets enforceable regulatory permissible exposure limits (PELs) on the amount or concentration of a substance in the air with the goal of protecting workers against the health effects of exposure to hazardous substances.[122] OSHA PELs are based on an 8-hour time-weighted average (TWA) exposure and are addressed in specific standards for the general industry, shipyard employment, and the construction industry.[123]

NIOSH, on the other hand, is part of the Centers for Disease Control and Prevention in the Department of Health and Human Services and was established to help assure safe and healthful working conditions by providing research, information, education, and training in the field of occupational safety and health.[124] NIOSH, acting under the authority of the Occupational Safety and Health Act of 1970 and

[117] Safe Cosmetics Act of 2010, H.R. 5786, 111th Cong. (2d Sess. 2010) (*available at* http://frwebgate.access.gpo.gov/cgi-bin/getdoc.cgi?dbname=111_cong_bills&docid=f:h5786ih.txt.pdf).

[118] *Id.*

[119] *See* Safe Chemicals Act of 2011, S. 847, 112TH Cong. (1ST SESS. 2011) (available at http://lautenberg.senate.gov/assets/SafeChem.pdf).

[120] *Id.*

[121] Centers for Disease Control and Prevention, *About NIOSH*, *available at* http://www.cdc.gov/niosh/about.html.

[122] Occupational Health and Safety Administration, Permissible Exposure Limits (PELs), *available at* http://www.osha.gov/SLTC/pel/.

[123] *Id.*

[124] Centers for Disease Control and Prevention, *About NIOSH*, *available at* http://www.cdc.gov/niosh/about.html.

the Federal Mine Safety and Health Act of 1977, develops and periodically revises recommended exposure limits (RELs) for hazardous substances or conditions in the workplace.

Both OSHA and NIOSH have defined exposure limits for both CNTs (also known as synthetic graphite) and titanium dioxide.[125]

	Carbon Nanotubes/Synthetic Graphite	Titanium Dioxide
OSHA Permissible Exposure Limit (PEL)	OSHA PEL for general industry: 15 mg/m³ TWA[126] OSHA PEL for maritime: 15 mg/m3 TWA[127]	OSHA PEL: 15 mg/m³ TWA[128]
NIOSH Recommended Exposure Limit (REL)	No established REL[129]	NIOSH REL for ultrafine and nanoscale TiO2: 0.3 mg/m³ [130] NIOSH REL for fine TiO2: 2.4 mg/m3[131] Revised NIOSH immediately dangerous to life or health concentration (IDLH) for titanium dioxide: 5,000 mg/m³ [132]

VI. EUROPEAN UNION

The EU has taken significant steps to define and regulate nanomaterials in the European marketplace. Like the United States, the EU currently regulates nanomaterials via a variety of different regulations, all of which have different definitions

[125] Centers for Disease Control and Prevention, Draft Document on Titanium Dioxide Posted by NIOSH for Public Comment, *available at* http://www.cdc.gov/niosh/updates/upd-11–23-05.html. (Titanium dioxide [TiO2], an insoluble white powder, is used extensively in many commercial products, including paint, cosmetics, plastics, paper, and food, as an anti-caking or whitening agent. It is produced and used in the workplace in varying particle-size fractions, including fine and ultrafine size.)

[126] 29 CFR 1910.1000.

[127] 29 CFR 1915.1000.

[128] NIOSH Pocket Guide to Hazardous Chemicals, Titanium dioxide, *available at* http://www.cdc.gov/niosh/npg/npgd0617.html.

[129] U.S. Department of Labor – Office of Safety and Health Administration, Chemical Sampling Information for Graphite, Synthetic (Total Dust), *available at* http://www.osha.gov/dts/chemicalsampling/data/CH_244000.html.

[130] Centers for Disease Control and Prevention, NIOSH Current Intelligence Bulletin: Occupational Exposure to Titanium Dioxide, *available at* http://www.cdc.gov/niosh/docs/2011-160/pdfs/2011-160.pdf.

[131] Centers for Disease Control and Prevention, NIOSH Current Intelligence Bulletin: Occupational Exposure to Titanium Dioxide, *available at* http://www.cdc.gov/niosh/docs/2011-160/pdfs/2011-160.pdf.

[132] Centers for Disease Control and Prevention, Titanium dioxide IDLH Documentation, *available at* http://www.cdc.gov/niosh/idlh/13463677.html.

of "nanomaterial." The EU has recognized the increased need for a more uniform definition of the term, because the significant lack of knowledge and information has led to disagreement and political struggles at the level of definitions.[133]

The EU Novel Food Regulation, for instance, which applies to novel food additives, food enzymes, flavorings, and certain food ingredients, has defined "engineered nanomaterial" as "any intentionally produced material that has one or more dimensions of the order of 100 nm or less or is composed of discrete functional parts, either internally or at the surface, many of which have one or more dimensions of the order of 100 nm or less, including structures, agglomerates or aggregates, which may have a size above the order of 100 nm but retain properties that are characteristic to the nanoscale."[134] The European Commission, in the regulation itself, admits the lack of conformity among the different definitions of nanomaterials published by different bodies at the international level and agreed that the Commission shall adjust and adapt its definition to technical and scientific progress and with definitions subsequently agreed at the international level.[135]

The EU REACH also regulates nanomaterials and has been compared with the United States' TSCA.

Nanomaterials are regulated by REACH because they are covered by the regulation's definition of a chemical "substance."[136] REACH therefore applies to nanomaterials as for any other substance, although there are no REACH provisions referring explicitly to nanomaterials. Under REACH, all chemical substances must be registered, and all manufacturers and importers of chemicals must identify and manage risks linked to the substances they manufacture and market.

Many nanoparent substances (e.g., silver, carbon, zinc oxide, silica, titanium dioxide, gold, aluminum) have been preregistered, and general registrations are planned for 2010. Several nanomaterials have been preregistered, including nanosilver and CNTs (unspecified, single-walled, multi-walled). Two main groups of nanomaterials will not be preregistered, however: (1) those based on polymers; and (2) those manufactured/ imported at less than 1 ton per annum. There are no specific nanosubstances yet registered by itself. As with the United States' TSCA, REACH has long been criticized as lacking clarity and therefore providing ineffective regulation of nanomaterials.[137]

133 European Commission Joint Research Centre, *Considerations on a Definition of Nanomaterial for Regulatory Purpose* (2010), *available at* http://ec.europa.eu/dgs/jrc/downloads/jrc_reference_report_201007_nanomaterials.pdf.

134 European Parliament legislative resolution of 25 March 2009 on the proposal for a regulation of the European Parliament and of the Council on novel foods, COM (2007) 0872 final (March 25, 2009), *available at* http://www.europarl.europa.eu/sides/getDoc.do?pubRef=-//EP//TEXT±TA±P6-TA-2009–0171±0±DOC±XML±V0//EN.

135 *Id.*

136 *REACH and nanomaterials, available at* http://ec.europa.eu/enterprise/sectors/chemicals/reach/nanomaterials/index_en.htm.

137 Scientific Committee on Emerging and Newly Identified Health Risks (SCENIHR), *Modified Opinion (after public consultation) on The appropriateness of existing methodologies to assess the*

In June 2009, the European Parliament approved an updated cosmetics regulation, which imposes stricter reporting and labeling requirements and imposes new safety assessment procedures.[138] Further, it redefines "nanomaterial" as "an insoluble or biopersistant and intentionally manufactured material with one or more external dimensions, or an internal structure, on the scale from 1 to 100 nm."[139]

EU regulations regarding nanoscale materials remain in disarray, as evidenced by the varying definitions of nanomaterial. Like the United States, the EU seeks to clarify its regulations as the market for nanoscale products continues to grow.

VII. CONCLUSION

Both the United States and the EU continue to grapple with the challenges of regulating a still-developing technology, which has begun to exceed its current regulatory confines. As the market for nanoscale products and materials continues to increase, the debate regarding the extent to which manufacturers, importers, and processors should bear the burden of proving the safety of their products will become increasingly pertinent to consumers and manufacturers alike. Currently, however, regulatory agencies at both the state, national, and international levels will continue to struggle to keep pace with the exploding market for nano-enabled products until comprehensive oversight of both the development and the sale of nano-enabled products and technologies – including defining what nanomaterials even are – can be enacted.

potential risks associated with engineered and adventitious products of nanotechnologies (2006), *available at* http://ec.europa.eu/health/ph_risk/committees/04_scenihr/docs/scenihr_o_003b.pdf; *The Synthesis Report on the public consultation of the SCENIHR opinion on The appropriateness of existing methodologies to assess the potential risks associated with engineered and adventitious products of nanotechnologies* (2006), *available at* http://ec.europa.eu/health/ph_risk/documents/synth_report.pdf.

138 Regulation of the European Parliament and of the Council on Cosmetic Products, PE-CONS 3623/09 (2009), *available at* http://register.consilium.europa.eu/pdf/en/09/st03/st03623.en09.pdf.

139 *Id.*

15

Regulatory Responses to Nanotechnology Uncertainties

Read D. Porter, Linda Breggin, Robert Falkner, John Pendergrass, and Nico Jaspers

Governments in leading industrialized countries are currently relying on existing regulatory frameworks for environmental, health, and safety regulation to cover nanotechnology risks. European Union (EU) and U.S. regulators generally have concluded that any risks posed by nanomaterials can be addressed using existing frameworks, but minor adjustments to specific regulations and their implementation are currently being made in order to close any potential gaps or eliminate uncertainties.[1] Identifying the appropriate response to uncertain risks is a difficult task for policy makers and regulatory agencies. They are faced with a high degree of scientific uncertainty and need to balance the costs and benefits of regulation as well as seeking a durable compromise between the often conflicting interests of scientific freedom, technological innovation, consumer safety, and environmental protection.

This article discusses how regulators in the United States and EU have addressed key uncertainties inherent to nanomaterial regulation in the context of chemical,

[1] *Nanotechnology* (in the singular) can be taken to refer to a wide range of different technologies. See the definition of nanotechnology in the American Society for Testing and Materials' "Standard Terminology Relating to Nanotechnologies," *available at* http://www.astm.org/Standards/E2456.htm (accessed July 5, 2009). In this chapter, we refer to "nanotechnologies"' and "nanotechnology," with the latter signifying the wider field of science and technology that encompasses the full range of nanotechnologies and applications. We refer to "nanomaterials" as a generic term for the structures, devices, and systems created through nanoscale engineering, including nanoparticles, nanostructures, and nanoscale substances, which have recently been defined by the International Organization for Standardization's (ISO) nanotechnology technical committee (TC 229). For terminology and definitions of nano-objects, see ISO (2008). *Nanotechnologies – Terminology and Definitions for Nano-objects – Nanoparticle, Nanofibre and Nanoplate*. A further distinction can be made between naturally occurring nanomaterials and (deliberately) manufactured nanomaterials. The latter are of primary concern in the context of this chapter. Another distinction can be made between transitive and non-transitive nanomaterials, with the former exhibiting "size-related intensive properties that differ significantly from that observed in fine particles or bulk materials," whereas the latter do not. When using the term "nanomaterials," this chapter implicitly refers to deliberately manufactured transitive nanomaterials.

food, and cosmetic regulation. We first discuss the key areas of uncertainty that plague efforts to regulate nanotechnologies and nanomaterials. We then consider how regulators on both sides of the Atlantic have responded to these uncertainties and identify common regulatory responses. We conclude by considering how regulatory responses have reduced uncertainty and suggesting further steps to effectively reduce uncertainty.

This chapter is based on the report of a project that was carried out in 2008–2009 by a consortium of research institutions from both sides of the Atlantic: the London School of Economics and Political Science (LSE) and Chatham House (the Royal Institute of International Affairs) in the United Kingdom and the Environmental Law Institute (ELI) and the Project on Emerging Nanotechnologies (PEN) at the Woodrow Wilson International Center for Scholars in the United States. The project, which was funded by a research grant from the European Commission and involved extensive consultation with experts and stakeholders in nanomaterials regulation, resulted in a comparative analysis of European and American regulatory frameworks in three areas: chemicals, food, and cosmetics. This chapter builds on the main project report, entitled *Securing the Promise of Nanotechnologies: Towards Transatlantic Regulatory Cooperation*.[2]

KEY UNCERTAINTIES

Regulators face a number of challenges in dealing with the potential risks of nanomaterials. These challenges are related to a series of uncertainties with regard to the development and commercial application of nanomaterials, hazards, and exposure pathways; the direction and speed of technological change; and the suitability and effectiveness of existing regulation frameworks. Understanding these uncertainties and reacting effectively and proportionally is a key imperative for regulators and policy makers as much as for industry and civil society.

Rapid Technological Change

It is common to differentiate between four different conceptual categories, or generations, of nanotechnologies.[3] As outlined in the U.S. Environmental Protection Agency's (EPA's) 2007 Nanotechnology White Paper,[4] the first generation of nanotechnologies focuses on manufacturing coatings, polymers, and more reactive catalysts, among others. A second generation includes nanoparticles for targeted

[2] Linda Breggin, Robert Falkner, Nico Jaspers, John Pendergrass & Read Porter, *Securing the Promise of Nanotechnologies: Towards Transatlantic Regulatory Cooperation* (London, UK: Chatham House, 2009).

[3] Roco, M. C. (2004). Nanoscale Science and Engineering: Unifying and Transforming Tools. *AIChE Journal* 50:890–97.

[4] EPA (2007). Nanotechnology White Paper, *available at* http://www.epa.gov/OSA/pdfs/nanotech/epa-nanotechnology-whitepaper-0207.pdf (accessed July 5, 2009). [*hereinafter* EPA White Paper].

drug delivery systems, adaptive structures, and actuators, for example. Both first- and second-generation nanotechnologies are currently in the research, development, and/or commercialization stage. Third-generation nanotechnologies, which may not be ready for commercial use for another decade, include novel robotic devices, three-dimensional networks, and guided assemblies. Even further into the future are fourth-generation nanotechnologies that may result in molecule-by-molecule design and self-assembly capabilities. Although first-generation nanotechnologies have mostly led to so-called passive nanostructures, second-, third- and fourth-generation nanotechnologies will lead to nanostructures that may perform an "active" function.[5]

EPA is not alone in predicting that future developments will include active nanomaterials and will converge with other technologies such as information, bio-, and cognitive technologies.[6] These second-, third-, and future-generation nanomaterials will develop in a way that is difficult to foresee. Regulators will need to monitor these developments and react flexibly to newly emerging risks. They will need to constantly expand their knowledge base, covering multiple areas of scientific and engineering inquiry, and develop flexible responses to a constantly changing technological environment.

How much funding and time will be required to test the nanomaterials flowing into the marketplace? Neither the Organisation for Economic Co-Operation and Development nor national regulatory bodies have provided public estimates, but a recent study indicated that assessing the risks of 190 nanomaterials now in production would require an investment of between $249 million (assuming optimistic assumptions about hazards) and $1.18 billion (assuming long-term in vivo studies of all nanomaterials).[7] The use of tiered testing strategies could reduce this sum, and the current low production volumes of some materials used primarily in research may reduce the need to test at all. But the risk assessment challenge is likely to increase in complexity and cost as more materials enter the market and, importantly, as second- and third-generation nanotechnology products and materials enter commercial production.

Commercialization Paths

It is difficult to predict precisely how nanotechnology will develop owing to the diversity of potential commercial pathways and the complexity of the nanotechnology value chain. However, the commercial promise of nanotechnology is beyond

5 Davies, J.C. (2009). Oversight of Next Generation Nanotechnology, Project on Emerging Nanotechnologies, Woodrow Wilson International Center for Scholars. 18, *available at* http://www.nanotechproject.org/process/assets/files/7316/pen-18.pdf (accessed August 18, 2009); Rodemeyer, M. (2009). *New Life, Old Bottles: Regulating First-Generation Products of Synthetic Biology*. Washington, DC: Synthetic Biology Project, Woodrow Wilson International Center for Scholars.

6 *See* EPA White Paper, *supra* note 4.

7 Choi, J. et al. (2009). The Impact of Toxicity Testing Costs on Nanomaterial Regulation. *Environmental Science and Technology* 43(9):3030–34.

doubt: increasing economic value of nanotechnologies in different market sectors, proliferation of innovations, as reflected in patent filings, and expanding investment in research by both private companies and national governments all suggest that nanotechnology is to assume an ever-expanding role in industrial society.

The growth of commercial products incorporating nanotechnology is difficult to measure, with projections for the future growth of commercial applications of nanotechnology ranging from $1 trillion to $2.5 trillion by 2015.[8] Because nanotechnologies are enabling technologies, such estimates do not always distinguish clearly enough between the more limited value added by nanotechnologies and the larger face value of products that "contain" nanotechnology product.[9]

An inventory[10] of consumer products containing nanomaterials, maintained by the PEN, lists more than 1,000 nano-enabled products that are currently on the market in 21 different countries. The vast majority of these products appear in the cosmetics, clothing, personal care, sporting goods, sunscreens, and filtration sectors and are available primarily on the U.S. market, with East Asia and Europe following in second and third place. The materials most frequently mentioned as being contained in products are nanoscale silver, carbon, titanium, silicon, zinc, and gold. Although the PEN inventory relies on self-identified products and may thus potentially overstate (but also understate) the true degree of commercialization of "nanoproducts," it is indicative of the wide range of commercial applications of nanotechnologies in consumer products.[11]

Nanosciences and nanotechnologies have wide-ranging and ever-expanding commercial applications. Existing products deriving added value from nanotechnologies include cars, clothing, airplanes, computers, consumer electronics devices, pharmaceuticals, processed food, plastic containers, appliances, and other products.[12] This diversity of commercialization has led some to consider nanotechnology a "general purpose" or "platform" technology like biotechnology and the internet.[13]

[8] Roco, M.C. and W.S. Bainbridge (2001: 3). *Societal Implications of Nanoscience and Nanotechnology* (Dordrecht, Netherlands: Kluwer); Lux Research (2010). The Recession's Impact on Nanotechnology, *available at* http://www.luxresearchinc.com/blog/2010/02/the-recessions-impact-on-nanotechnology/ (accessed June 1, 2011).

[9] See, for example, Michael Berger (2007), Debunking the trillion dollar nanotechnology market size hype, *available at* http://www.nanowerk.com/spotlight/spotid=1792.php (accessed July 5, 2009).

[10] *Available at* http://www.nanotechproject.org/inventories/consumer/ (accessed July 5, 2009).

[11] Analyses of the impact of nanotechnologies in different economic sectors are carried out by a range of private analysis and consulting enterprises including, for example, Lux Research and Cientifica. The EU-funded ObservatoryNANO (*available at* http://www.observatory-nano.eu/project/ [accessed July 5, 2009]) currently tracks scientific and technological trends in nanosciences and nanotechnologies and analyses "economic realities." In the interim review of its Nanoscale Materials Stewardship Program, the EPA identified "over 200 existing chemicals that are produced at the nanoscale for commercial and R&D purposes, of which 91 are likely to be manufactured for commercial purposes." EPA (2009:18). Nanoscale Materials Stewardship Program Interim Report, *available at* http://epa.gov/oppt/nano/nmsp-interim-report-final.pdf (accessed July 6, 2009).

[12] Lux Research (2008: 9). Overhyped Technology Starts to Reach Potential.

[13] Klein, J. (2007). Probing the interactions of proteins and nanoparticles. *Proceedings of the National Academy of Sciences* 104(7):2029–30; Lane, N. and T. Kalil (2005). The National Nanotechnology

Nanosciences and nanotechnologies will thus drive the development of a broad array of products and industries in various industry sectors ranging from manufacturing and materials to electronics and information technology and health care and life sciences. For instance, between 2004 and 2006, the value of manufactured goods and materials incorporating nanomaterials expanded from $13 billion to $50 billion, and in 2006, $1.5 billion worth of nano-enabled drugs were sold. Market research estimates suggest that by 2014 as much as 4% of total manufacturing and materials sector output may incorporate nanotechnologies, and 50% of manufactured output in electronics and information technology and 16% of manufactured goods in health care and life sciences may be nano-enabled.[14]

The growing importance of nanotechnologies can also be seen from the proliferation of scientific discoveries at the nanoscale and the associated explosion of patent filings. Between 1985 and 2005, the number of nanotechnology patents issued by the U.S. Patent and Trademark Office (USPTO) increased from 125 to 4,995 at a compound annual growth rate of 20%. As of 2005, USPTO also had a backlog of 2,714 published applications.[15] According to research supported by the U.S. National Science Foundation, in 2006 alone the USPTO published 1,156 nanotechnology patents. That same year, the European Patent Office (EPO) published 679 patents.[16]

Governments play a big part in promoting the research and development of nanotechnologies. In fiscal year 2010, the United States invested $1.6 billion in nanotechnologies-related research and development, in addition to independent funding by states.[17] The budget proposal for 2012 provides $2.1 billion to the National Nanotechnology Initiative (NNI), which would increase the cumulative investment in the NNI since its inception in 2001 to nearly $16.5 billion.[18] Under its Seventh Framework Programme (FP7), the EU plans to fund nanotechnology-related projects worth a total of €3.5 billion between 2007 and 2013, a near three-fold increase in funding over the 2002 to 2006 period,[19] in addition to the funding provided by EU Member States. Total global public and private funding for nanotechnology-related

Initiative: Present at the Creation. *Issues in Science and Technology, available at* http://www.issues.org/21.4/lane (accessed August 18, 2009).

14 Lux Research (2008). Overhyped Technology Starts to Reach Potential.

15 Owing to delays driven by the difficulty of assessing developments in novel technologies, the time it takes for USPTO to reach a decision has increased from an average of 33 months in 1985 to 47 months in 2005. Lux Research (2008). Overhyped Technology Starts to Reach Potential.

16 Chen, H. et al. (2008). Trends in Nanotechnology Patents. *Nature Nanotechnology* 3:123–25.

17 President's Council of Advisors on Science and Technology (2010). Report to the President and Congress on the Third Assessment of the National Nanotechnology Initiative, *available at* http://www.whitehouse.gov/sites/default/files/microsites/ostp/pcast-nni-report.pdf (accessed June 1, 2011).

18 National Nanotechnology Initiative (2011). Supplement to the President's 2012 Budget. *Available at* http://www.nano.gov/sites/default/files/pub_resource/nni_2012_budget_supplement.pdf (accessed June 1, 2011).

19 *See* European Commission (2007). Nanosciences, nanotechnologies, materials & new production technologies (NMP), *available at* http://cordis.europa.eu/fp7/cooperation/nanotechnology_en.html (accessed July 5, 2009).

research and development is estimated to have amounted to $18.2 billion in 2008 alone.[20]

Although the number of existing commercial products using nanomaterials keeps growing, uncertainty exists regarding future commercialization paths. Nanotechnologies allow for a broad range of product and process innovations without regard to sectoral boundaries. As the range of commercial applications expands, governments will have to address potential risks of nanomaterials in diverse regulatory contexts covering different industries and commercial applications, also involving "borderline products" that cross different regulatory contexts (e.g., cosmetic products with medicinal effects). This need not be a problem in itself but may add to existing uncertainty about the regulatory coverage of emerging nanomaterials risks.

Environmental, Health, and Safety Risks

With the commercialization of first-generation products of nanotechnologies proceeding at an ever-increasing pace, a gap has emerged between the development of nanotechnologies and our understanding of how nanomaterials interact with the environment and human health. Research into the environmental, health, and safety (EHS) risks of nanomaterials is being stepped up, but there is a growing recognition that, as Klein notes, "our understanding of the interaction of nanoscale objects with living matter, even at the level of single cells, has not kept pace with the explosive development of nanoscience in the past decades."[21]

A central problem in establishing whether nanomaterials pose a risk is that they may react differently to the equivalent material in bulk form.[22] A workshop on predicting nano–bio interactions organized by the International Council on Nanotechnology (ICON), for instance, found that "because nanoparticles change as they interact with living systems, it is unlikely that their physicochemical properties at any one stage in the life cycle alone will predict biological behaviour."[23] Moreover, "when a nanoparticle is put into a biological fluid or the environment, it becomes coated with bio-molecules in a complex and dynamic matter that is not well understood."[24] Existing approaches to researching EHS risks may thus not be sufficiently robust for establishing the safety of nanomaterials.

[20] President's Council of Advisors on Science and Technology (2010). Report to the President and Congress on the Third Assessment of the National Nanotechnology Initiative, *available at* http://www.whitehouse.gov/sites/default/files/microsites/ostp/pcast-nni-report.pdf (accessed June 1, 2011).

[21] Klein, J. (2007). Probing the Interactions of Proteins and Nanoparticles. *Proceedings of the National Academy of Sciences of the United States of America* 104(7):2029–30.

[22] Service, R.F. (2008). Nanotechnology: Can High-Speed Tests Sort Out Which Nanomaterials Are Safe? *Science* 321:1036–37.

[23] ICON (International Council on Nanotechnology) (2008). Towards Predicting Nano-Biointeractions: An InternationalAssessment of Nanotechnology Environment, Health and Safety Research Needs. *ICON Report*. 4. At p. 7.

[24] *Ibid.*, p. 8.

The potential risks associated with certain nanomaterials may depend on their chemical composition, their state of aggregation and agglomeration, the number of particles per unit mass, their physical form, the median size and size distribution, their surface area and surface charge, their solubility or miscibility, their state of dissolution, and their partition coefficient.[25] All these qualities are to be taken into account when categorizing and evaluating nanomaterials for potential (eco)toxicity.

Early results of research into EHS risks suggests that the safety of all nanomaterials cannot be taken for granted. Two recent studies by Takagi et al. (2008) and by Poland et al. (2008), for example, have indicated that some forms of multi-walled carbon nanotubes (MWCNTs) have the potential to cause mesothelioma in the linings of the lungs if they are inhaled and can migrate to the edge of the lungs. Further life-cycle analysis is needed to establish likely exposure levels of such materials, from factory workers to consumers and the environment. In the light of the first findings of such EHS risks, scientists have called for the development of better and more adequate testing methods.[26] Conventional toxicological methods are seen by some as too slow, too expensive, and not able to accurately capture all risks presented by new nanomaterial properties.[27]

Developing alternative research and testing methods for EHS risks of nanomaterials is complicated, however, by the multitude of nanotechnology applications, properties expressed, routes of exposure, and means of disposal. Case-by-case risk assessment of specific materials and their use patterns is needed. As Maynard notes, "nanotechnology more closely represents a way of thinking or doing things [. . .] than a discrete technology," which "makes it particularly difficult to discuss potential risks in general terms."[28]

In addition, the ongoing expansion of nanoscience and nanotechnologies is likely to produce novel nanostructures that may cause currently unknown forms of hazard. This is likely to further complicate the search for adequate risk regulation approaches, as the U.S. EPA has noted:

> The convergence of nanotechnology with biotechnology and with information and cognitive technologies may provide such dramatically different technology products that the manufacture, use and recycling/disposal of these novel products, as well as the development of policies and regulations to protect human health and the environment, may prove to be a daunting task.[29]

[25] *Ibid.*

[26] *See, e.g.*, SCENIHR (2009). Risk Assessment of Products of Nanotechnologie, *available at* http://ec.europa.eu/health/ph_risk/committees/04_scenihr/docs/scenihr_o_023.pdf (accessed July 7, 2009).

[27] Service, R.F. (2008). Nanotechnology: Can High-Speed Tests Sort Out Which Nanomaterials Are Safe? *Science* 321:1036–37.

[28] Maynard, A.D. (2008). Nanotechnology: The Next Big Thing, or Much Ado about Nothing? *The Annals of Occupational Hygiene* 51(1); Youtie, J. et al. (2008). Assessing the Nature of Nanotechnology: Can We Uncover an Emerging General Purpose Technology?. *Journal of Technology Transfer* 33: 315–29.

[29] EPA White Paper, *supra* note 4.

A lack of data on hazards and exposure pathways of certain nanomaterials, combined with uncertainty about the applicability of some existing testing methods, is a widely recognized impediment to the effective implementation of regulations. Risk regulation under conditions of uncertainty is, of course, not uncommon in areas such as chemical and food safety. Given the significant knowledge gaps on EHS risks of certain nanomaterials, however, it is too early to establish whether existing regulatory frameworks can and will be effective in the face of potential risks. Governments in various countries are currently engaged in more systematic efforts to promote research into EHS risks and the further development of testing methods, but given rapidly evolving nanotechnology research and commercialization, such efforts pose a continuous challenge.

Regulatory Frameworks and Capacity

Analysts have debated for some years whether current laws provide adequate oversight for certain applications of nanotechnologies or whether new legislative instruments are needed.[30] U.S. and EU regulatory agencies suggest that the existing regulatory framework, consisting of a range of laws and regulations, is broadly sufficient to deal with potential risks associated with nanomaterials and that only small adjustments or amendments may be needed to regulations and implementation guidelines in order to close any potential gaps.[31] This conclusion, however, remains a matter of debate, and even regulators who assert that their existing authority is sufficient recognize the need for the issuance of guidance and, in some cases, potential future amendments to existing laws. It is important to note that conclusions about the adequacy of existing frameworks largely depend on how legal authorities are implemented. Adequate guidance for implementation and the provision of the

[30] See, for example, the American Bar Association's Section Nanotechnology Project, which has produced a series of studies of different regulatory contexts (*available at* http://www.abanet.org/environ/nanotech/). *See also* Davies, J.C. (2006). *Managing the Effects of Nanotechnology*. Washington, DC: Project on Emerging Nanotechnologies, Woodrow Wilson International Center for Scholars, *available at* http://www.wilsoncenter.org/events/docs/Effectsnanotechfinal.pdf (accessed July 6, 2009); Environmental Defense Fund (2006). A Response to ABA's "Regulating Nanomaterials under TSCA Section 5.1": Why "existing chemical SNURs" won't suffice to protect human health and the environment, *available at* http://www.edf.org/documents/5421_EnDefNanoBriefing.pdf (accessed July 9, 2009); Taylor, M. R. (2006). Regulating the Products of Nanotechnology: Does FDA Have the Tools it Needs? Washington, DC: Project on Emerging Nanotechnologies, Woodrow Wilson International Center for Scholars. 5, *available at* http://www.nanotechproject.org/process/assets/files/2705/110_pen5_fda.pdf (accessed July 5, 2009).

[31] *See, e.g.* FDA (2007). Nanotechnology: A Report of the US Food and Drug Administration Nanotechnology Task Force, *available at* http://www.fda.gov/nanotechnology/taskforce/report2007.pdf (accessed July 5, 2009) [*hereinafter* FDA Task Force Report]; European Commission (2008). Communication from the Commission to the European Parliament, the Council and the European Economic and Social Committee: Regulatory Aspects of Nanomaterials, COM(2008) 366 final, *available at* http://eur-lex.europa.eu/LexUriServ/LexUriServ.do?uri=COM:2008:0366:FIN:EN:PDF (accessed August 18, 2009); and the respective Staff Working Paper, *available at* http://www.euractiv.com/29/images/SEC(2008)%202036_tcm29-173474.pdf (accessed July 5, 2009).

necessary resources for regulatory oversight thus become critical factors in developing effective regulatory responses. Uncertainty regarding the regulatory capacity of existing institutions in this area cannot be ruled out, not least because of the novel nature of nanomaterials risks and the limited experiences that regulatory agencies have been able to develop in this area.

One area that is a recurring theme in debates on regulatory capacity is the question of resources for the implementation of risk regulation frameworks. The challenges that novel technologies such as nanotechnology present require significant investment in human resources. Statutes are a necessary but insufficient condition for success if the regulators lack enforcement capacity, scientific expertise, and foresight. It is too early to say whether regulatory institutions on both sides of the Atlantic have sufficient scientific capacity to deal with the manifold challenges of regulating nanomaterials. What is clear, however, is that the public sector will increasingly have to compete with industry for talent in these emerging technology areas. The search for talent, particularly in the scientific area, thus needs to become a strategic priority for government, just as it is already in industry.

RESPONSES TO UNCERTAINTY

Regulators must decide a course of action even in the face of multiple uncertainties. In this section, we consider how regulators have acted to reduce these uncertainties in the context of chemicals, food, and cosmetics. In practice, despite distinct and diverse enabling authority, institutional practice, and political considerations, these regulators have evolved a similar suite of tools, including direct agency action, voluntary information disclosure programs, and mandatory information disclosure requirements. We elaborate on and introduce examples of each approach from the United States and EU in the sections that follow, with more detailed discussion on the mandatory information disclosure requirements. These descriptions cannot be, and are not intended to be, comprehensive descriptions of regulatory authorities or responses to nanomaterials. For a more detailed account, please refer to the complete project report.

In addition, the requirements discussed here are focused on regulators' actions to reduce uncertainties – not on the imposition of regulatory restrictions on products or substances. We note, however, that regulators have imposed few direct restrictions on nanomaterials, in part because of the substantial uncertainties involved in making risk management decisions. In this sense, the actions discussed in this section can be seen as a prerequisite to the development of regulatory restrictions, and increased investment in uncertainty reduction corresponds to more precautionary approaches to regulation.[32]

[32] For example, REACH explicitly states in its first article that "[i]ts provisions are underpinned by the precautionary principle," and it requires data generation and development before chemicals can be placed on the market. European Commission (2006: Article 1(3)). Regulation (EC) No. 1907/2006 of the European Parliament and the Council of December 18, 2006, concerning the

Direct Agency Action

Regulators have directly addressed uncertainties in two ways. First, they have considered the applicability of their existing regulatory frameworks to nanomaterials in order to determine whether these frameworks apply to nanotechnologies and nanomaterials, and what changes may be required to address emerging issues. Second, they fund and participate in research programs to advance knowledge about nanotechnologies.

Consideration of Agency Regulatory Frameworks and Resources

Every regulatory agency in the United States and EU that was considered as part of the project has begun to evaluate the adequacy of its regulatory framework and scientific capacity. Such evaluations reduce the uncertainty surrounding the adequacy of existing regulatory frameworks and, if deemed necessary, establish a plan for addressing gaps in existing authority and for responding to developments that may arise due to the resolution of other uncertainties, including EHS risk, commercialization, or technological change. Intra-agency efforts of this nature also commonly consider the adequacy of regulatory and scientific resources.

In the United States, both the EPA and FDA have considered how to apply their authorities to nanomaterials; we use the FDA here as an example. The FDA created a Nanotechnology Task Force to investigate "regulatory approaches that encourage the continued development of innovative, safe, and effective FDA-regulated products that use nanotechnology materials."[33] The Task Force issued its final report in 2007. In the report, the FDA recognizes that nanoscale materials may present unique health risks and benefits, but considers those risks to be uncertain. It has also acknowledged limitations in its ability to gather data to make risk determinations to support rulemaking.[34] As a result, the agency appears unlikely to regulate nanomaterials as a class. Instead, it will continue to apply its existing regulatory framework, considering nanomaterial risks as necessary to evaluate the safety of

Registration, Evaluation, Authorisation and Restriction of Chemicals (REACH). O.J. (L 396/1), *available at* http://eur-lex.europa.eu/LexUriServ/LexUriServ.do?uri=OJ:L:2006:396:0001:0849:EN:PDF (accessed August 18, 2009) [*hereinafter* REACH]. By contrast, TSCA has been characterized as containing a "reverse precautionary principle" that allows information to be gathered only when a risk is already known to exist. Farber, D.A. (2008:9). Five Regulatory Lessons from REACH. UC Berkeley Public Law Research Paper No. 1301306, *available at* http://papers.ssrn.com/sol3/papers.cfm?abstract_id=1301306 (accessed August 18, 2009).

33 FDA (2006). FDA Forms Internal Nanotechnology Task Force, *available at* http://www.fda.gov/NewsEvents/Newsroom/PressAnnouncements/2006/ucm108707.htm (accessed July 7, 2009).

34 Marchant, G. et al. (2007). Nanotechnology Regulation: The United States Approach, in G. Hodge, D. Bowman and K. Ludlow, *New Global Frontiers of Regulation: The Age of Nanotechnology* (Cheltenham, UK: Edward Elgar Publishing); FDA Task Force Report, *supra* note 24, at 18 (". . . ability to detect nanoscale materials in the body or in products regulated by FDA is limited, and development of appropriate analytical methods for classes of products and of nanoscale materials may require substantial effort.").

particular products. The agency's policy is thus likely to follow historical precedent for other emerging technologies, as well as its standing practice for review of products that contain natural (as opposed to engineered) nanoscale materials.[35] In addition, it is likely to issue guidance on particular subjects, as recommended by the Task Force report.

Similarly, the European Commission reviewed the regulatory aspects of nanomaterials and published its findings, along with a Staff Working Document, in June 2008. This review evaluates the relevant EU regulations and directives with regard to their coverage of nanomaterials and concludes that "current legislation covers to a large extent risks in relation to nanomaterials [. . .]. However, current legislation may have to be modified in the light of new information becoming available, for example as regards thresholds used in some legislation."[36] In February 2008, the Commission also published a code of conduct for responsible research in nanosciences and nanotechnologies in the form of a Recommendation.[37]

Funding and Supporting Research

Regulators may also take direct action to reduce uncertainty by funding and/or participating in their own or interagency or international research efforts related to nanomaterials. Support for research enables regulators to build internal capacity and resources and to better predict and respond to new types and uses of nanomaterials. Moreover, collaborative research projects both enable more effective advocacy for research funding and build knowledge networks that regulators may be able to access to address future regulatory needs. Finally, in addition to the small percentage of research funding directly related to EHS risks, interagency and intergovernmental cooperation on nanotechnology issues enables the creation of uniform standards and methodologies necessary for characterization of nanomaterials and their risks.

In the United States, most nanotechnology-specific research occurs at the federal level. In 2001, the government established the interagency NNI to coordinate this federal nanotechnology research. The Nanoscale Science, Engineering, and Technology Subcommittee (NSET) of the National Science and Technology Council (NSTC) is responsible for overseeing the NNI. NSTC was established by executive

[35] Marchant, G. et al. (2007: 196). Nanotechnology Regulation: The United States Approach, in G. Hodge, D. Bowman and K. Ludlow, *New Global Frontiers of Regulation: The Age of Nanotechnology* (Cheltenham, UK: Edward Elgar Publishing) (citing Sadrieh, N. [2005]. Perspectives on Nanomaterial-Containing Products. Presentation to Nanobusiness Conference.).

[36] European Commission (2008). Communication from the Commission to the European Parliament, the Council and the European Economic and Social Committee: Regulatory Aspects of Nanomaterials, COM(2008) 366 final, *available at* http://eur-lex.europa.eu/LexUriServ/LexUriServ.do?uri=COM:2008:0366:FIN:EN:PDF (accessed August 18, 2009).

[37] Commission of the European Communities (February 7, 2008). Commission Recommendation on a Code of Conduct for Responsible Nanosciences and Nanotechnologies Research, C (2008) 424 final, *available at* ftp://ftp.cordis.europa.eu/pub/fp7/docs/nanocode-recommendation.pdf (accessed 6 July 2009).

order in 1993 and is made up of cabinet-level departmental heads who coordinate interagency science and technology policy. The NNI's goal is to coordinate federal research and development by "serving as a central locus for communication, cooperation, and collaboration for all Federal agencies that wish to participate."[38] Twenty-five government departments and agencies participate in the NNI, 13 with individual nanotechnology research and development budgets, including the EPA but not the FDA. Only a small portion of these budgets are allocated to EHS research. Furthermore, the NNI's budget is the collective sum of each agency's nanotechnology budget; the NNI itself does not fund research. Instead, the NNI and NSET accomplish their goals by preparing and publishing federal budget supplements and research strategies, among other activities. The NNI released its strategy for nanotechnology-related EHS research in February 2008, and initiated public consultation for its revision in December 2010.[39]

On the whole, the major trends in European regulation of nanotechnologies are set at the EU level. However, countries that have heavily invested in nanotechnologies, such as the United Kingdom and Germany, play an important role in shaping these policy developments within the EU's decision-making system, making specific regulatory decisions where they have the authority to do so and generally promoting nanotechnology research and development and EHS-related research.[40] Specific agencies in the EU also have conducted prospective nanomaterials research. For example, the Scientific Committee on Consumer Safety (SCCS, formerly the Scientific Committee on Consumer Products [SCCP]) and the Scientific Committee on Emerging and Newly Identified Health Risks (SCENIHR), both managed by DG Health and Consumers, have formulated opinions on nanotechnology EHS risks.[41]

[38] *See* National Nanotechnology Initiative (2009). About the NNI, *available at* http://www.nano.gov/html/about/home_about.html (accessed August 9, 2009).

[39] *See* National Nanotechnology Initiative (2008). Strategy for Nanotechnology-Related Environmental, Health, and Safety Research, *available at* http://www.nano.gov/NNI_EHS_Research_Strategy.pdf (accessed August 9, 2009); NNI (2010). National Nanotechnology Initiative 2011 Environmental, Health, and Safety Strategy Draft for Public Comment, available at http://strategy.nano.gov/wp/wp-content/uploads/2010/12/DraftEHSstrategy-17Dec2010-to-post.pdf (accessed June 3, 2011).

[40] *See, e.g.*, Federal Ministry of Education and Research (Germany) (2007), Nano-Initiative – Action Plan 2010, *available at* http://www.bmbf.de/pub/nano_initiative_action_plan_2010.pdf (accessed July 6, 2009) (outlining strategy for evaluating the effects of nanomaterials on human health and the environment).

[41] Scientific Committee on Consumer Products (2007). Opinion on Safety of Nanomaterials in Cosmetic Products, *available at* http://ec.europa.eu/health/ph_risk/committees/04_sccp/docs/sccp_o_123.pdf (accessed August 18, 2009); SCENIHR (2005). Opinion on the Appropriateness of Existing Methodologies to Assess the Potential Risks Associated with Engineered and Adventitious Products of Nanotechnologies, SCENIHR/002/05, *available at* http://ec.europa.eu/health/ph_risk/committees/04_scenihr/docs/scenihr_o_003.pdf (accessed July 28, 2009); SCENIHR (2006). Modified opinion on the appropriateness of existing methodologies to assess the potential risks associated with engineered and adventitious products of nanotechnologies, *available at* http://ec.europa.eu/health/ph_risk/committees/04_scenihr/docs/scenihr_o_003b.pdf (accessed August 3, 2009) (arguing that "existing toxicological and ecotoxicological methods may not be sufficient to address all of the issues arising with nanoparticles").

These opinions followed the Commission's request for advice on specific risk assessment issues. The SCENIHR focused mainly on the appropriateness of existing risk assessment methodologies, whereas the SCCP addressed the safety of nanomaterials in cosmetic products. The European Food Safety Agency (EFSA, with respect to food and feed)[42] and the European Medicines Agency (with respect to medicinal products)[43] have also published opinions on specific aspects of nanomaterials safety assessment.

Voluntary Disclosure Programs

Most regulators have taken action to enlist regulated entities in the task of reducing uncertainties. By enlisting the private sector's expertise to develop and disclose information about nanomaterials, regulators can quickly reduce uncertainties relative to the types and commercial uses of nanomaterials and the EHS risks that targeted nanomaterials present. The resultant information can then feed into the agency's internal process of evaluating the sufficiency of its regulatory system and scientific and technical capacity. Information disclosure programs thus promise reductions of all types of uncertainty.

Regulators have introduced both voluntary and mandatory information disclosure programs; in this section, we focus on voluntary programs, which have been introduced in both Europe and the United States. Voluntary reporting may be attractive for agencies as a tool to avoid regulation or determine whether regulation is needed or to provide information that an agency might otherwise lack authority to collect. Industry, in addition, may support voluntary programs to avoid the imposition of legally mandated disclosure or review authority. Despite the incentives for participation, these programs have yielded less information than hoped in practice due to factors including confidentiality concerns and the complexity of disclosure requests.

U.S. Example

The EPA's Nanoscale Materials Stewardship Program (NMSP) was a voluntary reporting program for nanotechnology in the chemicals context. Consistent with EPA's prior use of voluntary reporting programs to collect EHS data, the NMSP still represents perhaps the most high-profile nanotechnology governance initiative that the EPA has sponsored to date.[44] Under this voluntary program, the agency sought to collect data to inform appropriate risk assessment and risk management practices

[42] EFSA (2009). Scientific Opinion: The Potential Risks Arising from Nanoscience and Nanotechnologies on Food and Feed Safety. *The EFSA Journal* 958:1–39.

[43] European Medicines Agency (2006). Reflection Paper on Nanotechnology-Based Medicinal Products for Human Use, *available at* http://www.emea.europa.eu/pdfs/human/genetherapy/7976906en.pdf (accessed July 29, 2009).

[44] *See* EPA, Nanoscale Materials Stewardship Program, *available at* http://www.epa.gov/oppt/nano/stewardship.htm (accessed July 6, 2009).

for nanoscale chemical substances.[45] The NMSP was divided into two parts. The Basic Program requested that manufacturers and importers provide information on their current use of engineered nanoscale materials. The In-Depth Program asked participants to partner with the EPA to identify data gaps, engage in testing, and develop new data.

In its 2009 Interim Report on the program, the EPA stated that as of December 8, 2008, 29 companies and trade associations had submitted information covering 123 nanoscale materials based on 58 different chemicals, and another seven companies had committed to submit information. Four companies agreed to participate in the In-Depth Program.[46]

The EPA concludes that:

> Most submissions included information on physical and chemical properties, commercial use (realized or projected), basic manufacturing and processes as well as risk management practices. However, very few submissions provided either toxicity or fate studies. Because many submitters claimed some information as confidential business information, the Agency is limited in the details of what it can report for any particular submission.[47]

It further concluded that "nearly two-thirds of the chemical substances from which commercially available nanoscale materials are based" and "approximately 90% of the different nanoscale materials that are likely to be commercially available" were not reported under the Basic Program. Furthermore, a number of the submissions did not contain exposure or hazard-related data, but "exposure and hazard data are two of the major categories of information the EPA identified in its concept paper for the NMSP that are needed to inform risk assessment and risk management of nanoscale materials." Finally, it noted that the low rate of engagement in the In-Depth Program "suggests that most companies are not inclined to voluntarily test their nanoscale materials."[48] As a result, EPA has stepped up its efforts to use mandatory reporting authorities, as discussed in more detail next.

EU Example

No EU entities have undertaken a voluntary disclosure program for chemicals, food, or cosmetics. However, several EU member countries have independently developed and implemented such systems. In the United Kingdom, the Department for

[45] EPA (2008). Notice: Nanoscale Materials Stewardship Program, *available at* http://www.epa.gov/fedrgstr/EPA-TOX/2008/January/Day-28/t1411.htm (accessed July 6, 2009).

[46] *See* EPA, Nanoscale Materials Stewardship Program, *available at* http://www.epa.gov/oppt/nano/stewardship.htm (listing participating companies and trade associations and the nanoscale materials covered by the reporting).

[47] EPA (2009: 9). Nanoscale Materials Stewardship Program Interim Report, *available at* http://epa.gov/oppt/nano/nmsp-interim-report-final.pdf (accessed July 6, 2009). [hereinafter NMSP Interim Report].

[48] *Ibid.* at 27.

Environment, Food and Rural Affairs (DEFRA) introduced the Voluntary Reporting Scheme (VRS) for Engineered Nanoscale Materials[49] in 2006, Europe's first such scheme. Since the end of the scheme's 2-year pilot phase in September 2008, DEFRA has been considering how to develop a future reporting scheme, not least because the voluntary project received only 12 submissions, representing about a third of the companies currently manufacturing nanomaterials in the United Kingdom.[50] In addition, Germany and Denmark have conducted targeted surveys of nanomaterials use that have obtained useful information.

Mandatory Disclosure

Where authorized to do so by relevant legislation, some regulators have developed mandatory information disclosure requirements intended to provide complete and accurate information on commercialization and EHS risks of substances and products containing nanomaterials. These requirements may be prospective, as in the case of notification to an agency before marketing a substance or product containing nanomaterials, or retrospective, such as an adverse event report.

Several authorities have created or proposed mandatory disclosures for nanomaterials or related products. France enacted the "Grenelle II Act" in 2010 to require periodical disclosure of the identity, quantity, and application of "nanoparticulate substances" by manufacturers, importers, and distributors[51] – a model under consideration for the EU's Strategic Nanotechnology Action Plan for 2010-2015.[52] Canada Health also recently issued a policy allowing the agency to require disclosure of certain types of information related to nanomaterials, including intended use and end products, characterization, physico-chemical properties and toxicological and other data, and risk assessment and management strategies.[53] Other European authorities have also proposed or expressed support for mandatory disclosures or nano-product registers, including the United Kingdom's Royal Commission on Environmental

49 *See* DEFRA, Nanotechnology-policy activities, *available at* http://www.defra.gov.uk/environment/nanotech/policy/index.htm (accessed August 3, 2009).

50 *See* Advisory Committee on Hazardous Substances (ACHS), Draft Minutes of the 31st Meeting of the ACHS held on 25/11/08, *available at* http://www.defra.gov.uk/environment/chemicals/achs/081125/minutes081125.pdf (accessed August 3, 2009); DEFRA, UK Voluntary Reporting Scheme for Engineered Nanoscale Materials, *available at* http://www.defra.gov.uk/environment/nanotech/policy/pdf/vrs-nanoscale.pdf (accessed August 3, 2009).

51 OECD (2010: 31). Current Developments/Activities on the Safety of Manufactured Nanomaterials, Series on the Safety of Manufactured Nanomaterials No. 26, *available at* http://www.oecd.org/officialdocuments/displaydocumentpdfv2/?cote=ENV/JM/MONO%282010%2942&docLanguage=En (accessed June 1, 2011).

52 European Commission (2010: 17/143). Report on the European Commission's Public Online Consultation: Towards a Strategic National Action Plan (SNAP) 2010-2015, *available at* http://ec.europa.eu/research/consultations/snap/report_en.pdf (accessed June 3, 2011).

53 Health Canada (2010). Interim Policy Statement on Health Canada's Working Definition for Nanomaterials, *available at* http://www.hc-sc.gc.ca/sr-sr/alt_formats/pdf/consult/_2010/nanomater/draft-ebauche-eng.pdf (accessed June 2, 2011).

Pollution (RCEP), Germany's NanoKommission, and the Belgian EU presidency.[54] The U.S. government has not proposed creation of analogous nano-product registers or other new nano-specific disclosure laws, instead modifying existing information disclosure requirements to better address nanomaterials – an approach exemplified by EPA's chemicals regulation discussed later in this section.

The relationship of mandatory disclosure requirements to regulatory action depends on regulatory authority. In some cases, such as the dietary supplement example cited below or the Grenelle II Act, mandatory disclosures are largely divorced from pre-market review or approval processes. However, mandatory disclosures are often first steps towards subsequent discretionary or mandatory regulatory action. The regulatory actions flowing from information disclosures can in turn be divided into discretionary and mandatory actions. In several cases cited below, agencies may, but are not required to, review and assess disclosed information and to prohibit or condition the marketing of a product or substance. In other cases, the regulator is required by law to review products before they are marketed.

The existence of mandatory pre-market review and approval frameworks is largely unrelated to a consideration of information disclosure. However, these frameworks are relevant to information disclosure in two respects. First, a higher degree of regulatory capacity is required to evaluate substances and products for pre-market approval than to simply collect information without evaluation. Pre-market approval requirements therefore increase uncertainty about the ability of regulators to implement these systems with respect to nanomaterials. On the other hand, agencies with pre-market approval mandates, such as EFSA and FDA, are likely to seek the necessary expertise and funding to respond appropriately to disclosures – thereby reducing uncertainty about the sufficiency of their regulatory capacity. Second, pre-market approval systems may provide incentives for regulated entities to gather and disclose information in order to avoid negative outcomes during safety assessment, resulting in reduced uncertainty about the EHS risks posed by particular substances or products. However, where approval systems do not generally require the generation of safety data and where agencies are unlikely to have independent data, as under U.S. chemicals law, regulated entities may have incentives to avoid testing that could indicate EHS risks. Such approval systems would not reduce EHS uncertainties and could even lead to misplaced faith in the safety of products or substances. Although experience with many regulations is insufficient to determine whether disclosures differ under mandatory and discretionary review authorities, early experience with

[54] RCEP (2008: 69–70). Novel Materials in the Environment: The Case of Nanotechnology; Working Group 3 of the NanoKommission (2010: 45). Review of Nanomaterial and Nanoproduct Regulation, *available at* http://www.bmu.de/files/english/pdf/application/pdf/nano_abschlussbericht3_en_bf.pdf (accessed June 2, 2011); Euractive (2010). REACH register to ensure traceability of nanomaterials, *available at* http://www.euractiv.com/en/food/reach-register-ensure-traceability-nanomaterials-news-497781 (accessed June 2, 2011).

EU food regulations – and in particular, EFSA's rejection of the petition to list silver hydrosol – suggests that further consideration of this issue is warranted.

U.S. Chemicals Example

Two principal laws govern chemicals regulation in the United States: the Toxic Substances Control Act (TSCA) and the Federal Insecticide, Fungicide and Rodenticide Act (FIFRA). The former provides authorities to regulate most chemicals, whereas the latter addresses pesticides in particular. In this section, we focus on TSCA, which was enacted in 1976 with three principal policy objectives. First, "adequate data should be developed" on the effects of chemicals on health and the environment, and the development of data "should be the responsibility" of chemical manufacturers. Second, the law states that "adequate authority should exist to regulate" chemicals. Third, this regulatory authority over chemicals "should be exercised in such a manner as not to impede unduly or create unnecessary economic barriers to technological innovation while fulfilling the primary purpose . . . to assure that such innovation and commerce . . . do not present an unreasonable risk of injury to health or the environment."[55]

TSCA includes several notice requirements. Section 5 of TSCA requires that manufacturers, importers, producers, and processors (hereinafter collectively referred to in this section as "manufacturers") of chemical substances notify the EPA at least 90 days before manufacturing or introducing a new chemical by filing a premanufacture notice (PMN). In addition, the statute requires that notice be provided before manufacturing or introducing a "significant new use" of a chemical.[56] For significant new uses of chemicals, however, the EPA must first issue a rule (Significant New Use Rule [SNUR]) before the requirements apply. Such rules must be based on the application of certain statutory criteria that determine whether a significant new use exists.[57] A SNUR does not impose regulatory restrictions on the chemical covered, but rather requires an entity that wants to produce or use the chemical, in a manner identified in the SNUR as a significant new use, to first file a Significant New Use Notice (SNUN) that is comparable to the PMN that is filed for new chemicals.[58]

55 15 U.S.C. § 2601.

56 15 U.S.C. § 2604(a); see also 15 U.S.C. § 2602(7), (11) (defining covered entities).

57 15 U.S.C. § 2604(a)(2)(A)–(D). These criteria include but are not limited to "the extent to which a use changes the type or form of exposure of human beings or the environment" and "the extent to which a use increases the magnitude and duration of exposure of human beings or the environment." In issuing a chemical-specific SNUR, the EPA may rely on its generic SNUR regulations, which set out categories of significant new uses, such as "any manner or method of manufacturing, importing, or processing associated with any use of the substance" without establishing a worker protection programme that includes, for example, certain personal protective equipment. *See e.g.* 40 C.F.R. § 721.63.

58 40 C.F.R. § 721.25.

The issue of whether nanomaterials are "new" or "existing" chemicals has been divisive. In early 2008, EPA stated that a nanoscale material with the same "molecular identity" as a chemical substance listed on the TSCA Inventory is considered an "existing" chemical substance, despite any differences in particle size or properties.[59] However, in October 2008, it published a Federal Register notice[60] in which it clarified that carbon nanotubes "are not necessarily identical to graphite or other allotropes of carbon" and if "a particular CNT [carbon nanotube] is not on the TSCA Inventory, anyone who intends to manufacture or import that CNT is required to submit a PMN (or applicable exemption) under TSCA section 5 at least 90 days before commencing manufacture."[61] In fall 2009, EPA announced that it planned to reconsider its original policy and subsequently announced that it would develop a significant new use rule to regulate nanoscale chemicals that are already on the TSCA inventory in their conventional form.[62] EPA has now issued SNURs for several nanomaterials, including for certain carbon nanotubes.[63] In all, EPA states that since January 2005, it has received and reviewed more than 100 new chemical notices under TSCA for nanoscale materials, including carbon nanotubes.[64]

In addition to requiring notice for new chemicals and new uses of existing chemicals, section 4 of TSCA provides the EPA with the authority to issue rules that require manufacturers, importers, and processors to undertake testing to "develop data with respect to the health and environmental effects" of certain chemicals, provided the agency first makes certain findings.[65] The EPA has not issued nanomaterial test rules to date. However, the agency states in its NMSP report that owing to "the limited participation in the In-Depth Program," of the NMSP, it will "consider how best to apply rulemaking under TSCA Section 4 to develop needed environmental, health, and safety data."[66] The report led to renewed calls for mandatory reporting

[59] EPA (2008: 2-3). TSCA Inventory Status of Nanoscale Substances – General Approach, available at http://www.epa.gov/opptintr/nano/nmsp-inventorypaper2008.pdf (accessed June 3, 2011).

[60] EPA (2008: 64946). Toxic Substances Control Act Inventory Status of Carbon Nanotubes, *Federal Register* 73:64,946.

[61] *Ibid.* at 64947.

[62] GAO, Nanomaterials Are Widely Used in Commerce, but EPA Faces Challenges in Regulating Risk 36 (May 2010), http://www.gao.gov/new.items/d10549.pdf (accessed November 22, 2010).

[63] EPA (2008: 65751–2). Significant New Use Rules on Certain Chemical Substances, *Federal Register* 73:65,743 (for siloxane-modified silica and siloxane-modified alumina nanoparticles); EPA (2011), Multi-walled Carbon Nanotubes; Significant New Use Rule, *Federal Register* 76:26,186; EPA (2010), Multi-Walled Carbon Nanotubes and Single-Walled Carbon Nanotubes; Significant New Use Rules, *Federal Register* 75:56,880.

[64] EPA, Control of Nanoscale Materials under the Toxic Substances Control Act (Apr. 2010), http://www.epa.gov/opptintr/nano/ (accessed November 15, 2010).

[65] 15 U.S.C. § 2603(a); *see also* Chem. Mfrs. Ass'n v.US Envt'l Prot. Agency 859 F.2d 977, 984 (D.C. Cir.1988) (upholding EPA's test rule).

[66] NMSP Interim Report, *supra* note 40, at 28.

and testing of nanomaterials.[67] After its release, the EPA stated in its Unified Regulatory Agenda that a Section 4 test rule "may be needed" for multi-walled carbon nanotubes.[68]

TSCA also imposes certain record-keeping and reporting requirements on manufacturers, distributors, and processors of chemicals. For example, they are required to maintain records of "adverse reactions to health or the environment" caused by a chemical and must submit copies of records if requested by the EPA.[69] In addition, manufacturers must immediately notify the EPA if they obtain information that a chemical "presents a substantial risk of injury to health or the environment."[70] In addition, in its NMSP report, EPA states that the agency "will consider how to best apply regulatory approaches under TSCA section 8(a) to address the data gaps on existing chemical nanoscale material production, uses and exposures."[71] Although EPA's Inventory Update Rule (IUR) requires certain information to be reported periodically pursuant to section 8(a), these reports are limited in scope and coverage[72] and may be subject to CBI claims. Furthermore, EPA has received reports related to nanomaterials under section 8(e), which, as discussed above, requires manufacturers to report to it substantial risk of injury to health or the environment. Many of the details are unavailable to the public, however, because the information is protected as confidential business information.[73]

In 2010, EPA initiated several actions to increase transparency. In August 2010, EPA issued a proposed rule, which has not yet been finalized, that would amend the IUR requirements to require more reporting from chemical manufacturers and also limit

67 Denison, R.A. (2009b). Nano Confessions: EPA Almost Concedes Mandatory Reporting and Testing are Needed. Nanotechnology Notes Blog, Environmental Defense, *available at* http://blogs.edf.org/nanotechnology/2009/01/ (accessed July 6, 2009).

68 General Services Administration, View Rule, Multiwall Carbon Nanotubes, *available at* http://www.reginfo.gov/public/do/AgendaViewRule?pubId=200904&RIN=2070-AJ47 (accessed August 4, 2009).

69 15 U.S.C. § 2607(c).

70 *Ibid.* § 2607(e).

71 NMSP Interim Report, *supra* note 40, at 28.

72 EPA's section 8(a) authority does not apply to small manufacturers and processors. *See* Environmental Defense Fund (2007: 22) Comments on EPA's *Concept Paper for the Nanoscale Materials Stewardship Program under TSCA* and *TSCA Inventory Status of Nanoscale Substances – General Approach*, *available at* http://www.edf.org/documents/7010_ED_WrittenCommentsonEPANanoDocs09072007.pdf (accessed July 6, 2009) (addressing the small manufacturer exemption). Furthermore, EPA only can require manufacturers and processors to maintain and submit "known" or "reasonably ascertainable" records and information about a chemical. 15 U.S.C. § 2607(a). In addition, reporting cannot be required for chemicals manufactured or imported "solely in small quantities for research and development." 40 C.F.R. § 710.30.

73 *See e.g.* EPA, 8(e) and FYI Submissions Received October 2008, *available at* http://www.epa.gov/opptintr/tsca8e/pubs/8emonthlyreports/2008/8eoct2008.htm (accessed July 6, 2009); *see also* Denison, R.A. (2008). Yes, Virginia, Inhaled Carbon Nanotubes Do Cause Lung Granulomas. Nanotechnology Notes Blog, Environmental Defense, *available at* http://blogs.edf.org/nanotechnology/2008/10/31/yes-virginia-inhaled-carbon-nanotubes-do-cause-lung-granulomas (accessed July 6, 2009).

the information that can be treated as confidential.[74] The agency also announced a "new general practice" for CBI claims in connection with Section 8(e) submissions. If the health and safety study involves a chemical identity that is already listed on the public portion of the TSCA Chemical Substances Inventory, EPA "expects to find" that the "chemical identity clearly is not entitled to confidential treatment." EPA explained that it "believes this new general practice will make more health and safety information available to the public."[75]

U.S. Food Example

Food safety in the United States is controlled by multiple laws that are implemented by several agencies, the FDA primary among them.[76] The FDA's authorities are drawn from the Food, Drug, and Cosmetic Act (FDCA) and Public Health Service Act (PHSA). The agency's precise legal authorities differ by product category and may include both pre-market approval of new products, including drugs, devices, food additives, and food packaging, and ongoing, post-market review of products sold to consumers, such as cosmetics, foods, food ingredients "generally recognized as safe" (GRAS), and dietary supplements. Thus information disclosure requirements for food products in the United States differ according to the FDA's statutory authorities.

The FDA regulates food additives under the FDCA, as amended by the Food Additive Amendments of 1958. These amendments were enacted to ensure public acceptance of the growing use of chemicals for food processing.[77] They were intended to balance the need for determining the safety of new additives against the benefits of promoting innovation in food science, without exposing to pre-market approval the majority of ingredients that had already been sanctioned for use or that were GRAS.

To obtain approval of a new food additive, a producer must submit a petition supported by data based on FDA testing requirements. The petition must demonstrate that there is a "reasonable certainty" that the additive "is not harmful under the intended conditions of use."[78] In evaluating the safety of an additive, the FDA considers the composition and properties of the substances, the amount typically

74 EPA, Proposed Modification to IUR Rule Fact Sheet (Jul. 2010), http://www.epa.gov/iur/pubs/Fact%20Sheet_IUR%20ModificationNPRM_08-05-10.pdf (accessed November 19, 2010).

75 EPA, Claims of Confidentiality of Certain Chemical Identities Submitted under Section 8(e) of the Toxic Substances Control Act (Jan. 2010), http://www.regulations.gov/search/Regs/home.html#documentDetail?R=0900006480a80fe4 (accessed November 19, 2010).

76 The total number of federal agencies with food safety responsibilities is far larger, encompassing "at least a dozen" agencies in total. Institute of Medicine and National Research Council (1998). *Ensuring Safe Food: From Production to Consumption* (Washington, DC: National Academy Press).

77 See Taylor, M. R. (2006: 19–20). Regulating the Products of Nanotechnology: Does FDA Have the Tools it Needs? Washington, DC: Project on Emerging Nanotechnologies, Woodrow Wilson International Center for Scholars. 5, *available at* http://www.nanotechproject.org/process/assets/files/2705/110_pen5_fda.pdf (accessed on July 5, 2009).

78 21 C.F.R. § 170.3(i).

consumed, immediate and long-term health effects, and various safety factors. If it determines that there is a reasonable certainty of no harm, it will approve the additive and issue a regulation that sets limits and conditions on its lawful use.[79] A petition is not required, nor does pre-market approval apply, to GRAS ingredients; as a result, the FDA may not be informed about the commercial use or safety characteristics of every GRAS ingredient.[80]

The food additive petition process does not currently explicitly consider particle size, although the FDA does evaluate the composition and properties of the material. This particle-size ambiguity creates uncertainty over how the FDA will treat petitions for approval of nanomaterials as food additives. The FDA Task Force Report recommends that the FDA issue guidance to help clarify what different or additional testing, data, and information may be required to support approval of petitions for nanoscale additives.[81]

Information disclosure requirements are different for dietary supplements, which are subject to notice provisions unattached to premarket review. Before the enactment of the Dietary Supplement Health and Education Act (DSHEA) in 1994, the agency regulated dietary supplements as conventional foods and food additives. The DSHEA established a unique framework for dietary supplement regulation, so that supplements are now subject to a different set of regulations from those governing conventional food products. Under the statute, the dietary supplement manufacturer, rather than the FDA, has the primary responsibility for determining that a dietary supplement is safe before it enters the market.[82] Generally, manufacturers are not required to register their products with the FDA, and dietary supplements are not required to undergo FDA review or obtain FDA approval before marketing. The FDA is responsible for monitoring the safety of dietary supplements once they are on the market and has the authority to take action against an unsafe dietary supplement only after it has entered commerce. It also regulates dietary supplement labeling and claims.[83]

The DSHEA limited the oversight of dietary supplements by the FDA, which lacks full pre-market review and approval authority and cannot remove dietary supplements from the market unless it can prove that they "present a significant

79 *See* FDA, Food Ingredients and Colors, http://www.cfsan.fda.gov/~dms/foodic.html (accessed July 7, 2009).

80 This is not to say that information need not be available for GRAS ingredients – rather, the information need not be notified to FDA. To qualify as GRAS, experts, qualified by their scientific training and experience, must evaluate an ingredient's safety for its intended use on the basis of objective scientific evidence and procedures – the same level of evidence required to demonstrate food additive safety. 21 U.S.C. § 321(s); 21 C.F.R. § 170.3; 21 C.F.R. § 170.30(b). GRAS determinations "ordinarily" must be based on published studies, which may be corroborated by unpublished studies and other data or information. 21 C.F.R. § 170.30.

81 FDA Task Force Report, *supra* note 24.

82 *See* Dietary Supplement Health and Education Act of 1994, Pub.L. 103–417, 108 Stat. 4325, (1994), *available at* http://vm.cfsan.fda.gov/~dms/dietsupp.html (accessed July 7, 2009). The Federal Trade Commission regulates dietary supplement advertising.

83 Ibid.

or unreasonable risk of illness or injury."[84] However, when it determines that a supplement poses an imminent hazard, the FDA can summarily remove that substance from the market. The identification of unsafe supplements has presented a challenge to the FDA, and the Task Force Report noted that "to date FDA has received only voluntarily submitted adverse events" for dietary supplements.[85] The Dietary Supplement and Non-prescription Drug Consumer Protection Act (DSNDCPA) of 2006 restored some of the FDA's authority by requiring responsible parties to report "serious adverse events" to the FDA.[86] This mandatory adverse event reporting for dietary supplements is based on the existing system that applies to drugs. Adverse event reports are not required to indicate whether the material is being used in nanoscale form. The FDA expects this authority to strengthen its ability to engage in post-market monitoring of dietary supplement safety.[87]

The FDA retains some authority over "new" dietary supplement ingredients (NDIs) under the DSHEA. NDIs include substances that have not been used in supplements previously and are not present in the food supply in the same chemical form. Without exception, producers must notify the FDA before marketing supplements that contain new ingredients – no GRAS exclusion applies to NDIs. In its notification, the producer must include information showing that the supplement "will reasonably be expected to be safe."[88] "However, the nature of the safety information on which the manufacturer may rely is not specified in the law, and there is no requirement that a manufacturer wait for a safety determination from the FDA before marketing the product."[89] This authority may require notification of new nanoscale ingredients that may be incorporated into dietary supplements. The Task Force has recommended issuance of guidance on the issue. A January 2009 report from the Government Accountability Office indicated that the FDA has begun to develop such guidance but could not provide a time frame for its finalization.[90]

U.S. Cosmetics Example

The FDA regulates cosmetics under the FDCA. As a result, although the specifics of cosmetics regulation are unique, the agency structures and processes governing it are analogous to those previously discussed for food. However, the FDCA grants the FDA more limited oversight authority for cosmetics as compared with other products, including drugs and most food products. The FDA's cosmetics authority

84 21 U.S.C. § 342(f).

85 FDA Task Force Report, *supra* note 24, at 15.

86 Covington & Burling LLP (2006: 2). The Dietary Supplement & Nonprescription Drug Consumer Protection Act, *available at* http://www.cov.com/files/Publication/e90c3bb3–3730-424e-aa060dc042550220/Presentation/PublicationAttachment/6fb63fa8–6257-49a5–81a8-dc2fdd891fc6/731.pdf (accessed July 7, 2009).

87 FDA Task Force Report, *supra* note 24.

88 21 U.S.C. § 350(b).

89 FDA Task Force Report, *supra* note 24.

90 GAO (2009). Report to the Congress. High Risk Series: An Update, *available at* http://www.gao.gov/new.items/d09271.pdf (accessed July 6, 2009).

does not include pre-market notification or review and is limited to labeling and post-market monitoring, with the exception of color additives, which are subject to pre-market review.

FDA recognizes that statutory limitations on mandatory disclosure have limited its ability to gather information about commercialization of nanomaterials. In its Nanotechnology Task Force Report, the agency notes that for "products not subject to premarket authorization by FDA, such as cosmetics . . . , the agency generally does not receive data, including safety data, before the products are marketed. Furthermore, there are no post-marketing reporting requirements for adverse events associated with cosmetics. Therefore, FDA receives only cosmetic adverse event reports that are submitted voluntarily."[91] The agency therefore uses voluntary industry initiatives to reduce uncertainty in the cosmetics context.

On the other hand, the FDA has responded to a specific request for regulatory action with respect to sunscreens, which are considered drugs in the United States but may be considered cosmetics in the EU. In 2006, the International Center for Technology Assessment (ICTA) and several other nongovernmental organizations (NGOs)[92] petitioned the FDA to amend its regulations to address nano-engineered particles in products over which it has jurisdiction, with a particular emphasis on sunscreens.[93] The FDA has not issued a final response to this petition, but on August 27, 2007, it proposed a rule to amend the OTC monograph for sunscreen, in which it solicited comments on the safety and efficacy of nanoscale particles in sunscreens.[94]

EU Chemicals Example

European chemicals regulation has recently been consolidated and integrated with the creation of a single new EU Regulation on the Registration, Evaluation, Authorisation and Restriction of Chemicals (REACH).[95] Having entered into force in June 2007, REACH is gradually replacing the patchwork of over 40 separate pieces of regulation that have hitherto covered different aspects of chemicals oversight in Europe. It has been described as the biggest piece of legislation the EU has ever undertaken,[96] and its full impact will only be felt once all of its elements have been implemented in the coming years.

91 FDA Task Force Report, *supra* note 24, at 15.

92 Friends of the Earth, Greenpeace, Action Group on Erosion, Technology and Concentrations, Clean Production Action, Center for Environmental Health, Our Bodies Ourselves, Silicon Valley Toxics Coalition.

93 International Center for Technology Assessment, *Citizen Petition to the United States Food and Drug Administration* (2006), *available at* http://www.icta.org/doc/Nano%20FDA%20petition%20final.pdf (accessed July 29, 2009).

94 FDA (2007). Sunscreen Drug Products for Over-the-Counter Human Use; Proposed Amendment of Final Monograph. *Federal Register* 72:49,070, August 27.

95 REACH, *supra* note 25.

96 *See e.g.* EurActiv, EU Environment Legislation 'Slow Or Incomplete', Says Review, *available at* http://www.euractiv.com/en/environment/eu-environmentlegislation-slow-incomplete-review/article-173904 (accessed August 3, 2009).

In addition, certain provisions relating to the classification and labeling of substances were previously covered by REACH but are now dealt with in a separate Regulation on Classification, Labelling and Packaging (CLP)[97] of substances. The new CLP Regulation, which came into force in January 2009, will replace the current rules on classification, labeling, and packaging of substances (Directive 67/548/EEC) and mixtures (Directive 1999/45/ EC) after a transitional period. It aligns European regulation with the UN Globally Harmonized System (GHS) and will provide the general framework for the classification and labeling of substances, including nanomaterials, independently of their quantity of production.[98]

REACH applies a "no data, no market" principle to the commercialization of chemicals that reflects its stated aim that manufacturers, importers, and downstream users "should ensure that they manufacture, place on the market or use such substances that do not adversely affect human health or the environment."[99] Whereas in the past, public authorities held the primary responsibility for carrying out comprehensive risk assessment, industry now must provide data and, in many cases, assessments of chemical safety in order to register its chemical substances.[100]

Registration of substances will proceed according to the annexes to REACH, which set out the scope of the information and data required and the time frame for submission. These provisions vary considerably depending on the quantity manufactured and potential toxicity of the chemical. Quantitative bands are set at 1 tonne, 10 tonnes, 100 tonnes, and 1,000 tonnes; the higher the band, or the more hazardous the substance, the more information is required. Substances produced or imported at levels below 1 tonne do not trigger the REACH registration requirement; however, such substances still could be *regulated* under REACH if listed as a substance of very

[97] REACH, *supra* note 25; European Commission (2008). Commission Regulation (EC) No. 1272/2008 of the European Parliament and of the Council of 16 December 2008 on classification, labelling and packaging of substances and mixtures, amending and repealing Directives 67/548/EEC and 1999/45/EC, and amending Regulation (EC) No. 1907/2006. O.J. (L 353/1), *available at* http://reach-compliance.eu/english/legislation/reach-legislation.html (accessed August 18, 2009).

[98] The subsequent discussion focuses mainly on REACH, but the REACH and CLP regulations need to be seen as complementary in creating the overall framework for chemicals regulation in the EU.

[99] REACH, *supra* note 25, at art. 1(3).

[100] The terms *substance*, *preparation*, and *article* have a very specific meaning in the context of REACH. *Substance* refers to "a chemical element and its compounds in the natural state or obtained by any manufacturing process, including any additive necessary to preserve its stability and any impurity deriving from the process used, but excluding any solvent which may be separated without affecting the stability of the substance or changing its composition." *Preparation* refers to "a mixture or solution composed of two or more substances," and *article* refers to "an object which during production is given a special shape, surface or design which determines its function to a greater degree than does its chemical composition." In line with common usage and secondary literature on REACH by the European Commission, including *REACH in Brief*, references to "chemical substances" in this text acknowledge the above definition of a "substance" in the REACH context. *See* European Commission (2007). REACH in Brief: What are the benefits and costs? What was the decision-making process? How will REACH be implemented?, *available at* http://ec.europa.eu/environment/chemicals/reach/pdf/2007_02_reach_in_brief.pdf (accessed July 6, 2009).

high concern subject to authorization or restrictions.[101] Information can be gathered through a variety of means, depending on factors detailed in REACH. These include use of existing data, modeling, and testing. In order to reduce industry costs and avoid unnecessary animal testing, REACH only requires new tests when it is not possible to provide the information using a permissible alternative.[102]

In addition, manufacturers and importers who place a hazardous substance on the market, either on its own or contained in a hazardous mixture, or who place on the market a substance that is subject to registration under REACH are typically required to notify the European Chemicals Agency (ECHA) of the identity, classification, and labeling of the substance. The information provided must include the forms or physical states in which the substance will be placed on the market.[103]

REACH also applies to substances in *articles*[104] that are produced or imported in an amount over 1 tonne per producer or importer per year, if those substances are intended to be released from the article during "normal and reasonably foreseeable conditions of use."[105] In addition, substances of very high concern that are present in articles above a concentration limit of 0.1% by weight and present above 1 tonne per year are covered by REACH, and safe use[106] instructions are required, unless exposure to humans and environment can be excluded during normal conditions

[101] Authorization and restriction schemes apply regardless of quantities manufactured or placed on the market. *See* European Chemicals Agency (2008). Guidance on Registration, *available at* http://guidance.echa.europa.eu/docs/guidance_document/registration_en.pdf?vers=26_11_08 (accessed July 7, 2009); *see also* European Commission, REACH and nanomaterials, *available at* http://ec.europa.eu/enterprise/reach/reach/more_info/nanomaterials/ (accessed July 7, 2009).

[102] Denison, R.A. (2007: IV-27 to IV-29). Not that Innocent: A Comparative Analysis of Canadian, European Union, and United States Policies on Industrial Chemicals. Environmental Defense, *available at* http://www.edf.org/documents/6149_NotThatInnocent_Fullreport.pdf (accessed July 6, 2009) (noting that REACH allows for registrants to adapt standard testing regimes, including use of alternative methods of testing, and to waive higher-tier testing requirements without any independent evaluation of appropriateness, unless the substance is later selected by the ECHA or a Member State for evaluation, before which time it can be manufactured).

[103] European Commission (2008: art. 5). Commission Regulation (EC) No. 1272/2008 of the European Parliament and of the Council of 16 December 2008 on classification, labeling, and packaging of substances and mixtures, amending and repealing Directives 67/548/EEC and 1999/45/EC, and amending Regulation (EC) No. 1907/2006. O.J. (L 353/1), *available at* http://reach-compliance.eu/english/legislation/reach-legislation.html (accessed August 18, 2009); see also ECHA (2009a). Questions and Answers on Regulation (EC) No. 1272/2008 on classification, labelling and packaging of substances and mixtures, *available at* http://echa.europa.eu/doc/classification/questions_and_answers_clp_20090526.pdf (accessed August 18, 2009).

[104] In an official publication on REACH titled *Questions and Answers on REACH*, the European Commission explains that "the [Chemical Safety Report] should also generically cover consumer use of substances as such, in preparations and in articles (e.g. plastics, textiles and toys) and subsequent waste handling." European Commission (2007). Questions and Answers on REACH, *available at* http://ec.europa.eu/environment/chemicals/reach/pdf/qa_july07.pdf (accessed July 6, 2009).

[105] REACH, *supra* note 25, at art. 7(1).

[106] A supplier of such articles "shall provide the recipient [. . .] with sufficient information [. . .] to allow safe use of the article including, as a minimum, the name of that substance." REACH, supra note 25, at art. 33(1).

of use including disposal.[107] The ECHA may require, however, the registration of a substance in an article at any time when it considers its release to pose a "risk to human health or the environment."[108]

Manufacturers or importers of chemical substances are required to produce a *technical dossier* that contains information on the properties, uses, and classifications of substances, in addition to guidance on safe use. Manufacturers or importers of substances in quantities over 10 tonnes also are required to provide a chemical safety report together with the technical dossier.[109] This must include a chemical safety assessment that considers not only the use of the substance on its own, but also its use in a preparation, in an article, and at all stages of the life cycle of the substance.[110]

General agreement exists among experts that nanomaterials are broadly covered by REACH, despite the fact that it does not explicitly mention nanomaterials. The European Commission, in its 2008 regulatory review, states unambiguously that "nanomaterials are covered by the 'substance' definition in REACH" and thus are subject to the same regulations as other chemical substances.[111] Thus REACH's registration requirements are generally applicable to nanomaterials, although the implementation of these requirements will play a critical role in determining how comprehensive this coverage will be.

In particular, uncertainty remains with respect to the issue of when nanomaterials should be considered separate substances from their bulk forms. The Competent Authorities Subgroup on Nanomaterials (CASG Nano) report of December 2008 states that "further work is needed to provide guidance for substances at nanoscale. In particular, the question needs to be clarified in which cases a nanomaterial is to

[107] *Ibid.* at art. 7(2)–(3). *See also* European Chemicals Agency (ECHA), Guidance Fact Sheet: Requirements for Substances in Articles (2008), *available at* http://echa.europa.eu/doc/reach/echa_08_gf_03_articles_en_20080801.pdf (accessed August 3, 2009).

[108] Decisions on whether a risk to human health or the environment exists and whether this risk is "acceptable" or "unacceptable" are taken in "comitology" procedures, where the Commission chairs a committee consisting of representatives of the Competent Authorities of the Member States. Scientific support can be provided by ECHA and may draw on EHS data collected through REACH. See Europa Glossary on Comitology, *available at* http://europa.eu/scadplus/glossary/comitology_en.htm (accessed August 3, 2009).

[109] However, classification and labeling obligations as outlined in the "Dangerous Substances" Directive (67/548/EEC) are not subject to the respective volume threshold. See European Commission (2001). Commission Directive 2001/59/EC of 6 August 2001 adapting to technical progress for the 28th time Council Directive 67/548/EEC on the approximation of the laws, regulations and administrative provisions relating to the classification, packaging and labelling of dangerous substances. *Official Journal of the European Communities*. O.J. (L 183/51).

[110] REACH, *supra* note 25, at Annex I. Annex I further states that such a safety assessment "shall be based on a comparison of the potential adverse effects of a substance with the known or reasonably foreseeable exposure of man and/or the environment to that substance taking into account implemented and recommended risk management measures and operational conditions." *Ibid.*, at §0.

[111] European Commission (2008: 4). Communication from the Commission to the European Parliament, the Council and the European Economic and Social Committee: Regulatory Aspects of Nanomaterials, COM(2008) 366 final, *available at* http://eur-lex.europa.eu/LexUriServ/LexUriServ.do?uri=COM:2008:0366:FIN:EN:PDF (accessed August 18, 2009).

be considered as a separate substance and in which cases it should be considered as a particular form of a bulk substance. As part of the preparations for such guidance, the Commission services are currently preparing a separate document in co-operation with the REACH Competent Authorities and its subgroup on nanomaterials."[112] The outcome of this process will inform whether and how nanomaterials trigger registration requirements and other provisions under REACH and CLP. For example, REACH holds registrants responsible for updating the registration dossier whenever the composition, use, knowledge of risks, or classification and labeling of a substance changes.[113] According to the European Commission, this means that "when an existing chemical substance, already placed on the market as a bulk substance, is introduced on the market in a nanomaterial form (nanoform), the registration dossier will have to be updated to include specific properties of the nanoform of that substance."[114] As a result, the European Commission acknowledged that it will need to carefully monitor the implementation of REACH and that current provisions such as quantitative triggers "may have to be modified" in light of experience with evolving implementation.[115]

EU Food Example

EU food and feed legislation has changed significantly over the past decade in the wake of a series of health and safety scandals, such as bovine spongiform encephalopathy, infected blood products for transfusions, and dioxin contamination of feedstock for chicken. These changes have brought about a strengthening of EU authority in food regulation, which covers food products and food production, packaging, and labeling, as well as the creation of the European Food Safety Authority (EFSA) as an independent European agency. Food regulation is now largely determined at the EU level, and national food laws in EU member states generally implement decisions taken by EU authorities. General risk management authority rests with D.G. Sanco, the European Commission's Directorate-General for Health and Consumers. Working closely with national authorities, the EFSA performs two main functions, which are the provision of independent scientific

[112] European Commission (2008: 10). Follow-up to the 6th Meeting of the REACH Competent Authorities for the Implementation of Regulation, *available at* http://ec.europa.eu/environment/chemicals/reach/pdf/nanomaterials.pdf (accessed July 7, 2009).

[113] REACH, *supra* note 25, at Art. 22.

[114] European Commission (2008: 10). Follow-up to the 6th Meeting of the REACH Competent Authorities for the Implementation of Regulation, *available at* http://ec.europa.eu/environment/chemicals/reach/pdf/nanomaterials.pdf (accessed July 7, 2009).

[115] European Commission (2008: 3). Communication from the Commission to the European Parliament, the Council and the European Economic and Social Committee: Regulatory Aspects of Nanomaterials, COM(2008) 366 final, *available at* http://eur-lex.europa.eu/LexUriServ/LexUriServ.do?uri=COM:2008:0366:FIN:EN:PDF (accessed August 18, 2009).

advice to risk managers and the communication of food-related risks to stakeholders and the wider public.

Although a complete review of EU food authorities is beyond the scope of this chapter, it is worth noting that these authorities commonly require premarket approval of food products – including, but not limited to, food additives, enzymes, flavorings, and supplements. The EFSA has expressed concern about its ability to effectively carry out its responsibilities given uncertainties related to nanomaterials. For example, the EFSA published its scientific opinion on the safety of silver nanoparticles in November 2008.[116] In response to an application to include silver hydrosols, a nutrient already in use in Europe and the United States, in the list of approved substances for use in food supplements, the EFSA declared that there was not enough evidence to determine the safety of nanosilver for use in food supplements. In its conclusion, the agency stated that the toxicological data were insufficient "to allow hazard characterization of silver hydrosol." Knowledge gaps regarding EHS risks thus prevented a definite regulatory decision, illustrating the importance of implementation to the question of how well the existing regulatory framework covers nanotechnology-related risks.

In addition to its provisions for pre-market review that have analogues under U.S. law, the EU also has enacted a Novel Foods Regulation, which has no U.S. counterpart. The Novel Foods Regulation (EC 258/97) applies to foods and food ingredients (except food enzymes, additives, flavorings, and extraction solvents) not consumed in the EU before May 15, 1997. It establishes a legal requirement for all novel foods to be approved before they are introduced to the market. Food producers need to submit a safety assessment for novel foods and, once they have received regulatory approval, are obliged to inform customers through labeling of any food characteristics or properties that "render a novel food or food ingredient no longer equivalent to an existing food or food ingredient." The label must also describe the method by which this characteristic or property was obtained. Although the Novel Foods Regulation was originally drafted to address genetically modified foods and feeds, which are today covered by Regulation 1839/2003, it was worded to apply to a broad variety of food products and is thus considered to be of central importance to the regulation of newly emerging nanomaterials in food products.

In January 2008, the European Commission adopted a proposal that would rewrite the scope of the Novel Foods legislation to explicitly include new technologies derived from nanosciences and to centralize the assessment and approval procedure at EU level. In a March 25, 2009 vote, the European Parliament endorsed the principles behind the European Commission's proposal and urged the Commission to introduce mandatory labeling of nanomaterials in the list of ingredients and to

[116] EFSA (2008). Scientific Statement of the Panel on Food Additives and Nutrient Sources added to Food. *The EFSA Journal* 884:1–3 (on a request from the commission on silver hydrosol as a source of silver added for nutritional purposes to food supplements).

include a definition of nanomaterials.[117] The European Parliament proposal also includes several specific requirements relevant to nanomaterials that would have required approval of nano-specific non-animal test methods before foods produced with nanotechnologies could be assessed or authorized for sale. This regulation could thus have slowed the commercialization of nano-enabled foods in the EU. However, the European Council's version of a revised Novel Foods Regulation, agreed in June 2009, while it also recognized that new test methodologies needed to be developed, did not make the authorization of foods produced using nanotechnologies conditional upon the development of such test methodologies.[118] Neither approach is anticipated to be put in practice in the foreseeable future, however, as Parliament was unable to reach agreement on aspects of the Novel Foods revision related to food from cloned animals.[119] As a result, the Novel Foods Regulation will retain its 1997 form, including those provisions that may require premarket approval of foods containing nanomaterials.

EU Cosmetics Example

Cosmetics are subject to less rigorous regulation than either food products or chemicals, just as in the United States. Under EU cosmetics authorities, information disclosures are required in certain instances, but are not mated to a mandatory product approval process. EU regulation of cosmetics is based on the 1976 Cosmetics Directive (76/768/EEC) and a patchwork of nearly 50 amendments that have been added over the past three decades.[120] Because of perceived legal uncertainties and inconsistencies[121] in the existing framework and a general desire to strengthen and harmonize cosmetics regulation, the EU recast the Directive into a new Regulation in November 2009, to take effect in 2013. Both the Directive and the new Regulation require responsible persons to submit information to the Commission before placing cosmetics products on the market.

[117] *See* European Parliament, Press Release, Novel foods, MEPs set new rules (2009), *available at* http://www.europarl.europa.eu/news/expert/infopress_page/067–52498-082–03-13–91120090324IPR52497–23-03–2009-2009-false/default_en.htm (accessed July 7, 2009).

[118] European Council (2009: recital 16a). Proposal for a Regulation of the European Parliament and of the Council on Novel Foods and Amending Regulation (EC) No. XXX/XXXX [common procedure] (LA) (First reading), 10754/09, *available at* http://register.consilium.europa.eu/pdf/en/09/st10/st10754.en09.pdf, June 27 (accessed August 9, 2009); *see also* Falkner, R., L. Breggin, N. Jaspers, J. Pendergrass & R.D. Porter (2009). *Consumer Labelling of Nanomaterials in the EU and US: Convergence or Divergence?* Briefing Paper. London, UK: Chatham House.

[119] European Council (2011). Conciliation on Novel Foods Failed, *at* http://www.consilium.europa.eu/uedocs/cms_data/docs/pressdata/en/lsa/120351.pdf (accessed June 3, 2011).

[120] An overview is available at http://ec.europa.eu/enterprise/cosmetics/html/consolidated_dir.htm (accessed July 8, 2009). A distinction is to be made between ingredients of cosmetic products, which are regulated by REACH (though not with regard to associated risks for human health), and cosmetic products themselves, which fall under the Cosmetics Directive.

[121] *See* European Parliament, MEPs Approve New Rules on Safer Cosmetics, *available at* http://www.europarl.europa.eu/news/expert/infopress_page/066–52333-082–03-13–911-20090323IPR52331–23-03–2009-2009-true/default_en.htm (accessed July 8, 2009).

Under the 1976 Cosmetics Directive, as amended, manufacturers must assess the safety of their products before marketing them, and in doing so, they must consider "the general toxicological profile of the ingredients, their chemical structure and their level of exposure." They are also required to notify the Competent Authorities in Member States when they place a cosmetic product on the market.[122]

The new Cosmetics Regulation contains more robust and specific information disclosure requirements, including discretionary regulatory review. Article 13 of the Regulation requires that submission to the Commission of specific information about each cosmetic production before it is placed on the market. This information specifically includes disclosure of "the presence of substances in the form of nanomaterials" and their identification and reasonably foreseeable exposure pathways.[123] This requirement also applies to products notified under the Cosmetics Directive.

In addition to Article 13, the Cosmetics Regulation contains a disclosure requirement specific to nanomaterials. Article 16 requires that, in addition to the notice provided under Article 13, cosmetic products containing nanomaterials must be notified to the Commission 6 months before being placed on the market. This notice includes, in addition to the identification of the nanomaterial, its specification (particle size and physical and chemical properties), an estimate of the quantity in products to be placed on the market per year, a toxicological profile of the nanomaterial, the safety data of the nanomaterial relating to the category of cosmetic product, as used in such products, and reasonably foreseeable exposure conditions. In the event that the Commission has concerns about the safety of a nanomaterial disclosed under this article, it can request the SCCS to provide an opinion on that nanomaterial's safety in the products and conditions specified. The SCCS must report its opinion within 6 months. If additional data are needed, the Commission may request it within a certain time from the responsible party. The Commission also is required to catalog all nanomaterials in cosmetic products on the market and to report to the Parliament and Council annually on developments in the use of nanomaterials in cosmetic products.

HAVE REGULATORY ACTIONS REDUCED NANOMATERIAL UNCERTAINTIES?

In this chapter, we have identified key nanomaterial uncertainties and considered how diverse regulators have employed strategies to reduce those uncertainties. We now conclude by considering whether these regulatory strategies have reduced uncertainties effectively. We note at the outset that experience with implementation of many information disclosure programs is limited. However, even the hesitant

[122] European Commission (1976: Art. 7a). Council Directive of July 27, 1976, on the approximation of the laws of the Member States relating to cosmetic products, 76/768/EEC, 1976 O.J. (L 262).

[123] European Commission (2009). Regulation (EC) No 1223/2009 of the European Parliament and of the Council of November 30, 2009, on Cosmetic Products (Recast). O.J. (L 342/59).

developments made to date indicate that some uncertainties are being addressed, whereas others may require alternative approaches.

Existing Regulatory Frameworks Are Generally Flexible Enough to Regulate Nanomaterials, But Regulators Lack the Basic Information Needed to Enable Risk Assessment

In their reviews of regulatory frameworks for nanomaterials, both EU and U.S. agencies have acknowledged that although nanomaterials are broadly covered by existing frameworks, scientific uncertainties remain to be resolved in order to strengthen the implementation of regulatory oversight mechanisms. The European Commission stated unequivocally in June 2008 that there is "a need for a rapid improvement of the scientific knowledge basis to support the regulatory work."[124] In similar vein, the EPA in its 2007 Nanotechnology White Paper declared that although the "overall risk assessment approach used by EPA for conventional chemicals is thought to be generally applicable to nanomaterials," ambiguities and uncertainties exist with regard to chemical representation and nomenclature conventions, the environmental fate of nanomaterials, environmental detection and analysis of nanomaterials, human exposure models, and toxicity testing.[125] Similarly, in the Nanotechnology Task Force Report, the FDA concluded that "[t]here may be a fundamental difference in the kind of uncertainty associated with nanoscale materials compared to conventional chemicals, both with respect to knowledge about them and the way that testing is performed." As a result, it recommended supporting efforts to enhance understanding of "biological interactions of nanoscale materials," "novel properties of nanomaterials that might contribute to toxicity," and "measurement and detection methods," among others.[126]

Recent scientific reviews also have underlined how persistent scientific uncertainties limit existing risk assessment approaches. In the area of cosmetics, for example, the EU's SCCP pointed to significant knowledge gaps and uncertainties with regard to available data and testing methods.[127] In its Nanotechnology White Paper, the EPA points to ambiguities with regard to chemical characterization of nanomaterials and knowledge gaps about the behavior of nanomaterials in the environment, among others.[128]

[124] European Commission (2008: 8). Communication from the Commission to the European Parliament, the Council and the European Economic and Social Committee: Regulatory Aspects of Nanomaterials, COM(2008) 366 final, *available at* http://eur-lex.europa.eu/LexUriServ/LexUriServ.do?uri=COM:2008:0366:FIN:EN:PDF (accessed August 18, 2009).

[125] EPA White Paper, *supra* note 4, at 30, 32, 33, 40, 51, 53.

[126] FDA Task Force Report, *supra* note 24, at 13–16.

[127] SCCP (2007: 5–6). Opinion on Safety of Nanomaterials in Cosmetic Products, *available at* http://ec.europa.eu/health/ph_risk/committees/04_sccp/docs/sccp_o_123.pdf (accessed August 18, 2009).

[128] EPA White Paper, *supra* note 4. FDA Task Force Report, *supra* note 24, at 13–16. The lack of a scientific basis for risk assessment will not necessarily stop other actors from trying to manage their exposure to

Creating a reliable science base is thus an essential first step toward reducing uncertainty on the EHS risks of particular nanomaterials and associated products. Many of the experts that we consulted have identified scientific gaps as the main area of concern for the effective implementation of existing regulatory frameworks. In order for regulation to work, regulators need data and scientific tools to develop a clear understanding of the nature of the materials that may cause harm and how to identify these materials, define the different types of risks involved, and establish appropriate testing methods and appropriate and effective methods of measuring nanomaterials in the environment, among others. In a rapidly changing field such as that of the nanosciences, where even the boundaries of what is considered to be a nanoscale material or structure are as yet ill-defined, it is of vital importance to establish those basic scientific tools as the basis for risk assessment and subsequent risk management.

Many of these scientific building blocks are as yet missing or have not been internationally standardized. Regulators and experts in the United States, Europe, and elsewhere are currently seeking to fill existing gaps and are working together in various international forums to create mutually agreed scientific standards. These efforts are focused on the following key areas, among others:

- Definitions: terminology, nomenclature, categorization
- Characterization: physical/chemical characterization of nanomaterials (e.g., length, shape, composition, aggregation, catalytic properties, surface chemistry)
- Metrology: measurement techniques and instruments
- Testing: safety testing and hazard evaluation methodologies

Developing common practices in these areas is a critical step toward more effective regulation; they are key building blocks of risk assessment. Such common practices play a key role in clarifying how existing regulations apply. They allow regulators to identify where more detailed implementation guidelines may be desirable that specifically focus on nanomaterials and to provide guidance to producers on special requirements for identification, reporting, and testing of nanomaterials in commercial use. Moreover, they enable regulators more fully to exchange information about human health and environmental impacts of nanomaterials.

risks. The insurance sector has been very clear that it views nanotechnology as a looming issue. Lloyd's Emerging Risks Team, for example, issued a report on nanotechnology that noted that "due to the potential impact to the insurance industry if something were to go wrong, nanotechnology features very highly in Lloyd's top emerging risks." Lloyd's (2007: 6). Nanotechnology Recent Developments, Risks and Opportunities. Similarly, Zurich Insurance's Canadian office ranked nanotechnology in the top tier of emerging global risks (along with climate change and deteriorating infrastructure). *See* Canadian Underwriter, Nanotechnology, climate change, infrastructure among top risks, November 22, 2007, *available at* http://www.canadianunderwriter.ca/issues/ISArticle.asp?id=76768&issue=11222007 (accessed July 8, 2009).

EHS Risks for Existing Nanomaterials Remain Uncertain, Even Where Data Generation and Risk Assessment Are Required for Pre-Market Approval

As discussed previously, significant uncertainty exists in the field of scientific definitions, characterization, metrology, and testing methodologies – "scientific building blocks." In this section, we discuss knowledge gaps with regard to the EHS risks associated with the production and use of nanomaterials. We treat such knowledge gaps separately from building blocks because, even after scientific building blocks have been created, regulators still face uncertainty about the potential risks to human health and the environment posed by nanomaterials in commercially traded products.

A number of authoritative scientific reviews carried out in recent years have revealed significant gaps in our understanding of how nanomaterials interact with the environment and affect the human body. As the Royal Society and Royal Academy of Engineering reported in their 2004 study, many important questions remain unanswered with regard to the specific properties of nanomaterials, their toxicity and environmental behavior, and levels of exposure throughout the life-cycle of nanomaterials. A more recent review by the United Kingdom's Royal Commission on Environmental Protection emphasized the continued knowledge gaps in the area of EHS risks of nanomaterials. Its 2008 assessment concluded that "there is a plausible basis for concern that some manufactured nanomaterials could present a hazard to human health and environment," and that "[h]owever good the research effort, significant uncertainties and areas of ignorance will remain."[129] Thus, although there is no evidence of actual harm from current applications of nanomaterials, uncertainty about the behavior of nanomaterials in the environment or in living organisms makes it difficult to know whether there are adverse effects and, if there are, the nature of such effects.

These uncertainties, in combination with uncertainty related to building blocks, have already begun to affect the use of nanomaterials in some products that require premarket approval. As noted previously, for example, in its scientific opinion on nanoscale silver for use in food supplements, EFSA declared that toxicological data were insufficient to allow hazard characterization of the substance.[130] Additional examples and efforts to reduce EHS uncertainties relative to particular nanomaterials and products are likely to appear in coming years due both to the build-up of pre-market approval petitions and notices and due to REACH implementation and potential EPA actions under TSCA. Ultimately, the effectiveness of regulators' efforts to reduce EHS uncertainties will depend on the implementation of mandatory

[129] RCEP (Royal Commission on Environmental Pollution) (2008: 55). Novel Materials in the Environment: The Case of Nanotechnology.

[130] EFSA (2008). Scientific Statement of the Panel on Food Additives and Nutrient Sources added to Food. *The EFSA Journal* 884: 1–3.

disclosure and pre-market approval provisions. Until these programs are more fully realized, however, it is premature to draw conclusions on their effectiveness.

Mandatory Information Disclosure Requirements Should Be Strengthened to Provide Comprehensive Information Related to Nanomaterial Commercialization

As mentioned previously, uncertainty exists not only about EHS risks of nanomaterials, but also with regard to the commercial use of nanomaterials and specifically what type of nanomaterial is contained in which intermediate or consumer products. Regulators on both sides of the Atlantic have also acknowledged that they currently do not have comprehensive knowledge about the presence of nanomaterials in commercially traded goods. Current regulations in the United States and EU contain reporting mechanisms for chemicals, certain food products, and – in the EU – cosmetic products. These mechanisms result in the reporting of nanomaterials under certain conditions, but these are not designed to generate comprehensive data on the commercial use of nanomaterials in different sectors and products throughout potential life cycles.

Likewise, voluntary substances reporting programs, which aim to generate data about both the commercial use of nanomaterials and potential EHS risks, are unlikely to fill commercial use knowledge gaps. Both the United Kingdom's Voluntary Reporting Scheme for Engineered Nanoscale Materials[131] and the U.S. EPA's NMSP had only limited success in generating data on engineered nanoscale materials that are being manufactured, imported, processed, or used.

Our research also has shown that many companies themselves are uncertain about the use of nanomaterials within their own industry. In part this reflects the competitive nature of the industrial innovation process; companies usually seek to protect their technological advances and prevent competitors from gaining knowledge about their use of new materials and processes. But it also reflects a general state of uncertainty in industry circles and beyond about the level of adoption of nanomaterials in internationally integrated sectors such as chemicals, food, and cosmetics. The globalization of production and trade has made it more difficult to establish a sound knowledge base on the commercial use of nanomaterials.

We conclude that existing attempts to establish comprehensive market registers are laudable but need to be taken further in the United States and at the international level. Several of our interviewees commented on the limitations of voluntary reporting requirements pertaining to commercial use.[132] Given the persistence of

[131] DEFRA (Department for Environment, Food and Rural Affairs) (2008: 9). Minutes of the Thirty-first Meeting of the Advisory Committee on Hazardous Substances (ACHS) held on November 25, 2008, London, *available at* http://www.defra.gov.uk/environment/chemicals/achs/081125/minutes081125.pdf (accessed July 8, 2009).

[132] *See also* Maynard, A. and D. Rejeski (2009). Too Small to Overlook. *Nature* 460(7252).

knowledge gaps about the commercialization of nanomaterials, we believe that governments on both sides of the Atlantic should strengthen existing mandatory reporting requirements and, where necessary, create new ones, with a view to gaining a comprehensive overview of the commercial use of nanomaterials. The idea of mandatory reporting is gaining ground in the debate on how to develop better knowledge on both commercialization of nanomaterials and their potential EHS risks, despite the challenge of protecting intellectual property rights and commercially sensitive information in such reporting schemes. The example of France's Grenelle II Act and similar proposed nano-product disclosure requirements may reduce uncertainties particularly but not exclusively related to commercialization of nanomaterials.

An Increase in Direct Funding Would Reduce Uncertainties Related to Environmental, Health, and Safety Risks

In our research, we found broad agreement among regulators and stakeholders on the need to promote research on the environmental and health effects of nanomaterials.[133] Given the pervasive nature of scientific uncertainty about nanomaterials and their potential EHS risks, it is not surprising that most of our interviewees generally advocate an extension of current research efforts into EHS risks of nanomaterials in an effort to reduce current gaps in scientific understanding. We conclude that, as a matter of priority, governments on both sides of the Atlantic need significantly to increase funding for direct research into EHS risks of nanomaterials.

Many interviewees commended ongoing efforts in this area, such as the EU's 7th Framework Programme and various U.S. research efforts, some of which can be tracked through the NNI.[134] However, some interviewees commented that these existing initiatives did not succeed in setting out a comprehensive research strategy on EHS risks or provide sufficient funds to support the agenda that they have created. In recent years, some improvements have occurred, including an increase in directed EHS funding from $68 to $117 million following completion of NNI's 2008 interagency EHS research strategy.[135] Despite improvements, funding still falls short of predicted needs, and integrated research efforts are likely needed to resolve EHS-related uncertainties. A 2010 review of NNI indicated a continuing need to link an EHS research strategy with "knowledge gaps and decision-making

[133] *See also* RCEP (2008: chapter 3). Novel Materials in the Environment: The Case of Nanotechnology.

[134] *See* NNI website, *available at* http://www.nano.gov/ (accessed July 8, 2009). For an overview of all EU nanotechnology funding programmes, see European Commission, *EU nanotechnology R&D in the field of health and environmental impact of nanoparticles*, *available at* ftp://ftp.cordis.europa.eu/pub/nanotechnology/docs/final-version.pdf (accessed July 8, 2009).

[135] President's Council of Advisors on Science and Technology (2010: xii). Report to the President and Congress on the Third Assessment of the National Nanotechnology Initiative, *available at* http://www.whitehouse.gov/sites/default/files/microsites/ostp/pcast-nni-report.pdf (accessed June 1, 2011).

needs,"[136] and interviewees also pointed to a lack of an implementation strategy for EHS research – both concerns that NNI intends to improve in its ongoing EHS research strategy revision.[137] Interviewees also noted a lack of international coordination of EHS research. Not all agree that research efforts can or should be directed at the international level, but we encountered considerable support among interviewees for better coordination of existing national or regional research strategies in a transatlantic context.

To Date, Regulators Have Not Meaningfully Addressed Uncertainties Related to Future-Generation Nanomaterials

Technological innovation is proceeding at a pace that governments are finding difficult to keep up with, and, although much of the current regulatory focus is on manufactured nanomaterials, few if any efforts are being directed at dealing with the regulation of emerging risks resulting from future generation nanotechnologies.[138] This result is unsurprising, as most of the regulatory tools deployed to reduce nanomaterial uncertainties work most effectively to produce information about existing materials and products, and some authorities, such as TSCA, were created expressly to avoid creating unnecessary barriers to technological innovation. Thus, in the absence of direct agency initiatives related to future-generation nanomaterials, it is not surprising that regulators have been slow to consider next-generation nanotechnologies.

CONCLUSION

The development of appropriate and effective regulation of nanotechnologies and nanomaterials requires regulators to resolve myriad uncertainties related to commercialization, EHS risks, and the adequacy of regulatory frameworks and capacity. This chapter has focused on the approaches regulators on both sides of the Atlantic have taken to reduce these uncertainties, and experience with these actions has been disappointing, despite the good faith efforts of regulators. Although there is some evidence that directed agency action to reduce uncertainty is improving, it is unlikely to

[136] President's Council of Advisors on Science and Technology (2010: xiii). Report to the President and Congress on the Third Assessment of the National Nanotechnology Initiative, *available at* http://www.whitehouse.gov/sites/default/files/microsites/ostp/pcast-nni-report.pdf (accessed June 1, 2011).

[137] NNI (2010). National Nanotechnology Initiative 2011 Environmental, Health, and Safety Strategy Draft for Public Comment, available at http://strategy.nano.gov/wp/wp-content/uploads/2010/12/DraftEHSstrategy-17Dec2010-to-post.pdf (accessed June 3, 2011).

[138] *See* Davies, J.C. (2009). Oversight of Next Generation Nanotechnology, Project on Emerging Nanotechnologies, Woodrow Wilson International Center for Scholars. 18, *available at* http://www.nanotechproject.org/process/assets/files/7316/pen-18.pdf (accessed August 18, 2009); and Rodemeyer, M. (2009). *New Life, Old Bottles: Regulating First-Generation Products of Synthetic Biology*. London, UK: Synthetic Biology Project, Woodrow Wilson International Center for Scholars.

meaningfully reduce uncertainty without further agency and private sector actions. Although regulators have actively considered the implications of nanotechnologies, efforts to date are only beginning to yield clarification of legal authorities and regulatory capacity. Voluntary information disclosure programs similarly have not yielded sufficient information to justify their continuation in some cases, and experience with the application of mandatory information disclosure requirements has been limited to date. In the U.S., completion of suggested guidance under the FDCA and regulatory action, such as test rules under TSCA, would improve understanding of agency capabilities in addition to providing needed substantive risk information. More information on the implementation of the EU data generation and submission requirements for chemicals, food, and cosmetics is needed to determine their effectiveness at reducing uncertainty.

Taken as a whole, regulators in both the United States and EU have taken positive steps to address uncertainties, but much work remains to effectively reduce each of the uncertainties identified in this chapter. Until these regulatory uncertainties are reduced, the overall regulatory processes may struggle to keep up with the pace of technological and commercial development in this area.

Index